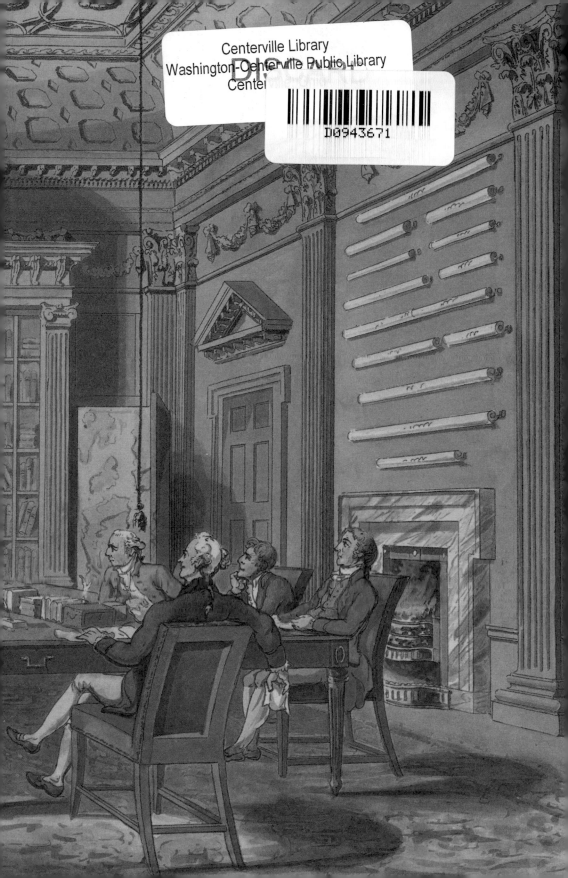

Britain Against Napoleon

ROGER KNIGHT

Britain Against Napoleon

The Organization of Victory 1793–1815

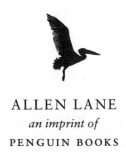

ALLEN LANE
an imprint of
PENGUIN BOOKS

ALLEN LANE

Published by the Penguin Group
Penguin Books Ltd, 80 Strand, London WC2R ORL, England
Penguin Group (USA) Inc., 375 Hudson Street, New York, New York 10014, USA
Penguin Group (Canada), 90 Eglinton Avenue East, Suite 700, Toronto,
Ontario, Canada M4P 2Y3 (a division of Pearson Penguin Canada Inc.)
Penguin Ireland, 25 St Stephen's Green, Dublin 2, Ireland (a division of Penguin Books Ltd)
Penguin Group (Australia), 707 Collins Street, Melbourne, Victoria 3008, Australia
(a division of Pearson Australia Group Pty Ltd)
Penguin Books India Pvt Ltd, 11 Community Centre,
Panchsheel Park, New Delhi – 110 017, India
Penguin Group (NZ), 67 Apollo Drive, Rosedale, Auckland 0632, New Zealand
(a division of Pearson New Zealand Ltd)
Penguin Books (South Africa) (Pty) Ltd, Block D, Rosebank Office Park,
181 Jan Smuts Avenue, Parktown North, Gauteng 2193, South Africa

Penguin Books Ltd, Registered Offices: 80 Strand, London WC2R ORL, England

www.penguin.com

First published 2013
002

Copyright © Roger Knight, 2013

The moral right of the author has been asserted

Set in 10.5/14pt Sabon LT Std
Typeset by Jouve (UK), Milton Keynes
Printed in Great Britain by Clays Ltd, St Ives plc

ISBN: 978–1–846–14177–5

www.greenpenguin.co.uk

For Jane

Contents

Abbreviations   ix

List of Illustrations   xi

Lists of Maps and Their Sources   xvii

A Note on Names   xix

Foreword   xxi

Introduction: A Hard-Working Generation   xxix

PART ONE
The Ever-Present Threat

1 The Arms Race and Intelligence 1783–1793   3

2 Pitt's Investment 1783–1793   21

PART TWO
Holding the Line

3 The First Crisis 1795–1798   61

4 Whitehall at War 1793–1802   96

5 Intelligence and Communications 1793–1801   122

6 Feeding the Armed Forces and the Nation 1795–1812   153

7 Transporting the Army by Sea 1793–1811   176

PART THREE
Defending the Realm

8 Political Instability and the Conduct of the War 1802–1812   213

9 The Invasion Threat 1803–1812   251

10 Intelligence, Security and Communications 1803–1811   285

11 Government Scandal and Reform 1803–1812   313

12 The Defence Industries 1800–1814   351

13 Blockade, Taxes and the City of London 1806–1812   386

PART FOUR

The Tables Turned

14 Russia and the Peninsula 1812–1813   417

15 The Manpower Emergency 1812–1814   433

16 Final Victory   449

Aftermath   467

Appendices

   1 Officials in Government Departments Involved
     in the War 1793–1815   475

   2 Reports of Parliamentary Commissions and Enquiries
     Relating to the Army and Navy 1780–1812   504

Chronology   517

Glossary   535

Bibliography   543

Notes   581

Index   637

Abbreviations

BL	British Library
Commission on Fees	'appointed ... to enquire into the Fees, Gratuities, Perquisites, and Emoluments, which are or have been lately received into the several Public Offices', *Reports* 1786–8
Commission of Military Enquiry	'appointed ... to enquire and examine into Public Expenditure and the Conduct of Public Business in the Military Departments' *Reports* 1806–12
Commission of Naval Enquiry	'appointed ... to enquire and examine into any Irregularities, Frauds or Abuses, which are or have been practised by Persons employed in the several Naval Departments' *Reports* 1803–6
Commission of Naval Revision	'appointed ... for Revising and Digesting the Civil Affairs of the Navy' *Reports* 1806–9
Committee on Public Accounts	'appointed to examine, take and state, the Public Accounts of the Kingdom' *Reports* 1780–87
Select Committee on Finance	*Reports* 1797–8
DHC	Devon Heritage Centre, Exeter
HL	Huntington Library, San Marino, California
HRC	Harry Ransom Center, University of Texas at Austin

NMM	National Maritime Museum, Greenwich
ODNB	*The Oxford Dictionary of National Biography* (Oxford, 2004)
SCC	Sim Comfort Private Collection
TNA	National Archives, Kew, London
TNA, POST	Post Office Archive, Mount Pleasant, London
WLC	William L. Clements Library, University of Michigan

List of Illustrations

Endpapers: Board Room of the Admiralty, by Augustus Pugin, with figures added by Thomas Rowlandson, 1808, coloured aquatint, from Ackermann's *Microcosm of London* (London, 1808–10), Vol. I, p. 16 (Bridgeman Art Library)

p. 139 Shutter telegraph cabin on the Admiralty roof, with shutter codes, print, after 1796 (British Museum)

FIRST INSET

1 Map of Britain, coloured engraving, illustrating the threatened invasion by Napoleon Bonaparte, by John Luffman, published 19 January 1804 (Bridgeman Art Library)

2 North view of the City of Westminster from the roof of the Banqueting House, engraving by J. T. Smith, drawn in September 1807 (Bridgeman Art Library)

3 Somerset House, by Augustus Pugin and Thomas Rowlandson, engraved by John Bluck, coloured aquatint, from Ackermann's *Microcosm of London* (London, 1808–10), Vol. III, p. 86 (1809) (Bridgeman Art Library)

4 William Pitt, by Thomas Gainsborough and Gainsborough Dupont, *c.* 1787–90 (English Heritage, Kenwood House, © English Heritage)

5 Henry Dundas, by Thomas Lawrence, 1810 (© National Portrait Gallery, London)

6 Lord Grenville, by John Hoppner, *c.* 1800 (© National Portrait Gallery, London)

7 Evan Nepean, unknown artist (Crown Copyright: image courtesy of the Ministry of Defence)

8 William Marsden, unknown artist (Crown Copyright: image courtesy of the Ministry of Defence)

9 George Phillips Towry, Victualling Board commissioner, by Philip Jean (© National Maritime Museum, Greenwich, London)

10 Captain James Bowen, Transport Board commissioner, British school (© National Maritime Museum, Greenwich, London)

11 Landing of British troops in Egypt, 8 March 1801, from James Jenkins, *Martial Achievements*, 1815, after William Heath (Bridgeman Art Library)

12 The landing at the Isle de France (Mauritius), December 1810: view from the deck of the *Upton Castle* transport, coloured aquatint after an original by R. Temple, published April 1813 (© National Maritime Museum, Greenwich, London)

13 Embarking troops and horses at Margate, *c.* 1800 (© National Maritime Museum, Greenwich, London)

14 Blackwall Yard from the Thames, by William Dixon, 1798 (© National Maritime Museum, Greenwich, London)

15 Charles Lennox, third duke of Richmond, in the uniform of the master-general of the Ordnance, by George Romney, 1795 (by permission of the Trustees of the Goodwood Collection)

16 General Sir William Congreve, by James Lonsdale, 1810 (© Royal Collection Trust/Her Majesty Queen Elizabeth II, 2013)

17 Prince Frederick, duke of York and Albany, by Benjamin West (Bridgeman Art Library)

18 General Sir David Dundas, probably by John Kay, 1806, watercolour (private collection)

SECOND INSET

19 William Pitt as the Cinque Port Colonel Commandant, by P. Hubert, published 28 March 1804 (Anne S. K. Brown Military Collection, Brown University Library)

20 Grand Review at Sandham (Sandown) Bay, Isle of Wight, 4 June 1798, by Richard Livesay, coloured aquatint (Anne S. K. Brown Military Collection, Brown University Library)

21 Cornhill Military Association with a view of the Church of St Helens and Leathersellers' Hall, 1799, by Edward Dayes, coloured engraving (Anne S. K. Brown Military Collection, Brown University Library)

22 Henry Addington, by William Beechey, c. 1803 (© National Portrait Gallery, London)

23 Lord St Vincent, by William Beechey (© National Portrait Gallery, London)

24 Charles Grey, by Thomas Lawrence, 1805 (courtesy of Sotheby's Picture Library)

25 Thomas Grenville, by John Hoppner, 1807 (Bridgeman Art Library)

26 Chatham Dockyard, by Joseph Farington, 1794 (© National Maritime Museum, Greenwich, London)

27 Plymouth Dockyard, by Nicholas Pocock, 1798 (© National Maritime Museum, Greenwich, London)

28 Martello Towers in Pevensey Bay, looking eastwards from Eastbourne, by William Westall, watercolour (© National Maritime Museum, Greenwich, London)

29 George O'Brien Wyndham, third earl of Egremont, in the uniform of the Sussex Yeomanry, by Thomas Phillips, 1798 (Petworth, West Sussex, © National Trust Images)

30 Banqueting House as Whitehall Chapel, by Augustus Pugin and Thomas Rowlandson, engraved by John Bluck, coloured aquatint, from Ackermann's *Microcosm of London*, Vol. III, p. 238 (1 December 1809) (Bridgeman Art Library)

31 The Board Room of the Board of Trade, by Augustus Pugin and Thomas Rowlandson, engraved by John Bluck, coloured aquatint, from Ackermann's *Microcosm of London*, Vol. III, p. 197 (1 October 1809) (Bridgeman Art Library)

32 A view of Copenhagen with the British Forces taking possession under the command of Sir Home Popham and General Murray, 7 September 1807, engraving published by J. Ryland (© National Maritime Museum, Greenwich, London)

33 The Last Act of the English, Copenhagen 1807, Danish engraving (© National Maritime Museum, Greenwich, London)

THIRD INSET

34 George Canning, by Thomas Lawrence, 1810 (by permission of the Governing Body of Christ Church, Oxford)

35 The *Cumberland* merchant ship engaging four French lugger privateers off Folkestone, 13 January 1811, coloured aquatint (© National Maritime Museum, Greenwich, London)

36 William Windham, by S. W. Reynolds, 1806, mezzotint (© National Portrait Gallery, London)

37 George Rose, by Sir William Beechey, 1802 (© National Portrait Gallery, London)

38 Spencer Perceval, by George Francis Joseph, 1812 (© National Portrait Gallery, London)

39 Lord Mulgrave, by William Beechey, 1807 (© National Portrait Gallery, London)

40 Lord Liverpool, by John Hoppner, 1807 (by permission of the fifth earl of Liverpool)

41 Lord Castlereagh, by Thomas Lawrence, 1809–10 (© National Portrait Gallery, London)

42 Norman Cross Prisoner of War Depot, Block House and the prisoners baking their own bread, by Captain Durrant,

watercolour (© Hampshire County Council Arts and
Museums Service)

43 The Emperor Napoleon and the empress accompanied by the
king and queen of Westphalia at the launch of the *Friedland*,
80 guns, at Antwerp, 2 May 1810, by Mathieu van Bree;
original in the Château de Versailles (Bridgeman Art Library)

44 Launch of the *Magicienne*, 36 guns, at Daniel List's Yard
at Fishbourne, Isle of Wight, 8 August 1812, unknown artist
(reproduced with the kind permission of the Isle of Wight
Heritage Service)

45 John Wilson Croker, by William Owen, *c.* 1812 (© National
Portrait Gallery, London)

46 John Barrow, attributed to John Jackson, *c.* 1810 (© National
Portrait Gallery, London)

47 George Harrison, by Charles Turner, published by and after
Thomas Barber, 11 November 1816, mezzotint (© National
Portrait Gallery, London)

48 Lord Palmerston, *c.* 1806 (by permission of the Master and
Fellows of St John's College, Cambridge)

49 Banquet given by the Corporation of London, 18 June 1814,
for the prince regent, emperor of Russia and king of Prussia,
by Luke Clennell (Bridgeman Art Gallery)

50 Fortress and Balloon in Green Park, coloured aquatint published
by Thomas Palser, 24 August 1814 (Anne S. K. Brown Military
Collection, Brown University Library)

51 Duke of Wellington, by Thomas Heaphy, 1813, watercolour
(© National Portrait Gallery, London)

52 Review of the Russian Army by European heads of state in the
Plains of Vertu, Paris, 10 September 1815, by F. Malek, original
in the Pushkin Museum (Bridgeman Art Library)

List of Maps and Their Sources

p. 58 British Offensive Strategy against Europe 1793–1814 (Mallinson, *Send It by Semaphore*, p. 157)

p. 95 Central London: Government Offices *c.* 1804–1812 ('Plans of all the Houses and Grounds within the Cities of London and Westminster and the Borough of Southwark held under leases from the Crown and also Public Offices and other buildings under the direction of John Fordyce, Esq., Surveyor-General of HM Land Revenue, by John Marquand and Thomas Leverton, finished in the year 1804', TNA, MPZ/10; Richard Horwood, 'Plan of the Cities of London and Westminster and parts adjoining showing every house, 1797', NMM, MID/6/11 & 12; Commission of Military Enquiry, *First Report*, p. 26; Crook and Port, *King's Works*, Vol. VI, pp. 537–71; Cole, *Arming the Navy*, p. 31; Philips, *East India Company*, p. 19)

p. 113 Somerset House Government Offices *c.* 1800 (Feilden and Mawson (Alan Robson), 'Conservation Plan for Somerset House Trust' (2008))

p. 138 Shutter Telegraph and Coastal Signal Stations 1796–1814 (Kitchen, 'Signal Stations', 337–43; Mallinson, *Send It by Semaphore*, pp. 83, 225–6)

p. 257 South-East England: Defensive Measures 1803–1810 (Clements, *Martello Towers*, pp. 20–30; Douet, *Barracks*, pp. 70, 75; Goodwin, *Military Defence of West Sussex*, pp. 70–71; Vine, *Royal Military Canal*, p. 53; Saunders, *Fortress Britain*, p. 131)

p. 258 East Coast: Defensive Measures 1803–1812 (Clements, *Martello Towers*, pp. 210–11; Douet, *Barracks*, pp. 70, 75; Kitchen, 'Signal Stations', pp. 341–2; Mallinson, *Send It by Semaphore*, pp. 83, 226; Saunders, *Fortress Britain*, p. 143)

p. 295 Post and Packet Services 1803–1814 (Robinson, *Carrying British Mails Overseas*, p. 76; Trinder, *Harwich Packets*, p. xii)

p. 358 Warship Building 1803–1815 (compiled by the author)

p. 442 The Service of the West Essex Militia 1803–1816 (Digest of Services, West Essex Militia, TNA, WO 68/257)

A Note on Names

As this book is concerned with over two decades of British history, and as many of the main politicians came from an aristocratic background or were promoted to the peerage, there were frequent changes of name. The following are the most important:

Henry Addington became Viscount Sidmouth on 12 January 1805.

Henry Dundas became Lord Melville in 1802 and was made first lord of the Admiralty in 1804. On his death in 1811, his son Robert Saunders Dundas became the second Lord Melville. In 1812 he was also appointed first lord of the Admiralty.

Charles Grey became Lord Howick in 1806 when his father was raised to the peerage as the first Earl Grey. On the death of his father on 14 November 1807 Charles became the second Earl Grey.

Robert Hobart was styled Lord Hobart in 1793, and on his father's death on 14 November 1804 became the fourth earl of Buckinghamshire.

Robert Banks Jenkinson became Lord Hawkesbury in June 1796 when his father was created the first earl of Liverpool. On the death of his father in December 1808 he became Lord Liverpool, and was appointed prime minister in 1812.

Admiral Sir John Jervis was raised to the peerage as Earl St Vincent after the battle of that name on 14 February 1797.

Charles Middleton, comptroller of the Navy Board between 1778 and 1790 and on the Admiralty Board from 1794 to 1795, was created

Lord Barham on 1 May 1805, from which point he was first lord of the Admiralty for ten months.

Dudley Ryder became Baron Harrowby on 20 June 1803 and the earl of Harrowby on 19 July 1809.

Robert Stewart became Viscount Castlereagh in 1796 and on the death of his father in 1821 became Lord Londonderry. As he was an Irish peer, he was a member of the House of Commons.

Arthur Wellesley was made Viscount Wellington after the Battle of Talavera on 4 September 1809, earl of Wellington on 28 February 1812 and the marquess of Wellington on 3 October 1812 after the Battle of Salamanca. He became the duke of Wellington on 11 May 1814.

Richard Wellesley, Arthur's elder brother, became earl of Mornington in 1781 on the death of his father. He was created Marquess Wellesley in December 1799.

Foreword

This story of the war effort against France begins in the 1780s, for the British government was preparing for conflict long before hostilities started in 1793. It continues for over twenty years, through the early 1800s when the First Consul and later emperor Napoleon, leading the French people and the many nations he subjugated, attempted to invade and conquer Britain. It ends in 1815, when the nations of Europe united for the last time to defeat him at Waterloo.

This is not a book about wholesale suffering and slaughter, starvation and devastation, which was the experience of large parts of the populations of central Germany, Russia, Spain and Portugal. Such was not the fate of British citizens; but they did experience more than twenty years of hard naval and military conflict, and, in consequence, significant casualties. Civilian Britain faced high taxation, social change and domestic unrest as well as long periods of intense political and public anxiety because of the threat of invasion when the emperor's dominance was at its height. The war against Napoleon was more extensive and expensive than that against Revolutionary France: in the words of John Cookson, 'a police action against a revolutionary regime had become a war of national survival.'[1]

I was brought up on the tradition of spectacular British naval victories in the French Revolutionary War, and the assumption that, although the war against Napoleon was protracted, final victory was inevitable. These images and memories are still very much with us. Most people (excepting a very few scholars) who read and think about the Revolutionary and Napoleonic wars today do not realize how vulnerable Britain was at this time; nor are they aware of how many years its soldiers and seamen had to fight, and of how much its civilians had to endure, to secure the survival of the country. It was a world war in all but name, enveloping Europe but also stretching as far as America and India, with ferocious fighting right to the finish, between two systems of government, each using every possible resource to overcome the other. A British victory was finally achieved but only through radical efficiencies in the nation's economic and political life: major reforms in the civil service, enormous growth in the quality and quantity of output by industrialists and farmers; and an acceptance of oppressive taxes by the rich and of military service by the less well off. Much of this is now forgotten. It may be that the horror of the Western Front in the First World War and the sheer size of the conflict in the Second World War have overshadowed the memory of the early-nineteenth-century French threat.[2] Perhaps this is not surprising, even though the French Revolutionary and Napoleonic wars lasted a generation, nearly four times as long as either of the two terrible twentieth-century wars. But the experience of the misery of what has been called total war, the changes that accompany it and the lessons to be learnt from it extend much further back than the conflicts of the twentieth century.[3] To the students of both, parallels between the Napoleonic War and the Second World War abound – in military and naval patterns of warfare, in stress among political and military leaders, in internal opposition and in distrust in relations with Continental allies. The most disturbing similarity is the plight of civilians on the Continent, displaced, ruined and starved by the campaigns of large armies.

There is much in the political world of Britain during the last fifteen years, too, that can be recognized in the period between 1793 and 1815. The danger to the state 200 years ago was more obvious and long-lasting, but unaccountable secret service dealings, the difficulties of judging incomplete intelligence and military operations of doubtful legality have a familiar ring. Echoes can be heard in some of the less benign consequences – of prolonged, unassailable parliamentary majorities, overconfidence, unminuted meetings, bitterly violent cabinet splits – though, as far as we know, no duels have been fought in recent times. The difficulties and compromises of coalition politics have lately been much in evidence, but 200 years ago similar political debates took place about the number of civil servants required and their cost, about the respective roles of the state and the private sector, and about the national debt and lax government accounting.

Yet these resemblances are not the reason why I wrote this book. Since my research student days I have been intrigued by the mechanics of eighteenth-century and early-nineteenth-century British government; and here I attempt to show these at work, in relation to the armed forces and to society as a whole, at a time when extraordinary pressures were placed upon them. My academic curiosity was further whetted by my career as an administrator in the National Maritime Museum, which, as an institution partly publicly and partly privately or commercially funded, was subject to fluctuating financial resources and shifting political expectations. Exercising the art of the possible was a day-to-day necessity. I thus identify with Professor Bruce Collins, who reflected on his career in academic administration in the acknowledgements for his recent book on these wars, *War and Empire*. His career, he writes, was 'an experience which has led me to be less ready to write loftily of military blundering and poor decision-making among those faced with uncertainty and confusion'.[4]

Since the scope of the book is very wide, and space is limited, I have omitted any explicit mention of debates among historians, and differing shades of interpretation, of which there have been many in the writing of the political, social and military histories of Britain in these years. Disagreeing with colleagues takes up too much space. For the same reason I have avoided the mention of recent concepts and code words used by the historical profession. The phrases 'fiscal-military state', 'contractor state' or 'network theory', for instance, cannot be found outside this Foreword: nor, indeed, the word 'trope'. Specialists in the period will be able to discern where I stand on most of these interpretations, and this book very obviously rests on the shoulders of the work of many scholars.

Though I have been thinking about some of the issues that this book addresses for more than forty years, its genesis came about, almost unconsciously, when I read Philip Harling's *The Waning of 'Old Corruption'* in the quiet of the Huntington Library in the course of a short fellowship there in 2007. It could have hardly been written, however, without the extensive scholarship and thoughtful writing, over forty years, of Piers Mackesy and the late John Ehrman.[5] The work of the present generation of naval historians, Michael Duffy, Roger Morriss and Nicholas Rodger, has been invaluable; so, too, have Rory Muir's and Christopher Hall's work on the government, strategy and the army, and John Cookson's on the militia and volunteers in Britain.[6] Dominic Lieven's recent book includes valuable work on the supply and logistics of the Russian Army between 1812 and 1813.[7] In these days of searchable internet databases, I would also like to mention how critically important books of reference have been to me. I have referred constantly to recent comprehensive compilations on the navy by Rif Winfield and on the army by Robert Burnham and Ron McGuigan.[8] It would have been impossible to navigate the government of the time without the *House of Commons* volumes, edited by Roland Thorne (1986), or the Office-Holders in Modern Britain series, compiled with exact scholarship by Sir John Sainty and Michael Collinge in the 1970s and 1980s.[9]

A word on the book's structure. Presenting twenty highly complex years of politics and warfare requires more than a simple narrative, particularly as the war grows in size and scope after the end of the Peace of Amiens in May 1803. The book's chapters become more strongly themed and cross-referenced in order to analyse what was happening on different fronts – intelligence, diplomacy, communications, supply, finance and technology. The first appendix lists ministers and the senior government boards; the second lays out the parliamentary commissions that reformed the administration of the army and navy in the Napoleonic War, and is of special relevance to Chapter 11.

Friends and colleagues who kindly read individual chapters have been enormously helpful. Patricia Crimmin, a source of sage advice for over forty years, cast a shrewd eye over the chapters on administration. Other chapters have also been read by Sarah Palmer, the founding director of the Greenwich Maritime Institute, and my recent partners there in the Leverhulme-funded project on the victualling of the Royal Navy between 1793 and 1815, Martin Wilcox and James Davey. Jonathan Coad, Huw Davies, John Houlding and Stephen Wood also generously gave their time to read various sections. Michael Duffy and Bruce Collins read the complete script in great detail at a late stage.

My warmest thanks to them all. Any errors that remain are of course my responsibility.

I have long pondered the distance between the two tribes of naval historians and military historians, and my thanks go to those who welcomed me into the history of the British Army in the eighteenth and early nineteenth centuries: Tom Bartlett, Hugh Boscawen, René Chartrand, Bruce Collins, Tim Cooke, Andrew Cormack, Michael Crumplin, Kenneth Ferguson, Alan Guy, Yolande Hodson and Stephen Wood, among others, have been helpful at all times. Kevin Linch at Leeds and the community of historians that he has gathered on his website 'Soldiers and Soldiering 1750–1815' have both instructed and entertained. The meetings of the 'Contractor State Group' at overseas conferences considering the comparative economic history of several nations have been continually stimulating. Among the participants of these meetings, I must thank Huw Bowen, Stephen Conway and Richard Harding, while Rafael Torres Sánchez and Sergio Solbes worked hard in organizing us all and publishing the proceedings. I have also benefited from unpublished work from Dan Benjamin, Bob Sutcliffe, Margrit Schulte Beerbühl and Anais Tissot-Pontabry. For help with references and points of interpretation I am indebted to Will Ashworth, Troy Bickham, Tim Clayton, Gareth Cole, Ken Cozens, Anthony Cross, Jeremiah Dancy, Helen Doe, Stuart Drabble, John Dunne, David Edgerton, John Hattendorf, Margaret Makepeace, Robert Malster, Maria Cristina Moreira, Keith Oliver, Jan Ruger, Tim Walker, Adrian Webb, Clive Wilkinson, Glyn Williams and Richard Woodman. The late Michael Stammers was always willing to proffer help and I shall miss his support in the future.

Old friends have helped too. Jonathan Coad guided me around the fortifications at Dover that used to be in his care when he worked for English Heritage. His tour of the Western Heights, normally closed to the public, gave me a dramatic insight into the anti-invasion measures of the time. Only when you stand on these huge fortifications, looking down at the old port of Dover, is it possible to appreciate their scale and their importance to the defence of Britain, and why governments of the day poured so much money into them. Alan Frost sent me some examples of informal, unminuted government decisions, the bane of eighteenth-century and, no doubt shortly, of contemporary historians.

My erstwhile colleagues at the National Maritime Museum have been most supportive, in particular Gillian Hutchinson, Pieter van der Merwe and Richard Ormond. Patricia Lynesmith made papers available at short notice at the Castle and Regimental Museum, Monmouth. Paul Catlow of the Somerset House Trust found invaluable plans of the occupancy of the offices in that great building 200 years ago. Sim Comfort allowed me to see a manuscript from his remarkable collection of eighteenth-century naval artefacts and papers. Robin Gilbert sent me the lively account of an invasion panic from his family papers. Alan Guy and Peter Boyden of the National Army Museum located an important unpublished paper by S. G. P. Ward, a soldier–scholar whose reflective authority is undiminished, even though he wrote more than a generation ago. To all these, I am grateful for their assistance.

I am very much in the debt of Stuart Proffitt, my publisher at Allen Lane/Penguin, who in the beginning helped me to frame the idea of this book, and who maintained steady encouragement and sure judgement throughout the years of its writing. My thanks also to my agent, Peter Robinson, and to Donna Poppy, who has been the most understanding and thorough of editors. Richard Duguid, Ruth Stimson, Stephen Ryan, Chris Shaw and Donald Futers have provided other forms of invaluable support. John Gilkes has very professionally turned my pencil-drawn tracings into attractive and I hope useful maps. Although acknowledgements for illustrations are listed separately, I would especially like to thank the present Lord Liverpool for providing an image of the Hoppner portrait of his great-great-uncle.

Documents and printed sources come from the National Archives, the Institute of Historical Research, the Bank of England Archives, the National Army Museum and the National Maritime Museum, and I am grateful as ever to the hardworking staff members who facilitated my research. I have also used material from earlier research projects over the last decade from the British Library and the Devon Heritage Centre at Exeter. During the writing of this book, most of the libraries and archives had long periods of restricted service or were closed for refurbishment; only the library of the Athenaeum soldiered on throughout, and I was willingly assisted there by Kay Walters, Laura Duran and Annette Rockall, particularly when they borrowed books for me from the London Library. Three more distant libraries had valuable manuscript collections, and permission to quote from them has come from the Huntington Library in San Marino, California, the Harry Ransom Center at the University of Texas at Austin and the William L. Clements Library, University of Michigan.

I have noticed that the authors of history books, in particular, enthusiastically acknowledge the support of their spouses, perhaps because these books take a long time to write and domestic disruption becomes a way of life. My wife, Jane, has accumulated my gratitude in industrial quantities. I have been especially fortunate that she studied history into her twenties before she had to drop the subject to take up another career. For this project she has been research assistant, document transcriber, conference attendee, intelligence expert and much else besides. She has read every word I have written, several times, pencil in hand. *Britain Against Napoleon* is dedicated to her, with love and thanks.

Charlton, West Sussex
October 2012

Introduction: A Hard-Working Generation

Work very hard and unremittingly. Work, as I used to say sometimes, like a tiger, or like a dragon, if dragons work more and harder than tigers. Don't be afraid of killing yourself. Only retain, which is essential, your former temperance and exercise, and your aversion to mere lounge, and then you will have abundant time both for hard work and company, which last is as necessary to your future situation as even the hard work ... Be assured that I shall pursue you, as long as I live, with a jealous and watchful eye. Woe be to you if you fail me!
– Cyril Jackson, dean of Christ Church, to Robert Peel,
1 April 1810, upon Peel's first appointment
in government as undersecretary for war
and the colonies, aged twenty-two[1]

In the late 1780s William Pitt, haughty, shy and still in his twenties, at the height of his political prestige as prime minister, would often ride down the Strand from Downing Street, turning right into the quadrangle of the newly built Somerset House. Some of his visits were for social and political dinners. Pitt's close ally, the forceful Scot Henry Dundas – treasurer of the navy from 1784 until 1800 and, much more importantly, home secretary in 1791 and then secretary of state for war in 1794 – had an apartment here. Lady Jane Dundas was 'at home on Monday and Friday evenings ... at Somerset Place', as the young George Canning was to note in his journal in 1794.[2] Many of Pitt's visits to Somerset House were, however, for business at the Navy Office, which administered the building and was responsible for the maintenance of

Britain's warships and kept the related accounts. The office was composed of 105 clerks and officials, housed in the most imposing part of the building, under the elegant cupola at the south end of the quadrangle.³ For a hundred years they had worked in a building in Crutched Friars in the City of London, designed by Sir Christopher Wren after the Great Fire, but by the late eighteenth century conditions were cramped, and the old building was in need of repair.

In May 1774 it was reported that large parts of the old Somerset House, built by Edward Seymour, first duke of Somerset, and appropriated by the crown after his impeachment and execution in 1552, were crumbling away and the building was close to collapse. George III agreed to its total demolition, and a radical decision was made to gather all the naval departments – at that point spread around different buildings in the City – in one place. Whose idea it was to create a 'government centre' is not known, though some attribute it to Edmund Burke, a consistent champion of the scheme. It appears to have been a pragmatic solution, rather than one of prestige, driven by the simultaneous decay of several different government buildings.⁴ The first plan for the site had been for a big, plain building that would accommodate all the naval departments as well as the Ordnance departments and the duchies of Lancaster and Cornwall, but the 'men of taste in Parliament' pressed for 'an object of national splendour'.⁵ Nevertheless, the administration of the navy had been made more efficient by the move, which started on 29 August 1786. The new Navy Office was conveniently close to the Navy Pay Office, the Sick and Hurt Office, and the Victualling Office, all in the new quadrangle, while the Admiralty was a mile away in Whitehall.

The more senior officials had living quarters in the building, since they might be summoned to business at any time of the day or night, which was why Dundas lived there. In office hours the prime minister would visit the comptroller of the navy, Captain Sir Charles Middleton, the senior of the seven commissioners of the Navy Board (which supervised the Navy Office, responsible not only for the dockyards and warship building, but also for purchasing naval stores such as timber, iron and canvas). The senior civilian on the Board was the surveyor of the navy, who oversaw the design, construction, repairing and refitting of warships in the dockyards or under contract. The management of the six home government dockyards also took much of the Board's time, although the larger yards – Chatham on the Medway, and Portsmouth and Plymouth on the south coast – had their own resident commissioners. The dockyard officers at the smaller yards – Deptford and Woolwich on the Thames and Sheerness at the mouth of the Medway – were responsible directly to the Board in Somerset House. The reach of the main naval offices in Whitehall also extended overseas. The Navy Board in Somerset House financed and managed bases in places such as Gibraltar, Halifax in Nova Scotia, English Harbour in Antigua and Jamaica.

Thus, when Pitt visited Middleton, the prime minister was by-passing his most senior cabinet colleague, the first lord of the Admiralty, Admiral Lord Howe, an isolated and difficult man. As comptroller of the navy, Middleton was responsible to the first lord, but, like his predecessors, exercised a considerable amount of independence. Pitt's business, however, directly concerned ships and their condition, for much needed to be done after the failures of the American Revolutionary War, which had ended in 1783 with the loss of the colonies. Pitt was interested in administration and its operational details, and Middleton lost no opportunity to press his reforming ideas upon him, though he was later to be disappointed by the degree to which Pitt dragged his heels in actually implementing them. The prime minister could easily become unnecessarily involved in minute detail, part of what has been called his 'government by enthusiasm'.[6] During the Dutch Crisis of September and October 1787, for instance, when relations with Lord Howe were at a particularly low ebb, Pitt and Middleton were corresponding over the smallest operational movements of regiments by sea.[7] Nor did Pitt's visits to Somerset House cease when Middleton resigned as comptroller in 1790. Middleton's successor was Sir Henry Martin, whose son recalled,

> It was no uncommon thing for Mr Pitt to visit the Navy Office to discuss naval matters with the Comptroller, and to see the returns made from the yards of the progress in building and repairing the ships of the line; he also desired to have a periodical statement from the Comptroller of the state of the fleet, wisely holding that officer responsible personally to him, without any regard to the Board.[8]

For most of the 1780s Pitt was without close political confidants in the cabinet, keeping his distance from his older colleagues. He conducted much business in unrecorded meetings and informal dinners. It was the young prime minister's habit to deal with a small group of bright, talented administrators in most departments, usually at undersecretary level, to supplement the established channels of the cabinet. Pitt had a superior and subtle intellect, adept at using the state servants skilfully: as one of his biographers put it, 'He worked with the grain and as a result became formidably well briefed.' John Fordyce, one of the commissioners for examining the Crown Lands, remarked to Henry Dundas in 1789: 'What I have found remarkably agreeable in any conversation I have had with Mr Pitt on business is not only the extreme quickness of his apprehension but the undivided and unprejudiced attention which he gives.'[9]

This circle of administrators with Pitt's ear ran across government. In addition to Middleton, it included Evan Nepean, undersecretary at the Home Office, whose extraordinary promotion to that role in 1782 by Lord Shelburne (previously he had been a humble purser and secretary to the port admiral at Plymouth) has never been wholly explained, though is probably attributable to Nepean's long experience in intelligence. Pitt also consulted William Fraser at the Foreign Office; James Harris, later Lord Malmesbury, from amongst the ambassadors; and Thomas Irving and William Stiles, former customs officials internally promoted to the Board of Customs, an important department upon whom all governments relied for its efficient tax-raising capacity. Irving was later to do much valuable statistical work as the inspector-general of imports and exports. Pitt also valued the advice of George Rose, secretary to the Treasury Board, and often talked with the young lawyer William Lowndes, who drafted complicated financial parliamentary bills for him.[10]

The decisions that Pitt and these officials took in the 1780s – on taxation and finance, investment in guns and munitions, fortifications, docks, buildings and ship maintenance – were to provide the critical underpinning of the long war effort that was to start in 1793. This was the group of men who would bear the diplomatic, financial and administrative burdens at the end of the 1780s, prosperous and optimistic years. None of them could have anticipated that the country was about to be plunged into over twenty years of bitter and costly fighting.

*

The majority of the British soldiers and seamen serving when Napoleon was finally defeated in 1815 were not even born when Pitt travelled down the Strand to visit Middleton in the 1780s. Of the public servants and politicians who were to take a major role in the Napoleonic War, only a few, such as George Rose and Evan Nepean, were in post before the start of the war in 1793. Some were not in government at all, such as the self-effacing Irishman William Marsden, who in the 1780s was a young man enjoying the scholarly life possible in London and acting as an East India Company agent. In his early years he had seen service in the Company and travelled widely. From 1796 he was to be second secretary and then in 1804 first secretary of the Admiralty.[11] Marsden's successor as second secretary, John Barrow, also travelled widely before working in government, but in the 1780s he was educating himself and tutoring young gentlemen in mathematics.[12]

Most of the future war leaders and decision-makers were still in their teens and early twenties, being educated at university. The most successful group was at Christ Church, Oxford, where early mutual acquaintance helped form bonds of trust and confidence as they moved into positions of national responsibility. The influential dean of the college, Cyril Jackson, selected those whom he helped on merit and gave them stern encouragement.[13] The formidable Lord Grenville was there, to be foreign secretary in 1791. He gave a helping hand to his contemporary Charles Arbuthnot, who, having started as a précis writer in the Foreign Office, rose to undersecretary, then ambassador to Constantinople and finally, in 1809, secretary of the Treasury. George Canning also knew Arbuthnot, describing him as 'pleasant, quick, gentlemanly and universally a favourite'.[14] Canning's character was more complex than his glittering progress through Eton and Oxford might suggest; the son of an actress, he was to find that the English elite never forgot what they saw as his somewhat disreputable origins, and he remained sensitive to this throughout his life. Nevertheless, under Pitt's patronage Canning became an undersecretary in the Foreign Office, a notably successful foreign secretary and, briefly in the 1820s, prime minister: he will be a central figure in this history. Canning was close to John Hookham Frere, who shone as a man of letters: 'an idle man,' Canning wrote in his journal, '[he] can accommodate his times to mine easily, and so of him ... I see more than almost any other human being.'[15] Frere had an indifferent career as ambassador to Portugal and then to Spain, and his communications, or rather lack of them, infuriated Nelson.[16] In 1808 he was blamed for having brought about Sir John Moore's advance on Madrid, when a retreat into Portugal had been the soldier's instinct: the decision ultimately led to the retreat to Corunna and Moore's death.

Two Christ Church men who were to become deeply involved in intelligence in the war were John King, undersecretary at the Home Office for fifteen years, and William Wickham, later spymaster, diplomat and chief secretary in Ireland. Wickham was a particular friend of Charles Abbot, who became a reforming politician with an eye for detail and then speaker of the House of Commons.[17] Two later prime ministers were also from Christ Church: Robert Banks Jenkinson, as Lord Liverpool in 1812, and the much younger Robert Peel, who started his illustrious career as undersecretary of state for war and the colonies in 1810.

Some future ministers acquired military experience while in their twenties. As the young MP for Rye, Robert Banks Jenkinson raised a regiment of the Cinque Ports Fencible cavalry in April 1794, and for a time could talk about nothing else, boring his friends. He tried to persuade Canning, recently elected as an MP, to join: 'He would have me take a troop in it as Captain. It would be good fun enough. But I do not feel the military disposition sufficiently strong within me – and so I have only bargained not to laugh at him about it.' Not long after, Canning and his friends played an elaborate joke on the young volunteer colonel by satirizing in verse some of his recruiting posters. Jenkinson took offence, and the quarrel between these old Christ Church friends was resolved only by the intervention of Dean Jackson.[18] The teasing and mischievous traits in Canning's character led to his colleagues and friends never quite trusting him, something that was almost to destroy his career fifteen years later.

Not yet in office, these young men had time for this sort of amusement. By contrast, the far more serious Robert Stewart, who became Viscount Castlereagh in 1796, took his early experience of hostilities as a volunteer in Ireland to heart. He wrote in 1795: 'Our regiment has learned its duty so fast, that they make now a very respectable appearance, and it has all been effected without flogging . . . I should like a military life.'[19] Significantly, in December 1796 Castlereagh experienced at first-hand the effect of military ineptitude and lack of intelligence when the army floundered about the southern Irish countryside in snow and intense cold, as the French invasion fleet approached Bantry Bay.[20] These young politicians were soon to be appointed to junior office, when they would discover the long hours required from an undersecretary.

In addition to gaining a formal education at one of the two English universities, ambitious young men went to the Continent in the ten years of peace before 1793 in order to learn French, a clear path to advancement. The 22-year-old Robert Stewart travelled to the Continent in 1791 and went again in 1792, when he confessed to an aunt that 'I understand French much better than I did, but am rather a greater coward ab[ou]t speaking it than ever.'[21] In addition to his Oxford studies, Robert Banks Jenkinson travelled in France and witnessed the fall of the Bastille, as did the irascible William Huskisson, who had his facility with French to thank for his first governmental post as superintendent of the Alien Office in January 1793.* Huskisson's fluency compensated for the inability of both Dundas (home secretary) and Nepean (undersecretary at the Home Office) to speak the language.[22] His main contribution was to be in tackling the immense financial problems that Britain had to face in the later years of the Napoleonic War. Similar financial talents were possessed by John Charles Herries, barely in his teenage years in the late 1780s, but who went on to study at Leipzig University in the 1790s. His knowledge of languages, combined with his accounting ability, was to be of critical importance when he was made commissary-in-chief in 1811 at the age of thirty-three. Equally important in the last two years of the war was Herries's close working relationship with Nathan Meyer Rothschild, the City banker who contracted with the government to provide enormous amounts of specie to pay the Allied armies. Rothschild was no more than a teenager in Frankfurt in the 1780s and did not arrive in England until 1799.[23]

* Huskisson's appointment arose out of meeting Pitt and Dundas at a dinner party, the introduction made by Lord Gower, who had been the last ambassador in Paris before the war (Melville, *Huskisson Papers*, pp. 1–4).

Ambitious sea and military officers also travelled to the Continent. Frederick, duke of York, George III's second son, on whom the king had settled a military career, went to Hanover in 1780 to study French and German, after which he was accelerated through the upper echelons of the army: he was a lieutenant-general by 1784 and a member of the House of Lords by 1787. When the war broke out the king insisted that the duke of York take command, aged twenty-nine of the first army expedition to Flanders.

At the same time a middle-aged Scottish colonel of Engineers, David Dundas, went to Prussia to observe the annual army manoeuvres in 1785, 1786 and 1787, from which experience, and translating from the Prussian textbooks, he published *Principles of Military Movements* in 1788. In 1792 he published *Rules and Regulations for the Formations, Field-Exercise and Movements, of His Majesty's Forces*, which led to the reform of the manoeuvres of heavy infantry regiments that had been abandoned in the American Revolutionary War; these manuals led to the mildly eccentric Dundas being called 'Old Pivot' throughout the army. Though largely forgotten today, no soldier in the two decades of conflict played a greater role in the defeat of Napoleon except for the duke of Wellington himself.

The young Arthur Wellesley, an impecunious Irish aristocrat, spent a lonely time at Eton between 1781 and 1785, but his talents and his knowledge of French developed when he enrolled in the French Royal Academy of Equitation at Angers in January 1786. A good knowledge of French was vital for a soldier: apart from its use in diplomacy, operationally it was essential to intelligence work and the interrogation of prisoners. By the time the war broke out, Wellesley had purchased commissions in six regiments, so that without having seen any action he nonetheless found himself lieutenant-colonel and commanding officer of the 33rd Regiment of Foot.[24] In the first year of the war, a rising young army captain, Harry Calvert, ADC to the duke of York in Holland, wrote home with advice to the parents of a young man about to get a commission: 'give the young hero as much French as he can possibly take, while he is in England. Languages are the <u>sine quâ non</u> to an officer who wishes to rise above the common routine of regimental duty; and I have myself felt very severely the misfortune of not understanding German.'[25]

Captain Horatio Nelson also went to France in 1784 to try to master the language, but fell in love, was rejected and came home without having learnt anything. He met a fellow officer while in France, Captain William Young, who became a talented linguist, and who was to play a distinguished administrative role in the wars, as well as at sea. Nelson chose not to meet another naval captain, Alexander Ball, who was residing in the same town, since Ball was wearing the newly fashionable epaulettes of which Nelson did not approve. Ball, a master of languages, ended his career as governor of Malta.[26]

As soldiers and naval officers these men were trained in the instant obedience of the quarterdeck or parade ground, and they tended to lack the dissembling arts and generally made poor diplomats. But both services needed able administrators and quite a number rose from the ranks of officers. In 1793 one young frigate captain, Thomas Byam Martin, met a young army officer, James Willoughby Gordon, who saw no chance for advancement and wished instead that he had entered the navy. But, as Byam Martin related, Willoughby Gordon

> attained to the highest rank in his profession, by self-acquired information in a great degree, and a constant persevering habit of reading and writing, so that he qualified himself for anything which good fortune might chance to throw in his way; and this occurred at no distant period, for his acquirements introduced him to the Duke of Kent, to whose staff at Halifax he was appointed secretary; and his readiness in the discharge of this duty led to a similar appointment under the Duke of York, and to his permanency, I may almost say, in office at the Horse Guards.

The two men next met in 1815, when Sir Thomas Byam Martin was deputy comptroller of the navy and Sir James Willoughby Gordon was quartermaster-general of the army.[27]

Apart from the uneasy Peace of Amiens – which lasted from March 1802 until May 1803, separating the war against Revolutionary France from the Napoleonic War – hostilities were maintained for a generation, four times as long as either of the major twentieth-century conflicts. In spite of a series of extraordinary naval victories, Britain made no impression whatsoever on French Continental expansion. It was apparent by 1805 that sea power alone would not beat Napoleon, though crucially it enabled Britain to escape defeat, expand its trade and continue to prosecute the war.[28] The long failure to secure victory was accompanied by food shortages, consequent social unrest and major financial crises. At two critical periods, between 1796 and 1798, and between 1807 and 1812, the British political system and the economy almost buckled under the strain. How this was avoided is a major theme of *Britain Against Napoleon*. Politicians, public servants, naval and army officers – all worked for the steady improvement and growth of Britain's political, financial, naval and military effectiveness.

This book is about these men and their contemporaries: how they operated and how they contributed to Napoleon's final defeat. It is neither a military nor a naval history; rather, it attempts to put the successes and failures of the army and navy into context, and explain how the two armed forces were supported. It examines the decisions of politicians, the quality of the intelligence available to them and the speed of their communications. It plots the improvements in the defence of the country by volunteers and militia, and the building of more extensive and effective fortifications. It assesses the country's industrial capability and the role of City finance, and describes how, towards the end of the wars, enough ships, artillery and provisions were provided to the ever-expanding navy and army as a result of a massively increased output, together with improved technology. At the same time, Britain supported Continental allies by sending them substantial amounts of gunpowder and small arms, as well as enormous financial subsidies. If the men who made these things happen had not worked as hard and as competently as they did, Britain would not have survived the onslaught of Napoleonic France.

PART ONE

The Ever-Present Threat

I

The Arms Race and Intelligence

1783–1793

In the month of March 1790, intelligence was received of an outrageous act of insult to the British flag, and cruel treatment of several Englishmen ... The din of war ran through the country like wild-fire ... The nation at large seemed animated by an indignant feeling ... It was with such feelings that the nation flew to arms after seven years of repose, not, however, the repose of idleness, for the time had been profitably spent in renovating and augmenting the fleet.
    – Lieutenant (later Admiral) Thomas Byam Martin on the British reaction to the Spanish capture of British ships and seamen at Nootka Sound in 1790[1]

In June 1783 the last shots of the American Revolutionary War were fired between Britain and France many thousands of miles from American shores at Cuddalore in southern India. The fight for American independence had lasted for over seven years, and Britain had fought the colonists in North America, and against France, Spain and Holland. Peace preliminaries had been agreed on 20 January, and the definitive Treaty of Paris was signed on 3 September 1783.[2] But though the guns may have fallen silent, this did not mean that mutual suspicion between Britain and France had lessened, even though for at least the first four years of peace all the combatant nations were licking their wounds after a costly war.[3] For the rest of the decade most of the nations of Europe were busily rearming. It was not one but several arms races, in a situation remarkably similar to that in Europe before 1914.[4] The central great-powers contest was between Britain and

France, with Spain potentially ranged alongside her Bourbon partner. However, Russia under Catherine the Great was flexing its muscles, expanding at the expense of Sweden in the Baltic and of Turkey in the Black Sea. By 1788 war had broken out in both these areas.

The British government's fear of a surprise French attack on India was constant through the early 1780s, not least because the French were building warships at a great rate. In Paris, however, the comte de Vergennes, the French secretary of state, seemingly triumphant after helping the American colonists detach themselves from Britain, felt that another war was inevitable, believing that the British would seek to avenge its loss of power and the American market. In 1784 he informed Louis XVI that the newly won peace was 'absolutely precarious'.[5] Vergennes was particularly worried about the recently built battle fleet with which Britain had ended the American Revolutionary War. When the peace treaty was signed, most of these great ships were ordered to stand in frame on the slips where they had been built, ready for the time when they might again be needed.

The immediate post-war years in Britain were ones of extreme political instability, and a feeling of weakness and recrimination prevailed. Parliament and the country had to swallow the bitter pill of the loss of the war and the colonies. After the fall of Lord North's government in March 1782, four different administrations were sworn in within twenty-one months. Eventually, out of the political chaos emerged William Pitt, second son of William Pitt, earl of Chatham, who had led the country for much of the Seven Years War. The Younger Pitt had been chancellor of the Exchequer in the earl of Shelburne's administration up to April 1783, and was able to form a government in December 1783 when support collapsed for the seven-month administration of the duke of Portland, supported by Charles James Fox and his old enemy, Lord North.[6] Nobody gave Pitt, still short of his twenty-fourth birthday, much of a chance: but he won the 1784 general election by a landslide, and those in 1790 and 1796, too. His premiership was to last eighteen years.[7]

The years of peace between every eighteenth-century war had always been devoted to rearming. After the Seven Years War, from 1763 to 1775, both the British and the French attempted to balance their severely dented post-war finances against the need for a warship-rebuilding programme. Both were disappointed with their respective efforts, though by spending lavishly the French managed to cut the British advantage in number of ships.[8] The fatal hesitancy of Lord North's government to mobilize enough warships in the early years of the American Revolutionary War left Britain in the weakest naval position it was ever to experience relative to the Bourbon powers of France and Spain, which, exceptionally, acted together in support of the colonists.[9] In spite of the strong showing of the navy during the last two years of the war, Britain's position would once again be weak if it had to fight a united France and Spain. Lord Howe in a letter in early 1786 drew the king's attention to, 'the extraordinary attention given by the other Maritime Powers of Europe to the increase of their naval strength, and the nature of their alliances'.[10] Pitt reduced the navy debt, which had stood at over £15 million in 1783, to £1.5 million in 1786, chiefly by converting the principal debt into stocks that were sold on the London market. He secured parliamentary approval for high levels of Naval Estimates and expenditure, at between £2 million and £3 million a year for most of the decade, because of the general rearming in Europe.[11]

Through the 1780s the combined battle-fleet tonnage of the two Bourbon powers exceeded that of Britain's by 35 per cent, a margin greater than that during the fatal early years of the American Revolutionary War, when Lord North's government had failed to rearm and mobilize in time.[12] Money was needed to improve the infrastructure and equipment of its armed forces, and the capital-intensive navy required the greater share, for the building of new ships and maintaining the condition of the existing fleet were critical. The building of a ship of the line was only the beginning. What counted were well-manned ships at sea, their holds full of provisions, gunpowder and shot. For the first time in the eighteenth century, the navy had a carefully calculated plan of maintenance.* It aimed for, and achieved,

---

* Charles Derrick, a Navy Board clerk close to Middleton, wrote of the 1780s: 'It was not forgotten, on the return of peace, what powerful fleets had on several occasions been opposed to ours . . . neither was it overlooked, that in order to combat with still greater success, in a future war, the same powerful enemies . . . great exertions must be made to put an adequate number of Ships into good condition' (Derrick, *Memoirs of the Rise and Progress of the Royal Navy*, pp. 180–81).

a hundred ships of the line, ready and effective at all times, their frames maintained to keep pace with the natural deterioration of oak-built ships, which meant giving thorough repairs to at least ten ships of the line and ten frigates every year, a rate of peacetime maintenance never attempted before. This would have been the main subject under discussion when Pitt made his regular visits to Somerset House to see the comptroller of the navy.[13]

Three departments of state – the Foreign Office, the Home Office and the Admiralty – monitored the war preparations of the French and other potential enemies.* Each ran its own intelligence network, and, as we shall see, intelligence-sharing between the departments could be sporadic and patchy. Information available to Foreign Office ministers was complemented by regular reports from diplomats in foreign capitals. Evidence of the activities of the spies and agents is not easy to come by, but some of the Treasury accounts recording payments to them still exist. Annual expenditure on intelligence by the Foreign Office was around £25,000 up to 1786, but, with the first of the diplomatic crises, over the Dutch in 1787, spending increased dramatically to £98,050; and in 1788 to £211,796.[14] The undersecretary at the Home Office, Evan Nepean, also ran a network of spies. The accounts reveal that between 1785 and 1789 he paid £14,576 to his agents, but there is no way of knowing the total amount expended by all departments.[15]

The third department that spent money on intelligence was the Admiralty. Most of its information on the French Navy came from observations by British warships off the main naval bases of Brest and Toulon. For the Atlantic coast the main source of intelligence came from Captain Philippe D'Auvergne, who commanded a squadron of small ships based in Jersey from the 1780s until almost the end of the Napoleonic War, and whose knowledge of the treacherous coast and

---

* Until 1782 there had been two secretaries of state who shared domestic business, while foreign affairs was shared between them on a geographical basis, commonly called the 'Northern' and 'Southern' departments. From 1782 the 'foreign' secretary managed foreign affairs, while the 'home' took over domestic and colonial business. Institutionally the Foreign Office took over the staff who had served in the former Northern Department, while the Home Office took those from the Southern Department (Sainty, *Foreign Office*, p. 1).

fast-flowing tides off the Normandy and Brittany coasts was second to none.* However, the Home Office, too, had Brest watched. Nepean's accounts, for instance, record a payment of £105 on 3 May 1785 to a James Johnstone, 'to defray the expenses of his Journey to Brest and other places on the coast of France'; on 24 May a Captain Le Geyt was paid £25.5s. 'for information on the proceedings of the French on the coast of Normandy'.[16]

Toulon, the principal base of the French Mediterranean Fleet, also had to be watched, and alarming rumours started early in the peace. The European-wide spy network, controlled from Rotterdam by a Dutch woman, Margrete Wolters, had been operational since the Seven Years War. She had agents not only in Paris but in all French and Spanish naval ports. She reported her intelligence to the Admiralty, but she had retired.† It reported in October 1784 that Toulon was expected to have thirty battleships ready by the next January.[17] Nepean immediately sent a naval officer, Captain Arthur Phillip – who was to command the 'First Fleet', which founded the British colony in New South Wales at the end of the decade – to investigate. Phillip reported that ten battleships were in the port, though they were not preparing for sea. Several frigates could be 'ready for Sea in a short time' and that the arsenal was 'in very good Order and very superior to what it was when I saw it before the War'.[18] He was paid £150 for his trouble.[19]

Gibraltar, which during the American Revolutionary War had been under siege by the Spaniards for nearly four long years, was another cause for concern. British access and trade to the Mediterranean depended upon it. The prime minister took a personal interest in the design and building of small, sailing gunboats for the defence of the Rock. Captain Roger Curtis, who had been present at Gibraltar during the siege, was sent on a secret mission to the Baltic at Treasury expense to obtain the best gunboat design from the Swedes, whose

* In the National Archives are 130 volumes of weekly naval and military intelligence reports between the 1780s and 1814 to the secretary of state for war. D'Auvergne also corresponded with the Home Office over distribution of money to French émigrés (TNA, WO 1 and HO 69).
† Through the 1790s she was still being paid an annual pension of £159 by the Admiralty 'for former services' (12 Nov. 1798, 12 Nov. 1799, NMM, NEP/3).

coasts were lined with inlets and small islands suitable for these small shallow-draught vessels, armed with a single large gun. He had discussions with the great naval architect Fredrik af Chapman, son of a British naval officer in the Swedish Navy, and admiral superintendent at Karlskrona Dockyard, then at the height of his prestige. Curtis brought back gunboat plans and in November 1787 these were laid before Pitt, several gunboats were built at Deptford Dockyard, and trials took place during the next year.[20] The defence of Gibraltar was never to be a problem in the coming wars.

A far bigger naval threat was posed by the French attempt at Cherbourg to build breakwaters to establish a safe anchorage for their fleet in the Channel. Had it succeeded, the danger to Britain in the Western Approaches would have been increased radically. The geography of the south coast of England had given the British the advantage in the Channel, because the naval bases at Portsmouth and Plymouth were accessible in most winds, approached by the Solent and Plymouth Sound, even though they were tricky to leave in strong south-westerlies. In addition, Torbay was a safe fleet anchorage, except in strong east and south-easterly winds. The French Fleet, on the other hand, could rendezvous only at Brest, facing west into the Atlantic, and thus could not leave in the prevailing westerly or south-westerly wind. The new harbour at Cherbourg would have been north-facing, enabling warships to use a south-westerly wind for a sudden descent on the British coast, while the same wind would have made it difficult for the British Fleet to get out of harbour.

However, French engineers faced what were to prove insuperable difficulties. Before the advent of steam power, which enabled the moving of rocks of greater size and the fixing of thicker and stronger piers, building a new harbour with only wind- and manpower was a difficult, often impossible, undertaking. The wooden cones with rocks inside them that provided the foundation of the piers needed to be strong enough to withstand fierce Channel tides and northerly winter gales. Work on new breakwaters at Cherbourg began soon after the end of the American Revolutionary War in 1783, and the first large 'cone' was sunk in June 1784. Ninety were planned. To emphasize the importance of the project, the site was visited in 1786 by Louis XVI.[21]

British interest in the project unsurprisingly extended across several government departments. When the negotiators for a proposed commercial treaty travelled to Paris in 1786, the foreign secretary wrote to the chief negotiator that, although the 'Government is already in possession of many particulars respecting the nature and progress of the works at Cherbourg, I shall very thankfully receive any additional information.'[22] D'Auvergne sent in regular reports to Lord Howe at the Admiralty, as did the young Captain Sidney Smith, who was travelling in France.[23] A senior naval captain and MP for Plymouth, John Macbride, also spent a day on the site in August 1787, reporting to Middleton that thirteen cones were in place and that five more were on the stocks. Macbride was impressed with progress, which he attributed to 'near about ten thousand men at work ... between four and five hundred stone lighters are constantly at work.' One French 64-gun ship had passed the winter there and had found it a good roadstead. The inner basin and outer fortifications had been improved. 'On the whole,' Macbride concluded, 'it is a wonderful undertaking; in my opinion it will answer.'[24]

Had further progress been made, the outcome would have been serious, but the winter gales of 1788 destroyed the timber work of the westward cones. Howe had always held that it would fail. He wrote to Roger Curtis: 'I shall have much satisfaction in ... disproving the evidence in favour of the undertaking.'[25] The French did not give up easily, however, and were still working on the project in December 1789. In late May, Captain Sir Andrew Snape Douglas, commanding the *Southampton* frigate, anchored by the breakwater. He reported in June 1789 to Lord Hood, commander-in-chief at Portsmouth, that three French regiments, 600 seamen and 'a considerable body of artificers' were still at Cherbourg, and he reckoned that the breakwater would be finished to the low-water mark by the end of the year:

> With regard to the success of the Digue [breakwater] and its standing to the end of time, I have as little doubt as I had at first I walked upon it, and could easily perceive that the stones were not at all moved or incommoded by the Sea, and it is so clear and well shaped on the inside that a ship of three Decks might lay alongside of it afloat. I have little doubt of Cherbourg becoming a place of refuge for an inferior fleet or a place of rendezvous to prepare an attack upon this Country if the French should ever be in a position to do so.[26]

With their state finances rapidly weakening, however, the French abandoned the project for many years at the end of 1789.[27]

In 1787 the nature of the peace changed when Pitt's government experienced its first diplomatic crisis. Hitherto Pitt had taken little interest in the Continent, concentrating on tax reform and government efficiencies.[28] A Dutch political crisis provided Pitt with his first foreign test. Though the Netherlands was a shadow of the power of a hundred years earlier, its strategic position and trade links, particularly in the East Indies, meant that nations would fight to ensure it did not fall under the influence of an unfriendly power. Internal politics consisted mainly of hostilities between the Orangeists, led by the stadtholder, and the Patriot Party, which had republican leanings. The former were supported by Britain and several of the Northern Powers, including Prussia, for the sister of King Frederick William II was married to the stadtholder. Tension escalated when the Princess of Orange was captured and held prisoner by the Patriot Party. The courts of Europe were shocked by the insult to a sovereign power. It was a precursor to the violence soon to erupt in France. Encouraged by Britain, the Prussians began to mobilize their army through the summer of 1787.[29] The French started to make preparations for war.

British officials naturally wanted to find out as much as they could about how the French were deploying their forces. In the late summer of 1787 Nepean twice sent an agent over to Dunkirk and Gravelines, and paid for several reports from observers at Brest and Toulon through the summer and autumn. Payments were also made to the master of a merchant ship from Sandwich in Kent for 'watching the motions of the French'.[30] All these reports can only have demonstrated how little the French were mobilizing their navy. But on 9 September intelligence was received in the Admiralty that French troops were preparing to embark in Dunkirk, Calais and Boulogne and to sail for the coast of Holland.* By now the Prussian Army was on the borders

---

* The French were also trying to discover how the British were reacting. At the end of Oct., Howe wrote to Hood at Portsmouth, warning him of two French agents who had reportedly landed on the Isle of Wight and who were expected to make their way to Portsmouth via Southampton (31 Oct.1787, NMM, Hood Papers, HOO/2/176).

of the Republic of the United Provinces, waiting to move, and it invaded on the expiration of its ultimatum on 13 September.

Only then did Pitt decide to act. On 19 September 1787 the government ordered twenty-seven ships of the line into commission.[31] In determining what steps to take next, Pitt did not restrict himself to advice from cabinet. On 1 October 1787 he called a typically informal meeting at Downing Street, writing a note to Admiral Lord Hood, his cousin and at that time commander-in-chief at Portsmouth: 'If you should have no particular engagement I should be much obliged to you if you could dine here today. Our Party is formed for the purpose of talking over operations abroad, in case they should soon become necessary.'[32] At the Admiralty Office in Whitehall, on 9 October, Pitt, Howe, the master-general of the Ordnance, the duke of Richmond and the lord chancellor, Lord Thurlow, agreed that Howe should issue orders to commanders of warships in the Channel to intercept French ships, 'and if he finds them steering towards that coast to do his utmost to take or destroy them'.[33]

Pitt was able to take a tough line with confidence, knowing how weak the French were financially.* Faced with a Prussian army already in Holland and with the British naval mobilization, on 27 October France backed down and signed a declaration stating that it would cease interfering with internal Dutch politics. Both Britain and France agreed to place their navies on a peace establishment at the level of 1 January 1787.[34] For France, this was a humiliating loss of face, and Vergennes's plans to build up French power and prestige were thwarted. When the crisis was over, Charles James Fox, Pitt's great parliamentary opponent, and who at this time was no friend to France, declared in the Commons that Britain should improve its 'marine, cherish and preserve it and all that belonged to that favourite service, and we might then consider the ambition of the House of Bourbon, its imbecility, or its power, as matters of equally trifling consideration'.[35]

---

* On 19 Aug. Pitt had attended a dinner party attended by Charles-Alexandre de Calonne, a former French minister, who had tried and failed to reform French government finances. He had fallen foul of the French *parlement* and was now seeking refuge in England. No better briefing on the weaknesses of French finances could have been had (Black, *British Foreign Policy*, p. 147).

The government ordered the British Fleet to be demobilized at the end of 1787, but, as usual through the periods of peace in the eighteenth century, Britain kept a considerable number of ships at sea, unlike any other European country. By mid 1788, 111 ships were in commission, manned by 18,243 seamen, with half a dozen ships of the line, acting as guard ships, at Portsmouth and at Plymouth, and a smaller number performing a similar duty at the mouth of the Thames. Smaller vessels cruised at Jamaica, the Leewards, Nova Scotia, the Mediterranean and Newfoundland, protecting British trade.[36] The 'First Fleet' voyaged to New South Wales. Despite inevitable wear and tear on the ships at sea, British officers and seamen (unlike the French) kept up their seamanship skills and ensured a steady flow of intelligence. For instance, in July 1788 Captain Henry Warre, commanding the sloop *Kingfisher* in Toulon, sent a detailed report to Philip Stephens, the secretary of the Admiralty, on the state of the French ships there. His visit included the usual elaborate courtesies between officers and gentlemen of the *ancien régime*. 'The Compte D'Albert, the "commandant marines",' he reported, 'was exceedingly obliging, and seemed to regret His Majesty's ships did not often visit Toulon, and expressed himself sorry his Orders were positive to prevent all Englishmen *whatever* from viewing the dockyard. Any other foreigners are permitted to see it.'[37] Warre, however, furnished Stephens with a detailed list of the French ships, including whether or not they were copper or iron bolted, and estimated completion dates for those being built, implying that the commandant had given him the information.

As revolutionary events unfolded across the Channel, Nepean's internal domestic surveillance began to feature in the Home Office secret service accounts. An entry appears in February 1788 for four guineas to be paid, as a counter-espionage measure, to 'Capt. Collett who is employed by the French Minister in obtaining accounts from time to time of the state of Equipments at Portsmouth and Chatham to induce him to discover such other persons as are employed in the same way'.[38] The Russian ambassador in London was watched because he 'and his attendants ... were concerned in enticing seamen into the Russian service'. Irishmen with suspected contacts with France were also followed.[39]

In late 1788, the government also used its intelligence machine to spy upon Opposition politicians at the time of the Regency crisis, when the king's illness (porphyria) appeared to be a permanent condition. The prospect of the prince of Wales as regent replacing the monarch seemed very real. Such an occurrence would bring the Prince's friends in Opposition to power and Pitt needed to know who was talking to the leaders of the Opposition. Accordingly, two men were employed by a Home Office agent, William Clarke, who had been instructed by Nepean to watch those 'who frequented the houses of the Duke of Portland and Mr Sheridan'. Portland had already briefly been prime minister and within five years would be home secretary in Pitt's coalition government. Richard Brinsley Sheridan, MP for Stafford, was another prominent Whig, whose oratory was much feared by the government although his overall political contribution was to be slight. The only government post he occupied in a long political career was as treasurer of the navy, appointed by the Whigs when they briefly came to power in 1806.[40] He was a witty, hard-drinking and erratic Irishman, perpetually on the brink of bankruptcy, who juggled the careers of dramatist, theatre manager and politician over thirty years, and was known as the 'King of Drury Lane'. On 6 December 1788, the two men employed by Clarke followed Sheridan all day around London, when he visited, among others, Josiah Wedgwood, the duke of Devonshire, Charles James Fox and Brooks's, the club at the centre of Whig politics. Sheridan's followers finally left off the chase at 1.30 in the morning when their quarry was at Mrs Fitzherbert's, in the company of the prince of Wales, the duke of York and the duke of Queensberry.[41] The use of Home Office domestic surveillance was to be put to more justifiable use in the years ahead, when it was directed against those British subjects with extreme radical and violent agendas and French émigrés with doubtful sympathies, and was to become a central feature of the intelligence war.

Another foreign crisis, completely unanticipated, hit Whitehall in January 1790, when news came that the Spanish had seized two merchant ships in Nootka Sound, to the west of what is now Vancouver Island, and had imprisoned and ill-treated the crew, an action Spain justified by claiming the whole of the Pacific as its own. At first Pitt was inclined to ignore the incident, but when the owner of one of the ships, John Meares, returned to London in April there was an outcry. British merchants had been trying to penetrate the Pacific since the late seventeenth century, and the trading community had long harboured a strong resentment of a palpably weakened Spain and its supposed monopoly of the South American and Pacific markets. Pitt believed that access to the Pacific was worth fighting for, and he knew that the British Navy, if well deployed, could not be withstood by the Spaniards. Spain's stance was based upon what it saw as British aggression; but success against Britain's superior forces would depend upon its Bourbon ally, France, and the French were now badly divided and very disorganized. After 1786 the French Navy had been increasingly debilitated by a lack of money, which eventually led to strikes by unpaid dock workers at Brest and Toulon in 1789, and unfinished and poorly maintained ships.[42] In the same year radical elements in Toulon, aligning themselves with the Jacobins in Paris, seized power in the town. In 1790 the Constituent Assembly rashly adopted a new and harsher penal code for French seamen; the French Atlantic Fleet at Brest mutinied, and unrest spread to the dockyard and town.[43]

British ministers felt a decision to challenge the Spanish was a risk worth taking. Parliamentary opinion was behind them. Scouting vessels were immediately sent to watch the French and Spanish naval bases: the 36-gun *Melampus* was positioned off Brest; the sloops *Zebra* and *Fury* off Cádiz and Ferrol; and *Hound* was sent to watch the Swedish Fleet in the Baltic.[44] At the same time, Pitt spoke in the House for the British right to trade in the Pacific, maintaining that the wider principles of access to it were now at stake. At the beginning of May 1790 the cabinet ordered the mobilization of the fleet, to be commanded by Lord Howe, and a press for seamen was authorized. The mobilizations in both countries continued through the middle of 1790. Pitt's plan was to threaten Spanish ports with a powerful Channel Fleet and, using the sea control that this afforded, transport troops to the West Indies, where they would both defend the British West Indies and, if necessary, attack Spanish settlements. Plans to foment rebellion in the Spanish colonies had been in existence since the 1740s but had never been implemented; but the idea of dissolving the control of Old Spain was revived by the presence in London of Francisco de Miranda, who twenty-five years later was to play a part in the founding of Venezuela, the Latin American republic. Although Pitt had several fruitless meetings with him, the idea of British help for liberating Spanish South American colonies was to recur during the Napoleonic War.[45] In May, France managed to order the mobilization of fourteen ships of the line in Brest and Toulon, but, because of the tangled state of French politics, unrest in their dockyards and lack of money, they were of no help to their ally. By contrast, forty British ships of the line were fitted out, and by the end of June twenty-five were at sea.[46] To match this, the French National Assembly voted in July to mobilize forty-five ships of the line, but, again, although the order went out from Paris, very little happened.[47]

In Spain, however, intelligence reports indicated that the armament was going well. Twenty-six ships of the line had been fitted out, though some assessments emphasized the lack of Spanish seamen. Anthony Merry, in temporary charge of the embassy in Madrid, reported that 'the quickness observed in arming here is much greater than it was expected the Spaniards could have been capable of.' Reports also came in of large purchases of salted provisions for the Spanish Fleet from as far away as Leghorn, and the British government had to take steps to prevent such shipments from Cork, which exported very large numbers of casks of salt beef and pork directly to Spain.[48]

On 4 July, Howe formally took command of the fleet at Spithead. On 30 July the cabinet, in order to intimidate Spain, ordered him to sail to Torbay, ready to get to sea and then cruise off Ushant. Meanwhile, the Spanish Fleet of twenty-six ships of the line had left Cádiz on 20 July, although it cruised in local waters to exercise the crews for some days. Howe put to sea on 14 August with thirty-one ships of the line and nine frigates. By the time he reached Ushant, the Spanish were off Finisterre.[49] Two potentially hostile fleets were cruising close to each other in the Western Approaches.

In late July the resolve of the Spanish had started to give way, and on 24 July they signed a declaration agreeing to reparations for the incident at Nootka, while leaving open the wider question of the rights of access to the Pacific.[50] The Spanish government informed the British that it was taking measures to discipline the Spanish officer who had seized the British ships in Nootka, but their requests for mutual disarming were refused by Pitt. Britain accepted the document without abandoning its claims on the Pacific. The Spanish did not give up, waiting to see if France would act on their behalf. But by the middle of 1790 the French Navy was paralysed and a mobilization against Britain was impossible, a situation well known to the British government.

Another diplomatic crisis was looming in the north, though it came to nothing. Pitt wished to warn Russia not to impose overwhelming terms on Sweden at the conclusion of the war between the two Baltic powers. In order to bring pressure to bear on Russia, Britain began to mobilize a second fleet. On 1 September 1790, Pitt ordered seventeen ships of the line to assemble under Lord Hood in the Downs, but a week later a despatch arrived in London from Stockholm announcing that a satisfactory Baltic peace had been achieved. The fifteen ships that had gathered in the Downs were ordered to Spithead, which they reached by 25 September, to await Howe's fleet. By October, the Navy Board and the dockyards had made ready no fewer than forty-three ships, and the Admiralty had ordered the raising of 55,000 men.[51] As Pitt and many others knew, neither the Spanish nor the French – in fact no other European power – could match either the speed of mobilization or a fleet of this strength.

On 9 October, with autumn storms increasing in frequency, Howe brought his fleet back to Spithead. He had previously sent a ship to Brest to check that the French were not commissioning their warships: it turned out that only one ship was anchored in the Brest Water outside the dockyard. After a month at sea, the Spanish Fleet returned to Cádiz. While conflict in European waters had been avoided, the British ships were still held in readiness. Preparations for an expedition to the West Indies had already been in hand, and on 6 October Rear-Admiral Samuel Cornish departed for Jamaica with six ships of the line and transports with troops for the garrison there, a significant force.

Pitt pressed home his advantage. On 13 October the British ambassador in Madrid presented an ultimatum to Spain, with orders to return to London within ten days – effectively a declaration of hostilities – if no reply was received. Under considerable pressure, the Spanish government agreed to almost all the British terms. The right of British traders to settle along the coast between Alaska and California and to fish in the Pacific was now established, long desired by merchants in

Britain, although the Spanish resisted the demand that merchants should be allowed to trade directly with Spanish America. The prime minister was informed of the capitulation on 4 November, and on 13 November the fleet was ordered to demobilize.[52] Pitt had won a considerable diplomatic victory, made possible by France's naval weakness and the rapid mobilization of the British Navy. He had gone a long way towards restoring British prestige in Europe, so badly shaken by the American Revolutionary War defeat in 1783.

The final mobilization of the ten years' peace, spurred by the Ochakov Crisis of 1791, was, by contrast, far from glorious for Pitt. The relatively easy successes in 1787 and 1790 had made him overconfident. The immediate cause of this complex dispute lay in Russian expansion to the south at the expense of Turkey. Both Austria and Prussia were concerned at Russian aggrandizement after its success against Sweden. Britain was also having difficulties in completing a commercial treaty with Russia: Catherine the Great's government was delaying agreement because of its suspicions of British diplomatic and naval intentions, particularly because of the alliance with Prussia that had come about during the Dutch Crisis of 1787.[53]

But Russia held all the cards in this dispute. As a self-sufficient Continental country it was not susceptible to British naval power, and the Russian Baltic Fleet would hardly come out of harbour to fight a superior British force. By contrast, Britain was dependent upon supplies of hardwoods, mast timber and hemp from the Baltic region in general, and from Russia in particular.[54] Such dependence upon Russia for naval stores, particularly mast timber and hemp, was increasing, and by the 1790s it was almost total.* A major factor in this complicated confrontation was thus the long-term British concern about the supply of vital war materials, one that had dominated the wartime

* In 1783 Britain imported over 11,000 great masts from the Baltic, of which 8,000 came from Russia. By 1793 this had fallen to 2,496, of which only 1,400 came from Russia, but wartime requirements over the next three years quadrupled demand, until in 1796 over 21,419 great masts were imported, 17,739 from Russia. The dependence on Russia for hemp was even greater: in 1793 Britain imported 27,000 tons of hemp and 10,000 tons of flax (Kaplan, *Russian Overseas Commerce*, pp. 216, 226–7).

strategy of British governments when dealing with the wider Baltic regions for most of the eighteenth century.[55] During the American Revolutionary War, the British Navy had been ruthless in capturing neutral shipping carrying these stores from the Baltic to its Continental enemies.* This British aggression had led to the 'Armed Neutrality' in 1780, when Russia, Sweden, Denmark and the Netherlands formed an alliance to protect their shipping; they stopped just short of hostilities, though the Dutch were forced into war against Britain, to their great cost.

Although in the two years following the end of the American Revolutionary War, Britain and France quickly replenished their dockyards, both nations were in search of new sources of supply. After 1783 the French developed alternative sources of timber from Cherson on the north shore of the Black Sea;[56] and they also came to an agreement with Sweden to secure timber from forests near Gothenburg for the use of the French Navy, an arrangement that resulted in the sale of the French West Indies island of St Barthélemy to the Swedes in 1784.[57]

Britain's search for other sources of naval stores was linked to wider considerations of the balance of power in Europe. Britain wanted a stronger Poland to counter Russian influence in Eastern Europe. One British diplomat stressed its importance to the foreign secretary in 1791: 'almost the whole commerce of the southern part of Poland, several articles of which, such as hemp, pitch, timber, etc., are of infinite consequence to a maritime power.'[58] Poland's borders at this time stretched far south to the western Ukraine, only a hundred miles from the mouth of the River Dniester on the Black Sea, and its trade depended on this and other rivers. Russia, however, had in 1788 captured from the Turks the fortress city of Ochakov, which dominated this area of the Black Sea coast.

Though encouraged by the Prussians and by Joseph Ewart, the envoy in Berlin, to take a more aggressive attitude to Russia, Pitt moved cautiously.[59] British diplomats tried to bring about an alliance with Turkey and Poland.[60] Again, a fleet was mobilized, and again Lord Hood was appointed to command. By the end of March 1791 thirty-three

---

* The French were forced in 1780 to invest in building a canal linking their northern rivers and the Seine to the Loire so that Baltic masts could reach Brest by some other way than the Channel route (Syrett, *European Waters*, pp. 126–7).

ships of the line were gathered under him in the Downs.[61] In late March the cabinet formed a plan to send fleets both to the Baltic and to the Black Sea to support the Turks, where Ochakov was to be attacked. But, beyond providing a naval presence in the Black Sea to put pressure on Russia, there was no clear objective.

At the end of March 1791 the matter had to be taken to the House of Commons so that money could be granted for further naval armament. The Opposition attacked the proposition thoroughly in both houses, arguing that the government had not justified the measures it was proposing. Although the ministry won the debate in the Commons, the government was shaken, and divisions appeared in the cabinet. Press attacks followed.[62] The Levant Company merchants, knowing the local conditions and the weather patterns, were against the plan of mobilization.[63] The argument dragged on through April and May, until the government finally backed down. By August a treaty between Russia and Turkey had been signed. Turkey remained vulnerable, and in the next four years Poland was to be partitioned twice.

Pitt had acted upon diplomatic advice alone; no one with naval experience had been available to him. Howe had gone three years before; Middleton had resigned the previous year; Hood was afloat. Instead, Pitt was advised by his brother, Lord Chatham, first lord of the Admiralty. A glimpse of the poor quality of Chatham's advice is afforded in the lame and contradictory letter about the Black Sea expedition that he wrote to Joseph Ewart at the end of May 1791, when the government had given up the idea of mobilization.

> The undertaking would be rather an arduous one, the navigation being so little known, and the prevalence of particular winds in the summer months, rendering the passage up the canal of Constantinople very precarious . . . I should see no objection as a military operation to this step . . . but . . . this plan has not been approved here from the consideration that the sailing of a squadron for the Black Sea would be considered, as tending to immediate hostility . . . and the old objection besides of expense recurs . . .[64]

This failure of foreign policy was quickly forgotten and overtaken by events in France during 1792. Pitt was still in a strong position. The British Channel Fleet was in a more or less continuous state of mobilization from 1790 to 1792; the French Fleet could not put to sea. The naval race had been lost by the French even before the worst excesses of the revolution took effect.[65]

By February 1792 Pitt felt he could reduce the Navy Estimates, the first time that he had done so since coming to office in 1783; yet even after some ships had been paid off, the navy remained in a state of readiness: 125 ships were still in commission between July and December 1792, manned by about 20,000 seamen.[66] Then, in April, war began on the Continent when France was invaded by Austria and Prussia. In September 1792 the French Revolutionary Army repulsed the Prussian Army at Valmy, and in November the Austrians at Jemappes, after which it occupied the Low Countries. The guillotining of Louis XVI on 21 January 1793 finally convinced Pitt that war between Britain and France was inevitable. Since British naval preparedness was far in advance of that of the French, the sooner it began the better, and on 1 February 1793 the prime minister manoeuvred the French into declaring war.[67]

When warned by Edmund Burke at a dinner party at Downing Street in September 1791 of the dangers to the old European order presented by the French Revolution, Pitt had replied, 'Never fear, Mr Burke: depend on it, we shall go on as we are until the Day of Judgement.'* The prime minister's ringing confidence was founded upon many years of work, and much expenditure of money, in putting Britain's navy on a strong footing.

---

* Witnessed by Henry Addington, Burke was reported to have replied, 'Very likely, Sir, it is the day of <u>no</u> judgement that I am afraid of' (Pellow, *Sidmouth*, Vol. I, p. 72; also quoted in Ehrman, *Younger Pitt*, Vol. II, p. 88; Mori, *Pitt and the French Revolution*, p. 101).

2

Pitt's Investment

1783–1793

Naval strength is not the growth of a day, nor is it possible to retain it, when once acquired, without the utmost difficulty, and the most unwearied attention. The English have proved by their conduct, for almost two centuries, the firmness and steadiness of their naval character. Whereas the maritime enthusiasm of the French has only occasionally taken place, and does not seem consistent with the bent and genius of the people.

– Sir John Sinclair, Thoughts on the Naval Strength of the British Empire (1782)

Pitt took over leadership of the country at a time of extreme political instability but also of rapidly growing economic strength. The population of Great Britain and Ireland increased from thirteen million in 1781 to fourteen and a half million in 1791, and to just under sixteen million by 1801.[1] Between 1783 and 1802 the British economy grew at an annual rate of very nearly 6 per cent, a greater pace than at any time during the previous century. Though the period of peace between the wars was a prosperous one for all Europe, other countries lagged well behind Britain's industrial and commercial development. The critical task for British politicians and administrators at this time was to translate this buoyant economy and newly created wealth into an efficient military machine, particularly the capital-intensive navy. What Pitt's government managed to achieve before war broke out in 1793 is the key to understanding how Britain survived to come through to eventual victory in 1815.

Since a large proportion of government income derived from customs duties, the health of overseas trade was prominent in the minds of government ministers, especially in relation to defence spending. Here Britain enjoyed the advantage of the largest merchant fleet in Europe, owning in 1786 over a quarter of the tonnage at 881,963 tons; the French came second, at just over a fifth, with 729,340 tons.[2] In 1780 about five or six million pounds of raw cotton were imported, mostly from the West Indies; during the following twenty years this figure multiplied more than eightfold, to over fifty million pounds. Exports of cotton goods were booming, and were to continue to increase after the start of the war in 1793: average earnings in the 1780s were £750,000; by the turn of the new century that figure was over £5 million, with growth continuing at the remarkable annual rate of 12.3 per cent until 1814.[3] Woollens earned the country £3.5 million a year. Fourteen million tons of iron and steel were exported; by the early years of the next century this had doubled.[4] Consistently the most important area of trade was northern Europe: the Netherlands, the German ports and the Baltic – with the last of particular significance, as it was the source of crucial strategic raw materials, such as timber, hemp and iron, as well as growing quantities of wheat. Exports to the area were increasing steadily through the 1780s and 1790s and were eclipsing every other trading region in the world.[5]

Exports of textiles and manufactured goods to North America and the West Indies, in return for cotton and sugar, was another pillar of this expansion, though the trade conducted by the East India Company ships was also important (they took the same cargoes, as well as munitions and ordnance for the Company's armies, and brought back silk and other luxury goods, tea, specie and, vitally, saltpetre from India for the manufacture of gunpowder). The West Indies produced sugar and other tropical products, consumed domestically; but the French held the lead in the West Indies sugar trade and profited from the re-export of sugar to the rest of Europe. Production in St Dominique (now Haiti) exceeded that of Jamaica and the other British islands, and in the 1780s made the merchants of Bordeaux, Nantes, La Rochelle and Marseilles very rich. At the end of the 1780s the sugar exports of St Dominique were more valuable than the total exports of the newly formed United States, but by then the French economy was so dependent upon the West Indies trade in sugar and coffee that when a slave revolt broke out in St Dominique in 1791, it was a major financial blow to France.[6] Nor had the victory of French and American arms in the American Revolutionary War translated into an increase in other trade between the allies across the North Atlantic, for the higher quality and lower cost of Britain's manufactures comprehensively, and remarkably quickly, re-established it in the export trade to its former colonies. For the four years between 1786 and 1789, trade between Britain and the United States was worth £2,567,000, whereas that between France and its former ally was worth only £56,000.[7] The French also failed to capitalize on the potential for the procurement of naval stores from the United States, for French naval shipwrights resisted pressure from their ministers to use North American live oak.[8]

Britain had the great advantage of being able to draw on the strength and innovations of private industry which benefited from government departments awarding contracts to industrialists and businessmen. By the 1790s, the state victualling and ordnance yards and dockyards alone had nowhere near enough capacity to achieve the increased levels of industrial production needed for prolonged war. Longer lines of responsibility threaded their way from the Whitehall offices, through officials in the state yards and out into the private sector. Much of the business in government offices involved drawing up contracts and overseeing the tendering process, while maintaining quality control over manufactured goods or primary foodstuffs delivered by contractors into the state yards. It took time to decide, when prices were fluctuating, whether to vary the terms of contracts, usually upwards, with merchants who were trading or with industrialists who were manufacturing goods. The government obtained advantages from its dealings with contractors: it needed the market expertise and flexibility provided by merchants and agents, and it profited from the innovations of private manufacturers, who were, in general, more creative than their counterparts in the state establishments.

Every sort of commodity and service was obtained for the state through contracts, which enabled Britain to accelerate production of shipbuilding, armaments, munitions, civil engineering, fortifications, army supplies and foodstuffs. With ships built of oak with a limited life, the navy's warship construction had to be continual to keep up the fleet numbers; and, in order to achieve this, it was necessary to engage the building slips and shipwrights of private shipbuilders. Once the war had started, the royal dockyards did not have the capacity to produce enough new ships, other than those of 90- and 100-guns, and had to concentrate upon refitting and repairing an ever-growing fleet (although far more ships were built by the royal dockyards after 1803 than in the French Revolutionary War). The Ordnance depended entirely upon contractors for its small arms and cannon. Army barracks had to be built and maintained, while uniforms, horses, forage and all sorts of supplies had to be procured. The Victualling Board needed fresh provisions, cattle, flour and biscuit and many other foodstuffs: between 1793 and 1815 the Board signed an estimated 10,000 contracts for every sort of provision, with over 1,000 contractors, from merchants to farmers, often men of no great wealth.[9]

An example of how closely the state and individuals worked together is provided by John Trotter, a contractor who had started in the American Revolutionary War by supplying the army with bedding.[10] At the end of the war in 1783 he persuaded the army, which was as usual looking for immediate economies, not to auction surplus equipment; he then purchased and warehoused every sort of item, which he was able to deliver back to government immediately when war broke out. By taking risks of this kind, his business flourished over the years, not least because of the bureaucratic rivalries between the War Office and the Office of Ordnance.* By 1807 Trotter was controlling 107 depots, and in the following year, most unusually, he was formally brought into government as storekeeper-general.[11]

---

* Trotter introduced the bell tent to the army, replacing the inferior ridge pole tent, although the new design was lampooned: 'But 'tis easier by far to compose and invent / By an English fireside than in Trotter's bell-tent' (Ward, *Wellington's Headquarters*, p. 15, quoting Anon., *An Accurate and Impartial Narrative of the War* (1795)). John Trotter was considerably more honest than his brother Alexander, whose financial dealings, as we shall see, caused a major political storm early in the Napoleonic War.

By contrast, another businessman of the period, the shadowy Jean-Jacques de Beaune, took risks with government business on both sides of the Channel. In London, from the mid 1780s to 1791, he negotiated a series of loans to meet the prince of Wales's debts, secured on the prince's hereditary revenue. He then moved to Paris, where in 1792 he became the sole contractor to the French Army, supplying horses, drivers and equipment. In the hysterical atmosphere of Paris under threat, he was accused of making excessive profits, arrested and guillotined in 1793.[12] After this the French turned away from putting out army supply contracts and opted instead for state control.

The tax revenues of the burgeoning British economy began to swell. Pitt steered measures through parliament that increased duties on luxury goods but cut those on tea so dramatically that smuggling it became unprofitable. He revived Walpole's idea of a 'sinking fund' of surplus revenue that would go towards redeeming the national debt, which had grown by 1783 to £243 million, held in government loan stock. Thus, every year from 1786 Pitt allotted £1 million to the sinking fund, with £1.2 million added from 1792. The fund was administered by independent commissioners, and legislation was put in place to protect it from raids by the Treasury.[13]

The prime minister also brought efficiency measures to both government and private business by simplifying taxes. He moved the collection of some taxes from the overworked Stamps and Excise Office to the Taxes Board. In an impressive exercise in simplification, the tangled and extensive customs duties were codified in the Consolidation Act of 1787, with widespread political approval. In achieving these improvements, Pitt had the assistance of officials such as William Lowndes, whose grasp of fiscal complexities helped him push complicated legislation through the Commons. As a result of this, and of the expanding economy, excise revenue increased by 50 per cent between 1782 and 1796, while the costs of collection fell.[14]

The machinery of government also needed reform, as demonstrated by the findings of two parliamentary enquiries. In 1780 Lord North had been forced to appoint a Committee on Public Accounts, which reported on the activities of government departments up to 1787. It found widespread sinecures held by officials and that some departments were totally inefficient. It proposed a radically new philosophy for government administration: that those holding government posts were there to serve the members of the public and should not exploit them for personal profit. Pitt agreed with the reforming principles of the commissioners appointed to the Committee on Public Accounts, as described in their *Seventh Report* of 1782: officeholders must 'be made into servants of the state and, through the state, of the public'; and a person in office 'ought not to be permitted . . . to carve out for himself an interest in the Execution of a public Trust'. But Pitt made sure such principles were never debated in the House.[15]

Pitt appointed the Commission on Fees, which completed its *First Report* in 1786, examined in detail the system of payment of government officials, and found an illogical and inefficient bureaucracy, staffed by officials on small salaries, whose incomes were swollen by the payment of 'Fees, Gratuities, Perquisites and Emoluments' paid by contractors, army and naval officers, and other interested members of the public. It, too, recommended far-reaching changes in the salary structure.* Though these ideas took root only slowly, they established themselves after 1800 as ground rules of the first importance for government administration.

Pitt's reputation as an honest man was unassailable, but the perceived greed of his followers gave the Opposition a stick with which to beat his government. Thus, long-term suspicions were held about the power of Henry Dundas, who controlled thirty-six parliamentary seats in Scotland and held the post of president of the India Board of Control from 1793 to 1801, in addition to his role as home secretary from 1791 to 1794 and then secretary of state for war from 1794 to 1801.[16] Pitt disappointed many of his followers when he did not act on the recommendations of the Committee on Public Accounts, which reported between 1780 and 1787, and the reports of the Commission on Fees, Gratuities, Perquisites and Emoluments in the Public Offices, made between 1786 and 1788.† Rather than publicly agree with these principles, Pitt simply abolished unnecessary sinecure posts under his control, especially in the Customs Department, when they became

---

* See Chapter 4, Chapter 11 and Appendix 1.
† See Appendix 2 for details of this and other parliamentary commissions.

vacant through the death of the incumbent.* These redundant posts slowly diminished in number, and the great reforming promise of Pitt's early years as prime minister inched forward only slowly.[17] Another result of Pitt's postponement of reform, which became the big political issue after his death, was the continuing weaknesses in auditing and accounting across government spending departments. The commissions of Naval Revision and of Military Enquiry had to tackle this problem urgently when it became critical for the financial health of the country. 'Honest Billy's' combination of intellect, political intelligence and unworldliness was timely and priceless, but he left it to others to achieve real reform. 'The image of his dedication to probity and efficiency, rather than his actual accomplishments, was in fact Pitt's greatest contribution to the eventual modernization of British government administration.'[18]

A further priority was to bring about long-term improvements in Britain's military strength to prepare for any future conflict, a demonstrable need after the failures of the American Revolutionary War. Both the navy and the Ordnance required capital investment, and the prime minister invested handsomely, spending a total of £64,549,000 in the nine years between 1784 and 1792.† Naval expenditure was not slashed, as was usual after an eighteenth-century war, and increased from just under £7 million in 1783 to £9,447,000 in 1784 and £11,851,000 in 1785; this enabled Pitt to cut the navy debt that had accumulated since the American Revolutionary War, clearing all navy bills up to June 1783.[19]‡ The finance that Pitt made available

* An example of a sinecure post: the 'Collector Inwards for the Port of London, salary of £736.13s.4d., with additional fees of £1,094.16s.6d., Patent for Life, 21 April 1734': this was paid to the first earl of Liverpool, for political services ('Account of All Places for Life or Lives Whether Held by Patent or Otherwise', Parliamentary Register, Third Series, Vol. XVI (1802), p. 529).

† This figure is made up of £39,964,000 for the navy, £19,511,000 for the army and £5,074,000 for the Ordnance, averaging per year £7,172,000 for all three services. The contrast with the first full year of peace after the Seven Years War is marked. In 1784, £13,852,000 was expended, nearly three times the amount of £4,663,000 spent in 1764 (Mitchell and Deane, British Historical Statistics, p. 580).

‡ The cost of the Nootka Sound operation was over £3 million. Bills were presented to parliament on 3 Dec. 1790: £2,465,521 for the navy, £224,017 for the army and £496,715 for the Ordnance Department (Pimlott, 'Administration of the Army', p. 335, quoting Parliamentary Reports, Vol. XXVII, pp. 38–43).

had an immediate impact. The number of dockyard workers was retained at wartime levels, avoiding the usual post-war wholesale discharge of a large proportion of the labour force. The workers were used immediately to dock and repair the existing fleet. Here Britain had a considerable advantage over its Continental rivals. At the end of the American Revolutionary War in 1783, a remarkable total of thirty-seven ships of the line were either building or on the stocks waiting to be launched, most of them by private shipbuilders under Navy Board contract.* Between 1778 and 1783 Britain built 164 warships measuring 126,812 tons, three quarters of which were built in merchant yards (132 ships totalling 94,806 tons). At the height of the war, between 1780 and 1783, merchant yards built no fewer than nineteen 74-gun ships, to add to the nine built by the royal dockyards. This was the first time that private shipbuilders had decisively showed their collective industrial capacity, a development that was to be of even more importance in the following decades.[20] This new capacity enabled the royal dockyards to concentrate on building the 90- and 100-gun ships, which were too large for merchant yards, since they had to be built in a dock and floated out, rather than launched from a slip. By 1793 three first-rate ships had been built and two were on the stocks; six second-rate ships had been completed and five were under construction. A carefully planned maintenance programme was also put in hand, with a target of ten major repairs a year (although this was exceeded). During the ten years of peace, 138 ships of the line were built or given major repairs. By the early 1790s the fleet was in good order, which enormously relieved the pressure on the dockyards in the early years of the French Revolutionary War.

* The Thames was hardly large enough for all these activities. The young naval captain Sidney Smith wrote in his diary on 26 Nov. 1787: 'Attracted to Rotherhithe by a ship launch . . . the Captain, 74 guns, from Limehouse and a large East India ship [the Triton] immediately after from the opposite side of the River near Cuckold's Point – much confusion among the shipping occasioned by a strong easterly wind bringing up some hundreds of accumulated coasting trade, the channel fairly blocked from side to side and much damage done to hulls and rigging as the plot thickened with strong breeze and flood tide. The Captain, in going off, ran down a wherry of gaping spectators – a collier in the group nearly dismasted and a man chucked by the fall of a topmast, upon which he was, over several sail of vessels into the water' (Pocock, Sir Sidney Smith, p. 11).

The royal dockyards, however, needed to be overhauled. Well before peace was signed in March 1783, Middleton, the comptroller of the navy, was in action and tightening control. The dockyards had been governed by a system of standing orders since 1660, but by this point so many had been issued that they were overcomplicated and often contradictory. Middleton simplified and clarified them, and during 1783 the Navy Board issued 255 revised standing orders to the dockyards, and in the following year 96.[21] These changes were accompanied by threats and sanctions to be applied in the event of shortcomings. Dockyard clerks were 'not to be promoted by rote but by ability'. Some at Plymouth were dismissed for embezzling coal, and in June 1783 the standing order that discharged them was ordered to be read out to clerks in all the yards, quarterdeck fashion: 'if there was trouble, clerks will be discharged without further ceremony.' Apprentices (and therefore the apprentices' wages) were taken away from more senior shipwrights in supervisory roles, and were awarded to working shipwrights, enabling the apprentices to be taught their trade properly. Information on workmen dismissed for embezzlement or similar misdemeanours was to be centralized in the Navy Office, and then re-circulated to other yards, so that a mechanism was in place that would stop offenders from entering another yard.[22]

Nobody could drive this amount of change through conservative institutions without attracting a great deal of unpopularity, and Middleton, knowing that he had the prime minister's support, made no attempt to avoid it. He was a complex mix of self-belief, ruthless ambition and evangelical righteousness, and he trusted no one to do a job as well as he could himself. These qualities were reinforced by an unusual degree of irritability, for he had gained a reputation for an ungovernable temper when serving at sea, which on at least two occasions involved violence upon crew members under his command.[23] He lacked standing with the sea officers because he had failed to distinguish himself before his long service ashore as an administrator.[24] Admiral Sir John Jervis complained tetchily of Middleton's 'cant, Imposture, loads of precedents, and scraps of stay Tape & Buckram' and 'the utmost extent of his abilities having gone no further than the forming of a swaddling system of morality for his ship's company'.[25]

He was no more popular with civilian administrators. The normally tolerant and mild George Marsh, clerk of the acts,* who had worked in the Navy Office since 1745, devoted very long passages of his diary to his frustrations with Middleton. Relations had been friendly for Middleton's first four years in office, but Marsh became disillusioned, as he noted in his journal on 30 May 1789, for Middleton 'made all the knowledge he got from others his own so that he was deemed by people in power the best and most able Commissioner of the Navy Board'; 'By his manner he appeared to be a religious, just man, but by his actions he proved himself the contrary . . . he was in general a deceitful, proud, despicable character. I must own his ungrateful and unchristian like conduct to me has occasioned me rather more uneasiness of mind, than I ever had before from any connections with public office.'[26]†

However, real progress was bedevilled by the poor working relationship between the Admiralty and Navy offices. A board of seven commissioners oversaw the Admiralty, headed by the first lord, and it was senior to the Navy Board that built and maintained the ships. Other subordinate boards included the Transport and the Sick and Hurt boards, while the Victualling Board provided food for the seamen, although in August 1793 it was made responsible for feeding not only the navy but also the army garrisons overseas.[27] Howe, the first lord of the Admiralty, and Middleton, the comptroller of the navy, at the head of the Navy Board, had always been at odds. The Navy Board had been established at least 200 years before the Admiralty and had long guarded jealously its status and expertise. For twelve years, from his appointment in 1778 until his resignation in 1790, Middleton dominated the Navy Board. Now a bitter struggle ensued between the occupants of these two powerful posts. Howe was even

---

* The title of the post was changed to the secretary of the Navy Board in 1796.

† Middleton was an early and fierce opponent of slavery and at his most active in the 1780s. In 1786 he and his wife persuaded Wilberforce to lead the attack on slavery. Middleton's house, Barham Court in Teston in Kent, became an important centre for the abolitionist movement. James Ramsay became Middleton's secretary, and in 1784 Ramsay published his first pamphlet attacking the slave trade. Other prominent members of the movement, including Thomas Clarkson, were brought together by the Middletons (Blake, *Evangelicals in the Navy*, pp. 63–7; Hague, *Wilberforce*, pp. 112–13).

more complex than Middleton, regarding the junior officer as an upstart, and was devoid of the political arts, cautious and unpopular with his fellow naval officers, and pilloried in the press. But the main bar to success was his inability to express himself.* After a wary start on his appointment in 1783, the first lord soon offended Middleton. The comptroller had always been consulted on senior appointments, but Howe soon appointed an assistant surveyor without reference to Middleton. The first lord then made a surprise dockyard inspection in September 1784, countermanded Middleton's orders and made criticisms that he sent on to Pitt. Completed warships that the comptroller had carefully kept on their slips, covered by a timber roof, so that their condition would not deteriorate, were ordered to be launched immediately.[28] This was a direct invasion of Middleton's territory and relations worsened.

In spite of these damaging bureaucratic battles, Middleton continued with the reform of the working conditions and payment of shipwrights, caulkers, smiths and many other trades in the dockyards. Schemes of task and job work, intended to provide incentives, rather than payment by the day, which had started in the 1770s, were firmly established throughout the six yards (though Plymouth resisted until 1788).[29] The comptroller also attempted to stop the age-old abuse of 'chips', pieces of wood discarded after work had been completed on the main timbers of a ship, which by custom the members of the workforce were allowed to take out of the yard. As the order pointed out, workmen spent time making up bundles and wasted a great deal of material, and it encouraged pilfering of other materials such as iron nails or pieces of copper. Only shipwrights and house carpenters, 'and to such of them only employed on axe work', were now allowed to carry waste timber out of the yard. Further, the yard officers were ordered

> to suffer no Person to pass out of the Dock Gates with Great Coats, large trousers or any other dress that may conceal stores of any kind.

---

* To junior officers Howe appeared mysterious and sphinx-like. In a letter of 28 Dec. 1794, Fanny Nelson wrote to her husband after she had met Howe, describing him as 'the most silent man I ever knew'. In June the next year, Nelson wrote back, telling her that a letter he had received from Howe was 'a jumble of nonsense'. Howe is still a mystery, for he destroyed all his personal papers at the end of his life (Knight, 'Howe', p. 280).

No person is to be suffered to work in Great Coats at any time over any account. No trousers are to be used by the Labourers employed in the Storehouses and if anyone persists in such a custom he will be discharged the yard.[30]

There were, however, limits to what the comptroller could achieve, in respect of this order at least, and he had to report failure to the Admiralty: the workforce at Portsmouth 'in a body refused complying with it ... and their determination seemed preconcerted as the officers could not discover any individual more active than the rest.'[31] Chips were eventually commuted to an increase in wages in 1801.[32]

Middleton also reorganized the administration of the immense quantities of naval stores in the dockyards. He issued detailed instructions about 'a great variety of species', according to Charles Derrick, a clerk in the Navy Office and very much one of Middleton's men, 'for the general magazines, at each of the Dockyards, and also at the several other Naval Stations, both at home and abroad. This was truly an original and great plan, no idea of the kind having probably been ever entertained at any former period.'[33] To speed mobilization, the ready-use stores were rearranged so that all the equipment for a particular ship was in one place in the storehouses, rather than being grouped by type.[34] Previous failures to maintain ships 'in ordinary' – those dismantled and moored out in the harbours or rivers – were tackled by the appointment of 'Superintending Masters' and the issue of new orders on the routine to be followed. Improved double moorings were laid for the ships. Stricter financial controls and accounting systems were set up. Estimates were expected to mean something. Middleton sent a standing order to the dockyards in 1784:

You are on the whole to observe that no excuse will be received for exceeding the Annual Grants, and no support will be given to any officer who attempts it ... we find the sums expended under the head of Ordinary in the last year to have exceeded the grants very considerably, by which inattention, this Board has been led into mistakes concerning the Service, the House of Commons and the Admiralty have been misinformed, and the public drawn in Expenses for which no provision has been made.[35]

Middleton battled for years to get the dockyard accounting punctual and accurate. In 1787 the Navy Board had to admonish the yard officers because 'it had yet to receive their reports on stores issued in 1784 and 1785, at which we are much displeased.'[36]

Middleton threw himself into another great work: the development of the docks and buildings in the royal dockyards. This was not an easy task, because the great cost of building the new docks at Portsmouth and Plymouth led to hesitation and delay, different plans being drawn up in 1785, 1786 and 1789 respectively. By the closing years of the eighteenth century the docks were hemmed in by buildings and workshops, for the dockyards had developed piecemeal over many years, and none, with the exception of Plymouth, was ideally laid out.[37] Nor were these his only problems, for the dockyards constituted a battleground between him and Howe. The comptroller lost the battle to continue to employ an expert builder, John Marquand, to supervise building contractors in the yard. The shipwright officers objected to this job being taken away from them, and Howe backed them: Marquand was dismissed.[38]

The dockyard-building projects that Middleton saw to completion are still in evidence today. Prompted by near-catastrophic fires at Portsmouth in the American Revolutionary War, and the poor condition of the rigging- and rope-houses at Chatham, the three great storehouses at Portsmouth were built in the 1780s. A new 1,000-foot-long rope-house was constructed at Chatham. Here the rope-makers twisted and tarred the yarn, and laid cables of up to 900 feet, the length needed to hold the anchor of a ship of the line. This impressive building served the navy until it left Chatham in 1984, and rope is still made there today. At Plymouth the most northerly dock was built in the 1780s, 250 foot long and with 27-foot clearance on the sill of the gate.* Even more complex was the rebuilding of the wet and dry docks at Portsmouth, which were to prove critical in the coming conflict (warships were floated into the wet dock, which was then drained so that essential maintenance on ships' hulls could be completed).[39] During the American Revolutionary War, the largest ships of the line

---

* It was lengthened further by 10 feet and was able to take the huge *Commerce de Marseilles*, which was captured at Toulon in 1793. The *Naval Chronicle* described it as 'the largest dock in the Universe' (Coad, 'Plymouth Dockyard', p. 195).

could be docked at Portsmouth only at spring tides, which occur every fortnight, and this had led to severe delays in refitting. Such was the wear and tear on these docks that by the end of the war in 1783 only one of the five was in working condition.[40] Further, the size of ships of the line had steadily increased through the century, resulting in deeper draughts: by this time a first-rate ship had a draught of about 22 feet, and a 74-gun ship about 20 feet, while some of the French and Spanish prizes captured after 1793 were even deeper.[41] Without the dockyard capacity to maintain and refit warships of all sizes, and to do so continuously, British naval power would have been severely curtailed.

The most important new dockyard buildings and docks were undertaken by the long-established partnership of the contractors James Templar and Thomas Parlby, who had been responsible for the major civil engineering works at Portsmouth and Plymouth since the expansion of the yards during the Seven Years War and whose first major contract had been for the Royal Naval Hospital at Plymouth as long ago as 1758. Both had humble beginnings: Templar had been a house carpenter and Parlby a stonemason. Generally, Templar supervised the construction of buildings and Parlby the docks, which were built in Portland stone and granite. The two partners developed formidable management skills, controlling a large workforce on several sites. The partnership was at its most productive at the time of the American Revolutionary War, during which they built up their own quarries, lime kilns, regional depots and transport system. Templar died in 1782, but Parlby, with some of the next generation of the family, continued to manage large projects during the 1780s, and the contract for the double dock at Portsmouth was awarded to him in 1787.[42]

These complex works, incorporating a large wet dock linked to four dry docks, went forward slowly, and were modified by Samuel Bentham in 1796. For the first time docking a ship of the line could be completed without the aid of spring high tides. At its completion in 1802 this system was the most modern in the world, with dock gates being replaced by a wooden, boat-like structure known as a caisson, hollow and watertight, which was floated across the mouth of the dock, then flooded and sunk and held in vertical grooves in the side of the dock. It thus kept water out of the dock, which was then pumped dry. Caissons may have been among the least acclaimed of Samuel Bentham's innovations, but they were one of the most important. By the 1840s they were made of iron and are still widely used today.[43] These four docks radically enlarged and speeded the maintenance capacity of the fleet. In 1793 the navy had fifteen single and double docks available in all six home dockyards; after 1801 it increased to nineteen single and three double docks. But the roots of the improvements to these crucial facilities lay in decisions taken and investments made many years before the outbreak of war.[44]

These pragmatic and practical developments were to prove of greater worth than the breathtaking schemes conceived by some Continental nations. The Swedes and the Russians, for instance, were developing plans for docks and basins at Karlskrona and Kronstadt respectively, which were huge, architecturally spectacular and had no chance whatsoever of being built: their size and cost were far beyond the resources of these states and their much less well-developed economies.[45] And the French dockyards were in a dismal state in comparison with their British counterparts. By the end of the decade not only were improvements and maintenance lacking, but they were so starved of funds that in October 1788 the authorities at Toulon took the desperate decision to close the gates of the dockyard for two days a week: only the discontent and violence among the workers there, facing economic deprivation from high bread prices, forced them to return to full working the following month.[46]

Important technological decisions were also taken by the navy on the copper sheathing that from 1778 had been fitted to all warships, and the advantages of the new sheathing were considerable. Ships' bottoms were kept clear of weed, enabling them to sail faster, giving British warships clear tactical advantages. It lessened the need for dockyard refits and thus reduced their time in port. It also provided protection from the *teredo navalis* worm, which had long ravaged ships' hulls in tropical waters and was now infesting those around the home naval ports. Risks had, however, been attached to the use of copper since experiments in the 1760s, when the corrosive effects of electrolytic action on the iron bolts that held the ships together could be clearly seen. Nothing was then known of the theory of electrolysis, or of how electricity was conducted by salt water between copper and iron.[47] The dockyards attempted to protect the heads of the iron bolts from the salt water by sealing them with tarred paper, but this turned out to be completely inadequate. Doubts began to surface about the whole process. Then in September 1782 four ships of the line returning from America foundered in a mid-Atlantic storm, with the loss of 3,500 lives.[48] Although nothing could be proved from the hulls of the ships, which were on the seabed, it was presumed that weakened bolts had given way. The Navy Board was forced to rethink.

The solution was provided by Thomas Williams, the principal government contractor and a well-capitalized industrialist, who possessed the metallurgical expertise that the government lacked.* In 1783 his technicians perfected a cold-rolled alloy bolt that was hard enough to withstand being driven by sledgehammers into a ship's hull, but was chemically similar to the sheathing, thus ensuring that the bolt would not waste.[49] Such an innovation could have been undertaken only by operating on a large scale, and coppering developments, as well as the supply of bolts, sheathing and nails, lay entirely in Williams's hands. During the 1780s he also had access to the supply of raw material, having gained control of the Parys and Mona mines in Anglesey. In addition to his factories in Birmingham, he owned several smelting works – his site at Ravenhead near St Helens in Lancashire was the one most involved in naval copper, where the braces and pintles that supported the rudder, and which could weigh up to a ton and three quarters, were cast in the new metal. The bolts were manufactured in Holywell on the banks of the Dee in a works powered mainly by large water wheels. The copper alloy was drawn through a number of grooved rollers that gradually diminished in size, so forming the bolt, which was then finished under an enormous tilt-hammer. An 8- or

---

* Thomas Williams (1737–1802) was a man of ruthless determination who dominated the copper industry. There was a widespread feeling, probably correct, that Williams held an unfair monopoly up to 1792, causing very high prices: he was an MP between 1790 and 1802, and took care to have himself appointed in 1799 to a select committee on the copper trade, which did not probe too deeply into his activities. When he died he left at least half a million pounds (Harris, *Copper King*, pp. xv–xvi, 108–36; Thorne, *House of Commons*, Vol. V, pp. 585–6).

10-foot bolt could be made perfectly round in a minute. Bolts for the larger ships could be 20 feet long. Operations such as these were at the very limits of pre-steam technology.[50]

After three years of debate by the Navy Board and the dockyard officers, in August 1786 the Admiralty finally ordered all guard ships (those warships permanently in commission, anchored at the naval bases) to be fastened with the new copper-alloy bolts, 'as fast as docks can be spared'.[51] Thenceforth every ship that came into dock had the new bolts and fittings driven into the hulls, a lengthy and costly operation that was largely complete by 1793. The new bolts were three times the cost of iron and the rebolting process cost £1,500 for each ship of the line, adding approximately 5 per cent to its total cost.[52] But the ships were now seaworthy.

However, it was impossible to keep the secrets of manufacture away from the French, whose constant efforts at industrial espionage in the British iron and textile industries were notable. In peacetime some contractors had little loyalty to the government. Before the American Revolutionary War, the coke-smelted iron process, pioneered by John Wilkinson at his works near Wrexham, had been exported to France by his brother William, who had set up the large cannon foundry at Nantes and then directed the building of the great coke-iron making plant at Le Creusot. Other industrialists were wary of having strangers in the factories, but clever ruses could get through slack security. Once the American Revolutionary War was over, the French government sent two artillery officers, de Givry and de Wendel, to look at areas of England that had achieved advances in munitions manufacture. They went to Williams's foundries in Cheshire and Lancashire, and then to Holywell to view the cold-rolled bolt forging process. De Wendel reported to his French masters that:

> we found that there was nothing difficult in getting a good view of English Manufactures, one needs to know the language with facility, not show any curiosity, and wait till the hour when punch is served to instruct oneself and acquire the confidence of the manufacturers and their foremen, one must avoid recommendations from Ministers and Lords which do little good and make contact with some of the principal industrialists who can open every door . . .[53]

The French thus learnt the coppering process. British expertise and production at its copper mines kept the country ahead of its rivals, but in the coming wars the clear advantage that had been enjoyed by copper-sheathed British warships in the American Revolutionary War disappeared.

Many other long-term worries about naval power exercised the minds of the Admiralty and the Navy Board. Quite apart from the vulnerability of supplies of hemp and mast timber from the Baltic, fears that the traditional supplies of British oak were running out had first occurred in the late 1760s.[54] By the 1780s the navy had difficulties in procuring the timber that it needed on the London market, challenged in particular by the East India Company's building of ever-larger ships. In March 1786 Middleton questioned the purveyor of Deptford Yard, Benjamin Slade: 'Why are the merchant yards plentifully supplied, while dockyards are so greatly distressed and the service much retarded?' Slade's six-page reply was a story of traditional practices, rigid naval pricing and the merchants' advantages with their access to ready money.[55] In 1792 Middleton presided over the Commission into the Administration of Woods and Forest, set up to investigate the reason for, and the extent of, the shortage of British oak. The commission found that timber prices had gone up, though not uniformly or disastrously; but, because opinion was divided as to the cause, the government took no action. Its report made the first official mention of the potential for the use of iron in the construction of wooden warships, a practice that the East India Company had already adopted. Nevertheless, the feeling persisted that the Company took a disproportionate share of scarce timber resources to build its ships.[56]

Progress in the maintenance of the fleet by the second half of 1785 can be measured, using evidence from the plethora of documents produced in reaction to criticisms made by Howe after his dockyard inspection. Pitt called for papers from Middleton and they arrived in quantity, together with a pronouncement from the comptroller:

Mr Pitt will observe, that the progress in bringing forward the fleet since the peace, and making provision for it against a future war has been very great, and that there is good reason to believe that by the end of 1786, there will be upwards of ninety sail of the line, including the present guard ships, fit for service, and as many frigates of twenty guns and upwards, exclusive of those now in commission.[57]

This was fair, although Middleton neglected to mention the very serious problem of the corrosion of the iron bolts. The dockyards received their first test in the successful mobilization of 1787 during the Dutch Crisis, when a large fleet was ready in a few weeks. George White, the veteran master shipwright at Portsmouth, wrote to Middleton 'to assure you ... that a more cheerful and Spirited Exertion was never shown by both Officers and men at this time to expedite the equipping of the Fleet'.[58] Middleton's dockyards passed muster because he had ensured that the machinery of naval maintenance had been thoroughly overhauled.

Tense personal relations were not limited at this time to the comptroller and the first lord of the Admiralty. In Somerset House, another of the subsidiary naval organizations, the Victualling Board oversaw the assembling and packing of provisions purchased under contract from merchants, agents and farmers, as well as baking bread and biscuit, and slaughtering cattle and pigs before salting the meat in casks. In England the main victualling yard was at Deptford, but substantial establishments were at Portsmouth, Plymouth, Dover and Deal, as well as all the major overseas bases, while there were depots at most ports.[59] This organization was also experiencing friction between its commissioners. This was chiefly caused by the case of Christopher Atkinson, a very large grain merchant and MP for Hedon in Yorkshire, who had been appointed during the American Revolutionary War by the Board as sole agent for the purchase of wheat for the navy from the markets. At first all went well, but as the war progressed Atkinson began to pad out his prices, telling the Board that he had purchased wheat at a higher price than he actually had. After a bitter row, the reformers at the Victualling Board eventually won the battle to prosecute Atkinson, by four votes to three, aided by the jealousy of other merchants at the London Corn Exchange. He was charged, went through the courts, and was given a year's prison sentence.[60] He had to stand in the pillory and was expelled from the

House of Commons. After another dispute in 1785 between the commissioners over a clerk who had divulged commercial confidences, a reforming Board member resigned in disgust when the Admiralty failed to support sanctions against the clerk.

From this point the Victualling Board slowly regained its reputation. The chief reformer was George Phillips Towry, who had started his career in the navy and been appointed as a Victualling commissioner in 1784. He had considerable success in stopping illegal payments to the clerks in the administration of contracts, and ensured that commissioners did not receive a premium from clerks as a condition of employment. Whenever a problem required the presence of a commissioner away from London, it was Towry who did the travelling.[61] This tough Scot, who was still at his post when he died in 1817 at the age of eighty-three, was one of the few exceptions to the dominance of young men in the British government and civil service.*

The Atkinson case fuelled public distrust of those who had made money from the American Revolutionary War. After the findings of the Committee on Public Accounts, which produced its reports between 1780 and 1787, transparency in government dealings was much debated, and Edmund Burke and others pressed for reform at every opportunity. One cause for public suspicion was that the Treasury had not openly tendered for contracts to supply the army, although it had done a reasonable job in administering them.[62] Another was the feeling that political influence was instrumental in gaining a contract. As a result, parliament passed Crewe's Act and Clerke's Act in 1782, which prohibited holders of government contracts from entering parliament. In general, these steps did help to restore confidence, although compromises were inevitably made. The Navy Board, for instance, allowed four MPs to transfer their contracts to silent partners. But the

* Towry was lucky as well as capable. Not only had he married into a well-connected naval family, which included a former secretary of the Admiralty, John Clevland. He also won a lottery prize of £20,000 (*Gazetteer and New Daily Advertiser*, 4 Dec. 1770). In 1789 Towry's daughter Anne, a great beauty, married, after three refusals, the ugly but talented barrister Edward Law (1750–1818). In 1802 Law, as first Baron Ellenborough, was made lord chief justice and a member of the cabinet, 1806–7. Their eldest son, also Edward (1790–1871), became the first Earl Ellenborough and governor-general of India.

owners of the great Crawley ironworks near Newcastle surrendered their government contracts so that one of their partners did not have to give up his seat.[63] By the 1790s, these safeguards had slipped, as most obviously demonstrated by the powerful and immensely rich contractor and MP Thomas Williams.

The last of the major departments with war responsibilities was the Ordnance Department. Both the navy and the Ordnance managed very large industrial concerns, staffed by thousands of employees, some of which were on distant stations; but their governing structures were quite different. The Board of Ordnance was a senior board, and most of its members were MPs, likening it to the Board of Admiralty; while the Navy Board, responsible for the dockyards and shipbuilding, was more junior, with only the senior member of the Board, the comptroller of the navy, representing the Board in parliament.* At the head of the Ordnance Department was the master-general, a member of the cabinet until June 1798.[64] The post did not have the seniority of the first lord of the Admiralty, who belonged to the inner group of cabinet ministers responsible for strategy and policy, and the master-general of the Ordnance was outside this inner circle. Thus the artillery and engineers under his command were sent to support army operations for which he was not politically responsible. A further complication for the navy was that the first lord wielded extensive naval patronage, appointing admirals to stations and captains to ships, some of whom were likely to attain great wealth through prize money. While the navy attracted political trouble, the Ordnance Department was remarkably free of it.

The master-general was always a senior serving army officer, and the Board of Ordnance, which reported to him, had to be able to run the rest of the department without him, for he might well be appointed to active service, as happened in the case of Cornwallis and Chatham. Indeed, there was a marked distance between the master-general and the Board. The Board ran the considerable business of manufacturing

---

* The nineteenth century would see the end of these dual responsibilities. The Navy Board was abolished in 1832 and the Admiralty took over its role. The post of master-general was abolished in 1855 and the army took over his powers and those of the Ordnance.

armaments for both the army and the navy, as well as overseeing the building of barracks and fortifications, work mostly done by contractors. Communication with the army was handled through the master-general, while the Board of Ordnance dealt directly with the navy. The Ordnance had its own devolved style, with a good deal of local autonomy, and less of its business was referred to London than in the case of the navy.[65]

The Board of Ordnance oversaw the manufacture of munitions of all kinds, including cannon, shot and gunpowder for both the army and the navy.* It employed good-sized industrial workforces in the gunpowder mills at Waltham Abbey and Faversham, at the gun wharves at all the home bases and in the powder hoys that delivered gunpowder to warships. Magazines stored gunpowder at Purfleet on the Thames, at Priddy's Hard on the Gosport side of Portsmouth Harbour and at Upnor Castle on the Medway, establishments that multiplied through the wars, with the number of old ships adapted as floating depots particularly increasing during the Napoleonic War.[66] At the Woolwich Warren, artificers and labourers manufactured brass ordnance, shot and small-arms ammunition, proofed the cannon received from contractors and loaded the ordnance transports. To their number should be added artillery personnel as well as convicts, who were housed in hulks moored in the Thames.[67] By 1805 the establishment was sufficiently significant to be called the Royal Arsenal, a change initiated by the king himself.†

The master-general commanded the country's fortifications and barrack building, together with the increasingly important mapping capacity of the Ordnance Survey. In 1784 the hard-working duke of Richmond was appointed to be master-general. Richmond's abrasive

---

* The number of guns supplied to the navy far outweighed those to the army. At Trafalgar the British ships of the line carried 2,148 cannon, while, at Waterloo, British artillery amounted to 204 guns, of a much smaller average calibre than those of the navy (Cole, *Arming the Navy*, p. 5).

† The *Gentleman's Magazine* reported that on 27 June 1805, during a royal visit, 'His Majesty noticed how little appropriate was the name to the place and suggested the propriety of changing it to that of *Arsenal*. The Master-General admitted the justice of the idea and instantly adopted it; henceforward, therefore, in compliment of His Majesty's suggestion, the Warren is to be called the *Royal Arsenal*' (quoted in Hogg, *Royal Arsenal*, Vol. I, pp. 522–3).

personality and unpopularity ensured not only that the separateness of his department was accentuated but also that his personal isolation grew.* His blatant appointments to Ordnance posts of family members and his neighbours who lived near his country seat at Goodwood in West Sussex offended public opinion, at a time when patronage and sinecures were beginning to be questioned. Lord Grenville observed that Richmond was 'ingenious and acute . . . and in diligence and perseverance rarely equalled' but 'In office, he laboured too much at detached objects and minute details, harassing to his inferiors and perplexing to himself.'[68] Richmond himself remarked ruefully to Edmund Burke: 'I pass in the world for very obstinate, wrong-headed and tenacious of my opinions.' He was indeed hot-tempered, inconsistent and quarrelsome: he fell out both with the duke of York and with Henry Dundas, and when in 1795 Pitt eventually ejected him from his post no one in government was sorry to see him go.[69]

Nevertheless, Richmond was a reforming master-general. From the time of his appointment to the department in 1784 he started to reorganize it, cutting staff and budgets.[70] Richmond first achieved a considerable improvement in fortifications. An immediate post-war priority was the defence of Plymouth, from which the civilian population had fled in panic at the approach of the combined French and Spanish fleets in the summer of 1779. Some improvements had been made during the American Revolutionary War, but in 1784 plans were made to fortify the dockyard 'against a regular siege'.[71] Accommodation was built in Fort Monkton at the entrance to Portsmouth Harbour. At the other end of the country a completely new fort was built at Fort Charlotte in the Shetland Islands, in response to the harassment of the north-west coast of Britain by American privateers during the war.[72]

However, Richmond's effort to build comprehensive land defences against French attack did not succeed, though he worked very hard to plan an effective scheme of fortifications along the southern coast of

---

* Richmond was also unpopular because of the source of his wealth, originally a grant made by Charles II to his grandfather, one of the king's many illegitimate children: a tax of a shilling on every cauldron of coal taken out of Newcastle. In 1800 Richmond commuted his coal duties to the government in return for an annuity during his lifetime of £19,000 (Olson, *Radical Duke*, p. 102).

England, which he put forward in parliamentary bills in 1785 and 1786. His obstinacy and his very obvious moves to muzzle opposition meant that the bills were given a rough ride and were rejected by parliament when they came to be debated. Instead, a board of fifteen army officers and ten naval officers was appointed, with Richmond as chairman, to examine every conceivable French invasion plan and the most effective fortifications for a counter-attack. Its report, which was considered by the cabinet in January 1786, was also systematically rounded upon when it came to parliament, mainly on the grounds that the master-general had packed the parliamentary committee with supporters, and that there had been what was seen as sharp practice with the evidence: Sheridan called the report 'a fortress of sophistry'.[73] It too was rejected, though only by the casting vote of the speaker. A slightly revised bill, which was put before parliament in May 1786, was also voted down.[74]

Attempts to improve fortifications were not confined to the British Isles: in the immediate pre-war years, an expensive scheme was completed in the West Indies. At the end of the American Revolutionary War the defences of English Harbour in Antigua were surveyed by two Royal Engineer officers, and plans for fortifications and barracks were submitted. General Thomas Shirley, the governor of the island, lobbied hard: he had been governor of Dominica when it had been overrun by the French, and he did not want to be caught again.[75] Although the Island Assembly contributed almost nothing to the cost, Shirley got his way, and the Ordnance Department paid. Fortifications and barracks were built at the cost of well over £100,000 by 1790. When the plan was completed just after 1793, fifty buildings had been raised around English Harbour. But no French threat to the West Indies subsequently materialized, and the artillery there never fired a gun in anger.

The production of gunpowder was also improved. In 1784 Pitt had wanted to sell the Faversham Powder Mills, being convinced that commercial powder merchants could make better and cheaper gunpowder. Richmond, at that point powerful in the cabinet, persuaded him otherwise, encouraged by Major William Congreve, then deputy comptroller of the Royal Laboratory at Woolwich, who argued that powder could be manufactured more cheaply and securely by the state. The mixing of the three ingredients of gunpowder was tricky and, of course, potentially dangerous. British strength at sea ensured a steady supply of good-quality sulphur from Sicily and saltpetre from India, which the French lacked. The third constituent of gunpowder was charcoal, which was to be burnt in quantity from domestic wood. Congreve was constantly experimenting at Woolwich with the proportions of the mixture, as well as milling and grinding methods, and keeping the powder dry. As a result, the strength of British gunpowder was to be greater than that of France or of Holland in the coming wars, as proven by comparative tests made by the depot at Purfleet in 1794 and 1795.[76]

Magazines and other buildings for examining the powder were completed in the early 1770s at Priddy's Hard, the ordnance yard on the far side of Portsmouth Harbour from the dockyard, and Richmond and Congreve increased storage capacity there and at Plymouth. In 1789 the Ordnance acquired a site at Tipner Point, on the east side of Portsmouth Harbour, and slowly built a further magazine housing 5,000 barrels, although it was not to be finished during Richmond's time as master-general.[77]* In the final development, again in 1789, the year in which Congreve was appointed comptroller at Woolwich, the private gunpowder-mills at Waltham Abbey were acquired.[78]

The most serious problem that Richmond tackled was the quality of the cannon supplied to the army and navy. The numbers that had burst in the American Revolutionary War was little short of scandalous, but not surprising since many of them were old, and most had been 'hollow cast' using the old three-piece moulding technique. Only in 1775 did the Board of Ordnance decide to purchase guns that were 'bored from solid' (i.e., the barrel was drilled out from a solid gun), thus disqualifying almost all the Sussex furnaces, a decision that marked the beginning of the end for Wealden gunfounding.[79] All iron cannon were now cast solid by contractors and the barrel then bored. The cannon contractors

---

* The establishment of powder for a first-rate ship was set at 522 barrels when commissioned for foreign service and 477 for Channel Service, each barrel containing 90 pounds of gunpowder (Cole, *Arming the Navy*, p. 80).

were mainly from the north of England, although one of the most important, the Carron Company, was based in Scotland.*

Until 1780 there was no satisfactory process of quality control when guns were accepted by government. In that year Captain Thomas Blomefield, an experienced artillery officer, was appointed inspector of artillery and superintendent of the Brass Foundry at Woolwich, with complete responsibility for 'proofing' guns before they were accepted and paid for by the Ordnance Department (proofing was the process of testing the gun by firing it with a set amount of powder). His most important reform was to introduce the 'thirty-round proof', in spite of resistance from the gunfounding contractors, who naturally wanted fewer rounds fired from their newly cast cannon. By applying high inspection and proofing standards, Blomefield ensured that all substandard or damaged guns were rejected. In addition, large numbers were repaired through a new French method called 'bouching', by which any worn and oversized vent was filled with a copper bolt, and a new vent bored through the bolt.[80] Given the difficulty in the late eighteenth century of casting iron to a consistent standard, his achievement in increasing quality is particularly impressive. He wrote to the Board in 1792:

> The Imperfections of Cast Iron as applied to Guns are the extremes of hardness and softness, the former quality producing brittleness and the later a want of tenacity and cohesion; great skill and unremitting attention is requisite in the process of smelting it from the Mineral . . . it can never be expected that Iron Guns can be uniformly cast of a requisite degree of perfection which renders it indispensable that this variable should be guarded against by constructing them of heavy dimensions . . . it would therefore, I conceive, be inadvisable to diminish the established Proof Charges . . .[81]

* In June 1786, Russia gained gunfounding expertise from Britain when the manager of the Carron Company, Charles Gascoigne, moved to St Petersburg, attracted by a Scottish admiral, Samuel Greig, who was in the service of Catherine the Great. Gascoigne reorganized the Russian ordnance industry, improving quality and quantity, staying until his death in 1806, accompanied by eleven Scottish workmen who remained with him until the end. He was much criticized by others in the industry, for there were laws prohibiting the export of skilled technologists that dated back to the reigns of George I and II (Cross, *Banks of the Neva*, pp. 241, 248, 257).

Through these means the standards of guns in the navy, coastal defence and the army were much improved, and the incidence of gun bursts in the wars to follow greatly reduced.*

It was also a period of great experiment with gunnery. Blomefield, given a free hand by the Board of Ordnance and encouraged by Richmond, designed a strengthened, standard gun (which eventually came to bear his name) while working with the contractor Samuel Walker of Rotherham, who from 1786 produced experimental guns for him. Of some nine cannon-founding contractors, Walker and the Carron Company of Scotland produced the most new guns, undertaking contracts in thousands of tons.[82] The French were particularly interested in coke-smelted cannon, and in 1784 managed to get Barthélemy Faujas de Saint-Fond, an expert on furnaces, into the Carron works, but precautions had been taken and he could not see everything, especially 'the place where the cannon are bored, which nobody was allowed to see', and his report relied on his memory, 'for it may be presumed that I was not at liberty to take notes of them in writing'.[83] And, away from the limelight, in 1787, an artillery lieutenant, Henry Shrapnel, gave the first demonstration of his spherical case shell, filled with shot, in front of the officer commanding Gibraltar. This antipersonnel weapon was adopted by the army in 1803.[84]

Richmond pushed through important innovations for the army and navy's small arms, too, using his main Birmingham contractors, Henry Nock and Jonathan Hennem. The master-general considered the standard 'Land Musket' to be outdated. A variety of European ideas were combined into 'The Duke of Richmond's Pattern', which was officially adopted as the new infantry weapon. Testing these innovations took time, and Richmond signed his biggest contract, for 10,000 of the new muskets, in December 1792, only just before the declaration of war. Had there been more opportunity to train the gunsmiths in the manufacture of the weapon, Britain would have begun the war with the most modern and efficient small arms in Europe. In the event, the Ordnance Department had to fall back on the old 'Land Pattern', and the East India Company came to the rescue with its

---

* Many other pieces of gunners' equipment had to be checked for quality before use. In all, 424 articles of equipment were required to fire naval cannon and issued to the gunner of each ship, from nails to powder horns (Cole, *Arming the Navy*, pp. 5, 143).

shorter, lighter 'India Pattern' musket, which was to serve as the standard British line infantry weapon until 1840.

Richmond did, however, succeed in regularizing the gun-cleaning tools for the private soldier. Each man received a worm, turnscrew, pricker and bush, and an annual allowance for emery, brick dust and oil. He also introduced a new steel ramrod for sea service muskets. Some of these innovations were long lasting, with a new type of screwless lock, developed by Henry Nock, remaining in use until the 1830s. In 1790 Richmond found a more advantageous contract for gun flints and switched to Brandon in Suffolk, where they are still made today.[85]

Richmond's ideas were not confined to manufacturing improvements. The origins of the modern Ordnance Survey can be traced to his time as master-general. He encouraged the scientific work of the 'Principal Triangulation of Great Britain', which had started under the direction of General Sir William Roy in 1783. Surveying instruments were refined and improved, chiefly through the instrument-maker Jesse Ramsden. There was always tension between the more purely scientific aspects of the trigonometrical national survey and the necessities of defence against invasion, which laid more stress on topography, but towards the end of the 1780s defence gained the upper hand and more resources were made available to it.[86] Between 1787 and 1791 Jersey, Guernsey and the Isle of Wight were surveyed and six-inch-to-the-mile maps were drawn; but when war was declared, the northward progress of the triangulation survey was halted and the emphasis shifted to the topographical surveys of the southern counties, vulnerable to invasion. Richmond expanded the number of skilled civilian surveyors and draughtsmen: by 1794 thirty-one were based in the Drawing Room in the Tower of London.[87]* This development was, however, the last of a considerable list of initiatives brought about by one of the most progressive, but also one of the most unpopular and now largely forgotten, masters-general of the Ordnance.

The much reduced peacetime army was governed very differently from the navy and the Ordnance, each of which had to manage large indus-

---

* The 'Trigonometrical Survey', or 'The Duke of Richmond's Survey', was not known as the Ordnance Survey until 1801, and that description did not appear in print until 1809.

trial operations throughout both war and peace. Until the outbreak of hostilities, neither a secretary of state for war, at cabinet rank, nor a commander-in-chief was appointed. The memory of power based on military force during the Commonwealth made any permanent concentration of troops anathema to all shades of political opinion throughout the eighteenth century, and the rejection of a standing army of any size was a long-established tradition. During the peace, therefore, the army was managed by a minister below cabinet rank: the secretary at war, who presided over the War Office in the Horse Guards and who presented the annual Army Estimates to parliament and authorized all expenditure of money.* During the 1780s this post was occupied by Sir George Yonge, an ex-diplomat whose extravagant tastes beggared him and whose erratic performance later in his career made him a laughing stock. The king, who worked closely with the secretary at war, especially on promotions, later said that Yonge 'was never a man of business'.[88] But he performed routine peacetime business well enough, managing finance and liaising with the king over promotions. In the Horse Guards, Lieutenant-General Sir William Fawcett, adjutant-general from 1781 to 1799, was responsible for discipline, training, military regulations and applications for leave of absence. Arrangements for the movement and quartering of troops in Britain were undertaken by the Quartermaster-General's Department, although the orders were issued by the secretary at war, as responsibility for general civil order was held in non-military hands.[89]

When Pitt took office in 1783 the army was in a poor state. Battalions, reduced to minimum size, had been sent off to Ireland for reasons of economy, and the military presence in the Mediterranean and Caribbean was negligible. In any case, the peacetime army was

---

* These arrangements worked well enough in peace, but in wartime, with a secretary of state for war additionally appointed to the cabinet, as well as a commander-in-chief, confusion was to ensue. The Commission of Military Enquiry, reporting in 1808, tried to find a solution, but could not even discover the constitutional basis of the secretary at war's powers, and concluded that his authority 'is not now to be traced to its origin, but must be considered as grounded, in most instances, on usage'. Working in general below cabinet level, the secretary at war received instructions from the Treasury Board, the secretary of state for war, 'or applies personally to the King's confidential Servants for their concurrence' (Commission of Military Enquiry, *Sixth Report*, 25 June 1808, pp. 278–9).

always thinly spread and dispersed in small groups in order to carry out its anti-smuggling role along the south coast, to the detriment of its training as a body. Until the establishment of a civilian police force in the 1840s, the army was as much the guarantor of civil order as it was an instrument of foreign policy.[90] In this respect, the first part of the decade following 1783 was reasonably peaceful, although the memory of London burning during the Gordon Riots of 1780 was still fresh.* Towards the end of the 1780s a new pattern of domestic disorder was emerging, in part prompted by rapid industrialization. The army was still required to attend to anti-smuggling duties: between 1786 and 1789, for example, the 38th Foot Regiment spent a quarter of its time chasing smugglers, while the 10th Light Dragons nearly 40 per cent.[91] But troops were needed at Nottingham and Leicester in 1787; two years later they were also called to Liverpool and Wrexham to quell industrial disturbances. In August 1789 a detachment of the 1st Dragoons was sent to Leeds, where the workers had destroyed some new wool-spinning machines.[92] In 1791 riots took place in Birmingham.

By the second half of the decade the army was becoming an effective peacetime organization.[93] The garrison at Gibraltar was augmented by early 1785, but it took the threat of war in the Dutch Crisis of 1787 for the government to increase those in the Caribbean and East Indies. Other significant reforms were made. Infantry battalions of eight companies were given an additional two companies, making them more tactically viable. Six new infantry battalions were raised

---

* Lord George Gordon, an incoherent, unbalanced but dashing ex-naval lieutenant and MP, put forward anti-Catholic sentiments both in and out of the Commons. In June 1780 he presented a petition to parliament for the Protestant Association, formed to combat Catholic influence. The confused and violent situation rapidly got out of hand and London was in the hands of the mob for five days, with much property burnt. Order was only restored by the 12,000 troops that had been hurriedly concentrated in the capital. The number of those killed was 285, and 175 were wounded; 21 executions followed, although Gordon himself was found not guilty of treason. In 1788 he was imprisoned again for sedition and ended his days in Newgate, where he converted to Judaism (Randall, *Riotous Assemblies*, pp. 200–206; Langford, *Polite and Commercial People*, pp. 551–2; Steven Watson, *Reign of George III*, pp. 235–9; Namier and Brooke, *House of Commons*, Vol. I, p. 514).

specifically for service abroad.[94] Recruiting improved, and the army became numerically stronger, reaching over 41,000 effective troops by 1790.*

In this year progress was brought to a halt by the Nootka Sound Crisis. As a war had not been declared, the army conspicuously lacked a commander-in-chief, and the secretary at war was now desperately overworked and not senior enough to put expeditions in hand without delays.† Eight battalions went to the fleet for trans-shipment to the West Indies, a move designed to defend British possessions against potential Spanish attack, which left the number of troops in Britain at a dangerously low level for national defence as well as for maintaining domestic order. In addition, not enough marines had been raised to man the mobilized warships and the War Office was repeatedly requested to supply soldiers for the task, which was to lead to a souring of relations between the War Office and the Admiralty. By November 1790, 2,436 troops were spread aboard thirty-three warships.[95]

Measures were taken to recruit quickly. Ireland's less developed economy made for easier recruitment and became an important source of army manpower. The government also did not hesitate to create 'Independent Companies of Foot', approved by the secretary at war and raised quickly by professional army officers, who saw the measure as a means to social and professional promotion. This decentralized system of recruitment was to become very successful.[96] 'Invalid companies' were taken up from Chelsea Hospital for guarding duties. However, in spite of these measures, the widespread dispersal of battalions in 1790, and the many months involved in returning them to Britain, meant that regular army units were not in place when the war started in earnest in early 1793. During that year the immediate requirement for tens of thousands of recruits, and their training, together with immediate operations in Europe, was to lead to a long period of failure by the army.

*

* In that year over 10,000 were stationed in England, 9,500 in Ireland, 1,600 in Scotland, over 6,000 in the East Indies, 4,700 in the West Indies, 4,200 in Canada and 3,250 in Gibraltar (Pimlott, 'Administration of Army', Appendix 6, quoting TNA, HO 50/362, fols. 553–5, 'Numerical State of the Army', 6 May 1790).

† See Chapter 4 for the army hierarchy in wartime.

With Paris descending into anarchy and the troops of Austria and Prussia preparing to invade France, the government feared that the influence of the radical ideas that were changing so much in France would spread to England. The difficulty was that purpose-built accommodation for troops hardly existed.[97] The only sizeable working barracks were the Royal Marine Barracks at Chatham, Portsmouth and Plymouth, which had been built in the American Revolutionary War to house the forces protecting the dockyards in case of invasion. The great barracks at Woolwich had been started in 1777, but were not finished until 1808.[98] In general, if troops moved about the country they stopped in towns and quartered in private homes. Widely dispersed castles, forts and dockyard barracks, highly unsuited for the concentrations of troops that were required, could house only 40,000.[99]

Henry Dundas, as the home secretary, rapidly brought together a plan for housing troops and secured the king's approval for the building of barracks at Hyde Park and Knightsbridge. At a meeting at his home in Wimbledon with Pitt and Sir George Yonge, he despatched Colonel Oliver De Lancey, who had put down the Birmingham riots in 1791, around the country to investigate the barracks in England. De Lancey reported back in June 1792:

> it is a dangerous measure to keep troops in the manufacturing towns in their present dispersed state, and unless barracks could be established for the men where they could be kept under the eyes of their officers, it would be prudent to quarter them in the towns and villages in the country, whence in case of emergency they would act with much more effect.[100]

Dundas moved quickly. He by-passed the Ordnance Department, usually responsible for the construction of barracks but with a reputation for delay when it came to building, and also avoided dealing with the duke of Richmond, with whom relations were bad. He authorized De Lancey, appointed to the new post of superintendent of barracks, to engage private contractors to build barracks for three troops of infantry and horse in Sheffield, Nottingham and Birmingham, and for six troops in Manchester. Before the end of the year, Coventry and Norwich were added to the list, and a seventh barracks was ordered at

Hounslow.[101] It was a hasty but necessary decision, in anticipation of civil unrest rather than of direct danger from an enemy.* Significant civil disturbances would occur during the war years, although they were primarily caused by food shortages, not French republican ideas.

The rapid improvements in public and private communication at home and abroad, brought about by Pitt's administration for reasons of economic efficiency, were to be critical for the war effort in the years ahead. Fortunately, the Post Office was another government institution that was radically reformed in the 1780s. Driven by the Treasury to cut costs, the postmaster-general in 1787, Lord Walsingham, privatized the packet service. He addressed the Lisbon and trans-Atlantic routes first, issuing plans and specifications for smaller packet ships to potential contractors. A particular feature of the new design was the simplified plan below decks for reducing the number of places where the crew could hide goods for illicit trading, which cut into customs revenue. Instead of state-owned vessels of 200 tons, manned by 30 men, those to America would now be 150 tons, and to Lisbon only 100 tons. North Sea packets were to be of 70 tons, crewed by 11 men, though this was increased in wartime to 17. Contracts awarded to the masters and owners were for seven, fourteen or twenty-one years, with six months' notice from either side, for a set rate of £1,350 a year. In spite of opposition from the packet captains, the measures went ahead. The home waters' routes to the Continent, with vessels from 70 to 100 tons, were also changed, and all packets became privately owned, contracted to the government.[102]

The land postal service was slow and inefficient and its income was not keeping pace with the growing volume of post. The prime minister's intervention in the affairs of the Post Office in 1784 caused a political storm. Pitt wanted to improve efficiency and increase

---

* This hasty arrangement was to lead to trouble a dozen years later, for De Lancey used Alexander Davison, friend and prize agent of Nelson, as his main contractor for barrack supplies. Instead of carefully drawn-up contracts, the business arrangements, involving vast sums of government money, were underpinned only by an exchange of letters between the two men over Christmas 1794. The Commission of Military Enquiry was to uncover financial irregularities. In 1808 Davison was imprisoned and De Lancey was lucky to escape the same fate (Downer, *Nelson's Purse*, p. 338).

revenue, and gave much support to John Palmer, whose idea was to replace the mounted post boys with high-speed, French-built coaches also designed to take passengers. Postal rates would be raised to pay for the improved services. But Pitt found that changing the ways of this 270-year-old government institution was more difficult than he had anticipated. On 21 June he summoned the Post Office officials to the Treasury and announced that the first mail coach would run from Bristol to London on 1 August.[103] Palmer was to be employed by the Post Office in a senior position and receive 2½ per cent on the surplus from his scheme. The surprised Post Office officials were less than enamoured by these ideas, and the meeting turned angry, causing Pitt to leave abruptly. The long-established secretary, Anthony Todd, spent the next five years trying to obstruct the scheme. Relations between the officials and the undiplomatic Palmer deteriorated, and Pitt became heartily sick of the business.

The introduction of Palmer's mail coaches in 1784 brought about a reliable and frequent post that exceeded the expectations of the populace. Before 1784 the post travelled between five and six miles an hour; by 1792 seven miles an hour was achieved.[104] By the end of the century mail delivery speeds had increased to between eight and nine miles an hour. All major postal routes had a daily delivery: Bath, for instance, would have the London evening papers the morning after they were printed.[105] The new Bristol coach completed its journey in sixteen hours, and within a year the coaches were introduced into East Anglia and the south-east. By 1786 they serviced the Great North Road.[106] With all other traffic giving way to them, and no turnpike charges, they were faster than any other means of transport and reached new standards of reliability and timeliness. By 1792 sixteen mail coaches were arriving and leaving London every day.[107] The net annual postal revenue rose from £196,000 in 1784 to £391,000 in 1793; and by the early years of the nineteenth century it was over a million pounds a year.[108]

For those who had been responsible for the main improvements in the machinery of war, the period of peace ended in personal disappointments. The unpopular Lord Howe was the first to resign. Facing the same problem as other first lords before him – that is, far more applicants for commands and lieutenants' posts than he had available – he froze all promotions in 1787. He was attacked in the press and in parliament, but lacked the fluency and the will to make a reasonable public case. In the House 'he assured their Lordships that patronage was not so desirable as might be imagined, and that he was sure, out of twenty candidates for an appointment, to disappoint nineteen, and by no means certain of pleasing the twentieth.'[109] Deeply unpopular, he resigned as first lord in 1788 over Middleton's trivial, but to him symbolic, promotion from captain to rear-admiral. Howe had precedent on his side when he argued that a rear-admiral should be serving at sea or at least available for service, but Pitt did not support him. In his stead, Pitt appointed his elder brother, John, earl of Chatham; although Chatham's loyalty could be relied upon, his lack of energy was to be a great disadvantage.

After eight years of bureaucratic infighting in the Post Office, John Palmer was forced to resign in 1792, although Pitt settled a handsome pension on him.[110] Richmond remained as master-general until 1795, but was politically sidelined and held no further public office. Middleton did not survive much longer than Howe. Frustrated by Pitt's reluctance to act upon the naval reforms that had been outlined by the Commission on Fees, he resigned suddenly, to the relief of his colleagues in the Navy Office. George Marsh heard the news as he arrived at Somerset House on the morning of 15 March 1790. He noted in his diary:

> Most of the clerks were in the Hall of the Navy Office to meet and tell me of it, as I went to it, expressing the utmost pleasure on the event . . . In general Captains in the Navy are the most unfit persons to be members of the Navy Board, as they know nothing of the civil department and are, too, from their education and habits, very absolute and consequential.[111]

'Absolute and consequential' they may have been, yet Middleton and Richmond (and Palmer, too) possessed just those qualities that peace-time administration needed. Driven, controlling and self-absorbed, and caring nothing for personal popularity, they forced through change not because it was politically advantageous to do so, but because they believed it was right and that it was needed. With the very substantial budgets provided by Pitt they were able to achieve a great deal. Through them and their deputies, fundamental improvements were made to the country's capacity to wage war, which was be called upon regularly in the next twenty-two years. At the same time government departments developed greater expertise in the letting and management of contracts; the relationship between the public and private sectors would provide the key to future British military and naval expansion.

The differences in 1793 between British and French political stability, economic growth and naval capability had never been greater. In the French naval bases, ships were in poor condition and the few seamen that could be mustered were in a state of insubordination. The mutinies of 1790 had resulted in the dissolution of the corps of French naval officers, while the risky and costly investment in the breakwaters at Cherbourg had come to nothing.[112] Britain may have lost the American Revolutionary War, but it won the peace that followed.

PART TWO

Holding the Line

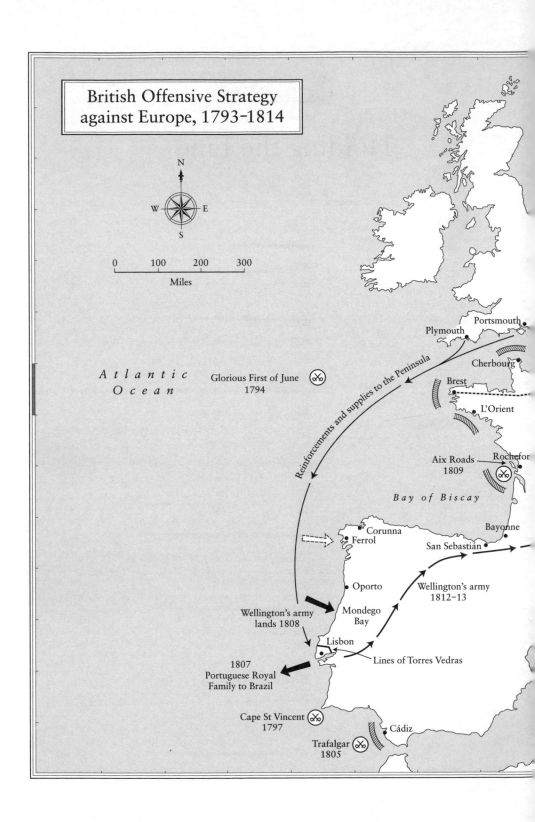

British Offensive Strategy
against Europe, 1793–1814

N
W E
S

0   100   200   300
Miles

Atlantic
Ocean

Glorious First of June
1794

Reinforcements and supplies to the Peninsula

Portsmouth

Plymouth

Cherbourg

Brest

L'Orient

Aix Roads
1809

Rochefor

Bay of Biscay

Corunna
Ferrol

Bayonne

San Sebastián

Oporto

Wellington's army
1812–13

Wellington's army
lands 1808

Mondego
Bay

Lisbon

Lines of Torres Vedras

1807
Portuguese Royal
Family to Brazil

Cape St Vincent
1797

Cádiz

Trafalgar
1805

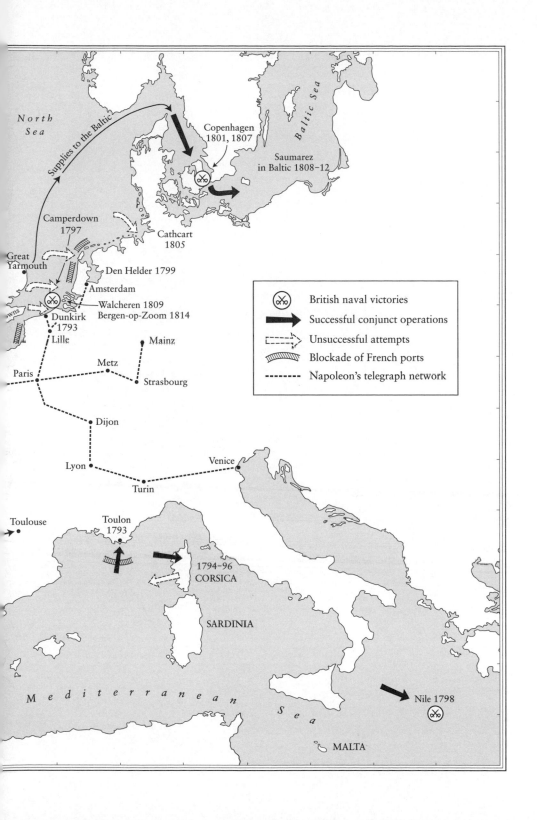

North
Sea

Supplies to the Baltic

Baltic Sea

Copenhagen
1801, 1807

Saumarez
in Baltic 1808–12

Camperdown
1797

Cathcart
1805

Great
Yarmouth

Den Helder 1799

Amsterdam

Walcheren 1809
Bergen-op-Zoom 1814

wns

Dunkirk
1793

Lille

Mainz

Metz

Paris

Strasbourg

Dijon

Lyon

Venice

Turin

Toulouse

Toulon
1793

1794–96
CORSICA

SARDINIA

Mediterranean

Sea

Nile 1798

MALTA

British naval victories

Successful conjunct operations

Unsuccessful attempts

Blockade of French ports

Napoleon's telegraph network

3

The First Crisis

1795–1798

Thus is the present War a new phenomenon, for, besides being a necessary War for self-defence, it is A WAR OF PRINCIPLE – a War in defence of all the Rights of Nations, against the Arbitrary Usurpations of a Gallic Mob.
– Robert Nares, *Man's Best Right: A Solemn Appeal in the Name of Religion* (1793)[1]

The exertion of France in her state of political insanity has as much exceeded the natural efforts of that country as the strength of the raving mad does that of a reasonable man.
– General David Dundas, 'Memorandum on Invasion', November 1796[2]

For two years, from late 1792, when war between Britain and France looked increasingly likely, reasoned parliamentary debate on the nature of the revolution in France was absent. The nerves of over-wrought MPs were frayed by news of French military success against Austria and Prussia, and by fear of French republican ideas and of domestic social change. The politicians postured to inflame public opinion. Pitt said of the French in January 1793 that 'their ambition was unbounded, so the anarchy, which they hoped to establish, was universal', and by June he had made it clear that he hoped for a change of government: 'the best security we could obtain, would be in the end of that wild ungoverned system.'[3] As many as 2,000 loyalist associations were founded up and down the country in 1792 and 1793.[4] William Windham, a moderate Whig, though with a personality characterized by extremes, went so far as to assert that Britain had been infiltrated by French sympathizers: 'In every town, in every village, nay almost in every house, these worthy gentlemen had their agents.' When pressed to negotiate with the French, Pitt argued that to accredit the republic by sending an ambassador would be an affront to British dignity. Edmund Burke argued that the acceptance of French principles would endanger 'our property, our wives, everything which was dear and sacred'. No stranger to histrionics, at one point he waved a dagger in the House, representing that it was one of 3,000 that had been ordered in Birmingham by the French.[5]

The ideological nature of the war fought between Pitt's government and the National Convention in Paris pushed both sides to perverse and exaggerated statements. Rumours of the killing of prisoners reached London, and in May 1794 the Convention passed a law declaring that prisoners of war were to be executed. According to Colonel Harry Calvert, in Holland with the British Army, the French decreed that 'no English nor Hanoverian prisoners shall be made ... not one of them ought to return to the traitorous territory of England ... Let the British slaves perish, and Europe be free.' The duke of York's immediate reply to this manifesto was moderate and honourable: 'mercy to the vanquished is the brightest gem in the soldier's character.' Ten days later Calvert reported that the Convention's orders had been completely reversed, and that any French soldier guilty of inhumanity to the British would be guillotined.[6] On 1 June, hundreds of miles out in the Atlantic, the British and French fleets met in battle. When the French ship *Vengeur du Peuple* sank, British seamen saved hundreds of the French crew: old traditions of humanity between enemies were not about to be swept aside.[7]

Extremism in parliament was matched by violence on the streets. By the last months of 1794 the government had to deal with serious domestic unrest; the wrath of the crowd was directed against the twin anxieties of impressment and the high price of food. Trouble had flared against crimping houses and recruiting offices.* On 13 July

---

* To 'crimp' was to entrap a man into the army or navy. Victims were often decoyed by prostitutes, plied with drink and when insensible enlisted into the army, navy or East India Company; alternatively the 'crimp' would lend money to seamen at extortionate rates, leaving them no alternative but to volunteer to obtain the bounty money

1795, during one of Pitt's dinners, rioters marched down Whitehall and gathered outside No. 10 Downing Street. One report mentioned that there were 12,000 people in the crowd. Stones were thrown through the windows, and one of Pitt's guests, the earl of Mornington (the future Lord Wellesley and elder brother of the future duke of Wellington), was hit on the shoulder. The crowd, beaten off by the military, flowed over Westminster Bridge to St George's Fields, to chants of 'Pitt's Head and a Quartern Loaf for Sixpence'. A suspected crimping house and a butcher's shop were attacked and furniture was burnt in the street.[8] Some of the rioters were trampled by the cavalry and two died.

Nor was London the only place to be affected by domestic unrest. Resistance to impressment into the navy led to violence in all the major seaports of the country. In dockside pressing disturbances, casualties were more likely to be members of the press gang than the men they were pursuing, very often in pitched battles.* Detestation of naval service was particularly strong in the north-east of England, an area that had little loyalty to the navy, and attempts to impress seamen there were complicated by a serious labour dispute between merchant seamen and shipowners that had started in October 1792 over rising food prices. At the outbreak of war in February 1793 the keelmen on the Wear blocked the river by mooring a double line of keels from bank to bank, a strike that was violently broken by a force of dragoons from Newcastle. In North Shields the press gang, without much support from the magistrates, was embarrassingly run out of town; as the report to the Home Office related: the sailors 'drove the Press Gang thro' the streets today with their Jackets turn'd, and their Hatts under their arms'.[9] It was little wonder that regulating officers and the lieutenants on impressment duty were faced with desertion

---

to pay back their debt. The term was also used to describe those who received a reward for turning in naval deserters, or one who, for financial reward, persuaded a seaman to leave one merchant ship to join another.

* At a time of rapid growth of trade, with merchant seamen fully employed at high rates of wages, the 1787 and 1791 mobilizations had provoked extreme resistance: 43 per cent of all press disturbances resulted in someone being killed or wounded, but by 1793 this occurred in only 11 per cent of disturbances (Rogers, *Press Gang*, p. 52).

from the press gang itself while on a raid, particularly if it was composed of naval seamen who had themselves been pressed.

Perhaps the attention of the government was distracted by violence at home, but from the start it underestimated the capacity of the French army to fight, assuming that the country had been fatally weakened by the revolution. Thus inexperience and overconfidence typified the British government's handling of the first seven years of the war. From the early 1790s Pitt's closest political confidants were Henry Dundas and Lord Grenville, Pitt's cousin, and this triumvirate largely controlled British foreign policy and war strategy between 1791 and 1801, ensuring that the cabinet supported decisions that effectively they had already taken. Occasional sharp disagreements occurred, with Dundas much keener to secure the colonies and sea power, and Grenville much more committed to the Continent; but mutual respect kept them together for the first phase of the war.[10]

Henry Dundas, the object of many of Pitt's visits to Somerset House in the 1780s and 1790s, was a boisterous and convivial politician, a manager of men and of Scottish parliamentary seats, whose route to power lay in building an unassailable political base in Scotland. One political ally thought he had 'the best social and public virtues, an affectionate heart as a parent, a husband and friend, and an unparalleled good temper'.[11] But his plain speaking, as well as his great power, made him enemies. He was very influential in the East India Company. From 1784 he was a commissioner of the India Board of Control, through which the government liaised with the Company, and from 1793 to 1801 was its president. Perhaps his least recognized achievement was as secretary of state for war in the second half of the 1790s: as the chief creator of a national defence force, he ensured that, by the end of the Revolutionary War, Britain was safer from invasion than ever before, and in possession of an increased military capability. Not for nothing has he been described as Britain's Lazare Carnot.[12] Pitt was closer to Dundas than to Grenville: 'every act of Dundas's', the prime minister wrote in 1794, 'is as much mine as his.'[13] This friendship brought Pitt relaxation, involving on occasion horseplay and copious alcohol, for Dundas had been brought up at the Scottish bar, notorious for its tradition of heavy drinking.[14]

Lord Grenville was the opposite: unpopular, cold and withdrawn, and he held his principles so securely that they translated into inflexibility.* In 1789 he became home secretary – a role that, until 1801, also had responsibility for the colonies – and then foreign secretary in 1791. George Canning, when meeting Grenville in 1793, thought he had less reserve than he had been led to expect by his reputation, and that it proceeded more 'from shyness than haughtiness. But he is a man not to be judged-of by once seeing.'[15] His hauteur made him enemies: years later, Lord Liverpool, the future prime minister, remarked of Grenville: 'He has no feelings for anyone ... he is in his outward manner offensive to the last degree.'[16] Grenville's strong character and considerable linguistic skills made him formidable in cabinet, especially on foreign policy. Only Pitt could overcome him in debate, and that with difficulty.†

However, these strong personalities were inexperienced; they avoided expert military counsel and logistical advice, and were unwilling to understand the limited capacity of the British military machine, which was to become well oiled only with war experience. Much was wrong with the command structure at the top of the army; as Harry Calvert described it, 'the system still prevailing of ordering from the Cabinet at St James's the active operations of the army in the field'.[17]

The Whig Opposition did not fail to attack the government's performance in the conduct of the war, but was divided, and Pitt did his best to drive a wedge between the different factions. The moderates were splitting from the followers of Charles James Fox. Of this radical group, Richard Brinsley Sheridan and Charles Grey were the most effective parliamentary orators, and they were bitter rivals.‡ Grey's

---

* Grenville was prime minister when the Slave Trade Abolition Act was passed in 1807 and a driving force behind it. He was present in May 1787 when Pitt had encouraged William Wilberforce to take up the abolitionist cause. Wilberforce in his old age remembered: 'after a conversation in the open air at the root of an old tree at Holwood just above the steep descent into the Vale of Keston, I resolved to give notice on a fit occasion in the House of Commons of my intention to bring the subject forward' (Hague, *Wilberforce*, pp. 144, 330–56). The 'Wilberforce oak' still exists and is a local landmark.

† As testimony to the care with which he prepared himself on any issue, Grenville's extensive map collection still survives in 131 beautifully tooled slip cases, with their original numbers, labelling and index (NMM, GREN, in the chart collection).

‡ See Chapter 1, p. 13.

character was contradictory: he was very ambitious, passionate, at times depressive and introspective, with a powerful need to be in charge that did not make him popular. Lady Holland, one of the greatest of the Whig grandees, described him as 'a man of violent temper and unbounded ambition'. He was also a man of extremes of mood: one woman friend noted that 'he is either very happy or very sad.'[18] He enjoyed a life of an apparently fulfilled domesticity, having no fewer than eleven sons and four daughters, yet he also kept a string of mistresses well into his sixties, among them Sheridan's young second wife, Hecca. Grey had made an immediate impact from the time of his first speech in the House in 1788, and both parties hoped that he would join them. His family connections, including those of his father, General Sir Charles Grey, were with Pitt's administration, but there was distance between father and son, and the younger man's career as a Whig politician was shaped by personal, rather than political, considerations. As Lady Holland commented, 'all the beauty and wit of London were on that side, and the seduction of Devonshire House prevailed.'[19] The chief attraction was Georgiana, duchess of Devonshire, who became his mistress and bore him a daughter. In this argumentative hothouse, Grey, Sheridan and some of the younger Whigs set up the Association of Friends of the People, which pressed for a radical agenda that included annual elections and greater democracy. Grey later regretted this impetuous, ambitious decision.[20] It was the start of a forty-year career, and although much of Grey's time was spent in Opposition, he was eventually to lead the Whigs as prime minister at their finest moment, the passing of the Great Reform Act of 1832.

Considering the advantages enjoyed by Britain, the war got off to a bad start. Critics of government could not, however, accuse Pitt, Dundas and Grenville of lack of energy. The government embarked on a bold diplomatic strategy when it put together the First Coalition in February 1793: Austria, Prussia, the Netherlands, Spain and Sardinia united against Revolutionary France. This coalition was supported by many British subsidies to Continental powers, the first of which was a payment to Hanover in 1793 of £452,000. Over the next twenty years there were to be over a hundred such financial transfers. They were naturally never popular with the country at large, but they were necessary to keep the nations on the Continent in the field against the French.[21]

In April 1793, British troops, commanded by the duke of York, were sent to Holland to defend it after the Austrian Netherlands had been overrun by French armies. A 'Flanders war' had never been planned and was embarked upon only to keep Austria, defeated at Jemappes, in the war. An improvement in Austrian fortunes at the Battle of Neerwinden in March was not, however, a sign of things to come. Dundas ordered an expedition to besiege the fortress-port of Dunkirk.[22] The British Army was still being regrouped after the wide dispositions made during the mobilizations of 1790 and 1791, but the rapid expansion of the army with untrained men limited its effectiveness. This led to damaging friction between Dundas and the duke of Richmond, who had not approved of the expedition to Dunkirk. Pitt was warned by Richmond not to throw away his army.* Recruits needed at least six months of training, and then they would still be raw, unable to face experienced troops.[23] Officers were appointed 'whose years and inexperience totally disqualified them for the situation', according to one officer in the field.[24] This lack of unity was felt even as far as the battlefield; as Calvert complained to a fellow officer:

> We want artillerymen, we want a general officer at the head of the artillery, we want drivers and smiths; we want three major-generals of infantry; we want a commanding engineer of rank and experience; we want a total reform in our hospital; we want, at least, two out of the four brigades of mounted artillery with which his Grace of Richmond is amusing himself in England . . .[25]

---

* Richmond's military advice to Pitt was correct, and the poor performance of the British Army in this war was due to lack of training, and also the subsequent decimation of experienced troops in the West Indies expeditions. It contrasted with the success of the British Army in the Napoleonic War, which was thoroughly trained before being committed to battle. Richmond left office as master-general in Feb. 1795. Lord Cornwallis, who succeeded him, reckoned that the newly arrived Portland Whigs had forced Pitt to sack the master-general: 'Notwithstanding his voluntary return to his duty in the Cabinet and, as I understand, his promise to behave better in the future' (Cornwallis to Colonel Ross, 26 Jan. 1795, Ross, *Cornwallis*, Vol. II, p. 281).

Without sufficient siege weapons (a failure of ordnance supply) York sat for two weeks in front of the walls of Dunkirk waiting for artillery and equipment to reach him. Outnumbered by approaching French armies, his army was defeated at Hondscoten. York suffered 10,000 casualties and lost much of his recently arrived artillery. Much blame was heaped upon the duke: appointed at the age of twenty-nine at the king's insistence, he was to prove brave but inexperienced. On one occasion, during the retreat in the winter of 1794/5, he was nearly taken prisoner.*

The calamitous expedition to Dunkirk did not divert the minds of ministers from the main strategy advocated by Henry Dundas of taking the French West Indies islands. The purpose was to weaken the wealth of France by capturing its islands and their sugar plantations. Stripping troops from England, Ireland and Gibraltar would enable Dundas to equip General Grey (father of Charles Grey the young Whig), who commanded the expedition, with over 16,000 troops. A departure date in the last week of September 1793 was set, time enough, Dundas believed, to take the French Windward Islands and St Dominque by the end of the year. At the end of August, Toulon had surrendered to Hood and the British Fleet, and was now defended by a thin force of British troops, with some help from Spanish and Neapolitan allies, both nations committed to stamping out revolutionary ideas. Dundas reckoned that there was enough time to bring 10,000 of the soldiers who had just been despatched to the West Indies back across the Atlantic in the spring of the next year to relieve the forces in Toulon.[26] He was encouraged in this impossibly ambitious plan by wildly overenthusiastic and overconfident despatches from Hood at Toulon, and was unwilling to listen to professional advice from soldiers or seamen or civil servants (who so early in the war had little experience of strategic planning or resource calculations). In the event,

---

* Lady Holland, while making her way home after travelling on the Continent, found herself near the army and was invited to dine with the duke: 'Almost all the persons immediately about the Duke are very young men, and as they live at headquarters, they fill his table and prevent him from inviting the general officers and colonels of regiments as frequently as it is usual for a Commander-in-Chief to do. This is one source of disgust ... The Duke feels this, and sometimes *expresses* himself hardily, when he ought to *act* with severity' (2 Nov. 1793, Ilchester, *Lady Holland*, Vol. I, p. 95n.).

Hood was forced to abandon Toulon in December 1793, withdrawing to Corsica with thousands of refugees on board his ships, though he did manage to capture and destroy thirty-two French ships of the line and stores before leaving. (The French naval effort in the Revolutionary War, in spite of the compensation of sixteen newly built ships, never recovered.[27])

In May 1794, following reverses, the Austrians decided to abandon their long-held possessions in the Netherlands. Dundas, worried about the invasion threat that might develop if the French occupied Ostend, ordered Major General Lord Moira to Ostend with command of a force of 10,000 men to defend the port at all costs. Bizarrely, he despatched Moira without any reference to the other commander in the field, the duke of York.[28] Soon after his expedition landed, it was re-embarked to aid the unrest in Brittany. By July, British forces were evacuated from the Low Countries. The expedition was witnessed by a disillusioned 25-year-old lieutenant-colonel, Arthur Wellesley: its mismanagement led him to attempt, unsuccessfully, to leave the army and find a civil post in government.[29]

Dundas persevered with the West Indies expeditions, which continued with enormous loss of life through disease until 1797, while Pitt and Grenville were forced to fall back on the long, slow process of coalition building with Continental powers. Howe's capture on 1 June of seven ships of the line in his battle with the French Channel Fleet, which was escorting a huge convoy of grain from America to Brest, was greeted with relief and rejoicing.* But anti-war sentiment was growing. By the end of 1794 Canning noted ambivalence in support for the war in the political circles that he frequented, discouraged by the success of the French armies: 'I heard . . . from young as well as old, of the changes that were working in people's opinions about the

---

* When the news arrived in London, George Canning was at the opera, which stopped after half an hour because of 'the bustle and hurry in the lower boxes . . . I never saw a finer or more affecting spectacle than the almost electric and universal sensation that seemed to pervade every part of the House – the transport and triumph which burst forth as soon as their astonishment had a little subsided.' He was much amused by the stony-faced silence with which the news was greeted in a box opposite, in which sat the Bouverie family – Whigs and therefore opposed to the war. 'The attention which they paid to the stage (rather than look about them to see rejoicing faces) was highly entertaining' (10 June 1794, Jupp, *Canning Letter Journal*, p. 121).

War, that I scarcely knew whom to consider as stout and safe.'[30] As a devoted follower of Pitt, Canning took immense care to persuade the waverers among his friends of the necessity of continuing the war. He recorded at great length in his journal the arguments he had with one of his Christ Church circle, Lord Boringdon, in January 1795. Boringdon was of the opinion that, while Pitt was the only leader fit to run the country, the war should still be abandoned: 'While he [Boringdon] continues to <u>vote with</u> Government in Parlt., because he wishes not to turn out Pitt, yet <u>talks</u> and <u>thinks against</u> them in private, because he wishes peace to be made.'[31] Canning employed his burgeoning eloquence in a conversation of several hours to change his friend's mind.

Howe's victory was but a single ray of sunshine in the dark prospect of 1794, made gloomier by further domestic unrest. The comfortably off in the grander parts of London, such as Mayfair or St James's, had been threatened several times by demonstrating crowds. By the end of October 1795 matters seemed to be out of control, and revolution spreading across the Channel, when the king's coach was jeered with shouts for 'Bread and Peace' as he went to open parliament. Afterwards the king returned to Buckingham House in a private coach, which the crowd again tried to stop, though he was rescued by the Life Guards. As the now empty state coach returned to the Royal Mews along Pall Mall, it was pelted with stones until every window was broken. Pieces broken from the coach were later sold for as much as sixpence in the street.[32] Within a matter of weeks Pitt pushed the repressive 'Two Acts' – the Treason Act and the Seditious Meetings Act – through parliament, and the oppressive domestic laws known by opponents as 'Pitt's Terror' had begun.*

In this atmosphere of crisis, the moderate Whigs, led by the duke of Portland, took fright. Already by December 1793 Portland (courted all the while by Pitt) had broken with Fox after two years of wrangling over the Whig Party's attitude to the French Revolution and to the war. Early the following year, together with William Windham, Portland

---

* The Treasonable Practices Act expanded definitions of treason to include attempts to coerce parliament, or attacks on the constitution, which were liable to seven years' transportation. The Seditious Meetings Act banned lectures or meetings of more than fifty people (universities excepted) unless permitted by local magistrates.

brought over sixty supporters to the government ('Alarmists', as they were called), making the prime minister's political authority unassailable. The realignment of 1794 effectively kept the Whigs from power for the next forty years, with the exception of one brief administration between 1806 and 1807 lasting only fourteen months.

The negotiations between the Pitt government and the Whigs were complex, with some existing ministers very dubious about the wisdom of a coalition government, particularly Henry Dundas, who, although he was Pitt's great friend and ally, had to give up the Home Office to Portland. Pitt wanted Dundas to take on a new department, as secretary of state for war. Dundas threatened to resign, believing that a new, separate department would lack power. He wrote to Pitt: 'All modern Wars are a Contention of Purse, and unless some very peculiar Circumstance occurs . . . the Minister for Finance must be the Minister for War.' Pitt pleaded, confessing to being 'really completely heart broken' at the prospect of Dundas resigning. Finally the king persuaded Dundas to change his mind. Ultimately his personal relationship with Pitt allowed Dundas to maintain his dominant cabinet position, and the doubts of the new secretary for war were never realized. In a political career lasting nearly a quarter of a century, he arguably played his most distinguished role in this post over the next seven years. The addition of the colonies to the department's responsibilities in 1801 lasted until the Crimean War.[33]

The Portland Whigs negotiated five cabinet places, two with senior war responsibilities. Portland took the Home Office and Lord Spencer became first lord of the Admiralty. In spite of his great reluctance to speak in public, William Cavendish-Bentinck, third duke of Portland, had already had a distinguished career in high office, and had nominally been prime minister in the short-lived Fox–North government in the early 1780s. As home secretary, he took a hard line in countering domestic unrest. A confirmed supporter of the theories of Adam Smith, he was always reluctant for the government to intervene in the markets to buy food for the populace, as it had to do in 1795 and 1796.

William Windham, though popularly tipped to be home secretary, reluctantly took the job of secretary at war. Pitt agreed that, although the position was not usually one of cabinet rank, Windham should attend cabinet meetings. Windham was rich, scholarly and popular, a sparkling conversationalist and orator: Macaulay was to call him 'the first gentleman of his age'.[34] Possessing great wealth, living in the east of the county of Norfolk, he hardly had his finger on the pulse of the country. As with many brilliant men, he was not a successful minister. He had a reputation for not attending his office, a disastrous trait since the role of secretary at war was essentially that of a bureaucrat, and his distaste for Dundas's brashness was unhelpful to relations at the centre of government.[35] Gilbert Elliot felt Windham was totally disqualified 'for any useful exertion, either in office or out of it'. Lady Holland was to label him 'more splendid than useful in public'.[36] The shrewdest judgement on Windham came from the Duchess of Devonshire: 'I think he is prejudiced and often led, and therefore unfit to lead others. If being well-meaning would alone do, he would do well.'[37] Windham's great passion in the 1790s was supporting the Vendéan royalists, and, largely as a result of his advocacy, an expedition of 3,000 royalist troops in fifty transports, escorted by warships under Sir John Borlase Warren, sailed in June 1795, and were landed at Quiberon, where they were cut to pieces by General Hoche. In parliament, Pitt defended the operation by pointing out that 'No English blood had been shed.' Sheridan replied, 'That is true, but English honour has been shed from every pore.'[38]

Lord Spencer was a noticeable improvement over Lord Chatham as first lord of the Admiralty, but had experience neither of government nor of the navy. Spencer also had a difficult time with some senior sea officers, the most serious incident being the court-martialling of Admiral William Cornwallis, who had acted with great distinction in maintaining the blockade of the French Channel ports and was to do so again. But this quarrel ensured that that gritty and useful admiral did not serve during Spencer's administration. The first lord also had little hesitation in securing the resignation of Admiral Sir Charles Middleton from the Admiralty Board in November 1795, to which he had been appointed by Lord Chatham in May 1794. Middleton had tried to block the appointment of a relatively junior flag officer that Spencer wished to make; Spencer insisted on passing over a naval officer whom Middleton had known and respected for many years.[39]* The strong tradition of automatic appointment by seniority rather than by merit was a significant weakness of both army and navy in the early years of the war. It would take some time to ease out the older officers and bring the younger and more vigorous ones to the upper ranks of both services.

Spencer acquired a reputation for giving way to the sea officers on the Board on matters of policy. The outspoken Dundas wrote to the first lord in 1798, exhorting him to: 'Exercise your understanding, and if your Board don't support your opinions and your measures, send them to sea or find others in their place.'[40] William Huskisson, undersecretary of state for war (with characteristic asperity) wrote to Dundas: 'The Plain Fact is that Lord Spencer wants firmness. He is not master at his own board, while Admiral Young, who is, has a little, jealous, overbearing mind, which opposes or thwarts every scheme he does not himself suggest.'[41] While Huskisson's judgement could be ascribed to jealousy between departments, Young, as a French-speaking, highly intelligent, punctilious young rear-admiral, did irritate others, in and out of the service, and was instinctively cautious. Lord St Vincent (as Admiral Sir John Jervis became in June 1797), commanding the Channel Fleet at the time, was critical of the principle of appointing professional naval officers as Admiralty commissioners in general and of Young in particular: 'It is incomprehensible to me why he keeps more than one Seaman at the Board, for they do nothing, but confound, impede & distract.'[42] (Although, as usual with St Vincent, he said one thing and did another: when he was appointed first lord in 1801, three sea officers and one civilian were on his Board.)

Although Britain began to lose the initiative in the French West Indies, Dundas maintained their conquest as top priority. After the expedition of 1793–4 under Grey and Jervis, a large force was assembled in the spring and summer of 1795 under Major General Ralph Abercromby and Rear-Admiral Hugh Christian. The deadline set for

* Middleton's remarkable reappearance in 1805 as first lord of the Admiralty at the age of seventy-nine was a political anomaly.

sailing from England was 15 September. Dundas ruthlessly stripped the best troops from units destined for other purposes in the Mediterranean and India and Spencer likewise took ships from the North Sea Fleet to escort the transports across the Atlantic.[43] The government needed 30,000 troops for the expedition, but it could raise only 18,000. The king refused point blank to release his guardsmen. All these preparations were dogged by misunderstandings between the admirals and generals, inter-service friction over discipline on board the transports and delays in assembling shipping.

Dundas, chafing in Whitehall, put back the sailing date until October, urging everyone to great effort. The expedition was certainly well equipped. Though late in arriving at Spithead because they needed repair, sixteen East Indiamen were invaluable as troop transports: to man them the Company raised 3,000 seamen at its own expense.[44] Their holds were loaded with the bricks needed for military buildings in San Domingo. Sixteen storeships carried twenty-four portable timber blockhouses. Eight ships of the line and ten frigates and sloops escorted twelve naval victuallers, eleven Ordnance storeships and four hospital ships. The 18,000 soldiers were carried by 110 transports. With them sailed merchantmen destined for the Mediterranean as well as the West Indies. The great convoy finally left Spithead on 16 November, a mild sunny day, but well into the season of dangerous autumn gales. Only a day later, when the ships were off Weymouth, a violent south-west gale struck. There were collisions, and some ships foundered. Most were driven back to Spithead, some swept all the way up the English Channel. Five ships went ashore on the Chesil Bank, where 249 officers and men were drowned, their bodies washed up on the beach.[45] The convoy had started with 236 ships but ended up on 29 January 1796 with 35.[46] The expedition was in tatters. A muster taken in February 1796 showed over 11,000 men back in Portsmouth, with 7,000 unaccounted for, presumed to be in the West Indies. Abercromby did not reach Barbados until 21 April 1796. Dundas had put too much of a strain upon Britain's war machinery.

Only in distant waters was there success, though not directly at the expense of the French, but rather of the divided Dutch nation, now occupied by France. Dundas's East India Company connections ensured that a small force was quickly off the mark in the early summer of 1795, sailing to secure the Cape and Dutch East Indies, having taken advantage of the presence of the fugitive Dutch stadtholder, the prince of Orange, in London to give authority to the expedition. The squadron was commanded by Vice-Admiral George Keith Elphinstone, with a force of only 3,000 men under General Craig; they had orders to sail on to Ceylon to take Trincomalee as well.[47] At the Cape, the Dutch were unprepared and morale was low: they had just over 500 infantry and 400 gunners. A bombardment was followed by lengthy negotiations, during which the British dug themselves into a good position. Food ran short for the invasion force, but Dutch resistance crumbled quickly. The Cape was taken on 16 September not in the name of the prince of Orange, but of the British crown. The Dutch felt deeply betrayed, and their local commander committed suicide.[48] Nevertheless, the next year Elphinstone was able to demand the surrender of an inferior Dutch squadron that arrived to try to relieve the Cape. Trincomalee, an immense, sheltered harbour in Ceylon, had fallen even more easily at the end of August.[49]

These small successes, though important for colonial security, were but sideshows to the main struggle in the West Indies. By October 1795, 52 regiments were either on their way to the islands or had already arrived; 53 were stretched out over the rest of the world, in the East Indies, the Cape, Canada, Gibraltar and Corsica, or on board warships, as there was also a considerable shortage of marines.[50] Eventually Abercromby achieved success in a confused and disparate war against French colonists, troops and rebels, where holding on to gains was almost as difficult as the initial assault on the French islands. St Lucia, St Vincent and Grenada were captured, Jamaica pacified, and the Dutch South American colonies were secured. In 1796 and 1797 a further, much smaller expedition was led by Abercromby, with Admiral Harvey as the naval commander. When Spain entered the war against Britain in late 1796, Trinidad became a target. It was captured in February 1797 with spectacular success and prize money. Spanish resistance there was minimal, but the Spaniards fought with courage and skill during the British assault on San Juan, Puerto Rico, forcing Abercromby to abandon the attack.

The abiding image of the West Indies campaigns is one of disease, which accounted for horrific British casualties. Between 1793 and

1801, 89,000 private soldiers and NCOs served in the West Indies. Half of them died: the exact figure was 43,747.* If discharges and desertions are included, the figure for losses is 62,250, a staggering 70 per cent.[51] The crews of transports and the navy also suffered badly. Such death rates among sea officers were never to be surpassed at any point in the French Revolutionary and Napoleonic wars.[52]

These great losses accentuated the problem of manpower shortages, something that was to dog successive British governments for twenty years of war, and affected both the army and the navy. By the middle of 1793 parliament had voted money for 45,000 seamen; a year later money for 85,000, although this figure was an intention and had no bearing on numbers actually aboard the ships. Impressment was responsible for only a small proportion of recruited seamen, at particular times of emergency: the King's Bounty, steadily inducing volunteers to join, proved to be more effective.† The real problem was competition for skilled seamen with a merchant marine that was still expanding and, because wages rose in wartime, paid better. An estimated 81,534 seamen in 1794 were employed in merchant ships, in comparison with the 83,891 in the navy.[53] In addition a relatively small number of privateers were also being fitted out at the start of the war, although they absorbed far fewer men. By 1795 parliament had voted money for 100,000 seamen. To meet the shortfall, in February of that year Pitt brought forward bills forcing shipowners to supply men to the navy, at one man for every seventy-five tons of shipping, hoping that this would raise about 18,000 men. Hostile reaction was immediate. In Whitehaven, for instance, the shipowners met at the Black Lion on 7 February 1795 to petition parliament, reckoning by the tonnage of their registered shipping that they would have to raise 761 men, and put forward persuasive arguments that this

* Similarly the French were reckoned to have lost 40,000 troops in their reconquest of San Domingo at the time of the Peace of Amiens (Holland Rose, 'West Indian Commerce', p. 37).

† The King's Bounty was £5 for an able seaman, £2.10s. for ordinary seamen and £1.10s. for landsmen. In addition, seamen would receive two months' wages on volunteering, so an able seaman would clear £7. For volunteers in London, the Corporation added £2 for an able seaman and £1 for an ordinary seaman (Dancy, 'Naval Manpower', pp. 149–50).

measure would 'annihilate our Coal Trade'.[54] It took far more time to raise men than the government had estimated. In March 1795 the government then tried to implement the Quota Acts, which required each county to raise a specific number of men for the navy.[55] This met smart opposition from the county members, and, though men were found, the process was still a slow one. The Acts were very complicated, with twenty-three different forms of orders and returns appended. The legal and administrative procedures involved parish overseers and justices of the peace, as well as the local Quarter Sessions, and in some cases parishes preferred to pay a fine, rather than raise their allotted number of men. The whole of Kent, for instance, a populous county with seagoing centres at Deptford, Woolwich, Chatham and Dover, raised just 500 men in 1796 and 1797, enough to man only a 64-gun warship.[56] It has been argued that these Acts were the first step towards conscription, but, if so, they were little more than a tiptoe.[57] The delays and complications of the quota system demonstrate why Great Britain could find no alternative to impressment when men were needed, however brutal it appeared then and still appears today.

It was a similar story with the land forces. Shortages of recruits at home were worrying.* In 1793 the army abroad numbered 18,194, though with the expansion of the war, particularly in the West Indies, it increased rapidly to 41,494 by 1794.[58] In the early years of the war recruitment was boosted by the Scots and Irish, who made up half the regular British Army in 1793 and 1794. With only one tenth of the population of the United Kingdom, Scotland provided a fifth of its military manpower, and of 56 regiments added to the line in 1794, 22 were Irish. Not surprisingly, however, particular difficulties were experienced in raising men for service in the West Indies. There was resistance from units already recruited in Essex and Newcastle, who

---

* In 1795 it was reckoned that 127,500 troops were required for the defence of Britain. A year later General David Dundas, then quartermaster-general of the forces, requested 16,000 cavalry and 100,000 infantry, compared to the actual numbers enlisted of 14,700 and 52,900. In 1796 there were still fewer than 10,000 volunteer infantry in England (Cookson, *Armed Nation*, pp. 26–7, 32). These figures broadly agree with Lieutenant-General Harry Calvert's, who reckoned in Aug. 1796 that there were 110,000 troops of every kind in Britain (Verney, *Harry Calvert*, p. 451).

refused to sign the muster book. In Ireland the atmosphere was even more tense. Loyal regiments had to be brought in to quell dissident troops protesting against embarkation in Dublin and Cork. In Dublin three days of riots in August 1795 brought city life to a standstill, with the soldiers ending their protest only when the cavalry, artillery and 2,000 militia faced them down. In Cork a full-blown mutiny did not give way until cannon were brought in: six mutineers were sentenced to be shot, and the NCOs were reduced to privates.[59]

The need for more troops became acute. Nevertheless, in the second half of the 1790s, recruitment eventually gathered momentum. In Ireland, after the invasion scares and rebellion in the country, the total of regular, militia and voluntary troops, which had languished at about 30,000 in 1797, reached over 100,000 by 1799.[60] This brought the theoretical strength of the home garrison throughout Great Britain and Ireland to about 100,000, and it varied between 65,000 and 110,000 troops for most of the French Revolutionary War.[61]

One consequence of the manpower shortage was a reliance on foreign troops. In 1799 one officer of the 60th Regiment recorded that battalions were composed entirely of foreigners: 'Russians, Poles, Germans, Italians, French, etc.: we had one Cingalese. These men were enlisted from the foreign brigade, viz. the Duc de Castre's corps, York hussars, chasseurs Britannique, le regiment de Mortemarte, and Prince Charles of Levenstein's corps etc.' The York Hussars, he added, 'were raised in Germany, and about 150 of them were Hungarians; their complexions very dark, and they wore large mustaches'.[62] If a French royalist was ever captured, his fate was death, as Harry Calvert reported after the surrender of Nieuport in 1794: '300 men of the Corps of Chartres formed part of the garrison, and I am afraid there can be no doubt in regard to the fate of these unfortunate men.'[63] Again, not surprisingly, the quality of these troops was poor, and they performed very badly in the West Indies, with high desertion rates. In 1797 Abercromby wrote to Henry Dundas in disgust: 'I clearly see that the German Regiments raised by adventurers will not answer. They are at best to be compared to the condottiers of the sixteenth and seventeenth centuries.'[64]

Backing up the regular troops were the traditional county militia regiments, which were used for invasion defence duties or to control domestic unrest, and subject to military discipline. They were established by annual Militia Acts passed by parliament, and raised by ballots held in local towns and parishes.[65] An individual could avoid service by paying for a substitute, of which there were many. The Oxford Militia in 1796, for instance, included 43 men from Coventry, Abingdon, Berkshire and even from distant Suffolk and Shropshire.* However, it was soon seen that the militia could be a good source of men for the regular army, and successive Militia Acts, starting with the first in 1796, began transferring men to the regular army, a process which was much expanded in the Napoleonic War.[66]

The early duties of the militia regiments were directed towards control of domestic order, and they were kept on the move so that fraternization with the local population was kept to a minimum. Inevitably in these early days, instances of the breakdown of discipline were numerous. When the price of flour and grain rose in 1794 and 1795, the militia food allowance of fivepence a day did not go far, and some units became involved in disturbances. During 1795 militiamen took part in sixteen food riots. In Portsmouth the Gloucestershire Militia forced butchers to lower their prices. Plymouth and Chichester suffered riotous behaviour by militia from Northamptonshire and Hertfordshire respectively. In Seaford in Sussex, the Oxford Militia, stationed there because of the invasion scare and responsible for order in the county, plundered meat from the populace.† The authorities took strong measures and five militiamen were hanged. In May 1795 Robert Banks Jenkinson and his regiment were ordered to Brighton to keep the peace when two soldiers of the Oxfordshire regiment were to be shot for rioting and pulling down flour-mills. Far from the light-heartedness of early 1794, Canning recorded that Jenkinson 'puts on a most formidable appearance of resolution'.[67]

Opinion of the militiamen was divided, their effectiveness dependent

---

* In Nov. 1796 the 'Berks., Bucks., Oxon. and Hants Original Militia Society Office for Providing Substitutes for the New and Old Militia' offered to find a substitute for an annual fee of one guinea (Horn, *Rural World*, p. 65).

† Militia regiments were kept moving to another county every nine months or so (see Chapter 9).

on local politics, the law and the determination of local magistrates.*
The duke of Gloucester, a professional soldier, was not confident of their
performance in the event of invasion, 'not from the men being bad, but
from the Ignorance of the Officers, and as they are well aware of their
own incapacity to command they will be diffident of themselves, and
Confusion will be constant'.[68] But, as the wars wore on, there can be no
doubt of the increasing usefulness of the militia, and the experience of a
military life was to be a great asset for recruits to the regular army.[69]

In Ireland, it was different. Deep-seated weaknesses in society were
perceived by Edward Cooke, undersecretary in Dublin Castle. In
1793 he wrote to Evan Nepean of 'a mountainous, poor, oppressed,
numerous and Catholic rabble with whom no gentry reside, among
whom there is no parish system . . . who have been and are ill-used by
their landlords'. His analysis was grim and proved to be correct: 'they
can only be kept down by power.'[70] Here, the implementation of the
Militia Acts caused violent and sustained disturbances, in contrast to
the previous peacefulness in Ireland. Food riots were unknown and,
until the beginning of the war, there had been much less domestic
unrest than in England.[71] Raising the militia caused disaffection
towards the British government, as well as divisions between Protes-
tants and Catholics. Attacks were made on soldiers who tried to enforce
the Acts, and loss of life became commonplace. During this period
militia regiments were formed but always with great difficulty. In
some areas in Ireland, militias could be raised by paid substitutes
alone and the ballot recruitment system was quietly abandoned.

There remained another way to avoid militia service: a man could
join the local volunteers. Volunteers were locally raised infantry and
cavalry, paid by the government and used at first for static defence of
government property or military installations. A minority of volunteer corps were formed in the industrial areas of the East Midlands,
Lancashire and Yorkshire, composed mainly of the middle classes,
who feared social unrest.[72] Only if the volunteers were called out to

---

* Ambivalence about the militia was heard around at least one London dinner table
in 1799. Lady Stafford reported to her son that one of her guests 'felt it not a Situation
for *a Gentleman now* to remain in a Militia Corps' (Granville, *Leveson Gower Correspondence*, Vol. I, p. 269).

active service would they be, as the Act of 1794 stated, 'subject to Military Discipline as the rest of His Majesty's Regular and Militia Troops', although no volunteers could be tried by court martial unless the court was composed of volunteer officers.[73] Volunteer recruitment proceeded slowly between 1794 and 1796, with 160 corps raised, including yeoman cavalry, mostly from the counties with the greatest threat of invasion. From 1794 volunteer regiments or battalions guarded and assisted the working of coastal batteries. Scotland raised nine volunteer Fencible battalions (the equivalent of English volunteers), then another sixteen with the first of the invasion threats in 1794.[74] Later the better-trained units supported the field armies in measures against invasion, the rest remaining in their localities undertaking guard, escort and police duties. This limited role was reduced in January 1798, when training budgets were cut, but the government was able to reverse its policy later in the year and set more generous allowances for training and service. Some corps were willing to travel away from their localities, while others prepared themselves for guarding prisoners of war or convoying army supply trains in the event of invasion. In London the government even incorporated the eight most efficient corps into the capital's garrison.[75]

The volunteers, however, were fair game to caricaturists and satirists, who made the most out of their portly efforts at marching or on horseback. One volunteer, Edward Law, later Lord Ellenborough, the lord chief justice, was mimicked on the London stage. A diarist noted that Law 'moved with a sort of semi-rotatory step, and his path to the place to which he wished to go was the section of a parabola'. He was turned out of the Lincoln's Inn Volunteers for awkwardness.[76] Yet much evidence points to considerable volunteer discipline and enthusiasm. When not on active service, which was almost all the time, discipline for the mass of the volunteers was self-imposed. In Dorset the Piddletown Light Infantry drew up their own rules. Rule 5 reads: 'Whoever Speaks, or Laughs in the Ranks, after the word attention is given, or until after the order stand at ease, to be fined Sixpence'. Rule 10: 'Whoever appears on Parade in Liquor, shall be fined Five Shillings.' Using his musket privately would cost a man 2s.6d. Fines were collected fortnightly.[77] These makeshift measures clearly had some effect, and the volunteers on occasion demonstrated considerable initiative.*

The manpower shortage ensured that the government was unable to contemplate any major initiatives. By the end of 1795 Pitt's cabinet belatedly realized that success was not likely to come easily or early, and concerns were growing about the possibilities of an invasion, for on 1 October 1795 France had annexed the Austrian Netherlands. Two major policy changes were initiated in 1796. The first was a serious effort at making peace with France. At the end of 1794, secret peace overtures from the moderate constitutional monarchist politicians had reached London. Convoluted negotiations with French opposition groups followed, conducted chiefly through William Wickham, transferred in haste from London to Berne in Switzerland.[78] The mood became more pacific in London. In the House of Commons, on 27 May 1795, Pitt signalled the end of the propaganda conflict that had marked the first years of the war, admitting that there might now be room for negotiation with Paris. He finally abandoned his hostile ideological stance on 8 December 1795.[79] James Harris, now the earl of Malmesbury, was despatched to Paris to negotiate with the Directory on 15 October 1796. In England there was support for peace, though some, including Edmund Burke, still opposed it. Malmesbury arrived in Paris on 22 October, taking a full week for the journey, which led Burke to make the witty, bitter comment that 'he went the whole way on his knees.'[80] Peace negotiations continued for two months, with Austria reluctant to be involved. Malmesbury resumed the talks in Lille in July 1797, but was finally ordered to leave in September 1797, when the French broke off negotiations and Malmesbury came home empty-

---

* In 1799 a French privateer was seen in Weymouth Bay taking the brig *Somerset*, on passage from Poole to Bristol. A captain in the Weymouth and Wyke Volunteers took some of his company, and some Sea Fencibles, on board a small cutter and gave chase, despite the fact that they were armed only with muskets and bayonets. They succeeded in retaking the *Somerset* and went on to make an unsuccessful attempt to capture the privateer, a brave decision in view of the privateer's superior guns over their own small arms (Clammer, 'Dorset Volunteers', p. 24). The recapture of a British ship by a volunteer army unit was unusual, to say the least.

handed. The constantly shifting political situation in France made it difficult to know if the French were ever serious. With the now-subdued Vendée no longer a threat to Paris, serious plans for French invasion attempts on Ireland were in hand, with a fleet and troops preparing in Den Helder and in Brest, while a flotilla was gathering at Dunkirk.[81]

The second major policy shift – to abandon the Mediterranean – stemmed from a weakening strategic situation in southern Europe. Led brilliantly by the dashing 27-year-old Napoleon Bonaparte, the French Army was overrunning Italy, and in August Spain changed sides, signing the secret Treaty of San Ildefonso with France and declaring war against Britain in October. In August the cabinet ordered Admiral Sir John Jervis, who had taken command of the Mediterranean Fleet in December 1795, to evacuate Corsica and to withdraw the fleet to Lisbon and Gibraltar, the latter potentially under threat from Spain. Jervis, who was ruthlessly instilling discipline in the fleet, was mortified by the order to retreat, received just when he had a real prospect of success against the weak Spanish Navy. Despite the cabinet's apparently decisive move, fissures were apparent, particularly the differences between Dundas and Spencer, whose inexperience was turned into excessive caution by the naval officers on the Admiralty Board. On 19 October the cabinet countermanded the previous order, intending to offer Corsica to Russia. Fortunately, Jervis received the second order too late, for his fleet had already evacuated the army from the island. He wrote to Spencer that it was 'a great blessing that the evacuation of Corsica had taken place before I received the orders to maintain the Viceroy in the sovereignty of it'.[82]

The government was also on the defensive financially, for by the fourth year of the war expenditure had increased to over £42 million, of which £28 million had been spent on the army, navy and Ordnance. Government income from taxes had hardly increased in recent years and in 1796 was £19.3 million.[83] Government credit was weakened, as shown by the fluctuations in the value of the 3 per cent Consols, the abbreviation for the 'Consolidated Annuities'. The price of this stock, always the best indicator of the financial health of the government, had stood at 81 at the beginning of the war in 1793, had slowly decreased in 1794 to between 72 and 63, but by 1796 had sunk to 53 and was to hit its lowest point in 1797, at the time of the naval mutinies, of 47½.* The chief loan contractor to the government, Walter Boyd, had become overextended, and began to fail, filing for bankruptcy in 1799.[84] Up to this point, Pitt's financial strategy was based on the assumption that the war was unlikely to last long, and that the imposed loans and rampant inflation in France would bring the enemy to the negotiating table.†

Now, with the peace talks faltering, Pitt risked the launch of a voluntary Loyalty Loan on 1 December 1796 – money raised from the public for government bonds issued at a generous percentage. Despite an atmosphere of foreboding, institutions and individuals responded readily and the issue was a success. The East India Company subscribed £2 million, the Bank of England £1 million. Members of the cabinet tried to raise a respectable amount to set an example. Within four days £18 million had been gathered, most of it from individuals spurred by feelings of national insecurity.[85] But it was still not enough, and Pitt needed to raise more by taxes. In January 1798 he introduced the Triple Assessment, a form of graduated income tax based on the assessed taxes of the previous year; by 1799 he had gone a stage further and brought in an income tax of two shillings in the pound on individuals with a total income over £200, with abatements for incomes between £60 and £200.[86]

The foundering peace negotiations were the precursor to another series of failures, most conspicuously at sea, where Britain was traditionally unassailable. It was difficult to maintain the blockade of the French Channel ports during the storms of the winter months, and the French began to undertake naval operations in winter. Between 1796 and 1806 seven French squadrons escaped from Brest and three left Rochefort, all but three of them in winter.[87] Senior British admirals could and should have done better, especially as victualling

---

* Van Sommer, *Consols*, 1793.–7. Consols were effectively the government securities of Great Britain. In 1752 many different stocks had been consolidated into a single stock bearing interest at 3 per cent.
† The cost of living in Paris, with indices at 100 in 1790, was said to be 5,000 in Nov. 1795, and the plight of the poor was desperate (Godechat, 'French Internal History', p. 288).

supplies were steadily improving through these years. From 1797 the Channel Fleet was led weakly by the unwell and demoralized Alexander Hood, Lord Bridport (the brother of Samuel, Lord Hood), now nearly seventy, who had long been second-in-command to Howe. Bridport's fleet was more often to be found sheltering in Torbay than off Brest. When he belatedly received his commission as commander-in-chief after Howe had gone ashore, he wrote a disgruntled letter to Lord Spencer, complaining about his situation and the number of ships at his disposal. Spencer passed it on to the king. The king, however, had no truck with either of the Hood brothers. Recalling that Bridport's brother Samuel had been dismissed by Lord Chatham for demanding more ships in the Mediterranean in 1794, His Majesty commented that 'it appears too plain that in his family self value is so predominant.'[88] Yet Lord Spencer kept Bridport in command of the fleet until April 1800, retiring him at the age of seventy-three. The dramatic and immediate improvement in close blockade brought about by his tough replacement, Lord St Vincent, served to underline Bridport's ineffectiveness.

In December 1796 Bridport's second-in-command, Vice-Admiral John Colpoys, cruising off Brest, was, through faulty intelligence, to make a mistake that led to the most dangerous single moment in the French Revolutionary War. Because the Admiralty was convinced that the Brest Fleet was heading for Portugal, Colpoys allowed a considerable French invasion force to slip through his blockade by returning to Portsmouth to resupply – but the French were making for Bantry Bay in Ireland. The young Castlereagh, commanding the Derry Militia as it hurried south, reported to his stepbrother, Charles Stewart: 'Colpoys could not venture so far from home as Portugal, his water being almost expended, but might well have follow'd them to Ireland.'[89] Colpoys should have ensured that he was never short of water.

The government in London hadn't the slightest idea what was happening. Commanded by General Lazare Hoche, the French expedition was a substantial fleet of 44 ships, 17 of them ships of the line, but with only 7 transports for 14,000 troops; each ship of the line had 600 troops on board, in addition to a crew of approximately the same size. The sailing ability of these hopelessly overcrowded warships was adversely affected, particularly when going to windward.[90] In the event, the winter storms proved too much for the French Navy, and after a week of gales they turned for home without landing. It was a near-run thing. Had the weather been more moderate, or the French leadership more daring, Cork, with its sheltered harbour, would have been open to an attack, its defences neglected by General Lord Carhampton, the commander-in-chief in Ireland. Since winter was the season when the quays of the city were piled with thousands of barrels of newly slaughtered beef and pork, and plenty of biscuit awaiting distribution, Hoche's army would have needed no resupplying, and could have held out against any attempt to dislodge it. Such a turn of events would have dramatically altered the course of the war. The episode created an expectation in ministers that the French would attempt an invasion of Ireland at some point in the future.

Lessons were quickly learnt. Spencer ordered Colpoys off station, and improvements were made to the system of blockade. Within government there was much concern at the lacklustre performance of the Irish military, particularly the slow movement of troops south to meet the danger, while the sour relations between Lord Camden, the Viceroy in Dublin Castle, and General Lord Carhampton, worked against efficiency.[91] But the government had denuded Ireland of regular troops: at the time of the attempt on Bantry Bay, only 2,000 regular infantry and 3,640 cavalry remained in the country, and the defence of Ireland rested on 17,000 militia troops. Of these, however, 10,000 were in the north, unable to march south to meet the French because of a discontented population and the threat of civil revolt.[92] Only the loyalist yeomanry emerged with any reputation.[93] The defence of Ireland had been on a knife-edge. From Dublin, Edward Cooke confessed to Lord Auckland that 'had a complete landing been effected, I fear that there would have been another tale'.[94]

The government now regarded Ireland as neither safe nor loyal. All the Irish generals were replaced, and in October Abercromby finally agreed, after much hesitation, to serve as commander-in-chief. He attempted to instil some discipline into the Irish Army by concentrating it in several centres, but this resulted in its losing much of its capacity to maintain civil order. Disputes flared between Abercromby and Lord Camden, the viceroy in Dublin Castle, unsure of their respective lines of authority.[95] Abercromby issued a 'General Proclamation' that scath-ingly referred to the army's 'state of licentiousness which makes it formidable to everyone but the enemy'. This was too much for Cam-den, who secured Abercromby's early return to England.[96] The United Irishmen in Ulster were systematically repressed, leading to a worsen-ing of relations and finally to outright rebellion in 1798. With such a sullen mood prevalent in Ireland, particularly in the north, a successful French invasion could have been disastrous for the British cause. As the duke of Portland remarked to Lord Camden: 'There is little distinc-tion to be made between indifference and disaffection.'[97]

Two months after the Irish emergency a ragamuffin French force of criminals and adventurers landed at Fishguard in South Wales. They were quickly rounded up by the local militia under Lord Cawdor, but the country was so jittery that the idea of a successful landing caused a run on the banks and the Bank of England was forced to suspend payments of bills into cash.* The 1797 Bank Restriction Act prohib-ited the Bank of England from issuing anything other than paper notes, and the export of gold was made illegal.[98] Britain thus came off the gold standard. Remarkably, the financial crisis did not lead to any change in British strategy. Not a great deal of specie had been exported, and most of the subsidies to allies had been remitted in bills of exchange.† The government borrowing continued. By the end of the Revolutionary War, the national debt was close to £700 million, more than twice what it had been when Pitt came to power in 1784.[99]

Notice was now taken of those who had been warning about the military threat to England itself. One such was Colonel George Hanger, who had published in March 1795 *Military Reflections on the Attack and Defence of the City of London*. He argued persua-sively that the British Fleet was no guarantor of defence, citing the 1779 fiasco in the American Revolutionary War, when the combined French and Spanish fleets had threatened Plymouth, and the British

---

* Some thirty of the Frenchmen escaped from prison near Pembroke, showing more initiative than during the invasion, and made their way back to St Malo, using Lord Cawdor's private yacht on the way (Lloyd, *Prisoners of War*, pp. 65–6).

† The great Austrian loan of 1795 of £4,600,000 had resulted in the transfer of only £1,193,000 in hard money; the rest was in commercial bills (Sherwig, *Guineas and Gunpowder*, p. 88).

Fleet was well to the west of the Scilly Isles. Hanger thought that the main danger was to the Thames on the Essex side, describing very exactly how invasion could be accomplished; and he urged that defence works should be thrown up around London.[100]

Systematic defence planning did not start until the second half of the 1790s, when agreement on the coastal areas most at risk from invasion was reached between the army, the Ordnance and the Home Office. Detailed assessments of the most likely beaches to be chosen by the French were made. There was not much likelihood of invasion west of the Solent, since a south-west wind which would assist an invasion flotilla from Brest or the Brittany ports would throw up heavy surf on beaches in the West of England. The main area of danger lay between Suffolk and the Solent, though the shoals of the inner Thames Estuary were seen as a natural defence. Immediate preparations on the south coast included provision for flooding the Pett and Pevensey levels.[101] A strategy of pre-emptive strikes against French ports was put forward by Henry Dundas in January 1798. Those ports in which shipping was concentrated, and where invasion preparations were suspected, were to be attacked.[102] The first successful raid took place in May of that year, against Ostend, led by Captain Sir Home Popham, blowing up the lock gates there, at the cost of the loss of the troops taking part, who could not be re-embarked because of a gale springing up.[103] Attacking ports where the French were making invasion preparations continued until the end of the Napoleonic War.

Only the victory of Admiral Jervis in February 1797 at Cape St Vincent brought relief to the gloom, when at last a rapidly improving Mediterranean Fleet dealt the Spanish Fleet a blow from which it never really recovered. But any feelings of confidence and safety that a successful navy might have engendered were quashed, when, less than three months later, mutiny broke out in the fleet at Spithead, a protest against over-zealous discipline and insufficient pay. There was little violence, and the men negotiated with the first lord of the Admiralty, who sped down to Portsmouth. Though the government publicly blamed subversive republican or Irish elements for the trouble, privately they acknowledged that, in Lord Spencer's words, 'the wages were undoubtedly too low in proportion to the times.'[104] The government largely agreed to the men's demands, and parliament started to draft legislation to enable the men to be paid more.* This took time, and the men at Spithead began to feel that they were being deceived. On 7 May, Admiral Colpoys, on board his flagship the *London*, ordered his marines to fire on the mutineers, killing several. He and his officers were captured by the seamen and confined to their cabins. Just when the lieutenant who had given the first order to fire was about to be hanged, a seaman who had been elected a delegate for the ship intervened. According to the intended victim, 'I had fifty pistols levelled at my head, and the yard rope round my neck, and by his manly eloquence procured a pardon from the delegates for the Admiral and Captain when everyone conceived it impossible that they could be saved.'[105] The lives of Colpoys, his captain and the lieutenant were all spared. It was a critical moment in the mutiny, and in the war. The mutineers at Spithead showed remarkable discipline and self-restraint. Afterwards Lord Howe travelled from Bath to the fleet, making his way from ship to ship, re-establishing trust by agreeing that unpopular officers should be replaced, probably exceeding his brief from the Admiralty.

The mutiny at the Nore, however, which broke out a month later, was much uglier, and the warships controlled by the mutineers blockaded the port of London, refusing entry to merchant ships. The first lord of the Admiralty, now at Sheerness, refused further concessions and stopped food supplies from going aboard the mutineers' ships. The government was worried that this disaffection would spread, and in the Downs and at Plymouth there were real signs of disaffection.[106] The mutiny eventually collapsed: Richard Parker, the leader, was hanged for high treason.†

* The seamen demanded equality with soldiers and their 'shilling a day'. In 1793 an able seaman received £1.4s. per lunar month, and ordinary seaman 19s. By 1815 these figures were £1.13s. and £1.5s.6d. and the unskilled landsman £1.2s.6d. (Lewis, *Social History*, pp. 300, 303).

† There were 'unpleasant symptoms', too, in one of the battalions of the Guards in London. An isolated instance among the artillery at Woolwich occurred on 27 May, and Pitt was woken in Downing Street by the accompanying gunfire (Fortescue, *British Army*, Vol. IV, Part 1, p. 530; Hague, *Pitt*, p. 404, quoting Wilberforce's diary).

Rebellion then spread to the ships under Admiral Adam Duncan at Great Yarmouth, whose ships were blockading the Dutch Fleet in the Texel, where troops destined for Ireland were embarking. One by one Duncan's ships sailed to join their fellows at the Nore. Here was an immediate strategic threat, but, worse still, the Nore mutineers threatened to sail up the Thames and hold the city to ransom under their guns. A worried Pitt wrote in early June to Spencer, asking for a chain and boom to be laid across the river from Tilbury to Gravesend to stop the mutinous ships (though the Ordnance Board reported that it would take two weeks to prepare one, and nothing was done).[107] Duncan persuaded the mutineers aboard his flagship the *Venerable* to return to their duty and the mutiny petered out. Duncan then, with remarkable presence of mind, went on to blockade the Dutch by anchoring his ship across the tide at the mouth of the Texel, making signals to an imaginary fleet out at sea, thus fooling the Dutch into believing that the British Fleet was at full strength. It was little wonder that Lord Spencer wrote on 14 June to tell Duncan that 'At the Trinity House dinner on Monday last, your health was drunk with universal applause. Your firmness on this occasion has indeed most deservedly secured you the approbation of your country.'[108]

Westerly winds prevented the Dutch from sailing out of the Texel through the summer of 1797, although the Dutch troops, accompanied by the Irish patriot Wolfe Tone, were embarked by July. Meanwhile, Duncan built up the number of ships in his fleet off the Texel. By mid August the Dutch, still in harbour, had run out of provisions, and the troops were disembarked.[109] Duncan rightly received further praise when he caught the Dutch Fleet off Camperdown in October, breaking their line and comprehensively defeating them, taking as prizes six ships of the line and six smaller ships. This put an end to any threat from foreign troops reaching Ireland from the North Sea.

Nevertheless, a serious Irish rebellion broke out on 24 May 1798. The army was reinforced, naval squadrons were stationed off the coast and experienced soldiers were now sent to Ireland. Lieutenant-General Gerard Lake, commander-in-chief, determined on ruthless suppression.* He was supported by Major General David Dundas, the experienced and thorough Major General John Moore, and the brilliant, headstrong Lieutenant-Colonel Robert Craufurd, who was deputy quartermaster-general. Craufurd felt that the Irish Militia was not ill-disciplined and that poor performance was the fault of the officers, 'more concerned with heavy drinking and nursing their packs of beagles than with learning the arts of warfare and attending to the welfare of their men'.[110] Craufurd's great fear was that the Irish rebels, if buttressed by the arrival of hardened French troops, would be irresistible: he had a good deal of respect for their fighting skills. By the end of the year Ireland was occupied by 100,000 soldiers, regulars, militia, volunteers and yeomanry. However, naive military tactics led the Irish rebels to occupy Vinegar Hill in County Wexford, but, after terrible slaughter by government artillery, they were defeated on 21 June in what proved to be the turning point of the uprising.

It was fortunate that the French found it impossible to land large bodies of troops in Ireland during 1798, for the small number that did manage it caused trouble enough. General Humbert landed at Killala in County Mayo in August 1798, when his troops behaved to the local population with traditional eighteenth-century civility rather than with revolutionary fervour. He quickly captured Ballina, Foxford and Castlebar – at the last engagement, the defeat of the militia was such an embarrassment that it came to be known as the 'Races of Castlebar'.[111] Humbert was later overwhelmed by British numbers at the Battle of Ballinamuck on 8 September, where he surrendered his small force of 844 men to Cornwallis. In contrast to the treatment of the Irish (almost all of whom were hanged), French officers and soldiers were treated as honourable prisoners of war. Rapid reinforcements were beyond the capability of the French Navy, which had to

---

* Lake ordered that no Irish prisoners were to be taken, following the example of General Hoche when suppressing the Vendéan rebels early in the war. At an engagement at Kilcullen David Dundas carried out these orders exactly, reporting that all 130 insurgents were killed, and none of his troops either killed or wounded. By contrast, at the Curragh a little later, he allowed the insurgents to surrender, for which he was criticized. Those United Irishmen who survived were imprisoned in Fort George near Inverness (Bartlett and Jeffrey, *Military History of Ireland*, p. 288).

overcome administrative delay and the British blockade; a squadron under Commodore Bompard tried to get away from Brest in August, but did not manage to do so until mid September. Sir John Borlase Warren restored some of the navy's defensive reputation when his squadron decimated Bompard's off Lough Swilly in October 1798; of the ten vessels in the French squadron, only three escaped capture.[112]

On 6 April the British cabinet took a decision that turned out to be both brilliant and decisive: to reinforce Admiral Lord St Vincent, now commanding the Mediterranean Fleet. Cruising with a powerful squadron off the south of Ireland, Rear-Admiral Sir Roger Curtis was given sealed orders that he was not to open until he was thirty leagues off the Irish coast. When he did so, he discovered that he was to take ten ships of the line down to St Vincent, who was blockading Cádiz. St Vincent immediately despatched ten of his own best ships, under the command of Thomas Troubridge, to reinforce Rear-Admiral Horatio Nelson, who was somewhere in the Mediterranean with three ships of the line, trying to find the great expedition commanded by Napoleon Bonaparte that had sailed from Toulon. The government, having misread intelligence reports, had been slow to realize that the bold French strategic move of 1798 was to strike at Egypt. Although Nelson was to miss the French fleet on its way to Alexandria, he destroyed it at the Battle of Aboukir Bay on 1 August 1798: his leading ships steered on the landward side of the anchored French ships which took them completely by surprise; only two of them survived and escaped. A relieved William Young wrote to Nelson on 3 October from the Admiralty: 'We have been drinking your health . . . and have lighted up our town till there was some chance of our burning it down.'[113] This overwhelming victory changed the nature of the war, bringing the Mediterranean under British control, opening up its trade, and encouraging Russia and Turkey into the war against France. The earl of Mornington did not restrain his praise when writing to Lord Grenville from India:

> I admire beyond all Greek, Roman, British, or any fame, the provident, bold, and (as it deserved) gloriously prosperous measure of reinforcing Lord St Vincent in the face of a menaced invasion and of an existing rebellion at home. Never was a public measure taken with more

wisdom or spirit. I cannot doubt that this success must awaken Europe.[114]

The Battle of the Nile was a glittering success, but there was little else for the British to cheer in the strategic situation at the end of 1798. The First European Coalition had collapsed. French power on the Continent was as strong as ever. In 1793 France stood alone against Europe: by 1796 Holland and Spain had changed sides to join her. Russia had contributed little to the Coalition, while Prussia, Sardinia and the Two Sicilies had retired from the fray.[115] Renewed war between Austria and France was expected over a long period, provoked by growing French domination of Italy and of Switzerland, which gave them access to the mountain passes between Germany and Italy, and undermined Austrian influence in the German states. War was declared in March 1799, by 'France recklessly, [and by] Austria with dogged resignation'.[116] It was followed by the formation of the Second Coalition against France, which Britain with all her former allies, signed on 1 June. No end to European-wide conflict could be discerned.

At least in the British administration the demands of a hard-fought war were beginning to clear out the dead wood. In 1794 General Lord Amherst, hero of the Seven Years War and commander-in-chief of the army, retired at seventy-six, to be succeeded in 1795 by the young duke of York, who, in contrast to his disappointing active fighting career, proved to be a tireless and able administrator. In the army, younger, talented and active men, such as Abercromby, Moore and Craufurd, were making their way to the top. Similar changes were taking place in the navy. Hood was sent as commander-in-chief, Mediterranean, in 1793, aged sixty-nine, and was dismissed a year later. Howe was sixty-seven when appointed as commander-in-chief, Channel Fleet. At the end of the four-day Battle of the First of June, not surprisingly, he was exhausted. He came ashore after the Channel Fleet was nearly wrecked in an easterly gale in Torbay in February 1795, but did not resign until May 1797, aged seventy-one. A handful of the most capable admirals of the older generation, such as St Vincent and Duncan, still flourished, and the solid Keith was to serve until the end of the Napoleonic War. Now Sir John Borlase Warren, Thomas Troubridge, James Saumarez and Richard Goodwin Keats were gaining seniority, while the younger Samuel Hood and Edward Pellew were making names for themselves as frigate captains. Nelson and his captains at the Battle of the Nile were on average ten years younger than those at the Battle of the First of June.[117]

At home, Pitt's political authority remained unthreatened, in spite of popular opposition to the war. But the reformer of the 1780s was, by the late 1790s, running a strongly repressive state, complete with Home Office spies and anti-labour legislation contained in the Combination Acts, of which that of 1799, 'to prevent the unlawful Combination of Workers', was the most severe. These were passed through parliament when there was great fear that southern England would be invaded, a fear that would not abate for the next ten years. At the same time huge sums of money were being spent on domestic fortifications, primarily at Dover Castle, and on the enormous increases in both the naval and military establishments.[118] To pay for all this, Pitt's efforts at raising taxes were beginning to bear fruit: by 1799 government tax income reached £31.7 million, in comparison with £19.3 million three years before.[119] The economy, which was growing vigorously and thriving, enabled Britain to carry on the fight.* Herein lay one of the differences from earlier wars in the eighteenth century, which had been curtailed by financial exhaustion after six or seven years. The pattern of hostilities against Revolutionary France remained the same: fleet actions in European waters, amphibious expeditions against the Continent, colonial warfare, defence against invasion and diplomatic coalitions with potential allies against a more powerful foe. What was different now was that the intensity and scale of the war against the French had dramatically increased.

---

* One modern estimate of real output of the total industry and commerce of Great Britain is that (with indices at 100 in 1700) it nearly doubled between 1780 (index at 197) and 1800 (at 387), while in the export industries it more than doubled. From 1785 per capita output increased by 9 per cent per decade (Deane and Cole, *Economic Growth*, pp. 78, 80).

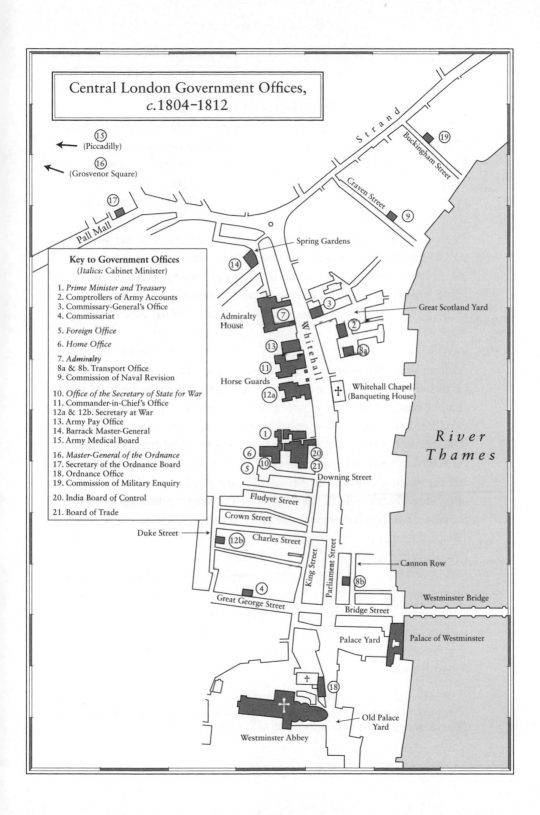

Central London Government Offices, c.1804–1812

⑮ ← (Piccadilly)

⑯ ← (Grosvenor Square)

Key to Government Offices
(*Italics:* Cabinet Minister)

1. *Prime Minister and Treasury*
2. Comptrollers of Army Accounts
3. Commissary-General's Office
4. Commissariat

5. *Foreign Office*
6. *Home Office*

7. *Admiralty*
8a & 8b. Transport Office
9. Commission of Naval Revision

10. *Office of the Secretary of State for War*
11. Commander-in-Chief's Office
12a & 12b. Secretary at War
13. Army Pay Office
14. Barrack Master-General
15. Army Medical Board

16. *Master-General of the Ordnance*
17. Secretary of the Ordnance Board
18. Ordnance Office
19. Commission of Military Enquiry

20. India Board of Control
21. Board of Trade

Strand

Buckingham Street

⑲

Craven Street

⑨

Pall Mall

⑰

Spring Gardens

⑭

Admiralty House

⑦

③

Great Scotland Yard

②

⑧a

⑬

⑪

Horse Guards

⑫a

Whitehall

✝ Whitehall Chapel (Banqueting House)

①

⑥

⑳

⑤ ⑩

㉑

Downing Street

Fludyer Street

Crown Street

Duke Street → ⑫b

Charles Street

King Street

Parliament Street

Cannon Row

⑧b

④

Great George Street

Bridge Street

Westminster Bridge

Palace Yard

Palace of Westminster

✝

⑱

River Thames

✝

Westminster Abbey

Old Palace Yard

4

Whitehall at War

1793–1802

The army, the navy, the public offices of government opened a career to numbers of every class, and by absorbing a very large proportion of the candidates for employment, created a corresponding briskness in agriculture, trade and professions.
– Joseph Lowe, *The Present State of England* (1822)[1]

A long war both required and caused the government bureaucracy to improve its efficiency. In the late eighteenth century, the civil service can be best described as a 'patchwork': parts of it were very competent and hard-working, while others were steeped in ancient precedent – unreformed, costly and, in some cases, useless. The Excise Department was widely held to be the most efficient, while the list at the other end of the scale included the Royal Household, the Seal Office and the Board of Works (which maintained government buildings).[2] The term 'civil service', conveying the idea of a coherent bureaucracy, governed by common rules and hierarchy, appeared for the first time only in a Treasury letter of 1816. 'Civil servants' were more commonly called 'officeholders', and the privileged who were awarded or inherited sinecures were known scornfully as 'placemen'.* Payments of fees and perquisites by outsiders to government officials in return for a service was a constant political irritant, particularly from the middle of the 1790s, the point at which the war initiated a great growth of government bureaucracy.

* However, the phrase 'civil servants in India' can be found earlier, in a letter of 6 May 1796 from Spencer to the commander-in-chief of the East Indies Station, Admiral Peter Rainier (Althorp Papers, BL, Add. MSS 75682, quoted in Ward, 'Rainier', p. 48).

At the centre of government was the Treasury, governed by a board of seven commissioners, whose first lord commissioner was the prime minister, the leader of the administration in office. The Whitehall policy departments such as the Foreign Office and the Home Office were relatively small. Those Whitehall departments with substantial spending, such as the Admiralty, Ordnance or Navy Office, or tax collecting responsibilities, such as the Customs or Excise, were managed by boards of commissioners, usually six or seven strong, appointed by the king.[3] Each of these boards ran its own office. The Treasury had a dual function, for not only was it the primary policy department, but it also supervised the Commissariat, which was responsible for supplying and provisioning the army, leaving control of the army, jealously guarded since the civil wars of the seventeenth century, ultimately in the hands of the prime minister. In 1797 the Treasury Department contained 142 clerks, of whom 85 served the Commissariat, but these numbers nearly doubled in the following seven years.[4] The army, being a decentralized, loose-knit organization composed of many regiments, dependent on the king for promotions and appointments, had no boards, though the secretary at war had 35 clerks in 1796; by 1806 they had increased fourfold.[5]

This loose system at the top of government, run on personal contacts, had its limitations, especially after July 1794, when the Portland Whigs left Opposition and joined Pitt's administration. If Pitt did not have a contact in a department, he remained 'uninformed and powerless'.[6] The prime minister could not order a minister to carry out a policy: only a decision of the whole cabinet could enable this to happen. All he could do was to persuade and to influence. The same was true of appointments, over which Pitt took great trouble, carefully selecting young men of talent.* He would encourage them by securing their appointment to select committees, or by giving them a chance to air their speaking talents – for example, by seconding the 'Address' in

* Pitt had intervened early in his administration to push for the appointment of Alexander Trotter as deputy paymaster of the navy, the man who eventually was to bring about the impeachment of his political master, and ex-treasurer of the navy, Henry Dundas. Pitt assured the banker Thomas Coutts that Trotter was 'a Person of whose character I had a very respectable Testimony . . . I do not know with certainty what his [Dundas's] decision will be' (Pitt to Coutts, 29 Dec. 1785, Pitt Papers, WLC).

answer to the King's Speech. His shrewdness at assessing the potential of young men was highlighted by their subsequent careers. Of thirty-four chosen by Pitt for the seventeen addresses in his first ministry, two were future prime ministers, Addington and Canning, and five became cabinet ministers. Indeed, Pitt encouraged and nurtured the early careers of the best part of two generations of politicians, stretching as far into the future as the earl of Aberdeen, who resigned as prime minister in 1855.[7]

In early 1795 Canning mused in his journal on the current gossip that he was likely to be given a seat on the Board of Admiralty, but he knew that it was unlikely: 'it must be an office in Pitt's disposal – and these Admiralty changes are solely and exclusively the province and choice of Lord Spencer – with whom I have nothing to do.' Some three months later Canning again, talking to Pitt, expressed his wish for office; Pitt 'lamented indeed that the number of efficient working offices, except those of the very first rank, was so small as to make the selection of such a one as I described out of very few indeed'. One vacancy existed at undersecretary level in the Home Office, which Pitt agreed to raise delicately with the duke of Portland.[8] In the event, early in 1796 Canning was appointed as undersecretary in the Foreign Office under Lord Grenville, which he hated; he referred later to 'the <u>disagreeableness</u> which I experienced during my Under Sec[retaryshi]p with Lord G'.[9] Pitt's use of informal influence was illustrated in early 1797, when the prime minister fell out with his foreign secretary over the peace negotiations with France, which Grenville opposed, a question debated with 'great violence' in cabinet. Pitt made use of his young man, obtaining information from Canning behind his foreign secretary's back, and altering Grenville's drafts for the king. They proved vital for winning the policy argument.[10]

A vignette of how the Treasury Board worked in practice has been left by Sylvester Douglas (later Lord Glenbervie), who was appointed to the Treasury Board in early 1797; he kept a diary full of gossip, and it is for this that he is chiefly remembered. Pitt was not present at Douglas's first Board meeting, but he was given the following brief beforehand by a fellow commissioner, John Smyth: 'You will find the office quite a sinecure ... Mr Pitt does all the material business at his own house, signs the papers, and then the other two Lords sign them of course. Other business the Secretaries judge of without carrying it to him.' In Pitt's absence, proceedings were dominated by the two secretaries to the Board, who had always been close to Pitt: George Rose, who had served the prime minister since his earliest days in office, and Charles Long, a cultured lawyer with modest political ambitions, who had been a friend of Pitt at Cambridge. According to Douglas,

> The book of matters then [came] before the Board, with the date written against each when the memorial letter, etc., was received, was then taken by Smyth, who read the items one by one, when Rose chiefly or Long mentioned something of the subject – or said Mr Pitt had, or would decide upon it – or that it must be postponed, on which Smyth ticked it off. In short to an ignorant person he would have appeared to be the Secretary and Rose and Long the Board ... On Thursday and Friday more formal Boards were held, for Pitt as well as Smyth and I attended ... Pitt's manner I thought awkward and not judicial, but his questions and observations were those so able a man might be expected to make. He seemed to have read the memorials with more attention than Rose, and not unwilling to show that he had.[11]

Though interested in administration, William Pitt was not one to hold to formal structures and reporting chains. He ran his cabinet ministers, formally known as 'His Majesty's confidential servants', very loosely. A perfunctory process had evolved for circulating Foreign Office papers between ministers, but there was otherwise little system.* In the 1790s the inner circle of ministers, Pitt, Dundas and Grenville, made the decisions, and much was done with Dundas alone at his home in Wimbledon. Dundas remembered that

---

* Despatches were made available in a cabinet room for ministers to read and memoranda in the Grenville papers in the British Library were initialled by ministers with recommendations (information from Michael Duffy, gratefully acknowledged). However, informality in decision-making was a hallmark of the times. Joseph Banks noted on some documents relating to the Macartney Embassy to China in 1792: 'As most of the business of arranging this Embassy was done in Conversation, the Parties being all in London, Little Curious Matter can be expected among these Papers' (Sutro Library, information from Alan Frost, for which I am similarly grateful).

> In transacting the business of the State, in forming our plans etc. we
> never retired to Office for that purpose. All these matters we dis-
> cussed & settled either in our morning rides at Wimbledon, or in our
> even'g walks at that place. We were accustomed to walk in the evening
> from 8 oClock to sometimes 10 or Eleven in the Summer Season.[12]

The prime minister preferred it that way, keeping his cards close,
using his access to the king to buttress his position. Besides, he did not
like writing letters, preferring to talk about a problem with the person
most concerned.[13] The first that Pitt's cabinet colleagues would hear
about the appointment of a new minister was when it was announced.
From the beginning of the war until the end of 1797 the conclusions
of only twelve minuted cabinet meetings were formally communicated to the king.* The cabinet had not developed into the official
discussion forum that it was later to become in the subsequent
governments of Portland, Perceval and Liverpool.[14]

Nor was Pitt very organized personally. The job of keeping him to
the daily schedule fell to his private secretary, Henry Legge, who
described his job as requiring 'Secrecy, attention to answering the Letters
civilly to those who desire to wait upon him, to be exact in recollect-
ing the Hours and Days that different People are appointed to come'.
And Legge added, 'Mr Pitt is the best temper'd Man in the World, and
the most pleasant to *work* with, for he is clear and patient, and likes
to make those happy with whom he has to transact Business.'[15] Among
his close circle of supporters, the shy and frosty public demeanour of
the prime minister disappeared.

As well as Treasury affairs, Pitt took on the overall control of foreign policy. The stress of these years made deep inroads into the health
of both politicians and administrators. It should not be forgotten that
when Pitt became prime minister in 1783 at the age of twenty-four, he
had already lived half his life. The intensity of the job of prime minister led to excesses of drinking, though it affected his performance only

---

* At one cabinet meeting in 1801, when Addington was prime minister, St Vincent
'finding nothing like business going on . . . got up, and said, if he was not wanted, he
must go away, as really he had <u>no time to throw away</u>, and so left the Cabinet' (28 Feb.
1801, Malmesbury, *Correspondence of the First Earl*, Vol. IV, p. 24).

marginally.* Public speaking did not, of itself, put a strain on Pitt. According to William Huskisson, 'he used to take a mutton chop and a glass of wine and water at three o'clock; nothing more.' The nerves of others were more fragile. According to gossip both Castlereagh and Liverpool 'took ether, as an excitement, before speaking'.†

Pitt as prime minister was subject to illness through stress, which might have induced his loss of judgement and bitterness which led to his bloodless duel with George Tierney in May 1798.[16] In the case of Henry Dundas, it was beyond the capacity of most mortals to take on the work that he set himself, in spite of the summer breaks that he took in Scotland. He also had some periods of breakdown in the mid 1790s, and was laid low by a throat infection in 1797, when Sylvester Douglas noted 'his most alarming symptom is want of sleep and a nervous affliction in his head'.[17] By 1800 he noticed 'a peculiar noise in his chest which corresponded to the beat of his pulse'.[18] He had had enough. He tried to resign as secretary of state for war, and did resign as treasurer of the navy in June 1800, persuaded to do so by his wife, who saw him for just ten minutes a day before bedtime.[19] Dundas only stayed on in government because of his loyalty to Pitt. He still had responsibilities as chairman of the India Board of Control, and remained at his comfortable quarters, for, as Pitt informed Windham, he did not intend to remove Dundas 'from the House in Somerset Place ... it is proposed that in future it should be considered as annexed to the office of the First Commissioner for India, instead of that of Treasurer of the Navy.'[20]

*

* It was, however, obvious on one occasion, which led to the memorable lines in an Opposition newspaper of a supposed conversation in the House between Pitt and Dundas:

> I cannot see the Speaker, Hal, can you?
> What! Cannot see the Speaker, I see two!

(Hague, *Pitt*, p. 308)

† The same source also 'asked Mr Wilberforce what made his fingers so black, and Mr Wilberforce told him that he was in the habit of taking opium before making a long speech; and "to that", said he, "I owe all my success as a public speaker"' (Fay, *Huskisson*, p. 71, quoting Lord Broughton, *Recollections of a Long Life*, Vol. III, 17 June 1827, pp. 203–4).

The right of appointment, or patronage, was the most important means of control and carefully cherished by the heads of the departments. Lord Spencer at the Admiralty dispensed patronage as many a Whig grandee did before him. His policy was described by Rear-Admiral Young: 'Lord Spencer's general wish is to employ as far he can distinguish, those Officers who are the most deserving of appointment, though the weight of influence will at times outweigh his good intentions.'[21] It did not, indeed, go unnoticed that relatives of Spencer's wife Lavinia made very good progress up the service; one rose from midshipman to captain in twenty months.[22] There were far too many applicants for any single post. Early in the war it was apparent that the navy had an excess of officers, for prize-money success and the increasing social status of the navy attracted many, and the mobilizations of 1790 and 1791 had brought a large number of commissioned lieutenants into the service in a short time. In 1794 Spencer brought in a centralizing scheme whereby young gentlemen midshipmen were appointed by the Admiralty as 'Boy First Class Volunteer',[23] and, although it was not immediately effective, it did eventually help the Admiralty to assume some of the authority that had previously resided with individual captains. The waiting room at the Admiralty was famed as a place where naval officers could spend a very long time waiting to see the first lord.*

Much was determined by the character of the minister within each department. Lord Spencer was popular, the administrative burden softened by his genial personality and the social charms of his wife. Marsden wrote: 'To-day we all dine with his Lordship; our Board is like one family. Business may, in former times, have been conducted as well in the Admiralty department, but certainly never so pleasantly or so smoothly.'[24] It was, perhaps, too comfortable, for Spencer's administration rested upon the hard work of the years of peace before the war: few ships were

---

* On one occasion the waiting room at the Admiralty was the scene of a remarkable tragedy, as William Young related: 'Captain Eaton who acted in the *Marlborough* came to town this morning to wait on Ld. Spencer . . . he was observed to be very wild and to talk very incoherently, and while he was in the waiting room, he drew his dirk and stab'd himself in the belly and in the neck, of which he died in a very short time; he appeared to be quite mad' (William Young to Charles Morice Pole, 21 July 1798, NMM, WYN/104).

built, and for additional frigates the navy relied upon French prizes: both maintenance and the lead over the French fell behind.[25]

But Spencer did ensure that administrative reform in the navy in Whitehall was implemented in the rapidly growing naval departments.* In 1796, on the basis of the recommendations of the Commission on Fees in the 1780s, the Navy Board was split into three committees: the Secretary's, Accounts and Stores, with the clerks reorganized to match the new structure. This changed the age-old practice of sitting as one Board, with every commissioner taking responsibility for all decisions, and resulted in greater transparency and efficiency. The first lord also established three important specialist units responsible to the Board of Admiralty. In 1795 the Hydrographic Office was founded, which improved the coordination of chart information, although the knowledgeable but difficult Alexander Dalrymple as the first hydrographer was not ideal. In the following year the inspector-general of naval works and the inspector of telegraphs were appointed, together with their support staff.[26]

The arrival of Lord St Vincent at the Admiralty in 1801, first lord in Addington's government, came as a rude shock. The admiral's curt manner, never far from the point of bullying, had terrified his captains at sea, and in Whitehall it caused deep divisions and long-lasting trouble.† He operated with a brusqueness more fitting to the quarterdeck than to Whitehall and its political niceties. *The Times* reported that the new first lord's hours of audience 'do not suit the generality of visitors. They are from 5 to 7 in the morning. After that he will receive no visitor.'[27]

Army business was conducted very differently. The duke of York was a natural bureaucrat, initiating a long period of reform and improvement, helped by his active appreciation of what was wrong

---

* In 1797 the naval departments together employed just under 400 commissioners, senior officials and clerks in Whitehall and Somerset House; by 1815 this had risen by over 50 per cent. The number of clerks in the Victualling Office in 1791 nearly doubled by 1805 (*Parliamentary Papers*, 1830–31 (92): *Public Offices Employment*, pp. 2–3).

† Witness his crude satisfaction in a letter to Nepean on one occasion when, on the Mediterranean station, he called his captains to account, giving them 'such a sit down, that, if it did not bring them to a stool, certainly made them piss and cry' (15 Aug. 1798, NMM, NEP/4, fol. 137).

with the army from his time in command of the army in Flanders.* As a member of the royal family, he was well beyond the ordinary reach of party politics. The real power and initiative, however, lay in the hands of the secretary of state for war, Henry Dundas. Yet a systemic failure was inherent within this department. Instructions would flow from the secretary of state's office in such detail that the commander in the field was deprived of initiative. There was little taking of professional advice in both the army and navy commands, and no general staff organization to bring information together to inform decisions. The duke of York, for instance, when he commanded the field army in Flanders in 1793 to 1795, and again in Holland in 1799, had little say in planning operations beforehand when in London.[28] How much a minister should listen to expert advice has always been a finely judged problem: Dundas himself should have listened more carefully to the military early in the war when he swept aside all difficulties, sending abroad late and costly expeditions.

As commander-in-chief, the duke of York was extremely active, applying himself to the defence of the country against invasion, which was anticipated following the return of the army from Flanders. During the summer of 1795 he was hardly in his office in the Horse Guards, completing a countrywide inspection from Plymouth to Sunderland, and conversing with the officers commanding the military districts and reviewing their troops.[29] He also started to introduce reform to the army; in Calvert's words:

> We want a total stop put to that most pernicious mode of bestowing rank on officers without even the form of recommendation, merely for raising (by means of crimps) a certain number of men ... to relieve deserving officers from the intolerable grievance of seeing men without merit, without family, or the smallest pretension to any military ability, pass over their heads ... solely through the medium of a rascally crimp.[30]

*

* Old Lord Cornwallis was not sanguine about the duke's appointment, writing privately in 1795: 'Whether we shall get any good by this, God only knows, but I think that things cannot change for the worse in that department' (Cornwallis to Colonel Ross, 31 Jan. 1795, Ross, *Cornwallis*, Vol. II, p. 284).

Whitehall was, therefore, the sum of the social, political and professional networks that threaded their way through parliament, the inns and the private houses around the centre of London, connecting military and naval men with politicians and administrators. Constantly shifting information and opinion about the war moved at times very fast through formal contact in parliament and the offices, but also through informal social occasions such as dinner parties, breakfast meetings and countryhouse visits. The complexity of George Canning's network sometimes bemused even him. He wrote: 'One loses sight of people so completely in this great town sometimes, that one hardly knows what becomes of one's most intimate acquaintances for days together.'[31] Many dining tables around Whitehall were the setting for the release of information and political negotiation. Some dinners were *ad hoc* affairs, occasioned by a debate ending early, and Dundas was an especially generous host with his apartments at Somerset House. After Canning had seconded the Address at the end of 1794, he supped alone with Dundas, and dined there several times in the years covered by his journal.[32] Some dinners reached across political groupings. Canning dined with the duke of Portland in February 1795, by then a coalition partner. The dinner was 'a mixture of all parties . . . [James] Hare being a Jacobin Oppositionist, [John] Crewe a moderate one, T[homas] Pelham an alarmist, out of place, the D[uke] an alarmist in place, and your humble servant a ministerialist. The dinner was exceedingly pleasant.'[33] A few months later Canning regretted that Pitt was neglecting his entertaining:

> By the way it is very bad style – that into which Mr Pitt has fallen this year – of not giving dinners. This is the second time since my coming to town that I have dined with him, and I can hear of nobody else that has done so oftener. It is very great remissness on his part, especially as his dinners are always good, and now and then pleasant.[34]

In order to further their careers, ambitious young politicians had to attract enough attention to be appointed as an undersecretary in an efficient department. They were the workhorses of government, part politician, part administrator. Some did not have independent incomes and needed a post to survive, while the better off could afford to choose. In 1795, the irascible William Huskisson viewed the prospect of being appointed to a new post, 'a kind of Under-secretary of the

India Department', with dismay. His inherited capital had now increased to over £16,000 with the prospect of more. 'Would it,' he asked his superior in the Home Office, Evan Nepean, to whom he was close at this time, 'be wise in me to throw away the best years of my life in the migratory and contemptible occupation of a Chief Clerk?'[35] A subtle distinction between those destined for higher office and the more junior secretaries was recalled by Canning at a dinner at Lord Grenville's, attended by Pitt and very senior politicians, at which Charles Goddard, Grenville's private secretary, 'in a proper, secretary-like manner, sat at the bottom of the table and helped the soup and the fish'.[36] But politicians at all levels, as well as the administrators, mixed socially at the receptions and balls given by politically influential hostesses, such as Lady Liverpool or the duchess of Devonshire.[37] The assiduous second secretary of the Admiralty, William Marsden could be tempted away from the office, even if he was not able to keep up with the fashion of the day. In July 1800 he confessed that he

> idled three or four hours at a breakfast given by the Duchess of Devonshire at Chiswick. It was by much the prettyist thing of this kind I have ever seen. I left Lady Georgiana Gordon, and many other smart ladies, dancing on the sod, at about six o'clock ... Windham and I were the only two who sported cocked hats. Lord Spencer said the admiration of the company was divided between these and the turban of Abu Talib, the Persian [diplomat].[38]

Marsden was careful to get back to the Admiralty to catch the evening post.*

It is difficult to assess the effectiveness of the 'placemen' who, in addition to their role as politician, accumulated sinecures to gain an income.

---

* The shrewd comments of this gentle and unpolitical man show him to be a prototype of the modern civil servant. He had outside interests and for many years was Treasurer of the Royal Society. He wrote to his brother, Alexander Marsden, 'I am going to meet a party of the Royal Society people, who are rather better company than your politicians' (4 Oct. 1806, Marsden, *Brief Memoir*, p.129fn.). When Marsden retired, he confessed to a former Admiralty commissioner: 'I never was in love with the business of the office but, like an honest man who marries an unamiable wife, I have always made the best of it, and endeavoured to do my duty' (24 June 1807 to Alexander Marsden, reporting conversation with William Young, Marsden, *Brief Memoir*, p.133fn.).

George Rose was perhaps the most successful, a man of limited talent, except for hard work. He rose from Treasury clerk in the late 1760s to Pitt's right-hand man in the 1780s, and through his career occupied many government posts around the Treasury, ending in 1807 as treasurer of the navy, in which post he died in 1818. Concurrently he accumulated a rich assortment of sinecures, including agent for Dominica, verderer of the New Forest and surveyor of the Green Wax Monies.[39] His obituary in the *Gentleman's Magazine* recounted that he was 'up early and late, and, with a total disregard of amusement, was always and totally in his business'. He was never far from the centre of power for thirty years, even though he was passed over by Pitt for those posts that Rose really wanted, when they were given to more talented men. He was MP for either Christchurch or Lymington continuously for thirty-four years and became very rich – with the result that he never escaped the taunt of 'placeman' from his parliamentary opponents. When he died, a fellow MP expressed regret that 'a man of such limited views should have so great influence'.[40] But administration needs hard workers, as well as brilliant men; and Rose had a conscience and worked hard not only for himself but for the underdog, as we shall see.

William Boscawen of the Victualling Board, on the other hand, never became rich. He had been to Eton and Oxford, was a practising barrister and classical scholar, but suffered from asthma all his life, which eventually killed him in 1811. In 1785 Boscawen, by his own account, was appointed by Pitt to the Victualling Board, but 'my acquaintance with Mr Pitt gradually drop'd and the interest of my family declined'.[41] However, he did become a commissioner of the Salt Tax from 1792 to 1798.[42] Judging by his obituaries, Boscawen was a popular man, and there is every reason to think that he was a conscientious member of the Board for his 26-year-period of office.[43]

By contrast, Mark Singleton was Irish and lucky. An army officer, he started his administrative career by the seemingly ill-advised move of eloping with the daughter of Lord Cornwallis, but was forgiven within a month, and was soon mixing in fashionable society and with the prince of Wales. He was, however, without an income, a problem solved in 1795, when his father-in-law became master-general of the Ordnance. Four months later the death of the principal storekeeper enabled Cornwallis to appoint his son-in-law to the post, while in

1796 the master-general set Singleton up as the member for Eye in Suffolk, controlled by the Cornwallis family, for which constituency Singleton sat, with some gaps, until 1820. He remained as principal storekeeper (bar the period of the Ministry of the Talents between 1806 and 1807) until 1829.[44]

Perhaps the least attractive of these examples was Edward Bouverie, the unprovided-for son of a well-connected aristocrat, the earl of Radnor. Bouverie was an MP from 1796 to 1803, and a groom of the bedchamber to the prince of Wales from 1787 until 1795. In 1794 he was wounded in a duel, brought about by the undue attention he had paid to the daughter of Lord Tankerville. For three years from 1803 he was a commissioner on the Transport Board, but then he served as a member of the Navy Board, a position that he kept to his death in 1824. He combined his work at the Navy Office with a place in fashionable society, acting in 1813 as escort to the handsome Lady Ellenborough, of which one observer remarked contemptuously, 'I could wish that she would select a less objectionable protector in public, as he has through life purported to play the part of Lothario, and is a very empty coxcomb.'[45]

Those who had served as secretaries to these boards were sometimes promoted, and they became senior rank politicians or commissioners on their board, allowing continuity of experience. Charles Long, for instance, second secretary to the Treasury Board, was appointed a commissioner in 1804 when Pitt returned to power. Philip Stephens had been secretary to the Board of Admiralty for thirty-two years before retiring in 1795, when Lord Spencer promoted him to the Board with a baronetcy. His experience made him invulnerable to political change, for he served under six first lords during his time on the Board. He even won the grudging respect of St Vincent, for naval tradition was one thing that this difficult admiral did honour. He wrote of Stephens: 'For though he has a cold Heart, and never went out of his way to serve any Man, except perhaps Sir Hugh Palliser, old habits with him and near Connexion with Lord Anson prompt me to be attentive to him.'[46] The king pressed for Stephens to continue in office when Lord Melville took over in 1804, though he finally retired in 1806, when he was just short of his eighty-third birthday, by which time one cabinet minister found him 'very far from infallible ... on points of Admiralty Law'.[47] Stephens served the navy for sixty-seven years.

Others became worn out at an early age. Nepean took his rheumatism to Tunbridge Wells for a cure during his brief spell as undersecretary for war between July 1794 and March 1795, leaving William Huskisson to run the office for him. He was to suffer from overwork and strain throughout these years. George Rose, when secretary of the Treasury, was ill for long periods in the 1790s, and Charles Long substituted for him. William Huskisson had a liver complaint in 1798 that took him to Cheltenham.[48] Spencer was convalescing at Bath during the summer of 1799 during a particularly difficult and busy period.[49] There is no doubting the long hours that were put in at crisis times in Whitehall. Marsden recalled that in September 1800:

> I sat in the board-room with Lord S, after his return from Wimbledon, till eleven o'clock. Admiral Young dropped in, and I remarked that it was the only public board whose members were so employed at that hour. Our armed associations, however, have the merit of more active service. They have been up for some nights.

On another occasion, Marsden became gloomy about the pressures of administration: 'I am sure that my continuance here will shorten my life.'[50] If the senior officials were kept long at the office, it can be certain that the clerks too had to follow suit.* At the Home Office Evan Nepean, when undersecretary, kept his clerks copying letters not only late into the day but also into the night.[51]

The subordinate naval boards of Whitehall were no less important to the war effort, and their hours were just as long as those worked by the major boards.[52] The Transport Board and Office were set up in 1794 (responsible to the Treasury) to charter merchant ships: these

---

* Before the war a Foreign Office clerk recalled that the office hours were 11 a.m. to 5 p.m. and 8 p.m. to 11 p.m., but that there were many idle hours. Lord Grenville revised the hours on 1 Apr. 1799 to 11 a.m. to 4 p.m., and on post nights from 8 p.m. until business was completed (E. Taylor, *The Taylor Papers* (1913), quoting TNA, FO 366/671: courtesy of Michael Duffy).

acted as transports for the amphibious expeditions, carried supplies
to overseas garrisons and victualled naval warships on blockade or on
foreign stations. This measure eliminated competition in the market
between the navy, Ordnance and army, which had bedevilled transport operations in the American Revolutionary War. Reform had been
pressed by Middleton at the start of the war and was adopted early in
1794, as Chatham informed him: 'I have seen my Brother, who
approves much of the plan suggested for the separate management of
the Transport Service, and seems inclined to its immediate adoption . . .
The greatest difficulty will be, I fear, to find a Sea Officer to be at the
head of it, possess'd of all the qualifications you so justly describe as
necessary.'[53] He was wrong. Captain Hugh Christian was appointed
as chairman for a year, but relinquished the post when he achieved his
flag and went to sea. He was followed by an Irishman, Captain Rupert
George. His duties included, he noted in 1807, 'attending the Treasury, Admiralty, Secretaries of State and Secretary at War, for their
respective directions'.[54] Responsible to the Treasury, George received
most of his orders from the secretary of state for war for expeditions,
while the Admiralty ordered transports for supplying warships.*
Before any transports sailed, his office had also to liaise with the Victualling, Ordnance and Navy boards. With so many masters to please,
George proved to be shrewd and sure-footed. His tenure lasted from
1795 to 1817 and in 1809 he was created a baronet.

The staffing of the Transport Office itself was small, since the main
business in London was contract tendering, but agents for transports
reported to the Board from afloat with every large convoy, and from
every naval base at home and abroad. These were commissioned naval
officers who had developed a specialized knowledge, usually with the
rank of lieutenant, although the senior agents were captains.

The workload of the Transport Board increased markedly by
1796, when, in addition to its main task of chartering transports, it
was given the responsibility for healthy prisoners of war, formerly

---

* The later inclusion of the expenditure of the Transport Board under the head of
Naval Expenditure has given rise to the idea that the Admiralty was its governing
board. The Transport Board eventually moved to offices in Dorset Court, Cannon
Row, near the south of Whitehall and close to the Treasury, a long way from the other
subordinate naval boards in Somerset House.

administered by the Sick and Hurt Office. A complex, countrywide organization had to be administered, although security at depots and prisons was the responsibility of the militia.[55] In 1796, for instance, there were 11,534 French prisoners in England and 4,932 British prisoners in France.[56] Due to exchanges with the French in the 1790s, numbers were kept down. Nevertheless, in 1799 there were 25,000 prisoners of war to feed and manage, and between 1796 and 1801 the cost of feeding and confining them was the considerable sum of £1,238,950.[57] The Office oversaw agents at each prison depot, and at each of the fifty to sixty parole towns in Britain, spread eventually over England, Wales and Scotland. A minority of prisoners were paroled, and these included commissioned officers down to ensigns and midshipmen and also the masters and subordinate officers of privateers and merchant ships over fifty tons. Those paroled gave their word of honour not to escape, and signed a form promising to obey the laws of the country, and not to engage in clandestine correspondence or to go outside the limits of their parole, usually a mile in any direction, without permission. If they broke their parole, they were sent to a depot or prison ship.[58]

The Transport Board then arranged 'cartels', merchant ships that would sail to France or Spain to exchange prisoners under a flag of truce. Difficulty in settling the numbers of prisoners to be exchanged were encountered with the French authorities, but negotiations with the Spanish agent were much more cordial.* As a result Spanish prisoners were relatively quickly exchanged. Between 1796 and 1802, the years of hostilities between the two countries, the numbers of Spaniards in captivity fluctuated, but totalled 4,536.[59] They remained in captivity for relatively little time: a minimum of two weeks and a maximum of six months. The task of administering prisoners was to be greatly increased during the Napoleonic War.

---

* The agent for transports responsible for cartels in Paris in 1797 was Henry Swinburne, who used his diplomatic immunity in a number of ways, as well as arranging for the exchange of prisoners of war. In May 1797 a cartel was to sail from Nantes, and he informed Lord Spencer '600 prisoners besides officers from different paroles are to go immediately from Brest.' By Aug. he reported that 'the number of British Prisoners at present in France is reduced to a few hundred.' Swinburne was still in Paris in Nov., anxiously awaiting his passport from the French authorities (Swinburne to Lord Spencer, 18 May, 14 Aug., 11 Nov. 1797, BL, Add. MSS 75813).

The Victualling Board constantly monitored prices in the food markets across the country, which meant that its members, like those of other boards, worked long hours. In his usual trenchant style, George Phillips Towry, the deputy chairman of the Victualling Board, wrote ('Private and Confidential') to Lord Spencer's private secretary, proposing that he and the chairman of the Board 'should have houses at Somerset Place'. He complained of the level of pay and house allowance, particularly unrewarding compared with that of the Navy Board: the situation was doubly unfair 'on account of their attendance upon the Board <u>every</u> <u>day</u> of the week'. He continued with a growing sense of frustration, and perhaps beyond the limits of official decorum:

> Indeed considering the sacrifices he has voluntarily made, in the bestowing his Patronage <u>solely</u> to friends of Government, and on giving his time entirely to public business, while the World is rapidly slipping from under him, without having one farthing to <u>add</u> to his fortunes. He hopes & trusts, that Lord Spencer will see his situation as worthy of attention, and will pardon him for his freedom upon the present occasion.[60]

With such a complex hierarchy and divided responsibilities, conflicts between departments were inevitable. Disputes between the Admiralty and the subordinate Navy Board have already been noted, but the Admiralty also failed to communicate as well as it might have done with the Ordnance Department, and there was little collaboration on forward planning, although relations between representatives of the two departments were better at the outports.[61] The Admiralty prepared its own estimates, which it brought before the House of Commons, receiving its revenue from the Treasury through the treasurer of the navy, and issuing navy, victualling and transport bills for paying its contractors. But the beginnings of Treasury encroachment can just be discerned at this time. A small example took place in 1799 when the stationery contract was removed from Admiralty control to the Stationery Office, which was answerable to the Treasury.[62] Each department fiercely defended its independence from the Treasury. In the last days of Pitt's government in December 1800, William Windham, secretary at war, complained to the prime minister of Treasury interference when allegations of irregularities in the War Office were investigated without his leave: 'the irregular and very unceremonious

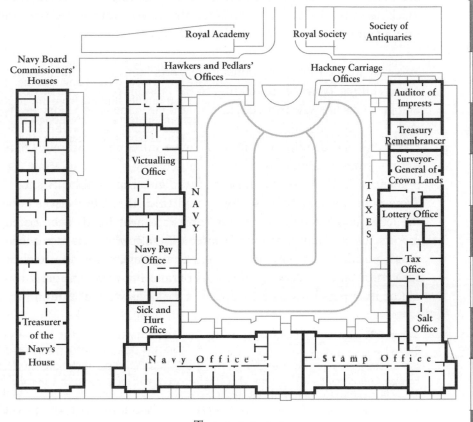

Somerset House Government Offices, *c.*1800

STRAND

Royal Academy — Royal Society — Society of Antiquaries

Navy Board Commissioners' Houses

Hawkers and Pedlars' Offices

Hackney Carriage Offices

Auditor of Imprests

Treasury Remembrancer

Surveyor-General of Crown Lands

Victualling Office

N A V Y

T A X E S

Lottery Office

Navy Pay Office

Tax Office

Sick and Hurt Office

Salt Office

Treasurer of the Navy's House

Navy Office

Stamp Office

Terrace

RIVER THAMES

way which the Treasury sometimes has of stepping into different Departments without any previous notice, publick or private, to those who
are at the head of them'.[63]

In spite of this friction, the government bureaucracy was of a considerable size and maturity. The number of clerks in almost every
department swelled by two or three times as the scale of war increased
towards 1815. Nor did this upsurge in numbers come any too soon.
Few of the departments with direct involvement in running the war
escaped the accounting backlog that was to clog up the financial
machine in the latter years of the conflict: they were undermanned
until the later years of the Napoleonic War.

Subordinate boards were constantly complaining to the minister
about staffing shortages in relation to the amount of work to be done,
and petitions likewise from clerks about their inadequate salary levels
had to be considered.[64] Of the clerks we know little beyond their
tasks, pay and conditions. Holidays were infrequent, although that
did not stop parliament in 1798 from debating a bill regulating 'the
number of holidays to be allowed clerks in certain public offices'.[65]
Promotion was largely by seniority.* Most of the junior clerks kept
the letter books (copies of letters sent) in a neat hand, and copied
reports for circulation around Whitehall. Only when clerks reached
senior positions did they draft letters or documents for ministers or
senior officials.† A clerk's tenure was permanent, and, if he grew too
old or ill, a pension was awarded; but sackings were not unknown.

---

* In the Foreign Office there were strong family links among the clerks. Thomas
Bidwell was chief clerk between 1792 and 1817, and another Bidwell was employed
concurrently, as were two Broughtons, two Rollestons and three Taylors (Collinge,
Foreign Office, pp. 60, 61, 75, 79). The Taylors were sons of a friend of Grenville's
father-in-law (information from Michael Duffy).
† In the Home Office there were thirty-four permanent clerks in post between 1782 and
1801, who entered the office between the ages of sixteen and nineteen, the sons of army
officers, the landed gentry, lawyers or clergymen. Some had been educated at Eton,
Harrow or Westminster. The Home Office could be a stepping stone to greater things:
thirteen of the Home Office clerks resigned when promoted to a variety of posts, such
as chief clerk to the Board of Trade, chief secretary to the government of Madras, or
an inspector at the Audit Office (Nelson, *Home Office*, pp. 47–50).

When Henry Dundas arrived at the Home Office he ensured that four inefficient clerks were soon retired. In 1795 one clerk, Edward Raven, letting his personal feelings get in the way of government policy, protested against granting pardons to criminals who agreed to enter military service. In 1800 Portland finally sacked him for failing to prepare pardons for some mutineers.[66]

By the end of the eighteenth century the system of payment to Whitehall clerks was outdated and inefficient, built up by precedent and ossified by custom over many years. The practice of fees and perquisites, strongly condemned by the Commission on Fees in the 1780s, and, as mentioned previously, studiously ignored by Pitt, led to anomalies and inefficiencies. The relationship between contractors and officials in the Whitehall departments, which awarded hundreds of contracts, was open to abuse. A timely 'present' could, for instance, ensure that a navy or victualling bill was made out expeditiously. In wartime, with business increased several fold, the resultant level of fees led not only to huge and inappropriate rises in incomes, but also to further 'presents' from those tendering contracts. These gifts were increasingly seen as illegal payments: by the end of the century they became known, at least by the Navy Board, as 'disgraceful transactions'.[67]

It is worth examining the position of one clerical post in some detail. William Pollock, the chief clerk in the Home Office, had been in the post since 1782. In 1793 he had no government salary at all, yet he had an annual income from his work in the Home Office of about £1,200. It was made up from a great variety of sources, including one half of the gratuities received from certain warrants signed by the king, five guineas a year from the East India Company, a commission on presents bought on behalf of newly appointed consuls (to be given to the ruler of the relevant country) and £100 in lieu of the privilege of franking letters and of franking newspapers to Ireland, formerly enjoyed by all clerks. He also received 10s. a sheet when he copied papers required by someone outside the Home Office. In addition, Pollock received £250 a year from the sinecure office of the clerk of the Crown in Quebec, stemming from the fact that the Home Office was responsible for the colonies until 1801.[68] Such anomalies could not be allowed to continue.* In 1795 the Home Office implemented the reforms recommended by the Commission on Fees, and thereafter Pollock received a fixed salary in lieu of these fees and perquisites, as did all clerks. His £1,000 a year was funded by a departmental consolidated fee fund.

This problem of personal fees was tackled head on by a zealous reformer and a stickler for detail, who did not fear to upset entrenched interests. Charles Abbot had been a prize-winning scholar at Christ Church, was very much an independent MP, sitting in a seat under the patronage of the duke of Leeds, with whom he had been at school at Westminster.† Abbot had defended Pitt's unpopular Assessed Taxes Bill, and as a result was made chairman of the Select Committee on Finance, which sat in 1797 and 1798. It produced thirty-six reports, very quickly, many of which were written by Abbot himself, the result of 'diligent but tactless investigations'.‡ 'He is a firm man and a very *little man*,' wrote Sylvester Douglas disparagingly; but after Abbot's election in February 1802 as speaker of the House of Commons he was to gain very general respect.[69]

* Sinecures could also flourish at a low level. The position of landlord of the Bunch of Grapes pub, which was built over the gateway of the Tower of London, was held in sinecure by the gentleman porter of the Tower, whose income was made up of rents from the public house and an adjoining bar. Both pub and gateway were in a ruinous condition by the late 1780s, but no one was willing to pay for the repairs. Further, the master of the Tower held that the pub 'was absolutely necessary for the garrison'. Five years later further repair estimates were obtained and the Treasury pressed for demolition. Finally, in 1797, local inhabitants petitioned Lord Cornwallis, the constable of the Tower, under 'the apprehension that some persons will be buried under the ruins'. The Bunch of Grapes was finally demolished, when the stumbling block was removed by the Treasury's agreement that the gentleman porter, who happened to be the bishop of Lichfield and Coventry, could be compensated by additions to his annual pension (Crook and Port, *King's Works*, p. 487).

† Abbot's half-brother was Samuel Bentham, from 1796 inspector-general of naval works. In 1795 Canning met him at dinner with Abbot, describing Bentham in his journal as 'a very sensible, well-informed man . . . a Col[onel] in the Russian Service – of two Regiments, one of which is at present quartered on the frontiers of China' (10 Nov. 1795, Jupp, *Canning Letter Journal*, p. 222).

‡ Abbot's next campaign was to improve and reform the records of church and state, badly stored in obscure locations. He established a Record Commission in 1799 and 1800 that noted the whereabouts and content of these archives, a remarkable effort in the middle of a war (Pugh, 'Charles Abbot', p. 326).

Abbot and the Select Committee made the scale of the problem public. The fees to War Office officials had increased between 1792 and 1796 by 800 per cent to a total of £43,000; in the Home Office by 350 per cent to £28,000. The annual salary of the clerk of the Cutting House at Deptford Victualling Yard was £135 in 1792; his fees alone came to £1,500 in 1797.[70] Under the spotlight of this sort of publicity, the departments had no option but to reform.

Not only money was involved in the abolition of fees, but also status. Three very senior Navy Board clerks protested to the first lord of the Admiralty that the changes had particularly singled them out, as the 'reduction of emolument from the alterations of 1796 were heavier than others, whereas in our hands, next to the Secretary, we know, and may without presumption say that the spring and power of the business of this great Office are.' The result was that it tended 'to do away that difference in rank, respect and profit'.[71] Gradually, department by department, both fees and presents were eliminated, although the payment of clerks remained a problem for over twenty years. When clerks were finally able to compare their salaries with those in other departments, they found they had cause to raise petitions, and much time was expended on these by senior officials and politicians.

Bureaucrats in Whitehall also had to be alive to the problems posed by labour disputes among the wartime workforce. In 1793 the home dockyards were manned by 3,000 skilled shipwrights and 8,000 labourers.[72] These large industrial establishments were prone to labour problems and wartime urgency was no bar to widespread strikes, most marked at times of high food prices.* Pitt's repressive legislation caused stoppages in the winter of 1795, when all grades of workers in the dockyards, unusually unanimous, suspected that the law was going to be used to declare a wartime strike treasonable. At Chatham Dockyard in November 1795 the entire workforce quietly walked out of the dockyard at lunchtime to sign a petition against the legislation, not returning until the next day.[73] Violent strikes took place in 1801 that had to be brought under control by the military. The shipwrights of the larger dockyards had considerable

* The victualling yards were much smaller. In 1800, for instance, their wage bill was just under a sixth of that of the dockyards ('Account of the monies . . . 18 Feb. 1801', NMM, ADM BP/21a, Navy Office).

bargaining power, particularly during the urgency of a mobilization, and the first months of every war of the eighteenth century saw them strike for better pay and conditions. Between 1803 and 1805 they petitioned the Navy Board seven times.[74] Workers in private shipyards were less likely to strike, but they did so during the Peace of Amiens, when the royal yards tried to lend the merchant yards some caulkers to break the dispute – with the result that the royal yard workers 'were driven back from the Merchant Yards in the Thames and have declined returning, although a Military Guard had been provided for their protection'.[75]

Administrative posts were also expanding overseas. During the French Revolutionary War a great many bases were added: dockyard officers were appointed to Ajaccio in Corsica in 1794; the Cape of Good Hope in 1795; Martinique in 1796; Port Mahon in Minorca when it was recaptured in 1798; Malta in 1800; and even, for a short time, Alexandria in 1801. The Ordnance and Victualling offices, too, had depots at these bases. An important group of British naval officials was positioned at Lisbon to organize support for the considerable number of British warships that was replenished and refitted there. A storekeeper was appointed to the East Indies squadron in Bombay and Madras, and a master attendant to Trincomalee. Where the fighting navy went, administrators were not far behind.

An example of a senior naval administrator appointed to a number of these foreign yards as the Navy Board resident commissioner was Captain Isaac Coffin. He had been injured while on active service and from 1790 was unable to serve at sea. Between 1794 and 1800, in rapid succession, he administered the bases at Ajaccio, Lisbon, Minorca and Halifax, Nova Scotia. He had a forceful personality, with the same mixture of distrust of his juniors and propensity to bully them as did his mentor St Vincent.[76] In 1801 he returned to England to become resident commissioner at Sheerness, where, with the first lord's backing, he carried out a thorough reorganization, on one occasion nearly losing his life when surrounded by furious yard workers.*

*

* The career of this tough but very effective administrator might have been ended by accident in 1797 in Ajaccio. A naval colleague recounted, 'While Coffin and I were close together working in his garden at Ajaccio a ball pass'd close over our heads that was fir'd at him by a Corsican Rascal he had discharg'd from the Yard . . . a common

The ability of government to formulate policies was to a large extent dependent upon the reliability and quality of the evidence at its disposal. Very important but less obvious measures were being put in hand to improve the information available to government, which were to shape political decisions in the years ahead. The first effort was devoted to finding how many people lived in Great Britain. Wartime costs were rising far beyond previous experience, so it was vital to know whether the country could shoulder the increased tax burden, raise sufficient capital and muster enough manpower. A long debate on the 'political arithmetic' of the nation had taken place in the 1790s, which divided economists into 'optimists' – those who estimated that between eleven and twelve million lived in the country – and 'pessimists' – those who reckoned the population to be no more than seven or eight million.[77] Charles Abbot played his part in this debate by promoting the Population Bill of 1800, which led to the 1801 Census and the first accurate statistics.[78] It silenced the pessimists, and reassured the political world that a sufficient tax base could be provided.*

Greater confidence was also generated in the estimates of national income as a result of the work of Thomas Irving, the inspector-general of imports and exports in the Customs department: he produced an accurate annual account by opportunely using the returns already collected by the department under the Convoy Act of 1798, which required merchants to declare the value of their cargo. Out of his work new calculations of the national income were revised upwards to £200 million a year.[79] We now know that trade figures were moving sharply upwards at the end of the century, but it was not obvious to contemporaries and Irving's work was of the first importance.†

---

amusement in that Island' (Captain Ralph Willet Miller to his father, 2 Mar. 1797, White, *Nelson's Year of Destiny*, p. 156).

* In a very different area, the growing awareness of the importance of accurate government information led the duke of York in 1797 to order all army commanding officers to compile casualty lists and report the names of the dead to the War Office (Lin, 'Soldiers' and Sailors' Families', p. 107).

† In the ten years between 1785 and 1794 British annual imports averaged £19.5 million and exports £14.2 million; in the next ten years, between 1795 and 1804, the figures were sharply increased: £24.3 million and £21.9 million (Deane and Cole, *Economic Growth*, p. 48).

The work of the Board of Agriculture and Internal Improvement from 1793, managed by its industrious chairman and secretary, Sir John Sinclair and Arthur Young respectively, also needs to be recognized. Young had a considerable reputation from his writing on political economy, and he had already drawn attention to the areas of uncultivated land in his 1773 work *Observations on the Present State of Waste Lands of Great Britain*. His energy and knowledge were now put to good use in centralizing information on agricultural output. The Home Office requested that the lords lieutenant of the counties provide crop yields for the harvests of 1794 and 1795.[80] In 1795 the Board published a report estimating that 7.8 million acres in England and Wales, or a fifth of the total, were uncultivated.[81] High wartime prices for foodstuffs encouraged investment. The enclosing of common and waste land in the wheat growing areas in central England increased, always controversial because of its impact on the lives of the agricultural poor.* Gross corn output rose from 19.8 million quarters in 1790 to 21.1 in 1800, and to 24.4 in 1810.[82] The state of the agriculture of each county was written up in detail and published, and improvements in breeding, crop rotation and ploughing were encouraged by landowners. The Board kept up a steady flow of agricultural reports and information beyond 1815.

Weaknesses in the government of the country still remained, notably in the neglect of accurate and up-to-date accounting, tackled only after scandals in the years following Pitt's death in 1806. The reforming effort would be redoubled when war resumed. For now there were few immediate diplomatic and strategic results. By the end of the Revolutionary War, French power on the Continent was as strong as ever. It is unsurprising that even the mild William Marsden reacted bitterly to the welcome given by the public to the Peace of Amiens, after nearly eight years of unremitting effort: 'I had occasion to witness, from the Admiralty Office, with no small indignation, the disgraceful scene of

---

* Young changed his opinions on enclosures after his early advocacy, writing in 1801: 'I had rather that all the commons of England were sunk in the sea, than that the poor should in future be treated on enclosing as they have generally been hitherto' (Horn, *Rural World*, p. 51, quoting Young, 'General Enclosure', *Annals of Agriculture*, Vol. XXXVI, p. 214).

the bearer of the French despatch being drawn in triumph, by an English rabble, about the parade at the Horse Guards.'[83] Twelve further years of war lay ahead, of a far greater scale and intensity than anything that had gone before, and it was only later in the Napoleonic War that the quiet labour of the politicians and administrators was fully recognized and came into its own.

5

Intelligence and Communications

1793–1801

You are in the daily habit of receiving the intelligence, and of combining it, and drawing your conclusions from it. I am therefore very much disposed to think that your ideas are more just than mine; and you may rest assured that I am decided to act upon your ideas (in which Mr Pitt perfectly concurs) rather than upon any doubts of my own.
    – Henry Dundas, secretary of state for war, to Lord
    Grenville, foreign secretary, on Grenville's certainty of a
    Dutch revolt against the French in 1799[1]

Wartime governments, in order to decide upon both defence and foreign policy, needed to know two vital things about the enemy: his intentions and his capability. Of course, when an army was in the field or a fleet was at sea, tactical intelligence was the responsibility of the general or admiral commanding. Policy, however, involved continual complex assessments, undertaken by a number of departments across Whitehall. In the 1790s it was never simple to find out what unstable French governments were planning; nor was it to be any easier to find out what the emperor was thinking during the Napoleonic War.

Assessing the enemy's plans depended upon information from diplomats, a task performed formally by the Foreign Office, which also ran secret informers, while agents worked covertly for the Home Office, the Admiralty or the secretary of state for war. In addition, William Windham, secretary at war between July 1794 and February 1801, had a great deal of contact with French royalist sympathizers in his efforts to stir up resistance in the Vendée in south-west France.[2]

The whole operation in the Vendée in 1795 was flawed because of over-optimistic assessments of the strength of the royalists: the evidence for their effectiveness came from the royalists themselves, leading to exaggerated claims, a classic intelligence mistake.

The Admiralty ran secret agents abroad to assess the state of readiness of the ships in the French north-western bases, but most information came from British warships blockading ports. Their captains were ordered to report any observations of the enemy fleet in port: their seamanship experience would pick up details such as the height of an anchored ship out of the water (that is, whether it was yet weighed down by guns or stores), or whether topmasts were in place or sails bent on the yards, which were firm indicators of the imminent departure of a ship. The luggers and fishing boats reporting to Captain Philippe D'Auvergne at his base in Jersey kept a continuous watch on Le Havre, Brest, L'Orient and Rochefort, looking for these sorts of clues, while his agents around the French ports would also pick up other telltale signs: concentrations of seamen, or leave being stopped, or other indications that an enemy fleet was about to leave port. He reported to both the Admiralty and the War Office.[3] Every source of information could help to build a picture of the capacities of the French and their allies. At the Admiralty, clerks compiled a classified index by geographical area into which every piece of intelligence was inserted.[4] In a general memorandum to the cabinet in April 1798 Lord Spencer described the system:

> All the intelligence received from time to time has constantly been circulated for the information of the Cabinet, and it is all entered in books (now forming a pretty voluminous collection) kept on purpose. A précis of the latest intelligence last received may easily be made out, and shall immediately be prepared if it is required; but no very great stress can be laid upon the inspection of any such partial extract, because it cannot always be known what degree of reliance should be placed upon any particular piece of information, and it is only from a general view and comparison of the whole that anything like a tolerable judgement of it can be formed.[5]

A few weeks later Henry Dundas sent some intelligence to Spencer from an American source, whose reliability was unknown: 'the only use such information can be of is by comparing with other channels and thereby judging of its probability.'[6] These principles remain the basis of central government intelligence assessment today.

Information on sightings of enemy-ship movements would be volunteered from all directions, often from merchants, whose business decisions depended upon the speedy conveyance of news; and sometimes it would come from that hotbed of commercial gossip and news, Lloyd's Coffee House.[7] Only fragmentary evidence has survived from these commercially driven international networks, but there is little doubt that they were efficient.[8] As well as information from agents and naval officers, fishermen and smugglers, material came from neutral ships, especially Americans, escaped prisoners of war and open sources such as French newspapers.

Intercepted despatches to and from French and other European governments were another fruitful source of intelligence, undertaken by the Secret Office in the Post Office. This department, complete with openers and decipherers, had been established in the seventeenth century and was never officially acknowledged; by 1793 it was funded by secret service money issued by the Treasury. Owing to staff shortages in other parts of the Post Office, the Secret Office had also been involved with internal security, but from 1798 it concentrated upon foreign posts and despatches, providing valuable information, for instance, about the United Irishmen. The Secret Office had agents at a number of foreign post offices, but it worked particularly closely with the 'secret bureau' in Hanover: in the 1780s staff of both institutions had exchange visits.[9]

Of course, both sides in this conflict were doing their best to get hold of enemy communications.* A constant fear of French spies within ministries dogged the life of ministers. There was nothing that we today would recognize as security clearances. James Bland Burges was told by a double agent not long into the war that a clerk in the Foreign Office was in French pay. For some periods Grenville had his

---

* In 1795 Lord Auckland tried to impress Pitt with his capacity: 'Such a system is always to a certain extent a double espionage, but it is become more necessary for us than it was even in the last war – in that war I obtained, thro' Americans, minutes of all despatches written by [Benjamin] Franklin deep from Paris; in one instance all the originals for Six months' (20 Jan. 1795, TNA, PRO 30/8/40/2).

despatches delivered to his home.[10] Very properly, negotiators at the peace talks in 1796 were circumspect about what they included in their correspondence. Granville Leveson Gower, writing to Lady Bessborough from Paris, ended one missive by saying, 'I am not sure that our letters may not be inspected by persons belonging to the Directory.'[11] In late 1798 Evan Nepean was warned by Richard Cadman Etches, a Dane who had worked as an agent for Catherine the Great, that a Frenchman named Gadole had been seen in London: '[previously] a principal commissaire in Belgium . . . I know him sufficiently to be confident that he will have Agents about all the Offices of Government more particularly the Marine from belonging to it in Paris.'[12] By 1801 the diplomat Arthur Paget was reporting from Vienna, after a visit through Paris, of a suspicion that French agents were deep into the British political machine: 'Mr Merry suspects that there is some sad foul play going on in our Fleets. The French, it is thought, have our private signals – Talleyrand has been heard to say that he has every determination of our Cabinet in eight days.'[13]

At the outbreak of war, the British secret service was a small internal surveillance organization headed by Evan Nepean, undersecretary at the Home Office.[14] It would rapidly grow into the Alien Office, which monitored entry of people into Britain after the passing of the Alien Act of 7 January 1793.[15] For the duration of the French Revolutionary War, this office – which dealt with both defensive home security and offensive spying on the Continent – was led and dominated by William Wickham. He was an expert linguist and member of the elite Christ Church group, known to Canning and others in the government, and rightly deserves his recently bestowed title of 'Master Spy'.[16] After a false start as a barrister, Wickham spent time in France and married into a well-placed Geneva family. The next step in his curious career was as a magistrate in Whitechapel, and while in this role he became involved in government security, trying to check hundreds of French émigrés who came flocking to London as the situation in France grew more volatile and dangerous. By August 1793 Grenville was employing him in secret activity in London.

Wickham also organized the surveillance of radicals in the London Corresponding Society, at that time the flourishing centre of British Jacobinism, by planting agents within it. On 8 May 1794 Wickham provided Pitt with clear evidence that some in the Society were bent on revolution, rather than on purely parliamentary reform. The government, alarmed that weapons were being stockpiled by potential revolutionaries, made rapid arrests, with Dundas steering the suspension of habeas corpus through parliament in two weeks, and the Society was broken.[17] As a result of this important report, Wickham was appointed superintendent of the Alien Office, working to the duke of Portland as home secretary. His job was, in Portland's words, not 'to omit any proper means of being well informed of the description and abode of all foreigners' and to ensure that the information given by the émigrés at the point of entry was 'the best and truest key to our Security with respect to the Aliens and even to their own'.[18]

At the same time as being engaged on internal security, Wickham was also working to the foreign secretary, Lord Grenville, intercepting and assessing foreign correspondence. Straddling the various ministries in this way made him the manager, for a short time, of an embryonic centralized intelligence assessment system.[19] However, in October 1794 the Foreign Office received faint peace feelers from moderate elements in the French government, and Wickham was abruptly sent on a secret mission to Geneva to follow up the French overture; he was to remain there until the end of 1797.[20] John King, formerly of Christ Church and now undersecretary at the Home Office, took on the oversight of the Alien Office.[21] As a result, separate ministries re-established their own networks. Secret service money was issued to each minister with a department engaged in defence or services business, so that he could maintain his own intelligence contacts. Putting together evidence to form accurate assessments of the enemy's intentions, therefore, came to depend upon exchanges of information and discussions at undersecretary and cabinet level. For instance, in January 1798, Canning sent from the Foreign Office to Nepean, by then at the Admiralty, an extract of a consul's despatch from Corfu about French ship movements.[22] But, as we shall see, internal jealousies between ministers, as well as resulting in an imperfect understanding of what information might be useful to others, could lead to a lack of timely circulation of intelligence around government. It was to handicap accurate judgements, which, in turn, led to faulty policy decisions.

Expenditure on intelligence went up sharply in wartime. Evan Nepean dispersed £50,571 on Home Office secret service business between June 1791 and March 1795.[23] Pitt was to explain to the House of Commons that overall secret service expenditure in 1795 totalled £150,000.[24] Money was transferred from country to country through the business houses of international bankers such as Boyd, Benfield & Co., or Herries, Farquahar & Co., each transaction passing through three or four houses, and often changing currencies as many times. Without the cooperation of the bankers, it is difficult to see how there would have been a secret service.[25] Every minister had to provide an affidavit confirming that he had 'disbursed the money entrusted to me for foreign secret service faithfully according to the intention and purposes for which it was given'. Lesser figures could also be entrusted with secret service money. Tom Grenville, the brother of Lord Grenville, who had been sent on a diplomatic mission, swore an affidavit for receiving such payments on 13 May 1800, 'at my house in Duke Street, Westminster'. It was countersigned by an official from the Auditor's Office.[26] This process did not, however, preclude the use of this money for purposes other than for the defence of the country. For instance, some of it found its way into the pockets of members of the Irish parliament, in an attempt to influence their votes on the Act of Union in 1801.[27]

There were some advantages to this decentralized arrangement, by which secret service money was divided among at least four ministries, as localized intelligence networks could be organized with the knowledge of only a few people. Personal links could be made in Whitehall between departments, and experience of handling intelligence transferred. Evan Nepean moved between three departments in a short time in the mid 1790s (he went from the Home Office in March 1794, to do a short spell as undersecretary to the secretary of state for war, and then in July 1795 became secretary of the Board of Admiralty). In 1797 and 1798 he corresponded with Lord St Vincent, at that time commanding the fleet outside Cádiz, and who was often in port in Lisbon. The admiral talked with Portuguese politicians, trying to divine the balance of the parties at the Portuguese court at a very tricky stage in Portuguese–French relations, which might have led to a treaty between the two countries. He interviewed one of

Nepean's agents, Joseph Wilkes, to arrange for intelligence to be sent to the British Fleet of the movement of Spanish warships in the harbour. Wilkes did not do well, and St Vincent complained to Nepean: 'Although every inhabitant of Cádiz was aware of the late move of the Spanish Fleet for days before it sail'd, Mr Wilke's emissary did not send the most trifling intelligence on that occasion.'[28] In July he discovered that Wilkes had been paid £5,000 from secret service funds.

> I cannot express my astonishment I feel at the extraordinary charge in the account you have enclosed from Mr Joseph Wilkes who has never rendered the most trifling Service to the Public . . . I have the strongest grounds to think they were traitorous – in any case they performed nothing – had they been efficient, one hundred pounds would have rewarded them amply.[29]

On another occasion, he vented his frustration to Nepean with an obsolete but still comprehensible insult: 'Mr Walker is an Imposter, and his intelligence not worth a Louse's Quin, therefore stop your hand in payment.'[30]

Additionally, the disadvantages of not having a clear overall intelligence hierarchy led to jealousies between agents in different networks. John Trevor, British minister to Sardinia, based in Turin, and Francis Drake, British minister in Genoa, both diplomats responsible for intelligence in their area, bitterly resented Wickham's influence with Lord Grenville, but the foreign secretary made it clear that Wickham had precedence within the Foreign Office.[31] Several departments and agents were involved in the Vendée, including Wickham for the Foreign Office, Windham as the secretary at war with links to the royalists, and the Admiralty.

Among those whom Evan Nepean at the Admiralty ran was the maverick naval captain Sir Sidney Smith – self-publicist, full of ideas, knighted by the Swedes for service there before the war, speaker of perfect French, a cousin of both Pitt and Grenville, both of whom trusted him, and extremely unpopular with his fellow naval officers, who very much did not.[32] Smith first came to the fore commanding a small naval squadron off Normandy, liaising with D'Auvergne in support of the operations on behalf of the French royalists in south-west

France. During 1796 Smith built up networks within France, carrying out counter-intelligence operations, and landing agents and money, off the coast under the cover of his role as a naval officer commanding a warship, with orders to capture French privateers.

In April 1796 Smith was captured with a fellow agent, John Wesley Wright, who was posing as his secretary, during a cutting-out operation at Le Havre about which mystery still remains. When the wind died the wherry being used for the raid was seized by French oared launches.[33] Smith was incarcerated with Wright in the Temple Prison in Paris and treated as a state prisoner, rather than as a prisoner of war, but he lived well, was allowed limited parole, and even managed to start up another intelligence network. He was supported by money from the British government through Henry Swinburne, the agent for transports in Paris, who had diplomatic immunity, as he was responsible for the exchange of prisoners of war.* The Directory regarded Smith's role in the burning of the dockyard at Toulon in 1793 as incendiarism because he was not acting under a regular commission at the time, only on written orders from Admiral Hood. His imprisonment was an embarrassment for the British government and complicated Lord Malmesbury's peace negotiations, which continued through 1796 and 1797. The French were intransigent, however, and would not listen to British arguments. Smith and Wright escaped in April 1798, a venture masterminded by Richard Cadman Etches, with the help of some clever travelling and disguise arrangements by royalists. Etches received £1,200 for his disbursements from Nepean's secret service accounts, and Smith £1,514.[34]

From his base in Switzerland, William Wickham, under the orders of Grenville at the Foreign Office, ran a variety of covert, cloak-and-dagger

---

* Another of Swinburne's tasks was to buy books from Paris booksellers for Lord Spencer, first lord of the Admiralty and a noted bibliophile. Their curious correspondence reads as though the war was almost not happening. Perhaps significantly, the purchase of books was always dealt with first in the letters, before prisoner of war business and Sidney Smith's welfare. The books, in Swinburne's name at the Transport Board, were sent via Calais and forwarded to Messrs Fector and Minet at Dover, who sent them on to London. Spencer paid for them through official channels: 'I shall remit the amount to Mr [John] March on your account' (12, 21 Feb., 14 Aug. 1797, Althorp Papers, BL, Add. MSS 75813).

operations in 1795, and was financing and trying to coordinate émigré royalists to seize France from the unstable Directory. The rapidly changing regimes in Paris were dependent upon the army, and indeed in the early years the survival of the Republic depended upon the French state being under military threat; it therefore made sense to try to suborn the generals. The most promising was the attempt to bribe Jean-Charles Pichegru, conqueror of Holland in 1794, who was by now disenchanted with the republicans, but the project was compromised.* Not all the cabinet in London, nor the king, were convinced that the restoration of the Bourbons would provide a stable government for France, which made Wickham's mission more difficult. The Austrians were similarly hesitant and as a result were running a timid military strategy. Wickham's efforts also have to be seen against the background of the disintegrating coalition against France. As his effectiveness depended ultimately upon the military success of the Allies, and France successfully countered attempts to overthrow the Directory in 1797 and 1798, his three-year mission was to fail. More than anything, he was hindered by the divisions and rivalries amongst those Frenchmen, especially between the royalists and the constitutional monarchists, who opposed the republicans, and he lost faith in his warring partners very early on.[35]

The effectiveness of intelligence depended not only upon trusted agents, but also upon the speed and security with which intelligence travelled across the world, and particularly across Europe, back to London. The traffic in despatches was heavy. British diplomats at the great courts of Europe were expected to inform London of developments once a week or every fortnight, and thus a great many ordinary diplomatic despatches were carried by post, in cipher. It is likely that these ciphers were not secure against French counter-intelligence.[36] Most of the ciphering and deciphering was done in the Foreign Office, a process dominated by the Willes family for over 120 years, of whom

---

* Pichegru was involved in a later conspiracy, imprisoned and murdered in his cell in 1804 (Sparrow, *Secret Service*, p. 293).

Sir Francis Willes was latterly the most eminent, retiring in 1807.* King's Messengers were entrusted with the most secret documents, sometimes running a shuttle service from the Continental courts to meet the English packet boats departing from North Sea ports.† Since, however, only forty messengers were on the establishment, controlled by the lord chamberlain, and they were expensive, other couriers could be informally pressed into service. King's Messengers were employed only for the most important messages and for carrying code books.[37]

In Whitehall the first port of call for incoming despatches was the undersecretary at the Foreign Office, who was responsible for getting them deciphered and preparing the official post for the secretary of state. It was a laborious and frustrating job, dominated by the uneven rhythm of the mails from the Continent. For most of the French Revolutionary War these came via Cuxhaven, on the Elbe Estuary near Hamburg, the centre for much Continental trade and postal traffic. A strong westerly wind would often prevent ships from leaving the port, resulting in a dearth of despatches; then, when the wind changed and the post eventually arrived, it would contain a backlog of accumulated packages. When relations between Canning and Grenville were at a low ebb, as they were for much of Canning's period as undersecretary between 1796 and 1799, the attention accorded to the pile of despatches could be scant, and some even remained unread.[38]

The speed and frequency of information that came by sea were thus wildly unpredictable, with delays of course caused by enemy action as

---

* Between 1716 and 1844 seven members of the family held office in the Deciphering Department of the secretaries of state, and, after 1782, the Foreign Office. The most remarkable of this family, apparently blessed with mathematical genes, was Edward Willes, appointed in 1716, who managed to continue his duties after he had been appointed Bishop of St Davids in 1742, and of Bath and Wells in 1743 (Ellis, *Post Office*, pp. 129–31; Sainty, *Secretaries of State*, pp. 51–2, 116–17).

† The life of a King's Messenger was hard and dangerous. One old Foreign Office hand recalled, 'the many instances in which they lost their lives by shipwreck, or were murdered; the innumerable cases in which they suffered bodily injury by being thrown from their horses or carriages; their sufferings from frost-bite, exposure and so forth' (Horn, *Foreign Office*, pp. 221–2, quoting Sir Edward Hertslet, *Recollections of the Old Foreign Office* (1901), p. 157).

well as by the weather. Contact with the Mediterranean was particularly difficult, since France and its allies lay across the lines of communication. Nevertheless, despatches could sometimes travel at remarkable speeds. The average running time from Spithead to Barbados was just under 39 days, and from Cork 42. The return journey from the Leewards to Spithead averaged 47 days, and from Jamaica, through the passage between Cuba and the North American continent, as many as 75. A large warship could expect to make Gibraltar from Spithead in 30 days, but the average for frigates and larger storeships, with their superior windward ability, was only 18 days.[39] Some naval frigates and cutters carried despatches very fast, if they had consistent heavy winter winds blowing from astern. In December 1800 the diplomat Arthur Paget reported from Palermo in Sicily that he had received a message from Admiral Keith at Port Mahon in Minorca in two days, a distance of nearly 500 miles, a speed that averaged out at ten knots. Paget rightly commented that it was 'an extraordinary passage'.[40]

With winds behind them, especially in the winter, even some ships not built for speed managed remarkably fast passages. Keith reported later in December that three ships with troops aboard took only three weeks to reach Malta from England.[41] In November 1799 the mast ship *Lord Macartney* and her escort, the *Lynx* sloop, reached the Downs from Halifax, Nova Scotia, in 16 days, a 2,000-mile journey; according to *The Times*, it was 'the shortest time ever known'. Even with the Gulf Stream pushing them along, the average speed of over five knots was unusual.[42] It was comparable with that of two fast, 16-gun sloops, *Bonetta* and *Shark*, which did the same journey in 16 and 14 days respectively in 1793.[43]

Communications depended even more upon the packet service run by the Post Office. Much depended upon the skill, knowledge and perseverance of the masters of these packets and their crews. Once the war started, constant communication with the Continent was vital for orders and intelligence, for trading merchants, for the transfer of specie and a limited passenger service, as well as the considerable post home from British seamen and soldiers abroad (generated by the Parliamentary Military Postage Concessions Act of 1796, which allowed them to send a letter for a penny, paid when posted).[44] The shortest route, from Dover to Calais, naturally had to be abandoned, and as a result no packet route became more important than that across the southern North Sea: the service ran from Harwich to the Dutch ports of Hellevoetsluis and Brill.* After the French invasion of Holland at the end of 1794, it had to shift its base from Harwich to Great Yarmouth, because Yarmouth's more northerly position required less windward sailing in the prevailing south-west or north-easterly winds.[45] Cuxhaven replaced Hellevoetsluis and Brill because landing was possible at all states of the tide.[46] Thus, the shortest passage for mail became Great Yarmouth to Cuxhaven, a distance of 240 sea miles. In the Napoleonic War, as we shall see, packets were required to travel much further north, as far as Sweden, as France gained control of more and more of northern Europe.

Autumn or winter conditions in the North Sea can be imagined: hard gales (usually from the south-west though sometimes from the north-east), when it would be cold and icy, fog or poor visibility, sluicing tides, and always the punishing, short, steep, grey seas when the vessel had to beat to windward. Neither coast was marked by much high ground to guide the master or pilot: shallow, dangerous sandbanks existed well out of sight of land. The master was required to measure his vessel's leeward drift when going to windward over a long period, and was without landmarks to fix a position. The amount of leeway would be unique to each vessel, so it was fortunate that the packets were very often owned by the masters, who were contracted to the Post Office. In fact, the knowledge of the masters and mates of the characteristics of their vessels and constantly sailed routes made their packets safer when crossing the North Sea than warships. Four of such larger naval ships were lost during the operations at Den Helder in 1799, the most famous being the 932-ton, 36-gun frigate

---

* The generally jaundiced public view of the North Sea crossing can be discerned from popular doggerel:

> Gravesend, Dover, Deal and Harwich
> The Devil gave his daughter in marriage
> And further to fulfil his will
> He flung in Hellevoetsluis and Brill
> (Trinder, *Harwich Packets*, p. 93)

Lutine, lost in November with all hands bar two on the Terschelling Sands, together with £140,000 in coin to pay the troops.[47]*

In spite of the considerable safety record of the packets, risks were manifold. There could be little heaving to under reduced sail in hard gales, for the post had to get through: sails had to be heavily reefed and the packet sailed hard. Ice across the Elbe was often so thick as to be impenetrable; dropping the mail at the island of Heligoland for later delivery by fishing boats was sometimes the only option. Capture by enemy privateers was the real danger, although during the French Revolutionary War this was more likely on the packet routes from Falmouth to Lisbon or Falmouth to the West Indies. The North Sea packets were generally manned by seventeen men, and the Post Office was urged to arm the vessels to defend themselves against privateers. John Bennett Bennot, the inspector of packets, was concerned about the expense, as well as the weight, which would 'retard them from getting away from the Enemy'. However, in 1797 he did request the postmaster-generals to obtain lighter carronades to arm the packets.[48] Sometimes cruising British frigates kept the enemy privateers off and, in the event, only five East Coast packets were captured in nearly ten years of operating in wartime before the Peace of Amiens.[49]

The log of His Majesty's packet *Prince of Wales*, one of the six vessels stationed at Yarmouth, reveals the details of life and navigation aboard a packet in the North Sea. For the year from September 1800, to take a sample, she made fourteen round trips from Yarmouth to Cuxhaven, with little variation in the course taken. Although she once made the passage eastwards from Yarmouth in a day, she averaged slightly over two days during the year; in September 1801, however, she took as long as five days against a north-east gale. Over three and a half days was the average for her return voyage, and she generally stayed about a week in Cuxhaven, waiting for mails from the agent or for favourable winds, during which her crew would undoubtedly have spent the time maintaining the vessel. If a King's Messenger arrived with an express despatch, the vessel would depart immediately, leaving

---

* The bell of the *Lutine* hangs to this day in Lloyd's of London, and is rung to announce a maritime disaster somewhere in the world. Only half the gold was eventually recovered.

the general post for the next vessel. In the year leading to the peace preliminaries of the Treaty of Amiens there was a noticeable increase in passages taken by King's Messengers, five being recorded in the log.[50] In August 1802, during the Peace of Amiens, she picked up the Danish negotiator Count Bernstorff and his suite in England, transferred him to an armed schooner on the far side of the North Sea and returned immediately. On 16 March 1801 the master, Anthony Deane, saw a vessel, 'and hearing several guns supposed she might be in some distress'. The sparse language of the log reflects his dilemma. He turned his vessel towards her, 'but coming on thick and blowing hard soon lost sight of her. At 4pm not knowing which way she laid with her head, night coming on & having the mails on board thought it most prudent to bear & continue our course.'[51] The wrecked ship was the 74-gun *Invincible*, which, soon after leaving Yarmouth, had struck the sands of Hammond's Knoll, off Happisburgh, at ten knots. Four hundred men were drowned.

For the individual passenger, journeys could be long and conditions gruelling, particularly if it was necessary to travel in winter. Tom Grenville, the brother of the foreign secretary, was appointed to a diplomatic mission to Berlin in November 1798. Even though a powerful frigate was assigned to convey him, the 24-gun *Champion*, over five times the size of a packet, he did not escape extreme discomfort. On his arrival at Yarmouth on 18 December 1798, a thick fog prevented his embarkation, and then an easterly wind prevented the frigate from sailing. When it reached the Elbe Estuary, the ship was damaged by the ice, and turned back, with the ice in her rigging making her almost unmanageable. On 29 December, Grenville was back in Yarmouth, considerably shaken. Five weeks after his first attempt he tried again, this time with the frigate *Proserpine*. She called for a pilot at Heligoland, where she was discouraged from making the attempt, but Grenville urged the man to press on. In the Elbe, ice had obscured the navigation marks, and a thick covering of snow the landmarks: the ship turned for home, then struck a sandbank. On the landward side of the ship the ice was solid, so she was abandoned by crew and passengers. In the intense cold, twelve men died and Grenville at one point found himself hauled from the icy water by the handle of a boarding pike. But his papers were intact. Eight miles away from

Cuxhaven, and on dry land, he set off across the tidal sands, but his guides had miscalculated: the tide raced in and Grenville's party were up to their waists in water, a blizzard blowing in their faces. They finally reached Cuxhaven in a state of exhaustion.* Sadly, Grenville's exceptionally dangerous journey had been made in vain, because his diplomatic mission in Berlin failed to bring the alliance between Austria and Prussia which he had been sent to achieve.[52]

When they eventually reached the Continent, those involved in conveying intelligence often found that their problems were only just starting. The roads in certain parts were extremely poor. One possible route for intelligence across Spain, from Barcelona via Madrid to Ferrol, was reported by John Hunter, the British consul in Madrid, to be 214 leagues distance, and could be covered by relays of mules in about twenty-five days, and costing 240 Spanish dollars, but the duration of the journey was dependent upon weather and the availability of straw and barley for the mules.[53] Another way to avoid France was through the mountainous parts of Austria, the path of diplomats and King's Messengers – an extraordinarily expensive route. A travel claim survives for Thomas Masterman Hardy, at that time a young captain returning to London from service in the Mediterranean in 1799, who travelled home from Leghorn via Vienna, Cuxhaven and Yarmouth. He purchased a post-chaise at Leghorn, sharing expenses with a King's Messenger, but the rough roads wrecked the carriage, and he was able to sell it for only £4 in Vienna. With 'expenses on the road' and the hire of post horses, he claimed the very substantial sum of £201 in expenses, but, according to the Navy Board's scale of expenses based upon rank, he was due just £145.[54]

In Britain, by contrast, the speed of communication by roads was steadily getting better, a development that was as important for the

---

* Lady Bessborough wrote to Leveson Gower of Grenville's terrible journey: 'The general anxiety about him and joy for his safety must be very flattering to him if he ever knows it. It was the highest of all honours, the homage paid to worth, for had either of his brothers [Lord Grenville and the Marquis of Buckingham] been in the same situation, neither their titles or their riches, or their places would have gained them half the interest that was shown for him' (Thorne, *History of Parliament*, Vol. IV, p. 95, quoting Granville, *Leveson Gower*, Vol. I, p. 242).

efficiency and costs of government and commerce as it was for ordinary people. Widespread road improvements had been achieved by turnpike trusts in the third quarter of the eighteenth century, a process that was continued during the war years, especially in the north of England. By the mid 1830s about 22,000 miles, a fifth of all the roads in the country, had been turnpiked or improved by other means.[55] Better roads were also, of course, useful for moving troops and artillery around the country, as well as for the carriage of valuable equipment for the war – such as the naval copper bolts manufactured in the north – whenever the reliability and speed of delivery were more important considerations than the cost, for coastal transport was far cheaper.

The government had a further method of moving information swiftly. Designed, built and manned by the navy in the mid 1790s, a system of shutter telegraphs radiated out from the top of the Admiralty building in Whitehall, putting ministers in touch with the commanders-in-chief at the Downs, Portsmouth or Plymouth in minutes. The first superintendent of telegraphs, a surveyor named George Roebuck, was able to build the first line of towers from the Admiralty to Deal in only four months. Such speed of construction was achieved because of the knowledge of the topography available from the accurate triangulation of the Ordnance Survey.[56] The optical telegraphs quickly became a new element affecting the timeliness of intelligence, for they were capable of sending rapid, detailed messages. The French had invented the system: by 1794 a line of telegraphs connected Paris to Lille. Information on the French system, including an alphabetical code found on a French prisoner of war, was shown to the commander-in-chief, the duke of York. An alternative system was quickly developed from the French model by the Reverend John Gamble, though the design adopted by the Admiralty was the invention of the Reverend Lord Murray.[57] Their operation involved the use of six shutters, which were turned rapidly; a distant observer would make note of each set of shutter positions, which represented a coded letter.

By January 1796 the first line of shutter telegraphs was operational. Charles Abbot noted in his diary on 4 February 1796: 'The telegraph at the Admiralty was finished this week, and signals conveyed to Deal in

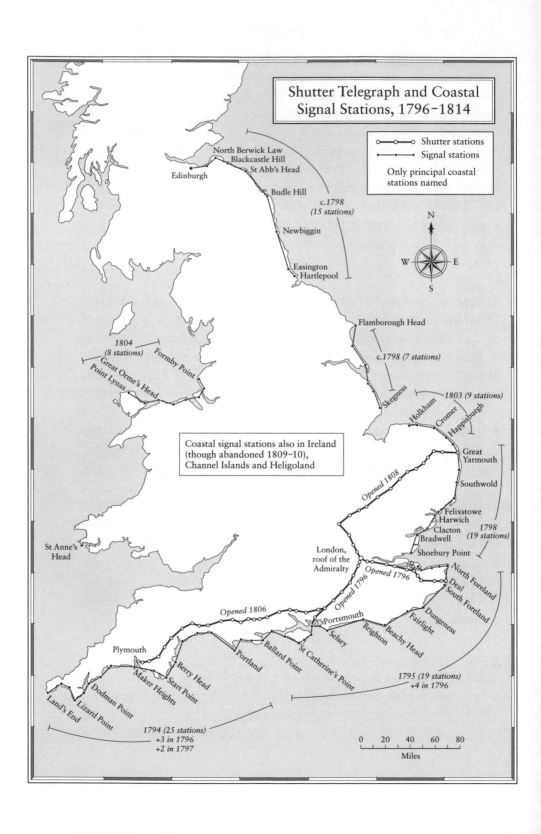

Shutter Telegraph and Coastal
Signal Stations, 1796–1814

Shutter stations
Signal stations
Only principal coastal
stations named

North Berwick Law
Blackcastle Hill
St Abb's Head
Edinburgh

Budle Hill

c.1798
(15 stations)

Newbiggin

Easington
Hartlepool

Flamborough Head

c.1798 (7 stations)

1804
(8 stations)   Formby Point
Great Orme's Head
Point Lynas

Skegness

Holkham   1803 (9 stations)
Cromer
Happisburgh

Coastal signal stations also in Ireland
(though abandoned 1809–10),
Channel Islands and Heligoland

Great
Yarmouth

Southwold

Opened 1808

Felixstowe
Harwich
Clacton   1798
Bradwell   (19 stations)

St Anne's
Head

London,
roof of the
Admiralty

Shoebury Point

North Foreland

Opened 1796   Deal
South Foreland

Opened 1806   Opened 1796
Portsmouth   Dungeness
Selsey   Fairlight
Brighton   Beachy Head
St Catherine's Point

Plymouth   Ballard Point
Portland
Berry Head
Maker Heights   Start Point
Land's End   Dodman Point
Lizard Point

1795 (19 stations)
+4 in 1796

1794 (25 stations)
+3 in 1796
+2 in 1797

0   20   40   60   80

Miles

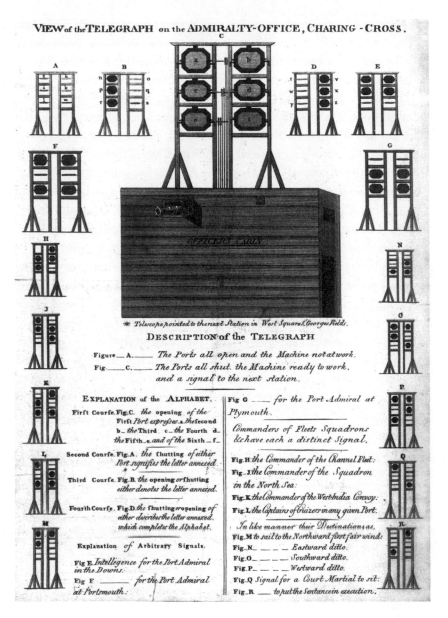

VIEW of the TELEGRAPH on the ADMIRALTY-OFFICE, CHARING-CROSS.

✳ *Telescope pointed to the next Station in West-Square S.t George's Fields.*

DESCRIPTION of the TELEGRAPH

Figure — A — The Ports all open and the Machine not at work.

Fig. — C — The Ports all shut. the Machine ready to work. and a signal to the next station.

EXPLANATION of the ALPHABET.

First Course. Fig. C. the opening of the First Port expresses a the second b — the Third c — the Fourth d — the Fifth e. and of the Sixth f —

Second Course. Fig. A. the shutting of either Port signifies the letter annexed.

Third Course. Fig. B. the opening or shutting either denotes the letter annexed.

Fourth Course. Fig. D. the shutting or opening of either describes the letter annexed. which completes the Alphabet.

Explanation of Arbitrary Signals.

Fig E. Intelligence for the Port Admiral in the Downs:

Fig F — for the Port Admiral at Portsmouth:

Fig G — for the Port Admiral at Plymouth.

Commanders of Fleets Squadrons & have each a distinct Signal.

Fig. H. the Commander of the Channel Fleet:

Fig. J. the Commander of the Squadron in the North Sea:

Fig. K the Commander of the West-India Convoy:

Fig. L the Captains of Cruizers in any given Port.

In like manner their Destinations as,

Fig. M to sail to the Northward first fair wind:

Fig. N — — — — Eastward ditto.

Fig. O — — — — Southward ditto.

Fig. P — — — Westward ditto.

Fig. Q Signal for a Court Martial to sit:

Fig. R — to put the Sentence in execution.

A print of the hut erected on the roof of the Admiralty, with the code for each letter around the edge. A fixed telescope can be seen trained on the next station. So much concentration was needed to make out distant signals that the 'glassmen' took turns of only five minutes.

seven minutes by the medium of thirteen intervening telegraphs.'[58] Within a year the line to Portsmouth was complete and communication could be achieved in fifteen minutes. The Portsmouth–London line was to be immediately useful during the Spithead mutiny: a message to Pitt of 13 May 1797 survives in his papers: '20 minutes before noon. Admiral gone to the *Royal William* to receive Lord Howe. His Lordship going off. 16 boats coming from St Helens.'[59] By 1801 the telegraphs were working so well that British warships off the French coast were able to signal directly to the Admiralty, via anchored signal ships and the flagship at the Nore.[60] When Nelson was bombarding Boulogne in August 1801, Thomas Troubridge at the Admiralty wrote to him: 'The telegraph tells us you are playing away at the Miscreants.'[61] This was the equivalent of modern-day 'real-time' intelligence.

The shutter telegraphs were complemented by another system started by the Admiralty in 1794, when it ordered the building of signalling stations around the coasts. Between five to seven miles apart, these stretched westward from the Solent to Land's End; and, in the following year, eastward from the Solent to the North Foreland.[62] The stations, of timber, were constructed very swiftly and completed about a month after the initial orders.[63] They were much less complicated than the shutter telegraphs, consisting of a single flagstaff, and could be used to send only short, prescribed messages, such as the sighting of a potentially hostile warship or privateer. Admiralty printed instructions to the naval lieutenants in command of each station were simple:

> You will find upon your arrival at the Station a temporary building or signal House, with two rooms, one for the accommodation of yourself, and the other for your two assistants . . . also a Telescope, one Red Flag, one Blue Pendant, and four Signal Balls.[64]

Once these two signalling systems were operational, the risk of a surprise landing by the French was very much reduced.

The coastal signal stations were intended primarily for sightings of enemy privateers, which constantly preyed on small merchant ships on coastal voyages. The most frequently used signals were those to ships off the coast, requesting a secret password so that ships could be identified as friendly. If anything suspicious was seen, a message was passed down the line of stations to the commanders-in-chief at Plymouth, Portsmouth or the Downs. There was much to report: attacks from smaller French privateers, rigged as luggers and very fast, especially to windward, were frequent. Within a month of the declaration of war in 1793, a British 16-gun sloop, the *Nautilus*, was chased into Plymouth Sound by two French 28-gun privateers; on the same day another privateer came within three miles of several large warships anchored there.[65] Incidents involving French privateers slowly increased until they peaked in 1797–8, though the danger of such attacks remained high until 1802.[66] The southern North Sea between Hull and London in the late 1790s was the scene of furious actions. Ships carrying butter, cheese and other agricultural products to London were captured in the winter of 1796, and the Cheesemonger's Company successfully lobbied the Admiralty for a warship escort.[67] In November 1799 the *Marquis of Granby* from Sunderland was captured by a French lugger (though she was retaken by her master, who had been set adrift in the ship's boat, once the privateer had gone off in chase of another English prize).[68] In the same month one of the ships managed by the coal merchant Michael Henley was captured off the North Foreland. The owner wrote to Henley: 'I must request therefore your assistance in procuring the Insurance of the vessel from Government.'[69] The danger of merchant ship losses to enemy privateers off the British coast was to be present until 1815.

At no point in the war did the importance of efficient communication and intelligence matter more than at its beginning, when there was a race to get the news of the declaration of war out to distant parts of the empire, ahead of the French. Those combatants who received the news first were given the advantage of surprise. The French had the edge when it came to communications with the West Indies, as they could start their voyage from Brest or from ports further south much more advantageously than the British, who had further to sail against the prevalent south-westerlies. Spread out across the Mediterranean, the French usually also had the advantage when getting news to India. However, the British position was improving. By 1798 Lord Mornington, governor-general of India, expected a monthly despatch overland, despite its expense (a single despatch cost nearly £800).

Even more critical was the speed of intelligence in May 1803 when news of the renewal of war was transmitted. The British consul in Alexandria, George Baldwin (whose salary was paid by the East India Company), ensured that it was sped on its way down the Red Sea to Bombay; and the British were able to march into the French enclave in Pondicherry before the enemy knew that war had been declared.[70]

The extraordinary journey of the resourceful Hugh Cleghorn to Ceylon in 1795 and 1796 illustrates the advantages and problems of the overland route in wartime. Cleghorn, at this point over sixty, was a nephew of Adam Smith and formerly professor of civil history at the University of St Andrews; he had also been a magistrate with William Wickham in London and worked for the Alien Office. In February 1795, Cleghorn suggested to Henry Dundas that, through private contacts, he should attempt to 'detach' a private Swiss regiment from its contract with the Dutch East India Company and to bring it into British service. Political allegiances were changing (the British withdrew from Holland in April) and by the middle of May 1795 the Dutch had been forced to come to terms with the French. Cleghorn knew that the owner of the regiment, Colonel le comte de Meuron, was 'extremely disgusted' with his Dutch employers. De Meuron had 1,200 well-trained men in Ceylon, Cochin and Batavia, and the regiment was, as Cleghorn described it, the 'chief European Force of the Dutch on the other side of the Cape'.[71] After conferring with the king, Dundas immediately approved.

Cleghorn left England within a fortnight, was in Hamburg on 7 March and in Neuchâtel by the end of the month, talking to the comte, who agreed that his regiment should change sides, and that he should set out for Ceylon with Cleghorn as soon as possible. The douceur of £5,000 suggested by Dundas proved not to be necessary: making good arrears of pay and the promotion of the comte above the rank of colonel were incentives enough. By 13 May they were in Venice, from where they took a ship to Alexandria, arriving in Cairo by 17 June. From Cairo, Dundas received one of his more exotic intelligence reports, Cleghorn ending the missive: 'I write under the continuous interruptions of camel drivers.' On 3 July, at Suez, the two men took passage on a pilgrim ship down the Red Sea, were shipwrecked and briefly imprisoned at Jedda, after which they took an

Arab ship to Tellichery on the Malabar coast in India, crossing the southern tip of India. They arrived in Ceylon, having made the passage in an open boat. By 13 October, Cleghorn had moved to Madras to make contact with the British East India Company. Two weeks later he was able to write to Dundas that the Meuron regiment had changed sides and that his mission had been successful, only eight months after he had first suggested it in London.[72] Trincomalee had already surrendered in late August, after a siege that had cost only fifteen British lives. After much negotiation, Colombo was to follow on 15 February 1796. It had been a virtually bloodless conquest. Though Ceylon as a whole was not under British control until 1815, after considerable bloodshed, Britain had secured the route to India, and, in Trincomalee, a most valuable naval base.

Cleghorn's journey illustrates the exigencies of long-distance travel in wartime and was smoothed not only by despatches from London to all the consuls likely to be in a position to help him, but also by government credit of £4,000, plus £1,500 for expenses, to be drawn on the bank of Sir Robert Herries. Government and the City thus combined to enable Cleghorn to travel fast and light. He drew £300 from George Baldwin in Alexandria on the way out and £350 from the British consul in Malta on his return journey (though here he had to spend some time in the lazaretto under quarantine). On the way back to England he journeyed from Naples to Corsica, at this time in British hands, where he delivered intelligence to Gilbert Elliot, the viceroy, before returning to Naples to undertake tasks for the ambassador, Sir William Hamilton, all the while dodging the French armies, on which he sent intelligence reports back to London, and visited Wickham in Geneva. By 14 July 1797 Cleghorn was back in London at an address in Old Cavendish Street.[73]

Successful episodes like this, however, which drew on efficient intelligence and communications systems, were few and far between in the French Revolutionary War, and the years between 1794 and 1799 saw a succession of non-events and failures. Planning for a landing at Den Helder took place during 1796, but, although Admiral Duncan planned to attack Den Helder in the summer of 1797, the mutiny at the Nore intervened, and nothing materialized until 1799. The French invasion attempt on Ireland in the winter of 1796 highlighted one weak link in the intelligence chain in Switzerland, where William Wickham's activities, by now well known to the French, were becoming untenable. The French brought pressure on the neutral Swiss to have him ejected, a threat increased by 70,000 French troops on the border at Basle, and communications became so difficult that he was virtually isolated. Two senior leaders of the United Irishmen, Lord Edward FitzGerald and Arthur O'Connor, went to Basle to consult General Lazare Hoche about arrangements for a projected invasion of Ireland. Wickham's agents lost them at the border, the revolutionaries completed their talks with Hoche, and the expedition to Bantry Bay was formalized.[74] Fortunately for Britain, as we saw in Chapter 3, defective French naval organization and confusion in the Directory ensured the expedition's failure.

The year 1798 saw the biggest blunder of British intelligence in the French Revolutionary War, for, in the successful invasion of Egypt, the French sprang a major strategic surprise. In February of that year Bonaparte was inspecting French troops in the Channel ports and was seen there by a British agent, but on 5 March the Directory decided that the young French general should lead the Egyptian expedition.[75] Several reports reached London in early 1798 of a very large armament of ships and soldiers at Toulon, but with no information as to the destination of the expedition. Intelligence gathering was being made more difficult by the British Fleet's having withdrawn west of the Strait of Gibraltar: St Vincent was commanding the Mediterranean Fleet off Cádiz. Receiving instructions from the Admiralty to re-enter the Mediterranean, he sent Nelson off on 8 May with three ships of the line, to find out what the French were up to, as we saw in Chapter 3. In the meantime, many theories and despatches were flowing into London as to the destination of the expedition: Ireland, Portugal, Naples, Sicily or Sardinia?

It transpired that each Whitehall department had its own theory. Consequently, none of the information held was distributed among, or discussed with, other departments, or at least not quickly enough to be of any use. The Foreign Office, as usual, had the earliest intelligence: that the French transports were being issued with biscuit for only 'three months' provisions' – sure evidence of the expedition's limited range and capability. The despatch containing this information came from Thomas Jackson, the minister in Turin, and was written on 31 March and passed on speedily to the Admiralty on 24 April, for the Foreign Office wanted warships in the western Mediterranean to encourage Austria to re-enter the war. Nepean, who was convinced that the French were intent upon Ireland, chose not to send the despatch on to the secretary for war, Henry Dundas, until 28 June.[76] Lord Grenville also received a long, reasoned letter, written on 16 April, from John Udney, the British consul in Leghorn, who had asked his merchant contacts for advice. Udney wrote persuasively about Egypt as the possible destination, and the concomitant threat to India.[77] Grenville did not pass on the contents of the letter.*

In late April, Henry Dundas received reports from another source – the Secret Committee of the East India Company – about what was likely to happen in India if the French successfully invaded Egypt.[78]† He also had information from Mauritius that the French were pulling together a force to mount an expedition against India. By the end of the month he had reached the conclusion that Egypt was Bonaparte's target, and so began to ask for reports from various experts on the effect that this might have and whether the French could break out of the Red Sea. Within the East India Company the conviction was growing that the French were going to head eastwards. On 9 June the Secret Committee of the Company wrote to the three presidencies at Bombay, Madras and Calcutta to say that Bonaparte was heading for Egypt, and that they were sending out 4,000 troops immediately. The commander-in-chief of the East Indies station, Admiral Rainier, took the precaution of sending two warships to cover the mouth of the Red Sea before he had definite intelligence of the French invasion.[79]

---

* A further problem was handling the vastly increased intelligence correspondence. Michael Duffy estimates that Foreign Office files doubled between 1783 and 1792 and between 1793 and 1802. There were three quarters more files and those much thicker than in the previous period. In 1793 Grenville appointed Charles Arbuthnot, a friend from Christ Church, as a senior précis writer to deal with this problem (Collinge, *Foreign Office*, pp. 41, 58).

† The Secret Committee of the Court of Directors of the EIC had considerable influence on the government's policy, and was the channel through which secret despatches passed between the Board of Control and the different centres of government in India (Philips, *East India Company*, p. 11).

Then the British had a stroke of luck. An agent for transports, Lieu-tenant William Day, was arranging a cartel for the exchange of prisoners of war in Genoa, a city that was still in theory neutral, though threatened by a French army. Day observed transports were being fitted for the French expedition, and his expert eye could tell that the merchant vessels being collected were not seaworthy enough for a voyage outside the Strait of Gibraltar, casting strong doubt on the possibility that the expedition was destined for Portugal or Ire-land. On 31 March, Day wrote to the Admiralty; and on 13 April he reported to Admiral Lord St Vincent off Cádiz that 120 transports for troops were preparing, as well as large casks, possibly for use as buoys in shallow water, 'but they [the transports] will be in a dreadful state whenever they put to sea'.[80] Day then went back to London at high speed by the land route, taking only two weeks, and immediately had an interview with Lord Spencer.[81] On 1 May the first lord wrote rap-idly, though still tentatively, to St Vincent that it was 'most probable that they are destined either for the coast of Spain or Naples, or (though I can scarce believe it) for the Levant'.[82] Crucially, there was no mention of Egypt – even as a possibility – and the omission of this vital word was to have a baleful influence on Nelson's efforts to find the French. Spencer's letter of 1 May was the last letter to reach Nel-son before he sailed up the Mediterranean.

However divided it was in opinion, the cabinet acted with unusual decision. On 1 May 1798 it decided to order ten battleships, under Admiral Sir Roger Curtis, away from the Channel Fleet to reinforce the Mediterranean Fleet under Lord St Vincent. The order was sent on 2 May. Curtis received it six days later as his squadron anchored in Beer Haven, a harbour off Bantry Bay.[83] On 19 May, Bonaparte's fleet departed from Toulon, escorting 280 transports containing 48,662 troops.[84] Curtis's ships from the Channel Fleet reached St Vincent off Cádiz on 24 May. The same day St Vincent sent off his ten best ships, provisioned for six months, under Captain Thomas Trou-bridge to reinforce Nelson. This effectively sealed shut the information window from London. By 8 June, Nelson was joined off Toulon by Troubridge and, with what was now a formidable squadron, he sailed south. He had, however, another source of intelligence, one that was more accurate than anything obtained officially, and to which he clearly paid a good deal of attention. A letter of 26 April from John Udney, whom Nelson had known from earlier service off the coasts of Italy, is still preserved in Nelson's papers:

> My private Ideas on the present situation ... their first attempt will be on Malta, from thence to invade Sicily to secure that granary and then Naples ... Whatever their views afterwards maybe ... time will shew ... I for my own part ... getting possession of Egypt; am convinced Buonaparte will hereafter & with more reason, in his unbounded enterprises, pursue the same scheme of Seizing and fortifying Alexandria, Cairo and Suez. If France intend uniting with Tippo Said against our possessions in India, the danger of losing half an Army in crossing the Desert from Egypt would be no obstacle.[85]

Udney's instincts on Bonaparte's destination were correct. The Knights of St John surrendered Malta to the French on 11 June, and for the rest of the month and July 1798 Nelson, still guessing, searched for the huge French Fleet. He headed eastwards for Egypt as speedily as he could, but overshot the French, slowed by their troopships and transports, which were sailing slowly along the coast of Crete before heading south to Egypt. Nelson reached Alexandria, missing the arrival of the French by only twenty-four hours. George Baldwin, the British consul in Alexandria, was absent on leave: had he been there, Nelson would have delayed for a few vital days.[86] Eventually, after doubling back to Sicily to reprovision, he caught up with the French ships of the line at anchor in Aboukir Bay on 1 August. Had Nelson known of the dawning suspicions of ministers in London about Egypt, the probability is that he and his powerful squadron would have caught and decimated Bonaparte's overcrowded warships and transports at sea before they landed the army. History would have taken a different course.

From May neither St Vincent nor Nelson had the information that was available in London. Spencer's letters carry no conviction and reflected the broad views of Nepean and the naval members of the Board.[87] The only cabinet minister with a different perspective was Dundas, influenced by his contact with the East India Company. To cap this inept performance, Spencer's urgent letter of 1 May from London to St Vincent off Cádiz was sent by a frigate that was then ordered to escort a convoy, thus arriving by the slowest means possible.

St Vincent complained to Nepean: 'What could have possessed you to put a letter of so much importance requiring the quickest despatch, on board a ship charged with a convoy?'[88] Dundas, with considerable justification, carried out a post-mortem of all intelligence received, which included a far from complete list from Nepean of despatches received by the Admiralty.[89] When Dundas finished his review at the end of September, he wrote a depressed letter to Grenville:

> I hate to indulge retrospective melancholy, but in this instance I cannot relieve my mind from it. If we had not been too incredulous as to the object of Buonaparte's armament, I think that such instructions would have been given to Sir Horatio Nelson as would have prevented him from leaving Alexandria, after he had once reached it in the auspicious and promising way he did.[90]

On 1 October, Dundas sent Nepean's list on to his undersecretary, William Huskisson, commenting, 'I shall drop that subject for the moment.'[91] Dundas thought, rightly, that a major failure had occurred and felt that Nepean had obstructed information about a possible Egyptian destination. Recriminations were checked by the news of the Nile victory, which reached London on 2 October. Yet Dundas did not forget: in May 1799 he had a clerk draw up a comprehensive list of fifty pieces of incoming intelligence during the summer of 1798.[92]

He did not get the improvement he was looking for, at least not immediately. The next year another major failure occurred when a large French Fleet of twenty-five ships of the line under Vice-Admiral Eustache Bruix left Brest and got past the blockading British Fleet and into the Mediterranean. The first intelligence signs that another big operation was under way were evident in early January 1799, when D'Auvergne in the Channel Islands picked up information on increased French activity. Unfortunately, at the end of that month he received, but overlooked, very solid information that the operation was aimed at the Mediterranean: he learnt that naval commissaries were travelling south through France by land to organize shipping.[93] The French also tried disinformation by planting false orders on a small French vessel, the *Rebecca*, picked up by the British lugger *Black Joke*, intended to point ministers' suspicions towards Ireland. The naval members of the Admiralty Board saw through the French ruse early, but that summer Lord Spencer was absent, taking the waters at Bath, and so the naval view was not reflected in discussions when the major decisions were taken by Pitt, Dundas and Grenville.[94]

On a foggy morning on 26 April 1799, Bruix slipped away from the one British frigate on station outside Brest. His orders were to destroy the dispersed British Fleet in the Mediterranean, and primarily to relieve the besieged French forces in Malta, Corfu and Egypt. The covering British frigate missed the French ships. The fleet was out, and once more the government in London did not have the slightest idea where it was going, assuming almost as a reflex action that it must be Ireland. Bridport and the British Channel Fleet were sent to cruise off the southern Irish coast. But Bruix went south and on 3 May appeared off Cádiz with twenty-five ships of the line, threatening the Mediterranean Fleet, at this point under Lord Keith, whose ships were dispersed: he had only fifteen battleships. In a rising gale Keith formed a line, but Bruix, conscious of the main objective of the mission, and the worsening weather, headed off into the Mediterranean; had he been bolder, he could have destroyed the smaller, dispersed British Fleet. Bruix then received further orders to help the French Army in Italy by ferrying supplies, after which he returned to the Atlantic, taking some Spanish battleships with him; he re-entered Brest on 8 August, having achieved nothing.[95] Britain had been lucky again, but signs of inter-departmental strain were contained in a letter written by Huskisson to a relatively junior naval captain, Home Popham, referring disparagingly to Nepean at the Admiralty:

> I trust that you will not be thwarted by the routine Oracle who presides over our naval operations, by having got the ear of our First Lord. I wish this self-important little man had the Emperor of Russia at his elbow, I think he would make him bestir himself a little more.[96]

Such frustration was symptomatic of the relations in Whitehall in the late 1790s.

In London, much hope was invested in the Second Coalition, signed in June 1799 with Russia, Austria and lesser powers, negotiated by Pitt and Grenville. The main British effort was an invasion of Holland at Den Helder in August, for which the British transported Russian troops from the Baltic to fight alongside their own. While the operation captured the remainder of the Dutch Fleet that had not been lost at Camperdown two years before, as a military operation it had little effect on the war. Intelligence assessments of the level of support that could be expected from the Dutch population were wide of the mark, due to the enthusiasm of Orangeists exiled in London. Etches, too, was over-optimistic from the reports from his network of agents at the Texel and other Dutch ports reporting on Dutch-ship movements.* He had been urging action against Holland over some years in his secret correspondence with Nepean.[97] Wickham returned to the Continent, where he presided over the disastrous involvement of one of his agents, the reckless and inexperienced James Talbot, who plotted to assassinate the Directory, an episode of which the higher echelons of the British government were unaware.[98] Before he had finished, Talbot had expended the huge sum of £377,807.[99]

In spite of enormous efforts and expenditure during the Revolutionary War, the verdict on the overall defence intelligence performance must be one of continual British failure, although it was offset by the inability of French naval organization and seamanship to take advantage of Britain's shortcomings. Ministers did not receive a coherent intelligence picture and suffered from lack of information about the reliability of sources; and when intelligence was available, it was often misinterpreted. Three main disadvantages were never overcome. The first was that Britain was facing an unstable regime. The cabinet did not come near to understanding the erratic minds of those who took strategic decisions during the rule of the Directory. French intentions were difficult to read, and complex situations were made yet more confusing by French counter-intelligence. The second major factor was Ireland. Time and again the judgements of ministers were skewed by their fear of a French invasion force combining with the rebellious population of Ireland. The weakness of Britain's Irish defence and the hostility of a large percentage of the population led the politicians into

---

* Etches took great pains to check the hydrographic details. 'I know the beach well,' he wrote to Nepean, 'from having made a practice when at the Helder of bathing every morning ... to convince myself, I am therefore confident that the troops might [be] landed from open Boats in safety' (21 Nov. 1796, NMM, NEP/2).

'mirror imaging' – erroneously thinking that the French were bound to do what they themselves would have done in similar circumstances. The third disadvantage was that the anti-republican elements in France with whom Britain tried to cooperate and whom it financed, the constitutional monarchists and the royalists, were bitterly divided. The groups hated each other as much as they hated the republican regime in Paris. The information they provided was often wildly optimistic and in some cases fraudulent, with royalists attempting to fool the British in order to ensure the next payment of British secret service funds. Within each group, the existence of several factions made coherent plans impossible. The French royalists, as Talleyrand was later to remark, 'learnt nothing and forgot nothing'.[100]

The year leading up to the signing of the Peace of Amiens in March 1802 saw some germs of improvement. The secret service had been hardened by a tough war in which it had taken on French counter-intelligence, with casualties on both sides.[101] Lessons had been learnt in Whitehall, and Henry Dundas's post-mortem was not wasted. The vast collection of intelligence in Whitehall was beginning to make a difference. True, Admiral Ganteaume broke out of Brest through the blockade with seven warships in January 1801 in a final attempt to relieve the French Army in Egypt, but once he got to the Egyptian coast he found British warships and retreated, like Bruix, having achieved nothing.[102] However, before the expedition to Copenhagen in March 1801, Admirals Hyde Parker and Nelson were well briefed by those who had served in the Russian Navy, including Etches, who supplied hydrographic information and charts. Nelson was warned that the shallowness of the water south of Copenhagen would mean that ships of the line would have to decrease their draught, by unloading their guns, to get through the Sound into the Baltic, which is exactly what Nelson's larger ships had to do.[103]

Pitt's ministers were strong personalities, frequently at odds with each other and driven by differing agendas.[104] Moreover, dependence on important individuals led to delay when ministers were frequently absent from London during the summer, when military and naval activity was at its height. The dispersal of authority led to the rise of over-powerful figures, particularly of Nepean, whose intelligence experience over twenty years gave him too much responsibility and a licence to spend secret service money without check. Consistent intelligence success would not come until the ministers around the cabinet table stopped involving themselves in interpreting intelligence, and concentrated on the policy decisions for which they alone were responsible.

6

Feeding the Armed Forces
and the Nation

1795–1812

Our Beef perhaps has been in salt for seven years. Our pork is good but very salt: our Butter, Cheese & Bread not good and to Crown all allowed only one Quart of Water per day for washing and drink. Its true we have a Quart of Grog a day, but those things is of little import at present. I am glad to inform you I am quite well both in health and limbs at present.

– James Whitworth, a 34-year-old landsman on
board H.M.S. *Portia*, a 14-gun brig sloop anchored in the
Yarmouth Roads, writing to his wife, 7 May 1812[1]

Complaining about rations was, and is, a time-honoured tradition, but to find direct evidence of a Napoleonic seaman's opinion of his food is rare. James Whitworth was bored after a month's cruising in the North Sea, and probably angry, because the ship's log shows that two days before he wrote the letter he had been given twenty-four lashes for disobedience, about which he failed to inform his wife. For a month the ship had been endlessly watching enemy shipping in the Texel. The *Portia* was anchored in the Yarmouth Roads, with a strong onshore wind that threw up surf, preventing the crew from landing. The fresh beef and vegetables that would be waiting for them on shore were thus unobtainable and the purser and cook were thrown back on casks of preserved rations to feed the 58-man crew. It was another week before the weather allowed fresh food to be brought aboard.[2]

The navy has long been notorious for issuing its sailors with bad food, a reputation honoured by the name given to the small beetle that infests bread and flour, called after the victualling yard on the west side of Portsmouth harbour at Weevil.[3] Yet, had this reputation been wholly deserved, the navy would not have been able to function: for the sheer physical effort demanded by sailing the ship meant that seamen needed to be well fed if they were to carry out orders effectively. They were required to manhandle guns weighing up to three tons, to furl heavy canvas sails and to haul up heavy anchors. Likewise, troops needed stamina for marching long distances, and for carrying small arms and personal equipment. All this required a generous supply of vitamins and daily calories.

Aboard a warship much depended upon the fair and methodical administration of food, a process heavily regulated by detailed naval instructions, and jealously watched over by the men. As a result, it was done with 'scrupulous fairness'.[4] Illnesses needed to be kept at bay because the crews lived in damp and cold conditions. Indeed, the improvement in the 1790s in the elimination of scurvy was critical for the maintenance of the blockade of the French naval ports. Lemon juice was issued as a preventive; this had as much to do with the determination of senior naval officers and better administration by the Victualling Board as with the advocacy of lemons by naval surgeons.[5] When the fleet was off Ushant, convoys of victuallers were escorted from Portsmouth and Plymouth by sloops and cutters.[6] Given that all supply operations depended upon wind-driven ships and were moved on land by horse-drawn wagon or canal boat, the scale and success of worldwide victualling for the navy and army were impressive.

The numbers of British soldiers and seamen who enlisted or were pressed between 1793 and 1815 were of 'an altogether different order of magnitude' from the figures of previous wars.[7] At their highest point, the armed forces were about three times larger than they had been in the American Revolutionary War. By 1801, to take one peak year, Britain was feeding 400,000 men in uniform (or, in the case of the 126,000 naval seamen, in clothes issued as 'slops'). The regular army, militia and volunteers totalled 248,000, of whom 90,000 regulars were serving abroad in distant garrisons from the West to the East Indies, from Canada to the Mediterranean.[8] Tens of thousands were discharged suddenly at the Peace of Amiens, but by the height of the Napoleonic War, numbers reached levels of between 11 and 14 per cent of the adult male population, or about three times the 'military participation ratio' of France.[9] At the same time, the population of Great Britain and Ireland was rising remorselessly, growing by more than 20 per cent over the period, increasing the difficulties of the feeding of the armed forces.[10]

To this should be added food provided for prisoners of war by contractors supplying the Transport Board and its agents in England. The prisoners were mainly French, but they were joined in time by Dutch, Danes and Russians as hostilities spread after 1803. Their rations were similar to those for British soldiers and seamen: a quart of beer, one and a half pounds of bread and a pound of beef a day. The system of exchanging prisoners broke down in the Napoleonic War, and the British captured many more prisoners than their adversaries; thus the number of prisoners of war to be fed increased relentlessly year after year. Prisoners were held on old warships moored at Woolwich, Chatham, Portsmouth and Plymouth, on which conditions were harsh. When numbers increased, some were confined in vast depots which had to be built quickly. The stone prison in the middle of Dartmoor in Devon, started in 1806 and completed in 1809, was designed to hold 5,000 but at one time housed 9,000. The wooden depot at Norman Cross, built in 1797, usually held up to 7,000. Porchester Castle, at the top of Portsmouth Harbour, and Stapleton near Bristol, confined the same sort of numbers. Those totals were to increase dramatically as Wellington advanced in the Peninsula, and when the war with the Americans was joined between 1812 and 1814.[11]

The Victualling Board ran the state victualling yards at home and abroad, and awarded contracts for the primary produce and processed provisions that fed the navy. The army was supplied by the Commissariat under the Treasury, but fresh food and oats for horses were procured at regimental level. Generally the majority of warships were stationed in the Channel Fleet or elsewhere in home waters, and at least half the seamen manned warships that were within reach of the home ports. Admiral Cornwallis commanded 30,000 men off Brest in late 1805. Only in the Mediterranean were there similar concentrations of seamen: by 1796 there were over 20,000 seamen there to be fed; exceptionally, in the summer of 1799 the fleets of admirals Keith and Nelson together contained 44,000. After Trafalgar the men under Admiral Collingwood increased year by year, until they peaked in 1810 at 33,000. A substantial fleet was kept in the Baltic under Saumarez for four years from 1808, although most ships came home in winter to escape the ice. The numbers of seamen on distant stations were much smaller. The East Indies Station, for instance, reached 10,000 in 1797 and 1806, and averaged far less, although Britain's establishment was larger than that of France.[12]

The army kept its stores at St Catherine's, quays immediately downstream from the Tower of London. From 1793 Pitt's administration agreed that the Victualling Board should have the responsibility for feeding the army abroad. By December of that year 10,000 troops had to be provided for in the West Indies and 20,000 for the Continent. The expeditions to the West Indies in the next five years comprised 89,000 soldiers.[13] The measurement of bread or biscuit alone required in 1801, at a pound of biscuit a day for each seaman, and a pound and a half for each soldier, amounted to 83,428 deadweight tons, distributed in 400,000 separate rations.[14] In addition salt beef and pork, pease, butter, cheese, vinegar, beer, wine, spirits and other minor items had to be procured. As much in the way of fresh beef and vegetables as possible was taken in ships that sailed from the home port. Often as many as thirty head of live cattle were carried on the main gun-deck when a ship sailed, and when these had been consumed fresh meat and vegetables were purchased abroad.

This enormous logistical task required skilled planning through the year. Usually late in the autumn, after decisions about the next year's campaigns had been taken in cabinet, the Victualling Board was informed of the number of men, where they were to serve and their requirements for the following year. The secretary of state for war and the Treasury issued the orders for the army, while the Admiralty, through the Navy Board, issued them for the navy. The Victualling Board had to liaise, again through the Navy Board, with the Transport Board, to ensure that enough transports were available to distribute the food. It had to buy well ahead for the requirements of both the navy and army abroad, and then account for its spending, an administrative task that lasted well into the Napoleonic War. It became even more difficult at the end of 1811 and the beginning of 1812, when the supplies of imported grain from the Baltic were disrupted by French dominance of the region.

Acquiring sufficient amounts of food and distributing it, particularly during the three periods of civilian food shortages and dramatic price rises (in 1795–6, 1800–1801 and 1809–10), was no easy task. Even before hostilities started in 1793 the country could no longer grow enough wheat to feed itself, and throughout the period the country had to import grain in large quantities, mostly from northern Europe. Poor harvests in 1792 and 1794 were followed by very cold winters. The 1795 yield averaged fifteen bushels to the acre, instead of the more usual twenty-four. The price of a sack of flour, which cost 44s. in 1794, rose to 83s. in 1795, nearly double, the result of real scarcity rather than market speculation. Appeals to the Privy Council for wheat supplies came from every county.[15] The inhabitants of some wheat-growing districts prevented the despatch of purchases made by large towns, sometimes involving considerable violence, until a law at the end of 1795 prohibited the obstruction of the free passage of grain within the kingdom. Bread riots were widespread from Lancashire to the Forest of Dean, from the south-west counties to East Anglia. In Birmingham a new steam flour-mill was invaded by rioters: two were shot by the militia.[16] Even in prosperous and peaceful areas there was trouble. In April 1795 a large crowd in Chichester in Sussex, swelled by people from the nearby countryside and some soldiers from the Herefordshire Militia, attempted to fix prices: they marched out to an adjoining village and forced a farmer to agree to bring his grain to market the next day at 5s. a bushel. Similar incidents took place elsewhere in Sussex and Kent. In Brighton about 200 country women demonstrated in the market, carrying a loaf and some meat on sticks, which they raised and lowered to demonstrate their demand for lower prices.[17]

In the face of these disturbances the government intervened in the market to alleviate the shortages. In 1795 Pitt and Dundas commissioned a well-capitalized London wheat factor, Claude Scott, to buy grain secretly from America and Canada for the general population, and also from Poland for the Victualling Board.[18] Merchants imported well over 300,000 tons of wheat, of which 95,000 tons came from

America.[19] The prime minister persuaded the East India Company to import grain into England from India, although the chairman was very aware that in dealing with 'a subject highly delicate and important in its nature' the Company should be seen to be obeying government orders.[20] The Secret Minutes of the Company record 'a verbal message from W. Pitt through the medium of W. Scott'.[21] The directors ordered twenty-seven ships to be sent from India with cargoes of grain, and rice began to be offered for sale during the second half of 1796. At the end of May 1796 the directors decided that 350 tons of rice were to be sold: 17,000 bags went up for sale on 6 July, 20,000 at the end of September and a further 20,000 at the end of December.[22] Apart from foreign wheat, naval and military food supplies imported into Britain from abroad included wine, brandy, raisins and olive oil from southern Europe. The West Indies provided rum, molasses and sugar.

Though there were some years of good harvests through the 1790s, by the end of the decade price rises were even higher than ever. A wet summer in 1799 produced a poor harvest, and price rises and panic set in. Parliamentary measures to prohibit the distillation of spirits, and articles in the newspapers encouraging a substitute for wheaten bread, such as a loaf of mixed wheat and potato, were ineffectual.[23] In 1801 disturbances in the countryside were less widespread than in 1794 and 1795, but there were other troubles: industrial recession, particularly in the textile industry, occurred at the same time. The urban centres of the South Midlands, Lancashire and Yorkshire were badly hit,[24] with hunger and illness rife in the northern industrial cities.* Over the winter of 1799/1800, soup kitchens were established in many northern towns through subscriptions; during the following winter vast queues were reported. Deprivation led to a serious fever epidemic and increased mortality in Leeds.[25] From Ireland, Edward Cooke reported to Lord Castlereagh: 'The soup-shops and House of Industry do much in Dublin, but the streets are crowded with beggars, and there is infinite distress in the parishes.'[26] In London rioting centred on the Corn Exchange in Mark Lane in the City. In the naval

* Continental states did not escape these shortages. For instance, the diplomat Sir Arthur Paget reported on the bread riots in Vienna in July 1805 (1 Aug. 1805, Paget, *Paget Papers*, Vol. II, p. 203).

towns of Portsmouth and Plymouth, crowds forced bakers to sell at what they thought a reasonable price and had to be dispersed by the authorities. One army officer wrote to the home secretary that 'in any other Country ... this ... would be called Famine.'[27] In October 1800 old Lord Liverpool was very gloomy when he wrote to Henry Dundas, foreseeing 'insurrections of a very serious nature, and that different Bodies of Yeomanry may possibly fight each other ... those of the Cities and great manufacturing Towns, who are adverse to the Farmers will fight those of the Country, who will be disposed to defend them.'[28]

Both these periods of shortages, 1794–5 and 1801, coincided with the concentration of demand for fresh food and provisions by the navy, required for the major amphibious expeditions setting out from British ports for the West Indies, the Mediterranean and the Baltic. This extra demand can only have helped to push up food prices, while the allocation of feed for horses had a marked effect on prices. Oats and hay for cavalry and army transport horses were procured locally when soldiers, militia or volunteers were in camp in Britain, and this would subsequently push up local prices. For overseas expeditions, fodder would be needed in significant amounts and at specific times at naval bases and other ports, all of which would have to be planned for in advance. Thus in July 1799, before the Den Helder landings, Brook Watson, the commissary-general of Great Britain, the senior Commissariat officer, ordered the Hamburg merchants Thornton & Power to purchase ten million pounds (4,464 tons) 'of good, sound, sweet heavy oats ... three million pounds of good fresh wheat ... three hundred thousand pounds of Rye meal ... and to deposit [them] in airy dry magazines contiguous to your navigation in order to prevent the necessity and expense of land carriage, which you are to keep secret'.[29]

The domestic market supplied most military provisions. Salt beef and salt pork were the staple diets, for they had a long shelf life. To provide the meat for salting and packing into casks, cattle were sent to London from every part of Britain as well as from the south of Ireland, while pigs were raised nearer London. Oats came from Scotland and the north of England, cheese from Cheshire, and wheat from the centre of England and East Anglia, to be processed into bread, biscuit and biscuit meal. Barley was made into beer, malt and vinegar. Butter came in casks from Ireland, which also began to export greater numbers of cattle to north-west England. As a result of this growing demand, the agricultural industry expanded substantially.

The largest purchaser in the whole country by far for all this livestock and produce was the Victualling Board in Somerset House. The main victualling yard and distribution centre was at Deptford, downriver from London on the south bank of the Thames. Although this was a considerable industrial site, its workforce was much smaller than those required for shipbuilding and repairing warships in the royal dockyards. In the victualling yard were bakers, slaughtermen, brewers, coopers and labourers. A government tide-mill to grind wheat was near by at Rotherhithe. From this central victualling yard provisions were distributed to other naval bases; warships and army transports leaving on a commission or on an amphibious expedition were supplied from the smaller state victualling yards at Dover, Chatham, Portsmouth and Plymouth. The agent victualler at these ports purchased stores such as bread or cattle on the hoof directly from local contractors; but these provisions were supplemented by large quantities of stores sent by coastal shipping from Deptford. Overseas garrisons and naval squadrons abroad were supplied by merchant ships, chartered by the Transport Board, which were convoyed directly from Deptford. Smaller depots, usually provided and manned by private contractors, were spread around Great Britain at ports such as Hull, Newcastle, Leith, Whitehaven, Cork and Falmouth, and these supplied smaller warships cruising in home waters or engaged in convoying around the coast.[30]

Most of the Victualling Board's food and services were provided by a variety of contractors that fell into three main groups. The first, usually based in London, consisted of a few well-capitalized commission agents, who bought very large amounts of wheat or live cattle for the Board, taking their profit on a percentage basis, but the Board was chary of this arrangement after the fraud exposed by the Atkinson affair in the 1780s. There was always a danger in giving a monopoly to one merchant, but the Board, nevertheless, allowed a small number of commission agents to dominate for large periods of the wars, a practice that for the most part provided what the Board required. In 1797, for instance, Edward Knight supplied over 40,000 quarters of wheat for the Board at Deptford and Portsmouth, although eventually he overreached himself and went bankrupt in 1809.[31]

Most contractors were of the second type, who supplied particular commodities to the Board for a specified period, usually with a six-month notice of termination from either side. These could vary from rich City merchants such as Sir Charles Flower, who supplied butter and cheese in great quantities, often in different partnerships, to small, independent merchants such as Richard Morris, who signed a one-year contract in October 1813 to supply onions, turnips, carrots, cabbages and potatoes to ships in Plymouth Sound from March 1814.[32] These contractors were chosen with care through competitive tendering, and the lowest tender was not always awarded the contract, because probity and credit standards had to be met.* They were well administered, and the Board carefully considered adjustments of the contract price when the market price rose out of the contractor's control.

The third category of contractor involved merchants who undertook to supply a ship or an army garrison with every type of provision at a particular port. 'Sea-provision contractors' had to be well capitalized and well organized. The merchant with the most contracts, at home and abroad, was Thomas Pinkerton, but his eventual bankruptcy demonstrates the way the government successfully managed to transfer risk to the private sector. At first all went well for Pinkerton. He held the contract to supply all the warships at Falmouth, Leith and Hull, but his biggest contract was for the Leeward Islands. In the first years he was in profit, but in the autumn of 1807 the commander-in-chief of the station sent some ships on the station without warning to Halifax, Nova Scotia, leaving Pinkerton with an unused surplus of

---

* Parson Woodforde recorded in his diary on 6 Oct. 1799 that he received 'a fine large Somerset cheese, a present from my nephew now with me, from a relation of his wife's at Mew near Stowton by name James Jules, a great dealer in Cheese and employed for Government in that way and is getting a good fortune by it . . . The cheese was about a Qr. of a Hundred Wht. with the King's Arms on the side of it' (Beresford, *Woodforde*, p. 476).

food. Deteriorating diplomatic relations with the United States, from which he purchased flour, rice and fresh beef, and rapid price rises when Jefferson's embargo of 1807 was imposed, increased his difficulties.* Having purchased at a high cost, he was left with provisions that had cost him dear when the embargo was lifted and prices dropped again. By 1810 all his contracts had been taken on by other contractors, and in 1812 Pinkerton was declared bankrupt. Another powerful contractor in these years was the truculent Basil Cochrane, who held the sea-provisions contract for the East Indies Squadron, based at Madras and Bombay. He was also to supply all ships in the East Indies. Not surprisingly, this was the most expensive naval station to supply, and profit and risks were correspondingly high. Cochrane's long-running dispute with the Victualling Board over the settlement of his payments continued for more than twenty years.[33]

The British victualling system relied upon the London Corn Market, in Mark Lane in the City, and the meat market at Smithfield, as well as other specialist merchants, some of them with international businesses, based in London. It was aided by an expanding and increasingly integrated agricultural industry. Greater demand for the military played its part in affecting prices, and contributed to periods of dearth. But the advantages that stemmed from a competitive market-based system, backed by the extensive London distributive and credit systems, with open and fairly administered contract tendering by government, gave the British advantages over their antagonists in both price and supply. Britain never favoured the monopoly of individuals or of the state, as did the forces of France and Spain, which, as we shall see, suffered from an inferior supply chain. Though there were occasional delays and difficulties, in general the British system was a remarkable success.[34]

The Victualling Board was crucial to this success, and its commissioners did not have an easy job. They naturally had to take account of the seasons, which dictated the optimum time and price at which to

---

* The United States Embargo Act, an early indication of worsening relations with Britain, prohibited American merchants from trading with Britain. See Chapter 15.

purchase wheat and cattle: most cattle were sold in the winter months. Some food processing could not take place in the summer: during warmer months beer could not be brewed in case it went sour; beef and pork could not be salted and casked because of the risk that the meat would decay. Foreign produce arrived in the London docks at particular periods of the year: tropical products such as sugar, rum and coffee, for instance, arrived in the autumn because the trade left the West Indies before the hurricane season in August and September. And the Board had to operate in domestic food markets in which price rises were politically sensitive. For protracted periods the commissioners sat for seven days a week, always on hand in case of unanticipated food-price movements. No longer could the Victualling commissioners take easy hours and be absent for parts of the week, as had been the case earlier in the eighteenth century.

The composition and expertise of this Board was therefore of supreme importance in determining the success or failure of Britain in keeping its armed forces operationally effective. After the Atkinson scandal of the early 1780s, the Board regained its reputation under the chairmanship of George Cherry until 1799, when he retired. The less effectual John Marsh, nephew of George Marsh of the Navy Office, then took over the chairmanship until 1808. Both had spent a lifetime in the administration of army or navy provisions, and were expert and honest.

George Phillips Towry was, however, perhaps the most remarkable of all the lesser administrators in Whitehall during the wars against Napoleon. Towry was just the man for a crisis, always ready to travel to sort out problems. His portrait when in his early sixties shows strong features with a personality to match. When St Vincent became first lord of the Admiralty in 1801, he sent Towry with clerks from the Victualling Office on a special mission to Lisbon to sort out the long-overdue accounts of the agent victualler there, David Heatley. The party was captured by a French privateer just before the packet boat reached Lisbon, but they were fortunate, as the Peace of Amiens was signed soon afterwards, and they were soon taken to Gibraltar and released. It was, nevertheless, an unusual distinction for the commissioner of a government board based in London to be captured by the enemy. Within days of returning to the office in Somerset House, Towry was off to Newcastle and Edinburgh to deal with a strike of bakers.[35]

While the Victualling Board had been given the extra responsibility of provisioning the army abroad in 1793, it no longer chartered merchant ships for government service; this duty was transferred to the newly constituted Transport Board in 1794. When long distances were involved, even within Britain, coastal ships were the economic option for transporting bulky agricultural products. It was quicker and much cheaper to move grain and milled flour downriver by barge. At the port at the mouth of the river the cargo could be offloaded on to a seagoing vessel, although merchant ships in this coastal trade averaged perhaps seventy tons and, being relatively small, could often extend their range upriver.[36] East Anglia and the counties to the east and north exported tens of thousands of tons of grain to London annually. Sailing barges from the Essex and Suffolk rivers, the Colne and the Blackwater, the Stour and the Orwell, the Alde and the Deben, brought wheat directly to the London mills, and barley and malt to the city's breweries, returning with manure from the thousands of horses in the capital as fertilizer for the fields. The River Bure connected the new steam flour-mills of Norwich to warships lying in the Yarmouth Roads, and to soldiers waiting to embark on transports there. The Ouse River and canal system, which reached deep into the heart of England, brought the local shallow-draughted vessels known as keels and wherries down to King's Lynn, where their cargo of wheat and barley would be sent on to London and Deptford.

Improved inland navigation benefited other agricultural products that went part of the way by sea. In the 1770s the Mersey and Severn and Trent rivers had been linked by canal, and in 1789 the Thames and Severn Canal was opened, giving agricultural products a considerable distribution network.[37] In Cheshire the River Weaver Navigation was used to transport rock salt to Liverpool for onward journeys of 600 or 700 miles to London and the East Coast fishing ports. By 1800, 150,000 tons of rock salt a year were leaving the Mersey for refineries elsewhere in the British Isles.[38] The opening of more canals was the key to bringing down the costs of bulk goods and ensuring predictable delivery.* Large numbers of Canal Acts were passed by parliament during the war years, and many waterways were under construction.[39] The Grand Junction Canal, which joined the Midlands to London, was started in 1793 and was operational, if not finished, by 1805; the Grand Union Canal was workable by 1806. To our modern eyes the canals of England look too narrow to be effective, but at the time they were built they represented a major improvement in efficiency. The advantage of inland water transport can be illustrated by the comparative cost of taking a 280-pound sack of flour from Reading to London: after the Thames navigation was improved in 1796 it dropped from 4s.6d. a load, the price by horse and wagon, to 6d. by barge.[40] England, with more accessible and sheltered coastal waters, kinder terrain and straighter rivers, fared better than France; Paris and its ports were ill served by the great meandering rivers of central France.[41] Such was the growth in canal traffic that in 1796 Pitt proposed to levy a tax on the carriage of goods by inland waterway, although after protests he dropped the idea.[42]

The movement of livestock from distant farms and pasture to the centres of population, to the victualling yards, and to the fleet and army at home was organized on a completely different basis. Pigs could not travel far, because they lost weight very quickly when on the move, and as a result they were intensively reared near London. Most were fed on the waste barley and malt from breweries, which were sited to the south of the city at Battersea and Vauxhall. The capacity of the London breweries was impressive: in 1781, 1.2 million barrels of strong beer were brewed annually; by 1815, 1.7 million.[43] By the time of the Napoleonic War, the malt and barley waste went to feed an estimated 40,000 to 50,000 pigs reared annually in and around London.

Cattle and sheep moved on the hoof, as a 'vast animal migration', extending over the whole of the British Isles.[44] By the end of the

---

* Although the sea and inland waterways were the most economical way to move agricultural products, the roads were improving and by 1800 the average wagonload had increased from four to six tons. Their main business was with goods of small volume and high value (Barker and Gerhold, *Road Transport*, p. 33).

eighteenth century an immense, loose organization of farmers, drovers and graziers, cemented by local systems of credit and trust governed by family or community, straddled the whole of Great Britain. Cattle in herds of perhaps 300 or 400 would travel twenty miles a day overseen by drovers on horseback. Those beasts with hundreds of miles to travel were given iron shoes like horses, although this posed a problem, because cattle, unlike horses, cannot stand on three legs, and they had to be laid on their side to be shod. Farmers would sell their animals to the drovers, who with their dogs moved them down what are still known today as drovers' roads along routes that had developed over hundreds of years. Little was written down: a drover would take away thousands of pounds' worth of animals, usually on credit, and not return for weeks.* Their destination would be a grazier nearer to market, who would buy the animals to fatten them. Anglesey cattle, for instance, were swum across the Menai Strait at low tide in herds, a boat on each side keeping them in line, taken to a local fair and sold on to drovers, who in turn drove them across country and sold them to graziers at Barnet Fair near London.

Scots cattle travelled to Norfolk for fattening and those from Ireland were shipped across the Irish sea to ports in the north-west, also heading to Norfolk. One estimate of 1794 reckoned that 20,000 fattened bullocks went from Norfolk to London annually, and that only a quarter had been bred originally in Norfolk.† In 1811, for instance,

---

* Perhaps the most impressive demonstration of trust was the tradition of dogs being sent home to Scotland or Wales from London on their own. One story involved a Welsh dog named Carlo who journeyed all the way back to Wales from Kent. His owner sold the pony that he had ridden on the outward journey, intending to go home by coach. He fastened the pony's harness to the dog's back and attached a note to it, addressed to each of the inns on the route they had followed, to request food and shelter for the dog, to be repaid on a subsequent journey. Carlo reached home in Wales alone in a week (Bonser, *Drovers*, p. 37).

† The only other livestock to be driven long distances were large flocks of geese and turkeys, generally from Norfolk, Suffolk and Cambridgeshire to London, and usually in Aug. after the harvest had been taken in. The journey was about a hundred miles and took about three months. Daniel Defoe tells a story of two aristocrats who bet on the pace of the two kinds of bird, a race that resulted in a win for the geese by two days. These drives were still taking place at the end of the century, although it was more usual for poultry to be transported in specially designed carts (Fussell and Goodman, 'Traffic in Livestock', p. 235).

44,553 cattle were shipped across the Irish Sea. Cattle from the East Riding of Yorkshire were driven to Hull for the use of the Victualling Office, a beast of sixty-eight stone losing about four stone in the process. Romney Marsh farmers, who always had plenty of grass for fattening, purchased Welsh cattle. A beast born in the south-west might spend the middle part of its life grazing in Herefordshire or Somerset, before being driven to Buckinghamshire for finishing, and thence to Smithfield.[45] Virtually every area in Britain contributed to feeding the great centres of population in London and the south of England, swelled as it was in war time by concentrations of seamen and soldiers.

A good many cattle went straight to the naval bases because the crews of ships were supplied with fresh meat when at anchor in Plymouth Sound, Spithead or the Nore. Live cattle, as already noted, were stabled on the upper gun-deck with the requisite amount of hay, particularly in ships sailing out to spend months blockading enemy ports. In 1808, at the port of Ystad in southern Sweden, Admiral Saumarez gave orders to the effect that if a British ship 'is in want of Live Bullocks, she is to hoist a white flag at the Main and fire one gun, when a supply agreeable to the following proportion with fodder will be sent to her.'[46] Ships of the line were given thirty cattle, frigates twenty and sloops twelve. The craving for fresh meat aboard could lead to discipline problems. At Malta in 1809 Admiral Collingwood took firm action against six midshipmen for stealing a cow from the shore and slaughtering it. 'It is disgraceful, but I will stop it if possible,' he wrote to another naval officer. 'They were marched with a file of marines to the Chief Magistrate in the middle of the day and are now in Prison. The inhabitants have a horror of them ... It requires exemplary punishment.'[47]

Constant high demand combined to create prosperity for farmers in the war years, their incomes estimated to have increased continuously by one or two per cent a year.[48] It was a period of investment and increased output, as illustrated by the case of West Sussex. The landscape of the South Downs was changed permanently: high wool and corn prices ensured that the scrub that had always naturally prevailed was cleared for wheat sowing and sheep runs. Arthur Young estimated in 1813 that 240,000 sheep were grazing on the Downs, and these immense flocks manured the land for high corn yields.[49] A keen interest in improving the stock of the local cattle at the annual Petworth Fair was stimulated by a series of valuable cups for the best bull, the first presented by the eccentric George O'Brien Wyndham, third earl of Egremont in 1795.[50]

From his seat at Petworth House, north of the Downs, Egremont exercised a more than benevolent ownership over his 110,000 acres and into the county beyond. He organized extensive and regular charity for the poor, especially in the years of dearth.[51] He mistrusted Pitt and kept out of national politics, though he was a member of the Board of Agriculture. He brought prosperity to the area by financing the Rother Navigation from the navigable River Arun to Midhurst at a cost of £13,300, completed in 1794, with eight locks raising the river by 54 feet, all the work done by his employees. This investment enabled more corn, flour and timber to be transported to the sea at Littlehampton, for onward shipment to Portsmouth; it also enabled lime for dressing the soil, much needed in the area, from the chalk pits at Houghton to be shipped upriver on the Arun (40,000 tons a year during the war years). In doing so, of course, the earl raised the value of his land adjoining the newly navigable river. It was chiefly through his efforts in 1811 that the Wey and Arun Canal was financed.[52] This could take barges from London to Littlehampton, by-passing the need for the sea voyage from London to Portsmouth, a route hazardous in winter and always subject to attacks from enemy privateers.*

Bulky primary produce and processed provisions, and other major commodities, such as coal, beer and fresh water, without which the navy could not have functioned, were transported by sea as well as by canal. Coal was needed for cooking on board. A first-rate ship might take as much as sixty tons in her hold at the start of a three-year commission, and the need for fuel was constant. Landing parties of seamen were constantly foraging for wood for the ship's oven when on

* Several schemes were put forward in the 1820s for a 'Grand Imperial Ship Canal' that would link the Thames at Deptford to Portsmouth, including one by George and John Rennie, big enough to take substantial warships as well as naval stores and provisions. In 1825 a committee to examine feasibility had among its members the secretary for war, the first lord of the Admiralty and the undersecretary of state for foreign affairs. A similar scheme to link London to Bristol with a ship canal also failed (Vine, *London's Lost Route*, pp. 98–109). Steam-powered vessels were eventually to overcome the vagaries of coastal transport by sail.

foreign stations. Beer was largely brewed in the state victualling yards, rather than by contractors, but it was tricky to handle and could go sour, and it was awkward and heavy to load on a ship, so wine or spirits were often issued instead.

Of all of the necessary commodities, fresh water was the most troublesome. Used in huge quantities, the deadweight tonnage of filled water casks that a ship took on board far exceeded all the rest of the provisions put together. The *Victory* had a capacity of 380 tons, but even she sometimes ran out of water.[53] When Nelson was returning across the Atlantic in pursuit of Villeneuve in 1805, some of the large water casks in the ship's lower tier leaked and on a calm afternoon in the middle of the Atlantic twenty tons had to be transferred from another ship.* The daily consumption of water for a first-rate ship of 850 men was a minimum of three tons. A 74-gun ship with 640 men would consume sixteen tons of water a week, while a 64 with 490 would expend fourteen.[54] Heavy casks had to be filled and hoisted aboard, then stowed securely in the hold. Water was needed not only for cooking but also for 'steeping' beef and salt provisions: the salt had to be leeched out of the meat before it could be cooked. Finding fresh, clean water was a constant preoccupation of naval captains when on foreign stations.

In the early years of the war even the well-established naval bases at Portsmouth and Plymouth could not provide enough fresh water for warships. Pioneering engineering was to improve the situation. It is here that we first meet Samuel Bentham, at this time the inspector-general of naval works, responsible for major improvements at both the western naval bases, and for many important naval technological

---

* On the same voyage in mid-Atlantic *Victory* also purchased forty-one head of live cattle from an American merchant ship (Knight, *Pursuit of Victory*, p. 494). Mid-Atlantic provisioning was not without risk, as recounted on another occasion by Lieutenant Gardner, when cattle were again purchased from an American merchant-man: 'As the Yankee had plenty for sale, and it being a dead calm, I loaded our boat with live and dead stock until she was pretty deep in the water. On our return, the sharks began to muster and the livestock began to ride rusty ... one of the boat's crew said, "Please, your honour if we don't cut the b—s' throats [meaning the livestock] ... their hoofs will be through the boat's bottom, as they are kicking like blazes, and here's a bloody shark close alongside us." However, we got safe alongside after a long tug' (Hamilton and Laughton, *Gardner*, p. 246).

developments in these wars. He came from a family of original think-ers and problem solvers: one of his brothers was Jeremy Bentham, the philosopher, to whom he was particularly close; and his half-brother was Charles Abbot. Samuel had entered the dockyard service at Chatham as a shipwright apprentice, unusual for someone from a family of rank, where he was frustrated by being forced to work with his hands rather than at the drawing board. Seeing that there was no easy route to promotion in Britain, he went to serve in the Russian Army, where he designed and built galleys for the Russian Navy, fought with distinction at the Battle of Kherson in June 1788 against the Turks, and by 1791 had attained the rank of brigadier-general. Untactful, pushy and obstinate, he was inclined to upset his fellow officers, one of whom was John Paul Jones, the American naval hero. When Bentham returned to England, he impressed Charles Middle-ton, who was anxious to accelerate the introduction of new methods and technology into British dockyards. In June 1795 Middleton wrote to the first lord of the Admiralty, Lord Spencer:

> The shipbuilding and Civil building have been too long committed to insufficient men. An opportunity offers of recalling it out of their hands, and as General Bentham is undoubtedly a man of first-rate abilities and of great experience in practical mechanics, I hope and trust they may be converted to the benefit of his native country instead of carrying them again into Russia.[55]

Middleton recommended that Bentham be given his own, independ-ent office, as inspector-general of naval works, to be responsible directly to the Admiralty Board – which was to prove a recipe for con-stant conflict.[56] When it came to persuading and convincing his colleagues, Bentham lacked two essential attributes, patience and flexibility, and this weakness was to blunt his effectiveness.

Bentham, nevertheless, brought confidence and innovation to engineering projects. At Plymouth the fresh-water supply problem was solved by the Plymouth Dock Water Company, which piped water from Dartmoor, although there were delays in 1798 over where to site the reservoir in the dockyard, as Bentham and the yard officers could not agree.[57] With the help of John Rennie, the civil engineer, improved water pipes were installed serving the wharves at the fleet rendezvous at Torbay. It was at Portsmouth that Bentham provided an imaginative solution and on a grand scale. By 1801 a deep well had been dug in Portsmouth Dockyard, lined to a hundred feet, with copper pipes driven further down. Fresh water was discovered at 274 feet, and it was steam pumped to the surface at the rate of 520 tons a day; pipes then took it to the edge of a wharf.[58]

Major works were also undertaken to store water at overseas bases in drier or tropical climates. Gibraltar was notably short of water, until six vaulted underground storage tanks were built between 1799 and 1804.* Water collected from the roof of the victualling yard was directed to the tanks, and purified as it flowed from tank to tank; from the lowest tank it was then gravity-fed to ships or boats in Rosia Bay. The local contractor, Juan Maria Boschetti, built them so well, of bricks sent out from England, that they were used by the Royal Navy for 200 years, and were in good condition when handed to the Gibraltar government in 2004.[59]

When the focus of the war moved in 1807 away from the Channel and towards the North Sea, the Victualling Board had to revert to more traditional methods to obtain enough water for seamen and troops. Costs and effort were much increased: a ton of water in a cask, delivered to a warship at Falmouth, was supplied by a contractor for 3s.10d.; yet the cost of delivering it to a ship in the Roads off Great Yarmouth was 7s.3d. Ships waiting in the Downs, or troopships waiting to sail to Walcheren, received water brought from the upper reaches of the Thames, a hundred miles away, where it was fresh above the level of the tide. Depot ships containing only water were moored in the Thames Estuary and were constantly served by half a dozen water transports. As thousands of tons were required at any one time to get a large fleet of warships away, it was little wonder there were delays.[60] Given a fair wind, the transports could make their journeys very quickly; but, when the wind blew from the wrong

---

* The lack of water for Abercromby's troops at Gibraltar on their way to Egypt in 1801 gave rise to a more than usually waspish comment from the duke of Richmond, out of office and still bitter, against the secretary for war: 'I suppose Mr Dundas drinks himself so little water that he does not consider it as at all necessary for an army' (Mackesy, *War without Victory*, p. 157, quoting Richmond to Lord Holland, 8 Feb. 1801, BL, Add. MSS 51802).

direction, they could not move. The problem for the coastal trade lay not so much in the length of the journey as in timing and safety, which were unpredictable.[61]

The timely arrival of victuallers for replenishment at sea was one of the main preoccupations of a naval commander-in-chief in these wars. On occasion shortages of food for frontline troops and seamen became critical, but these did not damage the overall war effort. In 1795 the troops carried by Keith's expedition to capture the Cape found themselves very short of food before they were luckily relieved by wheat arriving from India destined for Britain. Keith complained to Lord Spencer, the first lord of the Admiralty, about lack of information and supplies from Britain, 'nor a Morsel of Bread or flour, Rum etc so with 7000 troops to feed and a long voyage before me I have five days bread left, one week's Rum'. Spencer sympathized, but warned, 'it would however have been very satisfactory to us to have had a more accurate Return of what Stores of every Sort you found at the Cape, as we are at a loss to know what ought to be sent out for want of such Information.'[62] Victualling Board calculations depended upon precise information from those at sea.[63] In 1809 Admiral Strachan's squadron off Rochefort had to leave its station due to depleted rations, which led to questions being asked in parliament, but weaknesses in naval supply were usually few.[64]

When victualling was reliable, as it was most of the time, it brought about a real extension of British sea control. Adequate supplies of fresh food and processed provisions underpinned the whole British strategy of blockade of the French naval bases in the Channel from 1796 – one rendered highly aggressive in 1800, when St Vincent assumed command of the Channel Fleet and forced his captains inshore to impose a very close blockade. The warships were supplied by convoys of victuallers from Plymouth and Torbay, and instances of scurvy were negligible.[65]

Even more impressive was the supply of food to operations on distant stations. The most risky but successful combined operation of the French Revolutionary War was the Egyptian expedition, when, on 8 March 1801, an army of 14,000 under Sir Ralph Abercromby landed under fire at Aboukir and defeated the French. This force, together with the seamen on board the supporting naval squadron under Lord Keith, required 20,000 rations daily. The landing was at the limit of the range of supply, and the logistics gave Abercromby much anxiety. Only the capture of Malta the year before made it possible for adequate supplies to reach the expedition, though Malta itself, lacking self-sufficiency, also needed to be fed.* The other element essential to success was fresh produce and beef supplied by the Turks, as well as large quantities of biscuit, though they were slow to meet their promises.

Abercromby's plan was to rest his troops and organize his beach-assault drills with a stay of seven weeks in the superbly sheltered anchorage at Marmaris in Turkey.[66] Of course, the extra time this involved put more strain on the supplies. Commissary-General Motz, accompanying the expedition and charged with feeding it, regularly reported on his stock of food, and expressed his anxieties in his correspondence with the Treasury (his letters were forwarded to the Victualling Board by Treasury secretaries George Rose and Charles Long). His chief worry was a lack of specie to pay the Turks for local provisions, noting that one ship contained 20,000 rations for eleven days. A week after the landing he had enough bread rations for 92 days, 89 days' worth of meat and 83 days' of spirits, reckoning one pound of bread, one pound of meat and one gill of spirits per day. This would decrease to sixty days if the navy 'should continue to partake'.[67] The Board responded by sending out two convoys to the Mediterranean, ordered in February and June 1801: each convoy took over 3,000 tons of provisions.[68] The success of this expedition therefore depended, as always, upon a number of complicated and accurate calculations.

The war in the Baltic between 1808 and 1812 demanded an even greater victualling effort. The provisioning of Admiral Saumarez's fleet, manned by 16,000 seamen, was made particularly difficult by every Baltic nation bar Sweden being under French domination and therefore hostile. Most of the provisions were sent in victuallers from Britain, through the Greater or Little Belt, where the convoys were harried by Danish gunboats; by the end of 1808, 6,000 tons of

* An indication of how much was required to maintain the garrisons of Minorca and Malta was their combined monthly consumption of 80 tons of flour (Treasury to Victualling Board, Motz letter, 15 Nov. 1800, TNA, ADM 109/106).

chartered merchant shipping were required to feed the Baltic Fleet. In 1809 the island of Anholt at the mouth of the Baltic was occupied by the British Army because the water supply there was so abundant. Although the Swedes, too, were forced to declare war on Britain in late 1810, they continued to supply the British Fleet covertly, though they could manage no more than fresh beef, water and occasionally biscuit and citrus fruit. It was hardly surprising that this sparsely populated country could not supply more. When the British Fleet was anchored off almost any Swedish port, it temporarily doubled the local population.[69]

Saumarez's success in keeping open the Baltic trade, particularly the import of naval stores vital for British shipbuilding, owed much to a regular supply of provisions, without which this extension of British sea control could not have been maintained. The health of British seamen contrasted with that of the Swedish Fleet, which Saumarez visited in late 1808. He reported to the Admiralty:

> On board their ships I found 1500 Sick all much affected with scurvy, accompanied with dysentery, low fever, and a few Catarrhal complaints . . . all apparently sinking under general debility and despondency; in many instances amounting to insanity, which too frequently terminated in the unhappy sufferer committing suicide.[70]

Ashore, the admiral found that there were nearly 4,000 more Swedish seamen in a similar state of ill-health. By contrast, out of 11,000 sailors in the British Fleet at the same time, only 4 suffered from scurvy, 45 from rheumatism and 32 from venereal disease.[71]

During 1805, when the British were parrying every attempt by Napoleon to invade England, the advantage provided by good provisioning proved to be hugely important. The French and Spanish were at a constant disadvantage from lack of provisions, short rations and consequent sickness. Allemand's squadron managed to escape from Brest in April 1805, stay at sea for over five months, and return to Brest safely, but only with appalling sickness among his crews. Nelson, on the other hand, before setting off westwards across the Atlantic in pursuit of the French and Spanish fleets, managed to replenish his ships because he luckily ran into a victualling convoy not intended for him. On 10 May 1805, in one hectic night in Lagos Bay, near Cape

St Vincent, provisions were hoisted into his warships from the transports officially destined for General Craig in the Mediterranean.[72] On the way back, after the long chase over the Atlantic, the crews of the Spanish ships under Gravina's command suffered severely from sickness.

British ships enjoyed a similar advantage before the Battle of Trafalgar on 21 October 1805. Life was not easy for the French and Spanish crews in the ships of the Combined Fleet anchored in Cádiz Harbour. The only way food could be delivered in bulk from other parts of Spain to Cádiz was by merchant ships, but the port had been blockaded for many years by British warships, so supplies were short. The town had been subject to severe yellow fever outbreaks in 1800 and 1804. As the crews of French and Spanish had been unpaid for many months, morale was low and desertion high. On the flagship of Rear-Admiral Magon, the *Algésiras*, for instance, 37 per cent of the crew had scurvy.[73] The British Fleet, however, on blockade out at sea, was well provided for by a succession of victualling convoys from home, and fresh meat and vegetables from Lisbon and the North African ports. The result was that Nelson's seamen were better fed, and had greater energy and morale, than their French and Spanish enemies – evidence that the Victualling Board and its contractors had passed one of their sternest and most important tests.

7

Transporting the Army by Sea

1793–1811

When you consider that Transports are not commonly to be had at the present moment when they may be wanted, that to fit a Transport for service from the state in which she comes out of the merchant hands, is the work often of a full two months, and that Transports called for in a hurry can rarely be had without a great increase of price, and without exciting a degree of attention hardly compatible with secrecy ... The service will not so exactly meet as that the conclusion of one service shall correspond exactly with the commencement of another.

– William Windham, secretary of state for war,
to Lord Grenville, prime minister,
14 December 1806[1]

Statesmen and generals depended on the Transport Board to charter sufficient numbers of privately owned merchant ships from the market, needed to move the infantry, cavalry, artillery, ordnance and medical resources, along with wagons and food for thousands of soldiers and seamen. These ships took stores and provisions to warships blockading the enemy's ports, and to garrisons overseas, but the bulk of them supported amphibious expeditions, known then as 'conjunct operations'. They were the only way that Britain – excluded from the Continent from 1795 until the start of the Peninsular War – could directly assault France or its vassal states. But Britain was never to have much success in effecting difficult landings in force on Continental shores.

Amphibious operations were the most complex and costly operations attempted by the British state, and as such were overseen and coordinated by cabinet ministers. So many resources and so much money had to be committed that a decision to send an expedition could directly affect other areas of war strategy and policy. The authority to send an expedition lay with the prime minister, not only in his role as head of the government but also as first lord of the Treasury. He was advised by the secretary of state for war, the first lord of the Admiralty and, when appropriate, the master-general of the Ordnance.[2] If expeditions went badly wrong, it was usually due to mistakes or friction at this level of decision making.

With such a wide span of military and civilian involvement, it was essential to minimize conflict between government departments. This problem never entirely vanished, for control of the transports continued to be contested by the army and the navy, and indeed by the Admiralty and the Navy Board, throughout the wars. In July 1794 the Pitt government took the decision to reconstitute the Transport Board, which had not been in existence since 1717, and the Navy Board gave up the task of hiring transports, which it had undertaken for most of the eighteenth century, though not without protests.[3] As discussed in Chapter 4, the brief for the new Board was to hire transports for the army, navy and Ordnance, so that negotiations with shipowners or ship-brokers were handled by a single part of the government, the Transport Board; in the language of modern defence it was responsible for 'central procurement'. The hand of Charles Middleton at the Admiralty can be seen behind this move, for he wanted to remove the process of inspecting and surveying the ships to be hired from the hands of the dockyard officers.[4]

The newly constituted Transport Office was set up in Great Scotland Yard and then in Cannon Row, Westminster.[5] It led a near-autonomous existence, receiving a large majority of its orders from the secretary of state for war, rather than from the Admiralty Board, but it was financially beholden to the Treasury. The first chairman of the new Board, Captain Hugh Cloberry Christian, was soon promoted to rear-admiral to command the large expedition to the West Indies. This was still a relatively junior rank for a leader of such an enormous expedition, and army officers with greater seniority objected; the dispute did nothing to forward preparations and was solved only with difficulty by Lord Spencer.[6] As we have seen in Chapter 3, the expedition was catastrophically wrecked in the winter gales of 1794/5.* Christian was succeeded as chairman in 1795 by the shrewd Captain Rupert George, an able administrator.† Procedures evolved so that the responsibilities of each board were clear.[7] When a chartered ship had completed the loading of its cargo of provisions at Deptford, the master of the vessel would go to the Victualling Office at Somerset House to sign the bill of lading, from which point the ship and its cargo became the charge of the Transport Board.[8] Nevertheless, Rupert George became adroit at shifting the blame to the other boards – often the Board of Ordnance – when things went wrong, usually delays in loading and sailing vessels. A constant irritant was the tendency of admirals on overseas stations to retain the vessels that had sailed out with stores from Britain, which George took up with the Amiralty, and there were always problems when crew members of transports were pressed by the navy. His relationship with the secretary of state for war, who needed the largest amount of tonnage for transporting troops and army supplies, was generally very good.[9]

The navy, however, never stopped trying to regain control of the transports. As late as 1807 Captain Thomas Hamilton, a Navy Board commissioner, attempted to persuade Tom Grenville, the prime minister's brother, now first lord of the Admiralty, to oblige the commanders-in-chief to go through the Admiralty when obtaining transports, since 'the

* Evidence of the stress in getting this fleet off can be found in the account of a quarrel between Christian and a current commissioner on the Transport Board, Captain John Schank, as related by Sir Charles Saxton, commissioner at Portsmouth Dockyard, to Lord Cornwallis: 'the unfortunate & untimely dispute between Adm[ira]l Christian & Capt[ain] Schank, which (I am told) went to very indiscreet lengths (at this moment) on the part of the Admiral, Who Collar'd Schank, and then parted with a challenge from Schank, which they say the Adm[ira]l Accepted & promised to fulfil at his return from the Expedition' (Cornwallis-West, *Cornwallis*, p. 306).

† Witness his advice to Thomas Grenville, first lord of the Admiralty in the cost-conscious Ministry of All the Talents, when stating the estimate for transports in 1806 in Grenville's first Naval Estimates: the sum could be reduced, 'but perhaps it would be more convenient to Government, to have money in hand, than to run the risk of a deficiency, which might require a pre-mature calling of Parliament next year. I hope you will excuse the liberty I take in making these observations' (11 Nov. 1806, HL, STG 146 (28)).

hire of the Transports being paid for & regulated under the check of the Treasury, the Commanding Officers of the Navy abroad, are easily disposed to continue the employ of the Transports longer than ... if their conduct in this regard was continuously liable to the inspection of the Admiralty.' Hamilton claimed, fairly, that the retention of transports on foreign stations by the local commanders-in-chief led to shortages and high prices in Britain. A further advantage of naval control, Hamilton argued, in a pique of bureaucratic jealousy of the army, would be that the Transport Board would be 'empowered to expostulate with the Military departments, on many peremptory demands, if supported by the weight & authority of the Admiralty'.[10] The Transport Board thought otherwise, as did cabinet ministers, and the Board and Office retained their independence until 1817, when their functions were again absorbed by the Navy Board.*

The new Board implemented efficiencies immediately. The first was to use the registered tonnage required by the Customs Act of 1786 to calculate tonnage on which to base the chartering rate, as the tonnage registered with customs by the owners could be used for calculating payment, at so much per ton per month.† This procedure, which did away with the lengthy process of measuring the ship, was first suggested by Lieutenant James Bowen, the agent for transports at Deptford, who was to have a distinguished career in the Transport Service. Merchant ships were to be surveyed and valued in one operation by shipwright officers, responsible to agents for transports, who

---

* Senior naval officers were in two minds about the Transport Board arrangement, none more so than Lord St Vincent, who saw it differently when in power than he had when at sea. To Lord Spencer in 1797 he was of the opinion that the 'Transport Board [was] of no use whatever'. When he was first lord of the Admiralty he boasted to Henry Addington of 'having such a very efficient Transport Board' (30 June 1797, Corbett, *Spencer Papers*, Vol. II, p. 212; 17 Sept. 1803, DHC, Addington Papers, 152M/C1803/OZ93).

† The Merchant Shipping Act of 1786 required all ships above fifteen tons to register with the Customs Department. The process of measuring a ship was complex, displacement tonnage being calculated by multiplying 'the length of the keel by the breadth of the beam, and that product by half the breadth of the beam and divide the last product by 94'. However, there were many variations on this basic formula (Syrett, *Shipping*, pp. 111-12).

in turn reported to the Transport Board, and if the ships were not in good-enough condition they were turned down.

Attitudes and standards took a little time to change. Just when the new Board was taking over in 1794, the master of the *Lady Juliana* transport, recently returned from the West Indies, informed the owner that his ship had been subject to a very strict survey, and that the dockyard officers 'behaved with as much Friendship as I could expect from men of long acquaintance put under a new and perhaps troublesome Board'. Old customs still seem to have been followed, for the master found that it was necessary to pay 'a small fee in a proper place' to relieve him of the necessity of taking his mast out for repair, and he spent £6.9s. on wine for the master attendant and the clerk of the survey of Deptford Dockyard.[11] It was this sort of practice that Middleton was trying to eradicate.[12]

Of critical importance to the projection of military power overseas was the continuing growth of the British merchant fleet during wartime. In 1799 the French merchant marine, according to the Directory, had almost no ships.[13] By contrast, Britain in 1793 had over 14,500 registered ships measuring 1.4 million tons; by 1815 the total had grown by over 70 per cent, to just under 22,000 at 2.5 million tons.[14] Of these, however, only a small proportion was available to the Transport Board.* It relied on the market for procuring shipping, and thus had to follow the market price, and in times of particular shortage it had to increase the per-ton government chartering rate. An additional advantage for shipowners was government indemnification for loss against capture, although checks had to be put in place to guard against false claims, in particular to establish that a transport was actually in convoy at the time it was taken. A Transport Board order of 1 April 1797 required the master, in the event of capture, to provide a certificate

---

* Exactly how much shipping was available to the Transport Board varied from month to month and year to year. Of Britain's merchant ships 85 per cent were under 200 tons, too small for military use. Of the rest, the state of the economy, seasonal patterns of trade and shortages of merchant seamen conspired to complicate availability. At the height of government demand, in late 1808, the Board had chartered 1,012 ships, totalling 250,000 tons (an average of 247 tons each), at a time when the British Registry contained 22,646 ships totalling 2.3 million tons (an average of 102 tons) (Sutcliffe, 'Bringing Forward Merchant Shipping', pp. iii, 90–96, 310).

signed by the commander of the convoy that he 'believe[d] the Captures took place without any fault of the Masters'.[15]

In general, chartering a ship to the government during wartime was steadily profitable, based on rising freight rates. Short-term chartering provided employment for idle ships, while longer charters provided continuous income when trading opportunities were limited.[16] Michael Henley, a substantial shipowner and coal merchant from Wapping on the Thames, at one time had two thirds of his ships contracted to government, on which he showed good returns.[17] He owned more colliers than most shipowners, ships that had long been recognized as the most suitable for carrying troops, since they were broad and roomy, and of sufficiently shallow draught to get close to the shore when landing.[18]

This system was cost-effective to government, though some tried to prove otherwise. Lord St Vincent despised all contractors, none more so than the owners of the transports. In 1802 he wrote to a fellow member of his Admiralty Board of 'the fraud upon the public committed by the navy and transport boards, with the profligate percentage on the contracts'.[19] Yet chartering transports was cheaper than any other method of providing large amounts of tonnage, even though the judgement over whether to retain transports at government cost when not in use was very difficult. The cost to the Transport Board of chartering was usually about 7 to 8 per cent of the total naval budget.[20] When it became obvious that the war at sea was being won, some felt that merchant transports were far less effective than warships converted to carry troops. The relative merits were much debated. Lord Melville in a long speech in 1810 tried to persuade the House of Lords that little money was saved by chartering, using the example of the Egyptian expedition of 1801. The first lord of the Admiralty, Lord Mulgrave, replied to Melville providing officially calculated costs for the expedition: transports cost £12 per ton, and troopships £27; thus it cost £24 to transport a man to Egypt, but £55 to send him in a troopship.[21] Transports were usually chartered for two, three or six months 'certain', after which six months' notice could be given by either party. Freight rates were calculated at so many shillings per ton per month, with copper-sheathed ships gaining a higher payment than those that were merely sheathed in wood and tallowed.

To a warm climate, one soldier was carried for every two tons; to Gibraltar or the Continent, it was one man for every one and a half tons. A regiment of 700 men bound for the West Indies would therefore need 1,400 tons of shipping, and, with hired merchant ships ranging between 150 and 300 tons, on average each regiment required six transports.[22] The shipowner was contracted to provide a well-manned and well-equipped vessel. The crew had to number five men and a boy for every hundred tons.[23] They were given protections to keep the press gangs at bay, though a good deal of Transport Board time was spent in sorting out protests by owners who had lost their seamen in this way.

Equipment was of a higher quality than that for ordinary trade: a surviving specification for 1812, for instance, runs to four closely printed pages, itemizing rigging, reserve stores, navigational equipment and boats. If above 200 tons, four 3-pounder carriage guns or carronades were to be aboard; if below 200, then two only. Twenty rounds for each cannon had to be provided, as well as muskets, blunderbusses, pistols and swords.[24] Significantly, charters contained a clause by which ships could be retained by the Board or its agents, and they were not discharged from their contract until the vessels returned to Deptford or Portsmouth. In practice, the commander-in-chief on a foreign station, or the agent for transports on the station, could retain a transport at his discretion, with the result that some merchant ships remained on foreign stations for years at a time.[25]

The contracts bound merchant ships to obey the commands of the agents for transports, who were specialist commissioned naval officers, responsible to the Transport Board. These agents were based at every major British port, and eventually they constituted a worldwide network, either ashore or afloat with a fleet. They had a difficult job, as with any liaison role that involves pleasing several masters, but they were vital to the prosecution of the war. Dealing with impossible requests from more senior naval officers was perhaps even more difficult than responding to demands from army officers. In late 1795 the Transport Board transmitted a report to the Admiralty from James Bowen (by now a captain) from Cork Harbour, the great rendezvous for trans-Atlantic convoys, where he was 'having to attend to the quarrels of Young Officers of the Army, the masters of transports, Complaints about provisions, etc.'. He continued:

> We beg leave to assure their Lordships that, though our list of agents has swelled more than we desired and though every endeavor has been used to distribute them with œconomy as the requisite service would bear, we are, and have been, under great difficulty in procuring proper men, who considering the value and importance of their Trust, ought to be Officers of real Probity and Ability.[26]

The weight and complexity of this job, where seamanship and experience told more than a good education and social graces, was not to the liking of the relaxed Lieutenant James Anthony Gardner, who, for a short time, was appointed an agent for transports. He resigned when his transports were ordered to the West Indies after the war was resumed following the Peace of Amiens. His resignation, as he later recalled,

> gave great offence to Sir Rupert George ... However, ... I left a service that I never would accept of, had I my time to go over again, upon any consideration. For the short time I was in it I saw enough to convince me that if an officer did his duty, he would be like the hare with many friends; and if he acted otherwise, he must lay himself open to any puny whipster who might wish to take advantage of his good nature.[27]

Nor were the troubles of a transport agent over when his transports accompanied a fleet or were under convoy, for keeping the vessels together at sea was never easy, and had to be accomplished by signal flags. It was in the interests of masters to keep with the convoy, but in dirty, winter weather, or at night, ships could easily lose each other.* Neither masters nor naval officers liked the delays that

---

* Warships were much faster than transports. One army officer recorded that he sailed in a transport across the Bay of Biscay with a following wind, 'envying those who were fast running ahead of us. We were one of the sternmost vessels. Such is the superiority of the frigates over the best transports, that while the latter were going along with all sail set, the Frigates were running away from them under bare poles, obliged constantly to lie to, to enable the sternmost transports to come up' (Verner, *Reminiscences*, p. 12).

convoys inevitably caused, and transports were frequently known to slip away from the convoy at the end of the voyage to avoid the press gangs that habitually greeted them on arrival. Transport agents, as commissioned naval officers, also saw the masters of transports as socially inferior, which could lead to trouble, as illustrated by an altercation at the Texel in 1799, when William Dodds, the master of the *Eagle*, was ordered to berth in water that was too shallow. His protests to the agent were unavailing; and then, as Dodds informed his owner, Michael Henley:

> I then sayd if you will make water for the ship I will gett hur to the wharf he then put his hand to my brest and shouved me back and sayd be gon you scoundrell . . . another officer of the Navey came and pulled off my hat and throu it on the ground and sayd you fellow ought to keep of your hat when you speak to an officer of the Navey.[28]

It was not surprising that masters avoided the transport service as much they could, for it was a burdensome business, with its voluminous instructions and rules, and the necessity to keep a constant watch for convoy signals from the escorting warship. Another of Henley's masters claimed that he would much prefer to be the mate of any ship rather than the master of a transport.[29] Even so, merchant ships were forced to sail in convoy by the Compulsory Convoy Act of 1798, which ordered that all vessels in foreign trades had to sail in convoy, unless they were East Indiamen, Hudson Bay Company or on passages to Ireland.[30] By the terms of the vessel's charter party, a transport if taken when 'straggling' from a convoy would no longer be covered by government indemnity.

With French privateers brazen at various times, particularly in home waters, it made good sense for merchant ships to accept the delay because of the protection that a convoy afforded. One shipowner wrote to his master in May 1799: 'Whatever you do Do not leave the convoy on any account.' The same owner received a report in 1805 from the master of one of his ships having trouble in making his way into London down the Thames Estuary against south-west winds: 'Our commodore is really indefatigable and seems to have the welfare of the convoy much in view.'[31] When a convoy consisted of a great many ships – and some were numbered in hundreds – the senior transport officer, who might have junior agents for transports under him, would fly the equivalent of a commodore's broad pennant: 'a plain blue broad pennant at the main topmast head ... eight feet at the staff, and twenty feet long'. Such a flag was issued to Lieutenant Gardner: he called it, with disdain and professional embarrassment at having to ape the flag and rank of a full commodore, 'my swaggering blue pennant'.[32]

The first problem that faced the agents for transports was embarkation, a lengthy and complex process. The cavalry presented the greatest logistical difficulties, for these regiments required specially adapted horse-ships, together with others that transported only forage. Cavalry horses and provisions took up large numbers of ships, unsurprisingly, since senior officers took several horses each. (Two lieutenant-colonels commanding the 7th Hussars, embarking for the Corunna campaign in October 1808, each had five.) Baggage horses for carrying equipment and uniforms, and mounts for the groom and undergroom, were included in this number, as well as cavalry horses.[33] Majors had four, captains three and lieutenants two. In all, twenty-seven officers took seventy horses.[34]

Embarkation in the southern ports of England for Corunna in late 1808 demonstrates the difficulties for anyone attempting to organize this aspect of military transport. Six regiments and two troops of horse artillery, totalling 4,000 horses, were involved. First, the cavalry regiments had to march from their barracks to their embarkation port, each stage of the journey carefully planned by the Quartermaster-General's Department in the Horse Guards in London. The 15th Hussars took two weeks to march from their barracks in Woodbridge in Suffolk – via Romford in Essex and Kingston and Guildford in Surrey, then through Chichester in Sussex – to Portsmouth. The regiment was split up into squadrons, so as not to put too much strain on forage resources in the locality where the cavalry rested. In any case, the presence of a cavalry unit was enough to push up local oat prices, which were, anyway, at their highest for years.[35] The twenty-six transports required to take the regiment and horses rendezvoused in Stokes Bay, just off Portsmouth Harbour.[36] For the Corunna expedition as a whole, the anchorages of Portsmouth, Weymouth and Falmouth were all needed to muster the total number of transports.[37] Over 65,000

British, German and Spanish infantry, cavalry and artillery, and 7,155 horses, were carried in 522 transports, measuring 134,334 tons. In addition to 227 ships carrying troops, there were army victuallers, forage ships, ships carrying ordnance and camp stores, wagon train equipment, six hospital ships and one 'ship with rockets'.[38]

By definition, any movement of troops by sea involved the cooperation of the navy and the army, and, when this was not forthcoming, failure was likely and recrimination bitter. Nor, over twenty years of warfare, is it surprising that there were differing views of the conduct of these expeditions, varying from the condemnatory to the praiseworthy. Army officers were the first to give the Transport Service a bad name. Tension existed, in any case, between the services aboard chartered merchant ships when it came to the question of whether army or naval discipline should prevail when at sea. This gave rise to the 'Admirals' Mutiny' in October 1795, when the duke of York issued new regulations for troops at sea that appeared to remove them from naval discipline. All eight admirals in Portsmouth at the time signed an indignant letter of protest to Lord Spencer, who managed to persuade the duke to withdraw the new regulations, but the incident did not help relations between the services.[39] Moreover, army officers regularly criticized shipboard conditions and the small size and discomfort of the transports in which they found themselves.* In 1794, for instance, during the expedition to Holland, Colonel Calvert thought the tonnage of the transports quite inadequate and their condition unfit for the troops.[40] Another officer on his way to Spain in 1808 found:

> The vessel in which I was was a small Newcastle Collier, a wretched sailor, with more men and horses on board than she could well accommodate ... It was a universal complaint, the description of Boats that were hired as transports, not only were they wholly unfit for the service, but in many instances they were unsafe, as not being seaworthy.

* Small transports seemed always to have been overcrowded. One observer noted during the 1807 Copenhagen expedition that 'Transport no. 196 passed us, playing my favourite air the Lorette: she was much crowded with artillery men ... and had a large gun over her bow' (Chambers, 'Chronological Journal', p. 378).

1. *A Complete Representation of the Coast of England* (1804) helped disseminate public knowledge of the invasion threat. It gives the length of the sea passage from potential French invasion ports, and is framed by plans of eighteen of them, from St Malo in the south to Amsterdam in the north. Britain's military districts are delineated, each commanded by a general who reported to the commander-in-chief, the duke of York. The Southern Military District, seen to be the most vulnerable, was commanded by General David Dundas.

2. (*top*) *North View of the City of Westminster from the Roof of the Banqueting House* (1807). Westminster Hall (*centre left, back*) and Abbey, and St Margaret's, Westminster, can be clearly seen. Much of the activity in this book took place within this view. The terrace to the right housed the Board of Trade and the India Board of Control; the narrow entrance to Downing Street can be seen just beyond it. The classical block (*centre*) is no longer there.

3. (*above*) Somerset House was the centre of naval administration, where from 1786 all departments, apart from the Admiralty itself, were housed in offices to the right. (See plan on p. 113.)

4. William Pitt (prime minister 1783–1801 and 1804–6) in the late 1780s, when he was at his most confident, his face unmarked by the strain of the war. Pitt was not a natural war leader, and had to balance Dundas's forceful advocacy of a maritime and empire policy with Grenville's urging for coalitions with European governments.

5. (*below left*) Henry Dundas (from 1804 Lord Melville), secretary of state for war (1794–1801) and first lord of the Admiralty (1804–5), not long before his death in 1811. A convivial and plain-speaking Scot, Dundas provided much of the energy and drive behind the government's war policy, both during the formation of the volunteers in the 1790s and in his short period as first lord of the Admiralty. Though he was seventeen years older than Pitt, they were very close.

6. (*above right*) William Wyndham Grenville, Baron Grenville, foreign secretary (1794–1801) (*c.* 1800). Grenville's gaze, assured and even haughty, underlines his intellect and efficiency. Though a cousin of Pitt, they were frequently at odds, and Grenville did not join his second administration in 1804. After Pitt's early death, leadership devolved upon him, but his confidence seemed to melt away. His clumsy management of ministers was a major factor in the shortcomings of the Ministry of All the Talents.

7. (*top left*) Evan Nepean: served at sea during the American Revolutionary War and in 1782 had very early promotion to undersecretary at the Home Office; first secretary of the Admiralty (1795–1804), when he was one of the most powerful figures in Whitehall.

8. (*top right*) William Marsden: second, then first, secretary of the Admiralty (1795–1807). Marsden's tolerance and good nature, and marked lack of political ambition, allowed him to serve both Whig and Tory governments.

9. (*above left*) George Phillips Towry, a victualling commissioner for thirty-three years. Towry was an effective, tough, well-connected Scot and, as deputy chairman of the Board, more influential than his chairman. He was very active, travelling extensively on victualling business.

10. (*above right*) Captain James Bowen, a transport commissioner (1803–16) and much respected seaman. Howe appointed him master of his flagship at the Battle of the First of June, and St Vincent made him flag captain, Channel, in 1806. Bowen's administrative and seamanship experience were much in evidence in the operation to evacuate the army from Corunna in 1809.

11. (*top*) The successful landing of the army at Aboukir Bay, Egypt, under Sir Ralph Abercromby on 8 March 1801, which was opposed by French troops in the dunes. Behind the operation was a complex assembling of troops and the feeding of thousands of men on board many transports.

12. (*above*) The unopposed landing at Mauritius, December 1810. The taking of Mauritius in the middle of the Indian Ocean was also a considerable organizational feat, on this occasion aided by the lack of opposing forces and by calm weather.

13. The pier at Margate (*c.* 1800), on the north-east corner of Kent, was often used for the difficult task of loading troops and cavalry on to transports. Its location shortened the sea passage to the Continent, and allowed ships to sail in either westerly or easterly winds. Here three transports are being loaded, and a horse hauled up on the main yard of one of them before being lowered into its hold.

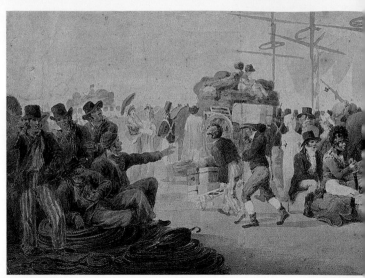

14. The shipbuilding slips and docks at Blackwall on the north bank of the Thames. In the foreground, two merchant ships are tacking towards London against a stiff breeze, but are helped by the flood tide, conditions that make for choppy waters.

We can date this view to 17 January 1798, because the painting celebrates the launch that day of the 74-gun *Kent*, the only warship to be built by the yard during the French Revolutionary War. All ships are flying a pre-1801 Union flag. The *Kent* can be seen centre left of the picture, flying large pennants (the Union Flag in front of the Royal Standard) that indicate an imminent launch. Admiralty barges can just be made out rowing down to witness the event.

15. (*top left*) The duke of Richmond, master-general of the ordnance (1784–95). Despite being the most difficult and quarrelsome of all politicians in the 1780s, Richmond instigated reforms that made a vital contribution to British military capability.

16. (*top right*) General Sir William Congreve, comptroller of the Royal Laboratory at Woolwich. Congreve had charge of the government powder mills at Faversham and Waltham Abbey, and was thus responsible for the supply of gunpowder to both the army and the navy.

17. (*above left*) The duke of York, commander-in-chief (1795–1809 and 1811–27). In spite of early military failure when promoted far too early by George III, he was made a full field marshal and commander-in-chief at the age of thirty-two, in 1795.

18. (*above right*) General Sir David Dundas (1806). This informal watercolour captures one of the characters of the army. He was an active major general in the 1790s and a formidable quartermaster-general in the crucial years between 1796 and 1803. After retirement, he stepped in, at the age of seventy-four, to replace the duke of York as commander-in-chief.

It is only necessary to look back to see the number of brave fellows who were lost, by being exposed to these old crazy unserviceable boats.[41]

Transports were worked hard, and their condition inevitably deteriorated. From Spain in 1810 Admiral George Berkeley complained to the first lord of the Admiralty privately that the transports were in 'so dreadful a state from being copper'd over iron fastenings, and being patched up for the sake of Hire, that some of them are actually not fit to trust to sea with Troops', and he reported that they had been surveyed and condemned.[42] A jaundiced view of these ships often came from sick and exhausted troops returning to England. Arriving in the Downs from Holland after the fighting in November 1799, the *Roebuck* transport was twelve days on the short passage, the troops 'under continual apprehension of the vessel being lost'. (Some of the soldiers had not had a change of clothes for ten weeks.)[43] But there were happier experiences. In 1801, on a voyage from Spithead to Nova Scotia, one young officer was more than satisfied that his men were comfortable, and he wrote to his mother:

> I must give you an account of a Transport, my party consisted of nine gentlemen, two ladies ... two children, and Betty the Maid. At meals all was delightfully formal, and immediately after, just the reverse: each followed his fancy, and I assure you the jargon that usually succeeded in nine feet square, provided all the charms there must be in variety; ridiculously comical as this was for a moment, fifty-three days would have indeed been heavy, if the men had not been excellent.[44]

Losses were caused, in the main, by winter gales. When shipwreck occurred with crowded ships, casualties were horrific, often exceeding those from sea battles. The Channel and the North Sea were particularly dangerous. Over 400 soldiers were drowned on passage from Yarmouth to the Downs during the operations against Copenhagen in 1801.[45] In November 1802 over 450 homecoming soldiers drowned when an old troopship, the Dutch prize *Vryheid*, lost her mast in the Channel and quickly broke in pieces on the beach off Dymchurch near Romney Marsh.[46] The seas during the voyage across the North Sea towards Copenhagen in the early autumn of 1807 were particularly

violent, and seven foundered with the loss of 400 soldiers.[47] Two transports were lost on the passage back to England from Corunna in early 1809, both wrecked on the Cornish coast: nearly sixty officers and men of the 7th Hussars, and their horses, were lost in the *Dispatch*, whose master was drunk in his berth; in the *Smallbridge*, over 200 soldiers belonging to the King's German Legion were drowned.[48] In a fresh breeze on a dark night in February 1811 a transport, without lights, was run down off Falmouth by a large frigate: 197 officers and other ranks, 15 women, 6 children and 6 seamen perished.[49] In the winter of 1809, however, the calmness of one master was much admired by an army officer when his vessel, returning from Corunna, got into difficulties on a lee shore off the Lizard, very near the infamous Manacles Rocks, two miles offshore. The army officer returned to his cabin and lay down on the floor, expecting the ship to strike, but it was saved by a fortunate shift in the wind. The master had prevented panic: 'I attribute our safety to the conduct of the Captain. His manner was so cool and encouraging to the sailors; not an oath was sworn, nor a harsh expression made use of.'[50] In general, however, the masters of these ships came under heavy criticism, and relations were worsened by the social distance between the gentlemen army officers and the masters, which significantly reduced real communication and understanding.

Yet these accidents must be set against the thousands of voyages that were made efficiently, in every year of both wars. In the French Revolutionary War alone, 135,000 troops were transported successfully from Britain to five theatres of war.[51] Historians have emphasized the failures of large amphibious operations, citing the consequent boards of enquiry, and indeed evidence of shortcomings is more readily accessible than that of successes. Enemy territory overseas was occupied and taken under British control in Newfoundland, the French and Spanish West Indies, Minorca and Malta in the Mediterranean, the Cape of Good Hope, and the French enclaves in India, Mauritius and islands in Indonesia. Often these territories were occupied by British troops stationed in nearby garrisons, using transports already present on the station. For instance, Madeira was occupied in 1801 by an expedition leaving from Lisbon, with a minimum of fuss and little publicity.[52] Most of these acquisitions were given back to

The owner of this considerable yard was John Perry, whose main business was to build and maintain the great East Indiamen (vessels the same size as a 74-gun ship) seen on the river bank in the left half of the picture, both in frame on the slips and in dock. In the right-hand half of the picture is a wet dock in which East Indiamen were repaired. The tall wooden structure (*centre right*) is the crane that hoisted masts in and out of the ships. Perry retired in 1803, and between 1802 and 1812, under Green, Wigram and Wells, this yard went on to build no fewer than ten ships of the line. No painting illustrates the maritime resources of Britain more graphically.

France under the terms of the Peace of Amiens in 1802, but they were again taken and occupied after May 1803. In all, between 1793 and 1815, at least fifty amphibious expeditions, some of them of no great size, took possession of hostile overseas possessions.[53] Most of the ships involved in these expeditions were merchant ships, amounting at times to a significant proportion of the British merchant fleet.* Such expeditions were in addition to the regular work of the transports in supplying provisions and stores to warships on blockade duties in home waters, and those serving on foreign stations and to an increasing number of overseas garrisons.

A typical example of a locally organized operation in the Mediterranean occurred in late 1805, when British troops under the command of General James Craig took part in the efficient and all but forgotten Anglo-Russian invasion of Naples. At Malta, in July, seventy transports, measuring 22,000 tons, were gathered, though with some difficulty, from all corners of the Mediterranean, with a view to conveying nearly 8,000 soldiers to Naples, from which the French had just withdrawn. An additional 13,000 tons of transports, sent from England, had to be provided to carry Russian troops from the Ionian Islands to Naples.[54] After two months of negotiations, the British troops withdrew, in the same transports, having secured agreement from the Kingdom of the Two Sicilies to occupy Messina in Sicily. It was an operation in which not a shot was fired; it concluded with a permanent British armed force in Sicily, which in turn ensured the security of Malta.[55] In the West Indies, at Martinique and Guadeloupe in 1809 and 1810, 6,000 veteran troops, with close support from the navy, overcame the local militia in ten days.[56] The worldwide movements of British troops in the Napoleonic War achieved such success that by 1811 France and its allies did not possess a single overseas territory.

Nevertheless, large expeditions in home waters were a problem from the start of the war and remained so to the end. After the first expeditions – to Holland in 1793 and to the West Indies in 1794 – the

---

* Losses of merchant ships and seamen were considerable. Between 1803 and May 1810 over 120 transports were captured or lost, 1,900 seamen perished and 1,700 were taken prisoner (Melville's speech, 21 May 1810, BL, Add. MSS 8807, fn. 6).

supply of merchant ships immediately began to run dry. By October 1795 the Transport Board had 717 ships under contract, with a total tonnage of 194,501 tons, but had produced only 60,000 to 70,000 tons for Admiral Christian's expedition, when 100,000 tons were required. By the middle of 1796, Rupert George was compelled to write to the Admiralty Board requesting that warships be used to transport troops, 'there being no adequate supply to be obtained from the several Ports of this Kingdom, or from Transports lately returned Home'.[57] The utility of 44-gun ships for carrying troops and stores had been suggested to Charles Middleton by an agent for transports in the late 1780s.[58] The Admiralty had already turned to medium-sized warships to fill the gap: as early as the first year of the war, in 1793, four 44-gun ships, each just under 900 tons, about three times as big as the average chartered transport, were adapted to carry troops and stores, which these warships did for much of the rest of their working lives through the wars. Twenty-two warships were adapted to this use before 1798, including five large 64-gun Dutch ships captured at Camperdown.[59] Additionally, in 1796, the Transport Board had to turn to the East India Company, with the support of Henry Dundas, as chairman of the Board of Control, hiring six large East Indiamen, measuring 6,500 tons.[60] In the hurry of remobilization after the Peace of Amiens in 1803, the Company also 'supplied Government with 10,000 tons [of] shipping armed free of expense in order to carry convoys to be employed as the Admiralty may direct'. These ships came under the control not of the Transport Board but of the Admiralty.*

Yet there was insufficient tonnage to meet peak demand. Following the great losses in the West Indies, no large amphibious expeditions

---

* Though the twenty-six EIC ships came free, they were indemnified against loss, and therefore needed valuing. Such was the hurry that they were ordered downriver immediately to Gravesend, and had to be surveyed and valued there by the Woolwich Dockyard officers: 'this disagreeable job has fell upon me and the other officers of this yard – and we have been down the river this fortnight past surveying the said ships' (John Tyson to Nelson, 26 Nov. 1803, NMM, CRK/13; Philips, *East India Company*, p. 113). John Tyson had been Nelson's secretary after the Battle of the Nile before coming ashore in 1802, when he was appointed clerk of the survey at Woolwich Dockyard (Knight, *Pursuit of Victory*, p. 674).

were attempted between 1796 and 1798.* At this time the Pitt government was trying to negotiate peace with France and had to deal with the naval mutinies at Spithead and the Nore, while Henry Dundas, as secretary of state for war, was building up the army after the West Indian débâcle. Towards the end of 1797, however, the decision was taken to convert many more older, medium-sized warships into troopships. They were refitted in the dockyards: the lower tier of guns was removed and accommodation for soldiers fitted in its stead. The first conversion was completed in April 1798: by the end of the year fourteen had been adapted, and by the end of 1800, with all the home dockyards undertaking the conversions, forty-three. By 1801 fifty-three troopships, measuring a substantial 52,000 tons, were available. The cost of the exercise was not negligible, for, in all, the conversions cost more than £270,000 over three years, at a time when the money voted to the Transport Office for 1801 for chartering transports was just under £1 million.[61] Significantly, these warships were not transferred to the Transport Board but, as with the East Indiamen, controlled by the Admiralty, their officers commissioned and their crews naval seamen. These troopships, however, were to prove no more popular than the transports. Henry Bunbury, a junior army officer, later recalled that 'It was a badly arranged service, and equally disagreeable to the officers of the army and the navy, who were always quarrelling.'[62]

Although no amphibious operations took place in 1798, the troopships were put to immediate use, because soldiers had to be evacuated from San Domingo, and many army movements to and fro over the Irish Sea were essential to deal with the rebellion. At the end of that year Henry Dundas wrote to Lord Spencer saying that he wanted to discuss improvements in transporting troops with him and Pitt. Among other things, he wanted vessels in readiness, bigger ships and changes to the naval discipline on board transports. Of the Transport Service, he commented: 'I have long thought it was radically erroneous.'[63]

However, the government was still unable to achieve the right

---

* Small expeditions in 1797 included Abercromby's to Trinidad and Puerto Rico; in May 1798 1,400 troops were involved in the raid on Ostend, while in November Duckworth and Stuart's expedition took Minorca.

balance of troops and ships for a successful amphibious operation. In 1799 a large, over-complex operation was mounted to invade Holland at Den Helder, to establish a bridgehead on the Continental mainland and to encourage the Dutch to resist the French. It was to be carried out with the assistance of Russian troops. Planning for this expedition had begun only in June, and it was, as usual, late in sailing. The duke of York, commanding the operation, was not appointed until early July. The landings took a month to complete: 'the soldiers had to wade and scramble out of the surf as well as they could . . . Everybody was out of humour, and out of heart,' Henry Bunbury recalled later.[64]

Sixteen British battalions were put ashore under Lieutenant-General Sir Ralph Abercromby on 27 August, seven on the following day, and thirteen between 12 and 15 September. Russian troops, conveyed by British transports (for they had no ships themselves), did not reach the Dutch coast from the Baltic until 19 and 23 September. The duke of York did not arrive until ten days after the landing of the first troops, taking a frustrating five days on passage from the Downs.[65] By the last week of September the troops in Den Helder reached the maximum at nearly 34,000, although 3,000 were sick; by 14 October this figure had risen to 6,500.[66]

The Anglo-Russian landings were far too slow and unloading was chaotic. Strategic surprise evaporated. The French and Dutch brought up reinforcements, destroyed bridges, flooded dykes and dug themselves in. The British Army performed well, landing skilfully and fighting immediately it landed, under difficult conditions through sand hills. However, its supplies were dangerously short. No storehouses or reserves of provisions were available. One old Dutch frigate had to be broken up for firewood because of the great shortage of coal. The British admiral, Andrew Mitchell, kept ten days' worth of navy provisions and handed over the rest to the army.[67] The main reason for this dire situation was the lack of sufficient transports. From a Transport Office memorandum circulated at cabinet level in 1800 we learn that no more than 296 transports, measuring 73,000 tons, took part in the operation, not counting the Admiralty troopships. Most of the transports made two and sometimes three trips from the Downs to Den Helder with soldiers, equipment and stores, landing in all

200,000 tons' worth of troops and equipment. The Transport Board commented that 'The troops and horses were more cram[m]ed into these ships than would be consistent with their health.'[68] Unsurprisingly, a heavy military defeat by a smaller French army ensued, followed by capitulation on 18 October 1799. Only the capture of the Dutch Fleet in the Texel in the early days of the operation prevented the expedition from being a total catastrophe.

Ministers, led by Henry Dundas, started to plan a major offensive against French territory even while the duke of York's forces were gathering for the Den Helder expedition. They still aimed high, planning to capture the naval base at Brest, a difficult and well-defended target, with no nearby sheltered bays for a fleet anchorage. The question was how large this operation should be and where it should land?* Planning was aided by a high level of intelligence for operations at sea, supported by an accurate map, but was thin on information on the countryside and rivers around Brest. The debate exposed how great were the fissures between ministers and departments, the divergent attitudes of the navy and army, and the lack of appreciation by the services of each other's point of view.

Lord Spencer wrote to Pitt on 2 September 1799, reflecting the opinions of his senior admirals when he put forward three planning principles: that as large a force as possible should be landed as quickly as possible; that it should be landed as near to Brest as possible; and that the landing place should allow direct communications between army ashore and the fleet.[69] Having rejected a large number of possible landing places as being unsafe for the fleet, Spencer suggested the compromise of Douarnenez Bay, the opposite side of the Rade de Brest from the dockyard. The contrary view of the army was expressed two weeks later by General Sir Charles Grey: the landing at Douarnenez, as he wrote to Dundas, appeared 'so full of difficulties, as to render it hardly practicable'. It is clear that Grey had no enthusiasm for this operation, correctly emphasizing the importance of choosing the right season of the year, and insisting that the only time to attempt it was

---

* The viewpoints of senior ministers in Nov. and Dec. 1799 survive in a letter-book, copied on the instructions, most likely, of Dundas. The letters are businesslike and precise, stripped of the usual polite flourishes, and give an unusually detailed insight into the process of reaching a major cabinet decision (Sim Comfort Collection).

spring, when the settled weather gave the fleet the best chance of staying at anchor in support of the army. His decided opinion was that not fewer than '70,000 actual effective men' would be needed to take and hold Brest. He based this upon the intelligence that the French had '37,000 men capable of bearing Arms without rendering the Men of war in harbour totally useless'. Besides, there would only be a narrow window in which to achieve it, as Brest was just six days' march from Paris, 'where there is always an immense body of Troops'.[70] Grey would have known that nothing like 70,000 troops were available for such an operation.[71]

Dundas was trying to devise an offensive strategy at a particularly complex time. Lord Grenville wanted the army to go to the Mediterranean to support Austria, but Austria was an ally in which Dundas had no trust. Dundas had his eye instead on securing Atlantic bases to enable trade with Spanish colonies in South America and, in truth, he did not possess a clear idea on how best to use the army.[72] The three ministers who decided foreign policy, Pitt, Dundas and Grenville, were never more divided.[73] By the end of November, William Huskisson, the undersecretary for war, produced a preliminary analysis of the shipping that would be needed to transport such an expedition of 70,000 men. In a letter of 30 November to Dundas, he suggested that the amount might be 160,000 tons (a gross underestimate, judging by the figure at which he finally arrived), to be ready by 1 March in the year it was to sail. But in order to obtain even this tonnage, ships in the Baltic trade would have to be taken up, which, Huskisson pointed out, would cause 'real distress to the commercial interests of this country'. Nor did he have much faith in taking up neutral shipping:

> Such ships are navigated and commanded by Neutrals (most of them Enemies at bottom) who have no Idea of the Service, are under no subordination, and have nothing of the necessary activity, exertion, or Seamanship for Services of this description; These Qualities might perhaps be found in the Americans, but they are not disposed or at liberty to engage in any such Service.[74]

This tightly argued report sowed doubts in Dundas's mind, as he wrote to Pitt from his home in Wimbledon, 'being quite alone all the day, I had full Opportunity to ruminate on the Subject, and the result was to make one more and more sceptical on the Question'.

Pitt, however, was not immediately persuaded by these doubts and replied, 'I should like to know the particulars on which Huskisson's Opinions are founded, but from all that I recollect, I cannot help thinking that the Expence at least if not the difficulty of providing the Transports is much overrated.'[75] Huskisson's final tonnage calculations for Grey's 70,000-strong expedition in his letter to Dundas of 18 December made the position devastatingly clear. The force would be composed of 60,000 regular infantry rank and file, with officers and sergeants, and 60 women to a regiment.* An infantry force of this magnitude would require seven regiments of cavalry, containing 4,000 rank and file, to which one would have to add officers, farriers, equipment, 12,000 horses and forage. When artillerymen, engineers, the medical Commissariat and members of the Quartermaster-General's Department were included, the total, according to Huskisson, would be 83,628 individuals, requiring no less than 350,000 tons of shipping, or

---

* 'Women only in the proportion of Six to every Hundred Men will be permitted to embark. They should be carefully selected, as being of good character and having the inclination and ability to render themselves useful' ('General Order for Troops Destined for Continental Service', 15 Apr. 1807, quoted in Glover, *Britain at Bay*, p. 130). In Sept. 1799 Lady Bessborough witnessed the embarkation of troops to Den Helder from Margate Pier, describing the dramatic scene to Granville Leveson Gower.

> You know only a certain number of women are allow'd to go, and they draw lots for it. One in particular wish'd very much to follow her Husband, but was told the number was completed and oblig'd to go on shore. She had an infant at her bosom, and another about a year old by her. She threw herself on the side of the Pier crying and sobbing almost to fits, and shewing every mark of agony while the remainder of the soldiers were embarking. As soon as they were all in, and the Anchor drawn up, she kept her eyes ste[a]dfastly fixed on the transport as it moved slowly up the Harbour. The soldiers were drawn up on the side waving their hands to their friends. Just as it turn'd round the Pier head she darted forward, threw the eldest child into the Arms of her Husband, and jump'd herself, with the other in her arms, amidst the shouts and acclamations of the Mob. The Soldiers received her and laid her gently on the deck, and the officer on board was so touch'd by her perseverance and despair that he permitted her to go. I cannot tell you how much this has struck my fancy; but we are in the midst of adventure here.

(Granville, *Leveson Gower Correspondence*, Vol. I, pp. 261–2)

at least a thousand ships. This total was the final proof that Grey's estimate of an expeditionary force of 70,000 men was a pipe dream, for at
no time between 1793 and 1815 did the British government come
within 100,000 tons of this figure.[76]

The British government had finally come to realize the limits of its
ambitions so far as amphibious operations were concerned. But it
seems extraordinary that it took seven years of war, until the last days
of 1799, to work out what was essentially an arithmetical sum, albeit
a complicated one. Had the Transport Board been represented in cabinet by a single, senior minister, the logistical limitations would have
been heard at that level. But Dundas, never a man to listen to advice
that contained problems, had planned the West Indies expeditions in
a vacuum and overstretched the system, driving them through to completion by sheer force of personality. He had not delegated enough,
nor trusted subordinates, nor allowed generals and admirals to plan
together, keeping detail in his hands that would have been better handled by others while he concentrated on strategy and wider political
issues. Now much wiser, Dundas realized that Brest was impregnable,
and he fell back on planning much smaller expeditions.

Still another element essential to amphibious success was a steady and
trusting relationship between the army and navy commanders. Dundas had a stroke of luck when planning his next expedition. General
Sir Charles Stuart, the energetic and ascerbic army commander-in-chief
in the Mediterranean (who had been brilliantly successful in taking
Minorca in 1798, dominating the dullard admiral John Duckworth,
responsible for transporting Stuart's troops), suddenly resigned on
being given orders with which he did not agree.[77] Sir Ralph Abercromby was appointed in his stead. A clash of personalities had been
avoided, as described by General O'Hara, the governor of Gibraltar,
who wrote to Admiral Lord Keith, commander-in-chief in the
Mediterranean:

> I am fully persuaded from the haughtiness of his [Stuart's] manner you
> never would have agreed; for tho' I believe he is a man of parts and enter-
> prise, he cannot possibly bear any difference of opinion from his own and
> [he is] certainly the least accommodating of any man upon earth. Sir

Ralph, on the contrary, I hold to be a reasonable, considerate, good officer, and listens with temper and patience to every proposal made to him.[78]*

In April 1800 Abercromby set sail southwards with 5,000 troops for the Mediterranean, though his orders were vague. An attempt to land at Belle Isle was abandoned. On 24 July the cabinet decided on attacks on Ferrol and on Cádiz. Both operations were a shambles: in neither were troops actually landed. Relations between Abercromby, the Scots general, and Keith, the Scots admiral, were distant. Of the scene off Cádiz, Colonel John Moore wrote to his father: 'It is not to be described the bad management and confusion which attended the assembling of the boats; it was increased by the ships being under sail.' Another army officer wrote: 'The business was most sadly bitched.'[79] Lord Cornwallis, the most respected senior general, wrote at the time that the army was 'the scorn and laughing stock of friends and foes'.[80] Rumours reached London that army and naval commanders over-seeing the aborted attack had been on different ships. Ministers knew well that it was the prickly and defensive Keith who was being diffi-cult. He received separate letters from Spencer and Dundas that had obviously been coordinated, since both mention the same points and were written on the same day; and the absolute requirement for cooperation between army and navy was stressed in each. The kindly Spencer was outspoken, but Dundas's letter was downright threatening. If it was true that the two commanders were on different ships, he wrote,

[it] is a new circumstance in a conjunct expedition, and appears to me calculated to lose many valuable hours which might be employed occasionally in connecting your ideas and concerting your future operations ... If unfortunately there does exist for it even the smallest foundation I must conjure both of you ... that you would extirpate from

---

* Colonel Bunbury described Abercromby as 'Mild in manner, resolute in mind, frank, unassuming, just, inflexible in what he deemed to be right ... An honest, fear-less straightforward man; and withal sagacious and well-skilled in his business as a soldier. As he looked out from under his thick, shaggy eyebrows, he gave one the idea of a very good-natured lion.' But Bunbury added, 'The General was a little too old for hard service, and he was extremely near-sighted' (Bunbury, *Narratives*, p. 45).

your minds every remnant of so pernicious a weed, which if allowed to grow into any magnitude will not fail ultimately to confuse the service in which you are engaged. If from such a course the fatal day of failure should arise, the public will not stoop so far from its chagrin and resentment as to enquire where the blame lay, but will consign to disgrace the fame of those who have brought so great a calamity upon them.[81]

The secretary for war could not make it more plain that, in the event of failure, it would be Keith who would shoulder any blame. Though relations between Abercromby and Keith were never close, cooperation now improved to such an extent that, five months later, they achieved brilliant success.

By March 1800 Keith had accumulated thirty-two chartered transports in the Mediterranean, totalling 10,545 tons, almost all in the Western Mediterranean: ten were at Gibraltar, unloading stores from England; three were troopships for the Minorca garrison; six victuallers and storeships were at Minorca, together with three carrying ordnance stores; and another five were at Palermo in Sicily, being used to bring men and stores to Malta.[82] The French garrison on the island had finally surrendered in September 1800 to the besieging British troops under General Graham, giving the cabinet, after much debate, the confidence to send Abercromby's forces to Egypt in an attempt to dislodge the French Army, which had occupied the country since 1798. It was a high-risk strategy, but the cabinet, pushed on by Dundas, now scented the possibility for peace, and a strong card was required for the negotiating table. On 19 November, Abercromby reached Malta, where the regiments and reinforcements were sorted out, and the sick taken off. Only three soldiers' wives per regiment were allowed to proceed with the 14,000 troops. Heart-rending scenes were acted out as those women not allowed to sail were put ashore when the signal was flown for sailing on 12 December.[83] Abercromby himself was not confident: 'I never went on any service entertaining greater doubts of success ... there are risks in the British service unknown to any other.'[84]

In the customary blowing winter weather in the Mediterranean, Keith took his warships and forty troop-carrying warships with

Abercromby's 14,000 soldiers eastwards from Malta, intending to anchor at Rhodes or in the Gulf of Macri.[85] Some soldiers had come from England and been afloat for many months, their sea journey broken only by short periods ashore. The *Inflexible*, a converted 64-gun ship of 1,385 tons, was crewed by 120 seamen, and transported 605 officers and men, leaving Dover on 14 May 1800, picking up more at Cork and Port Mahon.[86] The *Thisbe*, a 28-gun frigate of 596 tons – which before conversion to a troopship had had a full fighting complement of 121 seamen, now reduced to 89 – transported 286 troops of the 2nd Foot, commanded by the earl of Dalhousie. His soldiers were crowded and on two thirds allowance of provisions.[87] They lay under blankets, their clothes in tatters, for their replacement uniforms were aboard a storeship that had yet to arrive. Dalhousie cursed the ship's officers, 'vulgar blackguards, that would do anything to disoblige us or annoy a soldier'.[88] As the fleet sailed towards the coast of southern Turkey, where Keith expected Turkish reinforcements and supplies, morale was low.

Then their luck started to turn. Strong winds prevented Keith from reaching the Gulf of Macri, but the fleet fell in with the *Peterel* sloop, commanded by a young lieutenant, Charles Inglis, who had been cruising in the area. The spectacular Bay of Marmaris had not been surveyed and charted, but Inglis had been there a month before, so he volunteered to take the fleet in.[89]* The southerly wind made it a lee shore; the sloop's log records: 'Strong gales and squally with lightning and rain.'[90] It was a dramatic moment. The entrance to the Bay of Marmaris is narrow and hidden by perpendicular, lofty and rocky cliffs that plunge into water as deep as the cliffs are high. Inglis informed a brother officer, 'It was an arduous undertaking, considering circumstances – a gale of wind, hazy weather, a lee shore and dangerous coast. I fortunately pricked for the port within a quarter of a mile, although during the day we hardly ever saw half a mile ahead.'[91] According to Midshipman George Parsons, matters were very tense on the quarterdeck of the *Foudroyant*, Keith's flagship. He reported that the normally tight-lipped Keith shouted out,

* The Bay of Marmaris was eventually surveyed in 1811 by Francis Beaufort.

'God be praised for this great mercy!' ... uncovering and bowing his head with great devotion ... The entrance of Marmorice now became distinctly visible to all on deck, from the contrast of the deep still water to the creamy froth on the shore ... We now entered the spacious and splendid harbour, circular in its form, and more than twenty miles in circumference.[92]

The next night, Dalhousie and his officers celebrated Hogmanay ashore around a huge log fire, drinking to the new century. The brandy left them distinctly hung over the next morning.[93]

Fleet and army spent seven weeks there, waiting for supplies and reinforcements from the Turks, and for the wind to ease. On 20 January the troops were put on full rations. They put the time to good use by perfecting landing manoeuvres, Abercromby ensuring that army and naval cooperation flourished. During these weeks of recuperation, Keith carefully made several matters clear to Abercromby by letter. He would comply with requests for men to help the army, but,

The crews of the troopships are so short, and their anchors and cables so heavy in proportion to their strength, that your Excellency must be sensible, when their boats are employed in transporting provisions, water, etc., few, or no, men can be drawn from them; and from the transports and victuallers, nothing more can be expected than crews for their long boats, and others to tow them after which many of them will not have four men left on board.[94]

On 22 February 1801, Keith's fleet left the shelter of Marmaris Bay for Egypt. It totalled 175 ships: a handful of warships, forty troop-ships, many transports from England, the rest consisting of polacres, xebecs and feluccas gathered from the ports of Asia, the Aegean and the Adriatic.[95] Rough weather again prevailed, and the fleet did not sight the Egyptian coast until 1 March. Twenty miles from Alexandria, the plan was to land at Aboukir Bay, which they reached by 3 March. Unable to sail nearer the shore because of shallow water, the troop-ships and transports were anchored two miles out. On 7 March the *Peterel* 'Answered a general signal to cook three days Provisions for the troops etc.'[96]

The French Army commander, General Menou, had not taken the

threat of a British landing at Aboukir seriously and the local commander, General Friant, had only 2,000 infantry and cavalry at his
disposal, though he was confident of defeating a landing. He had
three iron cannon and a dozen field guns which would play havoc
with the boats filled with troops.[97] On 8 March, British regiments
were rowed ashore by ships' boats and landed in concentrated numbers: 3,000 men in fifty-eight flat-bottomed boats, supported on each
side by cutters with 6-pounders mounted in their bows. They were
followed by a second flotilla of eighty-four boats, each carrying thirty
men. The third flotilla consisted of fourteen launches, towed by
thirty-seven cutters, carrying the guns.[98] Under fire, several of the
boats were hit and sank. Colonel Henry Bunbury described the scene:

> So closely were our soldiers packed in the boats that they could not
> move, and indeed the strictest orders had been given that they should
> sit perfectly still. The seamen pulled steadily onward, the pace of each
> boat being regulated by that on the extreme right. In this calm order on
> they came, till they were within reach of grapeshot, and then the fire
> became terribly severe and destructive. Some boats were sunk, and
> many of our men were killed or wounded as they sat motionless and
> helpless.[99]

The wounded were ferried back to the two hospital ships. A naval
officer who was present blamed 'the confusion of the transport boats
on our left'.[100] But after their weeks of training, the troops remained
calm, and they formed up in perfect order on the beach.[101] The fighting was intense. The smaller French army was swept from the beach
and sand dunes in minutes, which was fortunate, since the wind was
too strong the next day to land more troops.[102] It was, however, novel
to see Frenchmen retreating: the restoration of the reputation of the
British Army had begun.

Almost seven years later, under a very different government, three conjunct operations took place that defined the rest of the war. The first,
against Copenhagen in August and September 1807, was a brilliant success, and benefited from a united cabinet solidly behind the pre-emptive
action. The possibility of hostilities against Denmark had long been
anticipated, and naval preparations had started a year before, when

Tom Grenville was first lord in his brother's short-lived Talents ministry. Grenville had the masters attendant of the dockyards survey the ships in ordinary and then refit 64- and 74-gun ships, which drew less water and so were suitable for the shallow Baltic. By the time his administration ended in April 1807, he had ordered twelve of them to Great Yarmouth, to be followed by four more, commanded by Rear-Admiral Keats.[103] Moreover, by the summer of 1807 Castlereagh, now secretary of state for war, also had troops at his disposal. A further 8,000 of the King's German Legion were already on the island of Rügen. A further 16,500 had been gathered in Britain intended for service in Germany. Thirty-eight warships were mustered in Yarmouth Roads, accompanied by 400 transports.[104]

Transporting the troops in high summer went smoothly, and Copenhagen was invested on 17 August by 24,500 troops. The Danes were surprised and indignant; the main Danish army was in Jutland because of the French threat, and forced to remain there by British naval ships.[105] Good relations between Admiral Gambier, the naval commander, and Lord Cathcart, the army commander, together with initiative from more junior officers, including Sir Arthur Wellesley, led to a successful operation. The three-day bombardment of Copenhagen and the deaths of numerous civilians sickened many, including the highly religious Gambier; and the legality of the pre-emptive attack was thought dubious, with George III, in particular, disapproving – but, in operational terms, the expedition could hardly have gone more smoothly.[106] Seventeen Danish ships of the line were seized and sailed back to England.*

The second operation was a success retrieved from a potential disaster, when warships and transports evacuated Sir John Moore's retreating army at Corunna in January 1809, the army which had

---

* The capitulation specified that Britain had only six weeks to get the ships out of Copenhagen, a lengthy task, since almost all of the Danish warships had neither rigging nor guns fitted. As Gambier was unwilling to strip his fleet of men to sail the prizes back to Chatham and Sheerness, the government swiftly advertised for seamen from the Greenland fishery, promising them a bounty, and guaranteeing freedom from the press and travel expenses back to their home port. According to the *Naval Chronicle*, 'upwards of 2,000 have already volunteered in the river, and in the eastern ports; and it is conjectured that many more will be collected for this purpose' (Tracy, *Naval Chronicle*, Vol. IV, p. 49).

been transported from England only months before. Moore was pursued by a French army under Marshal Soult, but a courageous rearguard action kept the French at bay, though Moore was killed. Rear-Admiral Sir Samuel Hood, with some warships and 227 hastily chartered transports, was sent from England to bring them off. The skill of the masters and crews of the transports, combined with the strength and tenacity of the crews of the naval pulling boats, was pointedly demonstrated. Three thousand troops were evacuated from Vigo, and 25,097 exhausted troops were taken off the beach at Corunna, with the French Army at their heels and the transports themselves under fire. Five transports were grounded and had to be abandoned, though the soldiers were transferred to other ships.[107] Four thousand barrels of gunpowder, just sent out from England, were blown up to avoid their being seized by the French. The explosion was witnessed by an army officer: 'a magnificent sight, but it did great damage to the city which rocked as with an earthquake and several men were killed by the explosion'.[108] Some cavalry horses were embarked, but most of them, worn out and lame, were shot on the shore. Another cavalry officer reported that 'Our loss may be well imagined when I mention that we embarked 640 horses and brought home 60.'[109]

The chief agent for transports was Captain James Bowen, specially appointed by Lord Castlereagh; one of the key factors in the success of this operation was the close cooperation between him and Hood. Bowen reported later to the Transport Board that

> The Tide being out when it commenced the troops were obliged to wade into the Boats up to their necks in water, the night was excessively dark, the transports were obliged to lie at a considerable distance, a gale of wind coming on as the tide flowed and the surf greatly endangering the safety of the Boats. To all this may be added the utmost efforts of a persevering enemy under whose fire more tremendous from its noise than from its effects. The latter part of the embarkation proceeded though he had not the satisfaction of sinking a boat or destroying a single man.[110]

Bowen praised the contribution of the transports and their crews, even though the well-crewed naval cutters and launches had made, according to Lord Melville in a speech in the House of Lords a year later, ten times as many trips as the boats from the transports.[111] The explanation for this, reported Bowen, was that the crews of the naval boats and launches had had rest and sleep:

> But the Agents and Crews of the Transports who had not this advantage supported the incessant toils of these first three days and two nights almost without refreshment, without rest and without a murmur and so exhausted at the conclusion as to be unable to pull to windward in the strong squalls. The general conduct of the transports has been highly meritorious notwithstanding the errors of a few: some stayed to get their allotment of troops long after the signal to weigh had been made.[112]

The wind got up in the final hours of the evacuation. Covered by the guns of the warships, the army rear-guard was embarked. Bowen brought off the last piquet of fourteen men of the 26th Regiment to Hood's 98-gun flagship *Barfleur*. As he did so, the French entered the houses of St Lucia, as Bowen reported, 'murdering stragglers'. The *Barfleur* crammed in 819 soldiers, small groups of officers and men from as many as twenty-three different regiments. Together with the crew of 500 seamen, a remarkable total of 1,371 men were on board.[113] The larger, 110-gun *Ville de Paris* had a crew of 600 but embarked 743 soldiers, making a total of 1,343, among them General Sir David Baird and his staff, 40 soldiers' wives and 7 children.[114] The boats of the 74-gun *Audacious* destroyed the beached transports and took off General Hope, his staff and stragglers, taking a total of 308 soldiers to Portsmouth. Among the rescued on this ship were 13 wives and children and 33 French prisoners.[115]

The warships made the journey in four or five days, with gales and fresh southerly winds behind them. The slower transports took longer, and fog in the Channel and a south-easterly gale provided one more hurdle for the exhausted troops. Anchored safely in a transport at Spithead on 25 January, Major Lord Carnock of the 15th Hussars wrote in his journal: 'Great apprehension entertained for the safety of the transports on account of the storm last night.'[116] A good proportion of the evacuated army was billeted in Hurst Castle, bleak and isolated, and bitterly cold in winter, at the western end of the Solent.[117]

The ordeal of the rescued soldiers was not yet over, especially for those crowded into the transports. One eyewitness described the disembarking soldiers, who had

> an appearance of much dirt and misery. The men were ragged, displaying torn garments of all colours; and the people of England, accustomed to witness the high order and unparalleled cleanliness of their national troops ... and never having seen an army after the termination of a hard campaign, were horror-struck.[118]

Six thousand soldiers required immediate hospitalization. Those who landed at Plymouth were taken straight to the military hospital, while those at Portsmouth were landed at Haslar Naval Hospital, where the army had leased wards from the navy.[119] Of 241 deaths at Plymouth, only twenty-five were caused by wounds; deaths from dysentery were twice those from typhus. According to the army surgeon James McGrigor:

> The sick and healthy being mixed together indiscriminately, it was no matter of wonder that the number of cases of fever landed in the last stages of typhus was great; in fact, it was enormous and it excited great alarm at Portsmouth and in the neighbouring country when an account of the mortality came to be noised abroad.[120]

In the Commons, only a week later, Hood was in his seat as MP for Bridport when the House expressed its thanks to the army and navy commanders for saving the country's main field army. All was quiet until Hood rose to reply: then 'the whole House burst into a roar of applause, so that he was quite delayed by it from beginning his speech.'[121] Doubtless the loudest acclamation came from the front bench, since a disaster to the army at Corunna would most likely have brought down the government. The saving of that army, the 'Dunkirk' of its time, was critical to the continuation of the war in Spain, at that time a very unpopular policy. Hood was awarded a baronetcy two months later.

The last of the amphibious operations, late in 1809, to transport an army to Holland, was a disaster. Early plans merely to capture Walcheren, and that island's port of Flushing, where Napoleon had five ships of the line building, developed into a much more ambitious plan of capturing and destroying the ships building in the heavily fortified and guarded dockyard at Antwerp. Its purpose was to destroy Antwerp Dockyard, sixty miles up the River Scheldt, which constituted a continuing threat to Britain because of its potential to build a great French fleet that might finally breach England's invasion defences. Planning of the expedition was held up earlier in the year by the parliamentary enquiry into the duke of York's alleged selling of promotions through his mistress: almost all the time of the House of Commons was taken up with this matter from late January until 18 March.[122] The duke's judgement and authority were sorely missed when he resigned. From the time of the first decision, taken in May – far too late in the year – by the duke of Portland's bitterly divided cabinet, this expedition was headed for failure.

The whole operation was driven by the secretary of state for war, Lord Castlereagh, but he was influenced by Captain Sir Home Popham, who had by now thrown off the disgrace of the failed South American expedition of 1806 examined in the next chapter. The close cooperation between the services, which had ensured the success of the Corunna evacuation earlier in the year, was lacking. The naval commander was the hot-tempered Rear-Admiral Sir Richard Strachan, described by a fellow officer as 'an irregular, impetuous fellow, possessing very quick parts'. During the action in the days after Trafalgar, for which Strachan is chiefly remembered, his impetuosity had led him to order his gunners to fire 'two guns shotted' at a British ship in order to encourage her captain to get into action with the enemy.[123] The sailors called him 'Mad Dick' because of the stream of oaths that came with his orders. During the operation, Strachan disastrously delegated responsibility for liaising with the army to Popham.

The choice for commander of the army was Lord Chatham, elder brother of William Pitt, who had been a lethargic and distant first lord of the Admiralty in the first years of the war, and was now master-general of the Ordnance. Why Chatham was chosen is something of a mystery: possibly it was a gamble for military success by a member of the government to prop up the ailing Portland administration. Chatham had fought in the siege of Gibraltar in the American Revolutionary War, and had done well during the Den Helder expedition under the duke of York; but for most of the last twenty-five years he had been, in the words of a soldier, 'accustomed to the routine of official duty, but without experience as a leader, and without the qualities necessary to the success of an enterprise which demanded decision of character and activity of mind and body'.[124] Little inter-service confidence was generated by the appointment of someone now considered by many a Whitehall warrior. A young naval captain, Charles Boys, observed from the Scheldt when he arrived, ''tis really a deplorable thing . . . to send Lord Chatham and a tribe of generals whose names are scarcely known out of St James's . . .'tis enough to make Mr Bull shake his head.' One exasperated colonel told Boys, 'Everything goes on at headquarters, as if they were at the Horse Guards; it did not signify what you wanted, you must call between certain hours, send up your name and wait your turn.'[125]

The expedition to Walcheren in 1809 was the largest to leave British shores in the French Wars, and it was late in sailing from the Downs. With transports still engaged in operations in Portugal, there were never enough available, and Rupert George, chairman of the Transport Board, suggested to Castlereagh that neutral ships should be requisitioned to make up the shortfall.[126] Not until 24 June did troops start to march to the five ports of embarkation, Deal, Dover, Chatham, Harwich and Portsmouth.[127] Easterly winds caused further delay.* Castlereagh travelled to the Downs, anxious to see the expedition off when it finally sailed on 28 July. Three days later he expressed early private doubts to his stepbrother, Charles Stewart:

> Without having any reason to complain of want of Exertion in any Quarter, the assembly and sailing of our armament was delay'd for a week. It is now all off, and <u>without an accident</u>, which is more than Ever happen'd in so large a Fleet. Indeed I believe so large a Fleet never before was collected, they amounted of above 600 sail, 260 of which, including gun boats were Ships of War. The Embarkation Returns (all sick left behind) was 43,700 men and officers . . . With such a Force, I should suppose the reduction of Walcheren can only be a question of Time, but the further operations of the Army Towards Antwerp, on which the fate of the Enemy's Fleet and arsenal depend, is much more questionable.[128]

* The numbers involved overwhelmed the local postal services. The Deal postmaster claimed that he had 20,000 letters for men in the expedition and arrangements had to be made for a special coach to carry the mail (Austen, *English Provincial Posts*, p. 87).

Horses and the difficulty of loading them were, as ever, a problem. For the Walcheren expedition, as late as 14 August, there were still over 300 at Ramsgate waiting to be embarked, and some never even made the journey.[129]

Lack of decision on the part of the army and bad communication between the services marked the expedition from the start. Two of the three planned landings were initially successful – on the island of Walcheren itself and further up the Scheldt on South Beveland, with its small fort at Batz – bringing the foremost British forces within fifteen miles of Antwerp. The main effort was now to capture Flushing. One group of the transports under Popham took shelter in the Roompot, to the north of the Scheldt, when they were supposed to be in Flushing.* The third landing, on Cadsand, on the south bank of the river, was postponed because of bad weather and then abandoned. The army then lost valuable time in bringing batteries up to reduce Flushing, already defended by 5,000 troops, and soon reinforced by 3,000 others who slipped over the river from Cadsand, which the navy failed to prevent. Flushing was eventually bombarded and set on fire, surrendering on 16 August, at the cost of 4,000 British casualties, though 6,000 prisoners were taken. The five ships of the line building there were destroyed.

The time lost by the British was used well by the French, who rushed reinforcements to the Scheldt and strengthened Antwerp's defences. The expedition advanced slowly to Batz, but with a lack of urgency that indicates that Chatham had early given up hope of gaining Antwerp. Before the end of August he and Strachan, with whom relations had deteriorated badly, decided that there was little chance of

---

* Sir Home Popham tripped up a final time in the House of Commons in the post-expedition enquiry, having assured the secretary of the Admiralty: '"Don't be alarmed; depend upon it, when I get up to speak I shall be so intensely listened to that you may hear a pin drop." He got up, carried the expedition triumphantly till it met with a gale of wind – and [said], "Sir, without the loss or damage of a single ship, I anchored the whole securely in the Room-Pot [the estuary to the north of the mouth of the Scheldt]." The security of a fleet of men-of-war afloat in the Cream-pot, raised such a general shout of laughter, that poor Sir Home's speech shared very much the fate of the luckless expedition' (Barrow, *Autobiography*, pp. 306–7).

success.* Rampant marsh fever hit the troops at the same time.[130] Chatham was still lethargic. One very critical naval officer wrote to an Opposition MP of what many had suspected: 'Nothing could have been more weak or more absurd than delaying the evacuation of the Island [Walcheren] after the great object of the Expedition was given up . . . I cannot help thinking that Lord C. never had any intention of attempting any more than was done.'[131]

By 17 September, 8,200 soldiers had been struck down with the virulent disease of marsh fever: they died at the rate of 250 a week. The fever was a potent mix of malaria, typhus, typhoid and dysentery. When units of the Walcheren troops arrived home, their approach to some towns, including Canterbury, Chichester, Horsham, Chelmsford and Ipswich, caused many of the population to flee the area. Some 36,000 men were admitted to army hospitals in 1809.[132] The permanent hospitals at Chelsea, Gosport, Plymouth, Chatham, Deal, Isle of Wight and Selsey had to be supplemented by temporary ones, which were established at Colchester, Harwich, Chelmsford, Dunmow, Bury St Edmunds and Southampton. At Ipswich the hutted camp known as St Mary's Barracks was completely given over to the sick.[133]

Public and press opinion was shocked and angry. The three-man Army Medical Board was ordered out to Holland to improve matters. Bickering among themselves, none of them went, not surprisingly in the case of the physician-general, Sir Lucas Pepys, who was nearly seventy and unwell.† At the beginning of 1810 the three officers were dismissed the service.[134] The casualties after Corunna in February

---

* Public scorn resulted in an epigram still remembered:

> Lord Chatham, with his sword undrawn,
> Stood waiting for Sir Richard Strachan,
> Sir Richard, longing to be at 'em,
> Stood waiting for the Earl of Chatham

† It was a period of high tension in the Army Medical Service (see Chapter 11). An army doctor and persistent critic of the Army Medical Board, Robert Jackson, thrashed the surgeon-general, Thomas Keate, with a cane, and received six months' detention for the attack (Ackroyd et al., *Advancing with the Army*, p. 30).

1809 were understandable, but not those resulting from the palpable neglect at Walcheren.

The transports had worked ceaselessly, but there were still not enough of them. Yet the Transport Board had done well, for it had succeeded in getting the expeditions off, albeit late, and in spite of the scarcity of merchant ships to support all the operations that the government had wished to launch. This considerable achievement was recognized by the award of a baronetcy to Rupert George.[135] Yet massive conjunct expeditions involving over 100,000 tons of merchant shipping were beyond the resources of the country, its inter-service relations or its communication systems. Cavalry was crucial to the warfare of the day. Napoleon made no precautionary moves to parry forces that did not possess a significant number of horses. The duke of York complained in 1806 that Continental armies never had less than a sixth of their forces as cavalry and some had as much as a quarter, but the British Army had little more than a tenth.[136] This 'shipping bottleneck' precluded direct and successful British intervention on the shores of France and its immediate neighbours. The army's demand for large expeditions to invade the Continent was a logical one. Captain Charles William Pasley of the Royal Engineers wrote a widely read book, published in 1810, called *Essay on the Military Policy and Institutions of the British Empire*, in which he argued for the use of large armies in order to avoid the 'unnecessary inadequacy of force'.[137] The strategic need for offensive conjunct expeditions, nevertheless, remained a pressing but unattainable priority until about 1810, by which time a secure foothold for British troops had been established gradually in Portugal, solving the problem of creating a bridgehead on the continent of Europe.[138]

PART THREE

Defending the Realm

8

Political Instability and the Conduct of the War

1802–1812

The distractions of the Cabinet have at last burst into open and public violence. It will scarcely be credited by posterity, that two of His Majesty's principal Secretaries of State should so far forget the duty that they owed to their Sovereign and the example they ought to give to the country in obedience to its laws, to fight a duel. Yet the fact is actually so . . . [It is] most serious that His Majesty should have committed the affairs of State to persons whose intemperate passions were so little under the controul of reason.

– *Morning Chronicle*, Opposition newspaper,
22 September 1809[1]

I will engage that there is not, even amongst the lowest of the people, a single man now to be found in England, who would not laugh to scorn any attempt to make him believe that one of the <u>parties</u> is better than the other . . . it was the disclosures made from 1805 to 1809, inclusive, that procured us this great and permanent good.

– William Cobbett, *Political Register*,
23 March 1816[2]

British politics during the French Revolutionary War had been notable for political stability and Pitt as undisputed prime minister, but this situation changed dramatically during the Napoleonic War. Between 1801 and 1812 parties were gripped by rivalries and riven by competing ideologies, all observed by an increasingly cynical public.

As Cobbett forcefully reminded his readers, political scandals reached a climax between 1805 and 1809. These five years saw three changes of prime minister, four secretaries of state for war and five first lords of the Admiralty. Leading the country in a war that grew in scale and complexity every year became more difficult; nevertheless, as each successive government became weaker than the one that had preceded it, the unity of the Opposition also declined.[3] The result was a period seldom surpassed for violent debates in parliament, broken careers and the settling of scores; at the same time, Napoleon was at the height of his power on the Continent after he defeated Prussia in 1806 and Russia in 1807, then bringing Russia into formal alliance with France by the Treaty of Tilsit in July 1807.

The instability began in February 1801, when Pitt, who had been in power for seventeen years, unexpectedly resigned over giving Catholics a role in the army and the navy, in the wake of the Act of Union, an issue that was to split British politicians for years. Pitt wanted to relax the rules by which Catholics were excluded: the king would not have it.[4] He turned to a close friend of Pitt, Henry Addington, to form a government. When speaker of the House of Commons, Addington had been dignified and effective, with a modest demeanour that suited him to this role. As a debater, however, he was indecisive and had no talent. Addington was not well born: his father had been William Pitt the Elder's physician, a profession that at the time did not enjoy much respect, and as a result the new prime minister was known slightingly as 'the Doctor'. Pitt's powerful friends, such as Henry Dundas, secretary of state for war, would have nothing to do with him, and Lord Spencer left the Admiralty. Addington invited Whigs into his government. The appointment that he came most to regret was that of Lord St Vincent as first lord of the Admiralty: St Vincent immediately demanded an enquiry into the running of the navy, which became the Commission of Naval Enquiry and the start of a process that drove a wedge between Addington and his eminent predecessor.[5]

St Vincent brought much unpopularity on the administration, and it did not take him long to become a political liability.[6] He selected as Admiralty commissioners two naval officers who shared his views. Captain Thomas Troubridge, lifelong friend of Nelson, was brave, but had an extreme and even violent personality. Like his chief, he never bothered with the subtle arts of politics, nor was he wary of its dangers. He was lucky to escape disgrace when he sold, it was rumoured, £40,000 of stock in March 1803, just before the news of a press for seamen became public; as such announcements always preceded the resumption of war, the price of stocks would fall. Both Addington and his colleague on the Board, Captain John Markham, defended him in the Commons, and the matter was dropped.[7] Markham had far more talent, was quick-witted and hard-working, and a competent speaker in the House of Commons, and when the Whigs came back into power in 1806 he served again on the Admiralty Board.[8] The new men at the Admiralty were convinced that the administration of the navy was corrupt to the core, and they brought brusque and unceremonious methods of management to an organization more used to negotiation, respect for precedent, and the push and pull of politics. No one denied that the administration could be improved, but imposing harsh and radical change at such a time was ill-judged. Looking to save money immediately, the Board cancelled shipbuilding and timber contracts, and further savings were made in the royal dockyards, where seven officers and 1,400 workers were dismissed. The result was an immediate loss of morale and near-paralysis of the dockyards and victualling yards.

Nevertheless, Addington's government achieved more than was expected, in spite of the new prime minister's homely and amateurish style.* The first decision was to sue for peace with France, which was highly popular in an exhausted and disorderly Britain. Wheat prices, 170 shillings a quarter in early 1801, fell to 60 shillings on 1 October when the peace preliminaries were signed.[9] Pitt, out of office, commented to Henry Dundas: 'I find Windham (as might be expected) in Agonies, but the rest of the World, as far as one can judge, very much delighted with the peace.'[10]

The negotiations at Amiens were conducted by Lord Cornwallis, and the final treaty was signed on 25 March 1802. The result was a

---

* The principal memory of this modest man is Canning's celebrated jibe:

> Pitt is to Addington
> As London is to Paddington

one-sided French diplomatic triumph, reflecting France's greater negotiating persistence, and the British general's weakness in an unaccustomed
role. British interest in Continental Europe was perfunctory. The status quo – French domination of Europe and Britain's hold on India
and maritime supremacy – was confirmed. France retained the territories it had overrun – Venice, the Rhineland and other northern
conquests – but agreed to evacuate Rome and Naples. All overseas
French possessions were returned and, in spite of the misgivings of
several politicians about the safety of India, the Cape was returned to
the Dutch.* Britain held on to Trinidad, formerly Spanish, and Ceylon, captured from the Dutch. Malta was to be returned to the Knights
of St John and its neutrality guaranteed, though the British garrison
and navy did not leave.[11] (The usefulness of Malta was much debated
in Britain, but the weakness of the Knights, emphasized by Spain's
confiscation of the Order's property there, increased British reluctance
to fulfil the terms of the Treaty. In February 1803 even Russia, fearful
of too much French power in the Mediterranean, advised Britain not
to abandon the island.[12])

   None of these diplomatic wranglings discouraged the immediate
resumption of social and commercial contacts between Britain and
France. The landed elite, deprived of the Grand Tour for a decade,
flocked across the Channel.† Charles James Fox went to Paris partly
as a political gesture, while the engineer James Watt travelled there to
seek business. William Wordsworth and J. M. W. Turner also visited.[13]
Not surprisingly after so long a war, relations between the two governments were still very sensitive. Captain Philippe D'Auvergne, on
leave from his intelligence activities in the Channel Islands, travelled

---

* Dundas wrote to Addington just after the treaty was signed: '[French] views with
respect to India are impregnated with a deep-rooted, systematick hostility to our interests in India and the symptoms of that hostility must break out almost before the ink
is dry . . . I say nothing of the Cape of Good Hope. You know a little of my sentiments
on that subject as it relates to the security of our political and commercial interests in
India.' A note by Addington on the back of the letter reads: 'Sentiments much changed
on reflection.' That was a little too late, though the Cape was retaken in 1806 (19 Apr.
1802, DHC, Addington Papers, 152M/c1802/OP25).
† During the Peace of Amiens 2,598 people travelled across the Channel to France
and 3,055 from France to England, although servants were not accounted for in the
official records (Morieux, 'Travelling across the Channel', p. 222).

to Paris, still pursuing his claim to his French title and lands. He was recognized and arrested, and only just escaped to England with the help of the British plenipotentiary, Anthony Merry, who briefly held credentials in the French capital until September 1802.[14] Merry's place was taken by Lord Whitworth as ambassador extraordinary and plenipotentiary, who arrived in Paris in November. His task was to continue negotiations with the French government, though he was not confident of his dealings with Bonaparte, first consul since 1799, writing to Sir Arthur Paget, ambassador in Vienna, at the end of April 1803 of 'the untractable character with which we have to do, I am almost inclined to despair'.[15] Bonaparte was making a series of expansionist moves, despatching a substantial French fleet to San Domingo to wrest back the island from the regime established by former slaves that had taken it over in 1791. He acquired Louisiana from Spain in 1801, and annexed Elba and Parma, rendering him dominant in northern Italy. He ordered an armed intervention in neutral Switzerland in February 1803. Just before war resumed in May 1803, Napoleon sold Louisiana to the United States, bringing the French Treasury much needed money.

Not surprisingly, the British government's distrust of Bonaparte remained acute. In spite of concern over the cost of the war, ministers were cautious about disarming. The regular army was set at 132,000, more than double the peacetime strength of the army after the end of the previous war in 1783. The 81,000 left in Britain and a further 18,000 in Ireland, as well as 48,000 militia, was more than any force that the French might be able to land with the vessels at their disposal.[16] Eight months after the signing of the Amiens Treaty, in November 1802, the British Navy still had 32 ships of the line and 217 smaller ships in commission, manned by over 50,000 seamen and marines.[17] Neither the fleet nor the army was put on a peace-time footing in the West Indies. In April 1803, a year after the signing of the treaty, Lord Hobart, the secretary of state for war, informed the Admiralty in a 'most secret' memorandum that the officer commanding the Leeward Islands squadron should obstruct the arrival of any troop reinforcements 'at any of the French Islands', though in the event none came across the Atlantic.[18]

The other area of concern was Egypt, which the government still felt was vulnerable.* At the end of 1802 the Mediterranean squadron, commanded by Rear-Admiral Sir Richard Bickerton, still consisted of eleven 74-gun ships, three 64s and forty-five smaller warships, with standing orders to keep the activities of the French warships in Toulon under surveillance. In March 1803 Bickerton received secret orders from Lord Hobart, over two months before war was renewed: 'The desires of the Chief Consul of the French Republic are still directed to the possession of Egypt and he is not unlikely to avail himself of any favourable opportunity that may offer.' If any French ships put to sea, Bickerton was to shadow them.[19]

Yet such was the confusion in the navy brought about by St Vincent's ill-judged measures for reform in the civil administration of the navy that Bickerton's sizeable squadron at Malta lacked supplies and provisions. Food had become scarce by June 1802: supplies from Sicily or North Africa alone did not suffice. In September men started to sicken, and by November scurvy cases were increasing rapidly. Dissatisfied at the conditions and their continued absence from England, the crew of one ship in the squadron mutinied; two men were hanged. Bickerton's ships were in poor condition, needing major refits in British yards. In January 1803 Bickerton described his situation to the Admiralty secretary, Evan Nepean, as 'nearly destitute'. In March 1803, he reported 403 seamen sick and 53 dead. St Vincent had ordered the closure of the naval hospital at Malta: the plight of the squadron would have been worse if the army hospital had not been available to treat the seamen. Provisions and stores did not arrive from England until 24 April 1803, only just in time for Bickerton to put his ships on a war footing.[20]

In the spring of 1803, Addington began to reason that if a resumption of hostilities was inevitable, they had better come sooner rather than later, and war was declared by Britain on 18 May 1803. He

---

* With good reason. The activities of the French colonel Sébastiani were reported by Captain Ross Donelly from Alexandria to Rear-Admiral Bickerton: Sébastiani, 'there is not a doubt, is come as a spy upon our actions, and a fomenter of disturbances. In a conversation which he had with the Pacha of Alexandria, and where General Stuart continued to have his interpreter, he with great pomp assured the Pacha that the Chief Consul had sent him to inform the Turk that he would take care to have him "reinstated in his dominions in Egypt"' (18 Oct. 1802, Admiralty in-letters, TNA, ADM 1/406).

spoilt the moment with an uncharacteristic and misjudged act of flamboyance, by making a dramatic late entry into the House of Commons to make the announcement dressed in the colourful uniform of the Woodley Volunteer Cavalry. His enemies jeered; his friends were embarrassed.[21] Thomas Grenville reckoned that Addington feared Pitt more than he did the first consul: 'He has no other courage than in comparison of those two apprehensions, by both of which he is alternately & sometimes jointly so beset as to have ample occasion for keeping all his little wits about him'; Grenville characterized the administration as 'this water-gruel government'.[22]

News from all quarters reported a familiar pattern of British reverses. The invasion threat now came from the Channel ports where Napoleon was massing his troops and building launches to bring them over to southern England. In June a French army walked into Hanover. In the north-east of England resistance to impressment erupted: a press gang was thrown out of Sunderland by seamen and keelmen, and the coal trade was brought to a halt.[23] In Dublin in July 1803 a brief and uncoordinated uprising, the last flicker of the 1798 Rebellion, was led by Robert Emmet, who had been amassing an arsenal of weapons in Dublin. The former spy chief, William Wickham, now chief secretary of Ireland, was in England when the outbreak occurred and the available intelligence was misread by his clever but uncommunicative deputy, Alexander Marsden (the brother of William, second secretary of the Admiralty).* Wickham's experienced intelligence office in London, dismantled at the peace, was sorely missed, but luckily the disorganization of Emmet's small band of conspirators exceeded that of the Dublin government. An explosion of Emmet's weapons burnt down a house, a disaster that caused him to bring the uprising forward; but the rebels were instantly intercepted by a patrol of soldiers that happened to be passing.[24] A handful of

---

* See Chapter 5, p. 127. It was Alexander Marsden who negotiated the bribes for Irish MPs between 1798 and 1801 to secure their votes for Union with the rest of Great Britain, using £30,000 of secret service money. The price of each Unionist was well known to Marsden. William Wickham, chief secretary at the time of Emmet's uprising, wrote to Lord Cornwallis, the lord lieutenant and commander-in-chief, of these MPs: 'With your Excellency and with me they have an air of uncomfortable greatness, but with him they quite shrink away' (Wilkinson, 'Union', p. 251, quoting Lecky, *Ireland*, Vol. V, p. 306n).

people were killed, and Emmet was immediately captured and condemned to be hanged.* Despite his failure, the public perception was that Addington's government had been taken unawares. William Cobbett thundered in the *Weekly Political Register*: 'The government of Ireland was as completely surprised as a drunken sentinel, who [sleeps] upon his post, and who requires a good bastinado to bring him to his senses.'[25]

Nevertheless, in spite of domestic criticism, it was Addington who caught Bonaparte off his guard by the sudden declaration of war. Half the French warships were committed to St Dominique, and the restocking of their dockyards at home with timber and other naval stores had not been completed. By June fifty British ships of the line were blockading French ports from the Texel to Toulon.[26] Unsuspecting French merchant ships fell to British warships as rich prizes. The only retaliation open to the French government was the decree of 22 May 1803: all Englishmen in France were to be arrested.[27]

Many were prisoners for years. One such was Walter Boyd, a loans contractor, trapped with his family, who did not see England again until 1814.[28] Robert Edward Clifford, however, managed to escape. From a prominent Devon Catholic family, Clifford had trained as a soldier in France, specializing in cartography, but came back to England in 1792. During the peace he had returned to Paris, where he posed as a disinterested mathematician and scientist, but in reality was a spy. He heard much talk of the projected invasion of England and relayed his information to a family friend, Lieutenant-General John Graves Simcoe, who was close to the prime minister. When war was resumed, it was rumoured in London that Clifford and a companion had been apprehended in Calais and executed by the French authorities, and his supposed capture was deemed sufficiently important to be debated in parliament on 23 May 1803, with the galleries cleared. Charles James Fox intemperately described Napoleon as 'the most stupendous monument of human wisdom' and that 'the execution

---

* Immediately before he was taken out to be hanged, Robert Emmet wrote a magnanimous letter to Wickham, absolving the Dublin government of guilt for executing the leaders of the rebellion. It has been claimed that the letter prompted Wickham's resignation as Irish chief secretary, though it is more likely that Wickham, in ill-health, had determined on leaving office before the rebellion (Durey, *Wickham*, pp. 184–6).

of the unfortunate Gentlemen, the subject of the debates, ought in no shape to be attributed to a cruel or savage temper in the Chief Consul but to Necessity, state Necessity, the law of the Wise & the Good in Every Age'. A radical dissenting MP, William Smith, went further, applauding 'the vigilance of Bonaparte [who] had foiled the intentions of His Majesty's ministers and called for their impeachment, since it was they rather than Bonaparte who were "the murderers of the two gentlemen".'* In fact, Clifford had just managed to escape on a horse-ship, accompanied by a substantial box weighing two hundredweight, full of maps of France. Within a week, he was dining with the prime minister.[29]

While the French imprisoned British visitors, Frenchmen caught in Britain were merely expelled.[30] But, as the war gained momentum, Britain changed tack and held on to many thousands of captured French seamen and soldiers, in the interests of manpower attrition; the traditional exchanges of prisoners of war between the combatants became a thing of the past as each side tried to wear down the other. Standing up to Napoleonic France demanded a completely different type of warfare from that of 1793 to 1802. The pressure and immediacy of war did not quell the divisions in the navy, dominated by continuing, vituperative arguments between St Vincent in the House of Lords and Captain Sir Andrew Snape Hamond, the comptroller of the navy, in the Commons. George Rose thought that Hamond acted 'with coolness, discretion and judgement' under the first lord's attacks, but, in June, Hamond declared with impatience that 'it was impossible to go on as things now stood'; he later modified this outburst to more appropriate parliamentary language, with understated irony: 'the Navy Board was not thought so well of by the present Admiralty as by their predecessors.'[31] In the spring of 1803 St Vincent's own morale plunged when he suffered prolonged illness, possibly malaria, which he had first caught in the West Indies, and he twice offered

---

* The account of this otherwise unreported debate, including the astonishing language of Fox and his supporters, survives in the Simcoe Papers. Smith continued: 'What becomes of the Ministers' pretended wish for Peace! . . . strict justice [had been done] between the wretched system of the wretched Ministers, & the Great Man of the People of France, the Liberator of Europe' (Ravenhill, 'Clifford', p. 168, quoting 13 Nov., Letters 1802, Simcoe Papers, Archives of Ontario).

Addington his resignation. Even though attacks on the first lord in parliament were frequent, the prime minister refused, because there was no one obvious to replace him.[32]

When the war resumed in May 1803, fourteen months after peace had been signed, the British dockyards were in disarray. For the last year of the Addington government, the demoralized administrators struggled. Short of timber and other stores and at the mercy of irate contractors, the dockyard officers grappled unwillingly with the first lord's new rules.[33] When William Marsden, the secretary of the Admiralty, accompanied St Vincent and the Admiralty Board on an inspection of Deptford Dockyard, they were 'pelted with mud by the women and boys', angered by St Vincent's stringent economies.[34]

St Vincent had not got long to go.* On 12 March 1804, Charles Arbuthnot, now an undersecretary at the Foreign Office, reported to Arthur Paget, the ambassador in Vienna:

> The general feeling seems to be that they cannot stand long. One bad Omen against them is that their friends who continue to give good Ministerial Votes . . . join as readily as the rest in bursting into fits of laughter whenever the Doctor gets up to speak. He is in truth a lost Man in the House of Commons, & as contempt is the worst evil that can befal[l] a Man, I sh[oul]d think it scarcely possible that a poor wretch so universally despised & laught at can continue much longer . . .[35]

Pitt took advantage of Addington's weakness and came out in open opposition in the Commons, choosing to attack over naval administration, since there was clearly a gulf between the prime minister and his first lord. Pitt took advice on naval matters from a wide spectrum of politicians, including Lord Camden, Charles Long and William Wilberforce; and from two naval officers, Admiral Sir Charles Middleton, the former comptroller of the navy and member of the Board of Admiralty, and Captain Sir Home Popham – and it was Popham who advised him to question St Vincent's blockade strategy, by

---

* As an indication of how much bad feeling St Vincent had stirred up in the navy, one naval officer wrote to Nelson six months later: 'The old Jesuit and his colleague Troubridge have been making a grand tour of the island . . . never was people so Cordially disliked by all kinds of people, their names are execrated by all parties' (Thomas Bowen to Nelson, 24 Sept. 1804, NMM, CRK/2/105).

advocating a concentration of effort on the building of gunboats for defence. This was risky, for Popham had misjudged general naval sentiment. Those naval officers in parliament who were not in favour of more gunboats were swayed by a forceful speech by Admiral Sir Edward Pellew, who condemned gunboats as 'the most contemptible force that can be employed'.* Pitt lost the motion, but it weakened Addington, and the government fell a month later on the question of the Army Estimates.[36]

Pitt returned to form another government in May 1804, though his political authority was a shadow of what it had once been, and from the start he and his ministers were under constant hostile attack from the Opposition, with Grey and Sheridan in the van.[37] Senior personnel changed again at the top of the Admiralty. Lord Grenville, now at some distance from Pitt, declined to join the administration. Henry Dundas, who had been ennobled in 1802 as Lord Melville, took over as first lord, immediately reversing St Vincent's policies. Stores contracts were quickly renewed; warships were sent to merchant yards for repair. Not least, Melville had to restore the loss of trust within the service. He wrote to Admiral Colpoys not long after he had taken over: 'There is not a day passes on which I do not receive twenty letters, claiming favour from me, because the writers have been ill used by Lord St Vincent ... and all I can with propriety do ... is deal with the Distribution of Naval Favours with as much fairness and impartiality as I possibly can.'[38]

To get more ships to sea, Melville took measures every bit as radical as St Vincent's, but in direct opposition to them, in particular employing far more contractors.[39] He also reorganized the ships on station and redistributed the inadequate number of ships available to him, with the aid of his knowledgeable private secretary William Budge. He kept most of the seventy ships of the line blockading the French ports, since Napoleon's army of invasion was now at its most threatening (see Chapter 9).† Melville ordered Admiral Cornwallis off Brest

---

* Between the general elections of 1802 and 1806, 36 naval officers held seats in parliament. MPs who had held regular army commissions numbered 125, but of those 71 were on half-pay or retired (Thorne, *History of Parliament*, Vol. I, pp. 310, 314).

† The first consul was crowned emperor on 2 Dec. 1804, though the British government never recognized this transition, and continued to call him Bonaparte or

to take no risks with his ships in the winter gales. The most controversial event of Melville's time as first lord was the order to seize the silver-laden Spanish frigates as they approached Cádiz from Mexico, even though Spain and Britain were not at war. This cabinet decision was unquestionably illegal, but it was decided on the basis of intelligence that Spain intended to declare war once the silver was safely in port.* Unfortunately, only frigates were sent to intercept the Spanish ships, and honour therefore demanded that the Spanish commander should fight back, since he was faced by ships of near-equal size. One of the Spanish ships blew up, killing almost all the crew, as well as the families of Spanish officers returning home to Spain.[40] Although war with Spain was virtually inevitable, and Britain was therefore extremely vulnerable at this point in the war, the interception of the Spanish treasure ships was widely unpopular. Melville was extremely distressed by the episode, for which he was ultimately responsible.[41]

He was, however, soon to resign, undone by domestic politics. Doubt was thrown on his integrity, when treasurer of the navy in the 1780s, by the publication of the *Tenth Report* of the Commission of Naval Enquiry in February 1805.[42] The report focused on the whereabouts of monies that should have been kept at the Bank of England but that had, in fact, been lodged in Coutts Bank by the paymaster of the navy, Alexander Trotter, who acted for the treasurer of the navy by virtue of a power of attorney. Suspicions were raised when both Melville and Trotter refused to answer some of the commission's questions. The practice of keeping money in a private account had been specifically prohibited in 1782, and had ceased in 1802.† The central issue was whether Melville knew of Trotter's activities in the 1780s and 1790s, or whether Melville had even profited from the

---

Buonaparte. In this book, however, he will henceforth be referred to as Napoleon or the emperor.

* For the complex world of specie and its transport across the Atlantic see Chapter 13.
† Charles Bragge Bathurst, treasurer of the navy 1801–3, was examined during the impeachment of Melville on 8 May 1806: according to his evidence, he gave orders 'during the course of the summer of 1802' to stop the practice of keeping small sums in Coutts or in any other private bank (Anon., *The Trial by Impeachment of Henry, Lord Viscount Melville* . . . (1806), p. 149).

arrangement. At the very least, he had been foolish in not keeping a proper check on a subordinate.*

The *Tenth Report* came to be debated in parliament on 8 April 1805, in an atmosphere of high political excitement, during a motion of censure brought by the brewer MP Samuel Whitbread. Opinions were divided: although many speakers saw the issue as important enough to be considered beyond party divisions, the debate was intense and virulent, for Melville had many enemies. Canning reminded the House that it was Melville who in 1795 had defended General Grey and Admiral Jervis after they had been brought before the House for their handling of prize money in the West Indies, and witheringly commented on the 'violence and invective' of a Whig attacker: 'I little expected that, in his present defenceless state, attempts to hunt him down would have been made by the kindred of Mr Charles Grey and the friends of Sir John Jervis.'[43] It was not an atmosphere in which sober judgement stood much chance.

The debate seemed to be going Melville's way, until late at night William Wilberforce spoke: he later recalled that when he rose to speak Pitt turned round from the front bench and looked at him: 'It required no little effort to resist the fascination of that penetrating eye.' But Wilberforce was not cowed and strongly condemned Melville, concluding, 'I really cannot find language sufficiently strong to express my utter detestation of such conduct.'[44] It was a decisive intervention, swaying perhaps, as some thought, as many as forty votes against Melville. The result of the debate was a tie, 216 votes to each side, thus ensuring that the speaker had to vote. Charles Abbot, 'white as a sheet' and after some minutes, cast in favour of the motion. The House erupted into 'huzzas and shouts' from the Opposition. Pitt was in any case not well, and was visibly shaken: according to one observer, he was brought to tears.[45] Melville's reputation was ruined, and he resigned from the government and from the Privy Council, his active political career over. He avoided a guilty verdict when the issue

---

* Dundas's slack superintendence of the staff of the Navy Pay Office was demonstrated by Adam Jellicoe, Trotter's deputy, who had also used naval money for a private investment. Dundas had spotted the discrepancy in the accounts, but had done nothing about it and Jellicoe continued in office. Jellicoe later committed suicide (Ehrman, *Younger Pitt*, Vol. III, 755n).

came before the Lords in a seventeen-day impeachment trial in April 1806: it was a spectacular theatrical event held in Westminster Hall that banished all thoughts of the war for the duration of its proceedings.*

But the war continued to be the most pressing issue and the swift appointment of a new first lord of the Admiralty was necessary. Pitt offered it to the home secretary, Robert Banks Jenkinson, Lord Hawkesbury, later to become the prime minister as Lord Liverpool, who thought it would be promotion: he wrote to his father, old Lord Liverpool: 'It is certainly the Office next to that of prime minister of the most Importance and of the Greatest Power and Responsibility.' But he refused it, pleading lack of seniority and of confidence that he would be able to calm 'that Party Spirit which has of late been spreading itself very widely in the ... Navy'.[46] No politicians or serving admirals seemed up to the job. The prime minister surprised friends and critics alike by appointing the veteran Admiral Sir Charles Middleton, who agreed to serve provided he gained a peerage: he became Lord Barham. He had, in any case, been advising Melville and his assumption of office was achieved with the minimum of fuss. The new second secretary to the Admiralty Board, John Barrow, later wrote that usually a newly appointed first lord would

> find some fault in the arrangements made by his predecessor, if it be only to change them, in order to show his own superior discerning. Lord Barham ... was satisfied for things to go on in their usual course, to remain quiet in his own room ... In fact, he never attended the Board; but when any doubtful question arose, one of the Lords or the Secretaries took his decision on it in his own room.[47]

This degree of delegation worked well, not least because of the experience of the junior lords of the Admiralty. Sir Philip Stephens, first

---

* Scaffolding and furnishings were provided by the unreformed Office of Works. The total cost was £8,188, of which the Office of Works spent £6,695. One spectator, Lord Campbell, commented: 'I never knew what earthly magnificence was till yesterday when I was present at Lord Melville's trial. Ye Gods! the Peeresses' box! A glory seemed to play round their countenances, and to shoot in vivid flashes to the extremities of the Hall' (Crook and Port, *King's Works*, p. 501).

appointed second secretary of the Board as early as 1759, and Sir Evan Nepean, who succeeded to the Board in September 1804 after his brief period of office in Ireland, had between them well over fifty years experience of attending the Board as secretary.* With Barham, they saw the Admiralty through the complex strategic moves of 1805.

In August, Pitt signed the Third Coalition with Austria and Russia, and the same month saw the arrival of Nelson in England after chasing the combined French and Spanish fleets to the West Indies and back. He put back to sea with refreshed ships, hoisting his flag on 14 September and by the end of the month had taken command of Collingwood's fleet, which was blockading the French and Spanish in Cádiz Harbour. With superior ships and sea-hardened crews, bolstered by leadership which stemmed from well-justified confidence, Nelson earned the overwhelming victory at Trafalgar on 21 October. He had promised Pitt the annihilation of the enemy fleet and he delivered it, though at the cost of his own life. News of the victory reached London in the early hours of 6 November. Three days later an ailing William Pitt experienced a last flash of popularity when he attended the Lord Mayor's Banquet. His carriage was hauled along by excited, cheering crowds. At the banquet he was hailed as 'the Saviour of Europe'. His speech was very short: 'I return you many thanks for the honour you have done me; but Europe is not to be saved by any single man. England has saved herself by her exertions, and will, I trust, save Europe by her example.' He was a very sick man, with what was probably a peptic ulceration of the stomach.[48] It was the last time that he spoke in public.[49]

Yet French control of the Continent had not been weakened by the great triumph at sea. A day before Trafalgar, one Austrian army was defeated at Ulm by the French and another ten days later at Caldiero in Italy. The rest of Pitt's coalition strategy failed: two amphibious expeditions that landed on the Continent, at Naples and in north

---

* Alexander Davison wrote to Nelson on 7 Jan. 1805: 'Nepean arrived yesterday from Ireland to the great joy of Lord Melville and will instantly take his Seat at the Admiralty Board. He will relieve the First Lord of much Anxiety and Trouble, as he will take the Labouring Oar: the principal business will now all be done by him' (NMM, CRK/3/159). By this time Stephens was eighty-two, and seen by some as past his best.

Germany, were completely ineffectual. Pitt tried to regain his health by going to Bath to drink the waters. Then, on 29 December 1805, came devastating news: a combined Russian–Austrian army had been utterly defeated by an outnumbered Napoleon at Austerlitz in his most brilliant victory yet. The result was that Austria was driven out of the war (although Russia continued its alliance with Britain until 1807). It was the end of the Third Coalition, and it struck a bitter blow to the depressed and sickly Pitt, now hardly able to eat.* Wilberforce was convinced that the news of this defeat physically affected the prime minister, already worn out and emaciated. Less than a month later, on 23 January 1806, Pitt was dead. His surgeon said later 'that Pitt died of <u>old age</u> at forty-six, as much as if he had been ninety'.[50]

Pitt's illnesses were well known, but he had always recovered. Those close to him were shocked. Pitt's cousin Lord Grenville, with whom there had been so many arguments, in 'an agony of tears' retired to his country seat at Dropmore for several days, though this retreat may also have had an element of political calculation. Fox, Grey and Sheridan withdrew a planned censure motion in the Commons and substituted a debate on 'the state of the nation'.[51] The political response that followed was complex. A private motion describing Pitt as 'an excellent statesman' was carried by 258 to 89. It was opposed by the ever unpredictable William Windham, former member of Pitt's cabinet, still smarting from the rejection of his ideas for attacking the Vendée in the early years of the previous war, who had criticized Pitt's handling of the French Revolutionary War and described Trafalgar as a defeat. With a greater show of unanimity, the House voted by a large majority the enormous sum of £40,000 to pay off Pitt's debts. Not the least of Pitt's exceptional qualities was his complete lack of interest in profiting from office. Even so, the parliamentary grant was sufficient only because friends chose not to reimburse themselves for their loans to him. Pitt's coffin lay in state in the Painted Chamber of the House of Lords, viewed 'by a vast concourse' of people. His

---

* It was at this point that Lord Mornington returned to England after his expansion of British power in India. His brother Arthur Wellesley warned him in a letter of 21 Dec. 1805 that no one was likely to take any notice of him: 'the public mind cannot be brought to attend to an Indian subject' (Davies, *Wellington's Wars*, p. 77, quoting Wellington's *Supplementary Despatches*, Vol. IV, pp. 533–41).

funeral at St Paul's on 22 February 1806 took place only six weeks after the great procession and ceremony for Nelson. Pitt's obsequies were more modest, though much the same music was sung and played in the two services. Nevertheless, three royal dukes attended, with the duke of York 'much affected'.[52]

Without Pitt's leadership, his ministry dissolved. His strong lieutenants of the 1790s were not only unavailable but had contributed to his political weakness: Melville was disgraced and Grenville had been estranged. After the usual period of negotiation, it was Grenville who now formed a new government on 10 February 1806, in alliance with the leading Whig Charles James Fox, who became foreign secretary. Since 1804 Grenville had wanted a ministry that would 'comprehend all the talents and character' in public life; and, although the term 'Ministry of All the Talents' was used ironically by opponents, it is nonetheless the term by which it has become generally known. Windham in particular believed that the new administration would be a fresh and less party-political government committed to reform, but it turned out to be the usual mixture of alliances and compromises. Indeed, it was a strange mixture of politicians altogether. Perhaps the most curious was the inclusion of the lord chief justice, Lord Ellenborough. Putting the most senior criminal judge in the cabinet was controversial, but it was part of the price of Lord Sidmouth's (as Addington now became) support.[53] The Foxite element in the new administration wanted reform and cost-cutting, as did Grenville, but he was politically weakened by the sinecures that were held by his family: it was hardly a good platform from which to launch his reforming programme.*

Throughout the Talents' brief period of office, the country was relieved of any threat of invasion by Napoleon, which had been looming for two years after the Peace of Amiens. In late August 1805 he

---

* Grenville had hesitated about accepting the role of prime minister and the post of first lord of the Treasury as he would be unable, because of conflict of interest, to draw his income from his long-held sinecure of auditor of the Exchequer. In the event Fox introduced a bill that put the income of the auditorship in trust as long as Grenville was prime minister (Jupp, *Grenville*, pp. 346–7; Harvey, 'Ministry of All the Talents', p. 623).

had led his armies away from the Channel ports and marched to central Europe, where he consolidated French power. He dominated central Germany, securing the dissolution of the Holy Roman Empire in August 1806, and was victorious over Prussia by the victories of Jena and Auerstädt in October 1806. In June the next year Russia was beaten at the Battle of Friedland and neutralized by the Treaty of Tilsit. Charles James Fox, now foreign secretary, tried to make peace with France, but his convictions about the greatness of Napoleon were shaken by negotiations with a militarily dominant emperor. It is difficult to discern a coherent strategy. Fox and Windham, the latter now secretary of state for war, avoided Pitt's policy of coalitions with the central European powers, and left them to their fate.[54] Instead, Windham enthusiastically embarked upon expeditions in the Mediterranean, in contradiction to all his earlier ideas, overwhelming more cautious ministers. Only Admiral Collingwood, left without interference, maintained a defensive position in the Western Mediterranean, keeping trade flowing and the French Fleet confined in Toulon.

The new government started cheerfully enough. Four days after the newly appointed first lord of the Admiralty, Charles Grey, arrived in his office, news of Sir John Duckworth's victory at San Domingo reached London: five French ships of the line had been captured or destroyed.* The secretary to the Board, William Marsden, recorded that 'It has put everyone (out and in), as you may suppose, in high spirits, and it is really a famous event.'† In January 1806 troops under Sir David Baird retook the Cape from the Dutch. The chief difficulty

---

* Grey became Lord Howick in Apr. 1806, when his father was promoted to an earldom.

† Marsden, however, was already beginning to feel the bureaucratic strain. The news of the victory came in the middle of the night. 'I had a terrible day of it – Was knocked up at three o'clock in the morning, when I had got about an hour-and-a-half's sleep, called up Mr Grey at four, having by that time arranged and docketed my papers, and drawn out a bulletin. I then worked till seven, and lay down in hopes of getting a little sleep, – but it would not do; so I returned to the office, and worked there till Mr Grey's dinner was ready.' Marsden tried again to resign when Grenville succeeded Howick, but Grenville would not let him go, as Marsden recalled, 'on grounds very flattering to me personally', but his health 'continu[ed] to suffer from the close confinement of office' (Marsden, Brief Memoir, pp. 126fn., 128–9; Rodger, Command of the Ocean, p. 483).

was not overcoming the defence, but in landing from the boats through the surf: forty-one soldiers from the 93rd Highland Regiment were drowned.[55] But these successes proved to be a false dawn. Three inept military initiatives followed and failed one by one. Duckworth was sent to the Dardanelles with a fleet to put pressure on the Turks in order to aid Russia. He passed the Dardanelles in mid February 1807, but was not the most subtle or diplomatic admiral, and failed to persuade the Turks. He should have had more help from Charles Arbuthnot, who by this time was ambassador at Constantinople; but Arbuthnot was tired, depressed and inactive. In early March the British Fleet had to withdraw under fire: Turkish guns and the swift current through the Narrows sent Duckworth away with nothing except casualties and damage to his ships.[56] A small expedition landed in Egypt in March 1807, the purpose of which was to forestall an unlikely French invasion, but it was twice defeated and ordered home by the next government.[57]

The third in this trio of misfortunes was an expedition foisted on the government by the extraordinary Sir Home Popham, who in early 1806 sailed from the Cape of Good Hope across the southern Atlantic to the River Plate, with the intention of occupying enemy Spanish territory. The idea for a daring initiative of this nature had been around for some years, but Popham was acting without direct orders.[58]

At first, surprise overwhelmed the Spanish, and Buenos Aires was captured in June 1806 and Montevideo in February 1807. When the news reached England, merchants hastened to fill ships with goods to trade with the newly acquired territory. However, military failure soon overtook the British expedition. Both cities were recaptured, and the attempt to retake Buenos Aires was thwarted by local Spanish volunteers, who compelled the surrender of Lieutenant-General John Whitelocke and his force of over 6,000 troops and seamen in July 1807. On the walls at Buenos Aires angry and mortified British soldiers scribbled: 'General Whitelocke is a coward, a traitor or both.' One of the disgusted officers wrote:

> History will record, and posterity with difficulty will believe, that such an army as ours capitulated with the rabble of a South American town,

and sold the interests of the country, and gave up the hard-earned
conquests of their brother soldiers, in order to secure a retreat which it
was most amply in their power to have made at their good pleasure . . .
Would to God the waters of Oblivion were as near at hand as are those
of La Plata![59]

The army and the public (particularly the merchants, many of whom
were ruined) demanded a scapegoat. Whitelocke was fortunate to be
merely 'cashiered, and declared totally unfit, and unworthy to serve
His Majesty in any military capacity whatever', as the sentence of the
court martial expressed it.[60] Many thought that his ineptitude was on
a par with that of Admiral Byng, who had been shot for cowardice in
1757. Popham, who was also court-martialled, claimed that he had
acted upon a verbal agreement that he had had with Pitt, who by then
had died; fortunately for Popham, the news of the military disaster
arrived only after he had got away with a censure.*

Windham's unsuccessful role in the conduct of the war overseas
was matched at home by his maverick treatment of all sections of the
army, in which he was influenced by the journalist William Cobbett.
In May 1806, with his first Army Estimates, Windham announced
reductions in the cavalry, Foot Guards and the artillery Royal Wag-
gon Train, reckoning to save £363,000 a year from these measures.[61]
In order to make the service more appealing and to boost regular
army recruitment, he limited the time that a man should serve in the
army to seven years, against the advice of the inspector general of
recruiting. Since 1802 legislation had prohibited militiamen joining
the regular army, due to opposition from the lords lieutenant and the
officers commanding the militia.[62] In order to encourage further army
enlistment, Windham suspended the militia ballot for two years, but
the measure failed. Lord Grenville complained privately to Charles
Abbot of 'Windham's utter unacquaintance with militia and county
affairs'.[63] As the legislation went through parliament, the king grum-
bled to Windham, as usual in the third person, that 'he has reluctantly

---

* Lord Melville admitted in Popham's court martial that there had been some discussion about a South American expedition. When asked whether Popham had been
appointed to any command authorizing him to attack South America, Melville replied,
'Certainly not' (Lowry, 'Popham', pp. 57–8).

acquiesced in the Change of a System with which He was Himself perfectly satisfied.'[64] The new measure made no difference to army recruiting and saved hardly any money: the army cost £18,581,000 in 1805 and £18,507,000 in 1806.[65]

Windham's policies towards the volunteers were both doctrinaire and counter-productive. He had always distrusted them, particularly fearing the democratic propensities of the urban regiments.* Yet he was the colonel of the Norfolk 4th Battalion, one of the most inefficient units in the country, which gave him, as Spencer Perceval pointed out cuttingly in debate, particular authority to denounce the volunteers as a useless extravagance.[66] As the volunteers were exempt from the militia ballot, Windham saw them as a hindrance to militia recruitment: in the Commons he referred sarcastically to the volunteers as 'painted cherries which none but simple birds would take for real fruit'.[67] Over 11,000 volunteers resigned immediately: the force that Addington and Pitt had fostered, and that the duke of York had made reasonably efficient, was virtually destroyed.[68] The secretary of state for war was not to be reasoned with. Lord Grenville, the prime minister, who was a lieutenant-colonel in the Buckinghamshire Yeomanry, asked Windham to soften his outspokenness to allay the fears of his many critics, to which Windham replied, 'I should only disgrace myself, without satisfying them.' Windham was in office for only just over a year but the confusion that ensued as a result of his decisions lasted until the following Tory ministry. Wilberforce, acutely, recorded in a notebook that 'Windham is a most wretched man of business, no precision or knowledge of details, even in his own measures.'[69]

It was, however, the Ministry of All the Talents that made the first really significant move in economic warfare, which had started almost immediately after the Peace of Amiens, when the French Army occupied Hanover in June 1803. The emperor had tried to exclude British trade from the Elbe, Weser and Ems, and prohibited not only imported British manufactured goods but also any from British colonies. In May

---

* Not without reason, for there are many examples of lack of discipline. For instance, in Brixham in Devon in 1801, the officers of the local volunteers organized disorder over high food prices (see Chapter 6). When war resumed, a press gang in Chester seized a member of the Royal Chester Volunteers for the navy: his fellow soldiers went after them to rescue him (Emsley, 'Volunteers', p. 44).

1806, frustrated after its failed peace moves, the government instituted what became known as the 'Fox Blockade', named after the foreign secretary, Charles James Fox. An order-in-council was issued that declared all Continental ports between the Elbe and Brest to be under a state of blockade, and that ships could trade with ports beyond this area only if they had loaded their cargoes in ports of countries friendly to Britain.[70] This 'paper' blockade did not conform to international agreements, by which a particular port had to be watched closely and continually by warships before it could be said to be in a state of blockade. The declaration of such a large area of blockade was justified, at least in British eyes, and it allowed warships to stop any neutral vessels in order to inspect documents and cargoes. Britain could hardly keep a squadron of large warships off every French port, but they did deploy large numbers of recently built small warships, which were kept at sea for long periods by improved victualling arrangements. The watch on the French and other Continental ports under their dominance was maintained by British frigates and the smaller brig-sloops, and captures were mostly of merchant ships.

Napoleon retaliated after his victory at Jena in October 1806. In November, the Berlin Decrees were issued by France. The preamble referred aggressively to the 'barbarian' British orders-in-council of May, and the text declared that all trade and correspondence by European countries, even neutral ones, with the British Isles was forbidden and any British goods being traded on the Continent were to be seized. Neutral ships that called in to Britain on the way to a French port were to depart without discharging any cargo; if the ship's master tried to conceal that he had done so, both the ship and the master would be seized.[71] The Continental blockade was thus started, economic warfare which was to endanger British trade and which was to last until Napoleon's downfall.[72]

In September 1806 Charles Grey, now Lord Howick, was appointed foreign secretary on the death of Charles James Fox, and Tom Grenville, who had been on the margins of power for many years, was made first lord of the Admiralty. A rich bachelor and bibliophile, mild and amiable, popular where his brothers were not, he nevertheless shared the Grenville family's characteristic coldness of manner, very marked when he spoke publicly. One young Whig, Francis Horner, noted his 'indiscriminate emphasis ... comes to have no more effect in one respect, than no emphasis at all ... at the same time ... your attention is fretted & worried by ... misplaced phrases & emphasis upon nothings'.[73] To Lord Grenville's disappointment, his brother failed to establish himself as leader of the government in the Commons. Tom Grenville felt that his close friend Lord Spencer would do better at the Admiralty if Spencer resumed his old post. 'I feel much disposed to doubt,' he wrote to his other brother, the marquis of Buckingham, 'whether I can be of any good service by entering into this <u>sea</u> of troubles which will engross all my time & annihilate me for the H of Commons.'[74]

Tom Grenville served as first lord for only twenty-one weeks. He never again sought high office, and soon after he left the Admiralty he even tried to give up his parliamentary seat. In spite of this diffidence, he chose his Board sensibly and dealt with some difficult senior appointments for admirals, at a time when the available talent was thin. He worked hard, six days a week, with office hours between ten and six in the evening.* With his private secretary, Edward Golding, he grappled conscientiously with the problem that beset every first lord of the Admiralty in these years: in spite of the increased number of ships in commission, the number of applications for promotions and posts vastly exceeded the numbers available. By this time, the attractions of the naval service had produced an upsurge in young officers, fostered by the practice during the previous war of captains making their own choice of the number of midshipmen they took to sea. The mechanics of appointing this surfeit of officers had also become absurdly over-centralized and even more oppressive than in the time of Lord Howe in the 1780s, when he had complained about it in parliament.

During his brief tenure, Tom Grenville received a daily average of twenty-one letters from correspondents outside government: over 60 per cent were applications for posts, ashore or afloat, in the navy. Not only had he to appoint sea officers, but marine officers, chaplains, pursers, surgeons, dockyard officers, Fencibles, lieutenants to signal

---

* Betsy Fremantle recorded similar working hours for her husband, Captain Thomas Fremantle, whom Grenville appointed to the Admiralty Board in Oct. 1806. The Fremantles moved into their Admiralty quarters, furnished with Fremantle's shipboard furniture, but had to move out after only three months when the Talents' ministry fell, to her great regret (Fremantle, *Wynne Diaries*, pp. 478–81).

stations. Applications were backed by senior admirals, MPs, old aristocracy, even the archbishop of Canterbury, but were mostly from the applicants themselves. Some were heart-rending, some angry and desperate, others cynical and political. Many clearly showed how much talent and experience was being wasted. He managed to appoint unemployed officers to newly commissioned warships: some ships were entirely officered by those who had hitherto been on half-pay.[75] In 116 working days at the Admiralty, he made 889 appointments, an average of just under eight per day.[76]

Away from this never-ending office task, Tom Grenville thought differently from his cabinet colleagues and made some shrewd strategic decisions. In late 1806 he decided to reduce the squadron blockading Rochefort to frigates only, the beginning of a shift of ships and men away from the Channel Fleet.[77] Difficulties with the United States, which was sheltering French warships in the Chesapeake Bay, were beginning to emerge. Grenville chose not to augment naval forces in Bermuda, because he had intelligence of the reported wretched condition of the French ships; as he wrote to his brother, 'besides which the French credit is so low that they can get no money to pay for the workmen, & their crews daily deserting'.

What he did do was to prepare suitable ships for operations in the Baltic, though, as he remarked to Buckingham as late as March 1807, 'My colleagues cannot be worked up with any Baltick interest in the present moment, tho' I think we should be striving there.'[78] In December 1806 he sent Henry Peake, the junior surveyor, together with the master shipwrights of Woolwich and Plymouth, 'to survey ships of war of 50 guns & upwards in the several Ports, to see how soon we can patch up an additional fleet of 10 or 12 sail for the Baltick in the spring'.[79] The day he left office, on 1 April 1807, he wrote to the marquis of Buckingham:

> I am lingering here in hourly expectation of my release . . . There is not an enemy ship at sea, & I may boast of having taken proper steps for an immediate supply of stores of hemp, etc., for 3 years, & I have added 300 artificers to the Dockyards, so that my account is reputably closed. Fremantle will have told you that I have also the credit in abstaining from making promotions for rank at the charge of the Board. I shall now breathe freely again.

Also on his last day in office he ordered sixteen smaller ships of the line, twelve of which were already commissioned, to assemble at Yarmouth.[80] These ships would form the core of the fleet used in the successful operation against Copenhagen. It did not take place until five months after he had left office, so Tom Grenville failed to receive recognition for the farseeing preparations that he had made.

Tom Grenville aside, the Talents' prosecution of the war had little to commend it. Lord Grenville confessed to his brother Buckingham when tired and depressed at the end of his administration, 'I want one great and essential quality for my station . . . I am not competent to the management of men. I never was so naturally, and toil and anxiety more and more unfit me for it.'[81] Divided and uncoordinated, the Talents fell in early 1807. Lord Grenville had again revived Pitt's 1801 initiative to appease Catholics and dissenters by enabling them to join the services. Again the king would not have it, and the demoralized government resigned.

The Tories in the new administration under the duke of Portland were more competent at running the war, but there were inherent flaws in this government, too. Portland was approaching seventy, suffering from gout and from a kidney stone, and had always been averse to speaking in public. Nor was he in control of his cabinet. The acrimonious atmosphere was worsened by the active intervention in affairs by the prince of Wales, who stepped into the vacuum caused by the declining mental capacity of the old king. Nevertheless, with Canning as foreign secretary, Castlereagh as secretary of state for war and Mulgrave at the Admiralty, it was a stronger team than the Talents. At the Admiralty, William Marsden managed at last to retire, succeeded by William Wellesley-Pole, brother of Lord Mornington and of Arthur Wellesley, as a fully political first secretary.*

*

* Mulgrave sent for the second secretary, John Barrow, to tell him of Wellesley-Pole's appointment over him. Barrow was pleased rather than disappointed: '[Wellesley-Pole] is an agreeable acquaintance, of great talent for business, and of an active turn of mind, and I am rejoiced in the prospect of having such a coadjutor' (Barrow, *Autobiography*, p. 299). Pole was a good administrator, but, as his subsequent career was to show, no leader.

This was ever a war of resources. In contrast to the French Revolutionary War, the army was given time to train from 1803 (at the same time it was on invasion duties) when war was resumed. There was a strong cadre of trained and disciplined troops around which to build an army. Castlereagh, as secretary of state for war, showed an immense capacity for concentration and for absorbing detail in this task. He immediately strengthened the volunteers, restoring their inspecting officers, and granted a bounty to militiamen if they would join the regular army. By using the bounty, nearly 28,000 men who were coming to the end of their five years' militia service were rapidly enlisted. Castlereagh restored the militia ballot and quickly brought it up to strength; he also created the local militia, which took over from the volunteers, which were slowly run down. His reforms were implemented swiftly, for soldiers were soon to be needed for overseas service.[82]

The whole nature of the war in northern Europe was changing. Napoleon, at the apogee of his power after signing the Treaty of Tilsit with Russia, could now turn his attention to overcoming Britain. He wrote to his minister of marine, Decrès, in July 1807: 'The Continental war is over. Energies must be turned towards the navy.'[83] He immediately took steps to try to secure the Danish and Portuguese fleets. The British, however, anticipated these moves remarkably quickly. On 14 July, Lord Mulgrave proposed to the cabinet that a large naval force should be sent to Copenhagen to prevent the seizure of Danish ships, to which Castlereagh suggested the addition of troops. British troops under General Lord Cathcart were already at Stralsund, the last Swedish territory on the southern shore of the Baltic: they had arrived on 8 July, ready to join Swedish and Prussian forces to advance south.[84] As we saw in Chapter 7, these forces came together quickly, and the bombardment of Copenhagen and the seizure of the Danish Fleet followed in early September. The misgivings over the attack on a neutral nation were debated in parliament, with William Wilberforce this time placing his moral authority behind the government.[85] Strategically it relieved pressure on Britain; Lord Hawkesbury, by then home secretary, wrote optimistically to the duke of Richmond: 'our left flank is now set completely at liberty.'[86]

But the government was less than successful in its attempt to follow up this victory. It ordered an expedition of 10,000 troops to Sweden to help King Gustavus against the newly hostile Russia. The army commander was to be Sir John Moore, an outspoken, talented soldier with firm Whig proclivities, though confirmed in his appointment by Castlereagh and the Tory cabinet. Escorted by twelve ships of the line under Admiral Sir James Saumarez, the expedition reached Gothenburg on 17 May 1808. Moore described his orders as 'inexplicit and contradictory'. Accounts of the prolonged negotiations between Moore and the Swedes read like a Whitehall farce. The 'mad' King Gustavus, distracted by the Russian threat to Finland, would not allow the British troops to land, and they languished for six weeks in the transports at anchor outside Gothenburg. Finally, Gustavus lost all patience with the negotiations and imprisoned Moore, who escaped in the disguise of a peasant, arriving back on board the flagship in the midst of a ball Admiral Saumarez was giving for the ladies of Gothenburg. Humiliated, Moore immediately took his forces back to England.

Almost at the same time, conflict spread to the south of Europe. In late November 1807 a French army under General Andoche Junot invaded Portugal. The Portuguese prince regent kept his options open until the last minute, but finally decided to flee to Brazil, escorted by British warships under the command of Admiral Sir Sidney Smith. His squadron sailed from Lisbon on 29 November, together with most of the Portuguese Fleet, the contents of the Treasury, the bureaucratic infrastructure of the Portuguese state and as many as 15,000 individuals. A day later, 1,500 French troops, after an immense forced march, entered Lisbon. In the words of their commander, General Junot, the soldiers were 'in bad order and worn out with fatigue'.[87] It was a graphic illustration of the speed and carrying capacity of ships, compared with the slowness and effort required for the movement of troops by land.

The vigour of the British, for which Canning as foreign secretary can take much credit, took Napoleon by surprise. It spoilt the emperor's master plan of wresting the maritime initiative from Britain and, at the same time, the focus of the naval war changed, for operations, ships

and men were moved away from the Channel to the North Sea and
Baltic, and south to the Mediterranean. Napoleon's shipbuilding programme in Antwerp was now causing concern as a new base from
which to launch a French invasion. The mouth of the Scheldt was
blockaded for twelve months a year, a complex operation commanded
with great skill by Admiral William Young: between 1809 and 1812 he
had between 40 and 80 warships under his command, the number
varying with the seasons and the assessed threat of breakout by the
French Fleet.[88] Young had detailed orders about which of several
courses to pursue if the French Fleet did manage to escape from the
Scheldt, with a view to protecting the Baltic or Ireland.[89] The new
invasion threat to Britain was now seen to be to the east coast, where
shallow waters created their own difficulties. A very large number of
British shallow-draught sloops, gunboats and gun-brigs were built
from 1803 onwards, needed not only for the shallow waters there but
also to meet a worldwide demand for convoys, sent to combat the
continuing depredations of French privateers, which were multiplied
from 1807 by the hostility of the Danes and the Dutch, and after
1812 of the Americans. As we shall see in Chapter 12, by the end
of the war successive administrations had ordered the building of
174 brig-sloops and 87 smaller gun-brigs, while 50 captured enemy
brigs joined the British Fleet.[90]

The number of British warships on the Channel Station therefore
declined dramatically. At the end of the French Revolutionary War
they had stood at 75 ships crewed by 38,000 seamen.[91] By September 1809 this figure had declined to only 30 smaller ships manned
by 7,000 seamen, which watched the naval bases of north-west
France. The Walcheren and Portuguese expeditions accounted for
51,000 seamen.[92] At the same time, Saumarez in the Baltic had 62
ships and just under 15,000 seamen.[93] This movement of operations
away from the Channel coast imposed a strain on naval administrators because of the difficulty of maintaining and provisioning the
warships. For more than a century investment had been concentrated in the facilities in the south and west of England, primarily
in Portsmouth and Plymouth. The east coast of England had no
deep-water ports, and assembling ships at the Nore and in the

Yarmouth Roads was very problematic – even dangerous in northerly and easterly gales.*

On the southern flank of Europe, Cuthbert Collingwood, commander-in-chief of the Mediterranean Fleet from the time of Trafalgar until his death in 1810, played a masterly defensive game. To maintain control of the Mediterranean he had, in 1807, 74 warships and over 25,000 seamen in his command, while the army numbered 31,000.[94] Toulon was blockaded to deny France free use of the Mediterranean, but Sicily was always a problem: it could not be given up, because it supplied Malta with wheat, but it would be impossible to supply enough troops to defend it.[95] In 1810 Napoleon tried one more time to seize it, but when he failed and it became clear that the island was no longer an objective, Britain was able to reduce its commitment there.[96] For a dozen years every one of Napoleon's moves in the Mediterranean was countered by Britain's ability to move troops and supplies faster by ship than he could move them by land.

The fortunes of Portland's cabinet continued to improve. The administration reacted quickly when it heard of the Spanish uprising against French domination in Madrid on 2 May 1808. Brutal suppression in Madrid by the French ensured that a country-wide revolt against the invaders was under way by early June. In spite of cabinet doubters, a decision to support the Spanish was taken with speed, and public approval of the new initiative was strong.[97] The pace of events increased. On 14 June, Sir Arthur Wellesley, whose talent was by now generally recognized, was given command of troops for Spain, which had been gathered at Cork originally for an expedition to aid General Miranda in Venezuela.[98] At the same time in London a complicated plan was put in hand to transport 12,000 Spanish troops under the marquis de la Romana from Denmark to Spain, right beneath the noses of the French. This operation was closely orchestrated from

---

* The provision of the very large quantities of fresh water required by warships was particularly difficult. Depot ships (so described for the first time) containing only water were anchored along the Thames Estuary by 1807, supplied by tenders that brought casks filled from the upper reaches of the Thames, beyond the reach of the salt water brought up by the tide (see Chapter 6, p. 171; Knight and Wilcox, *Sustaining the Fleet*, pp. 59–62, 197–202).

Whitehall, and carried out with admirable efficiency by Rear-Admiral Richard Goodwin Keats. Though not all the Spanish troops could be embarked, 9,000 of them landed at Santander in northern Spain on 9 October, neatly using British maritime predominance in the north and south of Europe to bolster the new theatre of war.[99] Further Spanish success followed. On 19 July a Spanish army beat a French force at Baylen, south of Madrid, forcing 18,000 French soldiers to surrender. On 1 August the force commanded by Wellesley landed at Mondego Bay in Portugal, a task that took five days on the open, sandy beach.[100] Three weeks later he defeated the French at Vimeiro. However, a weak armistice signed by the senior but politically inexperienced general, Sir Hew Dalrymple, at the Convention of Cintra allowed the French Army to be repatriated with both their arms and their plunder from the Portuguese. The signing away of a victory shocked a disbelieving Britain, causing a further political storm, and the generals were recalled.[101] A commission of enquiry was set up, chaired by General Sir David Dundas, now retired. Wellesley was implicated and lucky to get away relatively unscathed.

Little noticed in the uproar was the successful securing of a Russian squadron of seven ships of the line, which happened to be in the Tagus when the Spanish revolt began. As agreed at the Convention of Cintra, it was closely escorted to Spithead by seven British ships of equivalent rate. The Russian ships remained anchored there, crewless, neglected and rotting, until 1812; only two sailed again.[102] This marked the end of a disastrous year for Napoleon, which had begun with the prospect of his securing nearly a hundred ships of the line from the countries he now dominated; but those of Denmark, Sweden, Spain, Portugal and Russia were denied to him, mostly by decisive British actions.[103]

On land, however, the tide was still far from turning in Britain's favour. Napoleon marched with his army down to Spain at the end of 1808 and they carried all before them, causing Moore's army to retreat, and nearly trapping it at Corunna at the end of January 1809 (see Chapter 7). On the heels of this very narrow escape came a domestic scandal. Earlier in January the commander-in-chief, the duke of York, was accused in the Commons by a newly elected maverick radical politician, Colonel Gwyllym Wardle, of making appointments corruptly influenced by York's former mistress, Mary Anne Clarke. Whig

Opposition leaders were uncomfortable with the attack and advised Wardle to drop his accusations. Lords Grenville and Grey distanced themselves throughout, the latter considering Wardle 'an informer' who had 'formed an acquaintance and an intimacy with a vile prostitute to get into her secrets'.[104] Wardle was, however, encouraged by William Cobbett, who was using the episode to attack the influence of the crown, and to push for parliamentary reform. In debate, however, enough members voted against the duke's complete acquittal to force him to resign. Soon afterwards, Wardle was discredited.*

The case not only did the army political damage but deprived it for a time of the good sense and experience of the duke, who was reinstated in 1811. His place as commander-in-chief was taken for two years by General Sir David Dundas. This tough old soldier was not going to be pushed around by the new and very young secretary at war, Lord Palmerston, and it led to a long running dispute over finance and accounting between the Horse Guards and the War Office, just at a time when all energies should have been directed at the successful prosecution of the war in Spain.[105]

In spite of these strains, the government did not fall apart, because the Opposition was divided and failed to present itself to the backbenchers as a viable alternative government. A vote on the war in Spain in May 1809, for instance, was carried by the government by 230 votes to 111. A relieved Castlereagh wrote to his stepbrother, Charles Stewart, that the vote had

> put our friends in great heart, and given the Govt. much more weight than they have yet had. The Battle was last night waged for us ... the opposition were firing into Each other's Ranks into every direction:

---

* Mrs Clarke was paid £10,000 and given an annuity of £400 in return for the surrender of the duke of York's letters and the destruction of her prepared memoirs. During a court case in July it emerged that Wardle had sought out Mrs Clarke, and taken her to view some Martello Towers, in company with the military secretary of the duke of Kent, ostensibly in order to prepare a case against the military usefulness of the towers, but in reality to pump her about her relationship with the duke of York. This means of gaining his information ruined Wardle's three-month-old popularity and destroyed his career: he retired from parliament and took up farming (Thorne, *House of Commons*, Vol. V, pp. 486–8). The presence of the military secretary of the duke of Kent perhaps reflects the bad blood between the royal brothers.

Tierney at Burdett, Whitbread at Tierney, Bragge at Whitbread and Folkestone at Windham – nothing could indicate more Division on their part, or determined Union on Ours than this debate did.[106]

The Tory administration was soon, however, to be rocked. The failure of the very large expedition to Walcheren that set off late in the summer of 1809, as recounted in Chapter 7, was the nadir of the Portland government, and the consequent casualties among the troops caused indignation throughout the country. The disaster was debated in a two-month-long committee of the whole House of Commons. Before the troops came home, however, a duel was fought between George Canning and Lord Castlereagh. It laid bare not only the tension between the foreign secretary and the secretary of state for war – the two ministers most concerned with that formidable undertaking – but also the weakness of the cabinet ministers gathered around the sick and ineffectual duke of Portland. Canning's sharp tongue had made him enemies and created distrust, and he was regarded by the very aristocratic cabinet, and the king, as an outsider because of his background. Canning's supreme confidence in the power of his parliamentary oratory, and his impatience with those who did not think as fast as he did (so often the bane of very clever people) were the root causes of the dispute. He had his eye on the prime minister's job, for he knew that on 10 May Portland had tendered his resignation to the king, who had refused to allow him to go. In order to increase his influence in the cabinet, Canning plotted to move Castlereagh, whom he regarded as slow-witted, by sidelining him to some less important post. No one else in the cabinet had the nerve to tell Castlereagh what was going on.

The dispute culminated in September 1809 when the outwardly unemotional Castlereagh called Canning out, demonstrating his inward-seething anger when he pulled the trigger of a gun on Putney Heath. This duel was not a formal ritual for the restoration of honour, in which opponents fire into the air, but one in which Castlereagh, at least, fired to kill his opponent, a view supported by his call for a further round after both shots had missed in the first. Canning was hit by the second shot in the thigh. Had the ball deviated even slightly, it would have gone through an artery, leaving him dead, and Castlereagh in the dock for wilful murder.[107] Both ministers immediately resigned. Castlereagh, however, was soon rehabilitated and became foreign secretary in 1812. Canning was much in evidence at Westminster thereafter, but he never joined a ministry, and eventually withdrew to Lisbon as ambassador in 1814, giving the fragile health of his son as the reason for doing so. After the war, Canning reflected on how much he had missed:

> The station in Europe and in history, which I have thrown away ... having refused the management of the mightiest scheme of politics which this country ever engaged in, or the world ever witnessed, from a miserable point of etiquette, one absolutely unintelligible ... at a distance of more than six miles from Palace Yard.[108]

When his old mentor Canning left office in October 1809, William Huskisson followed two months later. Though junior at the Treasury, Huskisson was the most valuable of the financial ministers, and was a great loss to Spencer Perceval, who was then chancellor of the Exchequer under Portland. Throughout 1809 Huskisson had been in the thick of a great financial crisis: in March, Austria had declared war on France and without warning drew large amounts of money on the British Treasury, at a time when it was short of specie.[109] Huskisson was already concerned over the Treasury's heavy borrowing, and doubted whether the government would be able to raise enough taxes to pay the interest on the loans. A related problem was a shortage of silver and gold coin during the boom years of trade, particularly from the beginning of 1809 to the middle of 1810, when much of what the government had was required to pay the army in the Peninsula. Huskisson proposed cutting the budget of the army and navy by £2 million each, and the Ordnance by £1 million, but his recommendations were not accepted by Perceval and the cabinet.[110] In fact, the economy expanded in 1809 and 1810, and revenue from taxes exceeded estimates, so the government's credit was maintained and the immediate crisis averted.

The political situation was rendered even more unstable by the condition of the king. At the age of seventy-two, George III's mind had again given way, although no one expected the condition to be permanent. The role of the prince regent was formalized by parliament in

February 1811, with the proviso that he should do nothing irreversible for a year. After many years of friendship with the Whigs, it was expected that when the year was over, and if the king had not recovered, he would ask them to form a government. The Opposition was politically and personally divided: Grenville and Grey did not trust each other; Tierney, Sheridan and Whitbread similarly. The issue of Catholic emancipation, still much espoused by the Whigs, was still to cause them difficulties at court. The transition of the prince regent's loyalties from Whig to Tory was helped by the installation of a new and Tory mistress, Lady Hertford.

These factors intensified political feeling, and the stresses and fatigue suffered by ministers. The only exception was the vain and ambitious Irishman Richard, Marquess Wellesley, who had so greatly expanded British power in India. There he had enjoyed unbridled personal power and he never accepted the constraints of cabinet government. He was foreign secretary in Perceval's government, and contemptuous of that ascetic, evangelical prime minister. But Wellesley's laziness and inefficiency were breathtaking. He kept his ambassadors waiting for replies for months, not least because of his affairs. His brothers were infuriated by him. William Wellesley-Pole, by now chief secretary in Ireland, wrote to Arthur Wellesley in March 1810: 'I understand that he hardly does any business at his Office, that nobody can procure access to him, and that his whole time is passed with Moll', a well-known courtesan.[111]

Fortunately, others were more conscientious at this critical time. Castlereagh, reinstated in government as foreign secretary in February 1812, even with his immense capacity for work, found that he, too, had his limits, as he related to his step-brother Charles Stewart in April: 'I have been very hard work'd since I came in. A heavy Job in every Quarter. I don't recollect ever to have had so tough a task.'[112] The post of first lord of the Admiralty was, as we have noted, particularly strenuous. Tom Grenville's successor was Lord Mulgrave, an active soldier until 1801, who came to the post in 1807 when he was fifty-two.* It was not long before he was pressing Perceval to relieve

* In Jan. 1810 Tom Grenville wrote to his 56-year-old brother, the marquis of Buckingham: '<u>You</u> should <u>not</u> retire . . . mind and talents are fresh and vigorous tho' neither you nor I could stand the fatigues of such a session as the last in the House of

him of his office; as the prime minister told the king, 'the laborious duties of the Admiralty have been pressing for some time so heavily upon Lord Mulgrave's health, that he has told Mr Perceval repeatedly that it was impossible that he should be able to hold the office much longer.'[113] Perceval neatly sacrificed the less than energetic Lord Chatham after Walcheren: he was forced to resign as master-general of the Ordnance after an angry cabinet meeting. Perceval installed Mulgrave in his place, a post with much lighter duties than those at the Admiralty, and which he held until 1818.[114]

Mulgrave's successor as first lord, Charles Philip Yorke, also felt the ministerial strain. He had been made secretary at war in 1801, the best, according to the king, that he had ever had.[115] He had been less of a success as home secretary between August 1803 and May 1804, when he was overworked and had much to defend in parliament: accepting that office was, he said later, 'the most foolish thing I ever did in public life'. When the Talents were in government Yorke attacked Windham continually over the latter's military measures. Now, Perceval persuaded him to take the Admiralty, although Yorke had no great appetite for it and one observer thought that Yorke would be 'much too hot, and headstrong for such an office'.[116] But he did well, though he was never at ease in the post. He backed the ship-construction improvements advocated by Sir Robert Seppings against the conservative shipwright establishment and drove through the building of the Plymouth breakwater. He took his appointment duties seriously and, according to John Barrow, set a day aside to listen to naval officers, 'to their numerous tales of distress and disappointment, and too frequently to listen to them without the possibility of affording relief. Few, I believe, experienced this painful duty more strongly than Mr Charles Yorke.'[117] One MP thought that Yorke was 'a very humane, good man, and with a great deal more feeling than generally belongs to politicians'.[118] He was thus much affected by the loss of lives when three ships of the line, *St George*, *Defence* and *Hero*, returning at Christmas 1811 from the Baltic, were caught

Commons. There is too much serviceable stuff in you to lie down upon your pillow, & there is too little hope of quiet or prosperity in the country to justify either you or me in going to sleep when we ought to be upon duty at our posts' (16 Jan. 1810, HL, STG 38 (29)).

in a great storm and went ashore off Jutland and the Texel: in two days 2,000 men were drowned.[119] Yorke resigned in March 1812. He was fifty-eight and riddled with gout.

The home secretary, Richard Ryder, was the most unhealthy of all the ministers. Honourable but undistinguished, he could not, for instance, cope with defending in parliament his handling of the Luddite riots in Nottingham and York (which required a good number of militia units to bring under control) and the prime minister had to come to his aid in debate. From this point rumours abounded that Ryder would resign and he did so in May 1812, and took to his bed.[120]

The twelve months from the spring of 1811 had been the nadir of British fortunes. It was true that the French had been neutralized at sea, but on land the situation appeared dire. The Continent had experienced nearly two years of peace, on Napoleon's terms. For most of 1811 Napoleon had been gathering his forces for a massive invasion of Russia, and fears of an invasion of Britain were lessening, after long years of building defensive counter-measures. The French economy still seemed healthier than that of the British as the resources of more conquered nations came under Napoleon's control. His armies were stretched in the Peninsula, but at the beginning of 1812 a French victory remained the most probable result.[121]

In London the crisis also came at the same time and the cards that were played during these tumultuous months could have fallen another way. Had the prince regent not backed the Tories in an uncharacteristic attack of common sense in February 1812, the Opposition might have formed an administration. In the event, the prince abandoned the Whigs and put to lords Grey and Grenville an impossible proposition that they join Perceval's government, which they immediately refused. After so many years of political friendship with the prince, the Whigs were furious. But if Grenville had returned to power at this critical moment, Britain might well have changed course. In February 1812 Tom Grenville described his brother's 'deep despair' at finding 'that besides three and a half millions of deficit, there are forty-two millions of unfunded Exchequer Bills'.[122] Lord Grenville's inflexibility and his long-held belief that Britain could not afford to fund a war on the Continent could easily have led to a loss of nerve and an attempt to make peace.* Grey's view, on the other hand, was that not enough was being done by Perceval's government to support the army in the Peninsula. A Whig cabinet would therefore have been divided and at odds with parliament. In the middle of April 1812, Napoleon did in fact send a message proposing a peace treaty, with each side to retain its conquests.[123] The Tory government took the French overture for what it was, part of a delaying tactic to allow the emperor to make his preparations for the invasion of Russia. The Whigs might well have chosen to open negotiations.

Even so, Perceval's position was not strong and the prime minister also had to deal with the machinations of his foreign secretary, Richard Wellesley, who was manoeuvring to replace him.[124] Then, on 11 May 1812, Spencer Perceval was assassinated in the lobby of the House of Commons by John Bellingham, a depressed and deranged Baltic merchant who had been bankrupted by the trade blockades, and who blamed Perceval for his ruin. Even though he was not built on a heroic scale, Perceval's success in keeping his ministry together and nursing the country's finances had been critical. He was described by one MP as 'not a ship of the line, but he carries many guns, is tight built, and is out in all weathers'.[125]

It fell to Lord Liverpool, as Hawkesbury had become on the death of his father in December 1808, to form a government. He, too, was not a dominant character, and became irritable under the constant pressure (which was to earn him the nickname the 'Grand Figitalis').[126] Yet he was persistent, prudent, discreet and trusted. Forming his administration was complex and difficult. Yorke regretfully refused a post, saying that his health 'has greatly altered for the worse during the last two years and is attended with such unpleasant symptoms, affecting my spirits and nerves as well as my Frame'.[127] Castlereagh continued as foreign secretary, Lord Sidmouth became home secretary, Earl Bathurst the secretary of state for war and the second Viscount Melville, Henry Dundas's son, the first lord of the Admiralty.

---

* It is possible that Grenville's own precarious finances affected his capacity to grapple with these great debts at a national level.

Despite this unpromising start, the administration was to achieve success, which started in November 1812 at the general election, when Liverpool's supporters gained twice as many seats as the Opposition.[128] Few would have predicted when Liverpool formed his government that he would remain as prime minister for fifteen years.

9

The Invasion Threat

1803–1812

*Every town was . . . a sort of garrison – in one place you might
hear the 'tattoo' of some youth learning to beat the drum, at
another place some march or national air being practised
upon the fife, and every morning five o'clock the bugle horn
was sounded through the streets, to call the volunteers to a two
hours' drill . . . and then you heard the pop, pop, pop, of the
single musket, or the heavy sound of the volley, or distant
thunder of the artillery.*
– George Cruikshank, *A Pop-Gun Fired off . . . in Defence of
the British Volunteers of 1803* (1806)[1]

*The possession to an Enemy of Dover Castle [and] of the
opposite Entrenched Height and of the town and port . . . and
defended by 6 or 7,000 men would establish a sure communication with France and could not be easily wrested from his
hands. The conquest of this alone would be to him a sufficient
object could he arrive with means of immediately attacking it.
Its preservation to us is most important . . .*
– Henry Dundas, War Office memorandum, 1798[2]

Addington's cabinet had seized the initiative by its sudden declaration
of war on 18 May 1803. For a few weeks the British held it, but the
government knew that this might be very temporary. Napoleon's
dominance on the Continent and his 'Army of England' – a force,
when at maximum strength, of 167,000, concentrated in the French
Channel ports – left the politicians and people in no doubt of his

intention to invade. We will never know, if Napoleon's army had sailed, whether he would have managed to land his troops successfully or, even more problematic, to have kept them supplied. By the summer of 1804 just over 70,000 well-trained Frenchmen were encamped at Bruges, St Omer and Montreuil. With the reserves, Napoleon's army numbered 100,000. In concentrating such a large force, the emperor and his chief of staff, Marshal Berthier, were experiencing their own logistics problems.[3] Basins and breakwaters had to be built to protect the invasion flotilla from damage by the sea at several of the ports, including Boulogne, Étaples, Ambleteuse and Wimereux.[4] A year later, in August 1805, the emperor had accumulated enough landing craft in the Channel ports to carry 167,000 troops.[5]

The prime minister was more than aware of the dangers of civil disorder if the French Army reached English shores. The measures that he proposed to take would not have been half-hearted, as outlined in 'Memorandum of Circumstances to be Determined and Acted upon Previous to & at the Moment of Invasion', a document written before the Peace of Amiens in February 1801, the month in which he began his administration.* One passage reads:

> Strong Proclamations and strong General measures to be prepared and ready for the preservation of internal Quiet, and strong Examples must necessarily be made. Foreigners must be watched; Suspicious and Turbulent Persons secured ... Patrols will be everywhere established on the great Roads near the great Towns. The Towns, Counties and Districts of Counties, Committees of Magistrates will be formed and some constantly sitting (as well as Parochial Committees at the Church) to answer Requisitions and enforce Orders. The Supply of Markets must

---

* The list runs, in order: 'Reserve of troops in each District; General officers report on their Districts; Battalions and Light Infantry to be exercised; General Orders to be issued: Reserve Train of Artillery to be held at Woolwich; General Depots of Arms to be formed in each county; Plan for driving the country; Police powers; General Measures for Civil Order; Companies of Volunteers; Plans for the security of the Capital; Ordnance Magazines; Camp Equipage; Prisoners of War; Fortified Places; Naval Measures (in concert with the military, mouth of the Thames, Defence of the Coast of Essex, the floating batteries, Gunboats, Sea Fencibles); Proper cover arrangements if C-in-C leaves London; Retired and Half Pay Officers to report to County towns; Divisions of transports to be mustered to move troops; Troops from Ireland, Jersey & Guernsey to England'.

be kept open and protected, and any attempt to disturb them punished in the most summary manner.[6]

To anticipate the need to apply stern measures to discipline a truculent British population in the face of an invasion was wise, for in any case some of the government's anti-invasion measures were resisted. Almost immediately after the declaration of war, in June 1803, instructions were promulgated from Whitehall to the lords lieutenant of the counties to present an evacuation plan and consider how all food stocks, forage and livestock useful to the enemy could be removed or destroyed. This measure was stopped in its tracks by the protest of the duke of Richmond, the lord lieutenant of Sussex, a county seen as directly in danger of occupation. Richmond was also by then a field marshal, and sixth senior officer in the *Army List*, and his views held sway. On 7 and 8 July 1803, at the general meeting of the lieutenancy of Sussex, chaired by Richmond, and attended by General David Dundas as general commanding the Southern District, it was resolved unanimously to ask the king to reconsider laying waste 'one of the richest provinces in England'.[7] The general was reminded that anti-invasion measures had to work with local interests, and the scorched-earth plan was quietly shelved.[8]

Moreover, the alarm could too easily be raised and several invasion scares ran through the country, in the main caused by the mistaken lighting of primitive fire beacons.[9] Just how easily a town could be rendered panic-stricken is illustrated by a letter of late 1803 from Colchester from the author Ann Taylor to her sister:

On Tuesday night between 8 and 9 intelligence was conveyed by the telegraphs from Camp to Camp from there to Colchester and from Colchester to London that an enemy's fleet was off the coast . . . At this time the theatre and a book auction at Barlows were full but in one instant they were either depopulated or filled with cries and lamentations . . . The volunteers were flying to arms. The officers at the play were scampering out to gallop home to their camps . . . The scene would have been truly ludicrous, for in their great anxiety to be at their quarters in time all the horses, post-chaises, etc., in the town were hired within half an hour, crammed full of red coats and even in some instances two or three upon one horse tearing away to their different camps. The ladies in the theatre [were] shrieking and crying and tumbling out until there was scarcely a creature in the place. Women running out of their houses screaming murder and in fact a scene of most alarming tumult and confusion . . . and I am afraid that in case of many more alarms or of actual invasion, the demand for salts vinegar, etc., etc., will be more than our perfumers will be able to supply. However, in about half an hour signals were made to inform us that a mistake had been made by the first telegraph which announced an enemy's instead of a friendly fleet, and of course we all recovered.[10]

It was always assumed by the government that London was to be Napoleon's main objective. One of the prime minister's concerns was that the capital would be overwhelmed by refugees fleeing ahead of the French invading forces. Flour, rice and salted provisions, as well as 250 tons of biscuit meal, were stockpiled in depots in and around London, at places such as Fulham, Brentford and Staines. These emergency stores were sufficient, according to the commissary-general, Brook Watson, in a letter of November 1803, six months after the conflict had resumed, to the worried prime minister, 'to supply the whole capital a fortnight at the extreme extent of its consumption . . . and at the Mills in its vicinity is, I compute, at least equal to three weeks more. The Ovens within our reach are equal to Baking for double the number of inhabitants.' If really necessary, stocks of provisions held by the Victualling Board could also be used.[11] The Commissariat hired 200 teams of horses and wagons, extra Commissariat staff and storekeepers, and four master bakers with teams of journeymen bakers. As with preparations for other invasions that never came, of course, the effectiveness of these measures can only be guessed at.*

The prime minister's 1801 memorandum constituted a formidable list of tasks which overlapped with the defensive strategy of the commander-in-chief, the duke of York. The country was to be divided into seventeen military districts, each commanded by a general, who was supported by subordinate generals; the senior generals were responsible to the duke. Each district had a staff of officers from the

---

* Addington ensured that Brook Watson was awarded a baronetcy in Dec. 1803 for his efforts and his long career in the public service.

Adjutant-General, the Quartermaster-General and the Commissariat departments. All units, whether regular, militia, yeomanry or volunteers, came under the command of the general commanding the district.[12] The vital southern district, Kent with some of Sussex, was commanded by General Sir David Dundas, who gave up his post of quartermaster-general in March 1803. The duke of York and Dundas came to the conclusion that the most likely place for a French attack was on the east coast of Kent, rather than further south in Sussex, because of the east–west lie of the Downs, which would give British forces a natural defensive line. Canterbury, together with the nearby Boughton Hill, according to Dundas, was 'the key of the country', and he made Canterbury his headquarters.[13]

In broad terms, this thinking matched the judgement of Admiral Lord Keith, commander-in-chief of the North Sea Fleet, who did well over many years in what was a complex defensive command that required cooperation with the army. The comprehensive memorandum written by Keith to the duke on 21 October 1803 reveals how much thought and observation had gone into detailed naval planning, taking into account the direction of the wind, the sailing capacity and draught of the French vessels, and height of the surf with onshore winds on the threatened beaches. Every possible landing place was itemized from Cornwall to Scotland, the threat to each of them varying with a particular wind direction, and he considered each of the French ports and their capacity and tidal range. Keith discounted the West Country because of the rough sea conditions and the Isle of Wight: 'unless [the French] had the superiority by Sea, because it would not be easy to get off it to the Main, if we take the common precautions'. Concerning the shoreline of the Thames Estuary, it was 'difficult to speak with certainty of the sands ... Many of them are very little known; some of them are dry at low water and at an early time of the tide; but most of them can be crossed at High Water in Boats or small Vessels when the Weather is fine; but it requires skill for if the wind and tide are in contrary directions it must be hazardous ...' On balance, Keith argued, the attempt, if it came, would most likely be directed at beaches or bays in Kent or Sussex. In an easterly wind, for instance, the west side of Dungeness, with its steep shingle beaches, was ideal for landing troops from boats, or, with westerly winds, its east side or in Hythe Bay.[14]

Detailed plans were drawn up in 1803 for encircling an invading French army. These over-elaborate plans involved trapping the invading army 'in a net' in the south-east of the country, held there by very large numbers of volunteers from the north, with many forces converging on London. The logistics of such plans were very ambitious.[15] The principal planner was Colonel Alexander Hope, but the duke of York informally sent Lord Cornwallis details of the plans, who returned them with a blistering critique, and they were dropped.* The old general was critical of the current army command, remarking to his confidant, Lieutenant-General Ross, that Hope 'appeared formerly to me to be a good-humoured pleasant fellow, and I was partial to him, but his presumption, and the nonsense he has written, have much altered my opinion'.[16] A more public disagreement came from Colonel George Hanger, who published a revised version of his invasion warnings in 1804, again stressing that the likely choice of the French would be the Thames and the Essex coast, though he noted the improvements in the defences and militia to the east of London, as well as the building of many gunboats and small naval vessels suitable for the defence of the shallow rivers and creeks of Essex.[17]

The first critical issue was how to concentrate enough men to oppose a landing. In the opinion of the duke of York, 2,000 soldiers rushing the French boats 'in a contest of valour', as opposed to one of military skill, were worth three times that number later on.[18] However, rather than forming an extended line to attempt to contain the French as near the coast as possible, the duke's strategy was to delay the invading force as much as possible on its advance upon London. Breastworks were to be rapidly dug on the hills around south London, on Blackheath, at Nunhead, Penge Common and Norwood.[19] The outlying

---

* The well-born Cornwallis did not think highly of the eccentric Dundas, grumbling privately: 'The staff in Kent seems to be calculated solely for the purposes of placing the defence of the country in the hands of Sir David. However he may succeed with other people, I think he cannot persuade Mr Pitt and Lord Melville that he is a clever fellow; and surely they must have too much sense to believe that it is possible that a man without talents, and who can neither write nor talk intelligibly, can be a good General' (to Ross, 6 Aug. 1804, Ross, *Cornwallis*, p. 514).

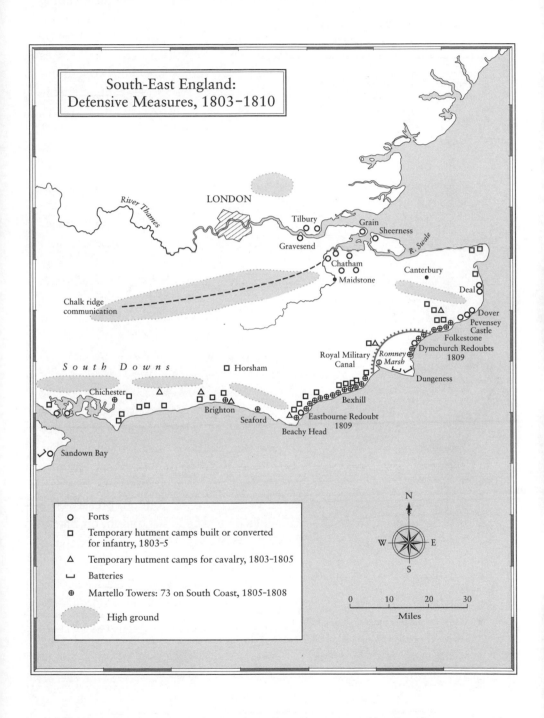

South-East England:
Defensive Measures, 1803–1810

LONDON

River Thames

Tilbury

Grain

Sheerness

Gravesend

R. Swale

Chatham

Canterbury

Maidstone

Deal

Chalk ridge
communication

Dover

Pevensey
Castle

Folkestone

Dymchurch Redoubts
1809

Royal Military
Canal

Romney
Marsh

South Downs

Horsham

Dungeness

Chichester

Brighton

Seaford

Bexhill

Eastbourne Redoubt
1809

Beachy Head

Sandown Bay

○	Forts
□	Temporary hutment camps built or converted for infantry, 1803–5
△	Temporary hutment camps for cavalry, 1803–1805
⊔	Batteries
⊕	Martello Towers: 73 on South Coast, 1805–1808
	High ground

N
W E
S

| 0 | 10 | 20 | 30 |

Miles

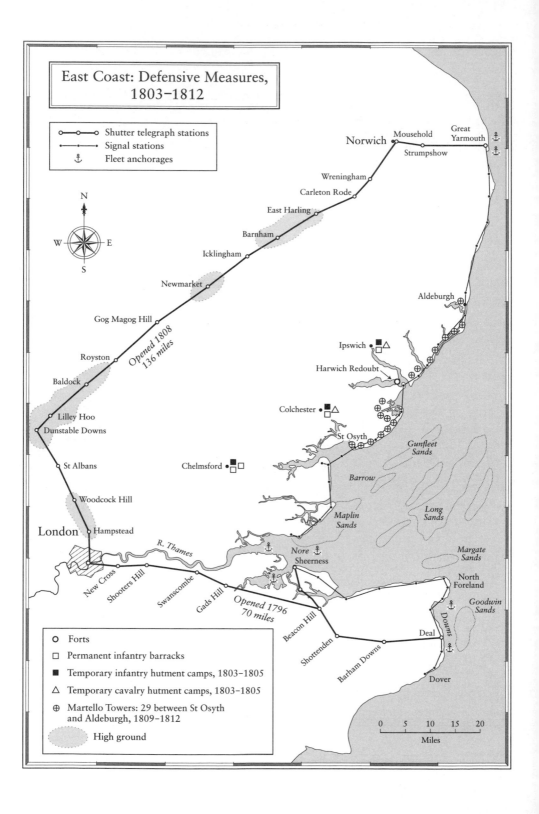

East Coast: Defensive Measures, 1803–1812

Shutter telegraph stations
Signal stations
Fleet anchorages

N
W — E
S

Norwich
Mousehold
Great Yarmouth
Strumpshow
Wreningham
Carleton Rode
East Harling
Barnham
Icklingham
Newmarket
Gog Magog Hill
Opened 1808 136 miles
Royston
Baldock
Lilley Hoo
Dunstable Downs
St Albans
Woodcock Hill
London
Hampstead
Aldeburgh
Ipswich
Harwich Redoubt
Colchester
St Osyth
Gunfleet Sands
Chelmsford
Barrow
Maplin Sands
Long Sands
Margate Sands
R. Thames
Nore
Sheerness
North Foreland
Goodwin Sands
New Cross
Shooters Hill
Swanscombe
Gads Hill
Opened 1796 70 miles
Beacon Hill
Shottenden
Barham Downs
Downs
Deal
Dover

○ Forts
□ Permanent infantry barracks
■ Temporary infantry hutment camps, 1803–1805
△ Temporary cavalry hutment camps, 1803–1805
⊕ Martello Towers: 29 between St Osyth and Aldeburgh, 1809–1812
High ground

0 5 10 15 20
Miles

garrisons at Portsmouth, Plymouth, Yarmouth, Hull and Edinburgh were strongly defended and had the capacity to withstand a siege for several weeks. But the overwhelmingly critical issue was to ensure that Dover Castle was held against assault, for it was central to the defensive plan agreed between the duke of York and General Dundas.[20] If Dundas's troops should be beaten on the coast, he was to withdraw them not to London but to Dover. 'In that strong position,' commented Colonel Henry Bunbury, on Dundas's staff in the Quartermaster-General's Department, 'he could have brought the enemy to bay', to give time for London to throw up its defences. If Napoleon went straight for London, Dundas's troops could then attack the French flank and its supply trains.[21]

After the sudden declaration of war, re-enlistment of regular troops, militia, yeomanry and volunteers went ahead at full speed through the spring and summer of 1803 and 1804.[22] Initiatives from different parts of the government caused some confusion: the secretary at war administered regiments that were enlisting regular soldiers, whereas the recruitment of both militia and volunteers came under the home secretary and the lords lieutenant of the counties.* Coordination of these efforts at local level, despite the involvement of the lords lieutenant, was not always effective. Justices of the peace, enforcing the militia ballot, had also to be mindful of the volunteers, which led to overlaps in enlistment between volunteers and militia. The duke of Richmond, lord lieutenant of Sussex, reported to the duke of York in August 1803: 'Much of the confidence that the lower orders of the people used to place in their magistrates has been shaken.'[23] Nevertheless, in fifteen counties, including Devon, the Isle of Wight, the Cinque Ports, Northumberland and Fife over 50 per cent of the male population, aged between seventeen and fifty-five, were wearing regular, militia, yeomanry or volunteer uniform. Kent and Sussex had 49 and 45 per cent respectively.[24] Additionally, between March 1803 and January 1804 the ranks of regular soldiers were increased from

---

* Jane Austen in *Pride and Prejudice* (published in 1813) made Lydia's admirer, Mr Wickham, the member of a militia regiment. The flighty Lydia's head was turned by a visit to Brighton, where 'she saw all the glories of the camp; its tents stretched forth in beauteous uniformity of lines, crowded with the young and the gay, and dazzling with scarlet' (Austen, *Pride and Prejudice*, Chapter 41).

52,000 to over 94,000. The navy had only shrunk to some 70,000 men during the peace, and by the end of 1804 it was again approaching 100,000.[25] Remarkably, by 1804 the two combined services totalled some 600,000 men, impressed, recruited or volunteered. The mobilization was to enlist between 11 and 14 per cent of the adult male population, about three times the 'military participation ratio' of France.[26] Although this peak could not be maintained, it nevertheless created an impressive force, and remained so until 1807, when William Windham, as secretary of state for war in the Ministry of All the Talents, controversially abolished the volunteers. He withdrew government financial assistance and abolished their exemption from the ballot, planning to replace them with universal military training, though he departed from office before this could happen.[27]

This rapid mobilization contrasted with the slow build-up from 1793 at the beginning of the French Revolutionary War, because well-tested mechanisms were now in place. The militia benefited most. Parliamentary Militia Acts passed in 1802 enabled 50,000 balloted men to be called up immediately, with an additional 25,000 to form the 'supplementary' militia.* So that each county fulfilled its quota, ballots and recruitment were supervised by a 'lieutenancies' command hierarchy based on the county, established by the 1803 Defence of the Realm Act. The lord lieutenant of the county was supported by deputy lieutenants who each controlled a 'subdivision'; in turn 'inspectors' administered each hundred (the medieval subdivisions within each county); and under the inspectors were 'superintendents' who oversaw each parish.[28] Counties were fined £10 per man missing if the quota was not met. Equipment, training and depots had to be arranged.

This complex system worked well because it had the support of the elites of the counties. The 1801 census and a new survey of counties had given the government a very clear idea of how many men aged between eighteen and forty-five were available, and thus liable for

---

* It cost about £12,500 in pay a year to keep the 676-strong Sussex Militia. The daily pay of militia officers was slightly less than that of the officers of the regular army infantry: e.g., lieutenant-colonel regular army 17s., lieutenant-colonel militia 15s.6d.; for lieutenants 6s.6d. and 5s.6d.; for surgeons 14s.1d. and 11s.4d. (Sussex Militia Pay Lists, Sept.–Dec. 1807, TNA, WO 13/2123; see also Burnham and McGuigan, *British Army against Napoleon*, p. 144).

militia service. In Sussex, for instance, the figure in January 1803 was 7,889 men.[29]* Parish ballots began as soon as war was declared, and those whose name had been drawn and who were able to pay for a substitute began to look for candidates. Roman Catholics and Quakers were banned from serving in the militia, but if they were drawn in the ballot they had to pay a fine, which in effect paid for a substitute.[30] As the pay of the militia was low, substitutes could charge a high fee and £40 was not unknown, but for periods they formed the majority in the militia ranks: of 26,000 men balloted between 1807 and 1808, only 3,129 served in person. Enterprising Scottish brokers advertised insurance against being called for service: for an annual premium of 10s.6d. a man could insure himself against the First Ballot, entitling the holder of the insurance to a sum to pay a substitute, should his name be drawn.[31] However, later militia legislation, when Castlereagh was secretary of state for war after 1807, substitutes were not allowed.[32] By July 1803 over 70,000 militiamen had been recruited, increasing to 85,000 by January 1804.[33]

The militia undertook routine internal security chores such as guarding military installations, and, on occasion, played an important role in keeping civil order. The quartermaster-general ensured the regiments were never stationary, so that militiamen did not develop sympathies with the inhabitants of any particular locality in case they were called upon to keep the peace. Nor did they serve in the county where they were raised.[34] The eight companies of the West Essex Militia battalion of 739 officers and men, for instance, were embodied at Chelmsford Barracks in April 1803, marched to Bradfield Camp in Essex for training and then to barracks at Harwich for the winter. In June 1804 the battalion was moved to Kent, where it camped at Sheerness; then to quarters at Rochester, Strood and Chatham; then, in 1805, to Portsmouth; then four companies embarked for the Isle of

---

* Resistance to any French landing near Bexhill in Sussex would have been very fierce, for it was here that the King's German Legion was based. Formed of thousands of Hanoverians who had fled their country after Napoleon invaded in 1803, this regiment played an important role in many operations, including a central part at Waterloo. These fine soldiers integrated well into the community. By 1814, when the regiment left Bexhill, there had been 108 marriages between Hanoverian soldiers and local women (Heizen, 'Napoleonic Wars in British and Hanoverian Memory', p. 1,410).

Wight, where they stayed until the summer of 1806, before the entire battalion moved inland.[35] Similarly, the Sussex Militia, during 1807, was moved at three-month intervals from Newcastle to Sunderland, to Hull and finally to Woodbridge in Suffolk, where it wintered at the barracks. The visibility of the regiment was maintained by visits to many towns in the north-east: duties included help with regular army enlistment as well as guarding local garrisons. On one occasion they provided a guard for deserters who were being marched from Newcastle to Carlisle.[36] In the warmer months, militia soldiers marched many hundreds of miles, and while they were not exposed to the dangers experienced by regular troops, and foreign service was avoided, they nevertheless had a strenuous war.*

The volunteers, who were never likely to move far from their locality, came forward in vast numbers, prompted by the 'Levy en Masse' Act passed in July 1803, which threatened 'to drill every able-bodied man whether he liked it or not'. (However, this Act was not to be enforced if sufficient volunteers were raised.[37]) A month later the 'August allowances' were promulgated, which laid down that volunteers were to be paid for twenty days' service, provided that their unit agreed to march to anywhere in the country in the event of an invasion. During the previous war, the volunteers from the Isle of Purbeck had agreed only to defend within five miles; but in 1803 their colonel offered 'the extent of the services to be in any part of Great Britain'.[38] By December 1803, 380,193 volunteers had come forward, 3.6 per cent of the population. In total, the volunteer body comprised 604 troops of cavalry, 3,976 companies of infantry and 102 companies of artillery.[39] The rapid response to the call to enlist in the volunteer regiments can also be seen as a move to evade more exacting militia service, for failing to join the volunteers left one open to the ballot.[40] The duke of York organized inspecting field officers to supervise training; the same officers served as staff for brigades of volunteers.[41] In October 1803 the king inspected a review of the London volunteer regiments in Hyde Park, over 12,000 strong, watched by a

---

* Private Robert Innard of the Durham Militia, returning home by coastal transport on a sick furlough from Portsmouth in Nov. 1808, was captured when the ship in which he was travelling was taken by a French privateer. He did not escape until Jan. 1814 (Rumsby, 'Militiaman', p. 251).

crowd estimated at 200,000. It was a day, the *Gentleman's Magazine* enthused, 'which afforded the most glorious sight we ever witnessed, without a single thing to excite the smallest regret' – a reflection of the general reassurance that these displays provided for the public.[42]

So rapid was the growth of the volunteer corps that it was some time before enough muskets and uniforms were available. In the first nine months of the war 103,572 pikes were issued to ensure that volunteers were not entirely empty-handed.[43] The Ordnance could supply only 150,000 reserve weapons, many of which were of non-standard issue and worn out, having been purchased abroad.[44] The home secretary, Charles Philip Yorke, in a confidential circular of October 1803 to all lords lieutenant of the maritime counties, advised that: 'A good fowling-piece, with a bullet-mould properly adapted to it, a powder-flask and ball-bag, together with a dagger or bayonet contrived to screw on the muzzle upon occasion, will prove a very efficient equipment for brave and zealous men determined to defend their country.'[45] Uniforms were another problem. General Henry Fox, inspector-general of recruiting, wrote to the adjutant-general, by now promoted Major General Calvert, noting that for the most part the volunteers were well clothed,

> but several want Great Coats and I am well informed by their Commanders that there are no possible means of obtaining a Fund sufficient to procure them . . . money has been thrown away in useless ornaments and appointments which might have procured comforts . . . I think that the Volunteers ought to be discouraged as much as possible in indulging in useless and ornamental dress . . .[46]

Sartorial standards did not slip, however, and in addition to their allowances volunteers funded their own finery. In Yorkshire the Halifax Volunteers were resplendent in scarlet coats faced with black silk velvet and silver lace, and the Grenadier Company sported bearskins. Not to be outdone, the headgear of some London regiments was equally dashing: the Somerset Place Volunteers wore light infantry 'Tarleton' helmets. The Light Horse Volunteers of London and Westminster wore scarlet Hussar jackets.[47] So did both the cavalry of the Dorset Volunteer Rangers and the county's volunteer infantry, though their coats differed. The rich green jackets of the rangers clothed the aristocracy and landed gentry; painted by Thomas Beach, their confident faces and posture are still evident in the many portraits that survive today.[48] Nor did the militia regiments go without finery. In 1808 the duke of Beaufort, colonel of the Royal Monmouth and Brecon Militia Regiment, ordered 'that each officer will provide himself with a Vulture Feather of the length of eleven inches of a similar pattern to that now in the possession of Captain Bridgwater'.[49]

In the counties the aristocracy and gentry took the lead in forming volunteer or yeomanry cavalry companies. In all, fifteen cavalry troops were formed in Sussex in 1803, three led by members of the aristocracy. The duke of Richmond at Goodwood had in 1797 set an example, as lord lieutenant, by raising the Sussex Yeomanry Horse Artillery, formed by prosperous farmers and tradesmen, consisting of 61 officers and men, two 3-pounder guns and two howitzers.[50] In 1794 the duke had not hesitated to give his neighbour, Lord Egremont at Petworth, some advice on the question of the volunteers. Like Richmond, Egremont's income was founded on coal, in his case yielding an enormous annual sum of £100,000 from an inheritance of mines in Cumberland. He was patron to many sculptors and artists, including Turner, and built up a renowned art collection, still to be seen at Petworth House today. With his 300 racehorses, Egremont was the most successful owner in the history of the Turf, winning the Derby and the Oaks five times. He provided horses, equipment and uniforms for the Petworth Yeomanry and was appointed colonel of the Sussex Regiment of Volunteers, but he protested to Richmond that a retired regular officer might be better equipped to command.* The duke disagreed: his advice to Egremont was that 'to stand forth as Commander was of more consequence than any practical knowledge of the cavalry business'.[51]

---

* An anonymous poem written about Egremont's troop took a cynical tone:

> Why does the baker on the saddle rise
> Who'd better stay at home and make mince pies?
> Is it to war with gnats and butterflies?
> Why does the grocer draw the ruthless sword?
> In hope to gain the custom of my lord.
> Why is the ploughshare to the cutlass bent?
> To bribe the steward to curtail the rent.

> (Hudson, 'Volunteers in Sussex', p. 176)

In spite of the impressive numbers of volunteers coming forward, the high targets set for the counties by government were rarely reached.[52] A particular difficulty in Sussex was to find officers for the volunteer infantry, which lacked the social cachet of the cavalry. In 1803 Viscount Gage, who commanded the Yeomanry Cavalry at Firle, described the problem to the duke of Richmond:

> The difficulty in procuring any officers in the district (for proper officers are out of the question) your Grace can have no conception of, almost all the young men of prosperity and influence being engaged in Captain Shiffner's or John Miller's troop of Yeomanry and I am sorry to add that I perceive the prevailing opinion of those who have not yet entered into either that the Cavalry is a preferable service.[53]

The social attractions of Captain George Shiffner's cavalry troop at Lewes or that of Sir John Riggs Miller at Ringmer clearly outweighed the public duty of acting as an officer of the less prestigious volunteer infantry, such as, for instance, the South Lewes Volunteers, which was so short of officers that the duke of Richmond was forced to put forward Mr Wimble, an ironmonger, for a commission. The unfortunate tradesman was, however, rejected by the colonel, William Newton, as 'not of sufficient property and situation in life to ensure subordination and good discipline'.[54] Infantry and coastal artillery volunteers might find a former regular to command them. The South Pevensey Volunteers, for instance, had as their sergeant-major an ex-sergeant of fourteen years' service in the 3rd Foot Guards; over 600 strong in 1803, they were likely to have been an impressive body of men.[55] As this part of the south coast is sheltered from the prevalent south-westerly winds, it was felt to be particularly vulnerable to invasion.*

Naval manning continued to be difficult. In ports all over the country resistance to the press gang by seamen stymied the navy's efforts to man its warships. Likely naval seamen joined the militia to evade the press, a loophole that in theory was closed by the Defence of the Realm Act of 1803.[56] Press-gang brawls were even more prevalent

---

* The North and South Pevensey legions were the largest in Sussex: between them eighty-five officers were listed in the 1804 War Office List of the ... Yeomanry and Volunteer Infantry (pp. 665–6).

than at the beginning of the previous war: seventy-five disturbances were reported in the newspapers between March 1803 and the end of the year. At Portland in Dorset, the quarrymen resisted the press gang and three local men were killed: the naval lieutenants commanding the press gang were charged with 'wilful murder' at the Dorset Assizes, though they were acquitted when the case was moved to the King's Bench.[57] The navy had a maritime equivalent of the volunteers, the Sea Fencibles, who were recruited, as *Steel's Navy List* had it, 'for the protection of the coast, either on-shore or afloat; comprising all fishermen and other persons occupied in the ports and on the coast, who, from their occupations are not liable to be impressed'.[58] Serving under the orders of Admiral Lord Keith, this force was relatively small, reaching only 30,000 by 1805. The Admiralty wanted more men to be recruited for both the regular navy and the Sea Fencibles, but was concerned that men who were needed in the navy were finding refuge by volunteering for the Sea Fencibles, by which means they were protected from impressment.[59]

On to the scene, briefly and rather incongruously, came Rear-Admiral Arthur Phillip, whom we last saw collecting intelligence at Toulon in 1784, since when he had commanded the First Fleet to Australia. Appointed inspector of the impress service, he was commissioned to report on the Sea Fencibles and impressment. For over a year Phillip travelled along the coasts of Britain, accompanied by a secretary. Not surprisingly, he encountered an immense variation in different parts of the country, with the militant Tynesiders and remote Norfolk furnishing the least number of Sea Fencibles. He also found a belief among the local seafarers that coming forward for the Fencibles would lead to impressment. For instance, in Eastbourne and Pevensey on the south coast, 63 per cent of the mackerel and lobster fishermen who enrolled for the Sea Fencibles were 'in general [a] very stout and able set of young men' whom Phillip felt should be in the navy. In Hastings he found the 'pilots' very rough, engaged in smuggling; 'they cannot be easily impressed,' he reported. Overall, he recognized that many seamen suitable for the navy were eluding him.* A subsequent investigation

---

* Phillip reported that over 16,000 seamen had been recruited in the thirteen months prior to Feb. 1805: 5,128 had been pressed, 5,978 had volunteered, together with 3,211 landsmen and 1,285 boys, and the magistrates had sent 559 vagrants and crimi-

into the problem by the pugnacious Rear-Admiral George Berkeley found widespread evasion in the West Country fishing ports, which exasperated him, as he reported to the Admiralty: 'exemption from the Impress & Ballot is now claimed as a sort of Right by these men, established by custom & riveted by the Sea Fencible System . . . every sort of service has been absolutely refused which could in the least interfere with their private occupations.'[60] Lord Keith went further, writing indignantly to the Admiralty in 1805 of the Sea Fencibles from Deal, Dover and Folkestone: '[they] regard themselves in a manner completely independent of the service, and as having a kind of prescriptive right to defraud the revenue and pillage individuals.'[61]

Naval establishments on land were guarded by their civilian employees. Over 4,000 volunteers guarded the six home dockyards, strategically critical sites. The Dockyard Regiment at Portsmouth, for instance, had a complement of over 1,000.[62] To those who spent their lives in these great industrial establishments, it seemed natural to agree with the Navy Board's statement that the 'Defence of the Magazines is Absolutely necessary.' John Tyson, Nelson's secretary at the time of the Battle of the Nile, and now clerk of the survey at Woolwich Dockyard, wrote cheerfully to his old chief: 'Little did I think after serving Thirty Years at Sea to have turned Soldier in my old Age. We have four companies in this yard and I have the Honor to be Captain of them.'[63] Each of the dockyards had its own volunteer regiment and the resident commissioner served as its colonel. The Admiralty issued the officers' commissions and, together with the Navy Board, debated the detail of the uniforms for the dockyard volunteers, revealing the importance that was attached to such conventions, and the small but significant differences that marked out the different ranks.*

---

nals (Frost, *Phillip*, p. 244, quoting TNA, ADM 1/581, fols. 86–9). Pressed men and volunteers from Shetland constituted higher than average per head of population, which was about 22,000 in 1801 and 1811. A modern estimate is that 5,000 Shetlanders served in the navy between 1793 and 1815 (Robertson, *Press Gang*, pp. 12, 26).

* 'A Close Blue Vest with White Buttons with the three Anchors: Blue Gaiters, Trowsers, Buttoned down the Leg; Plain Round Hats turned up on the left side with Loops and White Buttons as above: Black Cross Belts for side Arms and Pouch; Barred White on the Sleeve as other Regiments; Sashes Regulation' (1 Sept. 1803, NMM, ADM BP/23b).

Captains Sir Charles Saxton and Robert Fanshawe, respectively commissioners at Portsmouth and Plymouth dockyards, agreed with the uniforms proposed by the Navy Board, 'except the epaulets and Cocked Hat'.[64]

In the courtyard of Somerset House in 1804 the Somerset Place Volunteers drilled, formed 'Solely for the Defence of Somerset House'.[65] They were commanded by the Rt Hon. George Tierney, maverick politician and the current treasurer of the navy, but also lieutenant-colonel for the duration of the emergency. Under his command were eight companies totalling 380 officers and men. Among Tierney's officers were two naval captains, Henry Duncan and Samuel Gambier, members of the Navy Board, and George Phillips Towry, the long-serving vice-chairman of the Victualling Board, aged seventy-one.[66] Age was likewise no bar to another remarkable initiative by the pilotage and buoyage service, Trinity House. Eight old naval frigates were fitted out and armed to serve as blockships at the mouth of the River Thames near Tilbury, manned by the Royal Trinity House Volunteer Artillery and commanded by pensioned and half-pay officers, 1,200 strong, and safe from impressment because Trinity House was empowered to issue protections. To make the tedious duty bearable, only half the crew was aboard at any one time. This motley force was commanded by the deputy master of Trinity House, now appointed lieutenant-colonel, who had quarters aboard the *Trinity* yacht, which was assisted by two royal yachts. At a public dinner at the London Tavern on 3 October 1803, attended by the master of the Corporation, William Pitt, now honorary colonel of the new force, the officers were sworn in. George Rose described the scene:

> The sight was an extremely affecting one – a number of gallant and exceedingly good old men, who had, during the best part of their lives been beating the waves, now coming forward with the zeal and spirit of lads, swearing allegiance to the King, with a determined purpose to act manfully in his defence, and for the protection of the capital.[67]

The project continued for two years, although it attracted much criticism. Canning, out of office, made his view of the blockships known with a typically sharp squib:

If blocks could the nation deliver
Two places are safe from the French;
The one is the mouth of the river
The other the Treasury Bench.[68]

It is easy to write off the potential military effectiveness of the volunteers, for they were, like the Home Guard in the Second World War, never tested. There is no doubt, however, that, while the initial motive for the formation of the volunteers in the 1790s might have been fear of internal enemies, by the beginning of the Napoleonic War 'a patriotism developed that invoked defence and survival of the nation in the face of threatened conquest'.[69] Some, who were subject to military law and the Mutiny Act and received daily or weekly pay and had a higher military value than a private soldier – for example sergeants, trumpeters, buglers and drummers – were seen as belonging to the permanent establishment and therefore governed under military discipline. In November 1803 the Bank of England directors wished to settle a question on the discipline of the Bank's volunteers and asked their solicitors Freshfields for an opinion as to whether it was legal for trumpeters, buglers and drummers who received pay for their services, but who had not been 'attested' (sworn an oath of allegiance), to be subject to the Mutiny Act or Articles of War: the opinion of the lawyer, having 'perused 42 Geo III *c. 66* and 43 Geo III *c.* 121', was that they were liable. In 1804 a drummer in the third company of the Royal East India Volunteers was found guilty by court martial of desertion: a sentence of 500 lashes was reduced to 50 in consideration of his extreme youth. In the event, the officer commanding called a halt after four strokes and remitted the rest of the sentence.[70] Though these cases were rare, punishments did occur, usually for desertion.[71]

Some observers thought the standards of volunteers were high.[72] Colonel Hanger claimed that in general their marksmanship was good, comparing them favourably with regulars, and citing one experienced corps where the volunteers could 'throw three balls out of five into the target, at one hundred and one hundred and twenty yards'. He could furnish 'many more instances of their very superior skill in firing ball . . . I have seen many of their targets riddled.'[73] The

Light Horse Volunteers of London and Westminster impressed the young George Cruikshank: 'I once saw this regiment go through their exercise on a field-day on Finchley Common. A finer regiment of cavalry I never saw, nor have I ever seen regulars more perfect in the evolutions.'[74]* At the other end of the country, in Cornwall, the Artillery Volunteers, charged with the defence of Pendennis Castle overlooking Falmouth Harbour, and over 500 strong in 1803, were brought to an effective force through the command of an invalid ex-regular officer. In 1807 and 1808 their inspection reports read: 'Fit to act with Troops of the Line'. After 1809 they were absorbed into the militia. The report of 1810 read: 'The evolutions and firings were made with all the steadiness and exactness of regular troops.'[75]

Some regular soldiers were impressed by the volunteers. By March 1804 General Fox was able to report to Major General Calvert that 'I have the satisfaction in observing that there appears without exception a general zeal and order for the Public Service . . . the majority of them (both Cavalry and Infantry) are in my opinion fit to be joined to Regular Troops.'[76] Perhaps the most authoritative judgement came from old Lord Cornwallis, fretting in the country at the inactivity of retirement and not easy to please. In December 1803 he wrote to his old friend Lieutenant-General Ross that 'no man, whether civil or military, will persuade me that 300,000 men, trained as the volunteers at present are, do not add very materially to the confidence, and to the actual security of this country.'[77]

But politicians were divided over the merits of the system. Charles James Fox chastised the volunteers for their 'theatrical ostentatious foppery . . . fit for nothing but to be put on the top of a hill to be looked at'; nevertheless, in the general enthusiasm for springing to the

---

* In Dorset, in May 1804, during an invasion scare, two companies of the Dorset Volunteers infantry, those from Evershot and Sydling, refused to march past Dorchester, and their commanders reported: 'The remainder of the third battalion is so exasperated against these companies, that I could not propose their return to any quarters without risking the tranquillity of the place or without subjecting those companies to the probability of insult wherever they went.' The two companies were disbanded and their arms transferred to a new company, which sprang up immediately. It was an episode that illustrated the strengths but exposed the limitations of the volunteers (Clammer, 'Dorset Volunteers', pp. 23–4, quoting Internal Defence Papers, TNA, HO 50/102).

defence of the country, even he found it useful to appear in the uniform of his local corps.[78] William Pitt and Henry Dundas were colonels of prominent volunteer regiments: between them they commanded 5,000 men.* Liverpool and Palmerston were active supporters of militia or volunteer regiments and although Portland was too old and ill, his sons served in uniform. Lord Hobart, secretary of state for war in Addington's government, and his fellow cabinet member Charles Philip Yorke, both active colonels of militia regiments, were doubtful of the military capability of volunteers.[79] Among several published critics of the volunteers was the ex-soldier William Cobbett, who wanted a national citizen militia.[80] According to George Hanger, Cobbett had described the volunteers as 'nothing better than a rabble, blocking up the roads and preventing the regular troops from acting'. Hanger mounted a passionate defence of Pitt and of the volunteers, his wrath falling mainly on Cobbett: 'May the indignation of the British nation be poured down on the head of so daring and insolent an assassin of the public spirit.'[81]

Some fierce rivalries existed, too, among the volunteer corps themselves. In larger urban areas, such as Liverpool, volunteer bodies became politicized, while, of two volunteer corps in Manchester, one was exclusively Tory and another Whig, and on at least one occasion political differences led to a duel between commanding officers.[82] On another occasion two witnesses described a joint exercise at Wood Green in north London, 'when the Islington volunteers represented the English and the Hackney and Stoke Newington Volunteers the French. The Hackney Volunteers were so resolute not liking to represent the French, that the engagement nearly terminated with a real fight. A man . . . was stabbed with a bayonet in the thigh and several were wounded by cartridges.' The second witness continued:

> There was not the least understanding with the officers which company was to fire and [which] retreat, and they actually advanced and fired

* Pitt commanded the Cinque Port Volunteers from Walmer Castle, in which he lived as Warden of the Cinque Ports. The War Office commissioned a hundred-guinea telescope from William Herschel, the astronomer and telescope-maker, to be mounted on the walls of Walmer Castle to give early warning of invasion and particularly of aerial invasion by troops carried by Montgolfier balloons (Holmes, *Age of Wonder*, p. 200).

until their bayonets came into contact and the blood ran down their faces with the sting of powder. The Hackney corps added to put the Islington out of temper, for they took aim with their rifles and the wadding struck many of them and at last they got into great disorder. At this point a general brawl ensued that was only stopped by the Colonel plunging in on horseback where he begged them 'for God's sake to desist'.[83]

The volunteers, however, were an integral part of the duke of York's plan for the defence of the kingdom. In July 1803 the commander-in-chief sent an order to general officers commanding districts: 'the great object of the irregular Troops must be to Harass, alarm and Fatigue an enemy – nothing can more effectually contribute to this object than the operations of small bodies of men well acquainted with the country who will approach and fire upon the advanced Post of His army without ever engaging in serious action or hazarding themselves.'[84] The yeomanry cavalry would likewise have a secondary role: to enforce civil order, as specified in his memorandum by Addington. Henry Dundas informed Lord Grenville:

> The regular cavalry should be reserved for regular attack upon the enemy. The yeomanry cavalry should have their chief attention directed to preserve the internal quiet of the country. The provisional cavalry should be employed in driving the cattle, and such other business of a Hussar nature as may occur in each district.[85]

Regulars were to be used as front-line troops, for it would have been, in Colonel Bunbury's words, 'madness in the British to have risked a general battle in the field . . . our troops were not then of [sufficient] quality'.[86] In July 1804, for instance, over 18,000 regular troops were stationed in Sussex, with 20,000 more to be deployed within two days of an invasion, being brought to the fighting rapidly in a very few hours, as Bunbury adds, by carriages and fish-carts.[87] In this county alone sixteen temporary hutted camps were built to house infantry between 1803 and 1805, with another five for cavalry.[88]

In each succeeding month that Napoleon did not attempt the Channel crossing, confidence grew among the defending forces. In March

1805 Major General Henry Lord Paget wrote to his brother of his regulars, 'Mine will be a wonderful Regiment next year . . . Believe me that wherever the British appear, they will carry all before them.'[89] Colonel Bunbury reckoned that, had Napoleon invaded in the winter of 1803, his chances of success would have been far greater than in 1804, by which time defensive measures were far more advanced. Bunbury saw the high command from close quarters. He described the duke of York as 'indefatigable, energetic, and just', and noted that the duke had praised the 'able assistants in his Adjutant and Quartermaster-Generals, Harry Calvert and Robert Brownrigg' (the latter had succeeded David Dundas as quartermaster-general in March 1803).[90] As the invasion threat receded, the sceptics among the politicians began to feel that they were being proved right. In September 1804 the marquess of Buckingham wrote to his brother Lord Grenville on Addington's invasion measures: 'Sir Brook Watson [the commissary-general] is a most excellent ally in the military project of crying out for invasion; but charms he never so wisely, I cannot find one creature who believes it will be attempted.'[91]

It was easy for the Opposition to criticize, but the potential of the French invasion force could not be ignored, until Napoleon suddenly, on 23 August 1805, ordered the Grand Army to break camp and march to central Europe to counter a new threat from Austria. By early October the British government calculated that the immediate crisis was over. In the Treasury at Whitehall, William Sturges Bourne, senior secretary to the Board, requested Sir Brook Watson to recommend measures for dismantling the elaborate civilian provisioning arrangements. Watson proposed cuts worth £83,000 a year, a considerable sum, which indicates that the temporary measures in London were substantial.[92]

From mid 1805, a two-year interlude was enjoyed. Napoleon was preoccupied with campaigns in northern and eastern Europe until July 1807, when he signed the Treaty of Tilsit with the Russian emperor. Britain, for most of that period after the success of Trafalgar, with the Ministry of All the Talents in power, had the freedom to send British expeditions to recapture the Cape of Good Hope and the islands in the West Indies, although, as has been noted in Chapter 8, the opportunist attempt to take Montevideo and Buenos Aires was an abject failure. But in the middle of 1807, having secured Europe at the Treaty of Tilsit, Napoleon once again turned his attention to an invasion of Britain.[93]

The emperor's letters to his minister of marine, Denis Decrès, show how consistent was his intention of invading Britain. In March 1808, for instance, he wanted to concentrate invasion flotillas in Dutch ports rather than at Boulogne and Calais. In a draft plan sent in September 1810, he asked his minister: 'Let me know what sort of boats can be built at Dordrecht: I would like to build there a flotilla capable of carrying to Ireland or Scotland a force of four divisions, each of ten battalions or 8,000 men, making 32,000 infantry, 4,000 gunners and engineers and 6,000 cavalry and 120 field guns . . .' In August 1811 he was asking Decrès, 'Which is the port which should be preferred for assembling my squadron of the [Atlantic] Ocean? I see only two possible choices: Cherbourg or Brest. Which of these ports offers the most opportunities for a landing in England or Ireland?' Even after his return from the disastrous retreat from Moscow, he was still planning naval expansion. By now, his lack of reality on the resources available to him was palpable, but he had lost none of his ambition.* In July 1811 a long memorandum dated the end of June, containing the emperor's expansionist naval programme, appeared in *The Times* in London.[94] In Britain the fear of invasion never fully evaporated until Napoleon finally destroyed his army by choosing to invade Russia in 1812.

Alongside the formation of the militia and volunteers, coastal artillery and fortifications had been constructed. The fortifications, however, were not in a good state, and from the start of the Napoleonic War they were subject to improvement from several parts of the military machine, since responsibilities were confused. Permanent fortifica-

---

* Napoleon dictated in St Helena, 'After my talks with Alexander . . . Britain was to be forced to peace either by force of arms or reason. She was lost, despised throughout the continent: her action at Copenhagen had revolted all minds, and as for me, I sparkled with all the opposite advantages' (Hicks, 'Napoleon, Tilsit', p.126, quoting 14 June 1816, le comte de las Cases, *Le Mémorial de Sainte-Hélène, édition intégrale et critique*, Marcel Dunan (ed.) (Paris, 1951)).

tions were under the charge of the Board of Ordnance: from Selsey in Sussex to Cromer in Norfolk over fifty batteries and redoubts of various sizes had to be maintained and provided with cannon.[95] They were in the hands of the Board's chief engineer, whose title, in 1802, was changed by royal warrant to inspector-general of fortifications and works. Lieutenant-General Robert Morse filled the post in 1803, described by Lord Cornwallis as 'a good old fellow upon the whole, but no warrior'.[96] Large forts, or 'redoubts', were built at Eastbourne, Dymchurch and Harwich, each with ten guns, and not finished until late in the war.[97] However, the quartermaster-general in the Horse Guards was responsible for 'Fieldworks', i.e., works that were not permanent; but this could, and did, lead to friction with the Ordnance, for the definition of 'temporary' and 'fieldworks' was subject to wide interpretation.[98] Matters were further complicated in that temporary works also fell under the domain of the generals commanding the military districts; and the master-general of the Ordnance staked a claim as well, Lord Chatham grandly informing the secretary of state for war that

> Strictly speaking, all fieldworks merely should be communicated to me before the King's Pleasure is signified for their execution to the Commander-in-Chief, as involving great demands for men, guns, stores, etc., etc., except where they are so inconsiderable as to be defended and armed by the field train at the disposal of the general commanding.[99]

This struggle was never finally settled, and it was made more complex by Treasury control over funds, and army or Ordnance officers needed to go through a complex bureaucratic procedure before money could be spent on defence works. Land purchase was undertaken through the provisions of the Defence Act of 1803. Perhaps the most celebrated of the purchases at this time was that of the site at Shorncliffe near Sandgate on the Kent coast, recommended by General Sir David Dundas in 1804, where the light infantry, so distinguished later in the fighting in Spain, were trained by Lieutenant-General Sir John Moore.[100] A contract was signed to build a road running along the top of the North Downs between Guildford and Rochester, known as the 'Chalk Ridge Communication', to enable troops to move laterally across the system of roads. Though its track is not clear today, the work was completed by 1804.[101] To improve communications across the Thames, a raft, presumably hauled with ropes from each side of the river, was constructed between Blackwall and the Greenwich marshes, on the line of the present-day Blackwall Tunnel.[102] Rather more dramatic was the scheme to flood the Lea Valley to the east of London to stop an enemy advance after a landing on the Essex coast. A dam and a 'floating gate' were constructed at Four Mills, Bow, under the supervision of John Rennie, who considered that it would take twenty-six days stoppage of the river before the flooding was complete. Under his direction it was partially completed, but abandoned after the end of the first invasion scare in 1805.

The most renowned measure of these years was the building of the Martello Towers, best known because so many of them have survived. The idea of the towers stemmed from the experience of those on the headlands in Corsica, one of which, at Mortella Bay, caused British warships under Hood in 1794 considerable damage when they attacked the island, a result that was closely noted by General Dundas when he briefly commanded British troops there. These round towers were about thirty feet high with very thick walls to withstand bombardment; a single 24-pound gun was mounted at the top of each one. As a result of this effective performance, fifteen of these towers were built in Minorca when the island was recaptured by Britain in 1798.[103] A comprehensive scheme for the defence of the south coast of Britain was drawn up in the same year by Major Thomas Vincent Reynolds from the Ordnance Survey, based on his deep knowledge of the coast and country of southern England.* Reynolds listed 143 suitable sites for 'Martella' Towers between Littlehampton and Great Yarmouth, of which he considered 73 as 'urgently necessary', 48 'necessary' and 22 as 'desirable'. Detailed planning for building fortifications to counter invasion had been shelved in 1798 when the danger was thought to have passed and French energies had been put into the expedition to Egypt.[104] Developing fortifications had not been

---

* The Ordnance Survey had gathered a great deal of data but only one complete map of Kent had been published before the end of the eighteenth century (Hewitt, *Map of a Nation*, p. 152).

considered in 1801 when Napoleon started to build up his forces at the Channel ports during the peace negotiations before Amiens, even though Boulogne was bombarded by a flotilla under Nelson.[105] Now the threat was palpable. General David Dundas, based at the Horse Guards, and Lieutenant-Colonel Harry Calvert, the adjutant-general, became key figures. The towers were first urged on the House of Commons by William Windham in December 1803 when he was out of office, but disagreements between opponents and supporters of the new towers among the military led to delay in building. Henry Dundas, back in government in May 1804, revived these plans for tower defence and developed them into official policy.[106]

The debate over the building of the towers was reopened and settled at a conference at Rochester in Kent on 21 October 1804, attended by all the leading figures responsible for the military defence of the country: the prime minister, William Pitt, the secretary of state for war, Lord Camden, the master-general of the Ordnance, Lord Chatham, and the commander-in-chief, the duke of York. Generals Dundas, Brownrigg and Morse and Lieutenant-Colonel William Twiss, the chief engineer in the Southern District, were also in attendance, as was Lieutenant-Colonel Brown of the Royal Staff Corps, who was to be responsible for the building of the military canal. Viewing the proceedings with a jaundiced eye, unsurprisingly in the light of the bureaucratic divide, he wrote in his diary:

> At this meeting the expensive and diabolical system of Tower Defence was finally resolved on to an unprecedented extent ... but it was carried by the influence of the Ordnance people ... only whose opinions were by no means supported by reasoning ... Mr Pitt, from whom one would have expected a decided opinion, gave in to that of others ... without requiring (what indeed he could not have obtained) a satisfactory and well-digested plan of defence. All that was advanced was Tower, Tower, Tower ...[107]

Building started in the spring of 1805 under the supervision of the main contractor, William Hobson. A standard tower contained 700,000 bricks, of a distinctive dirty-yellow colour, most of them purchased by Hobson from the London brickfields; by placing the first orders quietly with smaller brickmakers, he managed to obtain a good price before the scale of the government requirement was known.[108] When work stopped on the south coast chain in 1808, 73 towers and two 11-gun circular forts had been built. A further 29 towers were built on the coasts of Essex and Suffolk, between St Osyth Stone and Aldeburgh, and one additional tower was added at Seaford in Sussex before all construction in southern England finished in 1812.[109] The final towers were built at Hackness and Crockness in Orkney in 1814 as protection for harbours against the depredations of American privateers.[110]

The towers were strong, with walls varying in thickness from six to thirteen feet, with the thickest segment facing seaward, the only direction from which there was likely to be a heavy bombardment. The bricks were bedded in hot lime mortar, a mixture of lime, ash and hot tallow calculated to withstand bombardment. A flat roof, supported by a central column from the base of the tower, carried the 24-pounder, mounted on a sliding traverse carriage that enabled it to fire through 360 degrees.* These towers had the potential to be devastating to boats carrying troops towards a beach, but success would depend upon the quality and training of those who manned them, and the support provided by other troops. When the question of who should man the towers had arisen during planning, Henry Dundas, over dinner at Walmer Castle with Pitt, is supposed to have said, 'Give us the towers and we'll find men!' Each tower required twenty-four men and an officer. Lord Chatham's idea was for them to be manned from a veteran battalion.[111] At Pevensey, in October 1804, the tower was commanded by a corporal and sixteen gunners from the eighth Invalid Battalion of

---

* Each tower was issued with a hundred rounds of solid shot, twenty each of case-shot, grape-shot, common shells, 8-pound cartridges, as well as half a hundred-weight of slow match and forty junk wads, and gunpowder. Of these, the case-shot was the most damaging anti-personnel ammunition, effective at 350 yards. The 'heavy' case-shot consisted of 84 6-ounce balls packed inside a thin metal canister, which burst on firing: a single round was almost as lethal as a volley of musket-fire from an infantry regiment. For short periods it was possible for an efficient gun-crew to fire three rounds a minute (Coad, *Dymchurch Martello Tower*, p. 12).

the Royal Artillery.* The towers were guarded by the militia. The Fife Militia, for instance, guarded the tower and redoubt at Dymchurch in 1806 and 1807.[112] In March 1807, when Windham abolished the volunteers, the South Pevensey Legion was disbanded, 'with the exception of the Eastbourne Company under the command of Captain Augur consisting of 120 privates'.[113] Windham's sudden announcement that the militia should take on all duties could not be implemented immediately, and coastal defence continued to depend upon volunteers.

Britain had used the lull of 1805 to 1807 to improve its defences. Early ideas of flooding Romney Marsh to render the country impassable were put aside because of doubts over the speed at which the Marsh would flood by opening Dymchurch Wall to the sea or by damming the River Rother. Instead, the idea of a canal with a defensive bank, from New Romney westwards across the top of Dungeness, with cannon at intervals, was put forward in September 1804 by Lieutenant-Colonel John Brown of the Royal Staff Corps, responsible to the quartermaster-general, and approval was given by Pitt immediately.[114] Not only would the canal act as a barrier to invading troops, but it could also be used to move defending troops and supplies along its length. The project was taken on by the Quartermaster-General's Department and classed as a 'fieldwork'; its construction was started by the contractors who had only recently finished excavating the London Docks, and supervised by John Rennie as chief engineer. In spite of employing hundreds of men, it proceeded very slowly, and the work was taken over by the Staff Corps under Brown.[115] With the help of other contractors, a work force of 1,500 men was assembled; and, when assisted by several small steam engines for pumping, progress was much faster, in spite of the difficulties of working through the cold and wet winter of 1805/6. By April 1806 ten miles of navigation had been completed, and in August of that year the dukes of York and Cambridge were towed in a small boat by horses along eighteen and a half miles of the canal in under three hours, at an average speed of seven miles an hour.[116] The canal construction was not without

---

* At a monthly cost of £39.12s.11½d., which included an innkeeper's allowance, beer allowance, as well as £2.7s.9¾d. towards the cost of the extra price of bread and meat (Pay Lists 1803–4, TNA, WO 10/528).

criticisms over its cost and perceived effectiveness. In October 1805 Lord Ellenborough, lord chief justice and soon to be in the cabinet in the Ministry of All the Talents, walked the length of the canal and then wrote to his friend Addington, now out of office: 'It will cost an enormous sum of money, and be, in my poor judgement, of no adequate use. An invading enemy will, by means of fascines,* get over it in any part they please in a very short time' – a harsh, inexpert judgement from a government opponent.[117] Though not yet complete, by mid 1807 the Royal Military Canal formed a tolerable military barrier.†

In different ways, other newly built canals had a beneficial effect upon Britain's security. The Grand Union Canal, connecting London to the industrial centres of the Midlands and the north, and its Paddington Basin opened in 1801. First, it enabled explosives to travel on a nationwide system of canals, rather than by coastal shipping, subject to the depredations of French privateers. The canal enabled the Ordnance to construct a major ammunition and equipment depot at Weedon Bec, built on a grand scale and fortified. Weedon is eight miles west of Northampton, nearer to Birmingham, the main manufacturing centre for small arms, and 120 miles from the nearest coast and thus much less exposed to French attack than Woolwich Arsenal on the Thames, east of the centre of London.[118] It was also identified as a possible place of refuge for the royal family and the government, if the French had landed and were threatening London. The canals could be used for moving troops efficiently as well. In December 1806 the Talents ministry sent two brigades of regulars totalling 5,000 soldiers urgently to Dublin. One brigade travelled from London by canal to Liverpool, where it was trans-shipped. The two brigades

---

* Fascines were bundles of sticks placed in trenches or ditches so that soldiers could cross the obstruction, used since at least Roman times,

† In Aug. 1807 an Act was passed establishing commissioners to maintain the canal and to authorize rates of toll. The expense to date was £143,081. In its early years it needed considerable subsidies for maintenance. Probably as a result of criticism over the great expense of an untested project, political heavyweights were appointed as commissioners: the prime minister, chancellor of the Exchequer, secretary of state for war, secretary at war, the speaker of the House of Commons and the commander-in-chief. In all, up to 1830, seven prime ministers gave advice on how to run the canal (Vine, *Military Canal*, pp. 80, 82–4, 227–8).

received their orders on 10 December and were in Dublin by 8 January 1807, a journey of less than a month for a large body of men.[119]

The expense of both the Royal Military Canal and the Martello Towers was insignificant compared with the costs of the works on the Chatham Lines and Dover Castle, upon which the defence of southern England ultimately depended. An 1804 estimate for eighty-eight Martello Towers came to £221,000.[120] Extensive work on the fortifications at Chatham and the building of Fort Pitt and Fort Clarence, part of the lines defending the dockyard, started in 1805 and continued until 1812.[121] Even more expense was incurred by the Ordnance on Dover Castle, which at times had a workforce of over 1,000, under the charge of Lieutenant-Colonel William Twiss. Using the massive medieval structure, but ruthlessly levelling parts of it, Twiss skilfully achieved 'a grafting operation', rather than building anew.[122] The works at the Castle itself were complete by 1803, but huge sums were expended for the rest of the Napoleonic War on the adjoining Western Heights that commanded the vitally important port of Dover, which had to be denied to the enemy at all costs. Fieldworks were improved, underground works and massive barracks were built. These sophisticated fortifications protected an 'entrenched camp' containing 5,000 or 6,000 troops, manning 139 large guns: in 1816 an estimated total cost of the works reached £402,999.* However, this sum did not include the London brick, which accounted for the largest proportion of the building materials, nor did it account for all the labour. During 1797, for instance, nearly 300 men from the East Suffolk Militia and the Montgomery Militia were employed on the works.[123] Twiss also put in a massive 180-foot-long shaft with three circular stairways to enable troops to be moved rapidly up to the top of the Heights or down to sea level. The work was continued through the war, but in later years funding became sporadic and they remained unfinished in 1815; Colonel William Ford, the resident engineer at Dover, complained of

---

* For cost comparison purposes, a contract-built 74-gun ship built in the Napoleonic War, complete and fitted, totalled between £80,000 and £90,000 (Winfield, *British Warships*, pp. 77–86).

the manner in which the great question of the fortifications of this country is treated by the Government. In a state of alarm expense is not considered; when that alarm subsides, we discontinue our operations; if the financial system is hard pressed, we are ordered to suspend our works, and the regular plan, which is conducive to the safety of the state is lost sight of in some more immediate and pressing service.[124]

As we have seen, the government was also continuously concerned at the potential for attack by the French on Ireland. Fortifications there were hardly less extensive than in England, where Dublin and Cork were the great prizes for an invader. Martello Towers were built around Dublin Bay even before those in England. Despite the fact that a French attack on Dublin from the sea was felt to be the least likely of the threats, the positions of fourteen towers had been selected by the middle of 1804, a contractor appointed and building complete by 1805. Lord Cornwallis, who gave up the post of master-general of the Ordnance in 1801, privately thought that the Irish towers were 'totally useless'.[125] After much debate, shaped by the invasion scares of 1796 and 1797, the west of Ireland was seen to be the most vulnerable. For hardened French troops, Dublin would have been only a week's march away, and the use by the French of the Grand Canal from the Shannon to Dublin could have shortened that time. Between 1804 and 1806, and then again from 1811 to 1814, batteries and towers were constructed along the line of the Shannon. As in England, the local reservists were trained to assist the artillerymen in working the guns.[126] At Shannonbridge, the nearest point to Galway Bay, work started on earthwork defences in 1804, and these developed into some of the most sophisticated fortifications of the age.[127] Barracks multiplied late in the war for troops garrisoned for internal security. From 1807 Martello Towers were built at the anchorages where the French might land, at Bantry, Galway, Lough Swilly and Lough Foyle.[128] The building of these extensive works continued until the end of the war, demonstrating that the fear of a large-scale French landing in the west of Ireland was still central to the defensive thinking of the British government until at least 1812.[129]

Altogether in the British Isles, including the two in Orkney, a total of 168 Martello Towers, of differing designs and materials, were built during the Napoleonic War. More were projected: at one point in 1804 a circular went out to district commanders to report any further sites that might be appropriate.[130] There were mistakes, and some, particularly on the Kent coast, were built too near each other, so that fire from their cannons would have badly overlapped. Opinion on their likely effectiveness in the event of invasion remained a matter of debate. Some thirty years after the wars, the duke of Wellington reflected: 'At all events, if they are nothing else, each of them is an excellent defensive guardhouse, which cannot be surprised and may be defended forever against anything but a regular attack by a superior force.'[131]

The effect that defensive preparations undertaken by Britain, from the arming the auxiliary forces to the building of fortifications, had on Napoleon's resolve to invade can only be surmised. He would have had to take into account the damage inflicted by the Royal Navy on his invasion craft and subsequently on French supply vessels. But a dozen years of unremitting military engineering from 1803 to 1815 unquestionably made the British Isles safer, and, as every year passed, an invasion therefore became a greater risk for the French. Even so, the threat posed by Napoleon from 1807 until midway through 1812, whether from his newly building fleet at Antwerp and other Continental ports under his control, or from an expedition to the west of Ireland, was still very much in the minds of military planners. As late as 1 January 1811 a 253-page Defence Report was drawn up whose authors were quite certain of Napoleon's intention to invade: 'These considerations must be too strong upon the mind of every reflecting Man and the disasters of successful Invasion too evident to need any illustration ... irresistible evidence from long experience that till Invasion has been attempted He will never be at rest.' The report proposed the need for 400,000 British militiamen in 800 battalions. Napoleon's army of only '60 or 70,000 men could never [even] subjugate the Country ... nothing short of five times the number ... could hold a probability of even temporary success.'[132]

This expanded number was almost exactly the size of the army that Napoleon prepared in 1811 for his invasion of Russia and that was destroyed during the retreat from Moscow in 1812. Had that disaster not struck the French, those huge British militia battalions might have been needed and the fortifications come into their own. Instead, by the end of 1813, after nearly twenty years of mobilization and construction, the threat of invasion had been overcome and the army was able to release most of its line regiments and deploy them overseas in the Peninsula and to the near Continent.[133]

10

Intelligence, Security and Communications

1803–1811

But for the justification of a hostile armament against Denmark we must look for other reasons. I trust however that the world will feel that we have them ... Intelligence from so many and such various sources of B[uonaparte]'s intention to force or seduce D[enmark] into an active confederacy against this country, leaves no doubt of his design. Nay, the fact that he has openly avowed such intention in an interview with the E[mperor] of R[ussia] is brought to this country in such a way as it cannot be doubted. Under such circumstances it would be madness, it would be idiotic ... to wait for an overt act.
– Scribbled memorandum by Spencer Perceval, chancellor of the Exchequer, undated [but 22 July 1807], on information that Napoleon intended to force Denmark to declare war on Britain, in the period before the operation against Copenhagen[1]

From the time of the resumption of war in 1803 after the Peace of Amiens, the intelligence battle between England and France began to take a different direction, as ideological conflict gave way to more traditional war between nations. As we saw in Chapter 5, in the 1790s espionage initiatives had attempted to foster an uprising in France. Though the Alien Office had played its part in counteracting the dangers to the state at home and in Ireland, its attempt to stir up trouble on the Continent was an expensive failure. The end of this phase of secret warfare was marked by an assassination plot against Napoleon by French royalists, uncovered in early 1804 by the French secret police, and implicating a senior French figure, General Jean-Charles Pichegru. Led and financed by Britain, the plot, when it was discovered, caused the British government acute embarrassment.[2] As a postscript to the plot, in March 1804 Sidney Smith's erstwhile fellow secret agent, John Wesley Wright, returned to Quiberon on the coast, south of Brittany, commanding a ship whose mission was to evacuate any survivors of the Pichegru plot; but Wright was betrayed, captured and imprisoned, again, in the Temple Prison in Paris. He was murdered in his cell on 28 October 1805.[3]*

This final attempt by Britain to foment counter-revolution ended in the death of Pichegru, and also that of the duc d'Enghien on 21 March 1804. The latter's offence was merely to be a Bourbon prince, and he had played no part in the plot against Napoleon. Further, he was captured on foreign territory and brought by French agents to France, where he was rapidly tried and executed. The emperor lost the propaganda advantage he had gained through the discovery of the plot to assassinate him: eliminating a young prince who was clearly innocent was unpopular, even in France. Nevertheless, Napoleon was able to consolidate his power, and British attempts to destabilize the French government ceased.[4] After these events both French royalists and their bitter rivals, the constitutional monarchists, were forced to take a lesser role. Some continued to provide information to Britain, although others also undoubtedly contributed to Napoleon's spy network in England.[5] Of the major French royalist political adventurers, only the comte d'Antraigues, who became close to George Canning when he was foreign secretary, remained useful to the British government.

Systematic collection and better organization were to be the hallmarks of intelligence analysis during the Napoleonic War, although an attempt in early 1803 to bring about the comprehensive integration of military intelligence was to fail. The idea of the establishment of the

---

* Evidence on the conspiracy is scarce owing to the wholesale destruction of Alien Office documents, a process that started in 1834. The diplomat Francis Drake, then based in Bavaria, was implicated in the assassination plot. After his death in 1821, Lord Hawkesbury, by then Lord Liverpool, purchased Drake's papers from his two sons, who were persuaded that it was in the national interest not to publish them, as Drake had requested in his will. The two sons received an annuity paid out of the civil list (Sparrow, 'Alien Office', p. 301; Durey, *Wickham*, p. 194). In 1836 the functions of the Alien Office were transferred to the Home Office (Sainty, *Home Office*, p. 5).

'Depot for Military Knowledge' was similar to that of the French in Paris, who centralized secret and open source military intelligence in their 'Bureau de Renseignments' and whose 'Topographical Bureau' held maps and plans.[6] The new quartermaster-general, Major General Sir Robert Brownrigg, formerly military secretary to the duke of York, had the commander-in-chief's support for the new measure, and it was approved by Charles Philip Yorke when he was secretary at war. The British version was to consist of four departments: Plans, Movements, Library and Topographical. Brownrigg also went further by proposing that the Secret Office in the Post Office and the Alien Office be integrated with foreign intelligence. The failure to establish the Depot was due to the prosaic reason of a lack of office space, as the duke of York later explained to Lord Castlereagh: 'The chief obstacle has been a want of sufficient accommodation to place in security and to arrange in order the valuable materials which were to be collected.'[7] There would have been enough space on the additional floor of the Horse Guards then being built, but it was not finished until 1805. For the moment, some military maps were drawn, but nothing further was done.*

In the last three years of the French Revolutionary War, William Wickham had briefly achieved what could be described as centralized, cross-government intelligence assessment.† Known as the Inner Office', with its network of Christ Church graduates, it had been broken up by Addington when he introduced peacetime economies.[8]

Wickham fell out of favour with Pitt, and was appointed by Addington as chief secretary to the lord lieutenant of Ireland in February 1802, in which post he spent an unhappy two years. It was during this period that Robert Emmet's one-day rebellion broke out on 23 July 1803, and, as we saw in Chapter 8, although Wickham was not himself in Dublin on that day, he was blamed for not having anticipated it. He resigned, citing overwork and strain. On the fringe of politics,

---

* The effective integration of tactical military intelligence was achieved by Wellington in the Peninsula, when British diplomats, naval officers and civilians cooperated closely (Ward, *Wellington's Headquarters*, pp. 29–30; Davies, 'Intelligence during the Peninsular War', pp. 205–6; 'Diplomats as Spymasters', pp. 40–50).
† Wickham returned from Switzerland in early 1798 and was made one of the under-secretaries of the Home Office from Mar. 1798 to Jan. 1801.

and now uncomfortable in it, he had no further part in the intelligence world.[9] The career of Evan Nepean, secretary of the Admiralty, and another important hub in the Whitehall intelligence machine, took a similar turn. He fell out with the naval members of his Board and, as his colleague William Marsden noted, 'having long found his official situation irksome', was appointed by Addington to follow Wickham as chief secretary of Ireland, a post for which he, too, was little suited.[10]

Information circulated around Whitehall with more system, purpose, verification and analysis than had been the case in the 1790s.* From the resumption of war, there was better cooperation between cabinet ministers and departments, the lack of which had marked the intelligence failures before Napoleon's conquest of Egypt in 1798. Detailed correspondence circulated around Whitehall, signed and annotated by each of the undersecretaries as he read a letter or memorandum before sending it on. The movements of the documents can be traced through the Foreign Office, Home Office, Admiralty and secretary of state for war. The Post Office was often included in this network, for its packets could pick up important information on ship sightings when at sea; and the Alien Office, interviewing passengers through the ports, would transmit useful intelligence through John King, undersecretary at the Home Office.

To handle this mass of information, greater system was used in the internal workings of each office, brought to a new level of collation and cross-reference by the indexing and summarizing of correspondence in great volumes known as 'Digests'.[11] The young Colonel Henry Bunbury – appointed military undersecretary to the secretary of state for war in late 1809 when Liverpool hurriedly succeeded Castlereagh – assumed a major role in summarizing intelligence from all sources for his chief. Although one of the most urgent issues was to discover how many reinforcements were to be sent to the French armies in the

---

* Not only with strategic and tactical intelligence, but also with navigational data collected by the Hydrographic Office. A good example of the need to centralize and analyse this sort of information was the requirement for accurate charts and navigational information on the Baltic, which before 1801 had not seen a British fleet for seventy years, but in 1807 and from 1808 to 1812 a large British naval presence was in the Baltic, and the quality and quantity of charts improved (Davey, 'Hydrographical Office', pp. 81–103).

Peninsula, Bunbury handled and processed every sort of intelligence destined for the secretary of state's office.[12]

Routine intelligence and security systems operated effectively. The Alien Act of 1796 limited entry to certain ports, under the terms of which persons seeking entry to Britain had to obtain permission from the secretary of state.* As ever, the navy maintained its watch on French ports. Philippe D'Auvergne, made a rear-admiral in 1805, and assisted by General Sir George Don, lieutenant-governor of Jersey, filed his voluminous intelligence reports from Jersey until he retired on half-pay in 1812. D'Auvergne now had a network of agents in every port from L'Orient as far north as the Texel. From them he brought large amounts of both naval and military intelligence together that were sent back to Whitehall.[13] The efforts of D'Auvergne's agents ashore were supplemented by the observations of the small warships under his command, which also harried French trade and pursued enemy privateers.[14] In the same way, a small squadron of gun-brigs, commanded by Captain Edward Owen from the *Immortalité*, collected intelligence when Napoleon was massing his invasion flotillas in 1804, and made a thorough nuisance of themselves along the French Channel coast by bombarding ports and taking any small enemy vessels that ventured out.†

---

* The account of a German traveller in 1810 showed how the screening of overseas arrivals worked in practice.

> On arrival at Harwich from Holland we dropped anchor, and a boat with custom officers pushed off from the shore with Mr Billingby the director of the Alien Office at their head. The former climbed aboard and began a personal search upon such persons who were likely to carry contraband goods about them … In the meantime Mr Billingby to whom a nominal list of passengers was delivered by the captain, began to call them over; and taking one half of us in his boat, made for the shore. They showed us into the White Hart Inn, and then took the boat again to fetch the rest. Our baggage was taken to the Custom House and there kept till our licences arrived, for which we had without delay applied to the Central Alien Office through our friends in London.
>
> (Trinder, *Harwich Packets*, p. 71, quoting *Letters from Albion to a Friend on the Continent*, 1814)

† In Aug. 1804 the *Immortalité* took on board a stranger for a fortnight when cruising off Boulogne, whose name, a midshipman recalled in later years, was never known, and whom 'I must still designate by the appellation of "Mr Nobody", the cognomen by which alone he was known to the midshipmen.' The ship kept close to the shore

The government also used smugglers to deliver and collect intelligence which often traversed the Channel and southern North Sea at speed, making it difficult for the authorities on both sides to keep developments of any sizeable operation secret. Information often travelled in vessels under ten tons, light rowing galleys, cheap to construct, manned by perhaps a dozen oarsmen, up to forty feet in length. In calm conditions these fast galleys could complete a Channel crossing under cover of darkness. No one knew French and Dutch waters and their dangerous tides better than the fishermen and watermen of Dover and Deal. Transmitting intelligence by these fast vessels was mixed with other business. Smuggled tobacco, alcohol and French lace and silk were still profitable in wartime, as were earnings from the transport of bullion and escaped prisoners of war, in both directions.[15] The Dover customs collectors complained to the customs commissioners in London that these boats were 'so finely constructed and manned with such expert rowers that few if any of the boats in the service of the Revenue are equal to them in swiftness'. In 1809 the Preventative Water Guard was founded, but it had only thirty-nine revenue cutters and sixty-two boats to patrol the entire English and Welsh coastlines.[16] Thus, contact between smugglers and fishermen on both sides of the Channel was hardly interrupted by wartime conditions, and carrying intelligence provided another source of business. Family links were strong between the ports of England, France and Holland. In 1804 Sir John Moore, at Shorncliffe on the Kent coast training troops, reported to the Home Office: 'There is hardly a family in Folkestone which has not Relatives settled at Flushing and there is a constant intercourse.'[17]

---

in order to give an opportunity of pursuing certain researches ... which ... he did with the greatest earnestness and coolness, unruffled and undisturbed by the showers of shot and shell that fell around the ship, splashing the water about her at every instant. The object of this scrutiny seemed to be to ascertain ... the fortifications around Boulogne, and the position and bearings of the different batteries which faced the sea, and also the exact distance at which the flotilla in the roads was anchored from the shore.

The crew were glad to see him go ashore back in the Downs, as he made the ship 'serve every day, whilst he was on board, as a target for our friends to amuse themselves by practising at' (Crawford, *Reminiscences*, pp. 59–60).

During the height of the invasion threat in 1804 and 1805, Lieutenant-Colonel Willoughby Gordon, the assistant quartermaster-general of the Southern District, maintained a network of spies with which he communicated by means of the smugglers through Flushing.[18] In 1811 the Foreign Department of the Post Office wrote to John Barrow to plead very strongly for the release of some smugglers who had been detained by a warship:

> a boat was coming from France as usual, the Master of which had French Newspapers for this Office ... regularly sanctioned and approved by the Post Master General and equally by Government, and it is always the rule when any intelligence is received to forward it to the secretary of State & afterwards to the public newspapers. The principal channels through which Intelligence is procured is by the means of Smugglers & it has generally succeeded ... it is of material consequence to the Govt to have a channel by which Intelligence may occasionally be obtained.

The secretary to the Board of Admiralty endorsed the letter: 'Their Lordships cannot interfere.'[19] Intelligence also flowed by this means in the opposite direction. In July of that year H.M. Gunboat *Locust* stopped a rowing galley, the *Apus of London*, just outside Gravelines. The master claimed that his vessel was on a secret mission ordered by John Wilson Croker, but gold and English newspapers were found aboard, 'and in two kegs with false heads', the naval commander reported to the customs officials at Dover, 'were also secreted a quantity of letters addressed to French merchants and various other papers – upon the discovery of which the master appeared very much agitated indeed.'[20]

Escaped prisoners or deserters often conveyed intelligence across the Channel, especially if they were sailors, and their information could be given some weight. One British seaman, Ralph Dunlop, who as a prisoner of war suffered 'cruel and harsh treatment, into an almost hopeless state, [he] with several others agreed to engage in the French service, in the hopes of being brought to the Coasts, to find an opportunity to escape'. His information after the action in the Basque Roads in 1809 was precise and detailed. Two years later D'Auvergne sent some intelligence gained from French sailors who had deserted from St Malo to Jersey, 'representing they were not paid for serving in the French ships of war and [were] very ill treated'. The deserters' information was corroborated by neutrals 'lately arrived at Guernsey'.[21]

Ordinary diplomatic and military communication had to be swift and reliable. Post Office packets carried despatches to the West Indies, the Mediterranean and across the North Sea, as well as domestic and commercial mail. These ships also transported the King's Messengers, who travelled the Continent, delivering particularly important despatches and cipher books to and from British diplomats at foreign courts. Those areas of conflict far from London, such as the Mediterranean, however, often experienced long periods without contact between politicians in Whitehall and admirals and generals in the field. Nelson became frustrated with lack of information during his long watch on Toulon between 1803 and 1805, and had to take a large number of independent decisions. During Collingwood's period as commander-in-chief from 1805 to 1810 he had to run his own Mediterranean-wide intelligence network, largely composed of the officers under his command, and as a result he developed a particularly acute strategic awareness.[22] He was, according to Thomas Creevey after reading his correspondence some years later, 'the prime and sole minister of England, acting upon the sea, corresponding himself with all surrounding states, and ordering everything upon his own responsibility'.[23] Nor was Collingwood a stranger to the subtleties of intelligence deception. His last success at sea, in October 1809, when his ships destroyed a French force that broke out of Toulon with supplies for the French Army in Barcelona, was triggered by a clever ruse in disguising the readiness of his fleet in Port Mahon, which he knew was being observed by someone he suspected of being a French double agent.* The action ended with the destruction of two

* A retired French officer, who had in the past given information to the British, was brought by a British frigate for an interview with Collingwood, with information about a French force that was shortly to sail from Toulon. The admiral, who already knew this, suspected that the Frenchman's intention was in fact to gauge the readiness of the British Fleet. He therefore ordered the fleet in Mahon Harbour to look as

French ships of the line and thirteen transports, while four were captured.[24]

In spite of British ascendancy at sea, it was a struggle to keep communications open with diplomats and governments on the Continent, especially in those countries such as Prussia and Austria that resented the overweening influence of the Napoleonic regime. Naturally, this was a difficulty that France avoided, as French conquests were mainly on the Continent: it had few sea communications and the advantage of internal lines. Merchants also faced problems. For almost all the Napoleonic War, European waters were packed with enemy privateers, not only from France and Holland but also from Spain, until that country turned against France in 1808. From 1807 Denmark and Norway were actively hostile, and between 1812 and 1814 bold and successful American privateers captured many British merchant ships in both North American and European waters (as we will see in Chapter 13). British Post Office packets also suffered considerably: between 1803 and 1808 ten Falmouth-based packets were captured by French privateers, and two by Spanish. After 1812 eighteen struck their colours to American privateers.[25] Packet losses were fewer among those working out of Harwich and Yarmouth to the Continental North Sea ports: seven were taken during the war as a whole, three of which were interned in Hellevoetsluis in Holland at the sudden outbreak of the war in May 1803.[26]

All packets were built for speed and sailed close to the wind, but they found well-manned privateers difficult to shake off. Debate was continuous within the Post Office as to whether or not the vessels should be more heavily armed, because guns added significantly to the weight of a packet and adversely affected its speed. In 1811 one

---

though every ship was refitting, with topmasts struck, sails unbent, scaffolding over the sides, painting and caulking in full swing. When the Frenchman had reboarded the frigate after his interview with Collingwood and left the island, the captains were immediately summoned and the fleet made ready, so that 'the whole fleet, which a few hours before seemed half dismantled, and all bustle and confusion, is now in perfect order, and only waits for the land-breeze in the morning to lift their anchors and proceed to sea' (Crawford, *Reminiscences*, p. 184).

Falmouth-based packet was chased off Finisterre but got away, as the packet commander related when applying to the postmasters-general for compensation to replace equipment: 'I was obliged for the preservation of the packet and to prevent the loss of H.M. mails and despatches, to knock out the stanchions, throw overboard the long boat, and run off my lee gun amidships in order to expedite the sailing of the vessel, which I am happy to say had the desired effect and after a hard chase of thirty-six hours we escaped.'[27]

As the war became concentrated away from the Channel, and conflict both on land and at sea moved further north, the importance of communications across the North Sea increased. As French domination spread north taking in the German ports and then Denmark, the packets were forced to take the mail by northerly and more distant and dangerous routes. In 1803 the Post Office struggled to keep the Cuxhaven route open, but increasingly the southern Danish ports of Husum and Tonningen had to be used for mail delivery, a distance of 240 miles. As a precaution postal agents were set up in Heligoland, from which mails were sent onwards to Hamburg and other German ports by fishing boats.* As the head of the Hamburg Post Office put it to a Post Office official in London in 1806, 'the way is the most sure and the only one that will continue to dure the longest time.'[28] An agent with credentials was also set up in Gothenburg in southern Sweden: the route flourished, although here the danger to packets was due to weather rather than to French predators.[29] For a short period in 1806 the Cuxhaven route was again possible, but in the summer of 1807, the year of the apogee of Napoleon's power, British hostilities against Copenhagen made the delivery of mail to Danish and German ports impossible. From 1807, the only route for mails to countries in northern Europe was from Harwich or Yarmouth to Gothenburg, a voyage of 480 sea miles, which necessitated sailing a round trip of at least a thousand miles. This compared with the peacetime route of

---

* The annexation of Heligoland in Sept. 1807 allowed travellers greater freedom to enter Britain, through the fast 'Bye Boats', sailing from Harwich and Yarmouth, licensed to sail without convoy, but they took profitable passengers away from the packets. In May 1811 the packet-boat commanders complained to the postmaster-general about the activities of these boats, requesting that their licences be restricted (Trinder, *Harwich Packets*, pp. 71–2).

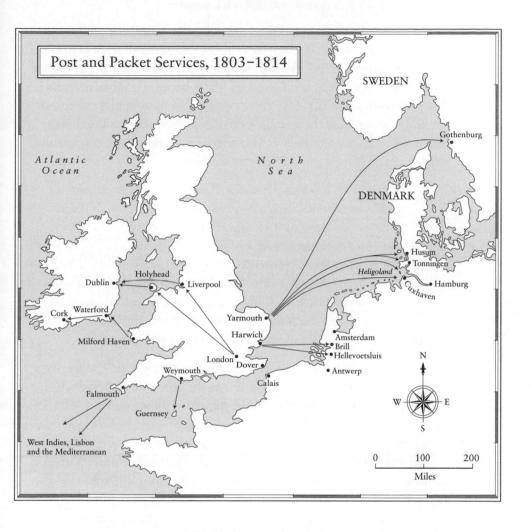

SWEDEN

Gothenburg

*North
Sea*

DENMARK

*Atlantic
Ocean*

Husum
Tonningen

Heligoland

Hamburg

Cuxhaven

Holyhead

Dublin

Liverpool

Cork Waterford

Yarmouth

Milford Haven

Harwich

Amsterdam
Brill
Hellevoetsluis

London

Weymouth

Dover

Antwerp

Calais

N

Falmouth

Guernsey

W——E

West Indies, Lisbon
and the Mediterranean

S

0   100   200

Miles

Dover to Calais of just over twenty miles, or Harwich to Hellevoetsluis
of 120 miles. As year by year the North Sea and the Baltic assumed
greater wartime strategic and diplomatic importance, the packet service had to stretch itself even further.

Only in summer was the Gothenburg route anything less than hazardous. The *Prince of Wales* packet, commanded by Captain Anthony
Deane, sailed there first in 1804, and made fifteen such passages in the
next three years, ten in summer, when the average time for the voyage
was eighteen and a half days. In winter the average time taken was

nearly doubled to thirty-two days. The longest round trip, in November and December 1805, took forty days, including nine days in port at Gothenburg delayed by bad weather.* Approaching the Swedish coast in February 1805 the *Prince of Wales* became trapped in the ice. The ship managed to get into clear water by dropping pigs of iron on to the ice, 'suspended from ye Bowsprit by Ropes Led through Blocks'. Off Sweden again a month later, Deane had an even worse time of it and tried to reach Marstrand, some way to the north of Gothenburg:

> At 3pm tack'd from a great Quantity of Ice, At 7pm a large ship ran foul of us, in a very thick fog, & stove in our Larboard Bow, broke our best Bower Anchor &&, At Midnight ye Fog clear'd away. At Daylight bore away for Marstrand, could not get in for Ice extending from ye Paternosters to ye Main, proceeded to ye Winga, to try at Chelsea Sound or at Wergo, these were also block'd up, At last came a Pilot who took us into a small harbour Call'd Fueto Sound, & at Noon went on shore with ye Mails, hir'd guides & over ye Rocks and Ice. At 8pm arriv'd & deliver'd ye Mails to ye Agent at Gottenburg.[30]

This wearying route, involving an eight-hour trek over the ice by a packet captain with a sack of mail, was the sole means by which the British government in winter could maintain direct contact with its diplomats and allies in the north of Europe, and merchants could conduct business with their Continental agents.†

These new long routes soon began to cost the packet masters money in broken gear and unbudgeted expenses. In 1804 all twelve of the Harwich masters signed a letter to the postmasters-general at the same time as submitting their accounts, asking for greater remuneration, for they were now sailing far further than they were contracted, as they expressed it: 'When no other vessels scarcely ever attempt it,

---

* The log of the *Prince of Wales* records thirty-seven round trips between Aug. 1804 and Sept. 1807, an average of just over a dozen a year: the vessel delivered mail to Cuxhaven (4), Husum (11), Tonningen (2), Heligoland (3), Marstrand (2) and Gothenburg (15).

† The importance of the route was underlined in 1807 by the transfer by warship through Gothenburg of £500,000 of specie to the emperor of Russia, 'payable to Messrs Harman', part of a sum that was due to Russia from the subsidy treaty of 1805 (Treasury to Admiralty, 13 Jan. 1807, NA, ADM 12/34; Sherwig, *Guineas and Gunpowder*, pp. 149, 366). (See Chapter 13.)

our constant exposure at sea and consequent exorbitant Insurance which we are compell'd to pay as well as the demands of seven, eight and sometimes nine pounds each voyage at the Custom House at Husum.' The postmasters-general secured the Treasury's permission 'to distribute One thousand Pounds in equal proportions among the twelve commanders on the Harwich Station'. Four years later the masters again applied for further remuneration; by this time the insurance charges were 'enormous ... six guineas per cent for six months from June to January against Sea Risque and nine guineas per cent for the same period against all risks': each master had to pay £267.15s. This time the request went straight to William Huskisson, the junior financial secretary of the Treasury, but also the MP for Harwich.* He was assured by the packet captains of 'our utter Impossibility to carry on the Public Duty unless some arrangement takes place to provide for the great losses we are daily suffering'. The twelve masters received a further payment of £3,000, to be split among them, though their request had to be considered on the basis of submitted detailed accounts and was granted only after some argument.[31] The packets derived income from passengers and bullion freight, as well as from providing the mail service.[32] It was clear, however, when the accounts were submitted, that they were losing money, and the Post Office's decision to reimburse their captains demonstrated the importance of sound contractual arrangements. Both government and packet-ship owners were aware of how much each needed the other, and that they both benefited from the arrangement.†

Though the Harwich packet masters and crew were considered

---

* Huskisson was MP because Harwich was a 'Treasury seat', with control over customs and Post Office patronage: he thus nominated packet captains to the postmasters-general (Thorne, *House of Commons*, Vol. II, p. 160; Trinder, *Harwich Packets*, p. 104).

† Transporting King's Messengers with diplomatic despatches had priority over ordinary mail. At Gothenburg in Nov. 1804 the *Prince of Wales* had just sailed for Harwich with the mails when after half an hour it had to turn back to port. The captain noted the delay in the log: 'Came a boat with an order to stop for Despatches which had just arrived.' In Jan. 1806 she sailed from Cuxhaven 'with Messrs Basset & Mills, two of HM Messengers'. In July 1807 the packet was returning to Harwich: 'Came a boat from Yarmouth and took ye messenger and Mail onshore' (*Prince of Wales* log, 27 Nov. 1804, 4 Jan. 1806, 10 July 1807).

privileged because of their long-held contract with government, in wartime they worked hard in sometimes terrible conditions. Captain Hearne, master of another *Prince of Wales* packet, took to the bottle in 1805 after long and exemplary service. Earlier in the year he, too, had sailed to Gothenburg and had been able to succeed in delivering the mail only after clambering fifteen miles over the ice. At one point, six masters were on shore, leaving their ships under the command of the mates, their seconds-in-command.[33] The Admiralty was well aware of these freezing and tempestuous winter conditions in the Skaggerrak and the Kattegat. When the agent at Gothenburg suggested in December 1810 that a naval sloop should be stationed off the port 'for the defence of the Packets' against Danish privateers, his request was refused. Croker annotated the letter: 'At this season of the year this appears highly dangerous.'[34] As soon as possible after the French withdrawal from Hamburg in March 1813, the Post Office there wrote to Freeling asking that the normal route to Cuxhaven be re-established, although the situation became confused when the French counter-attacked in May and reoccupied the city.[35] By the spring of 1814 the packets were ordered to try to land mail on the Dutch coast, but the Gothenburg route continued to be used until September that year.[36]

Relations between London and the Harwich packets contrasted with the ill-temper of the local packet commanders and crews at Falmouth, soured by attempts by the local Post Office agent to enforce regulations against smuggling. By long custom, every member of the crew of the Falmouth packets could earn money on his own account, returning from Lisbon or the West Indies with silks, wine and tobacco. From Falmouth, local women known as 'troachers' would pedal these wares around the countryside.[37] Feelings also ran high over naval impressment, for the Falmouth men accused the navy of overruling their traditional press protections. In 1810 mutinous packet crews at Flushing (Cornwall), across the harbour from Falmouth, were dispersed only by the reading of the Riot Act. The Post Office reacted by moving the packet contracts to Plymouth, which brought the dissidents to heel and the service was restored to Falmouth on 15 February 1811.[38] Significantly mail to the Mediterranean was disrupted by these difficulties. In October 1810 the first lord of the Admiralty, Charles Philip Yorke, remarked to Rear-Admiral Sir Samuel Hood, then at Port Mahon, that 'correspondence with the Mediterranean Fleet has been very uncertain & irregular for some months past.'[39] The postal service to the south was also interrupted towards the end of the war in April 1815, where George Canning, as the envoy in Lisbon, did not receive any mail from England for six weeks, and had to rely upon the Madrid newspapers quoting letters from Paris.[40] Yet, in general, as we have seen, the packet service worked well and its captains and crews kept going in often extremely hazardous circumstances. Without its efficiency, Britain would have found it very difficult to communicate and cooperate with its allies or to have kept trade flowing that was so necessary to the British effort against Napoleon.*

Defensive security was also vital and systems were improved as both naval and merchant fleets expanded. The first requirement was the identification of British ships at sea by 'private signal'. This numeral system was comprehensive, and included coastal signal stations, warships, revenue cutters, packet boats and every sort of merchant vessel. Every ship had a number that made early recognition possible from ship to shore and from ship to ship. Regular revisions incorporating the numbers allocated to new ships, and the cancellation of those captured or sunk, had to be distributed. Updating these numbers and private signals was a considerable and continuous administrative task undertaken by Admiralty clerks. On 10 November 1807, for instance, a full distribution of 740 copies of lists of the numbers allotted to additional ships were sent out by the secretary of the Admiralty; some were sent by the mail coach to Admiral Montagu, the port admiral at Portsmouth, who was to report to which ships he had given them; eighty went to Collingwood in the Mediterranean for distribution to the ships under his command.[41] A full renewal of private signals was issued on John Barrow's authority on 2 May 1809, to be distributed over the following six months to every warship worldwide: 'to

---

* Occasionally packets were ordered to transport horses for ambassadors or the military. Four horses belonging to Sir Robert Wilson, appointed as military commissioner to the Prussian court, were taken in Dec. 1806 by the *Auckland* packet, but the weather was so bad that no landing could be attempted and all four horses died (22 Dec. 1806, TNA, FO 33/36; Glover, *Wilson*, pp. 30–31).

commence on the Home Stations, the Baltic, the Coast of Portugal and as far as the Straits of Gibraltar on the 1st of June, within the Mediterranean, on the coast of America, and the West Indies on 1st July, the Cape of Good Hope and South America stations on 1 September and on the East Indies on 1 November next'.[42] Private signals were also distributed to the East India Company, and the signals for merchant ships clearing port were issued through 'John Bennet Jnr, Lloyds Coffee House'.[43]

Understandably, the Admiralty was concerned about security and it was always urging care on officers. If there was any reason to suspect that private signals had got into the wrong hands, a new signal book, or a part of it, would be issued through the port admirals and the lieutenants of signal stations. Those for 'H.M. Brigs, Cutters and Luggers employed cruizing on the Coasts of the United Kingdom commanded by Lieutenants' were renewed for this reason in July 1810.[44] Warnings to the Admiralty came from any quarter: as late as the spring of 1812 Freeling of the Post Office passed word back to Croker at the Admiralty that the captain of the *Sybille* had told one of his packet captains 'that the French are in possession of our Private Signals as he had a short time before chaced a French Brig of War with the Private Signal flying, which vessel escaped into the night'.[45]

Private signals from ships were linked to the coastal signal stations, another system of defensive security, thus allowing them to identify friendly ships. If a ship did not identify herself satisfactorily, the station would send a signal to the senior naval officer at Portsmouth or Plymouth along the south coast, or to Deal or Yarmouth on the east coast. The coastal stations had been dismantled at the peace in 1802 and the pockets of land on which they had stood returned to their owners; when war recommenced at the end of 1803 the land had to be re-leased and the stations hurriedly rebuilt.[46] Some clifftop stations were so exposed to the winds that during the months of peace they were 'very much out of repair'.* They were rapidly re-established and remanned.

---

* There was little trouble from the landowners. Only at West Wittering in West Sussex was there a difficulty because a naval captain had gone to 'great expense in fitting it up for his own Residence' during the peace. He agreed to move after pressing for 'some consideration' (Kitchen, 'Coast Signal Stations', p. 342; Mallinson, *Semaphore*, p. 136).

By contrast, the French used the peace to develop their communications network: they introduced a three-armed semaphore, invented by a French artillery officer called Depillion. It was much more visible and capable of sending any message than the British system, which consisted merely of hoists of flags and balls, based on the naval tradition, and used only numbers to represent prearranged set messages. By 1803 the new French stations were installed along the whole of the French Atlantic and Mediterranean coasts and helped the French to evade the worst of the British navy's close blockade of their ports. To counter this, British naval officers became adept at reading the French signal codes.[47] In 1808, for instance, a paper was found on board a French merchant brig by a British sloop off Boulogne with 'essential information for French vessels navigating without escort along the coast'. The document gave the sign of the semaphores for: 'The enemy is in sight of the Port and may intercept the French vessels in the course which they are now keeping ($\div$) [a division sign]. Then set at ($\cdot$) if safe.' The Admiralty sent the information to Rear-Admiral D'Auvergne in Jersey, ordering him to make the signals known to the commanders of his ships, 'with instructions to keep the same as secret as possible'.[48] Occasionally, the navy landed on the French coast and destroyed the telegraphs, to gain at least a temporary advantage. In 1808 Captain Lord Cochrane, in his celebrated cruise in the *Imperieuse* in the Mediterranean under Collingwood, raided and blew up the line of stations along the French coast between Catalonia and Toulon.[49]

By 1804 the Admiralty Board was pressing for a line of stations along the coast from Liverpool to Holyhead, and although this was not to happen until after the war for commercial reasons, a useful network of stations was built around Liverpool.[50] During the wars, lines of these stations were extended over the coast, in the north-east from Edinburgh to the Tees, in Yorkshire, Lincolnshire and along the north Norfolk coast, as well as in Ireland.[51] More were constructed around the coast of Essex and the Thames Estuary. By 1814, 138 had been constructed, with a further ten in Ireland. In 1810 the Admiralty set in motion trials of a semaphore system similar to that of the French.[52] Visibility was difficult on the flat coast of Essex for those who had to operate the coastal signal stations: it is sometimes impossible there to distinguish where sea and land begin or end, and hazy conditions often predominate in the spring and autumn. To shorten signalling distances, in 1811 a very leaky old ex-Danish gunboat, renamed H.M.S. *Warning*, was moored off Mersea Island with instructions to repeat signals over the estuaries of the rivers Colne and Blackwater between the Martello Tower at Frinton, East Mersea, and St Peter's Chapel on the Foulness Marshes to the south. The log of this humble warship demonstrates the difficulties that the signallers faced. Soon after commissioning at Sheerness, the long-suffering captain, Lieutenant Thomas Gill, 'found the vessel roll exceedingly heavy': in fresh breezes he had to order his crew to haul down the top mast and signal yard. He received '2 glass lanthorns with twenty pounds of candles for the purpose of showing a light to distinguish the *Warning* during the night'. After an unrewarding year peering into haze, and often being unable to make out signals, Gill sent his topmast and yard ashore, and his crew to East Mersea, 'as per Admiralty order', to help construct the new semaphore.[53]

Though this signalling experiment was clearly ineffectual, the need still existed to watch for invasion and look out for French privateers. The testimony of Lieutenant James Anthony Gardner illustrates the effort involved in trying to keep these channels of communication open. Gardner ended a modest naval career with eight years at the coastal signal station at Fairlight on the cliffs above Hastings between 1806 and 1814. Under him he had a midshipman, two signalmen and two dragoons who were to communicate with the nearest army commanding officer. He recalled:

> We had the strictest orders to be on the look-out by night and by day, in consequence of the threatened invasion ... I have heard many say that a signal station was an easy berth, and only fit for old and worn-out officers. This I flatly deny: and, without fear of contradiction, can safely say that I suffered more from anxiety at this station than ever I did on board of a man of war.[54]

The larger and more sophisticated shutter-telegraph stations, with London at the centre of their network, were designed as a speedy means of command and control rather than for defensive security like the coastal stations. But in this too Britain lagged behind France. The

French quickly built up a remarkable European-wide semaphore system, through which Napoleon knew what was happening in his vast empire. The 350-mile line between Paris and Brest had been completed in 1798, and by 1800 Lille, Metz and Strasbourg were all also linked with the French capital. At the height of his power in 1807, the French government in Paris was in contact with Brussels, Amsterdam, Mainz, Turin and Venice. Napoleon was, however, unable to maintain such efficient communications with Spain in the Peninsular War, as the stations were vulnerable to attack by Spanish forces and the guerrillas.[55]

Given reasonable visibility, the shutter telegraphs worked well. Orders were sent quickly to the naval bases, and the more important intelligence reports came through this means to Whitehall. As we saw in Chapter 5, the lines to Deal and Portsmouth had been built in the previous war and now further lines were constructed: London to Plymouth was ordered in 1805. As operations in the North Sea assumed more importance, this was followed by an order in 1807 for a line to Great Yarmouth. Both lines reached the coast by an inland route in order to avoid coastal fog, and were completed by 1806 and 1808 respectively.[56] In Ireland they were more expensive to maintain because of the need to defend them: the Treasury was given an estimate of £40,000 in 1804 for a line from Dublin to Galway for 'Signal stations with Defensible Guard Houses, Towers, etc.'[57] A line was built in Canada from Halifax to Frederickstown, although the plans of the duke of Kent, commander-in-chief of the Maritime Provinces briefly in 1799 and 1800, to achieve direct communication between Halifax and Quebec were over-ambitious and never completed.[58]

The effectiveness of visual telegraphs in Britain still remained susceptible to the reduced visibility caused by coastal mist and fog, especially in winter. A surviving telegraph journal for the inland London to Yarmouth line, for the periods December 1814 and January 1814, records that fog prevented transmission of messages for seventeen out of each month of thirty-one days, that is, 50 per cent of the time. On one occasion fog on the Plymouth line led to a spectacular misunderstanding. Many years later John Barrow, second secretary to the Admiralty, recalled the incident in 1812, after Wellington's victory at Salamanca. Sir Robert Calder, commander-in-chief at Plymouth, once threw the Cabinet into a state of alarm by a telegraph message . . . Despatches had been received from Spain, and Calder, anxious to convey the intelligence to town, sent up the following portion of a message; the rest was stopped by a fog: – 'Wellington defeated'; and thus it remained the whole day, to the dismay of those who knew only thus much of it. The arrival of Lord March (I think it was), in the course of the night, brought the account of a great victory over Marmont. The Admiral's head, like the weather, was somewhat foggy.* He meant to say 'The French defeated by Wellington', but unfortunately began at the wrong end.[59]

The importance of intelligence can be gauged by the impact that it had on policy. Good information was available on Napoleon's intentions in the weeks before the operation against Copenhagen in September 1807, as we saw in Chapter 7. But the assessments on the war-readiness of the Danes, taken earlier in the year, were largely unsound. For some time, as Napoleon tightened his hold on northern Europe, the British government had watched with trepidation his advance towards the Baltic: if France acquired the Danish Fleet, the strategic naval balance in home waters would swing back towards the emperor, while French control of the Sound would imperil the import of timber, tar and hemp from the Baltic ports, products upon which naval power and mercantile strength depended.

George Canning, who took over as foreign secretary on 25 March 1807, had been inclined to give the Danes the benefit of the doubt, but, as spring passed into early summer, an impression was gained, based largely on flawed intelligence, of the hostility of the Danish government.† Lieutenant-General the earl of Pembroke, recently

---

* The veracity of this story is enhanced by evidence of Calder's reputation. Among his detractors was Lord St Vincent, who described Calder's 'confused, wrongheaded & total incapacity to perform the duty of a first Lieutenant, much less that of a distributor of my orders' (to Evan Nepean, 3 Sept. 1798, NMM, NEP/4, fol. 147). Thomas Grenville took opinions on Calder in 1806: 'those who acquit him of want of courage dwell however very much upon his extreme indecision in critical situations' (to the marquis of Buckingham, 25 Nov. 1806, HL, STG 37 (34)).

† In Apr. 1807 Napoleon added disinformation by instructing his minister of marine to start activities at Brest that would appear to be expedition preparations: at the same

appointed on a special mission to Austria, was forced to take a northerly route to Vienna by French conquests and took a walk through Copenhagen dockyard. Although he knew nothing about ships and navies, he became convinced that the activity of Danish shipwrights indicated a mobilization, reckoning, as he wrote to Canning that night, that at least twenty Danish ships of the line 'were fit to go to sea with all their stores, etc., named and numbered'. Canning received the letter on 8 June. The British minister plenipotentiary in Copenhagen, Benjamin Garlike, had reported nothing to London, for the simple reason that there had been no unusual Danish activity. Canning, however, was intent on finding evidence of what he wanted to believe, and distrusted Garlike for his closeness to the previous government. He chose to blame Garlike for laxness, relieved him of his post and transferred him to Prussia. Tom Grenville, out of office and on holiday in Wales, received the news from Garlike and wrote to his brother: 'they have moved him from Copenhagen <u>almost in disgrace</u> to Memel because he would not write them word that the Danes were making hostile preparations at Copenhagen. He protests to me in his vindication that not the slightest preparation has been made by them.'* Grenville added in his letter to his brother Buckingham: 'They are really the shabbiest set of dirty politicians that was ever seen.'[60]

Then, on 14 June, Napoleon defeated a much larger Russian force at Friedland and brough Alexander I into formal alliance with France by the Treaty of Tilsit, signed on a raft in the middle of the River Nieman on 7 July, but Canning had already become convinced that pre-emptive action was needed. Alexander Cockburn, the British consul in Tonningen in Denmark, sent a message in the first week of July to the effect that France had already received permission from the Danes to occupy Holstein and that French troops were soon to be

---

time the minister was to inform the United Irishmen of an impending invasion to ensure that this false information was given the widest circulation (Munch-Petersen, *Copenhagen*, p. 95; Hicks, 'Napoleon, Tilsit', p. 128).

* Garlike's informant was Captain Beauman of the *Prins*, who had been to the dockyard on 25 July. He reported: 'there is not at present the shadow of the appearance of the equipment of any fleet, and it is impossible that any such could be made & hid from a naval eye. The state of the fleet is precisely the same as it has been ever since Lord Nelson's battle' (Grenville to Buckingham, 25 Aug. 1807, quoting Garlike's letter to him, HL, STG 38 (3)).

expected. This turned out to be inaccurate, though there was plenty of reason to think that it might have been the case. Nevertheless, it was a significant contribution to the cabinet's growing conviction, led by Canning, that force was required against Copenhagen. By 13 July it had decided that a strong fleet should go to the Sound; by 16 July Admiral Gambier had been appointed; and by the next day a letter had been sent from the cabinet to the king requesting the use of a conjoint force.[61] However, Castlereagh's secret instructions to Admiral Gambier stated the core of the government's position:

> the maritime power, position and resources of Denmark may shortly be made the instrument in the hands of France not only of excluding our commerce from the Baltic and of depriving us of the means of naval equipment, but also of multiplying the points from which an invasion of His Majesty's dominions may be attempted under the protection of a formidable naval force.[62]

A fleet of seventeen British ships of the line, accompanied by twenty-one frigates and smaller vessels, under the command of Admiral Gambier, and 400 transports with troops sailed from the Yarmouth Roads for Copenhagen on 26 July. Less than six weeks after Napoleon's victory at Friedland, British counter-measures were under way. On 7 September 1807 Copenhagen capitulated and surrendered seventeen Danish ships of the line, only seven weeks after the cabinet in London had taken the decision to act.[63]

The speed of these events in the days of sail, when men could travel no faster than a galloping horse or a ship with a fresh breeze behind it, was truly impressive. The pace was certainly too fast for Napoleon. (It is perhaps no coincidence that all this diplomatic and military action took place beyond the limits of the French telegraph system reaching out from Paris.) Rapid mobilization by the British was possible because a fleet was gathered at Yarmouth, made ready by the previous government; 8,000 British troops, the King's German Legion, were already in the Baltic on the island of Rügen trying to relieve the fortress of Stralsund in Pomerania, the last Swedish stronghold on the southern shores of the Baltic, which was besieged by the French; and a further 16,500 were ready in Britain. Troops were needed because the Danes had strengthened their coastal defences since the previous

Battle of Copenhagen in 1801, and a British Fleet could not now get near enough the city to bombard it.

This operation was not, however, free of further intelligence quandaries. On 21 July, the day on which the government finally decided to attack Denmark, Canning received a letter from the comte d'Antraigues, writing from his home near Richmond. The French royalist claimed that he had information from a senior Russian officer, Prince Troubetskoi, who was present at the negotiations at Tilsit, that Napoleon had secretly proposed a maritime league of France and Russia, hostile to Britain; and, while the tsar did not respond to this proposal, neither did he demur. If true, it would provide every justification needed for the decisive military action that the cabinet had just decided to take. The question was whether it was in fact true; or whether it was simply a move by d'Antraigues to secure himself a British pension.[64]*

This intelligence was utilized in the furious parliamentary debates that followed rather than during military planning. In early 1808 the Opposition attacked the government for its pre-emptive strike on Copenhagen and the consequent opprobrium that it had aroused abroad. To this, Canning stated that he had positive information of the hostile intentions of France, Russia and Denmark, though, in order to protect his sources, he was unable to give further details. (A rumour that a British officer was hiding under the table on the raft at Tilsit when the treaty was signed helped the government's case.) The Opposition could do nothing, as Canning's oratory was masterly, and by this time Russia, in any case, had declared war on Britain. Reaction outside parliament was broadly in support of the government. Even Tom Grenville had to admit privately in a letter to his brother, Lord Grenville, that, had the previous government been in power, they would probably have done the same.[65]

---

* D'Antraigues was a man of great charm and his European contacts were wide, but he was also a long-term royalist adventurer. Jane Austen, a stern judge of charm, met him some time later. She described him as 'a very fine looking man, with quiet manners, good enough for an Englishman ... if he would but speak English, I would take to him' (Munch-Petersen, *Copenhagen*, p. 121, quoting Deirdre Le Faye (ed.), *Jane Austen's Letters* (Oxford, 1995), pp. 184–5). D'Antraigues and his wife were murdered in their house in Barnes in London in July 1812 by a servant, who also took his own life, for motives that are still unclear (Sparrow, *Secret Service*, p. 347).

Further justification for the Copenhagen operation came from Napoleon's aggressive actions on the southern fringes of Europe. With the British navy still engaged at Copenhagen, the emperor sent an ultimatum to Lisbon demanding that Portugal should close its ports to Britain and declare war on its old ally, and sent an army south through Spain to reinforce his orders. Canning received the despatch while he was waiting for news from Copenhagen. 'Never was a time of so much anxiety,' he wrote to his wife.[66] He came to an agreement with the Portuguese ambassador in London, guaranteeing the safety of the royal family if they would withdraw to Brazil, with British naval and military help.

Yet still the British government worried about the threat of invasion. The source of the danger was the new French Fleet under construction in the dockyard at Antwerp. After the breathing space afforded by Napoleon's campaigns in eastern Europe which ended with the Treaty of Tilsit, British concern centred less on an invasion of the south coast, the perceived danger point in 1804 and 1805, than on the north and east coasts, and, as ever, on Irish shores. Exactly how much of a danger was posed by Napoleon's warship building at Antwerp, combined with the output of other dockyards under his control across Europe, has long been a cause for debate.* What is not disputed is that the scale of the emperor's naval ambition was such that British ministers had to take the threat seriously. Intelligence sources from Antwerp and Flushing included smugglers, pilots, special agents, a Swedish spy and an American, all corroborating significant amounts of naval activity. In late 1807 one British assessment reckoned that twenty ships of the line could be on the stocks in Antwerp, 'and the resources for building from the Black Forest through the Rhine inexhaustible'.[67] But there were always well-founded doubts that Napoleon could raise enough skilled seamen to man his completed ships effectively.[68]

---

* Naval intelligence reports still flowed in on the state of the docks and harbour of Cherbourg, which were continually building throughout the war (e.g., Captain Lord Beauclerk, H.M.S. *Royal Oak*, off Cherbourg, to C. P. Yorke, 27 June 1811, NMM, YOR/2). The outer harbour was opened in 1813, but the works were not properly completed until the middle of the nineteenth century. Only a handful of warships were built there before 1815 (Epin, *Arsenaux sous Napoléon*, p. 160).

Understanding the potential threat of the new dockyard at Antwerp was simple; what use the workforce was making of the extensive facilities was much more difficult. We now know that those ships that were built were constructed of green timbers, so that they would not have had a long life, but, even so, sixty-two French ships of the line and fifty-nine smaller rates were built in all French dockyards between 1803 and 1815.[69] The total workforce in Antwerp and other dockyards under French control peaked in 1807 at 24,000.* This total did not include the workforce in more distant dockyards under French control, such as Venice.[70] At its height, 4,000 artificers were working at Antwerp, among them shipyard workers from those countries that Napoleon had overrun: Italians, Dutchmen, Spaniards, Germans and even, by the end, Poles.[71] A further complication in estimating the threat was that every French naval establishment had a large complement of French convicts: Brest, for instance, averaged 3,000 through these years.[72] How much effective work they achieved could be no more than surmise.

It was, however, the weight of this intelligence that led to the disastrous decision to send the large expedition to take and destroy Antwerp in 1809 (see Chapter 7). Lord Castlereagh, the secretary of state for war, drove the measure through a divided and essentially leaderless cabinet, for the prime minister, the duke of Portland, was by this time very ill. On 21–22 May 1809 a rare check of Napoleon by the Austrians at Aspern–Essling, and the consequent optimism, enabled Castlereagh to persuade the cabinet into action in order to help Austria. Later, in the Commons, Castlereagh said of the decision to send the expedition that the Austrian victory 'had a preponderating influence with His Majesty's Government in the consideration of that question'.[73]

An array of intelligence had been gathered from army and naval sources for two years before the expedition sailed to the Scheldt. The tidal conditions, leading marks, possible landing places and anchorages were all known, as was the fact that sailing within the river, four miles wide at its widest point, brought ships within the range of enemy artillery on both banks. Information was also held on the number of

* Although this was double the number of the British royal dockyard workforce of 12,000 at the same date (Morriss, *Dockyards*, p. 106), the British Fleet by this time in the war was largely built in private shipyards.

regular and irregular French troops in Flushing; and how many were suffering from marsh fever and the state of the ships building there and those ready in the basin. Lord Mulgrave, first lord of the Admiralty, supported Castlereagh. But his minute to the cabinet of 25 March focused on the strategic necessity of striking at Antwerp, rather than the likelihood of success, and it demonstrated how much the threat of invasion was on his mind:

> the Scheld[t] Fleet is within a short distance of the vulnerable parts of the coast of England and conveniently situated for taking advantage of a leading wind that the British fleet in the Baltic would be exposed to an attack from the Scheld[t] and the existence of a strong fleet there would place in jeopardy all our Blockading Squadrons from Brest to Toulon . . .[74]

Senior army officers were virtually unanimously pessimistic on the prospects for the expedition. Such a weight of opinion from Lieutenant-Colonel James Gordon, General Sir John Hope, Lieutenant-General Robert Brownrigg and Major General Sir Harry Calvert should have been heeded, but Castlereagh ignored them. General Sir David Dundas, who had served in Antwerp in 1794, wrote to warn him that 'whatever way Antwerp is to be approached or taken, the service is one of very great risk, and in which the safe return of the Army so employed may be very precarious'.[75]

The cabinet, however, grasped at intelligence of a more encouraging nature. Several reports corroborated poor morale among the crews of the French ships blockaded in the Scheldt. An intercepted despatch of 7 December 1808 to Napoleon from Denis Decrès, the French minister of marine, contained an assessment of the possibility of keeping ships in the Scheldt, and of the expense of arming them and disarming them; he proposed laying them up for the winter, and sending all the crews to Toulon.[76] In late June intelligence was received that all troops and carpenters at Antwerp had been ordered to join the Grand Army.[77] No one considered the possibility of a rapid movement of troops to the area by Napoleon, swiftly brought about by his telegraph communications network from Paris, as well as the withdrawal of Austria from the war. The whole decision-making process demonstrated the way that politicians can shoulder aside intelligence when it gets in the way of the action they really intend to take.[78]

Yet, in spite of the major setback at Walcheren, by the spring of 1811 British intelligence had accurately begun to identify a plummeting in the morale of the French Navy, linked to reports of shortages of manpower. General Don in Jersey forwarded a report in May that 80,000 French naval conscripts were to be taken for limited service in Spain. Lack of naval manpower in Flushing was confirmed by observations of Admiral Young off the Scheldt on the state of the blockaded ships.[79] Young reported to Yorke in April a casual conversation between the master of the *Resolution* and a Dutch fishing boat on the mutinous state of the many nations that made up Napoleon's crews in Antwerp: 'There was nothing the crews of the French ships wished for as to go to sea, as they would certainly bring the ships to England.'[80] By early May, Young's judgement was firmer and more confident: 'From the apparent state of the ships there ... and from the disaffected state of their crews ... I should think it quite impossible for them to venture to put to sea.' And he added, 'in their present state, five [British] sail will as effectively blockade the Port, as five and twenty.'[81] By June, Young had obtained economic intelligence of interest: escaped prisoners had passed troops near Metz who were experiencing difficulties in obtaining supplies, as 'all Government Bills on Paris having lately been return'd protested ... what was procured was by requisition and force.'[82] By September he reported that French troops had been marched away from all parts of the coast. This was intelligence of real significance, indicating some serious weaknesses in French manpower and financial resources. Other messages coming out of France, however, indicated a continuing threat. In the autumn of 1811, credible information was provided for Charles Philip Yorke at the Admiralty that the French were planning an attack on the north of England from Antwerp, to which he attached some importance.[83] The government would not be able to lower its guard for at least another year.

Looking back now, it is apparent that the output of all the French dockyards began to fall sharply from 1811, through lack of money and because of the drafting of shipwrights and other workers into the army – dockyard companies fought at Wagram in 1809 and Dresden in 1813. The emperor's demands were becoming increasingly unrealistic. In January 1813 he ordered his navy minister to set his budgets to ensure that 104 new ships would be launched from French dockyards by 1815: eleven should be launched between March and June 1814 with the remainder the following year. The minister replied that he had 'fourteen ships on the stocks at Antwerp'. Napoleon made no attempt to understand why so little had been done, merely remarking to Decrès that 'You had reported much more work than you have done.'[84] A dictator had simply been told what he wanted to hear. The reality was that from 1812 to the end of the war only four ships of the line and five frigates were launched in all French dockyards. Numbers of workers and morale declined and sickness increased, as Napoleon stripped the yards of two thirds of their manpower to fight in the desperate defensive land battles in the last two years of the war.[85] As with other dictators in their final days, the gap between aspiration and capacity was enormous and the orders issued by the falling figure at the regime's centre, fantastical.

The threat posed by the potential capability of Antwerp perplexed the British government to the end. What was not clear at the time was that manpower was the problem vexing France. If the French had had the men, Antwerp had the capacity to build a force to threaten Britain. When peace terms were being negotiated in 1814, the British naval commissioner, Captain Thomas Byam Martin, was sent to inspect the city. He found that the newly constructed basins were large enough to hold forty-eight ships of the line and he reported to Castlereagh that the docks, slips and warehouses were of 'an extent of which we had no conception'.[86] The eye of a professional seaman, given the freedom finally to survey the dockyard facilities, understood the state of affairs all too well.

II

Government Scandal and Reform

1803–1812

Since I came into office I have proceeded on all questions of augmentation of salaries, on a strong impression of the importance of public economy ... I am aware that I have created much dissatisfaction by holding the public purse strings so close: but it is from an apprehension that without very rigid economy we can neither retain the goodwill of the public, nor hold out against the perseverance and resources of the enemy.

– Lord Mulgrave, first lord of the Admiralty, 1807–1810,
to George Rose, treasurer of the navy, 4 February 1809[1]

Our general opinion, indeed, on the conduct of Ordnance business, is that it is on the whole efficiently carried on; but that it is often executed on too great a scale, and without that attention to economy, which a due consideration of the large and unavoidable Expenses of the Nation imperiously demands.

– Commission of Military Enquiry, *Seventeenth Report*,
17 October 1811[2]

The growing scale and complexity of the war against Napoleon inevitably put an enormous strain on the bureaucratic machinery that underpinned the conflict. Numbers of officials and clerks in every government department swelled, and office space in Central London was insufficient. Office systems were weak, and appointments and promotion persistently relied on patronage, with the result that clerks with inadequate skills were often engaged. The abolition of personal

313

fees paid to officials and clerks, first recommended by the Commission on Fees in the 1780s and subsequently raised by the 1797–8 Select Committee on Finance (see Chapter 4), had been only partially achieved: no compensating payment of salary had been put in place and departmental staff were restive. Nor had any cross-government scales of payment emerged, which caused jealousies and tensions across departments. Yet the government did adapt and change, and financial and administrative reform gathered pace after Pitt's death in 1806. All ministries had to be committed to improving, in response to critics from within parliament as well as from the press (where William Cobbett, the radical and ex-sergeant-major of the 54th Regiment, was the most trenchant).[3] The process of reform was to take several parliamentary enquiries, highlighted by political scandal and occasional high drama, and driven by the imperatives and urgency of war.[4] One difficulty for successive administrations was that the radicals did not acknowledge what progress was being made.

It was not that the problems were unacknowledged. In 1806, for instance, at the beginning of the Whig Ministry of All the Talents, the chancellor of the Exchequer, Lord Henry Petty, told the House of Commons that unaudited accounts across government amounted to the vast sum of £455 million.* No other failure in government caused more wastage. Long-established procedures in the spending departments allowed both serving officers and civilian officials to retain large sums of public money in their private hands.[5] Problems of sinecures and the lack of transparency were also well known, while the obscurities and complications of Navy and Army Estimates precluded searching debate in parliament, since MPs hardly understood them. The Talents in their thirteen-month-long administration in 1806 to 1807 achieved very little in remedying these defects. When the Tories returned to power in 1807, they used the findings of two lengthy parliamentary commissions to bring the machinery of the army and navy

---

* An 'unaudited' account did not mean that a contractor had not been paid, but that his account had not been adjusted for any short measure or poor quality that might have been noted by the inspecting clerk or artificer when the goods were accepted by government (although in a minority of cases money could be owed to the contractor). Audited accounts were also made public, and, until that point, competitors did not officially know the price paid to the successful contract bidder.

to a pitch of efficiency equal to the immense task of surviving the dominance of Napoleonic France and eventually of overcoming it.

As the scale of the war increased, the government bureaucracy in London and the workforce in the state industrial establishments grew at a speed that inevitably led to serious strain. Following the collapse of the Peace of Amiens, the number of state employees more than doubled during the next dozen years of warfare against Napoleon. The expanding conflict generated greater amounts of correspondence, and an increase in the size and number of the volumes of accounts, personnel lists and records.* At the Treasury, for instance, there were just over 4,000 incoming letters for the first seven months of 1805; but ten years later, for the whole of the last year of the war, they numbered almost 20,000.[6] Between 1798 and 1804 in-letters to the secretary of the Navy Board doubled, from 7,983 to 14,420. To deal with this, the number of clerks also doubled, from 101 in 1796 to 204 in 1815.[7]

This was the pattern through all departments. The number of Ordnance Department officials and clerks nearly doubled between 1797 (117) and 1815 (227) at the centre of the organization, although throughout the country it employed a much larger complement, with 353 in 1797 but rising to 886 by 1815.[8] The Customs Department ended the wars with over 10,000 officials throughout the country and the Excise Department with 7,500. Officials and clerks in Central London in the navy, army and Ordnance departments multiplied over two and a half times, from 569 in 1797 to 1,476 in 1815. The complement of the War Office increased, in spite of attempts in 1805 and 1807 by the Treasury to control its numbers.[9] Departmental staffing costs rose in line with these increases (see Appendix 1). By 1812 the army's Commissariat had a staff of 53 in London, 20 commissaries-general and over 1,000 clerks serving abroad.[10] By 1815 the 'Return on the Number of Persons ... in all Public Offices or Departments' stood at 24,598 and their salaries cost £3.2 million.[11]†

---

* Some of the victualling-contract ledgers from late in the Napoleonic War, in the National Archives, are so heavy that it is not possible for a single person to carry them.
† For comparison, total government income in 1815 was £77.9 million and, in the same year, a 100-gun warship, H.M.S. St Vincent, was launched at Plymouth Dockyard at a cost of £110,549 (Mitchell and Deane, British Historical Statistics, p. 581; Winfield, British Warships, p. 12).

The large state industrial establishments followed suit. Swollen by the demands of a larger army and requirements to supply arms to Continental allies, the 1,500 workers in Woolwich Arsenal in 1800 had risen to 5,000 by 1814. Some of this large increase was due to additional artillery military personnel and a substantial number of convicts, housed in hulks in the Thames.[12] Deptford was the most important and largest victualling yard, and by 1813 it employed 1,500 men, although Portsmouth, with no space to expand, grew only a little between 1797 and 1815, from 553 to 616.[13] The six home dockyards ended the wars in 1815 with only a slight increase in their 3,000 shipwrights from 1793, but with nearly double the number of semi-skilled trades and labourers at 15,000.[14] Portsmouth was something of an exception because of the investment in complex machinery, and the consequent need for a highly skilled workforce: in 1793 the yard had 1,401 skilled men on its books; by 1813 this had risen to 2,466.[15] All the overseas dockyards had increased their workforces: between 1790 and 1814 Antigua had doubled, Halifax and Jamaica had substantial rises, while Malta, which had been acquired through conquest in 1800, added another 400 men to the total complement.[16] In addition, dockyard officers and clerks were appointed to Buenos Aires and Montevideo between 1806 and 1807, and to Rio de Janeiro, Mauritius and Penang between 1811 and 1812; additionally, a sizeable complement served in Barbados between 1807 and 1815.[17]

Although it is difficult to calculate an exact figure, by 1815 the navy employed between 20,000 and 23,000 civilian officials, clerks and workers, from Whitehall to the West Indies.* The overall figure for government civilian employees of the armed services would double that if those state servants who supported the army and the Ordnance were included. Yet an accurate estimate of the total industrial workforce that prepared Britain for fighting these wars can only ever be guesswork, for the massive expansion of output required did not come from the state yards. These great establishments were working hard to repair, refit and maintain the large and growing fleets for the navy,

---

* In parallel, the workforce in the East India Company's London warehouses more than doubled, from 1,393 in 1785 to 2,700 in 1813 (Bowen, *Business of Empire*, p. 264).

and the heavy guns and small arms and other equipment for the army; but it was the additional numbers of contractors and their employees in private yards, mills, warehouses and offices whose building, manu-facturing and trading led the country to victory.

The most mundane yet intractable problem was the shortage of government office space in Whitehall and elsewhere in London. An inefficient Office of Works, which had the task of building and main-taining government offices, did little beyond providing further temporary accommodation, although the area to the east of Whitehall around Scotland Yard was improved, and the Transport Office found a place there.[18] The War Office, Ordnance Department and Admiralty were responsible for their own works.* Lack of resources limited expan-sion. Edward Holl was appointed as surveyor and architect to the Admiralty in 1804, and his responsibilities ranged beyond London to as far as the dockyards, for which he designed many buildings; towards the end of the war he designed and built Sheerness Yard, with John Rennie, a project that lasted until Holl's death in 1823.[19] Another floor was added to the Horse Guards between 1803 and 1805 (as we saw in Chapter 10), and in 1809 a new site next to the Admiralty was found for the Hydrographic Office, with its heavy printing equipment.[20]

Those departments of the navy occupying Somerset House were not much better off. The grand new buildings that had opened in 1786 had never really been adequate. The Victualling Office, the first to complain, did so only five years after it moved there. The office had arrived with 65 clerks; by 1805 the complement had risen to 105, and George Phillips Towry, the deputy chairman of the Victualling Board, wrote to William Marsden, secretary of the Admiralty, to say that the situation had become intolerable. He had no private office and had to work at the Board table, 'subject to constant interruption ... nor has he any place in which to receive persons calling upon him on official business, except a small Slip without a Fire Place, which is likewise used as a Lumber Room.' Basements and garrets designed to store

---

* Inigo Jones's Banqueting House had been a chapel royal for some years, but in 1808 it was decided to convert it into a military chapel, designed to accommodate over 2,000 guardsmen (Crook and Port, *King's Works*, pp. 545–6).

books and papers were now occupied by clerks; offices designed for four or five clerks were now occupied by eight, nine or even ten. Many of them were under

> a constant necessity of writing by Candle Light during the whole day ... the Lobby for the Messengers which is but fifteen feet long by thirteen feet wide, is also the only place that can be used as a Public Waiting room for Merchants, Contractors and other persons attending at the Office; and it is besides unavoidably made use of as a Repository for the Secretary's Department.[21]

Relief came only when the Sick and Hurt Office was abolished in 1806, its responsibilities transferred to the Transport Board, and the Victualling Office could move into the vacated space.[22]

The only answer was to expand outside Whitehall. The headquarters of the army was at the Horse Guards, but the department spread across sixteen other buildings, such as the Recruiting Department in Duke Street and the Department of Accounts in Duke Street and Crown Street.[23] In 1808 the new office of the commissary-in-chief – centralizing all the army supply under one roof, 'Ireland and the East Indies excepted', but effectively created to ensure that the troops in the Peninsular War did not go short – found a home in Great George Street.[24] The Ordnance Department was widely dispersed: the master-general was housed near Grosvenor Square and the secretary's office, with its thirty-four clerks, in Pall Mall, where the Board of Ordnance met three times a week (these two offices were later combined). The bulk of the clerks, with the armouries and the Ordnance Survey, were housed at the other end of the capital, in the Tower of London. In the country as a whole the Ordnance was spread over 206 houses and 94 apartments.[25] Its messengers received substantial expenses if they had to travel out of London.*

In addition to the physical difficulties of working in crowded offices, the clerks, most of whom had had their fees taken from them, were

---

* A messenger travelling outside London would be 'off the stones', as it was termed, a reference to the lack of paved roads outside London. The commission registered its 'disapprobation' of the high rates of travel allowances (Commission of Military Enquiry, *Thirteenth Report*, pp. 11, 46).

constantly unhappy about their salaries, which had not been augmented to make up for lost income. A stream of petitions and memorials were sent up to the senior boards of all the three services complaining about the level of salaries, the increasing workload and, as the Navy Office clerks described it in 1803, 'the progressive advance in the price of every Article of Subsistence'. These complaints were contained in extensive documents sent up to the Board of Admiralty, in which the Navy Office clerks claimed that their equivalent pay had slipped behind that in other departments since 1796. Assuring their lordships of their loyalty, they justified their comments by stating 'that they have borne their share in the public exertion and sacrifice without complaint or satisfaction: but . . . they observe their salaries to be so much inferior to those of every office not only in the Naval but in every other public Department'.[26]

When the Talents came to power in 1806, it was the signal for another tranche of letters of complaint from the Admiralty clerks, who claimed that their duties were 'beyond those of all others, rigid, constant and laborious' (sentiments echoed in letters by the clerks of the Marine Pay Office).[27] Privately Lord Howick agreed, when he handed over the office of first lord to Tom Grenville: 'The truth is that they all I believe [are] very inadequately paid . . . this is a troublesome legacy I have left you.'[28] Another problem, recognizable today, was that clerks were tempted to leave government service by the higher salaries paid in the private sector: the Navy Board was informed, in late 1806, that one of its clerks on £80 a year had been offered £240 to work 'in a Mercantile House in the City'.[29] Petitions for greater pay came from the clerks in every dockyard through the following year, as well as from the naval storekeeper at Great Yarmouth, who wanted more salary and clerks for 'the increased business and responsibility of this Port'.[30] These problems began to be solved, as we shall see, only after 1808.*

---

* When Barham was first lord of the Admiralty in 1805 he was paid £3,000, of which £2,000 was paid out of the sale of old stores; as John Barrow commented, 'a shabby and incorrect mode of paying a great officer of state'. On his last day in office, Barham left a minute on his desk to put the first lord on the same footing as the secretaries of state. However, nothing came of it until 1812, when the first lord's salary was raised to £5,000 (Barrow, *Autobiography*, pp. 289–90).

St Vincent had been installed at the Admiralty just before the Peace of Amiens, convinced that the administration of the navy was wasteful and corrupt to the core. Although in most departments undersecretaries changed when Addington's government came in, the first lord retained Evan Nepean as first secretary. The mild William Marsden, the second Admiralty secretary, wanted to resign: Spencer and Nepean persuaded him that 'officers of the second class had ... [a] duty to carry on the public business with as little injury or interruption as possible from the change of principals'. After three years even the first secretary, Evan Nepean, who had started his career as purser on one of St Vincent's ships, wanted to leave and Addington appointed Nepean as chief secretary in Ireland to get him out of the maelstrom. In the opinion of John Barrow, the naval officers were to blame: 'Nepean had absolutely been driven out by the professional members of the Board.'[31] When Nepean left in January 1804, Marsden was promoted to first secretary, while the ambitious former purser, Benjamin Tucker, came in as second secretary, and was said to have a great influence over the first lord.*

The new first lord's ideological stance was reinforced by the extreme views of the inspector-general of naval works, Samuel Bentham, who also shared some of St Vincent's controlling and confrontational personality. Bentham saw society entirely 'through the eyes of mathematical computation' and believed that a complete change in the working methods of the dockyards was necessary.[32] He made the unrealistic proposal that every move of a worker should be standardized and measured, and claimed that, when working with wood, no personal judgement was required of the worker, thus making no allowance for the notorious unevenness of the material. Bentham wanted to eliminate the delegation of decision-making to the junior officers or to the workforce: according to his doctrine of 'individual responsibility', all business was to be controlled by an individual in

---

* George Rose reported a conversation with the king, who often stayed with Rose at his house, Cuffnells in Hampshire, as the royal retinue went down to Weymouth for the summer. The king thought that 'Lord St Vincent was governed by a worthless man of the name of Tucker, who had been his Secretary' (29 Oct. 1804, Harcourt, *Rose Diaries*, Vol. II, p. 181).

the centre of the dockyard, responsible to one man in London, rather than to a board of commissioners. The resulting increase of efficiency would do away with the need for contractors.*

St Vincent had three objectives: the reduction of the expense of government; greater efficiency by rooting out corruption; and getting rid of all naval contractors.[33] Unfortunately these three principles were contradictory. An anonymous informer told Henry Dundas that:

> For some time past it has been notorious that a system of terror has prevailed in the Dock yards. Spys have been set everywhere, informers have been encouraged and appointed to the places of those they accused so that no officer has any confidence in those that were acting with them. Their books and papers have been locked up and their minds agitated with some charge being laid against them before the Commissioners of Naval Enquiry.[34]

Matters got worse. Just as in the 1780s Middleton and Howe had been at loggerheads, so now St Vincent was very soon not on speaking terms with Sir Andrew Snape Hamond, the comptroller of the Navy Board, and all business was conducted in writing. The antagonism continued in parliament for some years, and the first lord would have abolished the junior board if it had been within his power.[35] Instead, St Vincent appointed Benjamin Tucker in November 1801, also an aggressive Whig, to a seat on the Navy Board, closely followed by Osbourne Markham, lawyer and brother of the Admiralty commissioner John Markham. The neutral Marsden kept his counsel:

> I believe I am as little *interested* in the success of either party as any one can be, and yet I feel a lively interest in all that passes ... I have not

---

* Samuel passed his ideas to his brother Jeremy, who incorporated them into his 'panopticon' prison, with a single prison officer in a central inspection lodge, 'seeing without being seen', enforcing 'direction and order'. When Samuel was sent to Russia by the Admiralty to oversee the building of warships for Britain in 1805, he designed and built a wooden panopticon in St Petersburg large enough to hold 3,000 workmen. The building contained wood-processing machines designed to be operated by unskilled peasants. The absolutism of Russia was more conducive to Bentham's frightening methods of control (Ashworth, 'System of Terror', p. 69; Morriss, *Royal Dockyards*, p. 213).

entered into one debate on the subject; but have read, and listened, and asked questions, with a view to assist my judgement.[36]

And of the Navy Board he wrote in December 1802:

> They are not faultless. Like most other Boards and Public Offices they have left many things undone; but the visitation did not bring home to them any act of corruption or malversation. It was then tried to drive them out by the most abusive letters that ever were written from one Board to another; but they were too prudent to gratify our gentlemen in this way.[37]

Marsden's moderation and pragmatism were, however, the exception in these years.

St Vincent persuaded Addington's reluctant cabinet to appoint a commission to examine naval abuses, although the first fraught meeting rejected the idea: 'Excepting my Lord Chancellor,' the admiral is said to have said afterwards, 'the whole cabinet has mutinied today! My commission is rejected! – but we'll read them a lesson out of the Articles of War, tomorrow, Sir!'[38]* But St Vincent had no parliamentary allies talented enough or committed enough on the Commission of Naval Enquiry to carry through anything approaching his radical ideas. The one reforming firebrand whom St Vincent wanted to appoint, Benjamin Tucker, was objected to at the last minute, and the commission was thus composed of Whig politicians or sympathizers of the second or even third rank.[39] Its chairman was Vice-Admiral Sir Morice Pole, recently elected an MP, whose wife was the cousin of John Markham. Pole's first known speech in the House, on 4 May 1803, was to answer criticism on the commission's apparent lack of progress.[40] Markham's brother-in-law, Ewan Law, lawyer and MP, was also appointed, but attended rarely; he wrote to a relative in 1804: 'The attendance on the office I hold is too much for me; I shall not be surprised if the new lord of the Admiralty [Melville], the old

---

* St Vincent was asked by the comptroller of the Navy Board, Sir Andrew Snape Hamond, if the commission was to be 'under the privy seal or parliament, and I rather inclined to the former, but upon further enquiry and consideration I decided for the latter' (St Vincent to John Markham, 14 Dec. 1802, Markham, *Markham*, p. 13). A parliamentary commission would make more political capital, while a privy seal commission could be implemented without debate by an order-in-council.

jobber, should procure a stop to be put to our enquiries; as far as I am personally concerned, I should heartily rejoice at it.'[41] These were hardly the sentiments of an avid reformer.

The reports of the Commission of Naval Enquiry, of which the first was published in May 1803, focused on known areas of weakness, such as casual corruption in the dockyards, badly administered contracts or insufficient quality control. The old principle of the senior dockyard officers acting as a single body in every matter, providing a 'check' on each other, had largely broken down by the 1790s as the officers' workloads had increased at the same pace as the dockyards'.[42] For instance, to ensure that the agreed number of cauldrons of coal was delivered to a dockyard, clerks and labourers, acting as 'coalmeters', counted in these very large deliveries. Through the years, over-friendly relations had been established that blunted the effectiveness of inspection. Money was paid as fees for the clerks, but food and drink also changed hands. The Commission of Naval Enquiry examined Plymouth Dockyard in detail: one merchant captain told the commission that after a voyage in 1803 he had left £5.11s.6d. for grog for 'Treating the Foremen, etc., which at that time you know well was a Custom'.[43] These misdemeanours and old customs were not, however, the fundamental problem. Content to score political points, the Commission of Naval Enquiry never attempted the reorganization and change of culture that the navy needed, failing to address the lack of accountability and muddled lines of responsibility, financial indiscipline, contractors' accounts not cleared, slack management and laziness, men too old for their jobs because of the difficulties of obtaining a pension. It should, however, be credited with opening up the whole question of maladministration. The reports of the commission caused sufficient debate to bring about the passing of two Acts of parliament in July and August 1803: the first improved the administration of the Chatham Chest, the money collection from seamen that funded Greenwich Hospital; and the second the distribution of prize money to seamen.[44] Reform after the Commission of Naval Enquiry made little headway, with the Navy Board's immediate response being to demand job descriptions for each of the commissioners.[45] There was even greater resistance to change from other offices, notably from the Victualling Board, which just ignored pressure to change.

Addington's government was forced out of office in May 1804, and Henry Dundas, ennobled as Lord Melville, was appointed first lord. Immediate changes were needed within the Admiralty. The radical second secretary, Benjamin Tucker, went immediately, and was replaced by the much travelled Lancastrian John Barrow. It was Barrow's talent as an author that had come to Lord Melville's notice, for Barrow had journeyed to China with Lord Macartney between 1792 and 1794, and spent some time at the Cape, where his reports and writing had impressed General Frank Dundas, Melville's nephew. The general had then taken Barrow to a dinner with Pitt and his uncle, where Barrow found that his views on the Cape of Good Hope accorded with those of the first lord. When Barrow later had his interview with Melville, he was urged to start at once: 'I need not say how much pressed Marsden finds himself . . . the sooner you put yourself into harness the better.' Barrow left the first lord's office and went straight to his new desk.[46] This was the start of a remarkable career, for, although Barrow lost his job briefly to Benjamin Tucker when the Talents came to power in early 1806, he resumed it in 1807 and did not retire for thirty-eight years.* A further personnel change was not so easy, and even Pitt was dragged into the business of replacing Osbourne Markham, who refused to be transferred to the Transport Board.[47] Markham had caused a furore among the rest of the Board by ostentatiously entering his own minutes into a private book in Navy Board meetings, noting the separate opinions of other commissioners. He would not be bound by collective decision-making and abstained from signing anything with which he did not agree, believing in the Whiggish concept of individual responsibility.[48] His patent to the Navy Board was revoked in July 1805.

Encouraged by Admiral Sir Charles Middleton, Melville set up his own commission, more ambitious than St Vincent's Naval Enquiry. On 8 January 1805 the Commission of Revising and Digesting the

---

* Tucker was not a popular man. When Tom Grenville took over as first lord in September 1806 he was loath to agree automatically to Tucker's continuing as second secretary. 'I shall try to keep him,' Grenville wrote to his elder brother, the marquis of Buckingham, 'but to such a forward position as 2nd Secretary, some of those whom I want as confidential at the board may object, & therefore as I before said, I cannot look to the livery till the Steward & Butler are agreed on' (4 Oct. 1806, HL, STG 37 (28)).

Civil Affairs of the Navy was established by Letters Patent under the Great Seal.[49] Middleton, appointed as chairman, surrounded himself with people whom he trusted, none of them politicians. He had worked on the Commission into Woods and Forests with John Fordyce, an able administrator who was the surveyor-general of crown lands,* and he made Fordyce's membership of the commission a precondition of his accepting the chairmanship.[50] Another trusted friend was the evangelical Ambrose Serle, a theological author, another experienced administrator and currently a commissioner of the Transport Board.[51] Two largely politically neutral admirals completed the commission, although neither was a friend to St Vincent. Admiral Sir Roger Curtis had been a follower of Howe, and had a good reputation as a staff officer. Rear-Admiral William Domett was a protégé of Lord Bridport, one of the Hoods; a highly respected seaman, aged fifty-three, he had come ashore because of ill-health. They were assisted by junior civil servants in their early twenties, two of whom, John Thomas Briggs and John Finlaison, were to rise to great eminence later in their careers. Finlaison, born in Caithness, the son of a fisherman, had come to London after an education in Edinburgh; at this time he was only twenty-three, but already demonstrating a formidable logical brain and an immense capacity for work.†

With the publication of the *Tenth Report* of St Vincent's Commission of Naval Enquiry, on 13 February 1805, attention was turned on the treasurer of the navy, and a real political crisis ensued, as we saw in Chapter 8, which led to the resignation of Lord Melville in May, succeeded by Sir Charles Middleton, now Lord Barham. Under political pressure, Pitt decided that the army and Ordnance departments also warranted a detailed enquiry. On 5 June 1805 the

---

* Nevertheless, on his appointment to the commission, the Whig Thomas Creevey moved in parliament for an enquiry into Fordyce's financial affairs, as the arrears on his land tax account remained unpaid. Fordyce was, however, warmly defended by Pitt (Thorne, *House of Commons*, Vol. III, pp. 789–90).

† The secretary of the commission was initially John Deas Thompson, but after his appointment to the Navy Board in July 1805 his place was taken by the Navy Office clerk John Thomas Briggs, later Sir John Briggs. John Finlaison was second clerk (NMM, MID/6/11). Finlaison's subsequent career gave further proof of his talents (see Appendix 2).

Commission of Military Enquiry gained the royal assent. No politicians were appointed to the new commission, only men with military, legal and financial expertise. The chairman was a serving major general, Hildebrand Oakes, though he was soon sent on active service as quartermaster-general, Mediterranean. His place was taken by another military administration specialist, Colonel John Drinkwater, who had acted as commissary to the 1799 Den Helder expedition. (He had sufficiently impressed William Windham to be offered the undersecretaryship of the secretary of state for war in 1807, though he declined.) With the backing of the prince of Wales, Drinkwater was to lobby very strongly for the post of commissary-in-chief in 1810, but had to make do with comptroller of army accounts, a post that he occupied until the office was abolished in 1835. As can be seen in Appendix 2, the other members of the commission were from the military, financial and commercial worlds. The *Morning Herald* was not sanguine about their success, noting in mock military style that they

> will require, that they be not only men of inflexible pretension, but of assiduity and unconquerable temper also; for . . . they will have to pass mountains, and labyrinths of figures, drawn up for years in great <u>martial</u> array, and to explore defiles of subtleties which nothing but patience and perseverance can possibly pass through.[52]

Seeking still to espouse the cause of reform, Pitt also approved a major restructuring of the Treasury, promulgated by a Board minute of 19 August 1805. The functions of the first and second secretaries were redefined in 1804 and their tasks separated, based on a plan submitted by Charles Long. The first secretary now became the parliamentary secretary, dealing with patronage and appointments; while the second secretary's responsibilities were solely financial.[53] The secretary to the Treasury at the time was William Sturges Bourne, another member of the Christ Church network. The department was still very small, with only thirty-six clerks, but the changes were radical. The existing four chief clerks were no longer to have generalized advisory roles, or to form a hierarchy governed by the anticipated yield of fees. Instead, they were to lead six separate sections, organized by function, which led to an increase of specialist knowledge. The first section, for instance, was to deal with war finance, and American, West Indian and Mediterranean business. The Treasury's Revenue Department prepared weekly, quarterly and annual revenue accounts for its Board. Though a dozen temporary clerks were taken on by 1809, it still remained small, and such was the pressure of work that by this time clerks were working on Sundays between ten and four o'clock.[54]

Perhaps the most important element of the Treasury reorganization was the establishment of a new non-political post of assistant secretary, under the first and second secretaries. George Harrison was appointed and was to take a critical role in further Treasury reform before the end of the Napoleonic War. The occupant of this position was forbidden to enter parliament, a step first suggested by the Commission on Fees in 1786.* Harrison was a 38-year-old lawyer who was an expert in taxation. As might be expected of a bright young man picked by an astute prime minister, Harrison made an immediate impact. Almost all Treasury business went through his hands, including the responsibility for the efficient transaction of the Board's orders. He signed directions for executing orders-in-council, and it was he who accepted bills of exchange drawn on the Treasury. He also served as a part-time legal counsel to the War Office. He had total control over the clerks (only he, for instance, could grant them leave of absence). Harrison's relations with every prime minister – in the prime minister's capacity as first lord of the Treasury – from Grenville to Perceval and Liverpool were excellent. The assistant secretary's human qualities and capacity for work transformed a position that might have been regarded as a superior clerkship into a confidential adviser to several prime ministers.†

---

* 'The line of duty committed to the Joint Secretaries seems of a nature too important to admit of sudden or frequent changes in office, and too laborious to allow of other avocations. For these reasons, we are of opinion that one of the said Secretaries, whose duty should be to attend to the current business of the Office, should be stationary in his situation, and be precluded from sitting in Parliament' (Commission on Fees, Second Report, p. 56). It was not until 1867 that the position came to be known as the permanent undersecretary.

† Harrison's hard work was notable. In 1812 he was confined to his house with gout, where, as he wrote to Perceval, he worked as hard 'at home as at the Treasury', aided by two private secretaries, 'without whom it would have been utterly impossible to have got through the business of the Office' (Gray, Perceval, p. 313, quoting 14 Jan. 1812, Perceval MSS).

The Whig Ministry of All the Talents came to power in February 1806. Building on Pitt's reforms, Grenville's work ethic continued to energize the Treasury. Charles Abbot reported that Grenville 'was determined to make the Treasury as remarkable for its punctuality in business as it had been heretofore for the contrary'.[55] Grenville's brother, the marquis of Buckingham, warned his relative, the newly appointed junior secretary William Henry Fremantle, not to 'relax in exertion' when he took up his post.[56] William Wickham, back from Ireland as one of Grenville's Treasury commissioners, built on and extended the previous government's reorganization. Efficiencies came to departments working directly to the Treasury, including customs and excise and the Post Office.[57]

With both sides of the political spectrum vying with each other in pressing for reform, one small department, the Sick and Hurt Office – under the Admiralty and responsible for sick and wounded seamen – itself became a total casualty. The *Seventh Report* of the Commission of Naval Enquiry, published in mid 1804, had been very critical of the administration of contracts at the Naval Hospital at Plymouth, and had found much fault with conditions on board the *Le Caton* hospital ship. More than anything the department was behind with its accounts, as were almost all departments; it simply did not have sufficient clerical staff. On 6 March 1806, in the dying days of his period of office, Lord Barham ordered the Sick and Hurt Office to transfer its books, papers and instructions to the Transport Board, which he had helped to create and which had a good accounting reputation.[58] Nevertheless, it eventually had to hire more clerks in addition to the complement of the Sick and Hurt Office to get through the backlog.

The Ministry of All the Talents was too short-lived to make much impact, yet reforming ideas were being developed by the little known members of the Commission of Naval Revision and of the Commission of Military Enquiry, who between them rewrote the regulations and accounting procedures by which the armed services were governed. These reforms were of critical importance to the conduct of the last eight years of war.

The Commission of Naval Revision worked away through 1806 and 1807, pointedly ignored by the Whig first lords who succeeded Barham, Charles Grey (who became Lord Howick in April 1806) and Tom Grenville.[59] The commissioners and the supporting clerks moved out of the Admiralty and into premises in Craven Street. Lord Barham, by now eighty-one, lived for most of the time away from London in the Kent countryside and left the bulk of the work to John Fordyce. Barham was much discouraged by the lack of interest taken by the Whigs as well as by the criticism of the commission in parliament by Grey and Samuel Whitbread.[60]* Grenville, for instance, refused to let Joseph Whidbey, the master attendant at Woolwich Dockyard, have a week's leave to advise the commission on the proposed new dockyard at Northfleet, for the first lord considered that the commission was acting beyond its brief.[61] The commission's report on the new dockyard was subsequently shelved and never published.[62]

The commissioners completed fourteen reports in December 1807, and in March of the following year John Fordyce wound up its business, a year after the end of the Whig government. Persuading Lord Mulgrave, who succeeded as first lord in April 1807, to accept their recommendations proved no easy matter.[63] In the event, the reports were implemented only after endless discussions between Fordyce and Mulgrave. The commission's secretary, John Thomas Briggs, observed that fear seemed 'to be a much more guiding principle with Lord Mulgrave than the spirit of amendment'.[64] Eventually the first lord's concerns were assuaged and eleven of the thirteen reports were adopted by an order-in-council, and published in April 1809.

In spite of this delay and lack of political confidence, the impact of the reports by the Commission of Naval Revision was considerable. The reports avoided political blame and concentrated instead upon providing new methods of administration, and criticism was trenchant. The *Tenth Report*, on the Victualling Office, made things

---

* Ambrose Serle wrote to Barham of the Whigs that 'an early termination of our commission would not be disagreeable to them' (19 Nov. 1806, NMM, MID/1/168).

absolutely clear on the first page: 'nothing short of a new system [is] likely to be effectual.' Much of the drafting of the reports had been left to the professionals and the clerks. For example, the *Eleventh* and *Twelfth* reports, on the Victualling service, were the work of the young second clerk of the commission, John Finlaison.

The Victualling Board and Office were reorganized on the lines of the other naval departments, which the Board had been resisting for a decade. Some of the senior officers at Deptford Victualling Yard were downgraded, so that their positions equated with similar roles in other yards, and radical clerical staff cuts were proposed. The duties of every officer were set out in detail, and the layout of every newly designed printed form and account was reproduced in the appendices.[65] A very efficient Victualling commissioner, Nicholas Brown, was appointed as first commissioner for accounts and cash. This complete overhaul was notably successful, and accounting time improved dramatically, resulting in the production of contractors' accounts, as well as their checking and auditing, in three weeks. By 1814 the Victualling Office had worked through the backlog of accountancy delays.[66] Operationally, an immediate improvement could be seen, for instance, in the early months of 1810. The previous year had seen a great strain in shipping thousands of tons of provisions to Admiral Saumarez's fleet in the Baltic, for the army in Spain and the Walcheren expedition had also to be supplied; some transports had left England for the Baltic with only partially filled holds. Better systems enabled the Victualling Board in London to take a long-term view, and two main shipments a year were now planned, with larger convoys of ships with full holds, rather than the hand to mouth planning that was prevalent before.[67]

In the dockyards outstanding issues on the pay and the organization of the shipwrights and other dockyard workers remained, and these complex difficulties were resolved by the energy and talent of another young man, John Payne, well known in the Navy Office for his organizing ability, who had become the chief clerk in the Navy Board secretary's office at twenty-seven. In 1809 he put forward a long memorandum to the Navy Board in which the confusing and differing interpretations that arose between the *Third* and *Eighth* reports on the dockyards – particularly over the calculation of task

The Right Hon.ble William Pitt

COLONEL Commandant of the Cinque Port VOLUNTEERS

To the Gentlemen Volunteers, the Corporations and other Inhabitants of
the Cinque Ports, This Plate is respectfully inscribed by their
Most obedient humble Servant Sam.l White

19. William Pitt as the colonel commandant of the Cinque Port Volunteers (1804). As warden of the Cinque Ports, Pitt lived at Walmer Castle, seen in the background. When out of office, between 1801 and 1804, he raised three battalions of volunteers and could often be spotted around East Kent wearing his uniform, riding many miles between different parades and throwing himself into manoeuvres and exercises.

20. (*top*) Grand Review at Sandown (or Sandham) Bay, Isle of Wight (1798). Sandown Bay was a vulnerable area for a potential invasion, low-lying and sheltered from south-westerly winds. A long line of troops can be seen marching along the beach, the red-coated militia at the front, and the blue-coated volunteers to the rear. In the foreground are riflemen in dark green, accompanied by a musician with a hunting horn. In the fort are volunteers with pikes, which had to be issued to the volunteers because of the shortage of muskets.

21. (*above*) Cornhill Military Association, founded in May 1798, was drawn from volunteers from the Cornhill Ward of the City of London. Such local organizations were abandoned when war was resumed in 1803, when volunteers in London were mostly concentrated into eleven large City regiments of Loyal London Volunteers. By autumn 1803 over 12,000 had come forward from the City, and over 14,000 from Westminster.

22. (*top left*) Henry Addington, prime minister from March 1801 to May 1804. Although he had been a fair and impartial Speaker of the House of Commons, Addington was a weak debater. From 1812, as Lord Sidmouth, he was home secretary in Liverpool's government.

23. (*top right*) Lord St Vincent, first lord of the Admiralty from February 1801 to May 1804. St Vincent brought to the Admiralty a quarterdeck style and a conviction that the administration of the navy was rotten to the core. His attempts at reform ended in a lengthy political furore, a navy with low morale and ships unprepared for the renewal of war.

24. (*above left*) Charles Grey, first lord of the Admiralty from February to September 1806, then foreign secretary until March 1807. Long years of fluent criticism of Pitt's government were not transformed into administrative and political capacity when in office.

25. (*above right*) Thomas Grenville, first lord of the Admiralty from September 1806 to April 1807. Grenville was a reluctant but conscientious minister. Some of his hesitancy is captured by this portrait of 1807, a contrast with the assurance of his younger brother, William Wyndham Grenville.

26. (*right*) Chatham Dockyard in 1794. Major investments had been made in the 1780s to renew the ropery and rigging-houses (*right*). These buildings were started in 1787, completed in about 1792, and still stand.

27. (*below*) Plymouth Dockyard in 1798. Substantial docks for refits and repairs of ships of the line are at left and centre, while a row of slips for the construction of large warships can be seen to the right. Moored on the River Hamoaze (*bottom*) are a store hulk and the yard mast crane with its reinforced mast, known as a sheer hulk (*centre right foreground*).

28. (*above*) Martello
Towers in Pevensey Bay,
looking east from
Eastbourne, with Langney
Point in the foreground and
the cliffs above Hastings in
the distance at right. This
stretch of coast was a
vulnerable open beach,
sheltered from the
prevailing south-westerly
winds. Although many
towers survive today, others
have been destroyed by the
sea or dismantled for
building materials. This
watercolour shows the
original, continuous line of
towers, which gave the
single 24-pounder guns on
top of each tower
intersecting fields of fire.

29. (*right*) The earl of
Egremont in the uniform
of the Sussex Yeomanry
(1798). The eccentric third earl suggested to his neighbour the duke of Richmond that a
professional soldier would do a much better job leading the volunteers. Richmond advised
that the earl's social standing 'was of more consequence than any practical knowledge of the
cavalry business'.

30. (*top*) Banqueting Hall in Whitehall (1809). Since so many soldiers were garrisoned in London, Inigo Jones's Great Hall was turned into a military chapel; the painted ceiling can be clearly seen. The civilian figures listening to the sermon were drawn by Thomas Rowlandson, who cannot help introducing an element of caricature.

31. (*above*) The Board Room of the Board of Trade (1809), which acted as a branch of the Privy Council concerned with commercial matters. Rather than frame policies, the Board monitored trade and collected statistics, important tasks during the economic struggle with Napoleon.

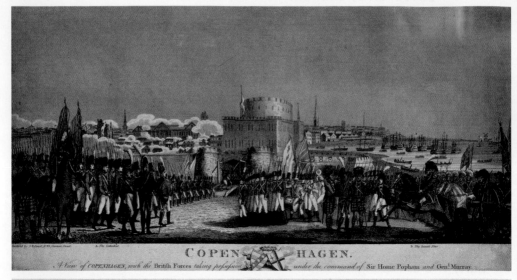

COPEN HAGEN.

A View of COPENHAGEN, with the British Forces taking possession under the command of Sir Home Popham and Gen.l Murray.

Engellændernes sidste Daad i Kiobenhavn 1807   *Le dernier Exploit des Anglois à Copenhague 1807*
fom en varig Triumph for Gambier, Cathcart, Popham &c   *ou le Triomphe de Gambier, Cathcart, Popham &c*

32. (*top*) British forces before they marched into Copenhagen, 7 September 1807. After three days of fierce bombardment, the Danes surrendered and an armistice was signed. Smoke can still be seen drifting over the houses, with the unprepared Danish Fleet moored in the background. British regiments in the foreground include Highlanders and (*centre*) the King's German Legion.

33. (*above*) *The Last Act of the English* (1807), a Danish view of the destruction of Danish warships in Copenhagen Dockyard. As the primary purpose of the expedition was to deny Napoleon the use of the Danish Fleet, every floating warship was sailed back to British ports. Here, British seamen have just pulled over the nearly completed ship at right centre, its back broken.

and job work for the different classes of workers – were resolved. After further Navy Board hesitation, and a consequent loss of patience by the new first lord, Charles Philip Yorke, the two reports were ordered to take effect on 1 January 1811.* Still there was confusion, and Payne was sent down to the yards, where he settled most of the issues in a matter of days, though at Plymouth he had to stay for two months. The measurement of work performed by the workmen was put on a more detailed and systematic basis by the use of a printed table; and the dockyard wages bill was reduced by 5 per cent. The Navy Board was therefore able to inform the Admiralty in June 1812 that 'the accuracy of the measurement and of the accounts may now be relied upon.'[68] Unfortunately the administrative talents of John Payne were lost to the navy, for he died suddenly at the age of thirty-two of meningitis.[69] His wife's petition for a widow's pension, which cruelly was not successful, claimed, without exaggeration, that Payne had 'new modelled almost the whole of the internal economy of the Dockyards'.[70] The copy of Payne's recommendations to accompany the petition runs to over a hundred pages.[71] Two years after his death his scheme of superannuation for the dockyard workers was adopted.[72]

The Commission of Military Enquiry took longer but was no less effective. Seven years and nineteen reports were needed to work through all the army and Ordnance departments.[73] Evidence gathering was thorough, under oath with witnesses present, questionnaires were used, and the commissioners visited all the establishments they were investigating.[74] Detailed appendices laid down comprehensive regulations and procedures that were to be implemented immediately. Just in case the notably independent regimental colonels thought that these new regulations did not apply to them, one paragraph in the *First Report* begins: 'And we do hereby direct and require the Commanding

* One direct result of the Commission of Naval Revision was that the Admiralty increased its control over the bases in the Indian Ocean, which had hitherto been complicated by the influence of the East India Company. From 1809 newly appointed resident commissioners at the Cape of Good Hope, Bombay, Madras, Trincomalee and Penang became responsible not only for the local naval yard, but also for the naval hospital and victualling (Day, 'Naval Power in the Indian Ocean', pp. 324–33).

Officer of each regiment . . .'[75] It was part of the process by which the colonels of regiments lost their autonomy and effectively became a layer of middle management during the war, even if their patronage within their own corps remained powerful.[76] A parallel process had been taking place in the navy: the powers of appointment of the captains of warships had been steadily curtailed, to be taken over by the Admiralty.

The *First Report* of the Commission of Military Enquiry appeared after only nine months, on the department of the barrack master-general. The commission thoroughly analysed its history and tabulated the accounts in a report of 113 closely printed pages. Oliver De Lancey had been hastily appointed by Pitt and Dundas to the demanding post of barrack master-general just before the outbreak of the French Revolutionary War.* In 1806 each one of nearly 200 regular, militia and volunteer barracks in Britain needed to be supplied with 120 items of equipment, such as furniture, bedding, utensils and tools, in various quantities.[77] By 1807 it was stated in parliament that there were 591 clerks in the Barrack Department.[78] De Lancey's accounts over fifteen years were a shambles: little auditing was done, and there were huge sums outstanding to his account at various times. Although his 'negligence' was exposed by the commission, the only action the government took was to seize his house in order to meet his liabilities.[79]

The primary purpose of the Commission of Military Enquiry's reports was to establish regulations and order, and it did this with a will. Not only were accounting forms and procedures specified, but detailed rules for matters such as cleanliness and order were laid down. Henceforth, for instance, all women were to be banned from barracks. However, the commission's examinations during the compilation of the *Third Report*, on the 'Stores and Services of the Barrack Master-General', led to the exposure of irregular financial dealings

---

* In 1804 the Treasury had tried to press Sir Brook Watson, the commissary-general, to take on the supply of the barracks. Watson refused this task, which he described as 'of a magnitude & Intricacy requiring the utmost attention', although eventually, after Watson's retirement, the Commissary-General's Department did take it on (29 Nov. 1804, commissary-general secret letter-book, TNA, WO 58/170).

and claimed the first political scalp. Alexander Davison, the chief contractor to the department, had supplied vast quantities of equipment, not by contract but merely through an understanding contained in an exchange of letters with De Lancey over Christmas 1794. A long investigation of discrepancies was led by J. C. Herries (of whom we shall hear more shortly), a young Treasury official and protégé of Spencer Perceval. It transpired that Davison had caused receipts to be forged and had also charged commission on items that he already had in his store. In December 1808 Davison was sentenced by Lord Ellenborough, the lord chief justice, at a court in Westminster Hall on thirty-six counts of defrauding the king. Apart from having to pay back a great deal of money to the government, Davison was sentenced to twenty-one months in Newgate Prison. It was a spectacular fall from grace, accompanied by a stream of hostile comment in the newspapers.[80]

This was a high-profile case, for Davison had flaunted his wealth, keeping a house in St James's Square, where he was, as it happened, a near-neighbour of Lord Ellenborough. Davison was well known for having been the prize agent of Lord Nelson and for having had medals struck for those officers and seamen who had fought in Nelson's victories. He had many friends in government: his character witnesses included Sir Evan Nepean and Sir Andrew Snape Hamond, as well as General Lord Moira, who had recently been master-general of the Ordnance during the Ministry of All the Talents; to Moira's embarrassment, he had only two years previously appointed Davison to the post of treasurer of the Ordnance. For the Portland government this successful prosecution of a previous Whig junior minister afforded a useful political advantage.*

* It went some way to compensate for an embarrassment for the Tories, the hushed-up disgrace of 'Honest Tom Steele', friend of Pitt, and joint paymaster of the forces between 1791 and 1804. Canning met Thomas Steele in 1793, describing him as 'perhaps the most popular man in Administration. I have never heard him mentioned without praise' (Jupp, *Canning Journal*, p. 29). In 1799 and 1800 Steele had appropriated over £20,000 without authority. He confessed to the Select Committee on Finance in 1807 and paid the money back with interest, but it was never known why and for whom he acquired the money, though apparently Pitt knew; even the cabinet in 1807 was not told (Thorne, *House of Commons*, Vol. V, p. 260).

Davison was not the last to be exposed. The military commissioners used their military, financial and legal expertise to great effect: no politician could have struck a shrewder blow to popularize and legitimize their task. This was a commission to be feared by soldiers and politicians alike. The *Ninth Report*, which looked into the administration of the West Indies army contracts and pay, could not have been more critical, for it found widespread corruption and recommended the indictment of several individuals: 'This evil has doubtless been of great magnitude, widely extended and deeply rooted.'[81] So effective was the commission that – after they had finished nineteen reports on the army and the Ordnance – five of its members were retained during 1812 to investigate the Office of Works, which maintained government buildings. The examination of the senior works officials took several weeks, the commissioners questioning each of them, under oath, for four hours at a time, over four successive days. They uncovered a complicated mess, spectacular overspending and ineffectual management. Soon after the presentation of the report to the Treasury, one of the commissioners, Colonel Benjamin Stephenson, was appointed surveyor-general of the King's Works, and brought about rapid changes in personnel and financial discipline in the department.[82]

As with the Admiralty, complications ensued at the War Office as a result of the publication of the Commission of Military Enquiry reports. It was decided that the secretary at war was accountable to the Treasury, which clarified many years of confused lines of responsibility. But perhaps the most interesting and effective measure was the appointment of an apolitical military undersecretary, in conscious imitation of Harrison's position at the Treasury. The post had been created by the Whigs in 1806, and filled by political appointees, but when Robert Dundas, Lord Melville's son, was in line to be given the job of secretary of state for war by Perceval in 1809, he expressed the wish to make an important change: 'Mr Dundas is further desirous that professional merit alone should influence the selection of an officer to fill this situation, and, when placed in it, that he should in no manner intermix in politics, or be a member of the House of Commons.'[83]

The candidate who came to fit the bill was Colonel Henry Bunbury, a tactful and conscientious administrator, only thirty-one years old, who had recently distinguished himself as quartermaster-general in the Mediterranean. His name had been put forward by generals Dundas, Brownrigg and Alexander Hope. When first offered the post, Bunbury was suspicious of its non-political nature, as he came from a strong Whig family and was due to receive a substantial inheritance that might have been imperilled by accepting office in a Tory administration. Only after an agonized correspondence with Hope and Brownrigg, and a written assurance that he would not have to take any part in politics, did he accept. In the event, it was Lord Liverpool who was made secretary of state for war, and who assured Bunbury that the undersecretaryship was 'purely military, entirely abstracted from all politics'.[84] The success of this appointment could be measured not only by the improvements brought about by Bunbury in his tenure of the office, which lasted until the end of the war, but also by his participation in a powerful cross-departmental committee advising on the supply of Wellington's army in the Peninsula, the other members being Colonel Willoughby Gordon, commissary-in-chief, and George Harrison. These able, young administrators solved the communication problem across departments and brought military experience and specialist knowledge, rather than politics, to this vital task.

However, the principal weakness uncovered by the Commission of Military Enquiry, as by the Commission of Naval Revision, was the unaudited accounts. With the press of war business taking precedence, examining and passing paymasters' and contractors' accounts had never been given priority. Though delay was endemic across all government spending departments, the War Office was the most dilatory. It presented the most difficult of tasks because of the dispersed nature of the army – with infantry and cavalry, and regular, militia and volunteer regiments, many of them at sometime having served overseas, and a plethora of contractors and agents supplying them. In 1801, only 460 of 9,546 accounts for the period 1798 to 1800 had been examined. In 1807, another parliamentary committee, that on Public Expenditure, was told that the paymaster-general's account for 1782 would be completed by Christmas 1807, while 'not one account of any Paymaster-General [had] been finally declared, nor made ready for declaration' in the past ten years.[85] When the young Lord Palmerston came to the office of secretary at war in

October 1809, some 40,000 regimental accounts were in arrears, stretching back to 1783.

The clerical staff of the War Office had been expanded several times in an attempt to deal with the problem but had made little impression. The Commission of Military Enquiry put its finger on one problem when it highlighted the short working day, which was from 11 a.m. to 4 p.m., and the War Office's hours were immediately lengthened.[86] After 1809 Palmerston as secretary at war put in hand a reorganization, and the Treasury sanctioned some expansion, increasing his staff to 144. The Commissary-in-Chief's Department had taken over the task of supplying the army in the Peninsula, and much remained to be sorted out between the new organization and the War Office.

Palmerston worked hard and expected the same from his subordinates. Improvements came slowly but money began to be saved.[87] Palmerston's zeal for reform led to difficult relations between the War Office and General Dundas, the temporary commander-in-chief, now very old and irritable, in the Horse Guards; both the prime minister and the prince regent were drawn in to arbitrate between these two very strong characters, even though there was a fifty-year difference in their ages. It took several years before the disagreements were resolved. Although the origins of this prolonged altercation were trivial, it did give rise to the question of whether the secretary at war had the right to demand financial information from the army.[88]*

As the system of accounts became more rigorous and transparent, cases of embezzlement came to light. Perhaps the greatest villain to be flushed out was Joseph Hunt, who had been a commissioner on the boards of the Victualling, Transport and Ordnance departments, and

---

* Palmerston also had to solve the problems of the Army Medical Board, from which all three members had had to resign in February 1810 after the medical disaster of Walcheren. Each member of the Board had been responsible for completely separate tasks, and its culture was to follow orders and take no initiative as a Board. Relations between the physician-general and the surgeon-general were governed by professional differences between physicians and surgeons. In 1810 the different functions of each member, imposed in 1798, were swept away. Three newly appointed commissioners, led by a director-general, were jointly responsible for every activity of the Army Medical Service, directly contrary to the principles of Benthamism (Ackroyd et al., *Advancing with the Army*, pp. 28–30; Howard, *Walcheren*, pp. 207–8).

latterly also MP for Queenborough. After his chicanery was exposed by the Commission of Military Enquiry, he resigned in January 1810 and fled to Portugal, with £93,000 of public balances in his possession. The Ordnance Department seized Hunt's house in south-east London, and he died in France in 1816. In another case, William Chinnery, a senior clerk in the Treasury, was found to have had almost £79,000 paid to him to defray official expenses in his capacity as a colonial agent.[89] The well-connected George Villiers, courtier and personal friend of the king as well as the paymaster of marines for many years, was the next to be caught, this time by the young John Wilson Croker, only a month into his appointment as secretary to the Admiralty in October 1809. Croker recalled many years later that, having paid 'a more minute attention to details than my two predecessors had happened to do, I saw reason to suspect a serious defalcation . . . and refused my signature to an additional issue of money till the last issues were accounted for'. Villiers exercised all the influence he could, 'pressed his royal patron to stifle my <u>capricious</u> opposition . . . all that was to be done to set all right was that I should sign the same routine order that my predecessors had always signed.'[90] Croker had to go so far as to offer his resignation to the prime minister, Spencer Perceval, rather than sign the order, and eventually he won the day. Villiers had indeed had something to hide. In January 1810 Perceval informed an astounded George III that Villiers's embezzlements up to 1804 amounted to £280,000. Further, his sureties of £10,000, lodged when he took office in 1792, had disappeared. The government seized the disgraced Villiers's house and estate; but as late as 1819 he still owed the government £220,000.[91] Croker's stand was significant, though one suspects he was fully aware of the extent of Villiers's situation before he made it.

A hardening of attitudes towards corruption and an intolerance of slackness throughout the departments were steadily developing, put more and more into relief through stricter systems and accounting. When, for instance, it was found in 1808 in the Victualling Office that the accountant for cash and all ten clerks in his department had been accepting presents from contractors, the Admiralty called in 'Mr Reed, Chief Magistrate of the Police Force': everyone involved was dismissed, though the press of business demanded that six of the junior clerks be reinstated.[92] The profound change of attitudes can perhaps be gauged by a small incident at Christmas 1812, when four of the Victualling Office messengers accepted a Christmas box of £5 each from a contractor. The Victualling Board minutes record: 'The Board highly reprobates such gross improprieties of conduct, entertained serious thoughts of instantly dismissing them altogether from the service of the Office.' Eventually the messengers were pardoned, their defence being that they did not think that Christmas boxes came within the strictures on taking fees and gratuities. Nevertheless, the Board fined the messengers £2 each.[93]*

This cultural shift was brought about in part by some radical changes of senior personnel. As a result of the reports by the two commissions, a good many senior officials in the administration of the navy and the army lost their jobs. This process was initially accelerated by the changes of government in 1806 and 1807, which brought about a rapid turnover of parliamentary government posts. When the Ministry of All the Talents came into power for thirteen months in early 1806, Lord Grenville needed as many offices in his gift as possible, for his coalition needed to reward not only his own followers, but also those of Fox and of Addington.[94] At least forty posts changed hands. Not only were all cabinet members replaced, but, unusually, every one of the five Treasury commissioners and six of the seven around the Admiralty Board table. All officeholders who were also MPs were changed, not only undersecretaries but also much more junior posts such as the clerk of the Ordnance, principal storekeeper and clerk of the deliveries. Furthermore, when the Tories returned to power under the duke of Portland thirteen months later, in March 1807, the posts changed hands yet again, and in only a minority of cases was the original Tory incumbent reinstated, with the exception of the junior Ordnance posts. Thus changes of administration effectively changed the incumbents of nearly forty posts twice over in quick

* In 1805 the master shipwrights of the royal dockyards protested to the Navy Board over the cessation of the ancient privilege of the presentation 'of a piece of plate on the Launching of a Ship in the respective Yards ... which is esteemed by us far above its intrinsic Value, arising from that Laudable pride which every man feels who has been the principal in conducting the executive part of the great machine a Ship' (Navy Board to Admiralty, 17 Apr. 1805, NMM, ADM BP/25a). Several of these handsome pieces still exist.

succession. Moreover, following the formation of the Portland government, ministers and undersecretaries were significantly younger, and subsequently more able to take the strain of long hours of administration and negotiation than the older men they had replaced.

William Marsden, secretary of the Admiralty, was the sole senior civil servant to remain in office when the Ministry of All the Talents came to power. He was the only undersecretary who had resisted going into the House.

> not only because I felt that I did not possess the talent necessary for distinguishing myself in a deliberative and popular assembly, where eloquence is the first and judgement the second requisite, but because I was satisfied of its being inconsistent with the effective discharge of my official duties in time of war, which required all my time and attention.[95]

This was a rational view, but it left the government without an MP in possession of authoritative and detailed naval knowledge. The Naval Estimates therefore had to be presented in the Commons by a member of the Board, Sir Philip Stephens, who had long been in Admiralty service as secretary. By this time over eighty, he had survived all the changes because he had the support of the king. Stephens finally retired in 1806 and Marsden in 1807.

At this point, the distinction between the political nature of the first secretary, appointed by the prime minister rather than by the Board, and the permanent official, then known as the second secretary, was formalized, just as it had been in the Treasury some years before. The new Tory secretary of the Admiralty was another Irishman, William Wellesley-Pole, a brother of the future duke of Wellington: he was forty-four and a highly competent parliamentary performer. One of the Board commissioners commented on Wellesley-Pole's 'energy and knowledge of business . . . [he] has done more for the Board in three weeks than ten years had done.'[96] He was followed in 1809 by a third Irishman, the 29-year-old John Wilson Croker, a Tory appointment whose tenure in office as secretary lasted for twenty-one years. His quick wit and forceful personality immediately established dominance over the Board. Croker described himself as the 'servant of the Board', but it was wryly observed by Charles Philip Yorke, first lord between 1810 and 1812, that 'it was precisely the other way round'.[97]

Two very young talents, both destined to rise to be prime minister, came into junior government posts in this period: Lord Palmerston was appointed in 1809 as secretary at war at the age of twenty-five.* No post in government required more drudgery or was more liable to make the young politician unpopular, especially among disappointed army officers. But it suited Palmerston. A week after he joined the office, he wrote to a friend: 'I continue to like this office very much.'[98] He stayed in it for nineteen years. A year later, at only twenty-two, Robert Peel was appointed undersecretary for war and the colonies by Spencer Perceval and immediately demonstrated a precocious debating talent.[99] Another able young man, Henry Goulburn, was brought on by Perceval and followed Peel in this office in his mid-twenties, the start of another distinguished career.

Unprecedented change was also in hand for those lower down the hierarchy. In May 1805 Lord Barham had written to William Pitt, 'Our naval boards are in such a weak state, that they cannot be relied upon for either advice or execution.'[100] Over the next three years, five out of the seven Navy Board commissioners were changed and five were ejected from the Victualling Board. The comptroller of the navy, Sir Andrew Snape Hamond, now sixty-eight, had written to Lord Barham in January 1806 of his 'long and painful illness' and expressed his intention to retire before he resigned when the Talents ministry came to power in February 1806.[101] Appointed in his stead was Captain Thomas Boulden Thompson, aged forty, a much admired officer, 'a solid, steady, good kind of man', who had lost his leg in 1801 at the Battle of Copenhagen.[102] One naval officer on the Navy Board was moved to be resident commissioner at Chatham, and another in his seventies was retired, as was old Sir John Henslow, the surveyor of the navy, who had come to the Navy Office as assistant surveyor as far back as 1771. It was in 1804 that the most distinguished dockyard

---

* Appointing bright young men attracted criticism, as in the scathing notice in the Opposition *Morning Chronicle*, 11 Nov. 1809: 'Next to the mismanagement of public affairs, the distribution of places to incapable men forms the most conspicuous part of the conduct of the present wretched Ministry. The appointment of Mr Croker to the Admiralty has attracted universal notice, and Lord Palmerston, as Secretary at War, and some say a Member of the Cabinet (though this we cannot believe) almost surpasses Mr Croker' (Brightfield, *Croker*, p. 35).

shipwright of the first half of the nineteenth century was given his first significant promotion. Robert Seppings was made master shipwright of Chatham yard at the exceptionally young age of thirty-seven: nine years later he had risen to be surveyor of the navy.

Lord Mulgrave, Tory first lord between 1807 and 1810, in spite of his initial hesitation over the findings of the Commission of Naval Revision, steadily implemented their recommendations.* In the opinion of John Barrow, who was able to observe him closely, Mulgrave 'possessed wit and humour in a considerable degree, and was always most agreeable at his own table; he was also an acute critic.'[103] (Captain Sir Andrew Snape Hamond, who, after retirement, was disappointed in his request to be appointed to flag rank, referred to Mulgrave's 'hasty and petulant disposition'.[104]) One way or another, Mulgrave was not a man to be trifled with: he continued to make changes in the navy in the same manner as the Whigs, but more brutally. In a single day, 3 December 1808, he either moved or forced five old or sick administrators to resign from the Navy and Victualling boards, all to be replaced by much younger men. The honest but ineffectual John Marsh, the chairman of the Victualling Board, was called in to see Mulgrave on 14 October 1808, when he was told, as he noted, 'to my great surprise' that, after forty years' service, he would be retired on three quarters of his salary.[105] Other casualties included William Budge, previously private secretary to Lord Melville, who had severe gout, and Robert Sadleir Moody, who had served in the Victualling Office for fifty years.[106] On the same day Samuel Bentham was appointed to the Navy Board as 'Civil Architect and Engineer'. Presumably Mulgrave implemented these new and controversial measures simultaneously to give them maximum political impact.

The difficult Alexander Dalrymple at the Hydrographic Office was tactfully told in May 1808 by William Wellesley-Pole that new

---

* A typical efficiency implemented by Mulgrave's Admiralty Board was to overturn long-established custom by sending orders directly to the Victualling Board, rather than via the Navy Board, 'for the purpose of giving celerity to the Victualling Board . . . to cause the utmost dispatch to be used' (Admiralty Orders and Instructions, 12 July 1808, TNA, ADM 2/154).

arrangements were to be put in place and that it was felt that, at his age, Dalrymple would not be able to fulfil the new duties. This was an unsurprising judgement in view of the hydrographer's stubbornness and lack of cooperation. The splenetic Dalrymple never got over the shock of this decision, and died a few weeks later, aged seventy-one.[107] He was replaced by Captain Thomas Hurd, ten years younger, a practical seaman and administrator, who transformed the system and operation of distributing charts to warships.* Some exceptions proved the rule. George Phillips Towry at the Victualling Board survived, although concerns were raised in the Commons when the changes were debated in March 1809. William Windham could always be relied upon to ask the awkward question: 'If age were considered a ground for removal, he would wish to know how Captain Towry was retained?' Towry was seventy-six at the time.[108]

The issue of age and efficiency was largely solved by an Act in 1810 that provided pensions for government servants.† The principle of superannuation had been approved by the 1797 Select Committee on Finance, and schemes had been in operation for some time in the customs and excise departments, and from 1801 in naval departments in London, with pension scales determined by length of service and behaviour. This government-wide scheme, controlled by the Treasury, was effective: immediately after its introduction, for instance, eight dockyard officers applied for their pensions.[109] It helped to develop uniform terms of employment, and to rid the government service of

---

* One former employee of the Hydrographic Office complained to the Admiralty Board of Dalrymple's 'want of a regular system of management', prolonged absences from the office and the general incompetence of staff: the advisory Admiralty Chart Committee persistently complained of lack of cooperation. Hurd's appointment brought about an immediate operational improvement. In the next six months he sent out 113 boxes of charts to ships on various stations, including thirty-three boxes to the Baltic. From 1809 onwards Admiral Saumarez's correspondence was free of complaints about the state of Admiralty charts (Davey, 'Hydrographical Office', pp. 94–5, 97, quoting John Cooke to Admiralty, 18 Dec. 1807, TNA, ADM 1/3522; Chart Committee to Wellesley-Pole, 26 May 1808, TNA, ADM 1/3523).

† Officials over sixty who had more than twenty years' service were awarded pensions equivalent to two thirds of their former salary; those who had served from ten to twenty years received half their salary (Harling, 'Old Corruption', p. 118). Similar principles of government superannuation still hold today.

the idea of office as property, supported by sinecures. Officials were on their way to becoming salaried and pensionable civil servants.[110]

The Commission of Naval Revision and the Commission of Military Enquiry brought about an improvement in clerks' salaries, established grades and seniority systems, and achieved parity between clerks at similar levels of responsibility in different departments. Those in the navy and the dockyards were established by orders-in-council in 1807 and 1808.[111] Lord Mulgrave did not, however, accept all the Naval Revision's recommendations, rejecting a £200 increase in salary for the Navy Board commissioners on grounds that have a modern ring: as he remarked to George Rose,

> I did not think that increase necessary, whilst so many eager candidates were pressing for the situation. If the Paymaster to the Treasurer of the Navy has his salary raised, will not the Commissioners of Victualling and Transport Boards, whose duties are so constant and laborious, especially the former, have a claim to a similar advance?[112]

Nevertheless, in 1811, in order to keep up the standard of applicants, the Navy Office had to establish a minimum salary for clerks, increasing from the basic level of £90 after two years and rising after twelve years to £200. Other offices followed this practice slowly, with most not reaching these levels of pay until after the end of the war.[113]

Sinecures and reversions, which allowed a select few to enjoy anomalous privileges and to accumulate a fortune for no effort at all, were further problems that were steadily being eliminated. The radicals continued to challenge the practice as fiercely as ever. In his address to the constituents of Westminster in 1812, Lord Cochrane attacked the marquis of Buckingham's sinecure as teller of the Exchequer. This sinecure was the equivalent, Cochrane pointed out, of the annual cost of all the navy's overseas victualling establishments, while another sinecure equalled the pensions to be paid for wounded naval officers: '1,022 Captain's arms or; 488 pair of Lieutenants' legs'.[114] Thomas Grenville warned his brother in late 1808: 'the encreased pressure of taxes in latter days has here produced in the people at large, & in Parliament too, a very jealous & feverish suspicion of offices & emoluments'.[115] Defence of 'inefficient' or 'irregular' emoluments' centred on the difficulties of bringing impecunious men of talent into politics. This could be argued in the cases of George Rose and George Canning, men who had received such benefit but were clearly hard-working. The problem had been tackled intermittently since the days of Pitt: by 1809 the number of placemen and sinecurists in the Commons had shrunk to eighty-four.[116] Sinecures were still, however, an emotional political issue.*

The sale of offices was another problem needing to be addressed. In the wake of the Mary Clarke affair (see Chapter 8), Perceval introduced the Sale of Offices Prevention Act in 1809, which made it 'highly penal to solicit money for procuring offices, or to circulate any advertisement with that in view'.[117] Civil servants were being appointed less now on grounds of party allegiance than on merit and appropriate experience. At the Victualling Board, for instance, John Clarke Searle had been appointed by Lord Howick, first lord of the Admiralty in the Whig ministry of the Talents; but Searle was promoted to be chairman of the Board by a Tory first lord, Lord Mulgrave. Searle, in turn, was able to persuade Mulgrave that a good candidate, Nicholas Brown, ex-purser and secretary to Lord Keith, should be appointed to the Board. Keith, who was Brown's main sponsor for such a post, had no connection to the ministry.[118] Brown was a notable success.

As the talents and specialist knowledge of senior officials improved, so did the skills of government clerks, as illustrated by the experience of the Commissariat. The first problem was to manage the expectations of the world outside the department. The first commissary-in-chief, Thomas Ashton Coffin, received letters of application for clerical posts containing bribes. For instance, he was offered £1,000 by a 'respectable merchant', who quoted testimonials from members of parliament; the prospective employee grandly announced that he would 'have no objections to any required duty or attendance'.[119] Coffin's successor, Colonel Willoughby Gordon, regulated promotion

---

* In 1810, just before he became first lord of the Admiralty, C. P. Yorke accepted the sinecure of a tellership of the Exchequer worth £2,700 from the prime minister. This had an immediate effect at the general election of that year. Yorke, the long-established member for Cambridgeshire, was roundly booed every time he tried to speak at the hustings, could not make himself heard and withdrew from the election (Harling, 'Old Corruption', p. 120; Thorne, *House of Commons*, Vol. II, p. 30; Vol. V, p. 671).

by establishing rules in 1809 whereby all clerks had to serve at least one year at junior level and for four years at higher levels.

The third occupant of the post, John Charles Herries, took reform much further. Herries came from a Scottish mercantile family and would likely have pursued a career in his father's bank, had it not bankrupted itself in 1798. He had been educated in Leipzig and was fluent in French and German, the latter eventually proving extraordinarily useful. Through the contacts of his father, Charles Herries, who was colonel of the Light Horse Volunteers of London and Westminster, a regiment full of politicians, the younger Herries secured a post in the Treasury.[120] He joined as a twenty-year-old copying clerk, and his assiduous work and talent made for a fast climb to high office. During the Addington ministry he became private secretary to Nicholas Vansittart, secretary to the Treasury, and in succession spent time in Ireland, wrote a pamphlet against William Cobbett and was offered a customs appointment by Grenville in Buenos Aires. On the fall of the Ministry of All the Talents, which Vansittart did not join, Herries was out of work. His father, still the colonel of the Light Horse Volunteers, wrote to Spencer Perceval, just appointed chancellor of the Exchequer, and Herries was taken on as his private secretary. A further succession of posts brought him to the position of commissary-in-chief in 1811, over which appointment Perceval had a battle with the prince regent to ensure that the post went to a civilian and not to Colonel Drinkwater, the chairman of the Commission of Military Enquiry. Herries succeeded in overseeing the extraordinarily difficult job of supplying Wellington's army in the Peninsula. When he took up the post he was thirty-three.

One of Herries's first projects, by arrangement with Charles Arbuthnot, by now secretary of the Treasury, was to institute a short examination in English and arithmetic for candidates for clerical positions in the Commissariat. The first results demonstrated the need for such tests. One candidate approved by the Treasury was found to have been court-martialled and cashiered from the army. Another, sponsored by a senior member of the government, was illiterate: he sought to impress his prospective employers by writing in his exam that he was 'lernging a letel French'. Herries wrote to Arbuthnot that 'I feel that I am getting into terrible hot water in consequence of my endeavours to purify this department.' In the War Office, Palmerston put every new entry clerk on probation for two months, after which a full report on the clerk's performance was considered. As a result, thirty-three probationaries were rejected between 1810 and 1833.[121] The consequence was an increasing status for the clerks, reflected in their inclusion in the *Army List* in 1812.[122]

Office systems were changed, in line with recommendations of the naval and military commissions. One of the first reforms that William Wellesley-Pole set in train in the Admiralty was the reform of record keeping, or, in modern terms, information retrieval. The compilation of 'Digests' had long been a favourite scheme of Charles Middleton from as far back as the American Revolutionary War and he had pressed it on Lord Melville when the latter had been first lord of the Admiralty.[123] During the course of the Commission of Naval Revision it became apparent that the Admiralty had difficulty in producing the documents that were demanded. When John Finlaison had finished his work at the Commission of Naval Revision he entered the Admiralty, where a new branch called the Admiralty Record Office was created.[124] By December 1809 it had six clerks, and by January 1813 an additional twelve supernumerary clerks were employed, with the result that papers were produced promptly thereafter.

Perhaps the most noticeable difference was felt by the House of Commons, which began to receive clear and readable accounts. In 1810, for the first time, a detailed, printed Naval Estimate of expenditure was presented to parliament.[125] Equally importantly, the senior government boards began to use up-to-date management accounts, which were a real help in formulating policy decisions. By 1812 the Navy Board, for instance, was providing the Admiralty with all manner of useful information: monthly cash accounts to date; yearly office and salary costs, with 'increase and diminution' from the previous year; ships in commission, as well as 'ships and vessels not mustered with reasons'. The total average costs of fitting out ships, broken down by rate, provided the Board of Admiralty with information that it had never had before. In October an account came before the Board of the costs of 'equipping the Russian ships for voyages to Russia, as against what money would be raised by selling them'. Perhaps the most remarkable was a table containing a breakdown of the annual costs of keeping different rates of ships at sea, on Channel or Foreign Service.[126] Such a concentrated analysis – encompassing information from across the organization and the Ordnance, and consisting of the costs of supply, maintenance, wear and tear, manning and provisioning, as well as Ordnance costs – would have been unthinkable in earlier years.

Significant improvements came, too, in the distribution of pay and prize money to families and widows of seamen and soldiers, as well as of pensions to veterans. There were pragmatic reasons for improving these systems. The strain on manpower was evident at an early stage in the war, and any measures that increased the support for service families would provide some encouragement for enlistment. The costs of poor relief, particularly near naval ports, were increasing, and money from the navy would alleviate the strain on local parishes. Statistics presented in 1812 to the House of Commons indicated that approximately a quarter of seamen and soldiers were heads of families.[127] The commander-in-chief, the duke of York, had already established a system of casualty returns in 1797, and for the benefit of widows the army issued in 1810 *Regulations for Ensuring the Prompt Payment of Sums Due to the Relatives of Soldiers Killed or Dying in His Majesty's Service*.[128] Customs, excise or tax officials would handle the payment on behalf of both services, after having been in receipt of documents from the Navy or the Army pay offices. Although soldiers may well have had the benefit of regimental generosity to fall back on, the army's systems did not have the sophistication that the navy's would eventually attain. Admittedly the navy's task was an easier one, since seamen were confined to a ship and were less dispersed than soldiers. Since 1728 the navy had a system of 'allotments' by which seamen could decide to send home a proportion of their pay for their families, though it did not work well.[129] The transaction would be witnessed by the commanding officer of the man's ship, who sent a signed, printed 'remittance' to allot some or all of the wages home, at the same time as the regular musters were forwarded to the Navy Pay Office in Somerset House. Identification of the wife or relative would be attested and a document signed by the local parish priest. Those wives or relatives who lived in London would come to Somerset House to be paid, while those who lived within five miles of a dockyard (and many of them did) would deal with the clerk of the cheque of each yard. The same system would also ensure the payment of prize money, and on the death of a seaman it would pay a lump-sum that included both prize money and wages that were due to a family. It was a complex arrangement and it needed the active engagement of those who administered it in London.

George Rose, made treasurer of the navy in 1807 at the age of sixty-three, set about making the payment of allotments and pensions efficient. This indefatigable worker had been a solid supporter of Pitt, close to the centre of power as senior secretary of the Treasury since the early 1780s, though never, to his disappointment, quite achieving cabinet rank. The treasurer of the navy was a relatively junior post, though well paid, one that was generally used to finance young up-and-coming politicians. Twenty years before, the Commission on Fees had damned the treasurer of the navy with faint praise, and the post had been the downfall of Melville in 1805.[130] Yet, when he was appointed in 1807, Rose strove to make something of the department and was determined to see a fair deal for seamen.* When he arrived in the office, as he recalled, he sent to 'every parochial clergyman in England, Scotland and Ireland, to the number of 15,000 or 16,000, complete information of the steps necessary to be taken by any of their parishioners who might have, or who might suppose they had, claims to wages or prize money, due for service of themselves or of deceased relatives'. In 1809 he dined with Lord Mulgrave and the Board of Admiralty to discuss his plan 'for ensuring regular adjudication and speedy distribution of the proceeds of prizes'. At that point, Samuel Hancock was appointed prize officer in the Navy Pay Office, and improvements followed. Hancock questioned, probed and picked up mistakes and provided information to Rose, who produced a report on prizes in 1811 pointing to the areas where payment was still delayed. Finding that his clerks were slow in answering enquiries, Rose

---

* A deeply humane side of George Rose can be discerned from a long list of causes he supported in parliament, including legal support for friendly societies in 1793, measures to alleviate unemployment, Poor Law relief (on which he wrote a pamphlet in 1802), apprenticeship regulation for all trades and a minimum wage for cotton weavers (Thorne, *History of Parliament*, Vol. V, p. 52).

divided the alphabet amongst the clerks in the inspection branch, assigning to each certain letters in it, that I might know with whom the responsibility rested, who should not perform his duty. That has been followed up by mulcts (which perhaps I had no right to impose) and reprimands. At one time I had the whole branch into my room, and stated to them, in the most impressive terms I could find language to express myself in, my fixed determination to dismiss the first person against whom a well-founded complaint should be made; on which I had remonstrances for having disgraced the branch ... My servants have general orders, never, under any pressure of business to refuse admittance to seamen or their relatives; or, indeed, to any poor enquiring person.[131]

It was an admirable effort for one so late in his career, and it was in tune with the spirit of the whole administration during the last years of the Napoleonic War.[132]

Nine years after the start of the war in 1803, much had altered in Whitehall and in the state establishments. The shock of the impeachment of the all-powerful Melville in 1806 made it clear that the old order was on the way out. From this point, change and improvement were continuous until the end of the war. The war departments of government doubled in size, their accounts were brought largely up to date, and money was saved. After twenty years of experience of war, thousands of contracts were made and managed with economy and efficiency. Annual parliamentary estimates actually bore some relationship to expenditure; and the public availability of accounts, now printed in Hansard, brought greater transparency to contemporaries and historians alike. Administrators in critical positions were younger and more energetic, and they supported their ministers with better information and systems. Military and naval officers who might have expected senior administrative posts gave way to efficient 'men of business'.[133] The internal disputes of administrators twenty years before had vanished. The tensions of the 1780s – for instance, between the first lord of the Admiralty, Lord Howe, and the comptroller, Charles Middleton, over naval promotions for officers who had come ashore and were administrators, and which had led to Howe's resignation – were long past. Expectations had changed. The promotion of two Navy Board commissioners, Thomas Boulden Thompson and Thomas Hamilton, to rear-admiral in 1809 while serving on the Board passed without comment. Faced after 1803 with a war of unprecedented scale, such old jealousies were outdated and inconsequential.

The productivity of the state industrial establishments was markedly higher, and they were free of strikes, in contrast with every eighteenth-century war since 1739; the throughput of warships at Portsmouth Dockyard, measured in 'ton-dock' days, more than doubled between 1793 and 1815.[134] Though contractors were mainly responsible for the increase in the rate at which ships and equipment were manufactured, the output of all industries increased sharply year after year until 1815, as we shall see in the next chapter. All this was achieved against a background of vituperative debates between politicians, frequent changes of political administrations and the taunts of the newspapers. A silent revolution had taken place across government: the quiet triumph of the 'men of business'.

12

The Defence Industries

1800–1814

It might be thought perhaps going too far to say that the battle of Trafalgar would not have taken place if the new mode of repairing ships had not been adopted . . . instead of 34 sailing of the Line, the Mediterranean Fleet would not possibly have exceeded 24 sail of the line at the time the action happened . . . by the ordinary method of repairing ships.
    – John Barrow to Lord Melville, February 1806[1]

The removal of soil, earth, or rubbish, the conveyance of stones, sand or lime, everything is done by little four-wheel carts, drawn by a single horse on iron-railways . . . The advantage which they represent is immense. England owes to them a part of her wealth. Never without them could coal, iron-ore, lime-stone, slate, and other raw materials, have been conveyed such distances, and nevertheless at a very trifling cost.
    – Captain Charles Dupin, *Narratives of Two Excursions to the Ports of England, Scotland and Ireland in 1816, 1817 and 1818*[2]

The account of the post-war travels in England by Charles Dupin of the French Corps of Naval Engineers is interesting not so much for what he observed but rather for what he thought was remarkable or impressive. To him the most surprising thing about Britain in 1816 was its prosperity. 'Everywhere throughout impoverished Europe', Dupin wrote, 'the commerce of England seemed to recede before our victorious banners. We imagined that Great Britain, exhausted, was on the

351

brink of ruin.'[3] He discovered how wrong this belief had been. Britain thrived on its war economy, since most of the considerable sums that the government raised in taxes and loans was spent in the domestic economy, while overseas trade, though disturbed for periods, hardly ceased.[4] Although the Napoleonic War was many kinds of conflict, it was not least a conflict between competing economies.

That Dupin in his first pages picked out the seemingly insignificant horse-drawn railways emphasizes the technological ingenuity that the British exercised before the wholesale application of steam power. Although most of British industry was powered by water, wind and horse-mills, many of the revolutionary changes brought about later by steam have tended to obscure its use during the Napoleonic War. According to a contemporary survey in London in 1805, 112 steam engines were already at work in London, used mainly for pumping, in public waterworks and docks, but also in breweries, distilleries and flour-mills. The new motive power was also beginning to be applied to manufacturing: a handful of London forges, foundries, machine-makers, roperies and a sailcloth weaving works accounted for fifteen engines, although they generated in total only 120 h.p.[5] The adoption of steam in industrial establishments was not straightforward. Early engines were not efficient, and before the rotary steam engine was introduced its only possible use in the dockyards was for pumping out docks. This task, of course, was not continuous, and thus the pump would have long periods of idleness, and was only marginally more economical to use than horse or human power. It was when steam began to be used for powering machine tools that it became an economic and practical proposition.[6]

Britain's industries made spectacular advances during the war. Cotton production increased three times between the mid 1790s and 1813; in the same period iron and steel manufacturing output increased fourfold. Investment in town improvements and new roads abounded, while house building, which had stagnated in the 1790s, flourished between 1810 and 1813. The great civil engineers, Thomas Telford and John Rennie, built canals, many of which were completed in the course of this war. Docks were dug at Dundee and Hull, and a graving dock on the Tyne, while London, which could already claim to be the greatest port in the world, opened the West India Dock on the Isle of Dogs in 1802, the London Dock in 1805 and the East India

Dock at Blackwall in 1806, as well as docks on the south side of the river.[7] The Pitt government's interest in such enormous projects, and the Treasury's intervention, were crucial factors in their construction.* Steam pumps kept the docks dry while building, and, when completed, the new bucket-ladder steam dredgers, invented by Samuel Bentham and operational by late 1802, kept them from silting up.[8] From the turn of the century the use of steam began to increase in the state dockyards. Other well-known figures of the Industrial Revolution had many dealings with state industries, including Matthew Boulton and James Watt, who built the first rotary steam engine. Henry Maudslay, from his engineering factory at Lambeth in South London, set new standards of precision engineering using lathes of his own design and making, but also produced steam engines, one of which, a 6 h.p. engine, he sold to the Woolwich Arsenal in 1809.[9] For harnessing this power, a price occasionally had to be paid, and steam caused some severe industrial accidents. At Woolwich Dockyard in December 1812, for instance, 'the machine used for bending and seasoning ship timber, unfortunately burst in consequence of being overcharged'. The explosion killed eight men, and another fourteen were dangerously hurt, suffering broken legs and thighs.[10]

Even where steam was not introduced, new machinery could make manufacturing more efficient, as in the improved rope-laying machines installed by Maudslay in 1811 in the Chatham Dockyard ropery.[11] Rope-laying had always been an extremely strenuous activity. Even so, 220 men were still required to lay a 24-inch cable, and only two could be laid a day before the men became exhausted.[12] However, such were the complications, including the risk of fire, that steam was not introduced into this process until 1837.†

Innovation in the production of military weapons was driven less by commercial competition than by the increasing scale of the war

---

* The government effectively bought off vested interests opposing the scheme. The Legal Quays were purchased by the crown, and the Consolidated Fund compensated those who lost income from the changes (Palmer, 'London's Waterfront', p. 12).

† One piece of Maudslay's original machinery used in the final twisting of the rope is still in its original place in the ropery at Chatham Dockyard, and was in regular use, after 173 years, when the navy left the dockyard in 1984. It is still used in demonstrations of rope-laying today (Coad, 'Chatham Ropeyard', p. 165).

and the fear of French power. Gunlocks to fire the long guns gave the British gunners a considerable advantage at sea, as, for example, in the slow Atlantic swell in the early stages of the Battle of Trafalgar; they were quicker, safer for the gunner and far more accurate at long range than the old slow-match still used by the French. The small, close-range British carronade, accurately machined to reduce 'windage' – the gap between the barrel and shot so that less powder was needed, thus making reloading quicker – was devastating. This small gun came to dominate British battle tactics and became known as 'The Smasher'.[13] Napoleon, frustrated by the lack of French carronades, issued reprimand after reprimand, writing in 1805 to his minister of marine, 'Here's ten years we are behind their Admiralty . . . I see no attention being paid to it.'[14]

The artillery saw another technological breakthrough when, in 1802, Colonel Shrapnel's bursting shells, or 'spherical case-shot' as they were known, were adopted. A fuse lit before firing exploded an inner casing full of small-shot as the weapon reached its target, making it generally effective as an anti-personnel weapon.[15] William Congreve's rockets had a chequered wartime existence. The son of William Congreve, comptroller of the Royal Laboratory at Woolwich, the younger William broke all the rules. He was not an army officer, but from 1804 he developed the rockets at his own expense, achieving a range of 1,500 yards. He courted advancement, at the cost of his own popularity, by successfully seeking the patronage of the prince of Wales, whose influence pushed Congreve's ideas forward over the heads of the professionals.

By 1806 Congreve was producing 32-pounder rockets that had a range of 3,000 yards, but accuracy was not a strong point. In October of that year the rockets were given a large and very fair trial in a night attack on Boulogne. The weather was moderate and the night very dark. Four frigates, nine sloops and seventeen gun-brigs were issued with over 1,500 rockets, of which 400 were discharged in half an hour, each vessel firing two at a time. The rockets caused much consternation among the French, and buildings were set on fire: but the invasion flotilla in the basin was unharmed.[16] Congreve argued that the rockets had sufficient range, but that the failure had arisen 'from a sufficient number not having been fired exactly in the direction for them', as he explained to the prime minister, Lord Grenville.[17] The rockets were next used at the siege of Flushing in 1809 during the Walcheren expedition, where they did great damage to the town, but not to the docks that were actually their target. One officer noted that they fell short and caused havoc among the British forward picquets; he also noted his general impression of Congreve, who 'had arrived too newly from the perfumed atmosphere of Carlton House to relish too close a proximity to the coarser smell of shot and powder'.[18] Charles Chambers, surgeon aboard the fireship *Prometheus*, observed that

> Congreve the rocket maker is become the jest of the whole Fleet, inso-much that every person is sporting wit upon him; some have conferred on him the appellation of Commodore Squib, etc.; he appears deter-mined to make himself conspicuous, as he wears a white hat and coat; consequence seems his leading characteristic, which cannot be won-dered at with a salary of £2,000 per annum, for an invention which hitherto has proved futile.[19]

The rockets failed on a number of counts: partly because of technical faults, and partly because they were operated by the Ordnance rather than by the regular army. Congreve became even more unpopular when he accepted, and styled himself with, a Hanoverian army rank. Yet, although his rockets were rightly regarded as risky, they were suc-cessful when maintained, tested and fired with care: the diary of William Laycock, a senior non-commissioned officer, demonstrates that he was clearly devoted to his rockets, journeying with them between 1808 and 1815 to Sweden, Portugal, Holland, Spain, Minorca and the Waterloo campaign. At the siege of Cádiz in 1810, for instance, Laycock's rockets set four French gunboats ablaze and destroyed them.[20]

Some of the military thought the rockets a dangerous development, 'teaching the French to burn our Navy', as Admiral William Young wrote in 1811 to Charles Philip Yorke, first lord of the Admiralty: 'They appeared to me to be the most dangerous experiments that we could make, and I should have been extremely glad to have prevented their being tried.'[21] Rumours of French experiments with 'Fire Balls' reached London, as an intelligence report from John Wilson Croker forwarded to Philippe D'Auvergne reported: 'all the French officers confirm that bad as your Congreve Rocketts are these will be ten times more mischievous.'[22] Congreve could claim, however, a late spectacular success at the Battle of Leipzig in 1813, when a 200-strong British rocket troop had an overwhelming moment: 2,000 enemy troops were panicked by the rockets and surrendered.[23] On 1 January 1814 a Rocket Corps was formed, a measure organized by the master-general of the Ordnance, Lord Mulgrave, with the patronage of the prince regent.[24] The following April, two Rocket teams proved their worth during the complex crossing by Wellington's army of the fast-flowing River Adour, near Bayonne: a French counter-attack by a force of 1,000 infantry was repelled. A guards officer wrote of the enemy panic after the first volley: 'Instantly the drums ceased, and the large column burst and fled in irretrievable confusion.'[25]

These weapons were developed pragmatically, as a result of trial and error. By contrast, theoretical approaches came to nothing in these years. The Society for the Improvement of Naval Architecture, founded in 1791, was a failure, at least in the short term, in its attempts to analyse the motion of a ship's hull through water, and to determine the nature of the friction that it generated. A series of expensive experiments bankrupted the Society, although the thinking behind it led to the establishment of the School of Naval Architecture in Portsmouth Dockyard in 1811, too late to be of any practical use in the prosecution of this war.[26] Less worthy, though more persuasive, were the dubious claims of Robert Fulton, a young American who tried to convince the French that he could build a submarine. In May 1802 strangers were ordered to withdraw from the House of Lords while their lordships were told about 'the improved construction of a Diving Boat in France . . . to blow up a first-rate man of war, with only fifteen pounds of powder'.[27] When the French rejected his ideas, Fulton came to England, and under an assumed name met senior members of the British government. This time the proposition was the design of underwater, explosive mines. The trial of one carefully staged demonstration was successful, but when tried against the French at Boulogne Fulton's mines failed. Paid off with a handsome sum, he returned to America to try to revive interest in his underwater weapon, and later found fame with the first steam vessel.[28] The civil engineer John Rennie met Fulton and thought him 'a man of very slender abilities though possessing much self confidence and consummate impudence'.[29] The same qualities were part of the complex character of Lord Cochrane, who in 1812 proposed 'Secret Plans' to the prince regent for the use of vessels full of sulphur and charcoal, to be burnt to the windward side of any port in which Napoleon's fleet were blockaded. This early form of chemical warfare was fortunately turned down by a committee chaired by the duke of York, and it remained only a theory for a hundred years.[30]

In the great scale of things, technological breakthroughs mattered less than increasing industrial capacity. Napoleon, in command of several countries with immense resources, chose this as his battleground. The issue was thus one of supply – how to produce enough war materials without loss of quality and, even more difficult, at reduced costs. Fortunately, the British government could turn to the burgeoning private sector. Privately owned shipyards, foundries and factories, as well as state establishments, built the ships and created the heavy weapons and munitions with which the army and navy fought against France, with the contractors manufacturing far more than the state. The proportion that came from the private sector was many times greater from 1803 than it had been throughout the wars of the eighteenth century. The iron foundries of the north of England and Scotland cast and bored the iron cannon for the army and navy; muskets and rifles were supplied by Birmingham gunsmiths; and uniforms and army equipment were purchased from private manufacturers. As we have seen, wheat was grown and pigs and cattle reared by farmers all over the country, and purchased at the market by the Commissariat or the Victualling Board. Almost all sea transport was hired under contract in order to transport stores or men to and from destinations in Britain or overseas. For contractors in war-related manufacturing – trade and the production of foodstuffs – war was a profitable business, though the government ensured that whenever possible financial risks were transferred to the contractor.

The relationship between contractor and state was least comfortable in the building of warships, the most complex and capital-intensive task of all. The Napoleonic War lasted longer and was of a much

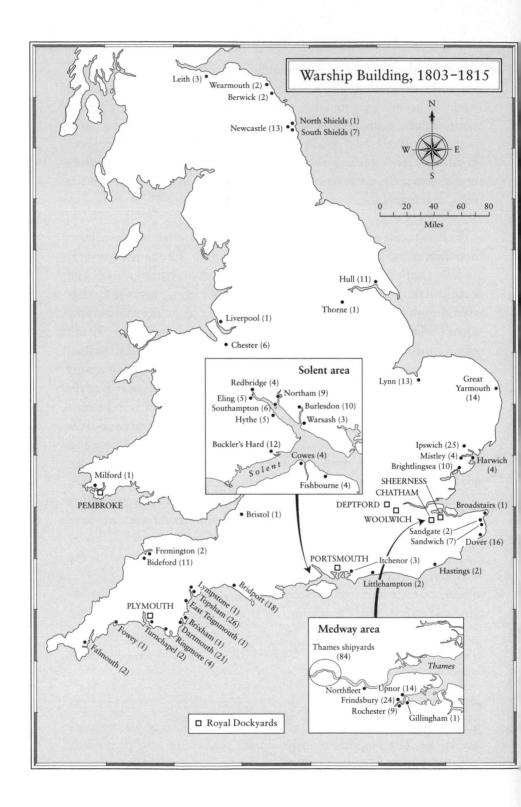

Warship Building, 1803–1815

N W E S

0 20 40 60 80
Miles

Leith (3)
Wearmouth (2)
Berwick (2)
North Shields (1)
Newcastle (13)
South Shields (7)

Hull (11)
Thorne (1)

Liverpool (1)

Chester (6)

Solent area

Redbridge (4)
Northam (9)
Eling (5)
Southampton (6)
Burlesdon (10)
Hythe (5)
Warsash (3)
Buckler's Hard (12)
Cowes (4)
Fishbourne (4)

Solent

Lynn (13)
Great Yarmouth (14)

Ipswich (25)
Mistley (4)
Harwich (4)
Brightlingsea (10)

SHEERNESS
CHATHAM
DEPTFORD ☐
☐
WOOLWICH ☐ ☐
Broadstairs (1)

Sandgate (2)
Sandwich (7)
Dover (16)

PORTSMOUTH ☐ Itchenor (3)
Hastings (2)
Littlehampton (2)

Milford (1)
☐
PEMBROKE

Bristol (1)

Fremington (2)
Bideford (11)

Lympstone (1)
Bridport (18)
Topsham (1)
East Teignmouth (1)
PLYMOUTH ☐
Brixham (1)
Turnchapel (2)
Dartmouth (21)
Fowey (1)
Ringmore (4)
Falmouth (2)

Medway area

Thames shipyards (84)

Thames

Northfleet
Upnor (14)
Frindsbury (24)
Rochester (9)
Gillingham (1)

☐ Royal Dockyards

greater scale than any previous conflict, and even the great size of the six home dockyards, which reached their maximum combined workforce of nearly 16,000 artificers and labourers by 1813, could not cope with its demands.[31] Where the private sector came into its own was in the accelerated building of warships. The capacity of the merchant shipyards to increase the navy rapidly to a completely different order of magnitude was remarkable. Between 1803 and 1815, 84 per cent of warships, or 72 per cent by tonnage, were built by private shipyards.*

This was not achieved until the disruption created by St Vincent's administration had passed. Sir Charles Middleton wrote privately shortly after the renewal of war that Britain was 'ill-guarded by Sea, & I still think the number of ships & other craft inadequate to the Service that may be required of them. But what is equally alarming, we have a worn-out fleet & no Timber to repair it.'[32] When Lord Melville came to the Admiralty in May 1804, a year after the resumption of war, not enough ships were at sea and radical measures were needed. The Navy Board and the dockyards had to be shaken out of the defensiveness and low morale that followed in St Vincent's wake. The new first lord also had to mend relations with the shipbuilding contractors, whom the previous administration had alienated, by quickly placing orders for new ships, and even sending some warships to private yards to be repaired, which had very rarely been done before. The priority, however, were those ships that needed to be repaired and immediately sent to sea, and here Melville drove through a radical idea against the Navy Board's wishes.†

---

* Of a total of 515 warships (337,579 tons), 433 (242,619 tons) were built in British merchant yards between 1803 and 1815 (Knight, 'Devil Bolts and Deception', pp. 5–7; Morriss, *Royal Dockyards*, p. 28).

† Melville's effectiveness during his year in office was helped by the experience of his private secretary, William Budge, a Home Office clerk, who had served in the navy as a midshipman during the American Revolutionary War, but had left the service afterwards in the ensuing peace because there were no prospects. Budge still, however, retained a keen interest in the navy, as his obituary notes: 'perhaps no individual, in any country, possessed a more accurate knowledge of the state of the different navies in Europe' (*Naval Chronicle*, Vol. XXXV (1816), p. 2). As was the custom for the private secretary of a first lord, Budge was appointed as commissioner of Victualling in 1805, retiring due to ill-health in 1808.

The traditional method of repair involved the laborious replacement of each rotten timber by a new one. Instead, Melville ordered twenty-three ships of the line to be 'doubled and strengthened with riders'. This was a method used by the East India Company, pioneered by its surveyor, Gabriel Snodgrass, who had in print virulently attacked dockyard standards of building and repair – hence new practices advocated from this quarter were going to be resented.[33] Instead of replacing the timbers, the yard gave the hull another timber bottom, laid over the existing one, while the internal timbers were strengthened with diagonal braces fastened with iron pieces. The new process was deeply unpopular among traditionalists, one of them being Rear-Admiral Thomas Troubridge, a member of St Vincent's Board. He had written in 1803: 'I have long reprobated riders. Every Taylor in the Country knows they destroy a Ship.'[34] The method, however, had the merit of enabling ships to be repaired in very fast time. Ships of the line needed to be docked for as little as two weeks, or perhaps a month, rather than several months. Melville faced a hard bureaucratic struggle to get the new measures adopted. He sent Sir Andrew Snape Hamond, the comptroller of the Navy Board, and Sir William Rule, the surveyor, down to Portsmouth and Plymouth to give orders directly to the yard officers concerning the new methods to be implemented, and the time within which they were to be repaired. Iron straps and standards were manufactured in Woolwich Dockyard, then taken by ship to the southern yards. Portsmouth was to repair eleven ships and Plymouth nine in a year. John Barrow wrote to Melville in early 1806 after the first lord had left office:

> As the measure of bringing forward ships from a state of ordinary by doubling and strengthening them with diagonal braces, according to the plan of Mr Snodgrass, is wholly your own, and was adopted in spite of a determined prejudice against it in every one of His Majesty's Dockyards, it may not be unsatisfactory to your Lordship to know the success of an Experiment which was undertaken in every department by something like compulsion and carried into effect with the utmost reluctance ... Not one third of the number could have been brought forward in the same time as by the plan of Snodgrass.[35]

This temporary measure was a risk, but proved to be a success. Nor were the twenty-three ships repaired in this way given easy duties. One of them, the *Caesar*, the 80-gun flagship of Sir Richard Strachan, led the squadron in a hard four-day beat to windward, chasing the French ships that had escaped from Trafalgar. All four were captured.

The country, however, also needed more small warships and needed them quickly. Frigates, brig-sloops and gun-brigs were the ships building on the slips of merchant yards. A gun-brig, for instance, was about eighty feet long, measured 170 tons, and could be built by an efficient yard in as little as six months.* Now that hundreds of small ships were required, the Navy Board had to use shipbuilders from all over the country, rather than those favoured on the Thames or in the Solent area. St Vincent had been convinced that the Thames shipbuilders had been colluding in raising prices, but the evidence points to increased labour costs affecting shipbuilding at the time of a boom. Another disadvantage for the shipyards of the Thames was that the work of shipwrights and caulkers was demarcated, while others in the country enjoyed greater flexibility of labour, with shipwrights sometimes doing the work of caulkers.[36] In any case, St Vincent placed no orders for major warships on the Thames, but he did place an order for two large frigates with Benjamin Tanner at Dartmouth, even though Tanner had never built anything of this size before. But St Vincent forced the Navy Board to select Tanner, as he had submitted the lowest tender.[37] As we shall see, this was pushing too far.

The Navy Board did not like the new policy of using many widely dispersed private shipyards, feeling that it had lost control over the quality of building. As market forces began to exert an influence on

---

* Much was demanded from these small ships, and they suffered considerable losses. In June 1805, for instance, three gun-brigs foundered in the Channel, without trace, and 350 men were drowned. Such losses were widespread (Grocott, *Shipwrecks*, pp. 196, 237, 285-7). The senior navy hated the new gunboats. Captain Graham Moore tried to reconstitute his frigate's crew, which had been temporarily dispersed into the gunboats, where the men 'have been obliged to play the part of advanced Picquets until the end of Dec[embe]r, very much exposed to the weather, not a little to the enemy's shot, and cooped up in a vessel not much bigger than a sentry box. It has ruined my ship's crew' (Moore to Thomas Creevey, 9 Jan. 1810, *Life and Times*, pp. 45-6).

the tendering process, the long-standing and carefully built relationships between the Navy Board and particular shipbuilders broke
down. The Board had always had more confidence in yards on the
Thames, in Essex or on the Solent near Portsmouth Dockyard, where
the building could be inspected regularly and conveniently. These
arrangements were safeguarded by the appointment of a senior royal
dockyard shipwright to the merchant yard as an 'overseer' to monitor
building standards. Now established shipbuilding businesses lost their
dominance and, though they still built for the navy, Barnard's, of Ipswich and the Thames (at this point directed by Barnard's widow,
Frances), and John Martin Hilhouse & Sons at Bristol were no longer
forces to be reckoned with.[38] On the other hand, the Board gained the
advantage of competition between the yards, which was at times
intense: between October 1809 and September 1813 a total of
140 warship-building tenders were received by the Board – with just
21 per cent successful.[39]

Shipyards in more distant areas of the country, including the
north-east, now tendered for, and were awarded, warship contracts.
Very small naval vessels were even built abroad, a practice against
which the Board had always fought. Private yards on the Medway,
hitherto spurned, were taken up, including that of John King of Upnor.
A surviving copy of the contract of 1812 for a 36-gun frigate built in
this yard is a hundred pages in length, and indexed, demonstrating
just how complex such hugely detailed specifications were by this
stage in the war.[40] Another Medway yard was that of Mary Ross, who
took over her husband's yard on his death in 1808. Under her notably
efficient management, the yard built nine ships, from a 74-gun to a
dockyard lighter, all within the specified contract time.[41]

Some of the Navy Board's fears were justified. To maintain standards, it instituted a sort of apprenticeship system for yards by starting
with orders for smaller ships: if a builder completed a gunboat satisfactorily, an order for a brig-sloop would follow, and then perhaps a
contract for a frigate. As contracts were effectively fixed-price, at a
time when prices were rising, under-capitalized builders could and did
bankrupt themselves. A fair proportion of these vessels were never
completed by their original builder.[42] An Admiralty document of
merchant-yard building times between 1801 and 1806 lists 238 as

'early', 23 'on schedule' and 240 as 'late'. Financial penalties for late delivery might be mitigated by the Navy Board for larger ships, but for smaller vessels penalties were levied in full.[43] Nevertheless, the overall performance of merchant yards was impressive, and they built their (admittedly smaller) ships faster than the royal yards.

In spite of mistakes and business failures, warship building in the twelve and a half years of the Napoleonic War was virtually double that of the previous four major wars of the eighteenth century. Between 1803 and 1815, 518 new warships measuring 323,136 tons, were built: 84 per cent of these were built by contract (72 per cent by tonnage). Private shipyards built 436 warships (228,176 tons), while the Royal Dockyards built only 82 warships (94,960 tons). (A further 52 (15,510 tons) were built in Bermuda, Halifax, Bombay and Penang.*) Great Britain possessed some 12,000 shipwrights and caulkers, a quarter of whom were employed in the royal dockyards.† The private-sector workforce was widely dispersed between 510 merchant shipyards, averaging sixteen shipwrights a yard.[44] Only ten ports had more than 200 shipwrights. The area around North and South Shields on the north-east coast saw the greatest concentration, with over 2,000. London and the Thames came a poor second, with just over 1,200, followed a long way behind, and in order, by Liverpool, Leith, Hull, Greenock, Whitby, Bristol and Great Yarmouth. Shipyards in all these areas, with the exception of Greenock, built warships for the navy, while continuing with their staple output of merchant ships. The east coast benefited from the heightened naval activity in the North Sea and the Baltic, with commercial ports fulfilling the role of minor fleet bases. In 1804 an influential dockyard officer, Joseph Whidbey, the master attendant of Woolwich Dockyard, recommended to Lord Keith, the commander-in-chief, that Leith be made 'an arsenal

---

* Between 1739 and 1802 there were 386 months of war, during which 694 warships were built in British merchant and state yards combined: output per month was 1.79 ships, or 1,305 tons. Between 1803 and 1815 there were 150 months of war, during which 515 ships were built and output increased to 3.43 per month, or 2,250 tons. (Knight, 'Devil Bolts and Deception', pp. 3–9).

† A country-wide survey was made in Apr. 1804 and returns were submitted to parliament: 8,675 shipwrights were employed in merchant yards (*Parliamentary Papers*, 1805 (193), Vol. VIII, p. 185).

in the Firth, where the expense would be very small and soon repaid in saving the expense on craft and time'.[45] By the next year, Leith had a naval storekeeper, and by 1806 a master attendant and a master shipwright.[46]

Great Yarmouth in Norfolk grew rich from the war and government contracts. Its population rose from 14,800 in 1801 to 18,000 in 1811, very much faster than the national average.[47] From the start of the Napoleonic War the Yarmouth Roads off the harbour entrance increasingly came to be used as a fleet rendezvous, where warships and convoys assembled to take on replacement spars and equipment, provisions, fresh meat and vegetables and water.[48] From there several major amphibious operations were launched, including the attacks on Copenhagen in 1801 and 1807.* Naval and Ordnance depots grew rapidly to service these fleets, and a small repair yard was established. The vessels supplying the fleet needed constant upkeep, and maintenance was often performed by one of the private shipyards. By 1804 there were fourteen in the town, manned by 237 shipwrights and caulkers.[49] Fifteen brig-sloops and gun-brigs were built here after 1804, their small size dictated by the shallowness of the entrance of the River Yare. Three 4-gun schooners, *Crane*, *Pigeon* and *Quail*, were launched in one day, on 26 April 1806, by Custance & Stone; all three had been ordered just four months before, on 11 December 1805. The speed with which these 56-foot vessels was built was exactly what the navy needed.

No area of the country exemplified this rapid expansion of naval shipbuilding more than Devon and Cornwall.† Before the Napoleonic

---

* One indication of the booming local economy comes from a participant in the 1807 Copenhagen expedition: 'The watermen are more exorbitant in their fare at Yarmouth than any port I ever was at, not excepting Deal. It is no uncommon thing for them to demand 30s. and 2 guineas for just rowing off to a ship, and if from certain exigencies they conceive your case to be desperate (such as your ship getting under weigh with a probability of being left behind, etc.) will with great deliberation impose a much larger sum' (Chambers, *Chronological Journal*, p. 429).

† Dorset, Devon and Cornwall shipyards built 90 warships (32,921 tons); on the Thames, merchant yards built 84 warships (79,947 tons); Solent area, 62 (30,007 tons); Medway, 48 (30,790 tons); Essex and Suffolk, 43 (15,919 tons); north-east England and Scotland, 40 (20,805 tons); Kent and Sussex, 33 (9,643 tons); Norfolk, 27 (4,373 tons); and other locations, 9 (3,771 tons).

War, the merchant shipyards of these two counties had never launched a ship for the navy; but between 1804 and 1815 they built sixty-eight warships, measuring just over 23,000 tons. Nor were these all small vessels, for the average size of these ships came to 340 tons, twice the size of a gun-brig. The 1804 survey lists 867 shipwrights working in fifty-eight Devon and Cornish shipyards, dispersed between thirty ports. Some of these were in tiny inlets, with a yard that employed only a handful of people, and so they were unable to take on government contracts; but other small ports, no more than villages fronting the sea, built sizeable warships. A Barnstaple shipwright called Richard Thorne moved his men three miles to the shore at Fremington, a hamlet on the south bank of the River Taw. From here he launched two ships: the *Delight* in 1806, 93 feet long, measuring 284 tons; and, in 1807, the *Ranger*, a 26-gun sloop, 111 feet long, 422 tons, one of the largest built in Devon. By contrast, Bideford, Dartmouth and Topsham were well established, building 57 warships between them. At Dartmouth, however, Benjamin Tanner, who had been awarded the contract for frigates in St Vincent's time, was caught out by underbidding at a time of rising timber prices. By January 1805 he was employing 200 shipwrights, but he had expanded too rapidly and with insufficient oversight: in February 1807 a critical point was reached when the *Thais*, an 18-gun fireship that he had built, was sent back to him on the grounds of poor workmanship, with a demand from the Navy Board for a return of all payments. He protested that he was 'thunderstruck at the sudden, unexpected and unmerited display of disapprobation'.[50] The Navy Board was instructed to act against Tanner for breach of contract, and he was driven into bankruptcy, with debts of £12,000.[51]

Someone who fared better was Robert Davy of Wear, just outside Topsham on the River Exe in South Devon, a shallow, silting river even in those days. Topsham's record was notable, for its three shipyards launched twenty-six warships, of nearly 9,000 tons, each ship averaging 340 tons. Davy had other businesses: lime-burner, coal and timber merchant, farmer grazier and even a little trading to Newfoundland, and was thus a businessman rather than a shipwright, for which trade he had not served an apprenticeship.[52] In August 1804 the local Exeter newspaper reported six warships building at Topsham.[53]

Davy's yard produced warships steadily through the war, accelerating production in the last three years. In 1813 he sent four 'government vessels' downriver in one tide.* The writer of a memoir on Davy recalled that

> He was so exact and prompt in completing his government contracts within the time specified, that he never had a complaint, while many others were <u>fined most heavily</u>. But when the Government offered handsome premiums per day during the hottest part of the war, just prior to the close of it, about say 1812 to 1815, to all those who would complete their contracts prior to the time stated, he received very large sums in that shape, having finished <u>all</u> his ships more or less before time.[54]

Shrewd and well capitalized, Davy took on no more contracts after 1814, when the naval shipbuilding boom came to an end. He was, in any case, in ill-health, although he lived to be a hundred.

The enlistment of these yards inevitably reduced building quality in some areas. Naval opinion was split and opinions strongly held, some arguing that speed of construction rather than quality was paramount. However, Nelson, out in the Mediterranean commanding the British Fleet, wrote a long memorandum on the subject, advocating the minority view.

> The gun brigs for the present service are not wanted to be built of such stout materials as those formerly, for the service being temporary, if they last a little longer that [sic] the French flotilla is all that is required: of course the vessels can be run up in a much shorter time than heretofore and being slighter will both tow and sail better.[55]

The question of quality was a complex issue, and views were inflamed by St Vincent's conviction that all merchant shipbuilders were rogues, and that their ships were built with 'devil bolts', shortened to save money, thus weakening the ship. He attributed the sinking of some

---

* One of them was the bomb vessel *Terror*, 102 feet long of 333 tons. These stoutly built ships came to be favoured for Arctic exploration because of their ability to withstand pressure from the ice. The *Terror* was selected for Sir John Franklin's ill-fated expedition in 1848. At the time of writing, maritime archaeologists are still searching for it.

ships directly to this alleged fault. The case of the *Ajax* is often cited as an example of poor building, but an examination of the case shows the contractors in a different light. In 1807 the Navy Board sued Samuel and Daniel Brent for £40,000, alleging that the ship suffered from bad workmanship and caulking, poor timber and low-grade ironwork. The arbitrators, however, dismissed the case and found that the only breach of contract was that the iron was not of 'best tough Swedish iron' but of 'rolled iron'. The shipbuilders were fined £450.[56] Another stick with which to beat the contractors was the 'Surveyor' class of 74s, all built by merchant yards, which, according to John Barrow, 'a facetious naval lord of a subsequent Board of the Admiralty called the "forty thieves"', though much of their unpopularity lay with their poor sailing qualities, the result of their design by the surveyors of the navy.[57]

The unprecedented shift to private shipbuilders enabled the extensive state dockyards and depots to fulfil several crucial tasks. The royal yards continued to build a few of the largest of the ships of the line, beyond the capacity of the facilities of any of the private yards, often building in a dock since these vessels were too large to launch down a slip.* Of the six great 120-gun ships built at Chatham and Plymouth dockyards, only the *Caledonia*, completed and commissioned in 1808 at Plymouth, saw any real service.[58] However, the royal dockyards altogether completed 82 warships, of 94,960 tons, between 1803 and 1815, averaging 1,160 tons, only a fifth of the number of ships constructed in private yards, but only less than a third of the merchant yard total if measured by tonnage.

Operationally the most important dockyard task was the docking, repair and refitting of ships returning from a commission, or taken

---

* Admiral Lord Collingwood did not think much of the designs of new large warships, writing in 1808 from the newly launched *Ocean* (90 guns): 'The new whimsies and absurd inventions of those who, having little science, would be thought to have it because they have an office from which science should proceed, has introduced many odd schemes in the construction of ships. And as this *Ocean* was intended to be perfection, unhappily they were all applied to her, and the consequence is that in a severe storm we had lately . . . she had like to have gone to pieces' (Collingwood to his sister, 17 Dec. 1808, Hughes, *Collingwood*, p. 259).

out of 'ordinary', and the maintenance of their hulls, spars, rigging, guns and equipment. Although the crew of a commissioned ship was continually employed in painting and carrying out maintenance jobs, the ships still needed regular docking.* Iron, still at a relatively early stage of its development, with a tendency to be brittle, was used not only for guns but also increasingly in the structure of wooden ships. Though a hardwood, oak was by no means indestructible and was susceptible to dry and wet rot. Three years between dockings was considered the safe maximum time between refits, although a winter on blockade, battered by gales, or a protracted period of service in the West Indies, could reduce that time considerably. William Marsden wrote to his brother Alexander from the Admiralty in 1805, 'I wish we had peace, and could lay our ships up in dock. They are worn down like post-horses during a general election.'[59] Keeping a vast stock of ordnance and a greatly augmented fleet fully operational meant that all these establishments had to run at full capacity.† By contrast, French ships, and those of France's allies, rarely left port.

As a cost-saving measure, timber masters were introduced into the dockyards through an order-in-council in May 1801, suggested by Samuel Bentham. These new officers were to cut the waste of timber in the yards, precisely measuring the work done by the shipwrights: 'he is not to trust to his eye, but to apply the straight edge of a batten or rule to ascertain the flatness.'[60] They also applied strict regulations when accepting timber from the merchants, which made for a good deal of contention because of the notorious difficulties involved in

---

* Maintenance of the docks themselves was also a problem, and wear and tear had reached a critical stage by 1800. Admiral William Young reported to Lord Spencer that the docks 'at Portsmouth will be shut up for at least twice as long as was reported, and the great dock at Sheerness is found to be so bad that it can no longer be used without considerable repair' (8 Oct. 1800, Althorp Papers, BL, Add. MSS 75847).
† The effective size of the fleet reached its maximum in 1809, when 709 ships, measuring 469,227 tons, were in commission, in which year 82 ships, of 116,422 tons, were building; 46 ships, 51,713 tons, were in reserve, or 'in ordinary' (Winfield, *British Warships*, p. xiv). Most British warship losses were from fire, foundering or wreck, rather than from enemy action. In the ten years from 1 Jan. 1797 to 31 Dec. 1806, 137 warships of all sizes were lost, at an average of 14 per year (Navy Board to Admiralty, 31 July 1807, NMM, ADM BP/27). Between 1807 and 1812 seven ships of the line were lost, an average of 1.4 a year (17 July 1812, NMM, ADM BP/32c).

evaluating such an inexact material. The contractors objected when large amounts were rejected, and even the appointment of agents to act on their behalf made little difference to these refusals by the dockyards. In addition, the hardwood shortage pushed prices up further, which St Vincent at the Admiralty declined to pay. As a result, the timber contractors supplied less and less timber, and reserves in the dockyards fell to a dangerously low level. War resumed in May 1803, and once St Vincent was out of office, and Pitt was returned to government, the problem could be alleviated by the paying of higher prices.[61]

Ingenuity had also to be exercised to overcome the shortage of hardwoods after 1803, which again pushed up the price of timber. The world was scoured for new sources: attempts were made to secure wood from southern Europe; two shipwrights were sent to South Africa to sample the hardwoods there; while ships sent out to New South Wales with convicts brought back timber that was tested in Woolwich Dockyard in 1805. Unexpected snags were found. The dockyard sawyers found the blue-gum trees, stringybark and mahogany from Australia so hard that it blunted their tools and they were put to 'additional expence of Files, and the necessity of frequently whetting the saws ... there is twice the labour in the Sawing compared to Oak Timber.'[62] As the men were paid by the task, the master shipwright asked the Navy Board for an increase in pay for the sawyers.

In 1804, after earlier experiments of 1795 and 1796, the navy began to build frigates from fir timber, which was cheaper because of the ease of working softer wood, and this in turn speeded building. Their anticipated life was only eight years, and, in spite of another round of fir shipbuilding in 1812, the frigates were not deemed a success.[63] Ships' timbers were reduced in size, and old ships were broken up in order to save good timber; but, after a period of experimentation that lasted the length of the war, new structural techniques were eventually found. These changes were introduced by a number of shipwrights, both in and out of the dockyard service, of whom the best known was Robert Seppings, who brought about an influential method of diagonal bracing very different from that proposed and adopted by Snodgrass.[64] In time, ships came to be built of teak in

India. The first of these, the 38-gun frigate *Salsette*, was launched in 1805, while the first 74, the *Minden*, was ordered in 1803, but had to await the completion of the building dock in the East India Company's Bombay yard in 1807, and was not launched until 1810.[65]

Additionally, the state yards acted as reception, storage and distribution depots for equipment and raw materials provided by contractors. Royal yard clerks and workers checked incoming stores: when the items were delivered, they were inspected for quality and quantity, according to the specification of the contract. The Artillery Inspectorate at Woolwich Arsenal, for example, developed and grew as a department that specialized in inspecting contractors' goods. As we saw in Chapter 2, Thomas Blomefield had started on the task of inspecting and proofing the nation's stock of heavy guns in 1780 and was on the way to completing an overhaul by 1793. By 1812 Blomefield's inspectorate had expanded to 102 personnel, with sixteen clerks, specialists and overseers, with smiths and labourers making up the total. The introduction of Blomefield's 'New Pattern' cannon made for a more reliable weapon, one able to withstand a greater rate of fire; replacement of the old guns was largely complete by 1810.[66] After a career of thirty-five years of heavy (and noisy) toil, with tens of thousands of cannon delivered by contractors passing through the inspectorate, Blomefield was rewarded with promotion to lieutenant-general of the Ordnance and a baronetcy.[67]

Cannon were provided by a small number of large foundries, with Walker's of Rotherham and the Carron Company of Scotland supplying cannon every year throughout the wars; ordnance expenditure with the Carron Company was the largest by some way.* Although eight other foundries cast iron guns for the government, these two companies dominated the market, and satisfied the large, continuous demand for shot.[68] The lack of competition was noted with some misgiving by the Commission of Military Enquiry. There were, however, risks involved.[69] In August and September 1804, for instance, a quarter of carronades supplied by the Carron Company failed their proof

---

* Carron's payments between 1803 and 1814 totalled £368,968, compared with £293,157 paid to Walker. The single largest annual sum was £63,735 paid to Carron in 1805 (Moss, 'Cannon to Steam', p. 475).

test at Woolwich Arsenal: 29 of a batch of 110. High costs and a manufacture from a difficult material, combined with a continuous rise in proofing standards imposed by the Ordnance, resulted in company failures, notably the Clyde Iron Works. By 1812 and 1813 only five companies, Carron and Walker's among them, were supplying the ordnance with cannon.[70]

Elsewhere in Woolwich Arsenal was the Royal Laboratory. In 1802 the Board of Ordnance had devolved to William Congreve (the elder) complete responsibility for the production of powder.[71] Elaborate proof testing of all powder, including that captured from the French, was conducted throughout the war, and improvements continued: building on the more powerful cylinder powder, introduced in 1787, the process by which charcoal was produced was further refined. This powder was superior to that of the French, who still had difficulty with their supply of saltpetre.[72]

The Ordnance Department had to take steps to increase quantity as well as quality. As the scale of warfare expanded, production had to increase several-fold. By 1807, with Napoleon astride Europe, demands from Britain's Continental allies for munitions became strident, even if they were not yet engaged in hostilities with Napoleon: 70,000 muskets were sent to the Baltic and 24,000 to Sicily; in April, Prussia's demands amounted to 40 howitzers and cannon, 10,000 muskets, three million ball cartridges and 100,000 flints, all of which were despatched within a month. Still the Allies demanded more. The Ordnance could not supply the 15,000 pistols that the Prussians wanted: it had only 2,000 in store.[73]

Contractors again came to the aid of the state to expand war production. The East India Company doubled imports of saltpetre from India, from 6,000 tons in 1808 to more than 12,000 tons in 1810.[74] Once the raw material had arrived in the country, the Ordnance supplied the merchants with saltpetre on payment of a deposit, but they were expected to procure sulphur and charcoal themselves. Imports of sulphur from Sicily and southern Italy subsequently increased: in 1807 well over 4,000 tons came from Italy, with Malta acting as a supply depot.[75] In 1793 at least 60 per cent of the gunpowder issued to the navy had been from private contractors, such as Charles Pigou at Dartford, or Edmund Hill, or Taylor & Co. at Hounslow.[76] But eventually state production expanded – great quantities of gunpowder were produced by the state mills at Faversham and Waltham Abbey – and the private sector was eclipsed: the proportion of powder manufactured by contractors fell to 40 per cent by 1809.[77] For the last few years of the war, the average annual consumption of gunpowder grew to 80,000 barrels of ninety pounds each.[78] The navy used by far the largest amounts of gunpowder and shot: at Trafalgar there had been 2,148 British cannon, a contrast with the 90 of much smaller calibre in Wellington's siege train at Vitoria. Three times the quantity of gunpowder and shot was consumed by the long bombardment of Copenhagen in 1807 than at Waterloo.[79]

State and contractor combined to speed up the production of small arms. In the last nine months of 1803 the army took delivery of only 40,000 muskets; in the twelve months of 1804, this rose to 167,000.[80] By 1805 the number of muskets, carbines and rifles produced reached 181,000 and by 1809, 270,000. In the two years to July 1810, Birmingham gunsmiths supplied no fewer than 1,045,000 barrels and locks for final assembly.[81] An Ordnance Board proof office for muskets and rifles was established in Birmingham in 1804, and this remained the chief area for contract small-arms manufacture. The new inspection regime, under Lieutenant-Colonel James Miller, enabled defective weapons to be detected on the spot.

The Ordnance expanded its own factories, in particular for the finishing of small arms. In Lewisham in South London an old Ordnance Department armouries building was updated, staffed with welders, lock-makers, grinders and polishers, all with highly specialized skills, mainly from the Midlands.* They assembled and finished gun barrels, gunlocks, rammers and bayonets. The lathes in this factory were powered by water, although the weak flow of the small River Ravensbourne in the summer caused problems; later a steam engine was added as the factory expanded. Fifty thousand sets of rifles, muskets and

* Some of the imported workers from Wednesbury in Staffordshire, north of Birmingham, brought the tradition of bull baiting to Lewisham, a matter which came before the magistrates at Blackheath, who ensured that it stopped. Local opinion of the incomers was not high, as recorded in a local history of 1815: 'the men being for the most part a low bred set of fellows from Birmingham, committed many depredations around the neighbourhood' (Macartney and West, *Lewisham Silk Mills*, p. 43).

components a year came from this mill. In 1811 the workshops at the Tower of London were moved to Lewisham, but the disadvantages of the site and the lack of capacity for expansion again caused the Ordnance Board to look elsewhere. A better site at Enfield, north of London, was selected, and, although this factory was to have a long and distinguished history, it did not come on stream properly until after the war's end; many workers from Lewisham were transferred there from 1816, the last of them by barge from Deptford Creek in 1818.[82]

The final assembly of ammunition, calling for great care and supervision, was undertaken by the state. By 1812 Congreve's workforce in the laboratory at Woolwich had increased to over 1,400, most of them engaged in assembling ball cartridges.* These men were paid by the day, rather than by piecework, because, as the Commission of Military Enquiry noted, that 'would be running a great risk of having the ammunition imperfectly made up'. It was soon realized that the output of ammunition from Woolwich was insufficient. In 1804 temporary 'Laboratories' at Portsmouth and Plymouth were established – assembly plants without the testing facility that was a function also carried out Woolwich.[83] In 1810, for instance, as a newspaper report ran, the *Amazon* frigate left Plymouth carrying 10,000 muskets for the Spanish patriots, 'and a proportionate quantity of musket ball cartridges, fit for their calibre, which were manufactured in the laboratory of the gun-wharf at this port, where 400 children are daily employed in forming and filling ball cartridges'.[84] Plymouth manufactured 70 million cartridges between 1806 and 1814. The War Office volumes record that the laboratory at Portsmouth made precisely 52,953,970 rounds between 1807 and 1814. In December 1813 it employed 353 people, of whom 294 were boys.[85]

---

* Another responsibility of Woolwich Arsenal was to supply the potent mixture by which fireships were set ablaze. On board the *Prometheus*, preparing for the Copenhagen expedition in 1807, two Arsenal workers installed barrels of sulphur, nitre and charcoal in the fire room, surrounded by barrels of charcoal and tar, to be lit by elaborate, hidden fuses. The *Prometheus* was new, fast and well appointed and was later converted to a sloop; she took Arthur Wellesley and his staff to Copenhagen (Chambers, *Chronological Journal*, pp. 372–3).

Another area of improvement in the Ordnance's performance lay in better distribution and storage, made possible by considerable state investment. The 2,440-foot-long wharf at Woolwich was built; the estimated cost in 1801 when it was started was £10,000, but it was not finished until 1813, by which time it had cost £197,000. The following year the accompanying complex of riverside military warehouses, known as the Grand Store, was complete.[86] Magazines were enlarged in old fortifications, such as Dorchester or Chester. In the forests of West Sussex, charcoal works were built at Fernhurst and Fisher Street. Some new establishments were small, as at Horsea and Stamshaw, on the north and east shores of Portsmouth Harbour, and St Budeaux, north of Plymouth Dockyard. Their task was to restore older powder by drying it and dusting it, for gunpowder degrades over the years. Horsea and Stamshaw together 'restoved and dusted' 13,000 barrels of powder during 1813, a vital task at this stage of the war.[87] The design of land magazines developed and became safer; Purfleet on the Thames and Upnor Castle on the Medway were expanded; at Great Yarmouth a magnificent magazine was built, where it still stands today by the River Yare, in the centre of the town, boarded up and neglected.

The amount of gunpowder and munitions stored at naval bases was substantially increased by the conversion of a number of old warships into floating magazines. Their use was expanded during the Peace of Amiens, as decommissioned ships sent back their surplus powder.[88] Powder 'hoys', used to transport munitions to ships lying off, increased in size, a change made possible by new piers and buoys. Distribution became safer and more dependable thanks to the newly built canals, and there was no longer a need to trust to the wind-bound vagaries of coastal transports.* In Northamptonshire, halfway up the Grand Union Canal, the Ordnance built a very large, fortified magazine at Weedon Bec,[89] which supplied much of the ordnance and

---

* Accidents did happen inland. In a strong westerly wind in Dec. 1802, four barges were about to 'shoot' (lowering sails and mast rapidly and relying on the tide to keep way on) the centre arch of London Bridge. The wind forced them together and they jammed under the arch. The centre barge was loaded with 21,000 bricks. Three sank after they got clear, though no lives were lost (Grocott, *Shipwrecks*, p. 135, quoting *The Times*, 15 Dec. 1802).

munitions to the expedition that left from Yarmouth to sail to Copenhagen in 1807. The magazine was finally completed by 1810.

This investment and expansion boosted production and the figures of munitions distributed from the summer of 1812 to Russia, Prussia and Sweden were now measured in hundreds of thousands; 120,000 muskets were sent to Sweden and Russia alone before the end of that year. In 1813 the Prussians received 100,000 muskets, with powder accoutrements and flints, an order that was repeated for Russia; and 40,000 were sent to Crown Prince Bernadotte in Sweden, together with uniform cloth. In the summer of 1813, for instance, one order to Sweden consisted of 2,000 barrels of gunpowder, 5 million musket cartridges, carbines, pistols, flints and 20,000 muskets. At the same time the army in the Peninsula had to be supplied: by the autumn of 1813, 201,000 muskets, 41,391 swords and 23.5 million cartridges had been sent.[90] Moreover, these exported small arms were probably superior to those produced in other European countries.[91] The difficulties experienced by the Ordnance in supplying the Peninsular armies at the start of the hostilities five years previously were now resolved.*

None of the credit for this great expansion can be laid at the door of the master-general from 1801 to 1806, the lethargic Lord Chatham. His predecessor, Lord Cornwallis, was scornful, writing privately in 1803: 'It is a cruel thing at this time that so important a department should be placed in hands so incapable and improper.' John Barrow at the Admiralty had no doubt who was responsible for the improvement in small-arms manufacture.[92] William Wellesley-Pole had been appointed clerk of the Ordnance in 1802, a post that he held (except during the Talents ministry) until he moved to the Admiralty as secretary to the Board in 1807 (as we saw in Chapter 11). According to Barrow, Pole 'had, by his attention and activity, brought the small arm department of the Ordnance to a degree of perfection it had never

---

* The total French production of muskets, carbines, rifles and pairs of pistols was 3,956,257, presumably including the production of French-occupied countries. Total British production 3,143,366 (Glover, *Peninsular Preparation*, p. 47, quoting Dupin, *The Military Force of Great Britain*, Vol. II (London, 1822), p. 175). More reliable are Ordnance figures that between 1793 and 1815, 2,834,485 India-pattern muskets were produced under Ordnance contract (Bartlett, 'British Army', p. 217).

before attained, and the Ordnance Department generally was greatly improved by his skill and vigilance'.[93] Even Lord Grenville, not known for issuing praise, reckoned that Pole was 'one of the most efficient men that ever filled the station he held at the Ordnance'.[94]

The search to reduce costs in war production was continual. It was the objective of cutting production costs that led to the building of the block mills at Portsmouth, often cited as the first example of mass, standardized production in the world, a project fully operational by late 1807. Blocks, or pullies, small and large, used mainly in the rigging, were a substantial part of a ship's equipment, and those in continual use wore out regularly. A 74-gun ship was equipped with 922 blocks for its running rigging and another 450 for working the guns. They were produced at the time by two contractors, Henry Taylor of Southampton and Bartholomew Dunsterville of Plymouth.[95] Three generations of Taylors had supplied most of the navy's blocks since 1759.[96] Their contract had been slackly administered, because no other manufacturer was apparently able to provide blocks in the quantities the navy required, nor had the Navy Board made any effort to find an alternative. The Taylors thus enjoyed a monopoly; by 1800 they had been allowed a 20 per cent increase over 1791 prices.[97]

Though pulley blocks appear to be simple to manufacture, a considerable number of woodworking processes were needed to complete them. Marc Brunel, a young émigré Frenchman, had designed a series of machines to do this, and in the 1790s had been in America hoping to interest manufacturers in his new method of production. Coming to Britain in 1799 to try his luck, he first turned to Henry Maudslay, who constructed a model of one of Brunel's machines.* Brunel married almost immediately he came to England, opportunely to the sister of the chief clerk of the secretary's office in the Navy Office. With his new brother-in-law's introduction, he took his ideas to the Taylors, but they chose not to consider them, confident that their horse-powered circular saws were sufficiently effective. Brunel secured an introduction to the inspector-general of naval works, Samuel Bentham, who took up

* These remarkable models still exist in the collections of the Science Museum and the National Maritime Museum.

the plans enthusiastically, having been working on the problem himself, though his ideas, with machines dependent upon wooden rather than the more rigid iron frames, were less sophisticated than Brunel's. In the spring of 1802 Brunel took his model to Lord St Vincent's Admiralty Board, which ordered Bentham to develop it and to build a mill at Portsmouth yard.[98] The main advantage was its ability to cut costs. Bentham and Brunel were eventually to deliver ships' blocks more cheaply, in greater quantities and faster than they were being manufactured by the Taylors.

Bentham combined these new production ideas with an immense construction project. Centred on a steam-pumping system for the dry docks at Portsmouth, it used an adjacent, large reservoir holding water that had been pumped out of the docks. Bentham thus created much needed space by building the new block mills over the reservoir. It was a complex project. Constructing the intricate woodworking machines for making the blocks also involved the active and long-term cooperation of Henry Maudslay in his factory in Lambeth in South London, where the machines were built. Manufacture would not have been possible without his precise machining of the screw threads from his screw-cutting lathes, or his practice of frequent and precise measurement, or the rigidity of construction of the machine conferred by the use of a metal framework.[99]

Thirty-eight machines for making blocks of seven to ten inches were ready by the end of May 1803, all of them to be driven by a steam engine, the power transmitted by a pattern of great overhead leather belts.* Installing the complex steam engine and the woodcutting machinery took another two years and further difficulties had to be overcome until the block mills were fully operational.[100] The Taylors were served notice that their contract was at an end in 1802, but it was renewed four times for limited periods between 1803 and 1805 because of the delays in bringing the dockyard block mills into production.[101] Bentham's continual and overconfident assurances about the early completion of the project did not help. Some idea of the level of

---

* Some of the block-making machines remained in production until 1966, and a small number are still in their original position in the now unused building at Portsmouth.

emotion that this engendered can be discerned from the bitterness of a letter from the Taylors to the Navy Board in November 1804:

> We are compelled to say, that We cannot suffer ourselves to be so completely at the service of General Bentham and a Frenchman who we have no trouble in asserting, will bring your Hon[our]ble Board into great trouble and difficulty, for if our Manufactory is suffered to decay, which will be the case whenever the Contract ceases, the Fleet will never again be supplied, for double the money now paid.[102]

The Taylors were wrong. As long as the project had high-level naval support, it would succeed, even though the set-up costs of the Portsmouth block mills were far in excess of any investment the private sector could have afforded. A further complication arose in 1805 when Bentham was ordered by Lord Barham, the first lord of the Admiralty, to travel to Russia to explore the possibilities of Russian dockyards building warships for the British Navy. No longer enjoying the support of St Vincent, Bentham suspected that he was being sidelined, for when he returned his post as inspector-general had been abolished, and he was given the title of 'Civil Architect and Engineer', though a seat had opened up for him on the Navy Board.[103] In his absence Bentham's assistant, Simon Goodrich, had been left in charge of the project. Goodrich handled the introduction of this new process with subtlety and firmness, very much better than Bentham would have done. Many difficulties interposed before the block mills came on stream, not least the training of dockyard workers in new practices, for they became machine operatives rather than craftsmen.[104] The power requirement was larger than had originally been estimated, and another steam engine proved to be needed. In spite of disagreements between Goodrich, the state employee, and Brunel, the contractor, the new machines were fully operational by 1807. In 1808 the navy used 154,285 new blocks of many different sizes, all produced by the Portsmouth block-mills with a workforce of forty-two day workers and fifteen piece workers, with a weekly wage bill of £89.[105]

The appearance of metal-processing mills in the dockyards through these years was another of Bentham's innovations, also brought to completion and into production by Simon Goodrich. The supply of copper sheets and bolts was taken back from the contractors. This industry had never been competitive, as both the mines in Anglesey and Cornwall, and the manufacture of the copper sheets, had been in the hands of a small number of industrialists since the introduction of the process, in particular Thomas Williams, until his death in 1802.[106] Dockyard practice before the late 1790s had been to strip the worn copper sheets off the bottoms of the ships in dock, clean them and return them to the contractor. At the start of the Napoleonic War the price of copper was rising again. Between 1803 and 1805 a smelting-and-rolling mill was built in Portsmouth Dockyard, driven through by Bentham, and by 1807 it was manufacturing 800 tons of rolled, recycled copper sheathing annually, as well as two thirds of the navy's bolts requirement.* A year later dockyard production had risen to 1,000 tons.[107] The wood- and metal-working mills brought changes in the dockyard workforce: the first 'millwright' appeared in the dock-yard pay books in 1805; by 1813 there were seventy-seven.[108]

This was the end of Bentham's reforms, for his influence was wan-ing. Instead, the Admiralty repeatedly sought the advice of John Rennie. Much of Rennie's work involved writing reports on the state of the country's dockyards, and, on the occasion when he inspected the pumps at Portsmouth in 1807, Goodrich commented acidly in his journal that '[Rennie's] observations convince me that he is deficient in experience and judgements about such matters or that he willingly slanders.'[109] Nevertheless, Rennie's opinion was increasingly influen-tial. Bentham wanted to construct a new machine for blowing air into the smith's furnace at Chatham. The issue came to the fore in 1807, when Bentham was away in Russia and the Navy Board, as it wrote to the Admiralty, 'consulted Mr Rennie, the civil engineer, for his opinion of the propriety of erecting this apparatus, and having received his answer, we are now of opinion that it will not be

---

* The dockyard-produced copper sheets were still politically disputed. An 1808 visit-ation had among the party Joseph Tucker, the master shipwright of Plymouth Dockyard, brother of Benjamin Tucker, St Vincent's one-time private secretary. Tucker criticized the Portsmouth-produced sheets as inferior to those from contractors. Goodrich noted on a letter sent to him: 'NB Mr Tucker's brother married one of Mr William's (the great Copper Contractor's) Daughters' (Coats, 'Block Mills', p. 78, quoting Henry Peake to Goodrich, 10 Feb. 1808, Science Museum, Goodrich Papers, SML, GA A234).

expedient to erect it, and have therefore given orders for providing bellows, as in other smitheries.'[110]

From the time of his appointment as inspector-general of naval works in 1796, Bentham had been used as an agent for change, independent of the Navy Board, but with some of its responsibilities. Although confrontation with the Board was inevitable, it was far from desirable, for, as the Commission of Naval Revision pointed out,

> when a difference of opinion arises, [it] occasions much altercation and correspondence, and frequently delays the execution of the Works. The appointment of an Inspector General of Naval Works, with powers independent of the Navy Board, produces an interference and counter-action of interests in the Dock Yards, which cannot fail to be injurious to Your Majesty's Service, by lessening the authority of the Navy Board in the eyes of their inferiors.[111]

From late 1808 Bentham continued to work as a Navy Board commissioner, but, as working in a team was contrary to his nature, he was no longer powerful. Pettiness and tension marred his last years: immediately there was a disagreement as to where Bentham was to sit around the boardroom table – in other words, a disagreement over seniority – which was not resolved until the Admiralty ruled in the Board's favour.[112] By 1812 Bentham had begun to absent himself from the Navy Office. His post did not long survive the appointment of the younger Lord Melville as first lord in March of that year. For the rest of his life Bentham's achievements went unrecognized.*

At heart, Bentham believed that the dockyards could be made so efficient that contractors of all sorts could eventually be dispensed with. Though he did encourage those under him to seek contact with private industry, Bentham's vision of state dockyards having minimal contact with the commercial world flew in the face of reality after the

---

* In 1813 Bentham sent to the Admiralty two lists of his measures. The first is of forty-one manuscript pages, the second of thirty-four (Bentham to Croker, from Hampstead, 30 Apr., NMM, ADM BP/33B; 24 Apr., BP/33C). He then published them as *Services Rendered in the Civil Department of the Navy* (1813). These individual technological discoveries and improvements represent a formidable achievement, even if the implementation of his management ideas came to nothing.

resumption of war in 1803. This would have required more docks and steam engines, new machine tools and a complete reorganization of the dockyard workforce, managed according to his principles of individual responsibility.[113] Bentham had flourished in the 1790s and under St Vincent, but the increased scale of the war had put demands on all parts of the state industrial machine that it could not meet alone. Like his erstwhile supporter Lord St Vincent, negotiation and trust were not part of Bentham's personality; he needed a position of power from which he could dictate and control. Negotiating with contractors was neither to his liking nor within his capabilities.

In spite of the contribution of the private sector, there was still pressure at various times to expand or relocate the state dockyards. Delays in getting ships away from the Thames yards during easterly winds had long been recognized as a problem. In 1806 Lord St Vincent advised Charles Grey, as first lord, to buy Pitcher's Yard at Gravesend, just where the Thames widens sufficiently so that a ship could, with the tide under her, beat out of the river. He further suggested that Deptford Dockyard could with profit be given over entirely to the Victualling Office.[114] Strong feelings on this subject were held by many naval officers. Deptford and Woolwich were 'almost useless', Admiral Berkeley wrote to the first lord in 1810.[115] Improvement plans and reports were compiled by John Rennie for the dockyards at Deptford, Chatham, Sheerness, Pembroke, Bermuda and Malta; there was even one in 1813 to improve the harbour facilities at Heligoland after it had been captured in late 1807. Many of these did not materialize, usually because they were too costly.[116]

The Commission of Naval Revision asked Rennie to write a report on all the dockyards, and the eminent engineer found the Thames and the Medway silting up, with some of the moorings in the Medway so shallow that warships were taking the ground at spring tides. He recommended that the Deptford and Woolwich yards should not be developed, and that a new dockyard should be built at Northfleet, near Gravesend. The government baulked at this major investment and, as a result, money was allocated to expand existing facilities at all the eastern dockyards except Deptford.[117]

The other great problem was where a fleet anchorage should be sited in the south-west. William Marsden wrote to his brother in 1804: 'What is your idea of the best plan for remedying the want of a safe and convenient anchorage for our Western Squadron? To improve Torbay by a pier? To improve Falmouth? To run out a pier at Cawsand, or a pier on the opposite shore by the Mewstone? . . . Something must be done.'[118] John Rennie was even asked to report in 1808 on the possibility of building breakwaters for moles in the Scilly Islands, but the estimated costs of over two million pounds were far too high.[119]

The debate focused on whether or not to build a major fleet base at Falmouth, an ideal harbour for the fleet blockading Brest to shelter in during strong westerly winds. The idea had been mooted from the beginning of the war, but the issue came to a head in 1806, when new ministers from the Ministry of All the Talents came to power. Admiral Sir John Borlase Warren and a captain named James Manderson were in favour.* Captain Thomas Hurd, soon to be appointed hydrographer of the navy, recommended that the new first lord should go ahead, reckoning that steam dredging would achieve a depth of six fathoms in quick order: 'it only remains to consider the expense of such an undertaking, the necessity of the thing being taken for granted.'[120] Against the project were the Cornishman Rear-Admiral Sir Edward Pellew, who called Falmouth 'that hole', and Lord St Vincent – as he wrote to Rear-Admiral Markham, 'the difficulty of getting out of Falmouth in winter time is so great that it cannot be depended upon; in other respects much may be made of it.'[121] However ingenious the proposals might have been, nothing could alter the fact that a frigate could sail close enough to the wind to beat out of the harbour in a south-westerly, but not a ship of the line. One neutral observer reasoned,

> that although it is the nearest port to Brest, and a very snug harbour to lay in, yet that the difficulty of working a fleet of battle ships out of it,

---

* Manderson was to publish a 150-page pamphlet extolling the virtues of Falmouth, addressed to the prime minister: *Twelve Letters Addressed to the Right Honourable Spencer Perceval* . . . (London, 1812).

on the wind moderating, in consequence of the Rock in the middle of the narrowest part of the entrance, it is a less eligible Rendezvous than Torbay.[122]

Moorings were laid, and further up the harbour a small stores depot at Mylor was established, but the Black Rock at the entrance to Falmouth Harbour was the main obstacle to building a new fleet base with which to prosecute the war in the Western Approaches.

The solution was eventually to be the building of Plymouth Breakwater, to halt the Atlantic swell that endangered shipping within Plymouth Sound. The initial ideas may have originated with St Vincent, and he certainly encouraged the project. John Rennie and Joseph Whidbey, master attendant at Woolwich, surveyed Plymouth Sound in March 1806.[123] They made a good team: St Vincent advised Tom Grenville that 'no two men understand each other better.'[124] They proposed a breakwater of just under a mile in length, east–west across the entrance to the Sound, to a depth of thirty-five feet. After some five years of debate, this huge project was pushed through by Charles Philip Yorke when first lord, despite resistance from Spencer Perceval, then chancellor of the Exchequer. John Barrow recorded that Yorke threatened resignation if the breakwater estimate was not accepted. '"Barrow, it is time for me to quit the Admiralty, and I shall do so very soon . . . On this score," said Mr Yorke, "I shall not yield, and the estimate shall remain and be produced in the state it is."'[125] The scheme was adopted by the Admiralty in January 1811 and authorized by an order-in-council in June 1812.[126] The quarries at Oreston near Plymouth were opened on 7 August 1812, and the first stones were dropped on the seabed that month. Joseph Whidbey oversaw the project, with the contractors working to him.* On 31 March 1813 the breakwater made its first appearance above the surface, when the tide was at low water springs.[127] The shelter it gave to shipping in Plymouth Sound in southerly gales was immediate. Nothing impressed the French naval engineer Charles Dupin more than this immense project. He left a description of the work on the breakwater,

---

* Whidbey was elected a Fellow of the Royal Society as a result of this work (Lambert, 'Science and Seapower', p. 17).

recording a scene at the nearby limestone (or 'grey marble') quarries managed by contractors. The stone was transported by horse-drawn trollies to barges, a cargo of sixty tons being loaded in fifty minutes, with a gang of eight men manning the winches and tackles. Dupin marvelled at

> those enormous masses of marble that the quarry-men strike with heavy strokes of their hammers; and those aerial roads or flying bridges which serve for the removal of the superstratum of earth; those lines of cranes all at work at the same moment; the trucks all in motion; the arrival, the loading, and the departure of the vessels; all this forms one of the most imposing sights that can strike a friend to the great works of art. At fixed hours, the sound of a bell is heard in order to announce the blasting of the quarry. The operations instantly cease on all sides, the workmen retire; all becomes silence and solitude; this universal silence renders still more imposing the noise of the explosion, the splitting of the rocks, their ponderous fall, and the prolonged sound of the echoes.[128]

From the quarries, the larger stones, some over five tons, were taken by purpose-built government barges with hinged sterns, and, inside the hull, trolleys on rails on an inclined plane, to aid the offloading of the stone into the sea. Smaller stones were taken by vessels provided by contractors, and every one was carefully placed when dropped. By 1816 an average of over 1,000 tons of rock were being sunk daily; in total, from the start of the project, nearly a million and a half tons were sunk. The greatest quantity of stone sunk in one week was estimated at over 15,000 tons. During the project the contract price for both quarried stone and transport was pushed downwards, so that the average cost per ton over the whole project was estimated at 8s.1¼d. The number of skilled men and labourers employed on the project never rose above 650.[129] By contrast, the French had employed 5,000 when they attempted to build the Cherbourg Breakwaters in the 1780s.

The Plymouth Breakwater underlined the country's naval strength – and its ability to persevere with an enormous undertaking after many years of a long war – better than any other project to that point. The British had combined financial and contract management with the new steam technology to great effect. The breakwater was not sub-stantially complete until 1847, and suffered storm damage in 1817 and 1824, to be repaired by a further half a million tons of rock.[130] But before the end of the war in 1815 it furnished the shelter for naval and merchant shipping that it had been designed to provide. It still resists the surging Atlantic swell today and protects the seaward approaches to the naval base at Plymouth.

13

Blockade, Taxes and the City of London

1806–1812

> To carry on the war on the present scale of expense with the
> ordinary means of the country . . . is <u>utterly impossible</u> . . . it
> follows therefore of <u>absolute necessity</u> that unless our expenses
> can be very greatly reduced we cannot continue to exist long
> as an independent nation.
>
> — George Rose, treasurer of the navy, to
> Spencer Perceval, just before he became prime minister,
> 11 November 1809[1]

How to finance the ever-expanding war was the central issue in British politics between 1806 and 1812. From 1793 to 1815, the army, navy and Ordnance cost a total of £830 million.[2] At the same time, £578 million of new funded debt was created to add to the national debt.[3] These amounts of money were quite unprecedented. When Lord Grenville left office in 1807 he was convinced that the country could not raise sufficient cash to finance a significant army on the Continent.[4] The Tory administrations of Portland, Perceval and Liverpool managed to prove him wrong. These governments had to perform four very difficult tasks simultaneously: to raise vast sums of money by taxes and loans; to ensure that trade flourished in order for money to be available for those taxes and loans; to pay the interest on a sharply escalating national debt and provide very large amounts of gold and silver to meet the expenses of Wellington's army in the Peninsula; and, finally, they had to subsidize their allies, through cash, credit and war materials, to keep the Continental armies operational and active against Napoleon. It was a close-run thing, but Britain held out until weaknesses started to appear in the Napoleonic juggernaut.

The first way by which ministers increased revenue was to persuade parliament that their proposed taxation measures were sound and reasonable. British citizens had always been taxed more heavily than those of other nations through the previous century, allowing the government to invest in a large and successful capital-intensive navy. Whereas taxation in Britain had accounted for roughly 20 per cent of national income, in France it ranged from 10 to 13 per cent.[5] Before the French Revolutionary War around £18 million a year was raised in taxes; but remarkably an additional £12 million on average was extracted every year between 1793 and 1815. After the shock of the financial crisis of 1797, Pitt took the art of raising revenue to a new level by persuading parliament to impose an income tax, for the first time in the country's history (as we saw in Chapter 3). From 1799 two shillings in the pound were to be paid on all incomes over £200; those with incomes between £60 and £200 paid less than two shillings.[6] The new tax raised a great deal of money: in all, £155 million before 1815.

Raising more taxes to contain the scale of borrowing marked a sharp change of course. Before the Peace of Amiens, loans to meet war expenditure from the City covered more than 70 per cent of military costs, but during the Napoleonic War they reduced dramatically to only 30 per cent, largely because of the contribution of income tax to government funds.[7] Income and property taxes were immensely unpopular, although during Addington's premiership the Treasury introduced the idea of taxing separate parts of an income, rather than the total, dividing it into 'schedules'. This allowed the parts to be taxed in different ways, and the innovation reduced the resistance to payment considerably.* Taxes were largely paid and collected efficiently: Pitt ensured that, while the propertied classes might oversee the process of tax gathering, assessment was carried out by salaried surveyors and

---

* In 1801 a tax rate of 2s. in the pound produced £5,628,813. After Addington's scheduling in 1803 a rate of only 1s. in the pound yielded £5,341,907 (Daunton, *Trusting Leviathan*, p. 184). Between 1806 and 1816 a country of fewer than 14 million people paid nearly £142 million in income taxes alone (Sherwig, *Guineas and Gunpowder*, p. 352).

commissioners, much to the displeasure of the Whigs. Thomas Creevey, diarist and backbencher, as well as briefly secretary to the India Board of Control between 1806 and 1807, wrote to the chancellor of the Exchequer, Lord Henry Petty, when he heard that there was to be little change when Grenville's government took power in 1806:

> of all existing Taxes the Property Tax is the most odious . . . most offen-sive to the general feelings of the country. It is Pitt's child, and it is worthy of him . . . The measure has all the air of the oppressive, unfeel-ing policy of the Grenvilles, and was I in your situation, I would have nothing to do with it . . . For the first year, at least, I would go on by loans and loans only.[8]

Not for the first or last time would an Opposition coming into power find its freedom of action circumscribed, and between 1806 and 1807 the Talents ministry retained income tax, as well as the bewil-dering array of indirect taxes already in place. At least twenty-one goods and services were newly taxed during these wars, including not only salt, beer and spirits, thread and lace, banker's notes, fire and marine insurance, auctions, ships' hulls and material, but also win-dows, carriages, stage coaches, farm horses, silk, hops, servants, newspapers, dogs, and even hair powder and armorial bearings. Some taxes were extraordinarily effective. Over the twenty-two years of war, foreign spirits yielded £30 million and domestic spirits £21 mil-lion; even the tax on farm horses amounted to over £9 million. Some new revenue-raising ideas did not work: hair powder was given up and armorial bearings were not used, though hunting continued in spite of the tax on dogs. The taxes on luxury hit the rich, but they submitted to the will of parliament, paying £345.5 million on all these items, the greater part of the immense grand total of £542 million paid in direct and indirect taxes between 1793 and 1815.[9] The elite's fear of military defeat and invasion ensured compliance with this tough tax regime.[10]

The need to raise government income continued to 1815. The last five years of the war saw a great crescendo of expense, swollen by the larger and larger subsidies paid to Continental powers to enable them to continue the struggle against Napoleon. Over the whole of both wars, £65,830,228 were paid to over a dozen countries, not only to the main Allies, Austria, Russia, Prussia and Sweden, and later Portugal and Spain, but also to Hanover and the smaller German states, Sardinia and Sicily. Over half this total was paid in the last five years of the war. In 1814 alone Britain spent £10 million; a small payment was even made to hitherto-hostile Denmark. The same amount was spent in the following year when over thirty European countries, great and small, shared in British subsidies.[11]

It was not until 1811 that Hansard printed a consolidated, easily understood table of annual public expenditure.[12] Total government expenditure came to just over £85 million. The largest share, £43 million, the cost of the army, navy and Ordnance combined, accounted for half that figure.* Alarmingly, interest on the national debt and Exchequer bills totalled only slightly less, at £35 million. The remainder consisted of civil costs and subsidies to Continental countries, the latter totalling 7.3 per cent of total expenditure. Government income from land-assessed taxes, property and income taxes (£26.8 million), customs and excise duties (£39.4 million), and profits from the Post Office (£1.7 million) raised only £69.2 million towards this outlay.† Thus there was a spending deficit of nearly £16 million, with the result that the government turned again to loans from the City.

Much business, therefore, passed between Whitehall and the City. As the war progressed, the mutual dependence of politics and trade was magnified, for the long-term threat of a French invasion drove public and private sectors together into a tighter embrace. Merchants required warships to escort convoys to protect their trade from enemy privateers while the government needed to borrow money from the City, as well as to purchase many of the critical commodities in which

---

* From a sample of three years, 1804, 1809 and 1810, it has been estimated that naval and military costs went proportionally towards pay, 50 per cent; food 16 per cent; shipbuilding 15 per cent; chartering of transports 5 per cent; clothing 4 per cent; arms and ammunition 4 per cent; building and construction 3 per cent; horses, barracks, stores and prisoners of war 1 per cent each (Rodger, 'Military Revolution to Fiscal-Naval State', p. 125, quoting O'Brien 'The Impact of Revolutionary and Napoleonic Wars 1793–1815, on the Long-Run Growth of the British Economy', *Review of the Fernand Braudel Center*, Vol. 12 (1989), pp. 335–95).

† There were other small sources of income which took this total from £67.9 million to the total of £69.2 million (Mitchell and Deane, *British Historical Statistics*, pp. 392, 396, 581).

City traders specialized, such as wheat and timber. The bonds were further strengthened by a significant number of bankers, insurers, merchants and industrialists holding parliamentary seats.*

The government's credit was constantly monitored by bankers and merchants to ensure that the paper money, issued since the financial crisis of 1797, would keep its value. In particular, bankers were always watching to see whether the amount of taxes collected was sufficient to cover the considerable sums required to pay the interest on the City loans. The 'Governors and Company of the Bank of England' since its foundation in 1694 had issued bank notes and settled Exchequer bills. It played a key role in engendering confidence, for its knowledge of the creditworthiness in the City was unrivalled: every merchant house of any importance kept an account with the Bank.[13] When the government floated a loan, competitive tenders from contractors were managed by the governor and deputy governor. Tenders from bankers or merchants, or usually groups of them, bidding to lend the government money were opened in their presence, in order, as George Rose expressed it, 'to guard against any partiality on the part of the Chancellor of the Exchequer'.[14] From 1805 George Harrison, the assistant secretary at the Treasury, held frequent meetings with the directors of the Bank.[15] There was plenty to talk about, apart from government loans: in early 1808 tough negotiations took place between the Treasury and the Bank over charges for managing the government's money. The Bank was paid £450 for managing every £1 million of unredeemed debt; by 1807 the Bank was being paid £265,000 a year. The Treasury ministers, Spencer Perceval and William Huskisson, persuaded the Bank to reduce charges, saving the taxpayer £65,000 a year. In addition, the Bank agreed to a loan of £3 million, free of interest, in acknowledgement of the excessive profit it had earned from handling the nation's money.[16]

This close relationship of government with powerful capital markets gave Britain a considerable advantage over France. Government and the bankers and international traders inhabited two parallel worlds, with intelligence, trading and credit networks largely independent

* Between 1803 and 1815 the number of City members of parliament fluctuated between 112 and 124, of whom approximately half were bankers, out of a total of 658 MPs (Thorne, *History of Parliament*, Vol. I, pp. 4, 318).

of national borders. No other city in the world had the power and the reach of London, the centre of many worldwide markets, supplemented by the burgeoning merchant communities of Liverpool, Glasgow and Bristol.[17] With large numbers of Continental merchants and bankers coming to London to escape the Napoleonic blockade, the City's international aspect became more and more pronounced. For instance, when, in 1807, eighty commercial houses in Hamburg failed, many of the firms that survived moved to London, Gothenburg or St Petersburg.[18] One recent estimate is that two thirds of all merchants in the City by the end of the wars were of Continental origins.[19] Several of these immigrants played crucial roles in raising money for the government for the purpose of prosecuting the war. The most notable was Nathan Meyer Rothschild, who arrived in Manchester from Germany in 1798 when he was twenty-one, to set up in the textiles trade, sending his bales of cloth back to his father in Frankfurt. He moved to London in 1808 and began banking there in July 1811.[20] Rothschild established a dynasty in London that still flourishes today.

The definitions of bankers and merchants were looser then than they are now. The House of Benjamin and Abraham Goldsmid became very rich in the 1790s by acting as bill brokers and dealers in the funds, and also underwrote insurance risks and contracted for public loans – the sort of role undertaken by a merchant bank today.* They also negotiated foreign drafts and remittances – in 1802 they were described as 'honourably and extensively known on the Continent as merchants particularly in the line of exchange, in which lucrative branch of merchandise the Goldsmids are unrivalled'.[21] Their wealth and the confidence that they engendered led them to be the leading intermediary between the City and the government, in effect acting as

---

* The system of redeeming government bills was reformed in a parliamentary Act of 1796, which limited the period of paying navy, Victualling and Transport bills to three months ('ninety days' sight'). Improved government accounting therefore enabled these bills to be paid with ready money, ending many years of incurring interest on unpaid bills. Before 1796 bills were paid 'In Course', or when the government made funds available for them, often years after the bills had been issued. This is the origin of the phrase 'in due course' (Cope, 'Goldsmids and the Money Market'; Binney, *British Public Finance*, p. 143; Beveridge, *Prices and Wages*, p. 527).

government brokers. Between 1797 and 1810 the government borrowed some £400 million through Exchequer bills: £70 million of these were issued by the Bank of England; the Goldsmids handled the balance of £330 million.[22] They also negotiated navy and Victualling bills for the government, as well as making up syndicates to contract with the government for loans. No City merchants came nearer to the centre of government until Rothschild in the last years of the war.

These men and their colleagues and rivals in the City needed strong nerves, for the wartime markets were at times very volatile, caused in part by the legislation of 1797 that had ordered the Bank of England to suspend the convertibility of the currency to gold, when the export of gold became illegal. Dealing in bank notes gave merchants flexibility in extending credit, although the conservative 'bullionist' critics, then and now, would say that it led to speculation. Despite this danger, more easily acquired credit was a great advantage in unstable wartime conditions, when communications were disrupted and trade delayed by the enemy at sea, and with the French in control of the Continental countries that Napoleon had annexed. Credit enabled merchants to anticipate future shortages and to build up reserves in their warehouses. But the unsatisfied demand that resulted from stockpiling pushed up prices, which then tumbled when the circumstances of the war changed and goods again became plentiful. Britain's floating exchange rate also increased risk and instability: the fluctuations inevitably led to speculation, a process accentuated by developments in other European countries and in the United States, which had also abandoned convertibility. (The trade outlook was bleak in 1807, for instance, which led brokers to increase their orders for cotton from America, though this did not stop serious shortages.) From 1808 to the early part of 1810 trade prospered; imports and exports rose again. In 1810 Liverpool handled 199,000 bales of cotton, a record for the decade. Boom led straight into bust, however, and from late 1810 to early 1812 the economic situation was again stagnant.[23]

However, in general, the British economy and the trade that went with it expanded, even though merchant shipping became the focus of economic warfare when each side imposed commercial blockades. If trade had not prospered, the very large taxes and government loans that were raised would have been beyond the capacity of the country.

But between 1792 and 1804 the value of British exports grew by just over 50 per cent, and imports by just under the same figure.[24] Cotton textiles led the export drive. By 1815 their value was six times greater than it had been in 1793. The development of domestic iron and steel manufacture began to shake the country free of dependence on imports; by the end of the war Britain was exporting between four and five million pounds of iron and manufactured products a year.[25]

Distant markets also played a vital role in maintaining Britain's economic strength. The 'Honourable' East India Company, as it was called, exported great quantities of goods from Britain, sending them out to India and China, after 1800, at an average annual rate of forty-two large ships, full of textiles, copper, iron, muskets, ordnance and general merchandise.[26] The help given by the Company to the war effort was immense. First, it acted as a procurement agency. In the frantic early years of the war after 1793, 162,900 'India pattern' muskets, already ordered by the Company, were purchased by the government for the army. Grain and rice were brought back from India to Britain, as were the vital and steadily increasing cargoes of saltpetre for the manufacture of gunpowder. Its ships were chartered to take troops to the West Indies. The Company also funded troops in India: the army that Lord Wellesley as governor-general used to extend British power increased from 192,000 European and native troops in 1805 to the enormous total of 227,000 in 1815.[27]

The second contribution of the East India Company was to swell the government's coffers through payment of high duties on Asian imports. This was a trade that employed not much more than 3 per cent of the tonnage of British shipping, yet transported 17 per cent of the total value of imports for home consumption, and yielded as much as 24 per cent of net customs and excise revenues on worldwide imports.[28] Customs and tea duties alone paid by the Company from 1806 were never less than £3 million a year, and averaged £3,745,961 between 1811 and 1815. The East India Company and the state had a complicated, many-faceted relationship and, unsurprisingly, the final accounts between the Company and the government for the war years were not settled until 1822. Some contemporaries regarded the Company as 'an integral part of the state'.[29]

*

In every respect, the functions of the state and private business were driven together by the demands of a prolonged war. In no other area was close cooperation between merchants and the navy more critical than in the defence of trade by the convoy system, for the privateers of France and other hostile countries were a constant menace. Imports into Britain, particularly of strategic goods, underwrote the entire British war machine. Large shipments of vital war materials had to be brought into the country – hemp came from Russia, saltpetre from India and sulphur from Sicily. Iron from Sweden became of less significance as the quality of British iron improved and output expanded. Timber, both hardwoods and pine and fir for masts, was transported from the Baltic, although alternative sources of timber were available, both in the Levant and in Canada.* The latter became an important source of both pine and oak when the supplies from the Baltic became expensive and difficult after the Continental blockade was declared in November and December 1806. In 1806 Danzig oak plank was £12 a load; by 1809 it was double that price, if it could be found at all.[30] The shipwright officers in the royal dockyards did not favour Canadian timber, reckoning it inferior to oak and pine from the Baltic. Tom Grenville as first lord of the Admiralty reported to his brother in November 1806: 'I am today almost <u>forcing</u> the Navy Board to encourage the offers of Quebec oak & masts, for our dependence on Dantzik must be hourly precarious.'[31] Very soon, however, Canadian oak was forced upon the shipwrights. In 1809 and 1810 Acts were passed that put prohibitive customs duties on Baltic timber, as part of the economic battle against Napoleon. Timber from the Baltic was priced out of the market. In 1805 four times as many loads of Baltic oak timber and plank had been imported as from Canada, and seven times as many great and middling masts sticks. By 1810 that had been more than reversed: seven times as many loads of Canadian oak were imported and fifteen times as many mast sticks.[32]

Nevertheless, the supply of timber and other materials of shipbuilding quality from the Baltic, and the trade more widely, remained

---

* The royal forests in England supplied about 4,000 loads annually to the dockyards, but oak was generally expensive on the British market. Had the Navy Board been prepared to pay high contractors' prices, there might well have been enough to satisfy the demands of the navy (Crimmin, 'Timber for the Navy', p. 192).

critical. In 1805, 6,000 merchant ship passages were made through the Sound to and from British ports.[33] In the years following, the value and volume of Baltic trade fluctuated widely, due to hostilities or to Napoleon's blockade, but in some years it exceeded the 1805 values, while towards the end of the war British exports to the Baltic doubled in value, although this reflected in part the post-1810 duties.[34] Free passage through the Sound or the Great Belt was maintained by the intervention of the British Fleet under Admiral Sir James Saumarez between 1808 and 1812.[35] Apart from keeping the Russian Fleet in port, the admiral's main task was to ensure that timber for masts, hemp for rope-making, hardwoods, tar and turpentine were extricated, in addition to the softwoods required for the building trades and the pit props used by the expanding coal and mineral mines. Cargoes of wheat became important during the years of shortage in Britain, though supply from northern Europe could never be relied upon. Shortages occurred after the poor harvest of 1810, at a time when the Continental blockade was at its most effective, exacerbated by the stockpiling of grain by the French in preparation for Napoleon's invasion of Russia in 1812. In such years imports of wheat from America made up the shortfall.[36] Of the naval stores, securing a sufficient supply of good-quality Russian hemp gave ministers the greatest worry, since no other sources around the world could furnish either the quality or the quantity. Eventually, the Navy Board agreed to buy hemp from India, contracting in January 1808 for 5,000 tons in that year, 7,000 in 1809 and 8,000 in 1810, but even these significant amounts were but a small proportion of the total requirement.[37]

The urgency and importance of the trade in essential war supplies necessitated close cooperation between London merchants and senior government officials. Isaac Solly provides one example. Solly was a long-established Baltic merchant whose ships had faced difficulties in getting out of the region in 1807. Thereafter he turned directly to the Navy Board for help.[38] In late 1808 he purchased hemp from Sweden under a secret contract with the Admiralty and had problems in getting his ships cleared from Gothenburg; so in 1808 and 1810 he successfully petitioned the Admiralty for special convoys specifically to protect his storeships.[39] When they were detained in Swedish ports, he wrote directly to the foreign secretary, who issued orders to his minister in Stockholm for the ships to be freed.[40] His appeals to higher and higher authority, and the readiness with which his requests were met, reflected the importance of the cargoes of his ships to the government. Without a continual supply of naval stores, the royal dockyards and the shipyards and rope-walks all over the country would have been starved of the means to renew or repair the warships and the merchantmen upon which the whole war effort depended.

A contemporary calculation reckoned that losses by the British merchant fleet from all causes were about 2 per cent per year between 1793 and 1815. In deep-sea trades, they could be as much as 5 or 6 per cent, half from enemy action and half from marine accidents. Convoys became compulsory by law after 1798, and this provision was more stringently applied after 1803.[41] The later years of the Napoleonic War saw less success for French privateers, as profits had dropped significantly from the good times of the 1790s.[42] British merchant ship losses peaked in 1810 at over 600, 3 per cent of the total of over 20,000 British registered ships for that year.[43] The Channel was the safest area: in 1808 losses represented only 1.5 per cent of all shipping, escorted or not.[44] Still, the French luggers came out from Dunkirk and St Malo. The revenue cutter *Swan*, for instance, was taken off the Needles in a calm in March 1807.[45] The French Channel ports also provided useful bases for the privateers of the new French allies, the Dutch and the Danes. In 1809 the master of a British cartel carried by a privateer into Calais observed a dozen privateers, of 12 to 16 guns, fully manned by Danes, Americans, Irishmen and Englishmen, ready to sail with the first fair wind.[46] The French corsairs, too, were having significant successes in the West Indies and the Mediterranean.[47]

By the middle years of the Napoleonic War, however, the British Navy had been re-equipped with more small warships, fast sloops, cutters and luggers that could be driven hard to chase the privateers, and convoys became regular and increasingly effective.[48] Four times a year, for example, the ships laden with fruit from the Ionian Islands and Greece rendezvoused at Malta, and were convoyed along the North African coast, keeping as far away from France as possible. At Gibraltar they were met by warships, to be escorted across the Bay of Biscay and thence to Britain.[49] These convoys, organized by Admiral

Collingwood, were thus an important factor in the increase of trade between Britain and the Mediterranean from 1807 to the end of the war.[50]

Sometimes, modest merchant ships not in convoy were able to defend themselves against privateers. In January 1811 the *Cumberland* lost her bowsprit and foremast after a rough Atlantic crossing and was apparently crippled; she nonetheless fought off four French luggers just off the coast between Dover and Folkestone, and in sight of a watching crowd. The *Cumberland* had a crew of twenty-six, while the estimated combined crews of the French luggers came to 270. As the French approached, the resourceful master ordered his crew below and armed them with boarding pikes. Initially twenty Frenchmen boarded the vessel. The master skilfully sheered his vessel away from their boats, and the crew rushed the boarding party with their long pikes, killing most of them while the rest jumped overboard. Three more attempts at boarding were similarly repulsed. In all, sixty privateersmen were reported to have been killed, and one British crew member was lost. As a reward, the Admiralty Board, 'as a mark of their satisfaction at the gallantry exhibited on this occasion', graciously granted the crew immunity from impressment for three years. The incident achieved modest fame, and prints of the action were soon on sale.[51]

There was less to celebrate on the occasions when the navy was embarrassed within sight of the British coast. In July 1810 John Barrow, visiting Ramsgate near Dover on Admiralty business, reported twice to the first secretary, John Wilson Croker, about losses off the Kent and Essex coasts 'at the height of summer and during fine weather', due to British naval complacency. On 18 July he reported that two colliers had been captured off the North Foreland while the captain of the nearest navy gun-brig had been sleeping ashore. Ten days later an ordnance hoy was taken near the Galloper Light; this time no action had been taken because of the caution of British sea officers, wary of both formidable French seamanship skills and fighting qualities, and deterred by what they regarded as the excessive time and effort required to secure prize money in the event of a capture. As Barrow reported confidentially, 'in the face of our whole squadron in the Downs, not one of which attempted to move ... it is mortifying enough to hear people publicly crying out, "Aye, this is what we get for paying taxes to keep up the navy: a French privateer is not worth capturing, she will not pay the charge of condemnation." '[52] 'This disgraceful situation,' pronounced a notice posted at Lloyd's, 'is beyond precedent.' Thus the problems of defending trade, with its successes and failures, led at times to angry exchanges between the navy and the commercial community.[53] Social tensions and professional jealousies also existed between naval officers and the masters of merchant ships that they were to convoy. Yet overall it was in the overriding interests of both parties to convoy trade effectively, and the low level of losses of merchant shipping during the wars indicates that they succeeded.[54]

The relationship between the mercantile community and the naval and merchant seamen who transported and protected trade had other dimensions, and their lives intertwined at several levels. Long absences of naval officers and seamen on service abroad created a need for shore-based support in the form of naval agents and prize agents, for by this time the complexities of administration and finance required full-time professionals to make sense of them. Almost all agents were based in London, with a very few at Portsmouth and the other naval bases. As the navy grew during the Napoleonic War, so did the number of naval agents.* Forty-six individuals or partnerships were operating as agents at their peak in 1810, exactly double the number that had been in existence in 1793.

The primary task of a naval agent was to draw an officer's or a seaman's pay at the Navy Pay Office in Somerset House. Publicans or traders might perform the task for seamen, but for the more complicated affairs of officers, specialized concerns developed, usually located around Chancery Lane and the Strand. Naval agents performed other services on a commission basis, such as investing in stocks, sending money to officers' relatives, or even buying lottery tickets. At any one time they could hold a great deal of money, enabling them to advance

---

* The extensive business of army agents likewise grew. Each regular, militia and volunteer regiment appointed a London agent, who performed the same functions as naval agents. The largest such partnership was that of Cox & Greenwood.

loans to their clients. Risks varied, as the income of naval officers largely depended upon the fortunes of war, and lending could and did lead some agents into financial difficulties.[55]

Prize agents, on the other hand, were appointed by an officer, a ship's company, a squadron or even a whole fleet to handle the progress of a case through the Vice-Admiralty Court and, for a commission, to distribute the prize money. Prize law was complicated and many cases were contested, leading to delays in payment of several years, especially if the prize had been taken on a foreign station. Although such activities were governed by Acts of parliament, many saw the business as open to abuse; it ran more fairly and efficiently after the 1805 Prize Act.[56] Plenty of money was made from prizes in the Napoleonic War by naval officers and seamen, though the previous high-value Spanish treasure ship captures were replaced as prey by the merchant ships of the various hostile powers after 1804.[57] Nearly half the prizes were taken by British warships with fewer than twenty guns.[58]

The merchant community also provided incentives for naval officers. After the Peace of Amiens the underwriters at Lloyd's set up the Patriotic Fund as an encouragement to naval captains, especially with regard to the defence of trade. Between 1803 and 1810 the fund's committee awarded elaborately decorated presentation swords or vases to those naval officers who had particularly distinguished themselves.* Perhaps the most celebrated defence of homecoming trade involved East India ships. Every year they would rendezvous at St Helena, from where they would be escorted home in convoy through the dangerous European waters. In February 1804, off the coast of Malaya, a fleet of unescorted East Indiamen from China, commanded by Commodore Nathaniel Dance, encountered the French Admiral Linois, who commanded a strong squadron. By forming a line, rather than fleeing, Dance's East Indiamen, of a size to be confused at a distance with ships of the line, hoodwinked the French:

---

* Eighty-two of these magnificent swords were presented (Comfort, 'Lloyd's Patriotic Fund'; *Swords and Dirks, passim*). In the French Revolutionary War swords had been presented by a more informal committee of City interests, founded in 1793, to encourage the capture of privateers, though naval officers who had quelled a mutiny during the disturbances of 1797 were also awarded a sword (Wood, 'Swords', pp. 189–91).

Linois did not risk an action and retreated.[59] By this subsequently much celebrated ruse Lloyd's escaped disastrous losses. Dance received a knighthood, and each captain, though he had displayed nerve rather than conspicuous bravery, received a sword of honour.

Individuals or groups in the private sector were usually quicker to recognize the service of seamen than the government. In addition to the presentation swords or vases, a lesser-known but admirable function of the Lloyd's Patriotic Fund was to provide relief for those injured while on active service and the relatives of those killed. For instance, during 1805, £105,000 was voted by the fund committee for the relief of officers, seamen and marines wounded or disabled and for 570 widows, orphans or other relatives of those killed.[60] The wealthy Alexander Davison, Nelson's agent, had medals struck and awarded them to those who served at the admiral's battles.* Substantial sums were also charitably given.†

From the promulgation of the Berlin Decrees in November 1806, Napoleon set out to attempt to control the whole of the European coastline in order to implement what was in effect a restructuring of Europe. French military and political expansion followed this escalation of economic warfare very closely.[61] The emperor was not attempting to starve Britain, for there were too many alternative sources of supply; rather, he was attempting to destroy the British economy by blocking trade with the Continent.[62] At the same time, he hoped to bolster the French economy by removing British competition from European markets.‡ Nevertheless, this bold move carried

---

* It was not until 1848 that the government recognized the contribution of seamen with the award of the Naval General Service medal.
† Lloyd's also donated £40,000 to the newly founded Naval Asylum, supported by individual donations from City merchants, for orphans of seamen killed in the war. The private sector led the government, although the asylum was enlarged and eventually given an annual parliamentary grant. The Naval Asylum became part of the Royal Hospital School in 1825 (Green, *Navy and Anglo-Jewry*, pp. 78–81, 86–7).
‡ Some areas and industries in France benefited considerably from Napoleon's Continental System. The shift of industry away from the Atlantic coast to the Rhine saw a growth in river traffic and industry, especially in the production of wool, cotton and silk textiles. Present-day Belgium and Alsace prospered. The transit of goods through

with it a self-inflicted wound: French foreign trade, which had been buoyant until 1806, declined rapidly (for reasons that will be discussed below); not until 1825 did its value exceed that of 1788.[63]

The British countered every one of Napoleon's provisions and more in a final order-in-council of November 1807, not only reiterating the blockade of 'all ports or places in the colonies belonging to His Majesty's enemies' but also stating that 'all goods and merchandise on board, and all articles of the produce or manufacture of the said countries or colonies, shall be captured, and condemned as prize to the captors'.[64] The first major consequence of imposition of the blockades of Britain and France was that diplomatic tension increased between the United States and both countries. The Americans claimed with justification that the neutrality of their ships was being violated, and passed the Embargo Act of 1807, which prohibited American trade with Britain and France, and led to an increase in tension between France and the USA. The French retaliated with the Bayonne Decree of April 1808, in which Napoleon ordered the seizure of all American ships in European ports. In 1810 there were persistent rumours in Paris that the United States would declare war on France.[65]

By now it was impossible for even neutral merchant ships to trade in Europe without subterfuge and false documents. The combined proclamations of the three governments rendered all trade as technically smuggling; yet the hostile powers themselves provided the means by which merchants could continue to trade across their borders. The main combatant nations promoted their own trade by issuing licences to shipping, so that contraband and forbidden goods could be carried – an arrangement that both the British and Spanish governments had allowed since 1797. Thus licences issued by the Privy Council's office in London protected neutral merchant ships from arrest by British warships and privateers. After the Peace of Amiens in 1803 a small number of licences were issued. Pressure from

---

Antwerp increased at the expense of the Netherlands: between 1807 and 1809 the volume of imports into Cologne from Holland fell by 87 per cent. The growing of sugar beet as a substitute for colonial sugar was encouraged by the French government (Crouzet, 'Blockade and Economic Change', pp. 571, 586–7; Aaslestad, 'Continental System', p. 116; Ellis, *Continental System*, p. 257).

the City, however, ensured that after the Berlin Decrees the number of licences rose sharply.[66]

A large part of the licensed trade was with the Continent, often under German or Prussian flags. Napoleon's 'Continental System' was therefore not proof against those determined to carry on trade. Merchants of all countries discovered new routes and methods to avoid customs officials of any country. Bankers in London and Kent were in touch with their French equivalents, often using trusted family networks, to finance smuggling across the Channel.[67] The government frequently made use of these informal and illegal lines of communication for its own purposes, such as sending bills of credit to a French bank to support British prisoners of war in France, or for more nefarious reasons, such as financing British intelligence agents abroad through a number of British banks, including Coutts.[68]

It was from 1807 that smuggling to the Continent grew to its greatest volume, most effectively from two offshore islands now in British possession. After its capture in 1800, Malta became an important centre for penetrating French-held territories bordering the Mediterranean. The island possessed 165 vessels in 1803; by 1811 this number had increased five times to 840. Traditional trade along the Illyrian coast via Trieste and Fiume was replaced by a trade in contraband.[69] In the North Sea, Heligoland, an Island off the coast of Germany, also came to prominence, even though it is no bigger than Hyde Park in Central London.[70] The British occupied the island in 1807, protecting it with a naval squadron, and it became a very efficient smuggling centre for transit of goods to the north German ports.

On the Continent itself, the small port of Tonningen on the west coast of southern Denmark enjoyed a remarkable if short renaissance: in 1809 over a hundred American vessels unloaded goods there, as did 281 British ships. The Rothschild family used this route to transport textiles into Germany: before the blockade Nathan had sent his bales of cloth from Manchester overland to Hull, to be shipped to Hamburg and thence by canal and road to Frankfurt. The family's agent in Hamburg, John Parish, was arrested by the French when the city was occupied in late 1806, on suspicion of handling British goods, but after six months the Hamburg house of Parish and the Rothschilds resumed business.[71] For a period the goods were exported to southern Baltic ports, principally to Lübeck, but thereafter the over-land route from there to Frankfurt was long and fraught with danger.[72]

Once landed, these goods could, of course, still be seized by French customs officials. Elaborate arrangements ensured that smuggled goods evaded discovery by the authorities. French restrictions had damaged Hamburg's normal port trades, resulting in very high rates of unemployment, experienced in all annexed Continental ports.* It was therefore not difficult to find people willing to engage in smug-gling: an estimated 6,000 to 10,000 people ferried contraband into Hamburg from nearby Altona. Goods were transported in double-bottomed carts; sugar was disguised as sand. At one point, the number of funerals passing between the two cities began to raise suspicions in the minds of French officials; when coffins were opened they revealed bags of sugar, coffee, vanilla and indigo instead of corpses. French military rule was intensely unpopular in the annexed territories, for troops were billeted at no cost to the French and swingeing taxes were also levied.[73] In such an atmosphere, officials could be persuaded, for a price, to look the other way – only an estimated 5 per cent of smuggled goods was actually confiscated.[74] Merchants had more knowledge, more persistence and more motivation to continue trade than those who sought to stop them, even though delays in delivery and payment caused extreme fluctuations in levels of business and difficulties with cash flow.[75]

As a consequence of smuggling and the dislocation of trade the cus-toms revenues of the French Empire plummeted from 51 million francs in 1806 to 11.5 million in 1809. In addition, lack of trade made life very difficult for French wheat farmers, unable to export any surplus crops. These two factors led to an acknowledgement by France that the Continental System could not maintain an absolute barrier to foreign trade. In August 1810 the French also began to issue licences, sold by the Ministry of the Interior to merchants and ship-owners: the exporting of grain, wines, silk and imported colonial

---

* By 1812 only soldiers, travellers and food were transported on the Elbe at Ham-burg. The textiles trade collapsed and most dockworkers were unemployed. Hamburg had 435 sugar refineries; only forty survived annexation. The plight of the Nether-lands was worse (Aaslestad, 'Continental System', pp. 124–5).

products was permitted, although import duties were set very high and the import of British manufactured goods was still prohibited.[76] French ports were granted more licences than those in annexed nations.* Extraordinarily, the amount of wheat exported to Britain was very considerable, with 74 per cent of British imported wheat coming from France in 1809 and 1810.† In 1810 and 1811 French licences issued for exporting wheat to England specified that the payment for the cargo should be in specie or bullion rather than in credit notes, for Napoleon was looking for every means to cut into British gold reserves, upon which credit ultimately depended. The export of gold from Britain had been illegal since 1797, but from 1808 to 1810 the pound depreciated against European currencies by as much as 15 per cent. If gold could be smuggled into France, British merchants would be keen to use it to pay illegally for cargoes that came in licensed ships, because a profit could be realized by using the gold instead of British bank notes.

These financial difficulties were exacerbated by the impact of Napoleon's blockade on the British economy. To reinforce his policy, in October 1810, just after the introduction of French licences, the emperor increased penalties for smuggling on the Continent. A new customs court was created to impose stringent penalties for handling British goods, including ten years' penal servitude or branding for the worst offenders.[77] Such severity was effective. Yet, even as Napoleon tightened his economic grip, the first major crack appeared in the edifice of the French Empire. The British blockade under Saumarez in the Baltic was succeeding in stopping Russian trade with France, and the Russian economy suffered a decline.[78] The tsar came under domestic pressure not only from Russian merchants but also from the nobility, who were bereft of luxuries such as coffee and sugar, and British manufactured goods. Concerned about the damage caused to Russian trade by the Treaty of Tilsit, the tsar opened Russian ports to neutral

---

* From 1810 to 1813 Bordeaux received 181 licences and 607 American permits; the corresponding totals for Hamburg were 68 and 5 (Marzagalli, 'Continental Blockade', pp. 28–9).

† In 1809 and 1810 the total of wheat exported to Britain from the French Empire was 1,497,616 quarters, out of a total from all sources of 2,023,112 quarters (Galpin, *Grain Supply*, p. 191).

ships on 31 December 1810. From that moment it became apparent that Napoleon would attempt to crush Russia.

An important subplot of the economic struggle between Britain and France – the need to accumulate gold and silver – remained of vital importance. Not only did gold reserves symbolize government and market confidence, but precious metals were the preferred means of payment for Continental subsidies, immediately convertible to military use, although many British loans were not made in scarce specie but with drafts guaranteed by the government.[79] But for naval and military operations specie was critical. At sea anywhere in the world a purser on board a warship could lean over the side of the ship to negotiate in silver dollars with traders in local boats for fresh meat or vegetables for the crew. Far greater amounts were needed to run a large army. Silver, in particular, usually in the form of Spanish dollars, was essential for many uses, not least for paying the troops. A soldier could buy extra rations, frequently a necessity rather than a luxury, and unpaid troops could quickly become a liability. Lack of cash could therefore have an immediate effect upon strategic and military decisions.

By contrast, Napoleon raised the money he required by punitive taxation of the nations that he had conquered, which paid dearly for military weakness. He forced Spain into signing the 'Treaty of Subsidies' in October 1803, money that Spain did not have in its Treasury, but needed to bring from Mexico. The first shipment was seized by the British in 1804, which action caused Spain to declare war on Britain.[80] As we shall see, the rest of the silver reached France by means of complex international mercantile networks. Extracting money from other Continental powers was easier for the emperor. Austria paid 75 million francs in 1805 and 164 million when defeated again. Between 1806 and 1812 Prussia provided a sum estimated at between 470 and 514 million francs. With this money, and in contrast to Britain, France maintained the convertibility of its paper currency to gold: it was essential that it did so, for its reputation for defaulting extended back to the last days of the *ancien régime*. In spite of the apparent stability of the French currency, foreign investors chose London as a safe and profitable home for their capital.[81]

The most complex of all the mercantile attempts to acquire specie, between 1805 and 1808, was the 'Hope–Baring contract'. Gabriel-Julien Ouvrard, one of the most respected bankers in Paris, took on the task of securing the money owed to France by Spain from the 1803 treaty from his own government. His efforts came to involve bankers from France, Spain, Holland, Germany, America, Mexico and Britain. Ouvrard travelled first to Madrid, and then to Amsterdam to negotiate with Hope & Co., one of the largest and most well-connected banks in Europe. As a result of successful negotiations, David Parish, Hope's agent in Hamburg, then travelled to New York in early 1806 to supervise the complex transactions by which silver was to be sent from Mexico to France via the United States, principally Baltimore. To pay for the specie, at least thirty-eight ships sailed to Vera Cruz in Mexico, carrying goods, particularly British textiles. The risk to neutral ships from British warships was too great to send specie across the Atlantic, so coffee, sugar and other tropical products were shipped to France as the means by which the French government was paid its Spanish subsidy.

For the final phase of the project, the London house of Barings was brought into the arrangement: a high degree of trust existed between the banking houses of the Hopes and the Barings, for they were connected by marriage. Sir Francis Baring asked for and received permission from the British government to ship the silver from Mexico, and even secured the services of a frigate to do so. For, although the specie was eventually going to the enemy, the merchants had secured a far more valuable asset from the Spanish government than a single cargo: British merchants could now trade with the Spanish American Empire. This concession came at a particularly propitious time, just as trade with the Continent became extremely difficult because of Napoleon's blockade. Thus it was that the last shipment of silver under the contract was undertaken by the British frigate *Diana*, which took on her cargo at Vera Cruz in June 1807. On board was Sir Charles Baring, who supervised the loading of silver to the value of £828,792, the largest single risk insured by Lloyd's during these wars.[82]

The acquisition of sufficient amounts of gold bullion and silver specie became more difficult in 1808 and 1809, when scarcity was exacerbated by merchant demand caused by the boom years of trade.

Another major specie contract was signed in mid 1806, with the Treasury paying for Mexican dollars procured by the merchants Gordon & Murphy, and the bankers Irving Reid, who had a further contract with the Spanish government.[83] Great profits could be made, but trade at such a distance with such valuable cargoes was open to fraud. Of a number of dollar-buying ventures that went wrong, the example of a former governor of Dominica and recently unseated Whig MP, Colonel Andrew Cochrane Johnstone, was the worst. He was one of the unscrupulous Cochrane family with a long career of corruption who in 1814 was tried with his nephew Lord Cochrane for attempting a spectacular stock exchange fraud. In Mexico in 1808 and 1809 Cochrane Johnstone exceeded his instructions and purchased dollars above the price agreed with the Treasury. When the money arrived in England, it was short, and a proportion of it was found in Cochrane Johnstone's private bank account. Spencer Perceval refused, rightly, to pay the commission on the transaction.[84]

Responsibility for the supply of specie during the period of the greatest shortage fell on the shoulders of the junior secretary at the Treasury, William Huskisson, whose financial grasp was unequalled. However, his reserved and distant manner did not endear him to those responsible for naval or military projects: he would deflect requests for specie by sending the applicant a long, written lecture on economics. Huskisson spent much of 1809 trying to secure Spanish dollars. Through agents he managed to obtain dollars worth £3 million from the Mexican government, and thereafter the total holdings of the Mexican Treasury. A further £6 million came from Mexican merchants, all against 'Bills on the Treasury of England in favour of the Spanish government'.[85] In Whitehall he prevented all other government departments from purchasing specie, since different agents bidding in the market pushed up the price.[86] To save the public purse, Huskisson sent as much specie as possible to the Peninsula rather than bills of exchange: dealing in gold was preferable because the rates of exchange had moved against the paper pound by as much as 20 or 25 per cent. The shortage of specie had reached such proportions in the autumn of 1808 that Huskisson told Perceval: 'I am afraid we can hardly expect that in the next three months our stores of bullion will be sufficient to keep up or replenish to enable us ... to continue our present exertions, and much less to increase them. We must therefore be cautious to what we commit ourselves.'[87] The cabinet decided that all available specie should be sent to Wellesley, and during the whole of 1808 the army in the Peninsula was sent £2,860,000 in specie, and £196,000 in bills of exchange.[88]

Pressure to obtain specie proved acute in 1809, given the continuing demand from the Peninsula and the cost of Castlereagh's planned expedition to Walcheren. Huskisson found Spanish dollars worth £125,000, but it was a struggle to raise even that amount.* He wrote to the commissary-general of the expedition: 'This sum, their Lordships [of the Treasury] are aware, will not be sufficient for the ordinary and extraordinary expenses of so large an army for any length of time.' Remarkably, Huskisson ordered the commissary-general to use coercion to obtain supplies from the local population, cutting across the strictly enforced principle that British troops paid for food and supplies, whereas the French Army did not. The army ignored Huskisson's strictures and bills of exchange were issued in Holland without authorization, at a considerable discount, but by the time that this became evident Huskisson had resigned from Perceval's administration.[89] The Walcheren expedition cost £884,275 in specie; by comparison, the Peninsula army during the whole of 1809 received almost £2,500,000 and it enabled Wellesley to stay in the field.[90]

The transport of gold and silver was always problematic. Warships were used to transport the major cargoes of specie that came from the port of Vera Cruz, much to the satisfaction of the captains, who would receive 'freight' money for their trouble.† Merchant ships under a

---

* It was later claimed that lack of specie was responsible for altering the expedition's objectives. Had more cash been available it would have been sent to north Germany (Gray, *Perceval*, p. 339, quoting *Parliamentary Papers*, 1810 (12): *Reports of Commons Select Committee*, Vol. VII, pp. 231–2).

† The question of whether a naval officer should benefit from the carriage of 'public treasure' had been much debated, and in 1801 had been stopped by the Admiralty. In 1807, however, it issued a partial repeal, and a 'gratuity' of a half of 1 per cent of the value of the specie was allowed to the captain (Lewis, *Social History of the Navy*, pp. 333–5). In late 1811 the senior officer at Rio de Janeiro, also a source of specie, proposed to the first lord of the Admiralty that warships carrying specie should be sent at regular intervals from Brazil, but the supply of specie remained disorganized (Vice-Admiral Michael de Courcy to C. P. Yorke, 4 Nov. 1811, NMM, YOR/3).

British licence were the more usual means, but could encounter difficulties from the British Navy. Often these ships were carrying other cargo not covered by the licences and were taken to a prize court on that account. Nor did the difficulties finish once a consignment of specie had reached England, for the army had to provide an escort overland. The usual Portsmouth-to-London route could be subject to delay. By 1812 the Treasury was sending specie in consignments up to the value of £100,000 by mail and stage coaches.[91]

Another drain on gold came through the Channel smugglers, who were encouraged by the French government to trade in illicit bullion. From 1810 to the end of the war, gold was transported across the Channel from Britain to France with French government approval and support. The gold reserves held by the Bank of England, which stood at £7.9 million in February 1808, declined over the next three years to £3.6 million.[92] By this time the gold came exclusively through Gravelines. Dunkirk and Wimereux had been the favoured ports in 1810, but, as some armament production was located near Dunkirk, this was seen as a security weakness. By an imperial decree of 30 November 1811, Gravelines was pronounced the only permitted port for English smugglers, and remained so until the end of the war. The movements of the smugglers were highly controlled by the French authorities, with the involvement of six ministries: interior, war, navy, finance, police and manufactures. Rules, restrictions and paperwork abounded, and the smugglers were confined to a guarded enclosure; security passes were issued to any Frenchmen entering the English quarter.[93] On the return journey the smugglers carried significant quantities of lace, silk shawls, bonnets, ribbons, leather gloves, brandy and Dutch gin.[94] All these elaborate measures assisted the French in their goal of disrupting the British economy. Smuggling was a sophisticated business, involving bankers on both sides of the Channel. From 1811 the Rothschild family were among them, operating on a large scale: in April 1812 Nathan sent six shipments of guineas to his younger brother James amounting to £27,300, in return for bills from several Paris bankers to the face value of £65,798.[95]

In addition to the export of specie and credit notes, military stores were also sent to Continental partners in enormous quantities. As we saw in the previous chapter, gunpowder and arms, primarily muskets, were shipped to Russia, Sweden, Prussia and Austria. It led to risky undertakings, such as the request conveyed by a London banker during the winter of 1810/11, Samuel Thornton, to the foreign secretary, Lord Wellesley, for the Russians, still formally allied to Napoleon, to be supplied with gunpowder and lead, a transaction that the prime minister approved. In July 1811 four merchant ships carrying 500 tons of gunpowder and 1,000 tons of lead, escorted by an 18-gun sloop, sailed to St Petersburg. The cargoes were consigned to Thornton's agent, who was instructed to exchange the cargo for 2,500 tons of hemp. When the ships arrived off St Petersburg, the Russians did not allow the cargoes ashore, and the goods probably found their way into Prussian warehouses.[96] By 1812, however, systematic shipments of field guns, muskets and gunpowder from Britain sailed north to Sweden and Russia. When the rising against Napoleon in eastern Europe took hold in 1813, the flow of arms and munitions to the Allies became a continuous stream. In November of that year Castlereagh announced in the House of Commons that 900,000 muskets had been sent to the Continent in that year alone, 'an exertion which reflected the greatest credit on the head and all the members of that department of the public service by which it was effected'.[97]

Yet, even as the French stranglehold showed signs of loosening, Britain encountered its worst economic crisis from the last months of 1810 to the autumn of 1812. Both imports and exports declined. Many merchant houses were broken by speculation. Government stocks went down. The value of 3 per cent Consols fell from 70 in 1810 to 65 in 1811 and to 56 in 1812. By 1812 the charges for government loans stood at £7.2s.0d. per £100, the worse terms, as William Huskisson pointed out in the House of Commons, since 1798.[98] The banking houses of Goldsmid and Baring had lent the government over £13 million. Confidence in the City was shaken when, in September 1810, old Sir Francis Baring died and two weeks later Abraham Goldsmid committed suicide and his bank failed.[99] Bankruptcies in the country nearly doubled, from just over 1,000 in 1809 to 2,000 in 1811.[100] Food shortages compounded Britain's problems. Yields from the harvest of 1811 were low, and 1812, when the weather was unsettled, proved no better. Large stocks of grain had to be imported and food prices spiralled. War expenditure increased and so did taxes; but government expenditure exceeded its income by nearly £16 million in 1810, as we have seen, by over £19 million in 1811 and by £27 million in 1812. To add to the gloom, on 18 June 1812 the United States declared war on Great Britain.

Unemployment in the Midlands and the north of England was accompanied by outbreaks of violence. The number of unemployed was remarkable, considering how many soldiers and seamen were needed to fight the war. In Liverpool some 16,000 were kept alive by charity during the winter of 1811/12, 17 per cent of the town's total population of 94,000.[101] In the industrial areas distress was translated into widespread unrest by Luddite protests against the introduction of the power loom, which had led to the discharge of skilled weavers. Disturbances broke out in many towns in the Midlands and Nottinghamshire.* The government passed an Act declaring that the destruction of the looms by rioters was a capital offence and moved the militia quickly to the centres of protest, taking the precaution of sending the Leicestershire, Rutland, Nottinghamshire, Northamptonshire and Warwickshire regiments to Ireland, in case they developed sympathies with the rioters. Thus early in 1812 the first battalion of the West Essex Militia Regiment, guarding prisoners of war at Norman Cross near Peterborough, was urgently ordered to Nottingham, travelling quickly by wagon and then by forced march. In May the troops went on to Newark on Trent, back to Nottingham and in early June to Mansfield, where they remained in quarters. In October the battalion marched to Leicester, where two companies were detached to Hinkley and two to Ashby de la Zouche.[102] The regiment was still in the Midlands in the middle of the following year, at Leicester and Derby, and later further north at Sheffield and Huddersfield. The disturbances were stopped by the end of 1813, but not before

---

* Wartime inflation exacerbated unemployment distress, and there is good evidence that wheat and other commodity prices reached a high point in 1812–13, suggested by one analysis as 62 per cent above the levels in 1792, and by another as 90 per cent, though all agree that inflation fell back after the war. The average price of wheat increased in each decade: at 47.9s. per quarter between 1781 and 1790; at 63.5s. between 1791 and 1800; at 84s. between 1801 and 1810; at 87.5s. between 1811 and 1820; at 59.4s. between 1821 and 1830 (Deane and Cole, *Economic Growth*, pp. 15–16; Hilton, *Dangerous People*, p. 7).

ringleaders had either been executed in York or condemned to transportation.

Spencer Perceval was determined not to give up office unless he was defeated in parliament in a vote of no confidence. His government suffered several defeats in the Commons, but he pushed ahead none-theless, managing to deal with the finance for the Peninsular War, hostilities with America, economic turmoil and severe domestic dis-order. This underrated prime minister, to his great credit, held his political and financial nerve. Together with the specie crisis of 1809, during which Perceval took the greatest political load, 1811 and the first half of 1812 were years of grave danger for the British state.

Only the decimation of Napoleon's army in Russia at the end of 1812 turned the tables. The dramatic weakening of the emperor's power changed the political situation in countries across the North Sea. Open revolt was unleashed against French domination in north Germany and Holland – encouraged, too, by the approach of the Rus-sian Army, which pursued the remnants of Napoleon's army across Europe. In February 1813, in Hamburg, tax collectors and customs agents were attacked by a crowd while smugglers were being arrested: the population had little to lose after years of impoverishment.[103] From that point the Continental System steadily unravelled. In April 1813, merchants in Heligoland smuggled an unprecedented amount of British goods into north Germany, in one month shipping 594 tons of sugar, 529 tons of coffee, 29 tons of tobacco, 7 tons of cocoa, 3.5 tons of tea and nearly 8,000 gallons of rum, besides manufactured goods worth nearly £30,000.[104]

With improving British fortunes, government confidence grew. The most immediate task was to ensure the payment of Wellington's army in Spain, which by the beginning of 1813 was desperately short of cash.[105] At this point the young banker Nathan Meyer Rothschild, who only four years earlier had been a textiles merchant in Manches-ter, came to the aid of the government. Through his father's influence in Frankfurt he came to manage a substantial amount of capital owned by the Landgrave of Hesse, now dispossessed by Napoleon, which Rothschild used to build up his own capital through commis-sions and manipulations of the exchange rates between the various European currencies. He was also lucky because in 1813 rival City bankers, for personal or financial reasons, were not in a position to help the government. Rothschild had the powerful advantage of an efficient family network of bankers throughout the capitals of Europe, but it was his ambition, his shrewdness, his cultivation of politicians, his nerve with fluctuating markets and exchange rates, and the security and speed of his communications across Europe that all contributed to his extraordinary rise to wealth and power.[106]

On 11 January 1814 the government officially charged Nathan Rothschild with the task of organizing the finance for Wellington's advance through France. He was to buy French gold in Germany, France and Holland, and transfer it to British vessels in the Dutch port of Hellevoetsluis, from where it would be taken to St Jean de Luz, on the French coast south of Biarritz. The enterprise was at Rothschild's risk, the commission 2 per cent of the sum delivered and was successful. This was the first of many of Rothschild's projects. By May 1814 the government owed Rothschild well over a million pounds; he was to earn much more on subsidies despatched to the Allies, business that Rothschild took over from other banking houses such as Barings. In 1815 the prime minister, Lord Liverpool, remarked of him to Castlereagh: 'I do not know what we should have done without him last year.'[107] Here was the highest degree of trust between government and the City. The relationship that most contributed to it was that between the banker and the British Treasury official, now the commissary-in-chief, John Charles Herries, who had the job of supplying Wellington's army. By March 1814 Rothschild was 'almost continually' in Herries's office in the Commissariat.

In April 1814 Herries left London for Paris to oversee a complex financial operation, in which strict confidentiality was of the utmost importance. Britain was still paying subsidies to the Allies, without which the European governments could not have kept their armies in the field and themselves solvent. These huge transfers from London had adversely affected the rate of exchange between Britain and Europe. Now that credit was officially available to Britain on the Continent, the government established a subsidy office in Paris, to be managed by Herries, from which transactions could be made to supplement those from London. Payments made in London and Paris could be balanced to ensure that speculators did not profit.[108]

A month after Waterloo, Herries returned to Paris to resume supervision of the payments of subsidies and British military expenses, and to clear up the complexities of the subsidies rapidly agreed during the urgency of the 1815 campaign. The Treasury arranged to finance the war effort by offering £30 million in 3 per cent bonds. The loan was allocated to Baring Brothers & Smith, and Payne & Smith, which put up a large part of the issue in Hamburg, Amsterdam, Vienna, Basle, Frankfurt and St Petersburg. Herries was able to use the proceeds of the sale of bonds for the payment of subsidies.[109] Only £1 million had to be sent from England to pay the subsidies.*

These immense financial responsibilities rested upon very young shoulders: in 1815, with their wartime achievements behind them, Nathan Meyer Rothschild was thirty-eight and John Charles Herries was thirty-seven.[110]

---

* The complexity of Herries's task was outlined in his letter of 1822 to George Harrison, which accompanied the final statement on the subsidies. The subsidies were paid

> by an arrangement entirely new which consisted principally in providing the Specie required for these Services thro' a single and confidential agency, by means of which it was collected with greater certainty and more economy; and much of the difficulty and embarrassment which had arisen in this branch of the Public Service was removed. The details of this arrangement embraced every mode by which foreign currencies could be obtained for British money or Credit, such as the purchase of Specie in all the markets of the world; the conversion of Bullion into coin at our own and at foreign mints; the coining of foreign money in England & the purchase of bills of remittance in such a manner as to conceal they were for a Public Account; the negotiation of British paper on the Continent at long date to avoid pressure upon the Exchange, etc., etc.
>
> (Sherwig, *Guineas and Gunpowder*, p. 329, quoting 28 Feb. 1822, TNA, Audit Office, AO 3/1088)

PART FOUR

The Tables Turned

14

Russia and the Peninsula

1812–1813

With respect to the language of people with regard to Lord Wellington, it is infamous & one cannot but deplore to what a length the liberty of the Press has arrived. People now are not satisfied because Lord Wellington has not utterly destroyed Massena and his army, and nothing will satisfy them but a great battle being fought. Yet these people some months ago declared that nothing was equal to the rashness of Lord W. even to attempt to resist Massena and his army . . .
    – Lieutenant-Colonel Sir Alexander Gordon from
        Portugal, to his brother Lord Aberdeen,
              22 December 1810[1]

A British Army on short commons is no easy thing to govern; already discontent and murmurs appear, transports are the cry. This is alas! the nature of our soldiers – heroic in action, full of spirits in advance and when he is well fed, but in retreat where subsistence is short, he becomes cross, unmanageable and too much disposed to give the thing up.
    – Brigadier-General Charles Stewart, adjutant-general in
        Spain, to his stepbrother Lord Castlereagh,
              6 August 1809[2]

Military events in 1812 in Portugal and Spain, 1,000 miles to the south of London, and in Russia, 1,400 miles to the east, sharply improved Britain's fortunes in the war against Napoleon. During 1810 and 1811 France had imposed peace on the rest of Europe, and the majority of new French troops had been sent to the Peninsula, with the result that the British Army had been pinned down behind the Lines of Torres Vedras, which protected Lisbon, and the Spanish were besieged in Cádiz. On 5 March 1811 they had begun to withdraw – and, when they did, Napoleon lost his great opportunity to crush the British Army.[3] The emperor now had other plans for his troops. On 29 December 1811 Wellington's Anglo-Portuguese army of 78,000 men advanced in severe wintry conditions from Torres Vedras. Wellington, despite the criticisms, had maintained his army behind the lines for two years, while Marshal Masséna's army had wasted away through hunger, sickness and desertion to only 40,000 effective troops.

Throughout 1811 Wellington had received accurate local intelligence that veteran French troops were being marched north for the projected invasion of Russia.* By January 1812 he had besieged and taken Ciudad Rodrigo, and Badajoz fell in early April, both key fortified towns in central Spain. The movement of French troops northwards accelerated: in March and April 1812 alone nearly 35,000 troops had been withdrawn.[4] In July, Wellington won a spectacular victory at Salamanca, and by August he had occupied Madrid. Although his army retreated just behind the Portuguese border for the winter, and the enemy was able to re-enter the Spanish capital, French power in Spain had been profoundly shaken. In the south the siege of Cádiz had been raised, and the French had abandoned Andalusia. Joseph Bonaparte's regime as king of Spain never recovered from these setbacks.[5]

Of even greater importance in the grand scheme of things were events in Russia, where armies three times the size of those in Spain were beginning the endgame of the Napoleonic War. On 24 June 1812 Napoleon crossed the border into Russia with his army of 220,000 soldiers.[6] He was opposed by three Russian armies totalling 241,000. The Russians retreated, bringing Napoleon to battle at

---

* A line of signal stations along the 29-mile length of the Torres Vedras defences could carry a message from one end to the other in seven minutes. Local intelligence was coordinated by a number of Spanish- and Portuguese-speaking intelligence-gathering officers, the most celebrated of whom was Major Colquhoun Grant of the 11th Foot, who was skilled at purchasing cattle outside the lines, then driving them in small groups at night through the French outposts (McGrigor, *Wellington's Spies*, pp. 122–4; Burnham, 'Observing Officers', pp. 74–5).

Borodino on 7 September, an immense but inconclusive struggle. The French had 587 guns, the Russians 624. The Russians suffered between 45,000 and 50,000 casualties, the French 35,000. After much debate, the Russian generals decided not to defend the capital and retreated. On 15 September, Napoleon entered Moscow and set up his headquarters in the Kremlin. Fires then were set all over Moscow, lasting for six days, some of them destroying vital clothing and equipment that would have been useful to the French. Exactly who started these fires has never been established, but significantly Moscow's 2,000-strong fire brigade had been evacuated. Critically, the Russian people perceived that the invaders were responsible for the destruction of the capital.[7]

The French emperor waited impatiently for the Russian government representatives to arrive to negotiate a treaty. They never came. On 19 October he and his army began the retreat from Moscow: had he waited only two weeks instead of a month his army would have reached Smolensk, where a large provisions depot had been established, before the snow arrived on 6 November. The French Army was not used to retreating under duress, and it was wretchedly ill-organized for doing so. It left Moscow with carts overloaded with the plunder of the soldiery, rather than with provisions: some food depots were destroyed as they left. No one had thought to provide winter horseshoes, a shortage that was responsible, in the opinion of one French officer, for more horse deaths even than hunger.* The consequent loss from hunger, hypothermia and frostbite of the soldiers, horses and equipment of the Grande Armée was the single event that lost Napoleon his reputation for invincibility, gave the Allies heart and presaged the emperor's defeat.[8] After the terrible crossing of the River Berezina at the end of November, by which time Napoleon had lost up to 40,000 men, his artillery and baggage, half of those troops who escaped were accounted for by the cold. Fewer than 20,000 of the troops who served in Russia fought again in a Napoleonic army.[9]

---

* In all, Napoleon lost 175,000 horses during the retreat from Russia. Replacing them in 1813 was to prove more difficult than finding more manpower, for, unlike the Russians, who had unlimited supplies of horses from the Steppes, the French supply was finite. Some French cavalry units had no horses at all in the following year's campaigning (Lieven, *Russia Against Napoleon*, pp. 257, 306–7).

These great campaigns in the far north and south of Europe were fought not only against the enemy but against harsh conditions. Large parts of both Spain and Russia are unforgiving landscapes, with extremes of heat and cold, poor roads and thinly populated countryside with low agricultural yields, unequal to feeding large armies. Spain, it was said, was a country where small armies were defeated and large armies starved, and the provisioning problem was far worse when an army marched through an area that had already been ravaged by campaigning.[10] The French forces hardly fell below 200,000, and were at their most numerous in July 1811 at 291,414. Wellington's armies did not exceed 80,000 until 1813, although it should not be forgotten that several dispersed Spanish armies and many bands of guerrillas fought on the side of the Allies. The French were never able to concentrate their forces because of the difficulty of provisioning. As Marshal Marmont observed in early 1812, 'The English army, provided in advance with large magazines, and adequate means of transport, lives everywhere equally well; the [French] Army of Portugal, without magazines, with little transport, without money, can only live by spreading itself out.'[11]

Thus the military advantages over the French gained in both Russia and the Peninsula were the results of a policy of prolonged tactical retreat, of evading an enemy that became weakened by starvation and exposure to winter weather. Tsar Alexander took his armies beyond Moscow, and Wellington withdrew behind the Torres Vedras Lines. In both cases the consequent wastage of the French Army proved to be the turning point in the military struggle. An essential element of military success, therefore, for the British and the Russians was an efficient Commissariat, forward planning, the establishment of food and equipment depots, and the securing of thousands of carts and the horses to pull them. Not the least of the improvements in the Russian Army in the years before Napoleon's invasion were found in the commissariat, for lessons in logistics and supply had been learnt from the campaigns after the Battle of Austerlitz in 1805, when the Russian Army all but starved. A ruthless requisitioning system, raising food and supplies from the Duchy of Warsaw, filled the thousands of carts as they followed the army. Commissars were appointed to ensure that local officials obeyed orders.[12] The Russians nonetheless found it difficult to keep their army supplied while in pursuit of the French in late

1812, because of the slow speed of their carts, which could not keep up with the army, and because the horses pulling them consumed great quantities of oats and straw. When provisions were plentiful, a Russian soldier was supplied with three days' rations and seven more days of dried black bread; but it required 850 carts to carry a day's food and forage for 120,000 men and 40,000 horses.[13] Kutuzov was criticized for holding his troops back in pursuing the French, but he reasoned that he could save his army and watch while the French soldiers were decimated by the cold. The Russian Army underwent great privations, but the sufferings and casualties of the invading army were terrible.

Britain played only a small part in Russia's great effort, but made timely provision of finance and munitions for the pursuit of Napoleon's army across Germany in 1813. In the winter of 1812, when the Russians were rebuilding their army, arming the reserve units that reinforced the field army in 1813, 101,000 muskets were sent from Britain (as we saw in Chapter 12). A request to Britain for a subsidy of over £4 million in December 1812 was successful, with £1.33 million immediately and £3.3 million to follow, which was significant in a country financed by depreciated paper roubles.[14] Britain's contributions of arms and finance to other European countries buttressed the emerging anti-French alliance, which was greatly strengthened when Prussia threw off its French alliance at the beginning of 1813.

The Allies in the Peninsula were totally dependent upon the British Treasury, and it was the operations of Wellington's army that generated the greatest political heat in London. Between 1809 and 1812 the Whig Opposition did everything it could to force the government to abandon the Peninsula, convinced that Britain could not afford to subsidize Portugal and Spain.* Powerful parliamentary speakers such as Grey, Whitbread and Sheridan continually spoke against retaining Wellington's army in the Peninsula. Lord Grenville's opinion was that 'Portugal so far from being the most defensible was the least

---

* Castlereagh had to reassure his stepbrother, Brigadier-General Charles Stewart, adjutant-general to Wellington: 'I can see you are all angry with us, that we do not protect you from Newspapers and Opposition Nonsense. I wish to God we could. The Army as well as the Govt suffers from the press – but be assured we do you Justice, and don't suppose we expect you to fly' (5 Aug. 1809, HRC, Londonderry MSS).

defensible of any country in Europe'; to his brother he wrote, 'We are reinforcing and defending Portugal, which to do is madness.'[15] Opposition newspapers such as the *Morning Chronicle* poured contempt on the prospects for military success in the Peninsula, but Lord Liverpool, secretary of state for war, secured a strong assurance from Wellington that Portugal could be defended, and he supported his general through thick and thin.[16] Nevertheless, by the autumn of 1810 the prospects did not look good, even to Lord Liverpool, who wrote to Wellington, 'Not one officer . . . expressed . . . any confidence as to probable success', and most were convinced of 'the necessity of a speedy evacuation of the country'.[17] But he still held firmly to the strategy of defending Portugal. By January 1811 Wellington's army had increased to 48,000 British troops. By October his intelligence told him that the French Army in Spain was in financial trouble, unable to pay new recruits or tend the wounded. He wrote to Liverpool, 'It is impossible that this fraudulent tyranny can last. If Great Britain continues stout we must see the destruction of it.'[18]

Against this background of vituperative political attacks, Liverpool and his successor as secretary of state for war, Lord Bathurst (after Liverpool became prime minister in June 1812), had to encourage Wellington.* The two ministers were patient and tolerated Wellington's complaints over criticism in the newspapers, his mistaken perception that he lacked the government's support and an inadequate supply of money. His scornful and contemptuous letters reflected, perhaps, the weight of responsibility on his shoulders.† As the war progressed, the politicians left its conduct to his military judgement, though Wellington continued to voice his frustrations. Liverpool's firm but open and conciliatory handling of his difficult

---

* Between Bathurst's appointment in June 1812 and the end of the war in 1814 he exchanged over 500 letters with Wellington (Thompson, 'Bathurst', p. 159).

† Wellington was quite extraordinarily critical of everything around him. His brother William Wellesley-Pole wrote to him in Aug. 1809, warning that 'You are not saying enough in praise of your officers.' Wellington did not take his elder brother's advice, writing back to him in Sept. 1810: 'The Army was and indeed still is, the worst British Army ever sent from England. The General Officers are generally very bad and indeed some of them a disgrace to the service' (Davies, *Wellington's Wars*, p. 123, quoting 22 Aug. 1809, Gwent Record Office, RP MS B/93; 5 Sept. 1810, A/34).

general was admirable. The prime minister had matured from his awkward and sensitive youth, and was proving an efficient adminis- trator, a powerful debater and a colleague trusted by his cabinet, party and the prince regent. Even Wellington eventually came to respect him. Liverpool was quick to pass on the intelligence he was receiving from Russia. As early as 27 October 1812 he informed Wellington that 'the situation of the French army must have become most critical. The season of the year must operate likewise against them in a degree incalculable.' He concluded correctly that Wellington could be confi- dent that the French could not reinforce their armies in Spain because of the events in Russia. In late December he wrote, less accurately, that he doubted whether Buonaparte (as he called Napoleon) could field any sort of army in 1813.[19]

It is difficult to see how Liverpool and Bathurst could have given Wellington greater support, for the fact remained that Britain did not have the strength to deliver a decisive blow.[20] It is never easy to mount a political defence of an army in retreat, and withdrawal to winter quarters after success at the end of the campaigns of 1810 and 1812 placed the ministers in a difficult position. Even though the Allied army, behind a strong defensive line, pinned down very large numbers of French troops that Napoleon needed elsewhere in Europe, this argument did not play well to critics. Defending the Torres Vedras Lines made great military sense, undermining the French Army, which suffered lack of food, shelter and supplies, but the House of Com- mons wanted an outright military victory. The message that the French were experiencing hunger and cold, and therefore wastage through disease and desertion, was not accepted as a valid strategy by the Opposition.

By November 1812 the cabinet began to see a clear connection between Napoleon's disaster in Russia and the operations in the Pen- insula. Bathurst wrote encouragingly to Wellington in November 1812, 'in whatever way the Campaign in the North may terminate, the French armies must suffer so much that they cannot hope to begin another, or make preparations for it, without such reinforcements from France, as will prevent her sending any considerable forces to Spain.'[21] Liverpool wrote at the end of December: 'The disposition to abuse the Government for the retreat from Burgos and Madrid might naturally have been expected in the actual state of political parties', but he assured Wellington that these attacks 'produced no effect of any consequence to the prejudice of those in whose hands the administration of the Government has been placed'.[22]

The following year saw even more slaughter in Germany and northern France, and the 1813 campaign proved to be a savage contest of manpower and reserves. But Napoleon's genius for extricating himself from tight corners continued. On his return to France from Russia, he rebuilt his army in the winter of 1812 and early 1813: 200,000 French troops, many of them untrained and untested, were fielded in the spring. Opposing this new army were only 110,000 of the Allied armies, but Austria and Russia had greater reserves of men than France. Between 1812 and 1814 the immense total of 650,000 Russians were conscripted, and a reserve army of 7,000 officers and 325,000 soldiers was formed. The Russian high command also gave priority to gathering horses, which were levied in some provinces in lieu of army recruits: from late 1812 nearly 50,000 were assembled. A further 14,000 reached the cavalry towards the end of the winter of 1812/13. Thousands more were available to haul carts. Old and tired horses were rested and rehabilitated away from the fighting.[23] These were resources which France could not match.

Though vastly smaller in scale, the war in the Peninsula was just as much a war of logistics, and Wellington's letters of complaint about scarce resources continued. At the end of 1813, from St Jean de Luz, he claimed that he was so short of supplies and specie that he could not move his army. Bathurst was also facing demands for men and equipment for northern Europe and for Canada, where Britain faced a hostile United States. He not only wrote to reassure Wellington that his needs were to be met before any others, but sent the military undersecretary, the tactful Colonel Bunbury, to explain to Wellington the cabinet's view of the plans and the outlook for the coming year. Although no record survives of their discussions, Wellington was almost certainly told the plans for Rothschild to provide specie for the troops: the risks of committing such a secret to paper were too high. Unsurprisingly, Bunbury travelled back with a stern memorandum from the commander-in-chief to Bathurst: he wished to keep his veteran troops, he needed more provisions and sea transport, and more support from the navy.[24]

The Tory governments had been committed to the Peninsular War since its start in 1808, and it was Liverpool's administration that began to reap success after its investment over several years.[25] Between 1808 and 1814 Spain received a subsidy that averaged just over £1 million a year, considerably less than the Portuguese subsidy, which was £1.5 million for the same period: in total Portugal received £10,605,689.[26] (Even this amount represented only 57 per cent of the total cost of keeping the Portuguese Army in the field; the rest was raised by the Portuguese government.*) Remarkably, monthly expenditure accounts were rendered from Lisbon to the British Treasury in London. The financial relationship, therefore, was as close as the military one, for many British officers served in the Portuguese Army, commanded by an Irishman, General William Carr Beresford. Over 60 per cent of the British payments went on pay, which included a 12 per cent increase in 1809.[27] However, Portuguese officers and men also received from Britain a full range of provisions from flour and bread to salted and fresh meat, salted fish, wine and spirits. The detailed accounts kept by the Portuguese Royal Treasury also reveal the longer list of help in kind, including uniforms, horse fodder, tents, bottles, bottle-straps, axes, new and second-hand blankets, and even firewood, which came with oil and flints.[28]

Provisions and stores for the British, Portuguese and Spanish armies were trans-shipped by merchant ships chartered by the Transport Board in London. Far from the battlefield, transports and their warship escorts brought essential supplies from Britain.[29] Between the summer of 1808 and the spring of 1814, the Allied armies in the Peninsula were supplied with reinforcements, munitions, food and stores by nearly 13,500 individual ship voyages from England to various ports

---

* The Portuguese government and army, supported by the British, became well organized, with an efficient Commissariat system. Portugal was not self-sufficient in cereals and depended upon imports from America. The Portuguese Army developed an effective transport system of ox carts, beasts of burden and small coastal and river vessels. As the war moved north, away from Portugal, capability had to increase. By 1813 the Commissariat required 54,891 draught oxen; by 1814, 67,782; and by 1815, 76,306 (Moreira, 'Contracts and the Role of the State', pp. 216–17).

in Spain and Portugal, escorted in 400 convoys.[30] In addition to this continuous stream of ships, wheat was procured from the Barbary States and Gibraltar; one very large consignment even came from Egypt. However, the really important alternative source of wheat and flour was the United States, shipped mostly from the Delaware River. This supply became critical during 1811 because of the failure of the harvest in Britain. The Lisbon trading house of Henrique Teixeira de Sampaio stepped up its imports of American supplies primarily of flour, but also of biscuit and maize (for horses), transported in neutral ships and using British licences. In 1811 seventy-one ships brought these cargoes to Lisbon in 529,105 barrels, accounting for nearly half of the Commissariat's issues of these provisions in 1811 and 1812.[31]

By late 1811, however, as we shall see in the next chapter, acute bread shortages were being experienced in Britain, and exports of wheat were prohibited. On 21 November, Liverpool informed Wellington that he could have no further wheat, but by that time enough wheat and flour had been stockpiled in Lisbon. Significantly, the supply from America continued while Britain and the United States were at war, such was the weak control of a divided United States Congress over the middle states. Eventually an American Act of 29 July 1813 prohibited all trade under British licences.[32] Six weeks before that, however, Britain had secured alternative supplies of grain by liberating the transport of wheat from the Baltic, after Napoleon's defeat in Russia.[33] When Wellington's army reached its greatest strength as it approached the French border in early October 1813, it was consuming forty-four tons of biscuit a day.[34]

An advancing army needed an efficient supply chain. The Russian Army's reached from Germany right back to Russia, and was ruthlessly and efficiently managed.[35] The supply of Wellington's army as it approached the French border was no less essential. The capture of Santander by Admiral Sir Home Popham in August 1812 gave the Allied armies a temporary convenient port before their retreat in the late autumn of that year, but it came into its own as the main supply depot after the Battle of Vitoria in June 1813.[36] Continuity and flexibility of supply gave Wellington a critical advantage over the French from the moment he landed in Portugal in 1808; as he described his first campaign:

I kept the sea always on my flank; the transports attended the movements of the army as a magazine; and I had at all times, and every day, a short and easy communication with them. The army, therefore, could never be distressed for provisions or stores, however limited its means of land transport; and in case of necessity it might have embarked at any point of the coast.[37]

For the taking of Ciudad Roderigo in January 1812, the siege artillery and its supporting stores went by sea. In March 1811 eleven transports moved this British heavy siege artillery 180 miles northwards from Lisbon to Oporto in twelve days; flat-bottomed boats then took the guns and equipment 50 miles up the River Douro to Lamego, taking six days. The final 130 miles by road was laborious and lengthy, a reminder of the efficiency of water transport. It took twenty-six days, and required 384 pairs of oxen and 1,092 country carts, making two journeys for shot and powder, and 200 carts for engineer stores.[38] After Ciudad Roderigo, the siege train moved on to Badajoz, which fell in early April.[39] However, in September and October, when Wellington invested Burgos, there were no such transport advantages, and little artillery: British infantry failed to scale the battlements, which remained unscathed; failure there was almost guaranteed.[40]

British sea control and a plentiful supply of merchant ships chartered by the Transport Board gave Wellington advantages in addition to a flexible and speedy supply train. Warships and transports were in use at every point of conflict along the Spanish coast. In June 1813, for instance, 255 ships were serving the army in the Peninsula: they were part of amphibious operations on the south-east coast at Cartagena, off the coast of Catalonia, Cádiz and Corunna, on passage to and from England. They created diversions, transported troops from Sicily, and landed arms to sustain guerrilla groups in the Catalan hills. Wellington told Rear-Admiral Thomas Byam Martin at the end of the war that 'If anyone wishes to know the history of this war, I will tell them that it is our maritime superiority that gives me the power of maintaining my army while the enemy is unable to do so.'[41]

Intelligence, as well as naval supremacy, played a vital part in the Peninsular War. Tactically the British often had the advantage, informed by a network of sympathetic informers behind enemy lines. The breaking of Napoleon's codes by Major George Scovell of the 57th Regiment of Foot gave Wellington an insight into the emperor's plans and, more often, into the relationships between the bickering marshals who commanded the French armies.[42] The hubs of these networks were the British ambassador in Lisbon, Sir Charles Stuart, and the ambassador in Madrid, Henry Wellesley, the fourth of the Wellesley brothers to play a major part in this war. The two diplomats cooperated closely with each other, running networks of agents the length and breadth of the Peninsula. The timeliness of intelligence was a problem over the great distances involved, but the navy both speeded and contributed to the process.[43] Its effectiveness and accuracy naturally varied from officer to officer. Off Cádiz, Vice-Admiral Richard Goodwin Keats sent reliable assessments to Wellington, while Sir Home Popham, 'given a choice between conflicting reports, chose that which most agreed with his estimation, or offered the most appealing prospects'.[44] In spite of such flaws, this transmission of intelligence was a significant advantage to Wellington; the French had nothing like it.[45]

The other operational British advantage was the supply and provisioning system. Unlike the French, who were an army of occupation and requisitioned without payment, British troops were under orders to pay for food and wine. The French armies had to disperse to find food and expended enormous effort in doing so, while foraging parties were always under threat of ambush from bands of guerillas. To some extent, Wellington's army also had to live off the land, for it could not depend only upon provisions from Britain; the pace of advance would have been constrained by the punctuality and volume of supplies from the sea. Plentiful supply engendered discipline, although British troops ran riot on occasion (the plunder and rape after the storming of Badajoz in April 1812 or after the siege of San Sebastián in September 1813 were dramatic, and shocked the officers who tried and failed to bring their men under control). Unsurprisingly, the British supply system was not perfect, especially at times of rapid advance: for instance, officers received tents only in 1811, and the enlisted men not until 1813.[46] When the British Army reached French territory, one officer recalled that 'Numbers of men were marching barefooted, and in vain did the captains of companies ride on before the line of march to the various towns in our route in order to purchase a supply of these articles, which they uniformly found had been put in requisition by the French.'[47]

Thus local flour, meat and fresh vegetables were essential to the British Army, and had to be purchased from Portuguese and Spanish farmers, for whom the preferred means of payment was the Spanish dollar. The shortage of specie caused Wellington and the politicians in London particular concern. By special arrangement with the Spanish authorities, Commissary Drummond went to Lima in Peru to purchase $3 million, but the main source of specie during these years was the traders of Lisbon. The paymaster-general's accounts record a total of £6,066,021 spent in the Peninsula during 1810, most of which was raised by bills of exchange.[48] Sooner or later, these bills would be redeemed in London. The lack of specie in the army was alleviated to some extent by a small number of British merchants who travelled up from Gibraltar through the Spanish countryside, purchasing British bills at a discount in return for silver, ensuring the Portuguese and Spanish farmers received cash, albeit at a lower price, for their produce; the traders would cash their bills in Lisbon at full value to realize their profit. Wellington did not like these merchants, and called them 'sharks', but they were essential to the local purchase system.[49] The situation improved by 1813, when the supply of gold and silver from Britain began to flow in greater quantity, helped by Rothschild's efforts.[50]

This crude credit system ensured the continuity of supply, as well as the cooperation of the Spanish populace, which was wearing very thin some time before the end of the war. Indiscipline and theft by British troops infuriated the Spanish. As the army moved towards the French border, and the threat from the French Army decreased, relations between the British and the Spanish deteriorated dangerously. After the taking of San Sebastián on the coast, mass pillaging led to the burning of the town, and subsequently to accusations from the local junta that this had been deliberate in order to maintain British trading supremacy. The Spanish authorities retaliated by withholding cooperation and hindering British supplies: imports were searched for contraband and delayed on their journey; the transport of supplies through the streets of Bilbao was banned because of damage caused to the streets by the wagons; Santander was quarantined because of supposed sickness. When the Allied armies invaded France in October 1813, which should have been a high point in the Anglo-Spanish alliance, violence erupted between British and Spanish soldiers.[51]

Yet, hard as Wellington's army had to fight as it approached French soil, it paled beside the immense, desperate conflict taking place in Germany, as the armies of Russia, Austria and Prussia, now acting together, pursued Napoleon. The campaign culminated in the three-day Battle of Leipzig in October 1813, the 'Battle of the Nations', when a total of half a million soldiers were involved on both sides, the largest battle ever fought to that date. The Allies had a significant advantage in numbers. The French defended the city of Leipzig but could not hold off three converging Allied armies. Total casualties are likely to have been in the region of 100,000 men. The Allies estimated their losses at 52,000 killed, of whom 22,000 were Russian. Napoleon retreated with only 70,000 effective troops, followed by 30,000 unarmed stragglers, and he had to abandon 300 guns and 900 ammunition wagons.[52] Napoleon and his much diminished army retreated across the Rhine into France on 2 November 1813.

Leipzig was not ransacked after the battle, for Tsar Alexander and the king of Prussia, who were present, prohibited plundering, and the Allied armies were in a state of high discipline. The aftermath of this great battle was nonetheless shocking. Removing the wounded and the dead from the battlefields around Leipzig took two weeks, a task undertaken by prisoners of war and the local civilians, who were conscripted into the task. It was almost a year before most of the sick and wounded soldiers left the area. The country was devastated, and it took years for the surrounding villages destroyed in the fighting to be rebuilt. Civilian starvation and exhaustion led to epidemics of typhus and dysentery: for some months after the battle in what was left of the city 700 to 800 a week fell ill with these diseases. In all, 13,500 citizens were infected with typhus; 2,700 of them died. This sort of horror was never visited upon the citizens of Britain.[53] Thus the Continental land war against Napoleonic France was essentially settled. By the end of 1813 the Allies occupied Germany east of the Rhine, and the 1814 campaign saw the invasion of France, which started in the winter in order to pre-empt Napoleon's efforts to reconstitute his army again. By the end of January the Allies had occupied a large swathe of northern France, ensuring that the area's manpower and food would not be available to Napoleon. He had some late success in fierce fighting and impressive manoeuvring north-east of Paris, when the extended supply lines of the Allies became fully stretched, making things very difficult for their armies. Eventually, however, he was beaten back, though the French put up a desperate defence of Paris, by superior numbers and better cavalry and artillery. On 30 March 1814 the Allies entered Paris and Napoleon abdicated soon afterwards.[54]

Without in the least downplaying the ferocity of the battles in both the north and south of Europe, the perseverance and courage of all the armies involved, the reorganization of the Russian Army, and the meticulous brilliance of Wellington and his staff, it is fair to say that these campaigns were ultimately decided not only by fighting qualities but by the efficiency of supply and logistics. It was a war through which only the healthy and tenacious survived.* Not the least of Wellington's personal accomplishments was to remain healthy for five years, withstanding the pressure of leadership, the rigours of campaigning, the unhealthy climate and the food. He never took any leave of absence, a feat perhaps attributable to his comparative youth. In 1808 he was under forty, while his staff officers were in their thirties, and those beneath them in the Adjutant-General's Department in their twenties.[55] Together they wielded a powerful combination of battle experience, stamina and youth. (As we have seen, only the politicians were younger.) The remorseless pressure of a long war demanded that these offices were filled by young men with brains and energy.

In war-free Britain, confidence had been rising steadily, and domestic unrest had subsided. In March 1813 the home secretary, Henry

---

* Between 1808 and 1814 in the Peninsula 8,178 British officers and men were killed, 37,765 wounded and 6,156 went missing. The chance of an officer being killed was 6.5 per cent, and of being wounded 29 per cent. For enlisted soldiers the percentages were 5.2 and 18 respectively. The chances of disease or accident were 3.6 per cent for officers and for enlisted men 11.3 per cent (Burnham and McGuigan, *British Army Against Napoleon*, pp. 213–14).

Addington, now Lord Sidmouth, wrote to his friend Admiral Sir Edward Pellew out in the Mediterranean:

> The present state of things, at home and abroad, is animating and encouraging to the greatest degree. I say, at home; for you may rest assured that the people are sound and firm. A most material and happy change, produced by various causes, has taken place in their temper and disposition within the last few months; of which almost every post brings proofs, even from those quarters where the spirit of insubordination and tumult was most prevalent.[56]

At the same time John Barrow recorded a general lightening of the atmosphere around the Admiralty Board table, citing the badinage between the commissioners.* 'We were in fact a merry Board-room group: Sir George Warrender and Sir Joseph Yorke were of themselves a host of fun, and Croker and I did our best to keep it up.'[57]

Such cheerfulness and levity were easier to achieve as the Opposition attacks on the cost of the war faded. Spencer Perceval's efforts to ensure the government's solvency and an expanding economy had kept the war on a sound financial footing. It was now widely accepted that the government and the Allies must aim for nothing less than the removal of Napoleon. In 1813 a newly elected Opposition MP, Sir Robert Heron, a blunt and uncompromising Whig, ever pushing for economy, saw little point in opposing the government, or discouraging it from pressing on with the war with 'the vigor for which . . . we must at least give them credit'. In February 1814 he reported: 'I have not yet attended the session of Parliament. There was in fact nothing to do. All agreed that every exertion must now be made to prosecute the war to an honourable termination and none of the measures of ministers have met with any opposition.'[58] At last parliamentary unity on how to fight Napoleon had been achieved.

---

* Warrender, who joined the second Lord Melville's Admiralty Board in Oct. 1812, was a talented amateur musician and a generous host, earning the nickname 'Sir George Provender'. Admiral Sir Joseph Yorke, brother of C. P. Yorke, was a jovial, quirky extrovert, who once woke up the Commons by beginning a speech: 'Mr Speaker, it has long been a disputed point among philosophers which is the greatest of two evils, "a smoking chimney or a scolding wife"' (Barrow, *Autobiography*, p. 320).

15

The Manpower Emergency

1812–1814

The drains of seamen which the American Lake Service has required has already greatly distressed us, and the supply of seamen is so inadequate to the current demands of the service, that . . . the ships in commission are too frequently short of complement, but not less than six sail of the line and sixteen frigates, with a great number of sloops and smaller vessels, are at this moment ready to receive men, and are lying useless because men cannot be supplied to them; and . . . three other sail and five frigates, besides sloops etc will be ready for men in the course of the present month.

– Lord Melville, first lord of the Admiralty, to
Admiral Lord Keith, commander-in-chief, Channel Fleet,
3 September 1813[1]

In the first years of the new century, the neutral United States had benefited from trading with both Britain and France. Its merchant fleet had expanded considerably, and it was a time of prosperity in the former colonies. Relations with Britain were friendly enough. British frigates, hunting French warships known to be in American waters, usually put in at Hampton Roads to take on provisions, and officers and crew went ashore in Norfolk, Virginia. On one visit in 1807 some British seamen from H.M.S. *Melampus* deserted and signed on with several American warships lying at anchor, including the 38-gun U.S.S. *Chesapeake*. The British Navy had always had difficulty in finding and retaining crews for its ships in North America and impressment had played a significant part in the breakdown of relations between the

colonies and London thirty years earlier. Vice-Admiral George Berkeley, no friend to Americans, and an impetuous man with a well-merited
reputation for lack of judgement, ordered the ships under his command to board American warships suspected of harbouring British
seamen. Now, with the pressures of war against Napoleon, skilled
seamen were even more valuable to Britain. In June 1807, under
orders from Berkeley, the 50-gun British warship *Leopard* then
attacked the *Chesapeake*, after a parley but without warning. The
American ship was manned by a new and inexperienced crew. Firing
lasted for ten minutes, until the *Chesapeake* struck her colours. Three
American sailors were killed, sixteen were wounded and the British
took away four of the crew who had deserted from the *Melampus*.
Admiral Berkeley's orders had gone far beyond the wishes of British
ministers, who eventually had to apologize to the Americans.[2] This
incident exacerbated deteriorating relations between Britain and
America. In January 1807 the British government had issued
orders-in-council that made trade with either Britain or France in
neutral ships, of which America had the largest merchant fleet, virtually impossible. An outraged President Jefferson addressed Congress
in firm tones that anticipated war.

As the president had insufficient ships to conduct any sort of hostilities, he retaliated by pushing an Embargo Act through Congress in
December 1807, which prohibited American merchants from trading
with Britain. In the event, the Act did more harm to United States
trade than to that of its intended target, and it almost crippled the
American economy.[3] At the same time the French were acting belliger-
ently against American merchant ships, which were frequently seized
in Europe for contravening the Continental System. However, in
1811 the president, by now James Madison, accepted French promises that the Continental System would be relaxed in the Americans'
favour.[4] No such conciliatory gesture was forthcoming from London,
but only argument about the definition of the citizenship of a British
or American sailor.* The British government's attitude to 'Cousin

---

* The United States relied on a period of residency, while other countries defined citizenship by place of birth. Differing interpretations of the nationality of many of those
seamen sailing under the flags of both countries meant that they could be claimed by

Jonathan', as the Americans were commonly called, passed from irritation to an unhealthy disdain. In such an atmosphere, it is unsurprising that further conflict emerged over the American Indians and other questions of the expansion of the United States westwards across the North American continent. Until 1812 exchanges continued in what was to be a vain attempt to avert hostilities.[5]

Significant opposition to the unenforceable Embargo Act came from New England, which had most to lose from it.[6] The political situation in Washington was complex, but on 18 June 1812 the Republicans, who had a limited political presence in that region, finally gained the upper hand and President Madison declared war on Great Britain, six days before Napoleon's army invaded Russia. There was little agreement across the states of America on the war, which made it difficult for the British government to read American intentions. The Republicans' war aims were unclear, though those of Thomas Jefferson were not: as early as 1807 he had suggested to Governor William Hull of Michigan that he should start planning an invasion of Canada with his local militia.[7] In the event, Hull's invasion of Canada in July 1812 was a disaster, but at sea the United States fared better. American privateers, often based in French ports, made significant inroads into British merchant ships during the first two years of hostilities.[8] Between August and December 1812, in three frigate actions – U.S.S. *Constitution* against H.M.S. *Guerrière*, the *United States* against H.M.S. *Macedonian*, the *Constitution* against H.M.S. *Java* – British ships, with the squadron under the command of Admiral Sir John Borlase Warren, were defeated by larger US frigates. These failures caused consternation to the public in Britain and embarrassed the government. The sense that the navy had become complacent was only offset in June 1813, when H.M.S. *Shannon*, commanded by a gunnery specialist, Captain Sir Philip Broke, forced the *Chesapeake* to surrender in an action that lasted only twelve minutes.*

To counteract the privateers, the British were forced to tighten their

---

either side as their own (Rodger, *Command of the Ocean*, pp. 565–6; Bickham, *Weight of Vengeance*, pp. 34–5).

* After the action the *Chesapeake* was commissioned as a prize by the Royal Navy, saw little action and was sold in 1819, when she was broken up and her timbers used for constructing a mill in Wickham, Hampshire, still standing today and called the 'Chesapeake Mill'.

convoy planning, and take draconian measures against the masters of
ships that ran from convoys. In early 1813 one master was prosecuted
and spent a month in the Marshalsea Gaol. The large American privateers were soon deterred by a ship of the line accompanying each
convoy across the Atlantic.[9] The main British strategy, however, was
to mount such an effective blockade of America's east coast ports that
the tonnage entering US ports collapsed from 715,000 to 108,000
between 1812 and 1814. Since the US Treasury depended almost
entirely upon taxes on imports and exports, by 1814 the federal government was effectively bankrupt.[10]

While the British strategy of commercial and naval blockades in
1812 and 1813 might seem to have been carefully planned, in fact the
Admiralty had little choice, for there were not enough seamen available to take more aggressive action. The secretary of state for war, as
well as the first lord of the Admiralty, were demanding levels of manpower that could not be satisfied. Soldiers were needed not only for
the defence of Canada, but also for an army that the government
planned to send to northern Europe. In November 1813 the Dutch
rose in revolt against French occupation, and a British military presence in the main theatre of war on the Continent was politically highly
desirable during the endgame against Napoleon.[11] Lieutenant-General
Sir Thomas Graham was sent to Holland with 7,000 troops, though
they were of very poor quality, having been previously rejected for
service in the Peninsula.[12] Strident demands for further forces were
still being made by the increasingly influential Wellington, now advancing northwards in Spain. In October 1813 he had 62,000 soldiers,
while another 11,000 were commanded by Lieutenant-General Frederick Maitland in the east of Spain, a total of 73,000 troops. Not since
the days of Marlborough had Britain committed such large numbers
to the Continent.[13] With so much at stake in Europe, the conflict in
North America was well down the scale of the priorities of Whitehall.
Parliament spent far more time debating financial problems and
domestic unrest, and indeed the problems of the royal family.* The

* Many hours of debate took place on the 'bullionist' question – whether Britain
should return to gold rather than have paper credit – while the troubled marriage of
the prince regent and Princess Caroline of Brunswick had again emerged as an issue,
coupled with the perennial problem of royal finances.

most consistently debated issues were the sufficiency of the army, the employment of foreign troops, and the principles of army and militia recruitment.

In 1813, therefore, Britain's ability to fight both the Continental and American wars was dangerously hindered by shortages of men. Naval manpower peaked in that year at 147,087 seamen borne.[14] From North American waters Admiral Warren pleaded for reinforcements.[15] Although ships and men deployed there had trebled by early 1813, they were too few, according to Warren, to blockade the immense eastern coastline of the United States.* From the Mediterranean, Admiral Sir Edward Pellew was also requesting more ships of the line to reinforce his fleet, which was blockading Toulon. Already reduced to twenty-six ships, it was potentially outnumbered by the French ships in Toulon, and the small British squadron watching Venice was similarly outnumbered. Pellew was told bluntly that he could have no reinforcements, because 'the exigencies of the public service at this time are so great.'[16] By autumn 1813 the situation had worsened. As the first lord of the Admiralty complained, ships were available but there were no crews for them.

The army, however, faced even greater problems. It required far more men than the navy, and, because recruiting was controlled and run by regiments, it was thus subject to the arbitrary nature of regimental repute. This was dependent upon many factors, including the battle record of the regiment and the character and standing of its colonel. Some regiments could put three or more battalions in the field, while others struggled to raise a single one.[17] As a result the duke of York as commander-in-chief lacked the ability to manage and to distribute manpower effectively. The remarkable fact is that throughout the twelve years of the Napoleonic War, with the exception of one year, 1807, when the army was least active, the regular army had never managed to recruit as many soldiers as it had lost through death, discharge or desertion and relied upon transfers from the militia to increase the establishment. An important factor in the manpower

* In Jan. 1812, on the North American station, there were twenty-three British warships crewed by 3,015 seamen. By Mar. 1813 the figure was sixty ships and 14,300 seamen (NMM website, based on Admiralty List Books, TNA, ADM/8).

struggle was the improvement in army and naval medicine. The sacking of senior army surgeons after Walcheren and new regulations in February 1810 improved qualifications and numbers of army surgeons. Higher standards and amputations quickly performed pushed up recovery rates.* Nevertheless, in 1810, for instance, the traditional recruiting deficit was nearly 14,000; for the following three years it averaged 10,000.[18] It was therefore an endless struggle to attract sufficient army recruits in the face of better-paid employment, a problem that worsened in periods of economic prosperity when industrial or merchant seamen's wages were forced upwards by demand. In 1806 the duke of York had briefed the newly appointed secretary of state for war, William Windham:

> On the Continent where there is comparatively speaking little or no trade or manufactures and consequently little means for the Employment of the Population otherwise than in agriculture, the Pay and advantages of a soldier are equal if not superior to that of the Handicraftsman and therefore is a sufficient inducement ... But in this Country where all Labor is so exceedingly high and where such inducements are held out to the Lower Class of the People either to engage in manufactures or to be employed at Sea ... the continual drain which is unavoidably occasioned by the common casualties of the Army, particularly in our Colonial Possessions, causes such an Annual Deficiency, as has as yet at least never been supplied by ordinary recruiting ...[19]

It was as well that the population of Great Britain and Ireland continued to expand: from the first census in 1801 (see Chapter 2) it was to grow by about 15 per cent a decade.†

---

* Of 1,242 badly wounded after the battle of Toulouse, 88 per cent walked out to convalesce or to rejoin their units. William Beatty, the *Victory*'s surgeon at Trafalgar, reported in Jan. 1806 that nine of the eleven who lost limbs during the battle had survived, and only six of his 102 convalescents had died (Crumplin, 'Surgery in the Royal Navy', p. 88; Brockliss, *Nelson's Surgeon*, p. 122).

† There can be no doubt of the utility of the census in calculating the potential strength of British manpower for fighting the war (Cookson, *Armed Nation*, pp. 95–9). The militia lists of 1804 show that there were 562,601 men between eighteen and thirty without children. If evenly distributed this would mean that there were 46,000 men of the ideal recruitment age of twenty (Linch, *Wellington's Army*, p. 150).

The position in France was very different. The French government demanded that all single men between twenty and twenty-five served, with the requirement of unlimited service. French peasant society resisted this and offered protection to several hundred thousand young men on the run who disobeyed the conscription laws or deserted.[20] Yet every year between 1808 and 1812 the French Army had available between 181,000 and 217,000 new conscripts.[21] Comparing British and French military manpower requirements is simplistic, as the French, potentially and then actually in 1813–14, faced the combined Russian, Austrian and Prussian armies, as well as those of Portugal and Spain; they, too, had allies, such as the Saxons. But Napoleon was beginning to suffer losses that were unsustainable. Between 1802 and 1815 the French officer-training schools turned out about 4,000 officers a year, but such numbers in any one year were not enough to replace the losses at the battles of Wagram and Borodino, and during the retreat from Moscow.[22]

Britain during this period, unlike Napoleonic France, never adopted conscription. In the last years of the war, the main method by which men were raised for the regular army was by attracting soldiers from the militia, by ballot and through bounties of increasing value that had been set by the nine Militia Acts between 1807 and 1814. The duke of Beaufort, colonel of the Royal Monmouth and Brecon Militia Regiment, reminded his troops in 1807 'that those Soldiers who are willing to Volunteer for Life are to receive fourteen Guineas, but those who enter for only seven Years ten guineas'.[23] Whereas in the French Revolutionary War 36,000 British militiamen had transferred to line regiments, in the Napoleonic War the figure was 110,000.[24] No other statistics better illustrate the great difference in scale between the two wars, nor how much the country had to dig into its resources to survive Napoleon.

Another measure that the army took to make up the shortfall was recruiting foreigners. From the first years of the Revolutionary War regiments such as the King's German Legion had fought for Britain. In the Peninsula the integration of the Portuguese Army under Wellington's command and military cooperation with Spanish troops, difficult though that was, were other methods by which British forces were bolstered.[25] Germans and Dutchmen were recruited into British regiments under Graham's command in Holland. In December 1813 Castlereagh proposed to the recently installed British ambassador to Holland that up to 1,500 Dutchmen could be found to 'make the British force more respectable', although nothing came of it.[26] Parliament took a great detail of interest in the issue of foreigners serving in the army, and Lord Palmerston, secretary at war, had to reassure the Commons regularly. He said in 1812:

> If any man would look at the map of Europe, and see what a proportion of its population the enemy had forced into hostility against this country, if he were also to consider the limited population of these two islands, and the extensive colonies we had to defend, and the navy we had to support, it appeared to him hardly possible that such a man could now adhere to the idea of not employing foreigners in our service.[27]

From 1808 until the end of the war, the army raised nearly 120,000 men by ordinary enlistment, and nearly 100,000 through the militia.* Yet by 1810 this system had run out of steam; in the adjutant-general's words: 'In the old militia the original institution is completely worn out by the introduction of a general substitution.'[28] By 1812 so many men had transferred to the regular army that the deficiency of the militia establishment was as high as 30 per cent.[29] In August 1813 Colonel Bunbury wrote to Bathurst: 'The volunteering of the militia into the Regular regiments has become extremely slack ... At the same time it is believed that a great Enthusiasm exists in the country ... and that the old militia would freely extend their service if they were employed with their own officers and to retain their peculiar advantages.'[30] By 1813 Britain was operating very close to the limits of its manpower with what was effectively a volunteer army.[31]

A final push was needed, and the government brought forward a 'New Military System', which became law in November 1813. The aim was to transfer 26,000 men to the regular army, encouraged by several

---

* Between 1808 and 1815 the army raised 117,275 men. The militia recruited 108,246, of whom 94,179 eventually transferred to the regular army (Linch, *Wellington's Army*, pp. 60–61). The West Essex Militia, which arrived in Dublin 500 strong in September 1813, soon after provided 300 volunteers for the regular army; the regiment had originally been embodied in 1803 with 700 recruits from balloting (West Essex Digest of Services, TNA, WO 68/257).

new measures. Militia officers were to be offered regular commissions; militiamen could volunteer as whole companies and be formed into provisional battalions under the command of militia officers for service in Europe; while up to three quarters of a militia regiment could be offered as a complete and separate unit. The 'peculiar advantages' to which Bunbury was referring were the family allowances that the militia enjoyed, but the regular army did not, and that were now to be retained by militiamen who transferred to the regular army. To add force to these measures, the government was given greater powers to call out the local militia and send it outside its own county for home defence reasons.[32] In January 1814 the regular army reached its peak at 233,837, by which time the militia had been reduced to 70,000.[33]

Success in these wars was not only dependent on the numbers of soldiers, but also on their experience and qualities of discipline. A benefit of the militia-transfer system was that it effectively resulted in a longer period of training, when perhaps a third of the army in the later years of the war had served previously in the auxiliaries.[34] This was significant. A transferred militia man could have spent two years in a second battalion at home before being despatched overseas to Spain. No inexperienced or old, worn-out soldiers were sent out to Wellington, which accounts for the exceptional endurance of his army (and contrasts with the soldiers being raised by conscription in France in 1813 and 1814). This regime was achieved by the efforts of the commander-in-chief, the duke of York, and General Calvert, the adjutant-general, who had become more influential in Whitehall.[35] The danger of the lack of trained manpower was starkly illustrated by the poor-quality troops commanded by Lieutenant-General Sir Thomas Graham in Holland. On 8 March 1814 Graham attempted a surprise attack on the French garrison in Bergen-op-Zoom. At first all went well, but in confused fighting the British troops lost momentum and were driven out of the town or taken prisoner. Graham had never wanted this command and was mortified at this failure, but neither the minister nor the army blamed him.[36]

The militia, however, was not an infinite resource to be plundered for men for transfer to the regular army, for it fulfilled many important tasks. The Luddite disturbances in the West Midlands which broke out in late 1811 and spread to Yorkshire in 1812 and Lancashire

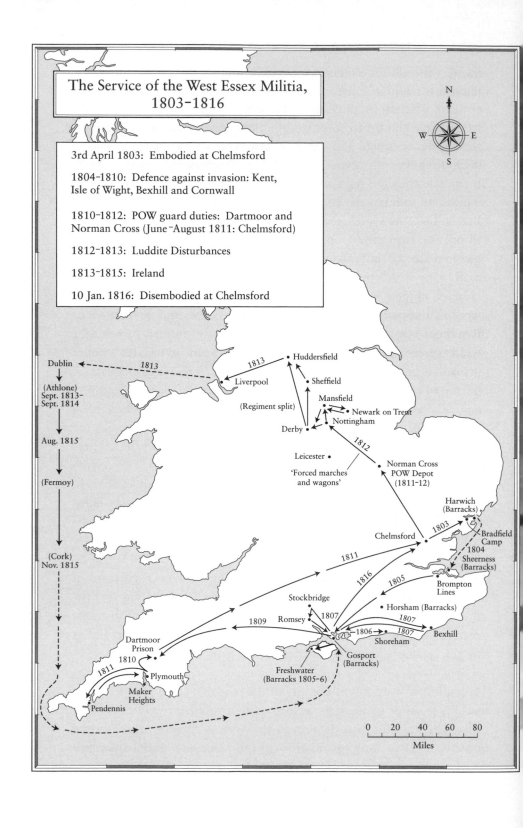

The Service of the West Essex Militia,
1803–1816

3rd April 1803: Embodied at Chelmsford

1804–1810: Defence against invasion: Kent,
Isle of Wight, Bexhill and Cornwall

1810–1812: POW guard duties: Dartmoor and
Norman Cross (June–August 1811: Chelmsford)

1812–1813: Luddite Disturbances

1813–1815: Ireland

10 Jan. 1816: Disembodied at Chelmsford

N
W E
S

Dublin ← *1813*

(Athlone)
Sept. 1813–
Sept. 1814

Aug. 1815

(Fermoy)

(Cork)
Nov. 1815

Huddersfield
1813
Liverpool
Sheffield
(Regiment split)
Mansfield
Newark on Trent
Nottingham
Derby
1812
Leicester
'Forced marches
and wagons'
Norman Cross
POW Depot
(1811–12)

Harwich
(Barracks)
Chelmsford
1803
Bradfield
Camp
1804
Sheerness
(Barracks)
1811
1816
1805
Brompton
Lines
Stockbridge
Horsham (Barracks)
1809
Romsey
1807
1807
1806→
1807
Shoreham
Bexhill
Dartmoor
Prison
1810
Freshwater
(Barracks 1805–6)
Gosport
(Barracks)
1811
Plymouth
Maker
Heights
Pendennis

0   20   40   60   80
Miles

in 1813 led to the redeployment there of militia regiments.* In case the regiments raised in these areas had sympathies with the rioters, the government wisely took precautions by ordering the local militia regiments to Ireland, their place taken by other regiments which were on shore-defence duties. They, in turn, were replaced by Irish militia regiments, manned by many Catholics, a move made possible by the Interchange Act (which allowed Irish militia to serve on English soil, and which had received the assent from the prince regent on 1 July 1811).[37] Latent suspicions of Irish Catholics were swiftly eclipsed by the need to provide manpower. George III, who would almost certainly have blocked the measure, was by now a sick and uncomprehending old man.

In Ireland itself, however, tensions between the populace and troops were still apparent. When the Royal Monmouth and Brecon Militia Regiment was quartered in Tullamore, though officers were made welcome by the local gentry, the soldiers were subject to 'frequent insults'. Regimental orders were promulgated in August 1813: 'If any person or persons approach at Night to ask Questions, the reply must be, "Stand Off I am loaded."' The colonel was 'confident of the very extreme caution they will Preserve whilst loaded in a Town, and he makes himself certain they will not fire unless compelled to do so in

---

* These riots were of considerable size. From Sheffield on 19 June 1812 Lieutenant-Colonel Lany of the East Devon Militia wrote to the newly appointed home secretary, Lord Sidmouth:

> Yesterday, being market day, an immense mob, principally women, assembled; and by a sudden rush emptied the market in a few minutes of all it contained. They next proceeded to all the shops where flour was sold, demanding flour at 3s. per stone, which had been selling, during the last fortnight, for 7s. . . . The 15th Hussars and ourselves have been constantly on duty since yesterday morning. I am sorry to say these lawless proceedings continue today; and parties are gone into the country to attack the mills, but are followed by dragoons . . . The Riot Act has just been read to at least 5,000, and Lord Fitzwilliam gave them five minutes to disperse, when, as they did not obey, the hussars charged down the street and cleared it immediately. We now have orders to fire if we meet with the least resistance. Thousands were added today to their numbers from the country . . . No lives have, as yet, been lost.
>
> (Pellow, *Sidmouth*, Vol. III, p. 88)

their own Personal Defence or to protect Property which may be intrusted to their charge'.[38]

The domestic peacekeeping tasks of the militia continued to be difficult and varied until the end of the war. Militia units played an important part in guarding prisoners of war while in transit, or when confined in depots or prison hulks. Many nations were represented: French, Italian, German, Dutch, American, Greek, Croat, Danish, Swedish, Norwegian and Polish prisoners.[39] Among the skilled men denied to the French war effort, for instance, were nearly 12,000 seamen from French privateers, some of whom had been incarcerated from the start of the war in 1803.[40] In Britain as a whole, prisoners of war totalled 52,649 by 1812, and 1813 saw a further swelling of the numbers as a result of British military success.[41] As Wellington advanced northwards in the Peninsula he sent 20,000 prisoners to England between 1811 and 1812.[42] More were to come in 1813 and 1814: at Plymouth in late 1813, 600 Frenchmen were housed on board *Vanguard*, Nelson's flagship at the Nile, and 700 in the *Temeraire*, the ship that had gone to the rescue of the *Victory* at Trafalgar. These prisoners had been captured at Bayonne and Pamplona, and did not have long to wait until the general repatriation in May 1814.[43] In the year of 1812, when war with the Americans was joined, few prisoners were captured, but in the following two years, when fighting took place in Canada, 14,500 American prisoners were sent to England, housed primarily in Stapleton near Bristol or on Dartmoor.[44] Relations between French and American prisoners could be marked by friction and violence.

As depots and hulks became more crowded, conditions deteriorated and tempers frayed. The worst incident took place at Dartmoor in April 1815. Somersetshire militiamen panicked and fired when confronted by a crowd of protesting American prisoners waiting to be repatriated. Sixty-three prisoners were wounded, of whom seven died.[45] The militia were needed to keep the peace between American and French prisoners and, on occasion, towards the end of the war, between those Frenchmen who retained their loyalty to Napoleon and those who supported the Bourbons: in December 1813 almost 600 prisoners on board the *Sampson* at Chatham came to blows over rival loyalties in France, and a Bourbon peace commissioner visiting a hulk in Portsmouth in April 1814 'had a large basket of filth thrown over him'. The prisoners involved in this second incident were the last to be repatriated. In Scotland in the same month at the Perth depot, as the local newspaper reported, 'six prisoners in the south prison of the Depot hoisted a white [Bourbon] flag, when almost the whole of their fellow captives clambered over the walls from the other prisons and threatened them with the most violent treatment. By the interference of the guard, they were saved from actual injury, and for their greater security were removed to the hospital.'[46]

To meet the increase of prisoners, the Transport Board and the navy adapted a dozen more old warships as prison ships, until by the end of the war thirty-four were in use. These overcrowded and unhealthy hulks were easier to guard than land-based depots, as they could only be reached by the oared launches or long-boats which took provisions aboard, or lighter gigs used for personnel. The government had, however, always been extremely worried about large concentrations of prisoners and the danger of mass escapes, and now the problem was growing. The mere presence of large prisons or depots could incite the local populace to unrest, particularly during periods of high food prices, when the consumption of food by so many prisoners was seen to be contributing to shortages. In 1814, for instance, 21,000 prisoners around Portsmouth consumed a hundred head of cattle a week.[47] Riots took place in Tavistock in Devon in 1812 over high bread prices, the crowd angered by the sight of great quantities of corn being sent to the prisoners at Plymouth and Dartmoor.

It is very difficult to calculate how many prisoners of war were confined in England, Wales and Scotland at the time of the greatest manpower shortages in late 1813. The five great land depots at Portchester, Stapleton, Norman Cross, Perth and the prison at Dartmoor held at least 40,000, and there were at least 20,000 confined in hulks at Portsmouth, Plymouth and Chatham. Several other establishments, such as Forton in Gosport or Millbay at Plymouth, took the best part of 40,000, and a significant proportion was always in transit from depots to hulks, escorted by the militia, or to the hospital ship in port. There were also a limited number of cartels, exchanging civilians captured aboard enemy ships. An approximate estimate of 100,000 prisoners of war in 1813 is conservative and there could have been many more.* Whatever the total, the significant fact is that tens of thousands of skilled French seamen and experienced soldiers were denied to Napoleon just at the time when he was most in need of them.

French prisoners of war did escape, even when they were hundreds of miles from the Channel. Between 1803 and 1814, 1,105 French officer prisoners of war who were allowed a degree of freedom by giving their word not to escape, broke their parole and at least 600 reached France over the Channel, assisted by smugglers.[48] French records show that between January and November 1811, 141 French officers made their escape, usually crossing from Deal and landing in Dunkirk, Boulogne and Calais, although some were taken further west from Dorset and Devon to Cherbourg. For the smugglers it was a risky though lucrative business, for up to 300 guineas could be charged. Thomas Moore was the most celebrated of these smugglers.[49] General Armand Philippon, the governor of Badajoz, had been captured in April 1812 after the siege of the city, and was taken to England, where he was paroled in Oswestry on the Welsh border. He successfully escaped in June, via Rye in Sussex.†

By 1813 even more prisoners were on the move, mostly northwards. In the previous year the government received information of a plot by French officers on parole to organize a mass break-out. It was rumoured that they would march on the large depots, release prisoners and occupy a port to give a French invading force a bridgehead.[50] The Transport Board took immediate action. Paroled officers were moved out of twenty-three towns in Hampshire and Devon, away from the

---

* The classic study by Francis Abell gives a figure of 122,000 (Abell, *Prisoners of War in Britain 1756–1815* (Oxford, 1914), pp. 117–18). An overall figure for 1793–1815 of a quarter of a million is given by Patricia Crimmin ('Prisoners of War and Port Communities', p. 17). It is difficult to obtain a figure at a particular time since the very detailed Registers are cumulative, but 'safe' averages of prisoners on ex-98-gun ships, for instance, can be calculated at about 700, and 600 for 74s (e.g., *Glory*, ex-98, *Ganges*, ex-74, Prisoner of War Registers, TNA, ADM 103/137, 103/150).

† A reward of £100 for his capture was put out, though without success, but the two smugglers who had taken Philippon to France were caught, as was the landlord of the Red Lion Inn, who was also the local postmaster. They were sentenced to two years in gaol and to stand in the pillory at Rye; as *The Times* put it, 'as near to the spot from where the French prisoners embarked so that they could see the coast of the country they favoured' (Crimmin, 'Channel's Significance', p. 76).

major ports, so that places such as Alresford and Bishop's Waltham, or North Tawton and Crediton, no longer had paroled prisoner-of-war officers living in the community. They were sent long distances, to towns in Wales such as Abergavenny or Welshpool. In addition, thousands of confined prisoners were moved away from the south of England to new camps and depots in Scotland, mainly from hulks on the south coast.* In 1811 only 500 or 600 prisoners were held in Scotland, but by January 1813 that figure had increased to between 12,000 and 13,000, held in depots near Edinburgh such as Valleyfield or Esk Mills. The largest was the stone depot at Perth, built in less than a year and completed by July 1812, and which was immediately full to its capacity of 7,000 prisoners.[51] Many were taken by one of the Transport Board's merchant ships from the southern English ports to Kirkcaldy or Dundee before a short march to Perth.

It took many months before the benefits of Napoleon's defeat in Russia in late 1812 could be translated into concrete advantage on the ground in America. But Admiral Saumarez's Baltic Fleet was steadily run down. By July 1814 seventy-two warships, including nine ships of the line, four 50-gun ships, twenty large frigates and thirty-nine sloops, were operating off the coast of the United States.[52] By the end of the war, thirty-two American warships, from sloops to large frigates, had been destroyed, captured or were blockaded in American ports, and over 1,400 American merchant vessels had been captured.[53]

Army operations were less successful, however, and Admiral Warren's successor as commander-in-chief, Admiral Alexander Cochrane, employed raiding and destruction tactics in an attempt to break the will of the Americans, bringing lessons from the vicious methods of warfare utilized in the Peninsula. In retaliation for the burning of York in Ontario by the Americans, a punitive British raid on Washington under Rear-Admiral Cockburn struck hard, using 4,500 lightly armed, fast-moving troops and marines. The British force burnt ships in the Navy Yard and destroyed government buildings, including the

* Liverpool's prisons contained no prisoners of war after 1803, although they had been in use in the eighteenth century. The proximity to Ireland and the vulnerability of the port to French attack might have been responsible for this decision (Lloyd, *Prisoners of War*, p. 244).

White House. It took only thirteen days to accomplish, and few casualties were sustained. This raid was a political rather than a military one, and it could not disguise the fact that British military resources remained stretched in North America.[54] Some of Wellington's best Peninsula troops were eventually sent to Canada, and as late as November 1814 the prime minister, Lord Liverpool, pressed Wellington to go to America to command the troops there, an offer that the duke refused: he feared the renewal of war in Europe and did not think that he could effect much improvement. He told Liverpool as peace negotiators were talking in Ghent: 'You can get no territory; indeed the state of your military operations, however creditable, does not entitle you to demand any.'[55] Liverpool ordered the negotiators to agree peace terms restoring the *status quo antebellum*, and the Treaty of Ghent brought the war to a close on 24 December 1814. The duke's instincts had been correct: on 8 January 1815, the British Army, unaware that a treaty had been signed, attacked New Orleans and was badly beaten.*

British government ministers disagreed about the result of this war. The young Henry Goulburn, undersecretary of war and one of the negotiators at Ghent, was furious with Liverpool for letting the Americans off, as he saw it, very lightly.[56] Primarily, however, there was relief that it was over, and, in any case, matters of far greater importance were being settled at the Congress of Vienna. Late in December 1814 the home secretary, Lord Sidmouth, wrote to his brother Hiley Addington:

> Preliminaries of peace are signed with America. This a great relief, though not in all respects a subject of exultation ... The war was too likely to become more and more unprofitable; and its continuance would have suspended our authority on the Continent of Europe, under circumstances the most critical. The good effects of the peace will soon be felt at Vienna.[57]

---

* Though this American victory came too late to affect the treaty, it created in American minds the belief that the United States had won the war (Bickham, *Weight of Vengeance*, p. 266).

16

Final Victory

The more I hear and see of the different Courts of Europe, the more convinced I am that the King of France is (among the great Powers) the only Sovereign in whom we can have any real confidence. The Emperor of Russia is profligate from vanity and self-sufficiency, if not from principle. The King of Prussia may be a well-meaning man, but he is the dupe of the Emperor of Russia. The Emperor of Austria I believe to be an honest man, but he has a Minister in whom no one can trust ...

– Lord Liverpool, prime minister, to the duke of Wellington, 23 December 1814[1]

The Allied armies finally marched into Paris on 30 March 1814, Alexander, emperor of Russia, and Frederick William of Prussia at the head of their troops.[2] The tsar immediately negotiated with Napoleon, who abdicated on 6 April and was granted the sovereignty of Elba, to which he retired. Lord Castlereagh, the British foreign secretary, Count Klemens von Metternich, the Austrian chancellor, and Baron Karl von Hardenberg, the Prussian chancellor, arrived ten days after the tsar and the king, so they could not reverse this fait accompli. Castlereagh, at least, realized that Elba was dangerously close to the coast of France, but no distant alternative such as the West Indies was available, as the Anglo-American War, which effectively encompassed the Atlantic basin, was only just coming to an end.

The Allies spent two months in Paris negotiating an agreement that would limit French power. Britain achieved its long-sought measure of security from invasion by ensuring that Antwerp and the Scheldt would be governed by an enlarged Holland. 'Our great object is Antwerp,' Lord Bathurst had written to Wellington in 1813. 'We cannot make a secure peace if that place be left in the hands of France . . . you may consider it almost as our *sine quâ non* as far as peace with us is concerned.'[3] Given the military situation, France was treated leniently. It renounced all claims over Holland, Belgium, Germany, Switzerland and Italy.[4] Louis XVIII was installed on the throne. Its frontiers were virtually the same as in 1792 and its colonies were returned, with the exception of Mauritius, Tobago and St Lucia.[5] Austria was to remain dominant in north Italy. Dutch overseas colonies were returned, with the exception of the Cape of Good Hope, which remained in British possession. For the loss of the Cape, Holland was compensated with a payment of £2 million, which was to be spent in erecting fortresses along the new border with France. The Treaty of Paris was signed on 30 May 1814. The larger problems of containing Russian and Prussian ambitions, and what to do with Poland and Saxony, were to be tackled at the meeting of the Allies at the Congress of Vienna, set for 1 July. The first stirrings of German nationalism, excited by the effort to throw off Napoleon, were at this stage barely visible.

For a time, however, the mood lightened. Early in 1814, at the prompting of Castlereagh, the prince regent had invited the Allied sovereigns to visit England, which they did in June. Tsar Alexander and Frederick William of Prussia crossed the Channel in the 74-gun *Impregnable*, escorted by the duke of Clarence, landing at Dover on 6 June. The Emperor Francis of Austria returned to Vienna, but was represented in London by Metternich. In attendance were Count Hardenberg, for Prussia;* the Russian foreign minister, Count Charles Nesselrode; and Alexander's Polish adviser, Prince Adam Czartoryski. The Allied sovereigns were mobbed and cheered by enthusiastic

---

* This was not the first time that Hardenberg had been in London. He was not Prussian, but from Hanover, and had entered the service of George III. In 1778 he had come to London in the hope of becoming the Hanoverian envoy in England, but had to resign because his wife began a scandalous affair with the prince of Wales, now, of course, the prince regent. Hardenberg then entered Prussian service (Zamoyski, *Rites of Peace*, pp. 54–5).

crowds and the tsar was particularly popular. According to Countess Lieven, the Russian ambassador's wife, there were never fewer than 10,000 people outside his hotel, blocking Piccadilly traffic. A sunlit river procession on the Thames in the royal barge, from Whitehall to Woolwich, was accompanied by barges and gigs, and cheering spectators.[6] There were many receptions and long dinners.[7]

Alexander grew weary of all the attention. He snubbed the prince regent, was rude to ministers and saw far too much of the members of the Opposition for the government's taste. He lost British goodwill, thus making it easier for Castlereagh to convince his colleagues of the potential dangers of Russian ambitions.[8] The vain, handsome and charming Metternich was, by contrast, hard-working and diplomatic, and courted the unpopular prince regent. The Austrian chancellor was taken aback by the fashions, manners and customs of London society, which, after a dozen years of separation by war, were now very different from those of Continental countries. He wrote home to his wife that London was more alien than Peking, adding that 'The women are for the most part of great beauty, but their clothes are a fright.'[9]

After three weeks the Allied sovereigns left London and travelled south to Portsmouth, escorted by the prince regent. The party first inspected the ships building and repairing in the dockyard, and then the block mills. Samuel Bentham took centre stage in showing the royal party around, to the annoyance of Simon Goodrich, who had been in charge of the mills for nearly ten years.* The next day the tsar and Frederick William inspected 7,000 troops on Portsdown Hill. *The Times* commented, with some exaggeration, 'Thus has ended the grandest scene perhaps witnessed in this or any other country.' The party then rode on to breakfast with the duke of Richmond at Goodwood, and afterwards to Petworth House to stay the night with the earl of

---

* Bentham took his fourteen-year-old son George, who wrote: 'My father ... though no longer in Office, was privileged as being the chief author of the most important establishments in the Yard, and was officially present among those who attended upon the Sovereigns[; he] had taken my brother, myself and Philip Abbot in the day before – we spent the night in the Office of the Master of the Wood Mills, and awaited in those Mills the Imperial and Royal Party. Alexander, on learning who we were, said some very civil things to us to our great gratification' (Coad, *Block Mills*, pp. 101–2).

Egremont. Next they travelled to Brighton, where the prince regent took his leave; and from there the sovereigns and their accompanying statesmen proceeded to Dover, where they took separate British warships to the Continent.[10] Alexander did not endear himself to the rest of the powers by insisting that the opening of the Congress of Vienna should be put back to 1 October, so that he would have time first to return to Russia.

On 29 June, the ministers of the four great powers each agreed to maintain 75,000 men under arms on the Continent for the duration of the Congress of Vienna, to be used only by joint decision.[11] Britain, with diverse demands on her manpower as usual, found this difficult: 20,000 troops had been sent to the war in America, and more were manning Mediterranean garrisons. In addition, parliament was anxious to reduce expenditure on the army: by the end of 1814, 47,000 men had been demobilized. In the Low Countries 15,000 Hanoverians were retained, but Britain still had only 33,000 on the Continent. An agreement was reached with the Prussians that they would maintain the number of troops by which Britain was short. For the eight months of this arrangement, Britain paid Prussia £355,333, effectively purchasing her manpower contribution.[12]

In London, victory celebrations continued. Lady Sarah Napier reckoned that 'eight hundred thousand souls were collected in and about London for two months, & that it is universally allowed that all went mad.'[13] The climax was the 'Grand National Jubilee' on 1 August. Lavish attractions were erected: in Green Park the 'Temple of Concord' housed 'transparencies';* a funfair was held in Hyde Park; a mock battle was staged on the Serpentine, with boats built at Woolwich Arsenal by Sir William Congreve, who had just succeeded to his father's baronetcy and to his post as comptroller of the Royal Laboratory at Woolwich. The prince regent's patronage ensured that Congreve played a major role in designing these attractions. He and John Nash designed a polygonal, timber-framed ballroom that was

---

* Transparencies were pictures made with translucent paints on materials like calico, linen or oiled paper, and lit from behind by candles. They were often produced in the eighteenth century at times of national rejoicing (Richard D. Altick, *The Shows of London* (London, 1978), p. 95).

erected to the south of Carlton House.* Congreve was also responsible for the fireworks, during which not only was a man killed, but
the Pagoda and 'Rialto' bridge in St James's Park were largely
destroyed by fire.[14] One MP remarked in the Commons that the mon-
uments were 'temporary in the strictest sense of the word since they
seemed to be made for the express purpose of being blown up'.[15]

The crowned heads and statesmen gathered in Vienna on 1 November
1814. The ministers were joined by Charles-Maurice de Talleyrand-
Périgord, now France's foreign minister. Talleyrand had become a
bishop at the age of thirty-seven, but had embraced the revolution.
He had then served Napoleon well, but fell out of favour and kept
his distance from the emperor.[16] He was the natural choice to represent the new Bourbon regime and, because of his cleverness and the
divisions among the Allies, quickly became a strong voice at the negotiating table. Talleyrand joined the Congress at its most stressful point.
Profound disagreements had to be solved over the borders of central
European countries, such as Poland and Saxony, which affected the
balance of power in Europe. A number of smaller nations, notably
Denmark and the states of Italy, also had differences with their neighbours. Britain had settled most of the matters it was most concerned
about in Paris, except for the issue of the abolition of the slave trade.
Pushed on by solid support from British public opinion, Castlereagh
worked hard to get those countries with maritime interests to agree to
abolition: Holland, Denmark and Sweden agreed; France, Portugal
and Spain, fearing that Britain was seeking overseas trade advantages,
refused. The British government would be pressing for this objective
for years to come.

The tsar dominated the Congress, not least because of his complex
personality, a mixture of autocracy and liberalism that made him very
difficult to read. He was convinced that only Russia could bring peace
and stability to Europe, but he was inconsistent and idealistic, and

---

* In 1818 the prince regent ordered 'the grand circular room in the gardens of Carlton
House' to be transported to Woolwich, where it was re-erected with a lead roof and a
central support. It was used to display war trophies and artillery models. Known as
the Woolwich Rotunda, it fulfilled this function until recent years, although at the time
of writing it now lies empty (Crook and Post, *King's Works*, pp. 318–19).

influenced by ideas of mystical religion.[17] The realpolitik was that Alexander had 200,000 troops stationed in Poland. The other great powers feared Russian expansion, and Castlereagh, Metternich and Hardenberg often tried to present a united front against the tsar, who wanted a kingdom of Poland under Russian control. The attempt to curb Russian power, however, failed: Castlereagh had overestimated the leverage that Britain and the other powers possessed. In London, Lord Liverpool and his government were concerned over Castlereagh's prominent role in negotiations over Poland. The politicians in Whitehall saw that Austria and Prussia were considerably weaker than Russia and Lord Bathurst, secretary of state for war, was ordered by the cabinet to write formally to Castlereagh to inform him that Britain would not go to war over central Europe. In this matter, Castlereagh was relying upon his strong financial position, on which the Allies were counting, as well as the fact that Britain's vital interests were not directly affected, both of which gave Britain's view a force and objectivity that those of the other powers lacked.[18]

Prussia's desire to appropriate Saxony, which had fought with France and now had to accept losses, very nearly proved to be the flashpoint of the Congress: the statesmen were unable to see a way around opposing views, and talked readily of renewed war. Negotiation became fraught, the participants exhausted.* In the midst of these complexities, news came on 1 January 1815 of the signing of the Treaty of Ghent, ending the war between Britain and America and strengthening Britain's position further: if it came to it, Britain was now in a position to go to war again. Castlereagh took some distinct risks. He confronted the Prussian negotiator Hardenberg with a secret, signed alliance between Britain, Austria and France, agreed on 3 January, to each put 150,000 troops in the field in the event of any

---

* The Austrian government spent 30 million florins on the Congress and its entertainments, which nearly bankrupted the country. The affairs of the major participants and the exploits of courtesans have become legendary. The dissolute exploits of Charles Stewart became the talk of Vienna, though his stepbrother Castlereagh, accompanied by his wife, was one of the few who was not distracted by the affairs, gossip and continuous parties. By the end of Jan. 1815, the British delegation had consumed 10,000 bottles of wine (Zamoyski, *Rites of Peace*, pp. 298–323; Bew, *Castlereagh*, pp. 373, 375).

attack by Prussia. A shocked Hardenberg backed down, and Prussia accepted only about a third of Saxony. A further month's negotiation drew a series of compromises from Austria and Russia that finally resolved the issue.[19] An agreement on Poland and Saxony was signed on 6 February 1815. By now Liverpool was urging Castlereagh to come home to explain what had been going on to parliament. The foreign secretary was relieved by Wellington, who arrived in Vienna on 3 February, and Castlereagh left for London on 15 February with his stock high, landing at Dover on 3 March. The arguments he presented in the House of Commons won him general support.

Before Castlereagh reached England, Napoleon had escaped from Elba. On 7 March 1815 the dramatic news reached Vienna.* No one knew where he was going. The Congress continued its negotiations, settling less critical matters such as the navigation of international rivers, the borders of Switzerland, details on the Low Countries and the states of Italy.[20] The Treaty of Vienna was finally signed on 9 June 1815.

Inevitably attention turned to military preparations. Relations between the Allies were ragged. Each of the four great powers had kept its armies at 75,000 men as agreed on 29 June 1814, although these troops were dispersed through Europe, positioned not defensively against France but rather against each other. However, under the renewed threat posed by Napoleon, the Allies pulled themselves together. On 13 March they outlawed Napoleon. Then came the news that the troops sent by Louis XVIII to arrest Napoleon had switched their loyalty back to the emperor. Talks in Vienna now became a council of war, held at Wellington's quarters. On 25 March each of the four major powers pledged to put 150,000 men into the field, to enforce the provisions of the treaties of Paris and Vienna, and to place Napoleon 'beyond all possibility' of ruling France. Russia's troops were too far away to be of immediate use, stationed mainly in Poland. Alexander offered to put 200,000 troops in the field with another 200,000 to come, and keep 150,000 in reserve – the British would

---

* When the news reached London on the same day, Lord Bathurst's house near Portland Place had its windows broken, and the same happened the next day to Castlereagh's house in St James's Square. The crowd was protesting at the discussion of the Corn Laws in parliament (Harvey, *Collision of Empires*, p. 175, quoting the *Annual Register* (1815), p. 23).

provide the finance for him to do so. (The Russian minister of finance warned Nesselrode that without British subsidies far greater than those paid in 1814, more war would bankrupt Russia.[21]) But neither Castlereagh nor Wellington wanted a huge Russian army in central Europe again and, in the event, the Russian Army, so critical in central Europe in 1813 and 1814, came nowhere near the fighting in 1815.

The British manpower deficit was calculated at effectively 100,000 men and subsidies needed to flow again to bring men to the battlefield. Troops kept in the field by British subsidies would count towards the British quota, but that did not necessarily mean that those troops would serve under Wellington. Fierce debates ensued with the Prussians over which German troops would fight with the British: they were likely to be men from the north German states, since they feared the power of Prussia. It was fortunate for the British that Wellington was in Vienna, where his political experience and talents were fully exercised in the bargaining for troops. Because of his great prestige, he was appointed to command the combined armies of Britain and the smaller powers, alongside the Prussians.[22]

Regiments were sent the news of Napoleon's escape as soon as it was known in London. Transporting British Army units to Belgium in a hurry was no easy task, with Wellington sending more and more demanding letters to Bathurst in London. By the end of May, Wellington had 36,000 troops, mostly British and the King's German Legion, with his headquarters in Brussels.[23] By June he had gathered a disparate force of nearly 68,000, more German than British, and with a considerable Dutch contingent.* British troops were still being transported across the Channel well into June.†

---

* British troops numbered 24,000, of whom 5,800 were cavalry and 3,000 in the Royal Ordnance in specialist roles. The Hanoverians consisted of 3,300 King's German Legion and 14,500 other troops, while Brunswickers contributed 6,000 and Nassau 2,900. The Dutch numbered 17,200 (Collins, *War and Empire*, p. 359; Davies, *Wellington's Wars*, p. 225).

† An undergroom described the process of offloading horses from a transport on to the beach near Ostend on 1 June: the ship swung forty horses in slings from the yards into the sea in one and a half hours, a rate achievable only after many years of practice, before the ship returned to England for more:

Napoleon gathered an army of 72,000 men and marched on Brussels, meeting Blücher, the senior Prussian general, at Ligny, where the Prussians fell back. On 16 June Wellington fought a defensive action at Quatre Bras against a hesitant Marshal Ney, and then fell back to Waterloo. Wellington skilfully deployed his disparate forces, defending the farmhouse of Hougement on his right in early attacks by the French, which failed. In the middle of the day Napoleon's artillery renewed their fire, but the Allied forces were positioned on a reverse slope, so that little damage was done. The great attack that followed on Wellington's centre nearly succeeded, but the French were stopped by point-blank volleys from British infantry. In the late afternoon Napoleon sent in waves of cavalry, but the squares of German and British infantry held. By six in the evening the French cavalry had given up exhausted, and the final attack by the Imperial Guard failed because Wellington had managed to assemble enough artillery to repel them and they disintegrated. In the end, Waterloo was as much a Prussian victory as it was a British one, for the arrival of Blücher's army swept the French from the field in confusion.[24] It was a desperate battle. The French lost 30,000, the British 15,000 and the Prussians 7,000. An unusually high number of senior British officers were casualties; almost all members of Wellington's staff were killed or wounded in the action.[25] When the prince regent heard the news of the victory, and of those who had fallen among his friends and acquaintances, he was moved to tears.[26]

This bloody battle proved to be the climatic end of hostilities. Napoleon surrendered to the British and was held on the *Bellerophon*, which anchored in Plymouth Sound from late July for eight days; he was

---

We had scarcely got safe on shore before we saw our horses swinging in the air, so that we were obliged to go again into the sea up to our middles to catch them as they came on shore. Two sets of slings were kept in use, so that while one horse was swimming between the ship and the boat having the slings taken off, another was swinging over their heads. It made the horses very fresh after such a long confinement . . . fancy between 20 and 30 ships discharging a somewhat similar cargo to the *Scipio*'s, all on the beach, the luggage thrown together in all directions, numbers of horses running loose . . .

(Chandler, 'Undergroom at War', pp. 217–18)

viewed every evening by a curious British public. On 9 August he sailed in the *Northumberland* from Torbay and after a passage of sixty-seven days reached St Helena. Castlereagh wrote to his stepbrother, Charles Stewart, on 4 December 1815: 'We have received intelligence today of Buonaparte's arrival at St Helena on 22nd October, he was out of sorts on landing.'[27] Behind this laconic irony lay over a dozen years of extreme risk and danger to Britain. After the start of the war in 1803 came a decade of dour struggle, with little to cheer the populace after the victories at Trafalgar in 1805 and San Domingo in 1806. The seizure of the Danish Fleet at Copenhagen in 1807 brought only muted applause because of its doubtful legality, and the successful retrieval of the Portuguese royal family and the Portuguese Fleet in November 1807 hardly seemed like a victory, important though these operations were. The same could be said of the dogged command of Collingwood, skilfully deploying the Mediterranean Fleet, and the efforts of the Baltic Fleet under Saumarez, which enabled trade to flow and military supplies to be delivered.[28]

This was not an age when ministers committed their ideas on long-term policy or strategy to paper.* The long strategy of naval defensive containment, backed up by the training and arming of large swathes of the population, seemed obvious and hardly needed clarification. Britain wanted to take offensive action against France and continuously sought the support of allies. Pitt's early policy of building alliances with those nations in danger of being overwhelmed by France was the correct one and persisted to the end. No single nation could have defeated Napoleonic France. There were many disappointments: before 1812, Napoleon managed to pick off individual countries, and coalitions frequently broke down. He was, after all, rarely bested on the battlefield in central Europe. However, Austria,

---

* Henry Dundas was an exception, for he had a naturally strategic mind. The rapid building of barracks in 1792 bears all the hallmarks of Dundas thinking things through, and all the decisions to do so were taken at his house in Wimbledon. He wrote policy and strategy papers on why Britain needed to trade with, rather than conquer, Spanish America in a long cabinet memorandum of 31 Mar. 1800, and on the potential effects of an escape of the blockaded French Fleet, 14 July 1804 (Hattendorf et al., *British Naval Documents*, pp. 344–50n, 350–51). His final contribution, in the last year of his life, was a long exposition in the Lords on the need to increase naval troop transports, rather than use smaller merchant ships.

34. George Canning in 1810, after his duel with Castlereagh and resignation from the cabinet in October 1809. Thomas Lawrence captures something of Canning's complexity and defiance.

35. (*top*) The *Cumberland* merchant ship engaging four French lugger privateers off Folkestone, 13 June 1811. This spirited action by a lone and damaged merchantman was witnessed from the cliffs near Folkestone, and became a minor sensation.

36. (*above left*) William Windham was a brilliant conversationalist, wit and dilettante, whose ministerial career demonstrated that brains without common sense can be disastrous. He was a lackadaisical secretary at war in the 1790s, but obsessively enthusiastic in his support for the Vendéan rebels in south-west France. His bizarre performance as secretary of state for war and the colonies in the Ministry of All the Talents tried the patience of his ministerial colleagues and gave heart to the opposition.

37. (*above right*) George Rose was a hard-working and devoted follower of Pitt, but a man of limited talents. He was at the centre of public affairs for thirty-five years, including secretary of the Treasury (1783-1801) and treasurer of the navy (1807-18), but to his great regret never achieved cabinet rank.

38. (*top left*) Spencer Perceval took over as prime minister after the death of Lord Portland in late 1809, with a divided cabinet, domestic unrest in the north of England and doubts about the country's ability to finance the Peninsular War. He held the government together at the cost of deep personal unpopularity, and was assassinated in 1812.

39. (*top right*) Lord Mulgrave, foreign secretary from 1805 to 1806, first lord of the Admiralty from 1807 to 1810 and master-general of the ordnance from 1810 to 1817. As first lord, Mulgrave drove through extensive naval reforms.

40. (*above left*) Lord Liverpool (prime minister 1812–27) was awkward, sensitive and querulous, perceiving slights where none were intended, but was also modest, conciliatory and trusted. He patiently handled Wellington's incessant demands from the Peninsula, and made an early, shrewd assessment of the consequences of Napoleon's retreat from Moscow.

41. (*above right*) Lord Castlereagh, secretary of state for war from 1805 to 1806 and 1807 to 1809, foreign secretary from 1812 to 1822, was perhaps the most driven of all the politicians of the era. Characteristically here, Castlereagh looks straight ahead, and with a level and unflinching gaze.

42. (*top*) *The Block House* and (*above*) *Prisoners Baking Their Own Bread* by Captain Durrant, presumably an officer in the militia. Land was purchased in 1796, structures (almost entirely of wood) rapidly erected and the first prisoners of war received in mid 1797. The site eventually covered forty-two acres. Between 1797 and 1814 an estimated 30,000 prisoners of war passed through.

43. (*top*) Antwerp: the launch of the 80-gun *Friedland* on 2 May 1810, watched by Napoleon and the empress, accompanied by the king and queen of Westphalia. It was a great public occasion, attended by thousands, and generated much propaganda, but the *Friedland* never left the Scheldt. At least five other large warships can be seen on the slips standing in frame.

44. (*above*) Fishbourne, Isle of Wight: the launch of the 36-gun frigate *Magicienne*, at Daniel List's Yard, 3 August 1812, with a contrasting lack of ceremony. List built two small brigs and two substantial frigates in this tiny inlet on the north coast of the Isle of Wight. The *Magicienne* was 145 feet long, mounted thirty-six 18-pound guns and had a crew of 264. She served off the coast of Spain before 1815, and subsequently in the East Indies and in the Mediterranean.

45. (*top left*) John Wilson Croker was a voluble and brilliant Irishman, appointed first secretary of the Admiralty in 1809 at twenty-nine. A fluent parliamentary performer, he made his name by forcing from office a senior official who had swindled the government out of substantial sums.

46. (*top right*) John Barrow, second secretary of the Admiralty for forty years (1804–6 and 1807–45). Barrow and Croker worked at the Admiralty together for twenty-one years, and became a powerful team.

47. (*above left*) In 1805, at 38, George Harrison was appointed by Pitt to the new non-political post of assistant secretary in the Treasury. With good sense and a tremendous capacity for work, he served five prime ministers until the end of the war and became a valued adviser to them all.

48. (*above right*) Lord Palmerston *c.* 1806, the year in which he left St John's College, Cambridge. He became an MP and an admiralty commissioner in 1807 and secretary at war in 1809. When he presented his first Army Estimates in early 1810, George Rose commented: 'I never heard statements made with more precision and clearness in the House of Commons.'

49. (*top*) Banquet given by the Corporation of London for the prince regent, the emperor of Russia and the king of Prussia, 18 June 1814. By this time Tsar Alexander had grown weary of attention, and relations among the royal party were tense. His sister, the grand duchess of Russia, who insisted on attending what was to be an all-male occasion, attempted to stop the singing of the National Anthem by threatening to have a nervous fit.

50. (*above*) Fortress and balloon in Green Park, with an army officer, presumably Sir William Congreve the Younger, supervising the setting up of fireworks, 1 August 1814.

51. (*left*) The duke of Wellington in a watercolour study which accurately conveys both his assurance and a degree of vulnerability. Quick-witted, fearless and physically healthy, he understood the virtues of flexibility, knew how to use intelligence and had a formidable grasp of logistical detail. He was, however, never willing to admit fault, and his political masters in London had a hard time with his constant complaints. But Wellington surely knew that he was the only man who could have lost the war in an afternoon.

52. (*below*) The review of the Russian Army in Paris, 10 September 1815. Tsar Alexander designed this great pageant to impress the Allied sovereigns and the duke of Wellington, mounted here with other rulers of European states. The Russians, unscathed by the casualties of Waterloo, fielded 160,000 troops that day, of which 28,000 were cavalry, and 540 guns. A senior British Army officer wrote, 'The sun glittered on their arms, and on the drawn sabres of the cavalry, to a distance that almost appears imaginary.' Another commentator exclaimed, 'Such a scene had never before been seen in Europe, and perhaps will never be seen again.'

Prussia and particularly Russia had large populations that could be offset against this; and, although Britain lacked such an asset, its wealth allowed it to subsidize its allies' armies and effectively purchase the necessary manpower.

After the Battle of Leipzig, the French populace no longer offered Napoleon its unequivocal support. The Napoleonic War had always been a war of manpower attrition, and it was fortunate indeed that the French emperor's miscalculations and spendthrift military gambling had the effect of cutting down his vastly superior resources. He had abandoned his army in Egypt in 1799 and had seen his armies in the Peninsula waste away. The enormous casualties sustained in Russia were followed by huge French losses in Germany in 1813. By 1815 the emperor, though the army was loyal to him, had lost the support of the French people, for the lives of too many young men had been lost in his wars. It has been estimated that the loss of nearly a million represents possibly a higher proportion of the population of France than were killed in the First World War.

Britain, for most of these wars, faced a strategic difficulty in going on to the offensive through what has been called the 'amphibious bottleneck'.[29] The sea gave Britain two advantages. It acted as a defensive shield against invasion and allowed the transport of goods and military stores cheaply and quickly. But the dependence upon wind and weather also made it extremely difficult to transport by sea an army that was large enough to gain ground quickly and achieve an element of surprise. The large amount of tonnage required for shipping horses for cavalry and for hauling wagons for equipment and provisions made for an unwieldy fleet. Those expeditions with over 100,000 tons of transports, such as those to the West Indies in the 1790s and to Walcheren in 1809, proved to be failures, expensive in both lives and money. The complexities of administration and the vagaries of the weather resulted in long delays, and landings on enemy territory often took place at the wrong season of the year. Castlereagh as secretary of state for war tried to create a 'disposable' force to be kept ready for deployment when wanted, but to have forces in reserve was beyond the resources of the country. On the two occasions when speed and success were achieved on the Continent, at Copenhagen in 1807 and the landing by Wellesley's army at Mondego Bay in Portugal in 1808, expedition preparations had already been made, the first by the foresight of Tom Grenville when first lord of the Admiralty, and the second by luck, for the army sent to Portugal had been intended for South America. Very large amphibious expeditions were beyond the administrative capacity of the country. France faced similar difficulties: even Napoleon flinched when his very large army was ready in 1804 and 1805 to invade England, and ultimately it was a risk that the arch-gambler was not prepared to take. Only when the great harbour at Lisbon, a city made safe from the enemy by the Torres Vedras Lines, was able to receive continuous supplies from transports did Britain have a bridgehead on the Continent firm enough to challenge Napoleon. Sending the British Army to the Peninsula in 1808 was politically very unpopular, exacerbated by early defeat and evacuation at Corunna in 1809. But Lisbon was successfully defended. Successive campaigns were fought against the weather and a tenacious French Army, with little quarter given. However, the populations of Spain and Portugal suffered terribly: by one recent estimate a million civilians died.[30]

The slow attrition of Napoleon's forces in the Peninsula developed into a winning strategy. Wellington's force of character and increasing success eventually gained political, then public, support. By his concentration on the defence of Portugal he gave the nation not only a string of victories but also a strategy for conducting the war on land; it was little wonder that decorations and rewards rained down on him. Even then, had Napoleon's ambition not outrun his resources, the British effort might not have been enough. By the time he gathered his enormous invasion force during 1811, his available manpower had reached its limit, for he had to draw troops from other theatres to make up an army. It is striking that Napoleon's fatal reverses occurred at the northern and southern extremes of Europe, in Russia and in the Peninsula, where campaigns were fought beyond the limits of his telegraph system. On the two occasions in 1807 when the British comprehensively outwitted the emperor, the capture of the Danish Fleet at Copenhagen and the evacuation of the Portuguese royal family and Fleet from Lisbon, the action occurred in places beyond his telegraphic reach.

As we have seen throughout the second part of this book, British ministers unsurprisingly suffered long periods of anxiety, particularly in the five years after the Treaty of Tilsit in 1807, when Napoleon was dominant in Europe. These years were less punctuated by adverse military setbacks than those of the first crisis period of 1795–8, but politically and financially they were more dangerous. Britain's Continental allies collapsed in the face of Napoleon's military prowess. The economic blockade proclaimed by Napoleon's Berlin Decrees in November 1806 caused a severe downturn in British trade. In 1807 Napoleon started to build a fleet of what he hoped would become 150 battleships to overwhelm England by sheer force of numbers, using the combined shipbuilding resources drawn from his vanquished opponents all over Europe. The threat of invasion, supported by a new French battle fleet building in Antwerp, led to a continuous and costly year-round British naval blockade off the mouth of the Scheldt, which was maintained for over four years.

The prolonged struggle was not without major British errors: political rivalries and crises, flawed intelligence assessments, overambitious war plans and the appointment of individuals who were clearly not up to the job. William Windham springs most readily to mind, hopelessly ill-suited to the administrative burdens of the office of secretary at war in the 1790s, and, it was said, not often in the office. He blundered about as secretary of state for war in the Talents ministry for thirteen months in 1806 and 1807: anything he put his hand to was doomed to failure. The incompetent sons of George III constituted another millstone around the nation's neck, with the honourable exception of the duke of York.*

Corruption and inefficiency in government persisted, but the humiliation and resignation of Lord Melville in 1806 served as a watershed,

---

* All the royal dukes had been given high military or naval rank and were keen to secure glamorous postings. Aside from the duke of York, only the duke of Kent saw some service, in the West Indies, and in the Maritime Provinces in Canada. During the Peace of Amiens he was governor of Gibraltar. The duke of Clarence, the future William IV, wanted to be commander-in-chief of the Mediterranean Fleet, a possibility of such disastrous implications that ministers kept the ill and exhausted Admiral Collingwood at sea with no leave until his death in 1810 (Bartlett, 'British Army', pp. 42–4; Rodger, *Command of the Ocean*, p. 555).

after which the pace of government reform increased. Under the relentless pressure of a great war, the British government machine had to regenerate itself almost constantly and become more efficient. The parliamentary system itself, so despised by Napoleon, was critical to this improvement, though it was at times a bruising experience for those participating in it. Ancient customs and patronage were sacrificed and sinecures diminished as men of ability rose to the top. The two lengthy parliamentary commissions, of Naval Revision and of Military Enquiry, which reported between 1806 and 1812, exposed corruption in the navy and army, but more tellingly revealed lamentable administrative incompetence and extraordinary delays in financial accounting. Fortunately, the recommendations of the commissions were adopted quickly.[31] Worn-out bureaucrats were retired, and new laws on superannuation were passed. The productivity of the state dockyards increased. Employees were paid promptly and labour disputes dwindled, a contrast with the French Revolutionary War. Technological improvements lessened costs. Relations between government officials and private contractors, governed by an increasingly sophisticated contract system, allowed government technicians and the officials who ran the Treasury, Army Commissariat and Ordnance, Navy, Transport and Victualling boards, together with the officers of the various state yards, to maintain and control quality.

Although contractors who make a profit out of war have never been popular either at the time or with historians, there were many benefits to the British government in this alliance between the state and commerce. Injections of capital and investment were much more easy and, when greater production was needed, as was demanded in the last five years of the war, the British economy surged at the height of what is generally known as the 'Industrial Revolution'. Purchasing of commodities by particular merchants for government use, usually on a grand scale, could be conducted relatively anonymously to avoid price rises, and imported commodities could be transported in neutral ships without difficulty. International merchants operated with daily knowledge of their market, buying or manufacturing with expertise far beyond the capacity of government officials.

The British economy and workforce had to supply increasing quantities of munitions, uniforms and supplies not only for British forces, but for the armies of the countries of Continental Europe that were to rise up against Napoleon and finally defeat him. Austria, Prussia, Russia, Sweden, Spain and Portugal all received critical supplies and money, without which they would not, and indeed could not, have taken up the fight against the French.[32] British manufacturers, shipbuilders, cannon-founders, gunsmiths and City financiers expanded production and distribution far beyond the capacity of the state's dockyards, victualling yards, and munitions and gunpowder factories. The owners of merchant ships chartered their vessels to government, so enabling distant parts of the world to be supplied, and troops to be transported in large numbers for amphibious expeditions. Agricultural contractors of every sort – from farmers, market gardeners, drovers, graziers, cattle and grain merchants to agents and wheat importers – achieved ever-increasing production and supply to fleet and army. All these efforts were possible because of what was, excepting a downturn in 1811 and early 1812, a dynamic, innovative and advanced economy.

Some have described these wars as 'total', judging their intensity, cruelty and scale as 'apocalyptic'.[33] Others regard them more soberly, seeing them rather in terms of the dynastic wars of the eighteenth century.[34] There is no doubt that the wars against France can be described as 'total' in the sense that they were a lengthy contest between two contrasting industrial economies and political systems. The use of wholesale commercial blockades as a central weapon of war prefigured their use in the twentieth century, and had long-term effect: twenty years of the British blockade of once prosperous south-west France left that region in a state of poverty from which it arguably did not recover until the second half of the twentieth century.[35] Britain escaped the ravages of occupation, and its economy was strengthened. Although the national debt was at extraordinarily high levels by 1815, manufacturing and extractive industries such as coal, iron and copper had been stimulated, shipyards were busy, agricultural prices were high and production developed, markets abroad had opened up, and trade had been maintained as a consequence of British control of the seas. The wars with France were as much conflicts between economies and their industrial capacities as were the twentieth-century wars with Germany that followed.[36]

The strategy of defensive containment led, almost by definition, to a long war. Of all the countries hostile to Napoleon, Britain alone fought France and its allies for the full twenty-two years, pausing only during the Peace of Amiens. The major problem, therefore, was the question of national stamina. Could Britain hold out, year after year, against a much more powerful enemy? This was why this period was the most dangerous for Britain. The financial strain in maintaining the war effort, both for the country and its allies, was almost intolerable.[37] But Spencer Perceval's government managed to continue to finance the army in the Peninsula, an all but unrecognized achievement. Perceval was a hardened politician, courageous and honest, who kept his nerve and led a fragile government at the most difficult of times. And at the time, as even the prince regent realized, there seemed no one else who could command a majority in parliament. Cut down by an assassin, Perceval has not received the credit for what he achieved, for he brought the country through a crisis every bit as menacing as that faced by William Pitt, and was famously described by Canning as 'The Pilot Who Weathered the Storm', and is still remembered as such today.[38]

At the centre of the British national effort was parliament. For all its faults, delays and doubts about costs and strategy, it was a better system of waging war than anything that could be mustered by a dictator, although, on the face of it, this would hardly seem to be the case. Between 1799 and 1812, from the years of Napoleon's rise to supreme power in France as first consul to his defeat in Russia, there were six British prime ministers, ten foreign secretaries, seven secretaries of state for war and nine first lords of the Admiralty.[39] But, while Napoleon had the advantages of continuity and speed of decision, he eventually lost a sense of reality. By about 1810 his ministers were telling him only what he wanted to hear. Just at the moment when the British government administration was jolted out of old ways, by getting up-to-date and complete information to parliament so that estimates and policy could be fully formulated and understood, Napoleon disappeared behind a cloud of illusion, ordering ships to be built by men whom he had sent to the army, to be paid for by an income that was disappearing as his control over his vassal states loosened and the Continental System disintegrated.

The British system certainly put great strain on both politicians and government servants. Parliamentary debates in this period of instability were often intense and language violent. The duel between Canning and Castlereagh in 1809 and the assassination of Spencer Perceval in 1812 were the most dramatic moments in a period fraught with drama. Aristocratic ministers, unused to the long hours of administration and opposition in the House, were particularly vulnerable to stress and fatigue, and regular visits for recuperation were made to spa towns such as Bath and Tunbridge Wells. Frequent changes of administration and vituperative debate resulted in tired and inept senior politicians. As war ministers only Pitt, Dundas, Canning, Castlereagh, Perceval and Liverpool passed muster. Among the incompetent must be counted the aged Portland, while none of the Whigs, especially Fox, Windham and Grenville in his later years, rose to the challenge. It was the younger politicians serving as secretaries and officials in the departments under them who provided continuity and strength. The contributions of Huskisson and Herries to managing state finances, of Harrison to the working of the Treasury, of Calvert, Palmerston and Bunbury to the reform the army, of Croker and Barrow to the efficiency of the navy, stand out among many, but certain things were common to all these men: youth, intelligence and formidable industry.

And then there were the twists and turns of the war itself, of which there are many examples that will be known to readers of this book, but that are outside of its immediate scope. Two, however, should be mentioned here. The most unexpected advantage came to Britain by the rising of the people of Madrid against French domination in May 1808, for it solved Britain's strategic problem of getting an army on to the Continent. The army that was sent at short notice was ready at Cork to go to South America, but instead landed in Portugal. It is sobering to reflect that, if this uprising had occurred a few weeks later, that expedition would have departed, and its commander, Arthur Wellesley, might very well have gone on to a relatively obscure career. Then there is the final gamble of Napoleon's escape from Elba. Had the British cabinet lost patience and refused to pay any more subsidies to its Continental allies, Napoleon might not have been defeated. After all the treaties and negotiations that had brought a kind of closure at Vienna, Britain might have withdrawn from Europe.[40] But the only time that an isolationist mood came over the British government was during the Ministry of All the Talents between 1806 and 1807, when Britain abandoned its central European allies. The combination of Grenville's economic caution and Fox's muddle-headed approaches to Napoleon led to a strategic vacuum, and a series of misguided overseas adventures, the purposes of which could only be that the ministry wished to be seen to be doing something. The subsequent Tory governments were both more determined and more clear-sighted, and parliament backed them, voting the necessary funds to continue the struggle.[41]

The historical headlines have been usurped by Napoleon and Wellington, the drama of Waterloo and the Congress of Vienna. The foundations of military victory, though, lay in the industrial capacity of cannon-founders, the expertise of gunsmiths in their machine shops, the diligence of shipbuilders and the makers of ropes, uniforms, gun-carriages and gunpowder, the hard work of those who toiled in the increasingly efficient agricultural sector, the merchant seamen whose ships transported vital stores and food, and the crews of packet ships who provided the means of communication throughout the year. In turn, none of this could have been achieved without the men who signed and passed contracts across tables in government departments, the civil servants who drafted documents and did sums in the backrooms and basements of Whitehall, and the international merchants and dealers who traded in the City. They were all needed as much as the tens of thousands of young soldiers and seamen who resisted, survived and finally overcame the threat from Napoleon.

Aftermath

I am by no means sure that the total destruction of the Emperor Napoleon and his army would be of such benefit to the world; his succession would not fall to Russia or any other continental power, but to that which commands the sea, and whose domination would then be intolerable.

– General Kutuzov, commander-in-chief of the Russian Army, to Colonel Sir Robert Wilson, British combat commissioner to the Allied Armies, when in pursuit of the French Army from Moscow, December 1812[1]

After Waterloo, Britain's military and diplomatic prestige was at a height reached neither before nor since. France was humiliated, occupied by hundreds of thousands of foreign troops, for whose food and accommodation the French government had to pay. The second Treaty of Paris of 20 November 1815 took France back to her 1790 frontiers. Savoy and several frontier fortresses were given up. An indemnity of 700 million francs was added to the costs of the occupying armies. The art treasures that the French had seized during the wars were repatriated: 3,000 statues and more than 2,000 paintings were returned to their former owners. The restored Bourbons were to be fatally weakened by association with this array of failures.[2]

The British armed forces that had contributed to the victory had suffered severe cuts long before the fighting ceased. At what was otherwise a moment for great satisfaction, the backbenchers in parliament, as usual worried about the size of the national debt, asserted themselves and rebelled when the Army Estimates went before the

House in 1816. The government was forced to abolish the property tax, which immediately reduced revenue by 20 per cent.[3] This was the start of a process that eventually led to a shrinking of the role of the state in the economy during the Victorian period, the years of 'laissez-faire' government.[4]

Reductions occurred first in the navy. Warships manned and in commission were cut in 1818 to a sixth of the total in 1814. Warships in commission fell from 713 in 1814 to 121 in 1818. The number of seamen 'borne' dropped by almost half, from a peak of 147,000 in 1813 to just under 79,000 by the end of 1815, a figure that was to fall much further in subsequent years.[5] By 1817 nearly 90 per cent of commissioned naval officers were unemployed and on 'half-pay'. For some, the employment situation hardly improved, which led to widespread suffering. A well-known cartoon of 1825, *A Mid on Half-Pay*, shows a haggard man blacking boots in the street, his midshipman's dirk lying broken in front of him.[6] But Britain had ended the war with over 600,000 tons of large warships, a figure that equalled the combined totals of France, Russia, the Netherlands, Spain, Portugal and the United States.[7] It was ironic that this tonnage was kept largely in reserve; yet the threat of commissioning it over the next forty years, until the advent of the steam warship, gave Britain its pre-eminent position in the world. It was a further irony that the prestige of the navy was not high in 1815, for it had played only a supporting, though vital, role in the last years of the war; this had brought it little glory, in contrast to the period up to the Battle of Trafalgar. Its reputation was not helped by courts martial after the Battle of the Aix Roads in 1809, a squabble between naval officers Admiral Gambier and Captain Thomas Cochrane. Cochrane did his service no favours when he was gaoled for a year in 1814 when found guilty of a stock-market scam.

On the other hand, the prestige of the army was high, not only because of its performance in the Peninsula and at Waterloo, but because of admiration for sacrifices made when success was elusive. Some regiments had suffered sickening losses, both on the Continent and overseas. Two examples can be taken from a long list. The Green Howards served from 1797 to 1819 in Ceylon, where nearly 1,500 had died, a loss of over 7.5 per cent a year from its established strength of 870 men.[8] At the failed assault on Bergen-op-Zoom in March 1814, two major generals and a brigadier were killed, and casualties were a startling 76 per cent of the force of 4,000 men.[9] After 1815 the government kept army numbers higher, and soldiers were discharged at a slower rate than the navy, from 240,000 soldiers in 1815 to 103,000 in 1828.* The militia ballots were ended by the Whig government in 1831; until then Tory governments had been cautious about reducing the means of tackling social disorder.[10]

The Central London offices of the navy and army quickly lost between 20 and 30 per cent of their staff. The Transport Office was abolished in 1817, with the pre-1794 arrangement re-established by returning responsibilities for chartering transports to the Navy Office. Within the army, the Barrack Office and Storekeeper-General's Office disappeared, their functions taken over by the Ordnance Department.[11] The post of commissary-in-chief was likewise abolished. By 1832 the Navy Office itself had been abolished by the Whig government, bringing all aspects of the administration of the navy under the Board of Admiralty. But most of the habits of sound administration established during the wars endured.

The country itself experienced prolonged economic disruption and destitution. Demobilized soldiers and seamen went home to find a much reduced labour market. Government contracts for shipbuilding, cannon and small arms ceased. Victualling contracts shrank dramatically, and lack of demand for naval and military provisions was instrumental in bringing down agricultural prices. The Midlands armaments industry was hit very hard, and the government tried to alleviate hardship there by the Poor Employment Act of 1817, which enabled funding to be advanced to public-works schemes such as canals, bridges and roads.[12] However, it was not effective, and serious violence soon broke out. In December 1816 in London a drunken meeting at Spa Fields in the City ended in an armed attack on the Tower. The 'Blanketeers', out-of-work weavers carrying blankets,

* In 1819, 64,000 men were stationed in Britain and by 1825 that number had fallen to 44,000 (Burroughs, 'Unreformed Army', pp. 162, 164).

marched from Manchester on London but were dispersed. Textile workers in Derbyshire rioted: three were executed and thirty transported. By far the worst, and best remembered, was the very large meeting at St Peter's Fields in Manchester in 1819, which came to hear the radical Henry Hunt speak on the need for universal suffrage and annual parliaments. Both regular army and volunteers were used to disperse the crowd on the orders of the magistrates. Eleven civilians were killed and 400 injured; it became known as the Peterloo Massacre.[13] The movement for parliamentary reform had stayed in the background during the war, but once the war was over it came to the fore and, in combination with the friction over the protectionist Corn Laws and the argument about Catholic Emancipation, set the political agenda for the 1820s, culminating in the Great Reform Act of 1832.

The Tories stayed in power for another fifteen years. Lord Liverpool remained prime minister until he had a stroke in 1827 and died the following year, aged fifty-eight. His old Christ Church friend George Canning succeeded him, but he, too, died after only 119 days in office, in August 1827, to be succeeded by Wellington, who was already a member of the cabinet as master-general of the Ordnance. William Huskisson's financial acumen ensured that he achieved cabinet rank, but his career was cut short in 1830 at the opening of the Liverpool-to-Manchester railway, when he accidentally fell into the path of Stephenson's 'Rocket'. After the end of the war, Lord Mulgrave declined quickly. By 1820 he was described as 'in the state both in look and power of a Man aged 90 though 64. He is so feeble that he cannot write a letter, and in his motion rather shuffles and creeps than walks.'[14]

Many of the younger politicians who had been so instrumental during the Napoleonic War rose to the top. In 1815 Robert Peel was chief secretary in Ireland, Lord Palmerston was secretary at war and Lord Aberdeen was present at the Congress of Vienna: all were future prime ministers. Henry Goulburn, one of the negotiators of the treaty of Ghent with the Americans, was to become chancellor of the Exchequer twice and was briefly home secretary. John Charles Herries, the commissary-in-chief until the abolition of the post in 1817, became chancellor of the Exchequer, secretary at war and president of the Board of Control.

The majority of the leading Opposition politicians were long lived.* The exception was Richard Brinsley Sheridan, harried by creditors, who died in poverty in 1816. Charles Grey, from his brief period as foreign secretary in 1807, was in Opposition for twenty-three years, but became prime minister when the Tory party split and Wellington resigned in 1830. Grey's brief premiership saw the passing of the Great Reform Act, but he retired in 1834 to Howick in Northumberland, living until 1845. Lord Grenville played little part in public life after he had led the Ministry of All the Talents, although he was made chancellor of Oxford University in 1809, an office he held until 1834. His hard-fought election at Oxford was managed by William Wickham, whom Grenville as foreign secretary had made his spymaster in the French Revolutionary War, and who now was a frequent visitor to Grenville's house at Dropmore Park in Buckinghamshire. Both died well into their seventies, Grenville in 1834 and Wickham in 1840, the latter's achievements totally forgotten.[15] The two Whig grandee bibliophiles had long, comfortable retirements after public service. Lord Spencer lived until 1834, Tom Grenville until 1846: Spencer's 40,000 books, notable for volumes on the evolution of printing during the fifteenth and sixteenth centuries, were sold in 1892 to the John Rylands Library in Manchester. Grenville reasoned that since the great part of his 20,000 books had been purchased out of sinecure income, he should leave them to the British Museum.

Admiralty officials, too, lived long. After his tempestuous spell as first lord, Lord St Vincent returned to sea during the Talents ministry, his final active command coming to an end in April 1807, at the age of seventy-two, but he had an active retirement which included staying in the south of France in his last years, until he died sixteen years later in March 1823.[16] William Marsden, first secretary, retired in 1807 at the age of fifty-three, when, as he commented, 'with the alterations in my habits of life, my health rapidly improved'.[17] His fears of

---

* William Windham had died in 1810 in bizarre circumstances. He was returning home late one night in July 1809 when he saw a fire in Conduit Street, where a friend had a nearby house containing a valuable library. He and others hurriedly emptied the books from the house, but in doing so he fell and bruised his hip, from which a tumour developed. He died after an operation to remove it (Rosebery, *Windham*, Vol. II, pp. 369–70).

a shortened life caused by the pressures of office were unrealized: he lived until he was eighty-one, dying in 1836. His successor as second secretary in 1804, John Barrow, continued long in office, until 1845. His working relationship with his senior, the first secretary, John Wilson Croker, in office until 1830, developed into a remarkable friendship. Barrow's eldest son married Croker's adopted daughter, and both families shared a house at West Moseley near Windsor that Croker bought in 1828.[18] Both pursued their literary interests before and after retirement, contributing to the *Quarterly Review*. Barrow wrote biographies of naval figures still useful and readable today, and his role in promoting the exploration undertaken by the Victorian navy constituted a career in itself. As second secretary he was largely responsible for commissioning warships for surveying and exploration purposes, particularly to the North-West Passage and Africa. He was an original member of the Royal Geographical Society, founded in 1830.[19]

The army administrators enjoyed honourable retirements. The duke of York died in 1827, survived by his elder brother, who had become George IV in 1820 and lived until 1830. General David Dundas, the soldier of the old school, who came out of retirement to take the place of the duke as commander-in-chief in 1809, died peacefully at Chelsea Hospital in 1820, aged eighty-five. Lieutenant-General Sir Harry Calvert remained adjutant-general until 1820, and could look back on a remarkable twenty-one reforming years in office. He died in 1826. Henry Bunbury, the military undersecretary who had combined so well with Herries to ensure smooth supplies to the Peninsula, and now promoted to major general with a KCB, retired from the army in 1832 and lived a comfortable rural life until his death in 1860. The third of those young officials, George Harrison, assistant secretary at the Treasury, was knighted, stayed in office until 1826, and lived until 1841.

The inventors fared less well. Samuel Bentham felt that he had been shouldered out of the navy, as indeed he had, and that his achievements had been insufficiently recognized. In 1814 he went to live in France, but returned to England in 1826. He died in London in 1830. His protégé Marc Isambard Brunel, whose talents had created the block mills at Portsmouth, poured his money into a factory in Battersea that produced boots for the army, mechanized on the same lines as the block mills, a logical direction for his talents. Peace in 1815, however, left him with a large stock of unsold boots and debts. After unsuccessfully petitioning Palmerston in the War Office for some relief, and suffering further financial loss because of the failure of his bank, Brunel was arrested and thrown into a debtors' prison in 1821. When it became known that Brunel was in correspondence with the Russian government seeking employment, powerful figures, including Wellington, intervened and his debts were paid by government. His career of invention and design continued, and he died in 1849, aged eighty-one.[20] William Congreve became involved in a financial scandal in 1826, after which he fled to France, where he died in penury in 1828 and was buried in the Protestant Cemetery in Toulouse. The French gave Congreve a funeral with full military honours.

These tales were, however, nothing to the tragedy of Lord Castlereagh, who became Lord Londonderry after the death of his father in 1821. The following year, depressed, unpopular and overworked, the foreign secretary cut his throat at his home at Cray in Kent. The cause of this suicide has generated much speculation – theories include blackmail, the appearance of the tertiary stage of syphilis, the latent symptoms of severe gout or even rabies – but there can be no doubting the contribution of overwhelming political pressure and a consequent well-documented mental debilitation. His obsessive work ethic was remarked upon by Wilberforce: 'If he had suffered his mind to enjoy such occasional remissions, it is highly probable that the strings would never have snapped as they did, from over-tension.'[21] Castlereagh's mind was officially pronounced deranged, thus enabling him as a suicide to be buried in consecrated ground. He was so unpopular that fellow ministers feared that disturbances might occur during a public funeral, but it passed off peacefully, and the foreign secretary was buried next to his mentor Pitt in Westminster Abbey.*

*

* Political pressure and overwork were the primary factors in the suicides of two of Castlereagh's most honourable political opponents, Samuel Romilly and Samuel Whitbread, who took their lives in 1815 and 1818 respectively. Both these deaths were known to have affected Castlereagh. Lord Ellenbrough suffered a similar severe mental decline before his death in 1818 (Bew, *Castlereagh*, pp. 538–57). The retrospective diagnosis of Castlereagh's possible syphilis is laid out in Hunt, *The Duel*, pp. 177–85.

By the efforts of all these men, and the nation as a whole, Britain had survived two decades of war, and was now safe from invasion. Its economy was powerful and growing, while those of the Continental powers were wasted and weak. The eyes of the government and governed had been on the Continent, but the most significant long-term change brought about by the Revolutionary and Napoleonic wars was a vast increase in British domination of the seas. Without planning strategically to do so, Britain now controlled the world's safest harbours, and developed naval bases and garrisons to guard them. In 1792 Gibraltar, Halifax in Nova Scotia, English Harbour in Antigua and Kingston in Jamaica had long been in British possession, and Sydney in Australia had been settled from 1788. By 1814 Britain had created a network of fourteen naval bases, including Malta, Corfu and Trincomalee in Ceylon.[22] Gibraltar, appropriated over a hundred years before in 1704, had no great harbour, nor had the Cape of Good Hope, both now British; but they were of such strategic importance that they, too, were secured, fortified and defended. Before the French Revolutionary War Britain had owned twenty-six colonies; in 1816 that figure was forty-three.[23] The 'empire', as it increasingly came to be called, was one of the unforeseen consequences of success in resisting the long siege of Britain by Napoleon.[24]

Appendix 1

Officials in Government Departments Involved in the War 1793–1815

(*) Member of Parliament concurrent with office. Naval and military ranks are those reached at the end of the period of office. Only the chairmen of junior boards are included in this appendix as space is limited, and commissioners on these boards are omitted.

The numbers employed in the offices and the total salary bill for the years 1797, 1805, 1810 and 1815 are taken from *Parliamentary Papers*, 1830–31 (92): *Public Offices Employment*.

The responsibilities and relationships between senior and subordinate government boards were not as simple as this appendix might imply. The Transport Board, for instance, is here positioned under the Admiralty, but the many masters of the chairmen of the Transport Board have been noted in Chapters 4 and 7. The position of the secretary at war was similarly complex, particularly in relation to finance and the Treasury. To give only one example, he was not responsible for barrack expenditure, yet he appointed all the deputy barrack masters-general and barrack masters (Commission of Military Enquiry, *Sixth Report*, p. 278). Anomalies had developed over time, and patronage and the right of appointment were not given up lightly.

TREASURY (Downing Street)

First Lord of the Treasury and Chancellor of the Exchequer

Salary 1797–1815: £5,000

William Pitt*	FLT: 26 Dec. 1783–21 Mar. 1801
	Chancellor: 19 Dec. 1783–14 Mar. 1801
Henry Addington*	FLT: 21 Mar. 1801–16 May 1804
	Chancellor: 14 Mar. 1801–10 May 1804

William Pitt*   FLT: 16 May 1804–23 Jan. 1806 (died in office)
                       Chancellor: 10 May 1804–23 Jan. 1806
Lord Ellenborough   Chancellor: 25 Jan.–5 Feb. 1806
William Wyndham Grenville, Baron Grenville
                       FLT: 10 Feb. 1806–31 Mar. 1807
Lord Henry Petty*   Chancellor: 5 Feb. 1806–26 Mar. 1807
William Cavendish-Bentinck, duke of Portland
                       FLT: 31 Mar. 1807–30 Oct. 1809 (died in office)
Spencer Perceval*   Chancellor: 26 Mar. 1807–11 May 1812
                       FLT: 6 Dec. 1809–11 May 1812 (assassinated)
Lord Ellenborough   Chancellor: 12–23 May 1812
Robert Banks Jenkinson, earl of Liverpool
                       FLT: 16 June 1812–20 Apr. 1827
Nicholas Vansittart*   Chancellor: 23 May 1812–31 Jan. 1823

Treasury Commissioners

Four serving at any one time. Salaries 1797–1815: £1,220

Edward James Eliot* 26 Dec. 1783–22 June 1793
Richard Wellesley, earl of Mornington* 19 Sept. 1786–3 Aug. 1797
John Jeffreys Pratt, Viscount Bayham (from 18 Apr. 1794 Earl Camden)
    10 Aug. 1789–7 May 1794
Richard Hopkins* 20 June 1791–3 Feb. 1797
John Thomas Townshend* 22 June 1793–28 July 1800
John Smyth* 7 May 1794–5 July 1802
Sylvester Douglas* (from 30 Nov. 1800 Lord Glenbervie) 3 Feb. 1797–
    9 Dec. 1800
Charles Small Pybus* 3 Aug. 1797–18 Nov. 1803
Lord Granville Leveson Gower* 28 July 1800–21 Mar. 1801
John Hiley Addington* 9 Dec. 1800–21 Mar. 1801
Nathaniel Bond* 21 Mar. 1801–16 May 1804
Lord George Thynne* 21 Mar. 1801–16 May 1804
John Hiley Addington* 5 July 1802–18 Nov. 1803
William Brodrick* 18 Nov. 1803–16 May 1804
Edward Golding* 18 Nov. 1803–16 May 1804
George Percy, Lord Lovaine* 16 May 1804–10 Feb. 1806

James Edward Harris, Viscount Fitzharris* 16 May 1804–10 Feb. 1806
Charles Long* 16 May 1804–10 Feb. 1806
Henry Wellesley* 16 May–7 Aug. 1804
George Spencer, marquess of Blandford 7 Aug. 1804–10 Feb. 1806
John Charles Spencer, Viscount Althorp 10 Feb. 1806–31 Mar. 1807
William Wickham* 10 Feb. 1806–31 Mar. 1807
John Courtenay* 10 Feb. 1806–31 Mar. 1807
William Henry Cavendish Bentinck, marquess of Titchfield* 31 Mar.–
    16 Sept. 1807
William Eliot* 31 Mar. 1807–6 Jan. 1812
William Sturges Bourne* 31 Mar. 1807–6 Dec. 1807
John Foster* 16 Sept. 1807–6 Jan. 1812
Richard Ryder* 16 Sept.–2 Dec. 1807
William Brodrick* 2 Dec. 1807–16 June 1812
John Otway Cuffe, earl of Desart* 6 Dec. 1809–26 June 1810
Snowden Barne* 6 Dec. 1809–5 Oct. 1812
Berkeley Paget* 26 June 1810–13 June 1826
William Wellesley-Pole* 6 Jan.–16 June 1812
Richard Wellesley* 6 Jan.–16 June 1812
Nicholas Vansittart* 16 June 1812–10 Feb. 1823
William Fitzgerald* 5 Oct. 1812–7 Jan. 1817
Frederick John Robinson* 5 Oct. 1812–20 Dec. 1813
William Lowther* (later Viscount Lowther) 25 Nov. 1813–30 Apr. 1827
Charles Grant* 20 Dec. 1813–25 Mar. 1819

Senior (Parliamentary) Secretary

Salary 1797: £6,000. 1805–15: £8,000

George Rose* 27 Dec. 1783–24 Mar. 1801
John Hiley Addington* 24 Mar. 1801–5 July 1802
Nicholas Vansittart* 8 July 1802–21 May 1804
William Sturges Bourne* 21 May 1804–10 Feb. 1806
Nicholas Vansittart* 10 Feb. 1806–1 Apr. 1807
Henry Wellesley* 1 Apr. 1807–5 Apr. 1809
Charles Arbuthnot* 5 Apr. 1809–7 Feb. 1823

Junior (Financial) Secretary

Salary 1797: £6,000. Salary 1805–15: £8,000

Charles Long* 26 Feb. 1791–9 Apr. 1801
Nicholas Vansittart* 9 Apr. 1801–8 July 1802
John Sargent* 8 July 1802–21 May 1804
William Huskisson* 21 May 1804–10 Feb. 1806
John King* 10 Feb.–2 Sept. 1806
William Henry Fremantle* 2 Sept. 1806–1 Apr. 1807
William Huskisson* 1 Apr. 1807–8 Dec. 1809
Richard Wharton* 8 Dec. 1809–7 Jan. 1814
Stephen Rumbold Lushington* 7 Jan. 1814–7 Feb. 1823

Assistant Secretary

Salary 1810: £3,000. 1815: £3,500

George Harrison 19 Aug. 1805–7 Apr. 1826

COMPTROLLERS OF ARMY ACCOUNTS
(Great Scotland Yard)

Salary £1,500 until 1806, then £2,000

Sir John Dick & William Molleson 31 July 1783–9 Jan. 1794
Sir John Dick & John Martin Leakes 9 Jan. 1794–9 Oct. 1802
John Martin Leakes & John Erskine 9 Oct. 1802–7 Oct. 1806
John Martin Leakes, John Erskine & John King 7 Oct. 1806–31 July 1811
John Erskine, John King & John Charles Herries 31 July 1811–24 Oct.
   1811
John Erskine, John King & John Drinkwater 24 Oct. 1811–3 July 1815

Comptroller of Army Accounts Office

1797: 13 clerks/£4,470
1805: 13/£5,520
1810: 30/£11,798
1815: 31/£12,065

COMMISSARIAT (No. 35, Great George Street)
Commissary-in-Chief

Ireland and the East Indies excepted

Salary 1810: £2,411. 1815: £2,379

> Thomas Ashton Coffin 1808–10
> Colonel Willoughby Gordon 1810–Oct. 1811
> John Charles Herries 1 Oct. 1811–16

By 1814, 136 Commissaries-General and 218 Deputy Commissaries-General with armies and in garrisons across the world

Treasury officials and clerks

1797: 142 clerks/£46,154 (of which Commissariat: 85 clerks/£14,341)
1805: 228/£73,450 (161/£33,744)
1810: 154/£67,684 (79/£17,177)
1815: 154/£78,638 (72/£20,403)

FOREIGN OFFICE
Secretary of State

Salary 1797–1815: £6,000

> William Wyndham Grenville, Baron Grenville 29 Apr. 1791–20 Feb. 1801
> Robert Banks Jenkinson, Baron Hawkesbury 20 Feb. 1801–12 May 1804
> Dudley Ryder, Baron Harrowby 12 May 1804–11 Jan. 1805 (retired due
>   to accident)
> Henry Phipps, Earl Mulgrave 11 Jan. 1805–7 Feb. 1806
> Charles James Fox* 7 Feb.–13 Sept. 1806 (died in office)
> Charles Grey, Viscount Howick 24 Sept. 1806–25 Mar. 1807
> George Canning* 25 Mar. 1807–11 Oct. 1809
> Henry Bathurst, Earl Bathurst 11 Oct.–6 Dec. 1809
> Richard Wellesley, Marquess Wellesley 6 Dec. 1809–28 Feb. 1812
> Robert Stewart, Viscount Castlereagh* 28 Feb. 1812–12 Aug. 1822
>   (marquess of Londonderry from 6 Apr. 1821)

Undersecretaries

Two in post concurrently. Salary 1797: £3,000. 1805: £4,500. 1810: £4,000. 1815: £4,500

James Bland Burges* 22 Aug. 1789–16 Oct. 1795
George Aust 20 Feb. 1790–5 Jan. 1796
George Hammond 16 Oct. 1795–20 Feb. 1806
George Canning* 5 Jan. 1796–1 Apr. 1799
John Hookham Frere* 1 Apr. 1799–25 Sept. 1800
Edward Fisher 25 Sept. 1800–20 Feb. 1801
Frederick William Hervey* 20 Feb. 1801–5 Aug. 1803 (Earl of Bristol from 8 July 1803)
Charles Arbuthnot 8 Nov. 1803–5 June 1804
William Eliot* 5 June 1804–25 Jan. 1805
Robert Ward* 25 Jan. 1805–7 Feb. 1806
Sir Francis Vincent 20 Feb. 1806–30 Mar. 1807
George Walpole* 20 Feb. 1806–30 Mar. 1807
George Hammond 30 Mar. 1807–11 Nov. 1809
James Edward Harris, Viscount Fitzharris* 30 Mar.–19 Aug. 1807
Charles Bagot* 19 Aug. 1807–16 Oct. 1809
William Richard Hamilton 16 Oct. 1809–29 Jan. 1822
Charles Culling Smith 13 Dec. 1809–27 Feb. 1812
Edward Cooke 28 Feb. 1812–5 July 1817

Foreign Office officials and clerks

1797: 24 clerks/£12,393
1805: 26/£17,860
1810: 31/£20,469
1815: 34/£23,592

Ambassador to France

(Diplomatic relations suspended 1792–1801)

Charles Whitworth, Baron Whitworth 10 Sept. 1802–12 May 1803
(Diplomatic relations suspended 1803–14)
Field Marshal Arthur Wellesley, duke of Wellington 8 Aug. 1814–18 Jan. 1815

Ambassador to Russia

Sir Charles, later Baron, Whitworth 29 Nov. 1788–6 June 1800
(Diplomatic relations suspended 1800–1801)
  Alleyne Fitzherbert, Baron St Helens 24 Apr. 1801–15 Aug. 1802
  Admiral Sir John Borlase Warren 5 Sept. 1802–9 Aug. 1804
  Lord Granville Leveson Gower 10 Aug. 1804–27 Jan. 1807
  Alexander Hamilton, marquis of Douglas and Clydesdale 27 Jan.–
    10 June 1807
  Lord Granville Leveson-Gower 12 June 1807–9 Nov. 1807
(Diplomatic relations suspended 1807–12)
  Edward Thornton, Minister Plenipotentiary 1812
  William Schaw Cathcart, Earl Cathcart 25 July 1812–5 July 1820

Ambassador to Austria

Sir Morton Frederick Eden 5 Feb. 1793–May 1794, 13 Dec. 1794–
    7 Aug. 1799
  Gilbert Elliot, Baron Minto 7 Aug. 1799–16 Sept. 1801
  Sir Arthur Paget 16 Sept. 1801–18 June 1806
  George Augustus Herbert, earl of Pembroke 14 May–3 Sept. 1807
  Benjamin Bathurst 14 Feb. 1809–? Oct. 1809 (disappeared, presumed
    murdered)
(Diplomatic relations suspended 1809–13)
  George Hamilton Gordon, earl of Aberdeen 29 July 1813–25 July 1814
  Lieutenant-General Charles Stewart 25 July 1814–29 Dec. 1822

Ambassador to Prussia

James Harris, Baron Malmesbury 24 Dec. 1793–6 Nov. 1794
  Lord Henry John Spencer 3 Jan.–3 July 1795 (died in office)
  Thomas Bruce, earl of Elgin, Nov. 1795–25 Jan. 1799
  Thomas Grenville, Extraordinary Mission 17 Feb.–31 Aug. 1799
  John Joshua Proby, earl of Carysfort 12 July 1800–24 Oct. 1801
  Francis James Jackson 15 Nov. 1802–2 May 1806
  Dudley Ryder, Baron Harrowby, 24 Oct. 1805–8 Jan. 1806
  (Diplomatic relations suspended 1806–7)
  Lt-General John Hely Hutchinson, Baron Hutchinson 23 Dec. 1806–
    20 July 1807

(Diplomatic relations suspended 1807–13)
    Major General Sir Charles Stewart 22 Apr. 1813–June 1814

Ambassador to Spain

    Alleyne Fitzherbert, Baron St Helens 9 June 1790–18 Jan. 1794
    John Stuart, earl of Bute 11 June 1795–10 Oct. 1796
(Diplomatic relations suspended 1796–1802)
    John Hookham Frere 14 Nov. 1802–22 July 1804
(Diplomatic relations suspended 1804–8)
    John Hookham Frere 19 Oct. 1808–24 Aug. 1809
    Richard Wellesley, Marquess Wellesley 11 Aug.–8 Nov. 1809
    Henry Wellesley 28 Feb. 1810–8 Apr. 1821

Ambassador to Portugal

    Robert Walpole 1772–16 June 1800
    John Hookham Frere Dec. 1800–19 Oct. 1802
    Lord Robert Stephen Fitzgerald 25 Nov. 1802–22 May 1806
    John Jervis, earl of St Vincent 26 Aug.–7 Oct. 1806
    Colonel James St Clair Erskine, earl of Rosslyn 26–7 Oct. 1806
(Portuguese Prince Regent to Brazil 1808: Percy Clinton Sydney Smythe,
Viscount Strangford, Envoy Extraordinary in Rio de Janeiro 23 July
1808–8 Apr. 1815)
    John Charles Villiers 20 Dec. 1808–11 Feb. 1810
    Charles Stuart 11 Feb. 1810–2 Apr. 1814
    Thomas Sydenham 7 July–23 July 1814
    George Canning 4 Dec. 1814–18 Apr. 1816

Envoy Extraordinary and Minister Plenipotentiary to Sardinia

John Trevor 16 June 1789–6 May 1797

Minister Plenipotentiary to Genoa and Parma

Francis Drake 15 Aug. 1793–4 Dec. 1795

HOME OFFICE (Whitehall)

The Home Office had responsibility for the Colonies from 1782 to Aug. 1801

Secretary of State

Salary 1797–1815: £6,000

Henry Dundas* 8 June 1791–11 July 1794
William Henry Cavendish Bentinck, duke of Portland 11 July 1794–
30 July 1801
Thomas, Lord Pelham 30 July 1801–17 Aug. 1803
Charles Philip Yorke* 17 Aug. 1803–11 May 1804
Robert Banks Jenkinson, Baron Hawkesbury 11 May 1804–1806
George John, Earl Spencer 5 Feb. 1806–25 Mar. 1807
Robert Banks Jenkinson, Baron Hawkesbury 25 Mar. 1807–1 Nov.
1809 (succ. as earl of Liverpool 17 Dec. 1808)
Richard Ryder* 1 Nov. 1809–11 June 1812
Henry Addington, Viscount Sidmouth 11 June 1812–17 Jan. 1822

Undersecretary

Salary 1797: £3,000. 1805: £4,500. 1810: £4,500. 1815: £4,569

Evan Nepean 1 Apr. 1782–11 July 1794
John King 3 Dec. 1791–16 Mar. 1806
John Beckett 18 Feb. 1806–28 June 1817

Non-Permanent (later Parliamentary) Undersecretary

Salary 1797: £3,000. 1805: £4,500. 1810: £4,500. 1815: £4,569

Thomas Brodrick* 17 July 1794–Jan. 1795 (died in office)
Post vacant 14 Jan. 1795–13 Mar. 1796
Charles Greville 14 Mar. 1796–1 Mar. 1798
William Wickham 1 Mar. 1798–5 Jan. 1801

Edward Finch Hatton 19 Feb.–18 Aug. 1801
Sir George Shee 18 Aug. 1801–17 Aug. 1803
Reginald Pole-Carew 17 Aug. 1803–29 May 1804
John Henry Smyth* 27 July 1804–5 Feb. 1806
Charles Watkin Williams Wynn* 5 Feb. 1806–5 Apr. 1807
Charles Cecil Cope Jenkinson* 30 Nov. 1807–1 Nov. 1809
Henry Goulburn* 27 Feb. 1810–20 Aug. 1812
John Hiley Addington* 20 Aug. 1812–22 Apr. 1822

Home Office officials and clerks

1797: 26/£14,770
1805: 32/£17,535
1810: 31/£20,772
1815: 31/£22,323

Superintendent, Alien Office (responsible to the Home Secretary)

Salary 1797–1801: £500

William Huskisson Jan. 1793–July 1794
William Wickham July 1794–5 Jan. 1801

ADMIRALTY OFFICE (Whitehall)
First Lord of the Admiralty

Salary 1797–1805: £3,000. 1812: £5,000. 1815: £11,000

John Pitt, earl of Chatham 16 July 1788–19 Dec. 1794
George John, Earl Spencer 19 Dec. 1794–19 Feb. 1801
John Jervis, Earl St Vincent 19 Feb. 1801–15 May 1804
Henry Dundas, Viscount Melville 15 May 1804–2 May 1805
Charles Middleton, Lord Barham 2 May 1805–10 Feb. 1806
Charles Grey* (Viscount Howick, 11 Apr. 1806) 10 Feb. 1806–
    29 Sept. 1806
Thomas Grenville* 29 Sept. 1806–6 Apr. 1807
Henry Phipps, Earl Mulgrave 6 Apr. 1807–4 May 1810

Charles Philip Yorke* 4 May 1810–25 Mar. 1812
Robert Saunders Dundas, second Viscount Melville 25 Mar.
1812–2 May 1827

Naval Commissioners of the Admiralty

Seven naval and civilian commissioners served at any one time. Salaries 1797, 1805: £9,000. 1810, 1815: £11,000

Admiral (Samuel) Viscount Hood* 16 July 1788–7 Mar. 1795
Vice-Admiral Sir Alan Gardner* 19 Jan. 1790–7 Mar. 1795
Vice-Admiral Philip Affleck 26 Apr. 1793–7 Mar. 1795
Vice-Admiral Sir Charles Middleton 12 May 1794–20 Nov. 1795
Vice-Admiral James Gambier 7 Mar. 1795–19 Feb. 1801
Rear-Admiral Lord Hugh Seymour 7 Mar. 1795–10 Sept. 1798
Vice-Admiral William Young* 20 Nov. 1795–19 Feb. 1801
Vice-Admiral Robert Man 10 Sept. 1798–19 Feb. 1801
Rear-Admiral Sir Thomas Troubridge* 19 Feb. 1801–15 May 1804
Rear-Admiral John Markham* 19 Feb. 1801–15 May 1804
Admiral James Gambier 15 May 1804–10 Feb. 1806
Captain Sir Harry Burrard Neale 15 May–3 Sept. 1804
Admiral Sir John Colpoys 15 May 1804–2 May 1805
Admiral Philip Patton 15 May 1804–10 Feb. 1806
Captain (George Stewart) Lord Galloway* (later Lord Garlies) 2 May
1805–10 Feb. 1806
Rear-Admiral John Markham* 10 Feb. 1806–6 Apr. 1807
Admiral Sir Charles Morice Pole* 10 Feb.–23 Oct. 1806
Captain Sir Harry Burrard Neale* 10 Feb. 1806–6 Apr. 1807
Captain Thomas Fremantle* 23 Oct. 1806–6 Apr. 1807
Admiral (James) Lord Gambier 6 Apr. 1807–9 May 1808
Vice-Admiral Sir Richard Bickerton* 6 Apr. 1807–25 Mar. 1812
Captain William Johnstone Hope* 6 Apr. 1807–30 Mar. 1809
Vice-Admiral William Domett 9 May 1808–23 Oct. 1813
Captain Robert Moorsom 30 Mar. 1809–3 July 1810
Vice-Admiral Sir Joseph Sydney Yorke* 3 July 1810–2 Apr. 1818
Rear-Admiral George Johnstone Hope 25 Mar. 1812–18 May 1813
Rear-Admiral Lord Henry Paulet 18 May 1813–24 May 1816
Rear-Admiral Sir George Johnstone Hope 23 Oct. 1813–2 Apr. 1818

Civil Commissioners of the Admiralty

Salaries as for naval commissioners

Charles George Perceval* (later Lord Arden) 31 Dec. 1783–19 Feb. 1801
John Thomas Townshend* 12 Aug. 1789–26 Apr. 1793
John Smyth* 27 June 1791–12 May 1794
Charles Small Pybus* 27 June 1791–25 July 1797
Sir Philip Stephens* 7 Mar. 1795–23 Oct. 1806
Thomas Wallace* 25 July 1797–10 July 1800
William Eliot* 10 July 1800–17 Jan. 1804
James Adams* 19 Feb. 1801–15 May 1804
William Garthshore* 19 Feb. 1801–17 Jan. 1804
William Dickinson* 15 May 1804–10 Feb. 1806
Sir Evan Nepean* 13 Sept. 1804–10 Feb. 1806
Lord William Russell* 10 Feb. 1806–6 Apr. 1807
William Edwardes, Lord Kensington* 10 Feb. 1806–6 Apr. 1807
William Frankland* 23 Oct. 1806–6 Apr. 1807
Robert Ward* 6 Apr. 1807–17 June 1811
Henry John Temple, Viscount Palmerston* 6 Apr. 1807–26 Oct. 1809
James Buller* 6 Apr. 1807–25 Mar. 1812
William Lowther* 24 Nov. 1809–3 July 1810
Frederick John Robinson* 3 July 1810–5 Oct. 1812
Horatio, Lord Walpole* 17 June 1811–5 Oct. 1812
William Dundas* 25 Mar. 1812–23 Aug. 1814
Sir George Warrender* 5 Oct. 1812–8 Feb. 1822
John Osborn* 5 Oct. 1812–16 Feb. 1824
Barrington Pope Blachford* 23 Aug. 1814–14 May 1816

Secretary to the Board of Admiralty

Salary 1787: £1,600. 1805–10: £6,000. 1815: £4,500

Philip Stephens* 18 June 1763–3 Mar. 1795
Evan Nepean* 3 Mar. 1795–20 Jan. 1804
William Marsden 21 Jan. 1804–24 June 1807
William Wellesley-Pole* 24 June 1807–12 Oct. 1809
John Wilson Croker* 12 Oct. 1809–29 Nov. 1830

Second Secretary

Salary 1787: £1,600. 1805–10: £6,000. 1815: £4,500

John Ibbetson 13 Jan. 1783–2 Mar. 1795
William Marsden 3 Mar. 1795–21 Jan. 1804
Benjamin Tucker 21 Jan.–21 May 1804
John Barrow 22 May 1804–9 Feb. 1806
Benjamin Tucker 10 Feb. 1806–5 Apr. 1807
John Barrow 9 Apr. 1807–28 Jan. 1845

Inspector-General of Naval Works

Samuel Bentham 25 Mar. 1796–28 Oct. 1807

Architect and Engineer of Naval Works

Edward Holl 3 Jan. 1804–28 Oct. 1807

Hydrographer

Alexander Dalrymple 13 Aug. 1795–28 May 1808
Thomas Hurd 28 May 1808–29 Apr. 1823

Inspector of Telegraphs

George Roebuck 23 Apr. 1796–23 Aug. 1816

Admiralty officials and clerks

1797: 45/£14,140
1805: 54/£24,390
1810: 59/£30,660
1815: 65/£32,059

NAVY PAY OFFICE (Somerset Place)
Treasurer of the Navy

Salary 1797–1815: £4,000

    Henry Dundas* 5 Jan. 1784–2 June 1800
    Dudley Ryder* 2 June 1800–21 Nov. 1801
    Charles Bragge-Bathurst* 21 Nov. 1801–3 June 1803
    George Tierney* 3 June 1803–29 May 1804
    George Canning* 29 May 1804–22 Feb. 1806
    Richard Brinsley Sheridan* 22 Feb. 1806–15 Apr. 1807
    George Rose* 15 Apr. 1807–13 Jan. 1818

Navy Pay Office officials and clerks

1797: 73/£16,435
1805: 104/£24,539
1810: 116/£29,319
1815: 120/£32,866

TRANSPORT OFFICE
(Dorset Court, Cannon Row, Westminster)

Chairman:
    Captain Hugh Cloberry Christian RN 1794–5
    Captain Rupert George RN 1795–1817

Commissioners:
    Captain James Bowen RN 28 June 1803–16
    Ambrose Serle 1794–1817

Secretary:
    Alexander M'Cleay

Transport Office, Medical Department

1810: 42 clerks/£9,180
1815: 41/£9,680

NAVY OFFICE (Somerset Place)
Comptroller of the Navy

Salary 1797: £10,700. 1805: £11,200. 1810: £13,200. 1815: £12,200

Captain Sir Henry Martin 29 Mar. 1790–1 Aug. 1794 (died in post)
Captain Sir Andrew Snape Hamond* 25 Sept. 1794–3 Mar. 1806
Captain Henry Nicholls 3 Mar. 1806–20 June 1806
Captain (Rear-Admiral 1809) Sir Thomas Boulden Thompson* 20 June
    1806–24 Feb. 1816

Surveyors of the Navy

Salary 1797: £10,700. 1805: £11,200. 1810: £13,200. 1815: £12,200

Sir John Henslow 11 Dec. 1784–24 June 1806 (Knt. 20 Mar. 1793)
Sir William Rule 11 Feb. 1793–21 June 1813 (Knt. 27 June 1794)
Sir Henry Peake 20 June 1806–25 Feb. 1822 (Knt. 25 June 1814)
Joseph Tucker 14 June 1813–1 Mar. 1831
Sir Robert Seppings 14 June 1813–25 July 1829 (Knt. 17 Aug. 1819)

Civil Architect and Engineer

Samuel Bentham 3 Dec. 1808–25 Dec. 1812

Surveyor of Buildings

Edward Holl 28 Nov. 1812–2 Nov. 1823

Assistant Surveyor of Buildings

Edward Holl 28 Dec. 1804–28 Nov. 1812

Navy Office officials and clerks

1797: 160/£32,890
1805: 171/£34,860
1810: 234/£54,910
1815: 225/£56,180

VICTUALLING OFFICE (Somerset Place)

Salary 1797: £1,045. 1810: £1,200

Chairman:
        George Cherry 10 Sept. 1785–27 Mar. 1799
        John Marsh 27 Mar. 1799–3 Dec. 1808
        Captain John Clarke Searle RN 3 Dec. 1808–20 Feb. 1822

Deputy Chairman:
        George Phillips Towry 4 Nov. 1803–12 Mar. 1817 (died in post)

Victualling Office officials and clerks

1797: 88/£12,582
1805: 112/£22,178
1810: 132/£28,288
1815: 168/£35,060

SICK AND HURT OFFICE (Somerset Place)

Office abolished 1806; functions transferred to the Transport Office

Commissioners

Salary: £500 and £65 for house rent

  Robert Blair 1790–1804
  Sir Gilbert Blane 1790–1804
  John Harness (transferred to the Transport Board in 1806)

Inspectors of Naval and Prison Hospitals

Dr Andrew Baird 1800–1806
Dr John Weir 1800–1806

OFFICE OF THE SECRETARY OF STATE FOR WAR
(Downing Street)

War and the Colonies from August 1801

Secretary of State

Salary 1797: £2,000. 1805–15: £6,000

Henry Dundas* 11 July 1794–17 Mar. 1801
Robert Hobart, Lord Hobart 17 Mar. 1801–14 May 1804
John Jeffreys Pratt, second Earl Camden 14 May 1804–10 July 1805
Robert Stewart, Viscount Castlereagh* 10 July 1805–5 Feb. 1806
William Windham* 5 Feb. 1806–25 Mar. 1807
Robert Stewart, Viscount Castlereagh* 25 Mar. 1807–1 Nov. 1809
Robert Banks Jenkinson, Lord Liverpool* 1 Nov. 1809–11 June 1812
Henry Bathurst, Earl Bathurst 11 June 1812–30 Apr. 1827

Undersecretary

Salary 1797: £1,500. 1805: £2,000. 1810: £4,000. 1815: £5,000

Evan Nepean* 11 July 1794–1 Mar. 1795
William Huskisson* 1 Mar. 1795–18 Mar. 1801
John Sullivan* 18 Mar. 1801–15 May 1804
Edward Cooke 15 May 1804–16 Feb. 1806
Sir George Shee 16 Feb. 1806–25 Mar. 1807
Edward Cooke 25 Mar. 1807–1 Nov. 1809
Charles Cecil Cope Jenkinson* 2 Nov. 1809–10 June 1810
Robert Peel* 10 June 1810–4 Aug. 1812
Henry Goulburn* 20 Aug. 1812–11 Dec. 1821

Military Undersecretary

Sir James Cockburn 27 Nov. 1806–25 Mar. 1807
Brigadier-General Charles Stewart* 25 Mar. 1807–1 May 1809
Frederick John Robinson* 1 May–1 Nov. 1809
Colonel Henry Bunbury 1 Nov. 1809–5 July 1816

War and Colonial Office officials and clerks

1797: 12/£6,850
1805: 16/£12,540
1810: 21/£16,265
1815: 21/£18,394

COMMANDER-IN-CHIEF'S OFFICE (Horse Guards)

General Lord Amherst Jan. 1793–Feb. 1795
Field Marshal Frederick, duke of York 13 Feb. 1795–18 Mar. 1809
General Sir David Dundas 18 Mar. 1809–26 May 1811
Field Marshal Frederick, duke of York 26 May 1811–28

Commander-in-Chief's officials and clerks

1797: 16/£2,558
1805: 27/£6,202
1810: 29/£6,516
1815: 29/£8,091

Military Secretary

Colonel Robert Brownrigg 1795–1803
Colonel William Clinton 1803–4
Lieutenant-Colonel James Willoughby Gordon 1804–9
Major General Sir Henry Torrens 1809–20

Adjutant-General

Lieutenant-General Sir William Fawcett 1781–99
Lieutenant-General Harry Calvert 9 Jan. 1799–25 Mar. 1820

Inspector General of Recruiting

1807 post abolished; duties to Adjutant-General

Major General Henry Fox 21 Oct. 1795–July 1799
Major General George Hewett 1803–Aug. 1804
Major General John Whitelocke 22 Nov. 1804–Mar. 1807

Quartermaster-General

Colonel George Morrison 1761–96
Lieutenant-General David Dundas 8 Nov. 1796–15 Mar. 1803
Major General Sir Robert Brownrigg 1803–8
Major General John Willoughby Gordon 1809–15

WAR OFFICE (Duke Street, Westminster)
Secretary at War

Salary 1797–1815: £2,480

Sir George Yonge* Dec. 1783–July 1794
William Windham* July 1794–Feb. 1801
Charles Philip Yorke* Feb. 1801–Aug. 1803
Charles Bragge 17 Aug. 1803–May 1804
William Dundas* May 1804–Feb. 1806
General Richard Fitzpatrick* Feb. 1806–Mar. 1807
General Sir James Murray Pulteney* Mar. 1807–June 1809
Lord Granville Leveson Gower* July–Oct. 1809
Henry John Temple, Viscount Palmerston Oct. 1809–May 1828

War Office officials and clerks

1797: 58/£36,617
1805: 127/£31,500
1810: 183/£46,776
1815: 208/£59,837

ARMY PAY OFFICE (Whitehall)

Joint Paymasters of the Forces

Salary 1797–1815: £4,000

Dudley Ryder* & Thomas Steele* 17 Mar. 1791–5 July 1800
Thomas Steele* & George Canning* 5 July 1800–26 Mar. 1801
Thomas Steele* & Sylvester Douglas, Baron Glenbervie* 26 Mar.
    1801–3 Jan. 1803
Thomas Steele* & John Hiley Addington* 3 Jan. 1803–7 July 1804
George Rose* & Lord Charles Somerset* 7 July 1804–17 Feb. 1806
Richard Temple* & Lord John Townshend* 17 Feb. 1806–4 Apr. 1807
Charles Long* & Lord Charles Somerset* 4 Apr. 1807–26 Nov. 1813
Charles Long* & Frederick John Robinson* 26 Nov. 1813–9 Aug. 1817

Army Pay Office officials and clerks

1797: 24/£11,340
1805: 41/£15,338
1810: 76/£21,388
1815: 81/£22,295

BARRACK MASTER-GENERAL (Spring Gardens)

Major General Oliver De Lancey 1792–1804
Lieutenant-General George Hewett Nov. 1804–6

Commission for Auditing Lt-General De Lancey's Accounts

Colonel Charles Herries 1814
William Bragge 1814

Comptroller of the Barrack Department

Osbourne Markham 1815

ARMY MEDICAL BOARD (No. 5, Berkeley Street, Piccadilly)

Physician-General:

> Sir Clifton Wintringham 1793–4
> Sir Lucas Pepys 1794–Feb. 1810

Surgeon-General:

> John Hunter 1790–Oct. 1793
> John Gunning 1794–98
> Thomas Keate 1798–Feb. 1810

Inspector-General of Regimental Infirmaries:

> Thomas Keate 1793–8
> John Rush 1798–1801

Inspector-General of Army Hospitals:

> Francis Knight 1801–Feb. 1810

Director-General:

> John Weir 1810–15
> Sir James McGrigor Aug. 1815–51

Principal Inspectors:

> Theodore Gordon 1810–?
> Charles Kerr 1810–?

ORDNANCE OFFICE (Tower of London and Pall Mall)

Master-General of the Ordnance

Salary 1793: £1,500. 1815: £3,000

> General Charles Lennox, duke of Richmond 5 Jan. 1784–23 Feb. 1795
> General Charles Cornwallis, first Marquess Cornwallis 23 Feb. 1795–
> 28 Aug. 1801
> General John Pitt, earl of Chatham 28 Aug. 1801–14 Feb. 1806

General Francis Rawdon-Hastings, earl of Moira 14 Feb. 1806–4 Apr. 1807
General John Pitt, earl of Chatham 4 Apr. 1807–5 May 1810
General Henry Phipps, Earl Mulgrave 5 May 1810–1 Jan. 1819

Lieutenant-General

Salary 1793: £1,100. 1815: £1,500

General Sir William Howe 6 May 1782–22 Nov. 1804
General Sir Thomas Trigge 22 Nov. 1804–11 Jan. 1814 (died in post)
Lieutenant-General Sir Hildebrand Oakes 1814–23

BOARD OF ORDNANCE
Surveyor-General

Captain George Berkeley* RN 1789–95
Colonel Alexander Ross 1795–1804
James Hadden 1804–10
Captain Robert Moorsom* RN 3 July 1810–Mar. 1820

Clerk of the Ordnance

Salary 1793: £600. 1815: £800

Gibbs Crawfurd* 1 May 1784–13 Oct. 1793 (died in post)
John Sargent* 11 Feb. 1794–30 June 1802
William Wellesley-Pole* 30 June 1802–22 Feb. 1806
John Calcraft* 22 Feb. 1806–7 Apr. 1807
William Wellesley-Pole* 7 Apr. 1807–29 July 1807
Cropley Ashley Cooper* 29 July 1807–14 June 1811
Robert Ward* 14 June 1811–29 Apr. 1823

Principal Storekeeper

Salary 1793: £500. 1815: £700

John Aldridge* 1 Mar. 1784–16 May 1795 (died in post)
Mark Singleton* 1 July 1795–22 Feb. 1806
John McMahon* 22 Feb. 1806–7 Apr. 1807
Mark Singleton* 7 Apr. 1807–8 July 1823

Treasurer

William Smith 12 Jan. 1784–13 Oct. 1803 (died in post)
Joseph Hunt Nov. 1803–Feb. 1806
Alexander Davison 20 Feb. 1806–7 Apr. 1807
Joseph Hunt* 7 Apr. 1807–30 Jan. 1810
Thomas Alcock 30 Jan. 1810–20 June 1818

Clerk of Deliveries

Salary 1793: £500. 1815: £700

Thomas Baillie 1 Mar. 1784–17 May 1802
Joseph Hunt 17 May 1802–10 Jan. 1804
Cropley Ashley Cooper* 10 Jan. 1804–12 Mar. 1806
James Martin Lloyd* 12 Mar. 1806–7 Apr. 1807
Cropley Ashley Cooper* 7 Apr.–29 July 1807
Thomas Thoroton 29 July 1807–31 Oct. 1812
Edmund Phipps* 31 Oct. 1812–1830

Secretary of the Board of Ordnance

Augustus Rogers 1794
Robert H. Crew 1794–1815

Inspector of Artillery and Superintendent of the Royal Brass Foundry, Woolwich

General Sir Thomas Blomefield 1780–24 Dec. 1822 (died in office)

Comptroller of the Royal Laboratory at Woolwich

Lieutenant-General Sir William Congreve 1789–1814 (died in office)
Sir William Congreve 1814–28

Inspector of Ordnance Shipping

Captain Thomas Dickinson RN 1781–1815

Inspector of Small Arms, Birmingham

Lieutenant-Colonel James Miller 1804–?

Ordnance Office officials and clerks

1797: 353/£46,031
1805: 606/£95,505
1810: 815/£140,237
1815: 886/£177,553

DUBLIN CASTLE
Viceroy/Lord Lieutenant

John Fane, earl of Westmorland 24 Oct. 1789–13 Dec. 1794
William Wentworth Fitzwilliam, second Earl Fitzwilliam 13 Dec.
　1794–13 Mar. 1795
John Jeffreys Pratt, Earl Camden 13 Mar. 1795–14 June 1798
General Charles Cornwallis, Marquis Cornwallis 14 June 1798–27 Apr.
　1801
Philip Yorke, earl of Hardwicke 27 Apr. 1801–12 Mar. 1806

Edward Clive, first Earl Powis 21 Nov. 1805 (did not go to Ireland)
John Russell, duke of Bedford 12 Mar. 1806–1 Apr. 1807
Charles Lennox, duke of Richmond 1 Apr. 1807–3 June 1813
Charles Whitworth, Viscount (Earl from 25 Nov. 1815) Whitworth
    3 June 1813–17 Sept. 1817

Chief Secretary

Salary 1797–1815: £4,153

Robert Hobart* 16 Apr. 1789–15 Dec. 1793
Sylvester Douglas* 16 Dec. 1793–12 Dec. 1794
George Damer, Viscount Milton 13 Dec. 1794–12 Mar. 1795
Thomas Pelham* 13 Mar. 1795–2 Nov. 1798
Robert Stewart, Viscount Castlereagh 3 Nov. 1798–24 May 1801
Charles Abbot* 25 May 1801–12 Feb. 1802
William Wickham* 13 Feb. 1802–5 Feb. 1804
Sir Evan Nepean* 6 Feb. 1804–22 Mar. 1805
Nicholas Vansittart* 23 Mar. –20 Sept. 1805
Charles Long* 21 Sept. 1805–27 Mar. 1806
William Elliot* 28 Mar. 1806–18 Apr. 1807
Sir Arthur Wellesley* 19 Apr. 1807–12 Apr. 1809
Robert Saunders Dundas* 13 Apr. –17 Oct. 1809
William Wellesley-Pole* 18 Oct. 1809–3 Aug. 1812
Robert Peel* 4 Aug. 1812–3 Aug. 1818

Undersecretary

Salary 1794–1805: £1,305. 1810–15: £1,846

Sackville Hamilton 7 Feb. 1780–6 Feb. 1795
Lodge Evans Morres 7 Feb. 1795–14 May 1795
Sackville Hamilton 15 May 1795–5 June 1796
Edward Cooke 6 June 1796–20 Oct. 1801
Alexander Marsden 21 Oct. 1801–7 Sept. 1806
James Trail 8 Sept. 1806–5 Sept. 1808
Charles Saxton (Bart 11 Nov. 1808) 6 Sept. 1808–4 Oct. 1812
William Gregory 5 Oct. 1812–1 Jan. 1831

Irish government officials and clerks

1797: 23/£11,496
1805: 23/£13,621
1810: 23/£12,596
1815: 25/£12,460

IRISH ARMY
Commander-in-Chief

Lieutenant-General Robert Cunninghame 1793–6
Lieutenant-General Henry Lawes Luttrell, second earl of Carhampton
    Oct. 1796–Nov. 1797
Lieutenant-General Sir Ralph Abercromby Dec. 1797–Mar. 1798
Lieutenant-General Gerard Lake 25 Apr.–20 June 1798
General Charles, Marquis Cornwallis 20 June 1798–27 Apr. 1801

Commander of the Forces

General Sir William Meadows 1801–3
Lieutenant-General Henry Fox 9 May–20 Oct. 1803
Lieutenant-General William Schaw Cathcart 20 Oct. 1803–1805
Lieutenant-General John Floyd 1805
General Charles Stanhope, earl of Harrington, Oct. 1805–Jan. 1812
General Sir John Hope 1812–13
General Sir George Hewett Dec. 1813–16

Irish Army officials and clerks

    1797: 29/£3,335

Including Commissariat

    1805: 1,090/£49,137
    1810: 1,064/£50,537
    1815: 259/£28,453

BOARD OF TRADE (Committee of the Privy Council for Trade and Plantations)

President

No remuneration

Charles Jenkinson, Lord Hawkesbury 23 Aug. 1786–6 June 1804 (cr. earl of Liverpool, 1 June 1796)

James Graham, duke of Montrose 6 June 1804–5 Feb. 1806

William Eden, Lord Auckland 5 Feb. 1806–26 Mar. 1807

Henry Bathurst, Earl Bathurst 26 Mar. 1807–29 Sept. 1812

Richard le Poer Trench, earl of Clancarty 29 Sept. 1812–24 Jan. 1818

Vice President

Dudley Ryder* 20 Oct. 1790–18 Nov. 1801

Sylvester Douglas, Lord Glenbervie* 18 Nov. 1801–8 Feb. 1804

Nathaniel Bond* 8 Feb.–6 June 1804

George Rose* 6 June 1804–5 Feb. 1806

Richard Grenville, Earl Temple* 5 Feb. 1806–30 Mar. 1807

George Rose* 30 Mar. 1807–29 Sept. 1812

Frederick John Robinson* 29 Sept. 1812–24 Jan. 1818

Board of Trade officials and clerks

1797: 19/£3,928

1805: 20/£5,790

1810: 20/£5,061

1815: 19/£5,835

INDIA BOARD OF CONTROL

President

Henry Dundas* June 1793–25 Apr. 1801

George Legge, Viscount Lewisham 25 Apr. 1801–6 July 1802

Robert Stewart, Viscount Castlereagh* 6 July 1802–11 Feb. 1806
Gilbert Elliot, earl of Minto 11 Feb.–15 July 1806
Thomas Grenville* 15 July–30 Sept. 1806
George Tierney* 30 Sept. 1806–4 Apr. 1807
Robert Saunders Dundas* 4 Apr. 1807–11 July 1809
Dudley Ryder, earl of Harrowby 11 July–7 Nov. 1809
Robert Saunders Dundas* (Viscount Melville, 29 May 1811) 7 Nov. 1809–4 Apr. 1812
Robert Hobart, earl of Buckinghamshire 4 Apr. 1812–4 June 1816

Secretary

Henry Beaufoy* 10 May 1791–3 July 1793
William Brodrick* 3 July 1793–19 Nov. 1803
Benjamin Hobhouse* 19 Nov. 1803–22 May 1804
George Holford* 22 May 1804–14 Feb. 1806
Thomas Creevey* 14 Feb. 1806–8 Feb. 1807
George Holford* 8 Feb. 1807–6 Jan. 1810
Sir Patrick Murray* 6 Jan. 1810–14 Mar. 1812
John Bruce* 14 Mar. 1812–20 Aug. 1812
Thomas Courtenay* 20 Aug. 1812–2 May 1829

GENERAL POST OFFICE (Lombard Street)
Joint Postmaster-General

Salary 1797–1815: £5,000

Lord Walsingham & earl of Chesterfield 13 Mar. 1790–28 July 1794
Earl of Chesterfield & earl of Leicester 28 July 1794–1 Mar. 1798
Earl of Leicester & Lord Auckland 1 Mar. 1798–27 Feb. 1799
Lord Auckland & Lord Gower 27 Feb. 1799–31 Mar. 1801
Lord Auckland & Lord Spencer 31 Mar. 1801–19 July 1804
Lord Spencer & duke of Montrose 19 July 1804–20 Feb. 1806
Robert Hobart, earl of Buckinghamshire & earl of Carysfort 20 Feb. 1806–5 May 1807
Earl of Sandwich & earl of Chichester 5 May 1807–6 June 1814
Earl of Chichester alone 6 June–30 Sept. 1814
Earl of Chichester & earl of Clancarty 30 Sept. 1814–6 Apr. 1816

Secretary

Salary 1797: £1,400. 1805–15: £1,200

Anthony Todd Jan. 1768–June 1798
Francis Freeling June 1798–July 1836

Inspector of Packets

J. Bennett Bennot 1791–1814

Post Office officials and clerks

1797: 957/£54,030
1805: 1,063/£65,998
1810: 1,129/£73,167
1815: 1,214/£83,380

SOURCES

Ackroyd et al., *Advancing with the Army*; *Army List*; Bindoff et al., *British Diplomatic Representatives 1789–1852*; Cole, *Arming the Navy*; Collinge, *Navy Board Officials 1660–1832* and *Foreign Office Officials 1782–1870*; Ferguson, 'The Army in Ireland'; Glover, *Peninsular Preparation*; Gregory and Stevenson, *Britain in the Eighteenth Century*; Institute of Historical Research, 'Officeholders in Modern Britain', www.history.ac.uk; Joyce, *History of the Post Office*; Judd, *Members of Parliament 1734–1832*; Lloyd and Coulter, *Medicine and the Navy*, Vol. III, pp. 4–5; Moody, Martin and Byrne, *A New History of Ireland*, Vol. IX; Sainty, *Treasury Officials 1660–1870*, *Officials of the Board of Trade 1660–1870*, *Admiralty Officials 1660–1870*, *Home Office Officials 1782–1870*, *Colonial Office Officials 1794–1870*; Thorne, *History of Parliament 1780–1820*; Watson, *Reign of George III*; *Parliamentary Papers, 1830–31* (92): *Public Offices Employment*, 'Number of Persons employed, and of the Pay or Salaries granted to such Persons in all Public Offices or Departments, and in the Year 1797, and in the Years 1805, 1810, 1815 and 1819; showing the Increase in each of those Years, as compared with 1797'.

Appendix 2

*Reports of Parliamentary Commissions and Enquiries
Relating to the Army and Navy 1780–1812*

COMMITTEE ON PUBLIC ACCOUNTS

**Reports of the commissioners appointed to examine, take and state the
Public Accounts of the Kingdom
Fifteen reports, 1780–87***

Commissioners

Thomas Anguish (equity lawyer; accountant-general of the Court of
 Chancery; died 1786)

Arthur Piggott (previously agent in Grenada)

Richard Neave (director of the Bank of England, 1763–1811; governor,
 1783–5)

Samuel Beachcroft (director of the Bank of England, 1760–73, 1777–96;
 governor, 1775–7)

George Drummond

William Roe ('provincial man of business from Bristol'; later on Board of
 Customs, 1788–1819)

General Sir Guy Carleton (former governor of Quebec; commander-in-chief,
 America)

Office: Office of Accounts, Surrey Street; Bell Yard

---

* *House of Commons Sessional Papers of the Eighteenth Century*, Sheila Lambert
(ed.), 2 vols. (Wilmington, Delaware, 1975); Torrance, 'Social Class', pp. 59–60, 68, 76.

REPORTS

1781

Third Treasurer of the Navy, completed 6 March

Fourth Paymasters-General of the Forces, completed 9 April

Fifth Richard Rigby, current Paymaster-General of the Forces, completed 28 November

1782

Sixth Treasurer of the Navy Pay Office and Pay Office of the Army, completed 11 February

Seventh Extraordinary Services of the Army in North America, completed 18 June

1783

Eighth Treasurer of the Navy and Auditors of Account, completed 23 January

Ninth Paymaster-General of the Forces, completed 31 March

Tenth Army Accounts in the Pay Office: Widows' Pensions and Chelsea Hospital, completed 2 July

1784

Twelfth Treasurer of the Ordnance, completed 11 June

COMMISSION ON FEES

Reports of the commissioners appointed by Act 25 Geo. III, c. 19, to enquire into the Fees, Gratuities, Perquisites and Emoluments, which are or have been lately received into the several Public Offices therein mentioned Reports, 1786–88*

Commissioners

Sir John Dick (comptroller of army accounts)
William Molleson (former comptroller of army accounts)

* *Parliamentary Papers: Commons Reports*, 1806.

Francis Baring (MP; banker; chairman of the East India Company, 1792–3; baronetcy, 1793)

REPORTS

1786

First　　Secretaries of State, completed 11 April
Second　Treasury, completed 20 June

1787

Third　　Admiralty, completed 27 December

1788

Fourth　　Treasurer of the Navy, completed 10 January
Fifth　　　The Commissioners of the Navy, completed 14 February
Sixth　　　The Dockyards, completed 10 March
Seventh　The Sick and Hurt Office, completed 20 March
Eighth　　Victualling Office, completed 17 April
Ninth　　　Naval and Victualling Departments at Foreign or Distant Ports, completed 1 May
Tenth　　　Post Office, completed 30 June

All reports ordered to be printed 15 July 1806

COMMISSION ON NAVAL TIMBER

Reports of the commissioners appointed to enquire into the state and condition of the woods, forests and land revenues of the Crown Reports, 1787–93*

Commissioners

Rear-Admiral Sir Charles Middleton (comptroller of Navy Board, 7 August 1778–29 March 1790; Admiralty Board commissioner, 12 May 1794–20 November 1795; first lord of the Admiralty, as Lord Barham, 2 May 1805–10 February 1806)

*　*House of Commons Journal*, 1787–93; *Eleventh Report*, 1792, pp. 264–374; Albion, *Forests and Sea Power*, p. 439.

John Call (MP; baronetcy, July 1791)
John Fordyce ((1735–1809) secretary to the commission; surveyor-general of Crown Lands, 1793–1809)

Office: Land Revenue Office, Scotland Yard

REPORTS

Eleventh   On how His Majesty's Navy may be better supplied with Timber, completed 13 February 1792

SELECT COMMITTEE ON FINANCE

Reports from the Select Committee on Finance
Thirty-six reports, 1797–8*

Chairman

Charles Abbot (MP)

Committee members

Henry Bankes (MP)
Dudley Ryder (MP)

REPORTS: COLLECTION OF THE PUBLIC REVENUE

1797

Seventh   Post Office, completed 19 July

REPORTS: EXPENDITURE AND AUDITING ACCOUNTS

1797

Seventeenth   Admiralty Board, Navy Board, Navy Pay Office, Marine Pay Office, completed 19 July
Eighteenth   Transport Office, completed 19 July

---

* *Parliamentary Papers: Commons Reports, 1797–8.*

Nineteenth Secretary at War, Comptrollers of Army Accounts, Paymaster-General, completed 19 July
Twentieth Barrack Office, completed 19 July
Twenty-first Office of Ordnance, completed 19 July

REPORTS: EXPENDITURE

1798

Thirty-first Admiralty, Dockyards and Transports
Thirty-second Victualling Office
Thirty-third Sick and Wounded Seamen
Thirty-fourth Chatham Chest, Greenwich Hospital and Chelsea Hospital
Thirty-fifth Army Expenditure
Thirty-sixth Secretary at War, Judge Advocate General, Commissary-General of Musters, the Military Governments of Great Britain

COMMISSION OF NAVAL ENQUIRY

Reports of the commissioners appointed by Act 43 Geo. III, to enquire and examine into any Irregularities, Frauds or Abuses, which are or have been practised by Persons employed in the several Naval Departments, etc. Reports, 1803–6*

Commissioners

Vice-Admiral Charles Morice Pole (MP)
Ewan Law (MP; lawyer)
John Ford (lawyer)
Captain Henry Nicholls, RN (comptroller of navy, 3 March–20 June 1806; later Admiral Sir Henry Nicholls)
William Mackworth Praed (serjeant-at-law)

---

* *Parliamentary Papers: Commons Reports*, 1803–6; most of these reports are printed in *Parliamentary Debates*; Albion, *Forest and Sea Power*, pp. 439–40.

Secretary

John Williams (Navy Board clerk; subsequently appointed by Thomas
    Grenville to be clerk of the cheque, Sheerness, 6 February 1807)

Office: Great George Street

REPORTS

1803

First	Naval Storekeepers at Jamaica, printed 12 May
Second	Chatham Chest, printed 6 June
Third	Block contract, Coopers Contract, printed 13 June
Fourth	Prize Agency, printed 18 July
Fifth	Sixpenny Office, printed 10 August

1804

Sixth	Plymouth and Woolwich Dockyards, printed 2 May
Seventh	Naval Hospital at East Stonehouse: *Le Caton* Hospital Ship, printed 11 July
Eighth	Victualling Department, Plymouth: Embezzlement of the King's Casks, printed 16 July

1805

Ninth	Receipt and Issue of Stores at Plymouth Yard, printed 16 January
Tenth	The Office of the Treasurer of His Majesty's Navy, printed 13 February
Eleventh	The Issue of Navy Bills for the purpose of Raising Money; Loss arising from the mode of paying the Interest of Navy and Transport Bills; Money impressed by the Navy Board for Secret Naval Service, printed 11 March

1806

Twelfth	Purchases of Hemp, Masts and Fir Timber on commission by Mr Andrew Lindegren, for the service of His Majesty's Navy from 1795 to 1799; Transfer of Contracts; and also Observations, by way of a supplement to the First Report

of the Commissioners of Naval Enquiry on the Memorial of
the Principal Officers and Commissioners of His Majesty's
Navy, in answer to that Report, printed 22 January

Thirteenth Contracts for Victualling Sick Prisoners of War, printed 15 May

Fourteenth Royal Hospital at Greenwich, printed 30 June

COMMISSION OF NAVAL REVISION

**Reports of the commissioners appointed in January 1805 for revising and
digesting the civil affairs of the navy
Fourteen reports, 1806–9***

Commissioners

Lord Barham (first lord of the Admiralty until February 1806)
John Fordyce (surveyor-general of crown lands)
Admiral Sir Roger Curtis
Rear-Admiral William Domett (Admiralty commissioner, 1808–13)
Ambrose Serle (commissioner of the Transport Board, with responsibility
for prisoners of war)

Secretary

John Deas Thompson (May 1805–February 1806; Navy Board commissioner,
15 July 1805–29; succeeded by John Thomas Briggs: clerk, Secretary's
Office, Navy Board, 29 May 1798–7 December 1807; second chief clerk,
7 December 1807–11 December 1808; secretary to Committee of
Accounts, Victualling Board, 1808; private secretary to first lord, 1830;
accountant-general of the navy, 1832; knighted, 1851)

Office: No. 30 Craven Street

REPORTS

1806

First Instructions for the Resident Commissioner and Principal
Officers of the Royal Dockyards, completed 13 June 1805,

---

* *Parliamentary Papers: Commons Reports*, 1806–9.

ordered by the House of Commons to be printed 4 February
1806

Second   Instructions for the Inferior Officers, Royal Dockyards,
completed 6 February, printed 3 April

Third   Instructions for the Surveyor of the Navy and his Assistants;
Education of Shipwrights; Plan of Education proposed for
Apprentices; Inferior Apprentices; Scheme of Task Work; Job
Work, completed 24 June, printed 16 July

Fourth   Navy Office: Navy Commissioners; Comptrolling Payments;
Inspector-General of Naval Works; Accounts; Contracts;
Salaries of Commissioners; Secretaries; Offices; Salaries of
Clerks, completed 9 July

Fifth   Instructions for the Resident Commissioners and Officers
at His Majesty's Naval Establishments Abroad, completed
2 August

Sixth   Instructions for Officers at the Outports, Deal, Harwich, Leith,
Falmouth and Kinsale, completed 4 December

1807

Seventh   Instructions for the Governors, Lieutenants, Physicians,
Surgeons, Agents, Stewards, Dispensers, Chaplains, Store
Matrons, Porters and Overseers of Labour of the Royal
Naval Hospitals at Portsmouth and Plymouth, completed
26 February

Eighth   Instructions for Task Work in the Dockyards (not published)

Ninth   Transport Office: Branch relating to the Transport Service;
Miscellaneous Services; Branch for Sick and Wounded Seamen;
Branch for Prisoners of War, completed 25 June

Tenth   Victualling Office: State of Accounting Arrears and reorganiza-
tion of the Office; Duties of the Committee for General
Business; Duties of the Committee for Cash and Store
Accounts; Duties of the Chairman; Duties of the Secretaries;
Contracts, completed 11 August

Eleventh   Victualling Yards: Useless and Erroneous Books, Accounts and
Returns; Deptford; General Remarks; Instructions and Regula-
tions for the Yard Officers; Employment of Artificers, Labourers
and Others; Contracting for Works and Stores; Supplies and
Accounts; Instructions for Master Butchers, Master Brewers,
Master Millers and Granary Men, Master Bakers and Inferior
Officers, completed 22 December

Twelfth   Victualling Yards Abroad: Instructions for the Agents of
              Victualling Establishments Abroad; for Receipt and
              Examination of Provisions and Stores; for Issues of Provisions
              and Stores, completed 22 December
Thirteenth   Transport Board: Instructions to the Resident Agents for
              Transports; Regulations to be observed by all Masters of Ships
              and Vessels employed and hired in His Majesty's Transport
              Service; Articles for Government of Officers commanding His
              Majesty's Armed Transports; Instructions to the Inspecting
              Agents, Shipwright Officers and Storekeepers for the Transport
              Service at Deptford; Instructions to the Surgeons, Agents,
              Dispensers at the Foreign Hospitals; Agents for Prisoners of
              War at Home and Abroad, to the Surgeons and Dispensers at the
              Depots for Prisoners of War at Home, completed 22 December
Fourteenth   Secret Report on Timber, never printed*

Fourth–Fourteenth reports ordered to be printed by the House of
    Commons, 11 April 1809

COMMISSION OF MILITARY ENQUIRY

**Reports of the Commissioners appointed by Act 45 Geo. III, c. 47, to enquire
and examine into Public Expenditure and the Conduct of Public Business
in the Military Departments
Nineteen reports, 1806–12**[†]

Commissioners

Major General Hildebrand Oakes ((1754–1822) chairman, but left the
    commission when appointed quartermaster-general, Mediterranean,
    11 July 1806; later Lieutenant-General Sir Hildebrand Oakes)
Colonel John Drinkwater ((1762–1844) succeeding chairman; later Sir John
    Drinkwater Bethune; army officer, military author)
Colonel F. Beckwith (dies before the First Report is completed)
Samuel. C. Cox (master in Chancery)
Giles Templeman (lawyer; captain, Law Association Volunteers, 28 July 1803[‡])

* In MSS in TNA, ADM 106/3110 (Morriss, Royal Dockyards, pp. 205, 231).
† Parliamentary Papers: Commons Reports, 1806–12.
‡ Volunteers List, 1804, p. 436.

Henry Peters (merchant)

Charles Bosanquet (wealthy West Indies merchant and author; gazetted in the London Light Horse Volunteers, 1794; lieutenant-colonel, London and Westminster Cavalry, 7 February 1799; 1809 member of Lloyd's; from 1823 to 1836 chairman of the Exchequer Bill Office; retired to Northumberland, where he became lord lieutenant)

Colonel Benjamin Charles Stephenson ((c. 1766–1839) later Major-General Sir Benjamin Stephenson; entered Hanoverian service, 1788; transferred to the English Army, 1796; deputy judge advocate, SW District, 1803–5; groom of the bedchamber to the duke of Cumberland, 1806–10; surveyor-general of the Office of Works, 1814–32; third commissioner, 1832–4; second commissioner, 1832–9)

L. Bradshaw

Office: No. 17 Buckingham Street, Adelphi

REPORTS

1806

First	Office of the Barrack Master-General: Arrears of the Barrack Office Accounts; Mode of issuing and receiving money; Measures proposed for a speedy Settlement of Accounts, completed 20 March, printed 21 March
Second	Establishment of the Barrack Office, completed 17 July, printed 18 July
Third	Office of the Barrack Master-General: Stores and Supplies, completed 24 July, printed 22 December

1807

Fourth	Office of the Barrack Master-General: Buildings, completed 28 February, printed 3 March

1808

Fifth	Army Medical Department, completed 8 January, printed 26 January

Sixth   Office of the Secretary at War: Establishment of the War
Office; Regimental Accounts; Agency and Clothing, completed
24 June, printed 25 June

1809

Seventh   Office of the Secretary at War: Department of Foreign
Accounts; Chaplain General, completed 10 December 1808,
printed 20 January 1809

Eighth   Office of the Secretary at War: Miscellaneous Accounts
Department, completed 6 January, printed 20 January

Ninth   Army Expenditure in the West Indies (Act 41 Geo. III, c. 22),
completed 28 March, printed 14 April

1810

Tenth   Royal Military College, completed 14 August 1809, printed
26 February

Eleventh Departments of the Adjutant-General and the Quartermaster-
General, completed 10 October 1809, printed 26 February 1810

Twelfth   Office of the Ordnance: Treasurer of the Ordnance, completed
27 February, printed 27 February

1811

Thirteenth Master-General and the Board of Ordnance, completed 22
February, printed 27 February

Fourteenth Office of the Ordnance: Estimates, completed 8 March,
printed 29 April

Fifteenth   Office of the Ordnance: Fortifications and Buildings; Barracks;
Small Gun Department; Shipping, completed 4 June, printed
23 July

1812

Sixteenth   Office of the Ordnance: Contracts; Royal Laboratory;
Inspector of Artillery; Royal Carriage Department, completed
2 August 1811, printed 9 January 1812

Seventeenth Office of the Ordnance: Military Accounts; Field Train
Departments; Royal Artillery Drivers; Deputy Adjutant-
General Artillery; Medical Department; Royal Military

Academy, Woolwich; Trigonometrical Survey of Britain, completed 17 October 1811, printed 9 January 1812

Eighteenth   Office of the Commissariat, completed 17 March, printed 20 March

Nineteenth   Royal Hospital Chelsea; Commissary-General of Musters; Royal Military Asylum, completed 25 March, printed 26 May

1816

General Index to Reports, 1806–12, printed 23 February

Chronology

1789

14 July: Fall of the Bastille

1791

6 July: Austria issues 'The Circular' calling on the crowned heads of Europe to restore liberty to the French royal family

3 September: The French constitution voted

1 October: The Legislative Assembly sits in Paris

1792

January: Founding of the London Corresponding Society

20 April: War between France and the First Coalition

21 May: British Royal Proclamation against seditious meetings and writings

10 August: March on the Tuileries; Louis XVI deposed and taken prisoner

31 August: September massacres start in Paris

September: French armies occupy Savoy and Nice, part of the Kingdom of Piedmont

20 September: **Battle of Valmy:** French artillery defeats Prussian troops under the duke of Brunswick and the threat to Paris lifted

21 September–26 October 1795: National Convention

6 November: **Battle of Jemappes** near Mons: French Army marches into Brussels

16 November: French decree opening the navigation of the Scheldt, exclusively awarded to the Dutch by the Treaty of Münster (1648) and guaranteed by Britain as recently as 1788

19 November: French edict that appears to promise support to the disaffected in other countries

21 November: British government introduces Aliens Bill, enabling it to regulate the movement of people in and out of the country

1 December: Ministers decide to issue a royal proclamation calling out the militia and assembling parliament

1793

January: Russo-Prussian partition of Poland

7 January: Aliens Act passed

21 January: Execution of Louis XVI

1 February: France declares war on Britain

13 February: Formation of the First Coalition of Britain, Austria, Prussia, the Netherlands, Spain and Sardinia, against France

14 February: British capture Tobago

18–21 March: **Battle of Neerwinden**: Austrians under General Prince Josias of Coburg and British under the duke of York defeat General Dumouriez; French driven from the Austrian Netherlands

25 March: Anglo-Russian treaty – twelve ships of the line, six frigates, to help Royal Navy

5 April: Dumouriez deserts to the Austrians; Committee of Public Safety formed in Paris; first French Army conscription, which causes insurrection in the Vendée

April: British expeditionary force to Flanders commanded by the duke of York

April: British attack Martinique, part of San Domingo, Pondicherry (India) and Miquelon (off Newfoundland)

16 April: Dundas orders an expedition to Dunkirk

25 April: Anglo-Sardinian treaty

25 May: Anglo-Spanish treaty

31 May: French National Guards surround the Tuileries; expulsion of the Girondins

12 July: Anglo-Neapolitan treaty

28 July: Allied victory at **Valenciennes**: Allied Army on French soil

15 August: Duke of York begins march on Dunkirk

27 August: British naval force under Lord Hood occupies Toulon

30 August: Anglo-Austrian treaty

6 September: French attack on the duke of York's army at Dunkirk

8 September: **Battle of Hondscoten**: French defeat British and Hanoverian army, and raise the siege of Dunkirk

15–16 October: Jourdan defeats the Austrians at **Wattignies**

16 October: Marie-Antoinette executed

26 November: Expedition commanded by General Grey and Admiral Sir John Jervis sails for the West Indies

19 December: Allied evacuation and partial destruction of Toulon: thirty-two French ships of the line and three frigates captured by British; Hood sails to Corsica with 7,500 Toulon citizens

December: Force under Lord Moira sent to Brittany to help the Chouans

1794

7 February: British landing in Corsica

22 March: British capture of Martinique

4 April: Capture of St Lucia – lost June 1795, recaptured May 1796

19 April: Treaty of subsidy: Britain and the Netherlands to pay a subsidy to Prussia (which received £1,226,495)

20 April: French surrender Guadeloupe

May: Habeas Corpus Acts, trials of members of the London Corresponding Society

17–18 May: French victory at **Tourcoing** over Allies in Low Countries. Austrians decide to abandon their possessions in the Netherlands

22 May: Surrender of Bastia in Corsica to British troops

1 June: **Battle of the First of June**

17 June: Henry Dundas orders 10,000 men under the earl of Moira to defend Ostend

26 June: French Army defeats British, Dutch and Austrians at **Fleurus**, re-occupies Brussels; British and Dutch retire to Holland; Austrians fall back behind the Meuse

June/July: Height of the Terror in Paris

July: Portland Whigs join Pitt's administration in coalition

16 July: French telegraph line between Paris and Lille opened

28 July: Robespierre executed

10 August: Surrender of Calvi in Corsica to the British

30 August: Valenciennes and Condé recaptured by the French

9 October: General Charles Pichegru commanding the Army of the North pursues British, Dutch and Hanoverian armies, takes Nimeguen and occupies Amsterdam

19 November: Treaty of amity, commerce and navigation signed between Britain and the USA (Jay Treaty) in London

24 November: Duke of York relieved of his command of British forces in Flanders

31 December: Brest Fleet sails for an Atlantic Cruise – four French ships of the line founder

1795

5 January: Austro-Prussian treaty

End of January: French conquest of the Netherlands complete, British troops withdraw; Stadtholder flees to England

9 February: French treaty with Tuscany

February: Britain finally concludes a formal alliance with Austria after two years of fighting as allies

13 February: Channel Fleet under Lord Howe almost wrecked in Torbay

13–14 March: Admiral Hotham's inconclusive **'First Action'** against the French Fleet off Genoa

5 April: Franco-Prussian peace under Treaty of Basle: Prussia now a second-rate power

14 April: British Army evacuated from Holland

4 May: Convention on loan with the emperor signed in Vienna (£4.6 million)

16 May: Holland makes terms with the French

17 June: British expedition sails to aid the French royalists (Chouans) in the Vendée in south-west France

13 July: Hotham's **'Second Action'** off the French coast near Toulon

22 July: Treaty between French and Spanish, also at Basle

17 August: Capture of Malacca from Dutch

12 August: Order-in-council establishes the Hydrographic Office

22 August: New constitution, in which the Directory replaces the Jacobin regime

29 August: Treaty between French and the Landgrave of Hesse-Cassel; France breaks First Coalition

30 August: Capture of Trincomalee from Dutch

16 September: Capture of the Cape of Good Hope by Admiral Elphinstone (Lord Keith) and General Sir James Craig

1 October: Annexation of the Austrian Netherlands, incorporated into the French Republic

5 October: Insurrection of 13th Vendémiaire in Paris, Napoleon's 'whiff of grapeshot'

October: 'The admirals' mutiny' at Portsmouth over the issue of whether soldiers afloat should be under naval discipline

7 October: Loss of the British Levant convoy to the French squadron under de Richery off Cape St Vincent

October: Rebellion in the Vendée crushed, the end of hopes for an early restoration of the Bourbon monarchy

3 November to 1799: The Directory rules in France

16 November: Rear-Admiral Hugh Christian's convoy sails for the West Indies, but is soon blown back by gales

1 December: Sir John Jervis takes command of the Mediterranean Fleet

December: 'Pitt's terror' launched with the 'Two Acts' (Seditious Meetings and Treasonable Practices Act; Seditious Meetings and Assemblies Act) rushed through parliament: also Irish Insurrection Act

1796

27 January: Shutter telegraph between the roof of the Admiralty in London and Deal completed

29 January: Rear-Admiral Christian's convoy to the West Indies again driven back by winter storms and returns to Spithead

February: Colombo taken by Captain Hyde Gardner; Admiral Peter Rainier takes Amboina from Dutch in the East Indies

12–16 April: Bonaparte's victories at **Montenotte** and **Dego** in Piedmont

10 May: Bonaparte takes the bridge at **Lodi** against the Austrians

15 May: Bonaparte enters Milan and occupies Piedmont and Lombardy

17 August: Capture of Lucas's Dutch squadron in Saldanha Bay, South Africa

19 August: Secret treaty of San Ildefonso between France and Spain

31 August: Admiralty orders the evacuation of Corsica

8 October: Spain declares war on England

22 October: Malmesbury peace mission to France arrives in Paris and leaves 21 December; returns to Lille, 4 July 1797; returns to Britain, 18 September 1797

17 November: Empress Catherine dies: Russian policies reversed and Russian squadron serving with British recalled

1 December: Pitt's voluntary Loyalty Loan raises £18 million in four days

16 December: General Lazare Hoche's expedition sails from Brest for Ireland

22–9 December: French Fleet arrives in Bantry Bay, but fails to land troops and leaves Irish waters

1797

15 January: French defeat Austria at **Rivoli**

28 January: Rear-Admiral Pierre Sercey's squadron declines to attack an East India convoy in the Bali Straits

2 February: Fortress at Mantua falls to Napoleon: end of Austrian resistance in Italy

14 February: **Battle of Cape St Vincent**: British Fleet under Jervis defeats Spanish

18 February: Surrender of Trinidad by Spanish, destruction of three ships of the line and a frigate, one captured

22 February: Small French force lands at Fishguard in Pembrokeshire but surrenders immediately

February: Bank crisis, temporary suspension of cash payments by the Bank of England

16 April: Outbreak of the naval mutiny at Spithead

18–30 April: Failed British assault on San Juan, Puerto Rico

12 May: Outbreak of the naval mutiny at the Nore and in the Yarmouth Roads

16 May: Convention on loan with Austria signed in London (£1,620,000)

22–23 July: Nelson's unsuccessful attack on Santa Cruz, Tenerife

4 September: Coup d'état of 18 Fructidor, the Directory's political crisis, forestalls a royalist seizure of power in France

11 October: **Battle of Camperdown**: Dutch Fleet defeated by Admiral Duncan

17 October: Treaty of Campo Formio: Austria makes peace with France; Britain only survivor of the First Coalition

November: Pitt's Finance Bill proposes income tax and new indirect taxes

1798

April: Outbreak of undeclared 'quasi-war' between France and the USA

April: Seizure and imprisonment of the Committee of the London Corresponding Society

6 April: Cabinet decides to send fleet to the Mediterranean

8 May: Nelson, off Cádiz, is sent by Admiral St Vincent into the Mediterranean accompanied by two other ships of the line

19 May: Bonaparte's expedition sails from Toulon, gathering more transports from Italian ports

20 May: British raid on Ostend led by Captain Home Popham: the locks destroyed, but troops unable to evacuate and are captured

23 May: Outbreak of rebellion in Ireland in Kildare

8 June: Thomas Troubridge with ten ships of the line joins Nelson off Toulon

11 June: Bonaparte's expedition captures Malta from the Knights of St John

21 June: Irish rebels defeated at **Vinegar Hill**

28 June: Lacking intelligence, Nelson reaches Alexandria for the first time, ahead of Napoleon

1 July: French Army begins landing in Egypt

21 July: Bonaparte's troops defeat the Egyptian Army at the **Battle of the Pyramids**; enters Cairo 23 July

1–2 August: **Battle of the Nile**: Nelson's squadron captures or destroys eleven French ships in Aboukir Bay, only two escaping

6 August: French expedition under General Humbert leaves Rochefort bound for Ireland

15 August: Tsar offers 60,000 troops for the Rhine in return for British subsidies

22 August: General Humbert lands at Killala in Mayo with 1,000 men

8 September: Humbert surrenders at Ballinamuck

16 September: Departure of second French expedition to Ireland under Commodore Bompard, intercepted off Lough Swilly in October by a squadron under Sir John Borlase Warren

September: Final British evacuation of San Domingo

14 November: British capture of **Minorca**

1 December: Formal treaty between Britain and Naples signed; army of Naples marches on Rome, but soon retreats

1799

27 January: Spanish Rear-Admiral Alava declines to attack an East India convoy near Macao

3 March: French forces in Corfu capitulate to Russians and Turks

7 March: Jaffa occupied by the French Army under Bonaparte

12 March: France declares war on Austria

19 March: Bonaparte begins siege of Acre

April: Pitt introduces income tax of 10 per cent

26 April: Bruix slips past British blockade of Brest with twenty-five ships of the line intending to relieve the French armies in Egypt

27 April: French evacuate Milan; Russians under Suvorov take city 29 Apr.

3 May: Bruix passes Cádiz without attacking Keith

3 May: Tippoo Sahib, sultan of Mysore, killed at the **Battle of Seringapatam**

7 May: Prussian offer to Britain of an offensive in return for subsidy

20 May: Bonaparte abandons the siege of Acre

1 June: Formation of Second Coalition of Britain, Russia, Austria, Turkey, Portugal and the Two Sicilies, against France

8 August: Bruix re-enters Brest with the combined French and Spanish fleets

23 August: Bonaparte sails from Alexandria to return to France

27 August: Anglo-Russian landing in Den Helder in north Holland; surrender of the Dutch Fleet

19 September: British troops under the duke of York win the **Battle of Bergen**

12 October: Duke of York runs short of supplies, signs armistice 18 October and agrees to evacuate north Holland

9 November: 18 Brumaire Coup: Bonaparte overthrows the Directory and establishes himself in power

1800

24 January: Convention of El Arish negotiated by Sidney Smith and the Turks with Kléber for the evacuation of the French Army; not ratified by the British government

April: Second Coalition collapses

21 April: Admiral Lord St Vincent takes command of the Channel Fleet

14 June: Bonaparte's victory over the Austrians at **Marengo**

2 July: Ireland becomes part of the British state as the Act of Union passed and Irish parliament abolished

25 July: British arrest a Danish convoy off Gibraltar

26 August: Failed British amphibious attack on Ferrol

29 August: British Fleet off Copenhagen forces an agreement with Denmark over neutral trade

5 September: French garrison in Malta surrenders to the British under General Graham

30 September: Franco-American 'quasi war' ended

3 October: Cabinet decides to send 14,000 troops under Abercromby to Egypt

6 October: Aborted landing at Cádiz by the combined operation commanded by Sir Ralph Abercromby and Lord Keith

16 December: Formation of the Second Armed Neutrality hostile to Britain, signed by Sweden, Denmark, Russia, supported by Prussia

24 December: Attempted assassination of Bonaparte in the rue Saint-Nicaise

1801

1 January: Act of Union between Great Britain and Ireland comes into force

15 January: Armistice between France and Austria

23 January: Ganteaume breaks British blockade, sails from Brest with seven sail of the line, heading to Egypt to relieve French troops; reaches Egyptian coast but turns for home when he sees British ships

9 February: Peace of Lunéville between France and Austria: Austria is driven out of the war

16 February: Resignation of Pitt's government

8 March: British Army under General Abercromby lands in Aboukir Bay under fire; warships and transports commanded by Lord Keith

12 March: Sir Hyde Parker and Nelson sail from Yarmouth for the Baltic

19 March: Addington's government decides to sue for peace

21 March: **Battle of Alexandria**: British victory over the French but General Abercromby killed

21 March: Treaty of Aránjuez between France and Spain: Spain cedes Louisiana to France

24 March: Assassination of Tsar Paul I

28 March: Treaty of Naples

30 March: Prussians occupy Hanover

2 April: **Bombardment of Copenhagen** by British Fleet under Admiral Sir Hyde Parker and Nelson

17 June: Britain signs convention with Russia

6 July: **Battle of Algeciras**: Rear-Admiral Saumarez unsuccessful against Linois, British ship captured

12 July: **Battle of the Straits**: Saumarez successful in night action

15 August: Nelson's unsuccessful attack on Boulogne

2 September: Menou capitulates at Alexandria

1 October: Preliminaries of Peace of Amiens signed between Britain and France

1802

25 March: **Peace of Amiens concluded:** Britain returns former French and Dutch colonies except Trinidad and Ceylon; the French retain their conquests except Rome and Naples; Malta undecided

29 June: British general election

2 August: Bonaparte appointed first consul for life

11 September: Annexation of the Kingdom of Piedmont to the French Republic as six new departments, followed in 1805–8 by that of Republic of Genoa and Tuscany and Parma

29 December 1802: royal assent given to bill to set up a Commission of Naval Enquiry

1803

30 April: USA purchases Louisiana and New Orleans from France

18 May: **Britain declares war on France:** Napoleonic War begins with king's order-in-council

May: French retake **San Domingo**; British troops under General Grinfield reconquer Tobago, St Lucia, Demerara, Essequibo and Berbice

22 May: French decree: all English males in France aged between eighteen and sixty to be prisoners of war

5 June: French occupy Hanover

23 July: Emmet's insurrection in Ireland

19 October: Secret Franco-Spanish military alliance

2 December: Establishment of the 'Armée d'Angleterre' at Boulogne

1804

7 January: British capture the Diamond Rock, Martinique

14 February: **Battle of Pulo Aor**, South-east coast of Malaya: by forming a line of battle, Commodore Nathaniel Dance of the East India Company fools the French Admiral Linois into thinking that his unescorted East Indiamen are warships; Linois retreats

21 March: Execution of the duc d'Enghien

12 May: Addington government resigns; Pitt forms a government

18 May: Bonaparte declares himself emperor of the French

6 October: Spanish treasure ships attacked off Cádiz

2 December: Coronation of Napoleon at Notre-Dame
12 December: Spain declares war on Britain

1805

11 January: Britain declares war on Spain
11 January: Missiessy sails from Rochefort for the West Indies
14 January: Villeneuve sails from Toulon but is driven back by a storm
28 March: Missiessy leaves Martinique to return to France
30 March: Villeneuve sails again from Toulon
April: Treaty of St Petersburg between Britain and Russia
10 April: Villeneuve and Gravina sail from Cádiz for the West Indies
19 April: Troops under Sir James Craig sail in convoy for the Mediterranean
11 May: Nelson leaves the Spanish coast in pursuit of Villeneuve and Gravina
16 May: Villeneuve and Gravina reach Martinique
26 May: Napoleon crowned king of Italy in Milan
June: Commission of Naval Revision ordered
5 June: Commission of Military Enquiry receives royal assent
11 June: Villeneuve's Franco-Spanish Fleet leaves the West Indies, Nelson
  sailing in pursuit two days later
17 July: Allemand sails from Rochefort
20 July: Nelson arrives back at Gibraltar after failing to catch the French Fleet
22 July: **Calder's Action** indecisive off Cape Finisterre
3 August: Napoleon arrives at Boulogne to take command of the army of
  invasion
9 August: Third Coalition of Britain, Russia and Austria is completed
11 August: Villeneuve sails from Ferrol for the Mediterranean
26 August: The Grande Armée breaks camp at Boulogne, abandoning the
  attempted invasion of Britain, and sets out towards the Rhine
28 August: Sir Home Popham's expedition to the Cape sails from Cork, with
  Sir David Baird in command of the troops
28 September: Nelson resumes command of the Mediterranean Fleet off Cádiz
8 October: Treaty of Naples
19 October: The French and Spanish Combined Fleet sails from Cádiz
20 October: Austrian Army surrenders at **Ulm**
21 October: **Battle of Trafalgar** and death of Nelson
30 October: French victory over the Austrians in Italy at **Caldiero**
4 November: Strachan's Action: four French ships of the line from the Trafalgar Fleet captured
November: Napoleon enters Vienna

20 November: Anglo-Russian expedition reaches Naples

2 December: Napoleon defeats Russian–Austrian Army at **Austerlitz**, driving both out of the war; news reaches London on 29 December

12 December: General Lord Cathcart, commanding 26,000 troops on expedition to north Germany, lands at Cuxhaven; sails home, having achieved nothing, on 15 February 1806

13 December: French squadron under Leissegues and Willaumez sail from Brest

26 December: Treaty of Pressburg between France and Austria

1806

10 January: Troops under General Sir David Baird recapture Cape of Good Hope

19 January: Withdrawal of British forces from Naples, reaching Messina in Sicily on 22 January

22 January: Death of William Pitt

6 February: Vice-Admiral Sir John Duckworth's victory off **San Domingo**

10 February: Grenville and Fox form an administration, the 'Ministry of All the Talents'

15 February: Craig's troops disembark at Messina and occupy the forts; on the same day Joseph Bonaparte proclaimed king of Naples and Sicily

May: Order-in-council promulgates a blockade of French ports between Brest and the River Elbe

28 June: Beresford captures **Buenos Aires**

4 July: British victory at the **Battle of Maida** in southern Italy

July: Confederation of the Rhine constituted

18 August: Jérôme Bonaparte proclaimed king of Westphalia

13 September: Death of Charles James Fox

14 October: **Battle of Jena** and **Battle of Auerstädt**: Prussians lose 25,000 men and 200 guns

27 October: Napoleon enters Berlin

8 November: Capitulation of Magdeburg

21 November: Berlin Decrees announce the blockade of Britain

28 November: French Army enters Warsaw

1807

7 January: British orders-in-council issued

3 February: General Auchmuchty captures **Montevideo**

7 February: **Battle of Eylau**: drawn battle between Napoleon and the Russian Army

19 February: Duckworth passes the Dardanelles in an effort to pressurize the Turks so as to help the Russians

17 March: British forces land in Egypt under Major General Fraser Mackenzie but to no purpose

24 March: Fall of the Ministry of All the Talents, formation of the duke of Portland's ministry

April: Convention of Bartenstein between Russia, Prussia and Sweden

14 June: **Battle of Friedland**: Napoleon overcomes a much larger Russian army, which leads the tsar to make peace with Napoleon

22 June: *Leopard–Chesapeake* incident

23 June: Convention of subsidy with Sweden signed at Stralsund (£1,100,000)

7 July: Franco-Russian agreement signed at Tilsit

10 July: General Whitelocke's attack on **Buenos Aires** fails disastrously

4 September: British capture Heligoland

7 September: British attack on **Copenhagen** leads to the surrender of the Danish Fleet of seventeen ships of the line

October: Treaty of Fontainebleau between France and Spain

11 November: Order-in-council further strengthens British powers of seizure

23 November and 17 December: Milan Decrees

29 November: British squadron under Sir Sidney Smith escorts the Portuguese Fleet and royal family from Lisbon to Brazil, hours before a French army under General Junot occupies Lisbon

2 December: Russian declaration of war on Britain becomes known in London

22 December: US Embargo Act

26 December: British occupation of Madeira

1808

27 February: Invasion of Spain by French troops

23 March: French forces enter Madrid

17 April: Bayonne Decree orders the seizure of American ships in European ports

2 May: Spanish revolt in Madrid against French rule

May: Joseph Bonaparte becomes king of Spain

10 May: Sir John Moore's army leaves Great Yarmouth for Sweden, arriving off Gothenburg on 17 May

21 May: British take Torshaven, Faroe Islands, and dismantle the fortifications

15 June: Siege of Saragossa begins

25 June: Shutter telegraph line from London to Great Yarmouth commissioned

15 July: Moore and his army arrive back in the Downs from Sweden

19 July: A Spanish army soundly beats a French army at **Baylen**, south of Madrid, forcing 18,000 troops to lay down their arms

1 August: General Arthur Wellesley commands a force of 9,000 British troops, which lands at Mondego Bay, Portugal

11 August: La Romana's Spanish troops begin the voyage from Denmark back to Spain, transported by the British

21 August: Wellington defeats Junot at **Vimeira**

25 August: Anglo-Swedish Fleet fights the Russians off Hango Head

30 August: Convention of Cintra

9 October: La Romana's 9,000 troops from Denmark land at Santander

4 December: Surrender of Madrid to Napoleon; Junta Suprema Central flees to Seville

1809

January: Treaty of the Dardanelles between Britain and Turkey

January: Committee appointed to investigate the duke of York's involvement in the sale of army commissions

9 January: Anglo-Spanish treaty of alliance

16 January: **Battle of Corunna** and evacuation of Moore's army

21 February: Capitulation of Saragossa

24 February: Surrender of Martinique

15–17 March: Duke of York's case debated in the House of Commons

18 March: Duke of York resigns as commander-in-chief, replaced by General Sir David Dundas

11 April: **Basque Roads** action: French lose four ships of the line

20 April: **Battle of Abensberg:** Napoleon defeats the Austrian Army

22 April: Arthur Wellesley assumes command of British troops in Portugal

12 May: Wellesley drives Marshal Soult out of Oporto

13 May: Napoleon enters Vienna

21–22 May: **Battle of Aspern–Essling**: Austrians catch Napoleon's army crossing the Danube and inflict rare defeat

5–6 July: **Battle of Wagram**: French defeat the Austrians, although not decisively; leads to an armistice

13 July: British capture of Senegal

28 July: Wellesley's victory at **Talavera**, after which British forces retreat to Portugal

28 July: Walcheren expedition sails

21 September: Duel between George Canning and Lord Castlereagh

14 October: Peace of Schönbrunn between France and Austria: Austria driven out of the war

25 October: Collingwood defeats French convoy bound for Barcelona

30 October: Death of the duke of Portland: Spencer Perceval forms an administration

13 November: British East India forces destroy Ras al-Khaima

19 November: Spanish defeat at **Ocana** leads to French conquest of all Andalusia except Cádiz

23 December: Final British evacuation of Walcheren

1810

6 January: Treaty of Paris between France and Sweden

6 February: Capture of Guadeloupe

17 February: Annexation of Rome to French Empire, with provision that Napoleon's heir shall bear title of king of Rome

19 February: Surrender of Amboina to the British in the East Indies

19 February: British treaty with Portugal (ensuing subsidies: 1810 – £1,237,518; 1811 – £1,832,168; 1812 – £2,167,832; 1813 – £1,644,063; 1814 – £1,500,00)

1 April: Marriage of Napoleon and Marie-Louise of Austria

9 July: The Netherlands is annexed to the French Empire

9 July: Capture of Réunion by British expedition

19 July: Norwegian ships take a British convoy off the Skaw

5 August: Trianon Tariff allows the import of colonial goods into France rather than total prohibition

9 August: Capture of Banda Neira, Moluccas, by British

23 August: British defeat at the **Battle of Grand Port, Mauritius**, in which three British frigates are sunk

27 September: **Battle of Busaco**: Marshal Masséna defeated

10 October: French Army stopped by the lines of Torres Vedras outside Lisbon

18 October: Fontainebleau Decree tightens up French blockade restrictions

17 November: Sweden declares war on Britain

3 December: Surrender of Mauritius

13 December: French annex north-west Germany (Hamburg, Bremen, Lübeck and Hanover); French Empire now consists of 130 departments

31 December: Alexander I opens Russian ports to neutral shipping

1811

5 February: Prince of Wales given virtually full powers as prince regent after George III's illness

5 March: French retreat from Torres Vedras towards Spain

March: Beginning of the Luddite disturbances in the West Midlands

13 March: **Battle of Lissa** in the Adriatic: William Hoste's squadron victorious

6 June: Reinstatement of the duke of York as commander-in-chief debated in parliament

4 August: British landing on Java

18 September: Surrender of Java

24 December: Loss of the *St George*, *Defence* and *Hero*, returning from the Baltic, in a storm on the Jutland coast

1812

January–September: Luddite disturbances spread to Yorkshire and Lancashire; frame-breaking made a capital offence

19 January: Wellington takes **Ciudad Rodrigo**

11 March: French shortages lead to food riots in Caen

7 April: **Badajoz** falls to Wellington after a long siege

April: Height of the Luddite disturbances

8 May: French impose price control on grain

11 May: Murder of Spencer Perceval; Lord Liverpool forms an administration

18 June: USA declares war on Britain

24 June: French Army invades Russia

22–23 July: Wellington wins the **Battle of Salamanca**

12 August: Wellington enters Madrid

16 August: Detroit surrenders to a British force

19 August: USS *Constitution* captures HMS *Guerrière*

7 September: **Battle of Borodino:** inconclusive, with huge casualties on both sides; Russian Army retreats

15 September: Napoleon enters Moscow

19 October: Napoleon begins the retreat from Moscow

18 December: Napoleon returns to Paris

1813

3 March: Treaty of subsidy with Sweden (£1,320,000)

27 April: American expedition captures and burns York (present-day Toronto)

1 June: *Shannon–Chesapeake* action

21 June: Wellington wins the **Battle of Vitoria,** driving French from northern Spain

26–27 August: Napoleon defeats the Allies at **Dresden**

8 September: **San Sebastián** surrenders to Wellington

10 September: US victory of Put-In Bay, Lake Erie

29 September: Americans recapture **Detroit**

5 October: Defeat of General Procter at the **Battle of the Thames** by US troops under General Harrison

8 October: Wellington's army enters France

16–19 October: Napoleon defeated at the three-day 'Battle of the Nations' at **Leipzig**

8 November: Allied peace terms offering Napoleon his throne and France's 1792 frontiers are rejected

19 December: British take Fort Niagara on Lake Ontario

1814

1 March: Treaty of Chaumont with Austria (subsidy £1,064,882), Prussia (£1,319,129) and Russia (£2,169,982)

8–9 March: Lieutenant-General Thomas Graham's force defeated at Bergen-op-Zoom

31 March: Allied armies enter Paris

6 April: Abdication of Napoleon

10 April: **Battle of Toulouse** won by Allies under Wellington

27 April: Surrender of **Bayonne**

3 May: Bourbon dynasty restored by Louis XVIII's entry into Paris

4 May: Napoleon arrives on Elba

24 August: British troops capture Washington, burning public buildings, including the White House

11 September: US naval victory of **Plattsburg**, Lake Champlain, halting a British invasion attempt

1 November: Opening of the Congress of Vienna

24 December: Treaty of Ghent ends Anglo-American War of 1812

1815

8 January: Before the news of the peace reaches **New Orleans**, British troops defeated after an unsuccessful attack on the town

1 March: Napoleon escapes from Elba and returns to France: beginning of the Hundred Days

March: Riots in London against the passing of the Corn Laws, which prohibit the importation of foreign wheat unless the price of home wheat is at or above 80 shillings a quarter

6 April: Riot at Dartmoor Prison: nine American prisoners of war killed, twelve seriously wounded and forty-two with lesser injuries, caused by Somerset and Derbyshire militias

9 June: Treaty of Vienna

18 June: **Battle of Waterloo**

22 June: Napoleon's Second Abdication

7 July: Allied armies enter Paris

14 July: Napoleon surrenders to the Royal Navy

9 August: Napoleon sails for St Helena

October: Disturbances at Hull, Sunderland and South Shields during the seamen's strike

16 October: Napoleon in exile on St Helena, where he dies 5 May 1821

20 November: Second Treaty of Paris: formal end of the French War

Glossary

able seaman: The most expert and highly paid seaman on a warship.

adjutant-general of the forces: Based in Horse Guards in Whitehall, responsible for issuing orders to the army, maintenance of discipline and ensuring that troops were properly armed and clothed.

admiral: Flag officer commanding a fleet or squadron, senior to a vice-admiral, who was in turn senior to a rear-admiral; a port-admiral was a flag officer commanding ships in and around a naval port.

'alarmist': Name given to those Whigs who initially opposed the war, but who, led by Lord Portland, supported Pitt's government in coalition from 1794.

battalion: A body of infantry of between 900 and 1,000 men, officers included, usually two to a regiment, though in a few regiments there were more. Battalions rarely served together in the same theatre of operations.

bill: A negotiable payment order for goods or services issued by the navy, Victualling Office, Ordnance Department or Commissariat.

blockade: The blocking of a hostile port by warships, lying off, to prevent the movement of enemy naval or merchant ships. A 'paper blockade' was one declared by a belligerent to exist, but not enforced.

block mills: Mills in Portsmouth Dockyard built to house steam-driven machine tools, designed by Marc Isambard Brunel, which manufactured ships' (pulley) blocks.

bounty: A sum of money paid by the government as an inducement to join the army or navy.

breastworks: A general name for temporary fortifications, consisting of a parapet and trench, that offered protection to infantry.

bullion: Gold or silver bars, but also applied to coin.

bush: Equipment for cleaning a musket.

carbine: A firearm of smaller than musket calibre and generally shorter in length, used by cavalry.

carronade: A short, light naval gun, which fired a large shot with low velocity, very effective at short range, manufactured by the Carron Company near Falkirk in Scotland.

cartel: A written agreement for the exchange of prisoners of war, or the ship used in the exchange of prisoners.

cauldron or **chaldron:** A measurement of coal by volume, weighing about 1 ton, 6 hundredweight.

caulkers: Skilled shipyard workers who drove oakum, or untwisted rope, together with pitch, into the seams between the planks of the hull or the decks of a ship to make it watertight.

Chatham Lines: Fortifications and forts around the dockyard at Chatham.

chips: Pieces of unused dockyard timber, allowed by custom to be carried out of the yard on the shoulder of a dockyard worker; abolished in 1801.

Commissariat Department: The government organization responsible for supplies and provisions for the army, as ordered by the secretary of state for war but reporting directly to the Treasury.

commissary-general: An officer of the Commissariat attached to army units and garrisons worldwide.

Consols: Short for 'Consolidated Annuities', the government securities consolidated in 1752 into a single stock bearing interest at 3 per cent. Their market price was taken as an indication of confidence in the government and the current economic situation.

corsairs: Name generally applied to privateers or pirates of other nations.

crimp: Someone who engineered the recruitment of seamen or soldiers for private profit.

diagonal bracing: Strengthening a ship by means of additional timbers called riders. Sometimes called cross-bracing.

Downs: The anchorage off Deal in Kent, inside the Goodwin Sands, sheltered from westerly winds.

drover: Someone who herded and drove cattle or sheep to market, often for many hundreds of miles.

embody: The term for calling out the militia to active duty (regular regiments were permanently on duty). When a militia regiment was embodied, it came under the provisions of the Mutiny Act, was subject to standard military discipline and received pay. When its services were no longer required, the regiment was disembodied.

emolument: The profit from office or employment.

establishment: The authorized strength of officers and men of an army unit, which could be changed as the war continued; for the navy, each ship had an establishment determined by its rate.

fees: Payment to officeholders by a beneficiary for carrying out or expediting a duty, such as making out a navy bill.

felucca: Small Mediterranean vessel of six or eight oars, or a narrow, decked galley-built vessel with lateen sails.

firelock: General term for a soldier's musket; also the lock on a firearm, which consisted of the priming pan and the hammer holding the flint, by which the gunpowder charge in the barrel was ignited (see also **gunlock**).

freight money: Money earned by a ship's captain for carrying specie.

general: Holding the rank below field marshal and above that of lieutenant-general, who was senior to major general.

graving dock: A dry dock used for cleaning and repairing the hull of a ship.

grazier: The middleman who purchased cattle or sheep from the farmer, fattened them for sale and brought them to market.

Green Wax Monies: Fines exacted for non-compliance of orders from the Exchequer, named after the colour of the seals affixed to the documents.

gunlock: A flintlock mechanism adapted for fixing to a cannon barrel, by which the weapon could be fired (see also **firelock**).

heave to: To bring the ship to a standstill, by setting the sails to counteract each other.

howitzer: A short-barrelled field gun, designed to fire explosive shells at a high angle of elevation and at low velocity, so as to drop them on to a target.

hoy: Small coastal vessel, used for carrying goods and stores to and from a ship.

hulk: An old warship laid up and put to various uses, including storing gunpowder or other stores, or prisoners of war.

impress or **press:** To recruit seamen forcibly by means of a press gang, acting on the authority of a press warrant issued to empower a named officer to impress seamen.

jobber: One who used a public office for improper gain.

keelmen: The crews of the barges on the rivers in the north-east of England that brought coal from the mines to ships for onward transport.

landsman: An unskilled volunteer or pressed man aboard a warship.

leeway: The lateral drift of a ship to leeward when sailing into the wind.

Letter of Marque: A licence issued by the Admiralty allowing a privately owned ship to attack the shipping of a hostile nation named in the document.

licence: A permit issued to a ship by the Privy Council to allow trade with the enemy in a particular commodity, making an exception to a blockade already established; used also by other nations.

lugger: A small fore-and-aft rigged vessel, with two quadrangular sails.

magazine: A reinforced building designed to store gunpowder as safely as possible; also used to denote any store of provisions or military equipment.

mast ship: A merchant ship adapted for carrying masts or fir or pine trees, loaded through ports cut into the stern.

militia: Non-regular army units raised by each county through a ballot system held in towns and parishes, to serve only within the British Isles; their main tasks were invasion defence, guarding prisoners of war and keeping public order.

musket: The standard infantry long arm, discharged from the shoulder, with a flintlock ignition and capable of being fitted with a bayonet.

navy agent: A civilian based usually in London, although a few were in the main naval ports, who attended to the financial affairs of naval officers, essential, as the officers served at sea for long periods (see also **prize agent**).

Nore: Anchorage at the mouth of the Thames, and also a wider area constituting the naval station in the southern North Sea, where warships would be under the commander-in-chief at the Nore.

order-in-council: Issued by the Privy Council with royal assent, bypassing parliament.

ordinary: The part of the Naval Estimates used to fund routine activities, including ships in reserve and the crews to maintain them: hence 'ships in ordinary'.

ordinary seaman: A semi-skilled seaman, between able seaman and landsman.

packet: A merchant vessel contracted to the Post Office to carry mail.

panopticon: Jeremy Bentham's name for a circular prison constructed so that a single warder centrally placed could observe all the prisoners in their cells. The government purchased land at Millbank to build one, but it was never started and the scheme was abandoned in 1812.

parole: A formal promise made by a prisoner of war, almost always an officer, not to try to escape, or to refrain from taking up arms against his captors for a stated period; in return, the prisoner was allowed freedom within stated boundaries.

perquisite: Any casual emolument gained in addition to a salary or wage.

pintles: Vertical pins pointing downwards, fixed to the rudder while hanging on the sternpost of the ship, allowing the rudder to turn.

placeman: One who holds a government post, used derogatively if one or more sinecures was enjoyed.

plenipotentiary: A diplomat given full powers to negotiate.

poleacre: A three-masted ship of the Levant, carrying square sails on the main and lateen rig on the mizzenmast.

pricker: (1) Infantry equipment consisting of a short, stiff length of wire, with a small horsehair brush, to dislodge gunpowder residue from the touch hole or priming pan of the musket; (2) a bronze spike used to clear gunpowder residue from the vent hole of a cannon barrel.

privateer: An armed vessel of any nation carrying a Letter of Marque issued by that country's admiralty, permitting it to capture enemy ships and cargo and sell them in that country's prize court.

prize agent: A civilian who specialized in securing prize money on commission from the prize courts for an individual naval or army officer, or other ranks (see also **navy agent**).

prize money: For the navy, the profits arising from the sale of prizes, either cargo or the vessel itself, and distributed in a strict ratio by rank. The army could earn a much more limited amount of prize money from captured equipment.

proof: A test, usually at Woolwich Arsenal, to check the soundness of cannon made under contract before acceptance and payment by the Ordnance Department; this consisted of firing 30 times.

quartermaster-general of the forces: Based in the Horse Guards in Whitehall, responsible for organizing the marching of army units, in particular the routes and times.

rammer or ramrod: A cylindrical wooden block fixed to the end of a rod, pushed down the barrel of a cannon to compress the charge before the ball was inserted; also, when made of iron or steel, used for firearms.

rate: The six divisions of warships arranged according to their size and weight of armament (100 guns = a first rate). The establishment of the complement of officers and seamen was decided by the warship's rate.

reef: To reduce sail to allow for heavy weather.

regiment: A body of soldiers in the regular army, differentiated by the type of troops, such as cavalry or Foot Guards, commanded by a colonel; in the case of the militia or volunteers, associated with a county or London district.

regimental agent: Appointed by the colonel of the regiment, based in London (or Dublin for Irish regiments), to act as the link between the War Office and the colonel on financial matters, functioning as bankers for individual officers as well as providing news and other services.

regular army: Permanent, full-time units, subject to the Articles of War and other disciplinary or legal constraints; also empowered to commandeer quarters in public houses and impress transport.

resident commissioner: A commissioned naval officer, responsible to the Navy Board, in charge of a royal dockyard at home or abroad.

reversion: The right of succession to an office or a place after the death or retirement of the holder.

riders: Additional internal ship timbers bolted to the frame of an old or weakened vessel in order to strengthen it.

rifle: A firearm with a spirally ground bore, giving the ball a rotating movement in the air; more expensive but more accurate than a musket.

Sea Fencibles: Volunteer force of fishermen and seamen gathered and paid by the government for the defence of coasts and ports during the French invasion threats.

semaphore: A visual signal structure, consisting of a tall upright, with one or more arms moving in a vertical plane.

sheer a vessel: Suddenly to alter course, or to use the tide, to swing the vessel away from something.

shot: Usually a solid metal ball discharged from cannon, but naval variants included bar-shot, chain-shot and grapeshot.

sinecure: An office to which no work or duties were attached, yet for which there was a salary or emolument.

'sinking fund': First set up in 1724, a fund formed by periodically setting aside revenue to accumulate capital to reduce the principal of the national debt.

slip: An inclined piece of ground running into water, on which a ship was built and from which it was launched.

slops: Ready-made clothing and equipment issued by the purser to seamen aboard a warship.

specie: Silver or gold coin, mainly Spanish dollars.

springs: The highest and lowest sea level reached at spring tides, which occur twice a month, when the position of the moon affects the magnitude of the tidal range. High-water springs could be the only time when it was possible to float a large warship out of dock.

station: A geographical sea area in which all British warships would be commanded by an admiral (e.g., commander-in-chief, Mediterranean).

transport: A merchant ship of 200 tons or over contracted to the Transport Board for the carrying of stores, equipment or provisions; also the chief means of transporting troops by sea (see **troopship**).

transport agent or **agent for transports:** A commissioned naval officer responsible to the Transport Board, positioned at a naval base or port, or who sailed with a convoy.

troopship: A medium-sized warship with some guns removed and converted to troop-carrying (see **transport**).

turnscrew: A Y-shaped tool issued with every musket; screw-driver blades were on two of the arms and a spike on the third.

verderer: A judicial officer of the king's forests who dealt with trespass and other misdemeanours.

volunteers: Infantry or cavalry army units consisting of individuals who served voluntarily, and largely at their own expense. In London, infantry units were raised by organizations such as the Bank of England; in the country, units were commanded by the local aristocracy and gentry. Though mostly committed to the defence of their county or local area, during the invasion threats of 1803–5 many units volunteered for duty further afield.

windward ability: The ability of a sailing vessel to point into the wind, achieved most efficiently by fore-and-aft rigged ships and hardly at all by square-rigged merchant ships.

worm: An instrument for servicing muskets, designed to be screwed on to the slim end of the ramrod of a firearm or cannon, enabling a ball or wadding to be extracted from the barrel of the weapon.

xebec: Small three-masted Mediterranean vessel, found along the coasts of Spain, Portugal and the Barbary states.

yeomanry cavalry: Tended to be rural volunteers, usually from the farming community, who formed mounted units for service in their own county.

Bibliography

DOCUMENTARY SOURCES

Readers will discern from the number of secondary works listed below that this book rests largely on the work of others. The subject addressed is so large that it could absorb many years' work in the archives and appear in several volumes. I have, therefore, had to use original documents sparingly and pragmatically.

I have a large amount of notes from previous projects, among which are some that have survived unused from my time as a research student forty years ago. If the book is over-rich in the details of naval administration, this is because of my many years of reading and working among the archives of the National Maritime Museum, as well as familiarity with the papers of Charles Middleton (NMM, MID) and those of the shipowner Michael Henley (NMM, HNL). The other NMM references are to the personal papers of naval officers such as Lord Keith (NMM, KEI), Lord Hood (NMM, HOO) and Sir Charles Morice Pole (NMM, WYN). I also made use of the museum's letters written to Nelson (NMM, CRK) in the collection purchased by John Wilson Croker in 1817 on behalf of the government, when ministers in the Liverpool administration were concerned that compromising documents about the admiral might be published. My recent work on the victualling of the navy between 1793 and 1815 left me with unused material from the British Library relating to Lord Spencer from Althorp (Add. MSS 75792); from Pitt's papers in the National Archives (TNA, PRO 30); and from Addington's in the Devon Heritage Centre (DHC).

I have also specifically used collections that are less well known. These include, from the National Maritime Museum, Evan Nepean's intelligence letters (NMM, NEP/2 and 3) and the papers of Charles Philip Yorke (NMM, YOR) for his period as first lord of the Admiralty. Less often used, too, is the official correspondence from the Navy Board to the Admiralty contained in NMM, ADM BP, which consists of loose papers and enclosures of an awkward size that were left unbound, and that are of particular interest. The same can be said for the analysis of the planned expedition to take Brest in

Sim Comfort's collection (SCC). For similar reasons, I was tempted to buy from a dealer's catalogue the log of the North Sea packet *Prince of Wales*. These logs are very rare because the vessels were owned by contractors and documents hardly ever survive, unlike those for naval ships.

In the United States, I consulted the papers of the first Lord Melville at William L. Clements Library at the University of Michigan at Ann Arbor; in the Huntington Library I used the very full records of Tom Grenville's brief time as first lord of the Admiralty in the Stowe–Grenville Collection (STG); and on a family visit to Austin, Texas, by chance I came across a small collection of letters written by Lord Castlereagh to Charles Stewart, his half-brother, in the Londonderry MSS at the Harry Ransom Center at the University of Texas.

Only when I needed to illustrate particular points in detail did I turn to the National Archives (TNA). I looked up various episodes in the Admiralty in- and out-letters, and the Minutes of the Board (TNA, ADM 1, 2 and 3). Clive Wilkinson pointed me to the Abstracts of Logs in TNA, ADM 7, made by Admiralty clerks for the purpose of recording the times taken for voyages, from which averages could be calculated. Occasional use was made of the muster books (TNA, ADM 36) and captain's logs (TNA, ADM 51). I made time to check the War Office in-letters in WO 1/361 relating to the Hugh Cleghorn episode, which, although others have written about it, was so extraordinary that I wanted to see the evidence for myself. The Commissariat out-letters in TNA, WO 58, made interesting reading and in a few cases I made use of the Treasury papers (TNA, T). Details for the militia and the volunteers came from the muster and pay books (TNA, WO 13) and the records of militia regiments (TNA, WO 68). I also took advantage of a speaking engagement at the Monmouth Castle and Regimental Museum to look at the regimental order-books of the Royal Monmouth and Brecon Militia (RMRE).

Printed Sources

Aaslestad, Katherine, 'Revisiting the Continental System: Exploitation to Self-Destruction in the Napoleonic Empire' in Philip G. Dwyer and Alan Forrest (eds.), *Napoleon and His Empire: Europe 1804–1814* (London, 2007), pp. 114–32.

— 'War without Battles: Civilian Experiences of Economic Warfare during the Napoleonic Era in Hamburg' in Forrest et al. (eds.), *Soldiers, Citizens and Civilians*, pp. 118–36.

Acerra, Martine, Merino, José, and Meyer, Jean (eds.), *Les Marines de guerre européennes XVII–XVIIIe siècles* (Paris, 1985).

Ackroyd, Marcus, Brockliss, Laurence, Moss, Michael, Retford, Kate, and Stevenson, John, *Advancing with the Army: Medicine, the Professions and Social Mobility in the British Isles 1790–1850* (Oxford, 2006).

Albion, Robert Greenhalgh, *Forests and Sea Power: The Timber Problem of the Royal Navy 1652–1862* (Cambridge, Mass., 1926).

Anderson, J. L., 'A Measure of the Effect of British Public Finance 1793–1815', *Economic History Review*, 2nd Series, Vol. 27 (1974), pp. 610–19.

Andress, David, *The Savage Storm: Britain on the Brink in the Age of Napoleon* (London, 2012).

(Anon.) *A List of All Officers of the Fencible Cavalry and Infantry; the Militia; the Gentlemen and Yeomanry Cavalry; the Volunteer Infantry; and the Cavalry and Infantry Associations* (War Office, London, 1801, 8th edition).

(Anon.) *A List of the Officers of the Gentlemen and Yeomanry Cavalry, and Volunteer Infantry of the United Kingdom* (War Office, London, 1804).

(Anon.) *The Trial by Impeachment of Henry, Lord Viscount Melville ...* (London, 1806).

Armstrong, John, 'The Significance of Coastal Shipping in British Domestic Transport 1550–1830', *International Journal of Maritime History*, Vol. 3 (1991), pp. 63–94.

Arnold, James R., 'A Reappraisal of Column versus Line in the Napoleonic Wars', *Journal of the Society for Army Historical Research*, Vol. 60 (1982), pp. 196–208.

Arthur, Brian, *How Britain Won the War of 1812: The Royal Navy's Blockade of the United States 1812–1815* (Woodbridge, Suffolk, 2011).

Ashworth, William J., '"System of Terror": Samuel Bentham, Accountability and Dockyard Reform during the Napoleonic Wars', *Social History*, Vol. 23 (1998), pp. 63–79.

— *Customs and Excise: Trade, Production and Consumption in England 1640–1845* (Oxford, 2003).

Aspinall, A. (ed.), *The Correspondence of George, Prince of Wales, 1770–1812*, 5 vols. (London, 1963–71).

Åström, Sven-Erik, 'North European Timber Exports to Great Britain 1760–1810' in P. L. Cottrell and D. H. Aldcroft (eds.), *Shipping, Trade and Commerce: Essays in Memory of Ralph Davis* (Leicester, 1981), pp. 81–97.

Atkinson, C. T., 'The Proposed Expedition to the River Plate in 1798: Contemporary Letters of Colonel Robert Brooke, Governor of St Helena', *Journal of the Society for Army Historical Research*, Vol. 36 (1948), pp. 69–76.

Austen, Brian, *English Provincial Posts 1633–1840* (Chichester, 1978).

Austen, Jane, *Pride and Prejudice* (London, 1813; repr. 1995).

Aylmer, G. E., 'From Office-holding to Civil Service: The Genesis of Modern Bureaucracy', *Transactions of the Royal Historical Society*, 5th Series, Vol. 30 (1980), pp. 91–108.

Bailey, De Witt, and Harding, David, 'From India to Waterloo: The India Pattern Musket' in Guy, *Road to Waterloo*, pp. 48–57.

Baker, H. A., *The Crisis in Naval Ordnance* (London, 1983).

Baker, Norman, *Government and Contractors: The British Treasury and War Supplies 1775–1783* (London, 1971).

— 'The Treasury and Open Contracting 1778–1782', *Historical Journal*, Vol. 15 (1972), pp. 433–54.

Balleine, G. R., *The Tragedy of Philippe D'Auvergne* (Chichester, 1973).

Bamford, Andrew, '"Injurious to the Service Generally": Finding Manpower for Northern Europe 1813 and 1814', *Journal of the Society for Army Historical Research*, Vol. 90 (2012), pp. 25–43.

Bamford, Paul Walden, *Forests and French Sea Power 1660–1789* (Toronto, 1956).

Barker, Theo, and Gerhold, Dorian, *The Rise and Rise of Road Transport 1700–1990* (Cambridge, 1993).

Barnard, John E., *Building Britain's Wooden Walls: The Barnard Dynasty c. 1697–1851* (Oswestry, Shropshire, 1997).

Barney, John, 'North Sea and Baltic Convoy 1793–1814: As Experienced by Merchant Masters Employed by Michael Henley', *Mariner's Mirror*, Vol. 95 (2009), pp. 429–40.

Barrell, John, *The Spirit of Despotism: Invasions of Privacy in the 1790s* (Oxford, 2006).

Barritt, M. K., *Eyes of the Admiralty: J. T. Serres, an Artist in the Channel Fleet 1799–1800* (London, 2008).

Barrow, Sir John, *The Life of Richard, Earl Howe* (London, 1838).

— *An Autobiographical Memoir* (London, 1841).

Bartlett, C. J., *Castlereagh* (London, 1966).

— and Smith, Gene A., 'A "Species of Milito-Nautico-Guerilla-Plundering Warfare": Admiral Alexander Cochrane's Naval Campaign against the United States 1814–1815' in Flavell and Conway, *Britain and America Go to War*, pp. 173–204.

Bartlett, Keith, 'The Development of the British Army during the Wars with France 1793–1815' (Durham Ph.D., 1997).

Bartlett, Thomas, 'An End to Moral Economy: The Irish Militia Disturbances of 1793', *Past & Present*, Vol. 99 (1983), pp. 41–64.

— '"The Invasion that Never Was": Naval and Military Aspects of the French Expedition to Bantry Bay 1796' in Murphy, *The French are in the Bay*, pp. 48–72.

— and Jeffrey, Keith, *A Military History of Ireland* (Cambridge, 1996).

Bath and Wells, Bishop of, *The Journal and Correspondence of William, Lord Auckland*, 4 vols. (London, 1861–2).

Baugh, Daniel A., 'Why Did Britain Lose Command of the Sea during the War for America?' in Jeremy Black and Philip Woodfine (eds.), *The British Navy and the Use of Naval Power in the Eighteenth Century* (Leicester, 1988), pp. 149–69.

— 'Great Britain's "Blue-Water" Policy 1689–1815', *International History Review*, Vol. 10 (1988), pp. 33–58.

— 'The Politics of British Naval Failure 1775–1777', *American Neptune*, Vol. 52 (1992), pp. 221–46.

Beckett, Ian F. W., 'The Amateur Military Tradition in Britain', *War and Society*, Vol. 4 (1986), pp. 1–16.

— 'The Militia and the King's Enemies 1793–1815' in Guy, *Road to Waterloo*, pp. 32–9.

Beerbühl, Margrit Schulte, 'Crossing the Channel: Nathan Mayer Rothschild and His Trade with the Continent during the Early Years of the Blockades (1803–1808)', *The Rothschild Archive* (2007–8), pp. 41–8, http://www.rothschildarchive.org/ib/articles/AR2008Blockade.pdf.

— 'Supplying the Belligerent Countries: Transnational Trading Networks during the Napoleonic Wars' in Harding and Ferri, *Contractor State*, pp. 21–34.

Bell, David A., *The First Total War: Napoleon's Europe and the Birth of Modern Warfare* (London, 2007).

Bellesiles, Michael A., 'Experiencing the War of 1812' in Flavell and Conway, *Britain and America Go to War*, pp. 205–40.

Bergeron, Louis, *France under Napoleon* (translated by R. R. Palmer) (Princeton, 1981).

Berkeley, Alice D. (ed.), *New Lights on the Peninsular War* (Lisbon, 1991).

Beveridge, Sir William, *Prices and Wages in England from the Twelfth to the Nineteenth Century* (London, 1939; repr. 1965).

Bew, John, *Castlereagh: Enlightenment, War and Tyranny* (London, 2011).

Bickham, Troy, *The Weight of Vengeance: The United States, the British Empire and the War of 1812* (New York, 2012).

Bickley, F. L., *The Diaries of Sylvester Douglas, Lord Glenbervie*, 2 vols. (London, 1928).

Bindoff, S. T., Malcolm Smith, E. F., and Webster, C. K., *British Diplomatic Representatives 1789–1852* (London, 1934).

Binney, J. E. D., *British Public Finance and Administration 1774–1792* (Oxford, 1958).

Black, Jeremy, *British Foreign Policy in an Age of Revolutions 1783–1793* (Cambridge, 1994).

Blackmore, Howard, *British Military Firearms 1650–1850* (London, 1968).

Blake, Peter, 'The Siege of Flushing 1809: A Success within the Failure of the Walcheren Expedition' (University of Greenwich M.A. thesis, 2008).

— *Military Superintendents of the Royal Gunpowder Mills* (Waltham Abbey, 2011).

Blake, Richard, *Evangelicals in the Royal Navy 1775–1815: Blue Lights and Psalm-Singers* (Woodbridge, Suffolk, 2008).

Blanning, T. C. W., *The French Revolutionary Wars 1787–1802* (London, 1996).

Bond, Gordon C., *The Grand Expedition: The British Invasion of Holland in 1809* (Athens, Georgia, 1979).

Bonser, K. J., *The Drovers: Who They Were and How They Went: An Epic of the English Countryside* (Newton Abbot, Devon, 1972).

Bordo, Michael D., and White, Eugene N., 'A Tale of Two Currencies: British and French Finance during the Napoleonic Wars', *Journal of Economic History*, Vol. 51 (1991), pp. 303–16.

Boucher, Cyril T. G., *John Rennie 1761–1821: The Life and Work of a Great Engineer* (Manchester, 1963).

Bourne, Kenneth, *Palmerston: The Early Years 1784–1841* (London, 1982).

Bowen, H. V., *War and British Society 1688–1815* (Cambridge, 1998).

— *The Business of Empire: The East India Company and Imperial Britain 1756–1833* (Cambridge, 2006).

— 'Mobilizing Resources for Global Warfare: The British State and the East India Company 1756–1815' in Bowen and Enciso, *Mobilizing Resources*, pp. 81–110.

— 'Trading with the Enemy: British Private Trade and the Supply of Arms to India *c.* 1750–1820' in Harding and Ferri, *Contractor State*, pp. 35–56.

— and Enciso, A. González, *Mobilizing Resources for War: Britain and Spain at Work during the Early Modern Period* (Pamplona, Spain, 2006).

Bowen, H. V., Lincoln, Margarette, and Rigby, Nigel (eds.), *The Worlds of the East India Company* (Woodbridge, Suffolk, 2002).

Boyden, Peter B., *Tommy Atkins's Letters: The History of the British Army Postal Service from 1795* (London, 1990).

— ' "System of Communication throughout Each County": Fire-Beacons and Their Role in the Defence of the Realm 1803–1811' in Guy, *Road to Waterloo*, pp. 126–31.

Bradley, P. Brendan, *Bantry Bay* (Dublin, 1931).

Brandon, Peter, 'The History of the South Downs Landscape' in Gerald Smart and Peter Brandon (eds.), *The Future of the South Downs: Landscape, Ecology, Land Use and Conservation* (Chichester, 2007), pp. 42–53.

Breihan, John R., 'The Addington Party and the Navy in British Politics 1801–1806' in Craig L. Symonds (ed.), *New Aspects of Naval History* (Annapolis, Maryland, 1981), pp. 163–89.

— 'William Pitt and the Commission on Fees 1785–1801', *Historical Journal*, Vol. 27 (1984), pp. 59–81.

Brenton, Edward Pelham (ed.), *Life and Correspondence of John, Earl of St Vincent*, 2 vols. (London, 1838).

Brewer, John, *The Sinews of Power: War, Money and the English State 1688–1783* (New York, 1989).

Brightfield, Myron F., *John Wilson Croker* (Berkeley, California, 1940).

Brockliss, Laurence, Cardwell, John, and Moss, Michael, *Nelson's Surgeon: William Beatty, Naval Medicine and the Battle of Trafalgar* (Oxford, 2008).

Brown, David, *Palmerston: A Biography* (London, 2010).

Bruce, Anthony, *The Purchase System in the British Army 1660–1871* (London, 1980).

Buckingham and Chandos, Duke of, *Memoirs of the Court and Cabinets of George the Third*, 4 vols. (London, 1853–5).

Bunbury, Charles J. F. (ed.), *Memoir and Literary Remains of Lieutenant-General Sir Henry Edward Bunbury, Bart.* (privately printed, London, 1868).

Bunbury, Henry, *Narratives of Some Passages in the Great War with France from 1799 to 1810* (London, 1854).

Burnham, Robert, 'British Observing Officers of the Peninsular War' and 'British Bridging Operations in the Peninsula' in Muir et al., *Inside Wellington's Peninsular Army*, pp. 71–83, 226–74.

— and McGuigan, Ron, *The British Army against Napoleon: Facts, Lists and Trivia 1805–1815* (Barnsley, South Yorkshire, 2010).

Burroughs, Peter, 'An Unreformed Army? 1815–1868' in Chandler and Beckett, *Oxford History of the British Army*, pp. 161–86.

Butel, Paul, 'Revolution and the Urban Economy: Maritime Cities and Continental Cities' in Alan Forrest and Peter Jones, *Reshaping France: Town, Country and Region during the French Revolution* (Manchester, 1991), pp. 37–51.

Campbell-Smith, Duncan, *Masters of the Post: The Authorized History of the Royal Mail* (London, 2011).

Camperdown, Earl of, *Admiral Duncan* (London, 1898).

Carnock, Major Lord, *Cavalry in the Corunna Campaign* (Society for Army Historical Research, Special Publication No. 4, 1936).

Chaloner, W. H., 'Salt in Cheshire 1600–1870', *Palatinate Studies: Chapters in the Social and Industrial History of Lancashire and Cheshire* (Chetham Society, 1992).

Chalus, Elaine, 'Elite Women and Social Politics', *Historical Journal*, Vol. 43 (2000), pp. 669–97.

Chamberlain, Paul, 'Marching into Captivity: Prisoners of War during the Peninsular Campaign 1808–1814' in Berkeley, *New Lights on the Peninsular War*, pp. 221–9.

— *Hell upon Water: Prisoners of War in Britain 1793–1815* (Stroud, Gloucestershire, 2008).

Chandler, David G., 'An Undergroom at War: Edward Healey 1815' in Chandler, *On the Napoleonic Wars* (London, 1994), pp. 214–29.

— and Beckett, Ian, *The Oxford History of the British Army* (Oxford, 1994).

Clammer, David, 'Dorset's Volunteer Infantry 1794–1805', *Journal of the Society for Army Historical Research*, Vol. 89 (2011), pp. 6–25.

Clayton, Tim, *Tars: The Men Who Made Britain Rule the Waves* (London, 2007).

Clements, Bill, *Martello Towers Worldwide* (Barnsley, South Yorkshire, 2011).

Clowes, W. Laird, *The Royal Navy: A History from the Earliest Times to the Present*, 7 vols. (London, 1897–1903).

Coad, Jonathan, 'Chatham Ropeyard', *Post-Medieval Archaeology*, Vol. 3 (1969), pp. 143–65.

— 'Hurst Castle: The Evolution of a Tudor Fortress 1790–1945', *Post-Medieval Archaelogy*, Vol. 19 (1985), pp. 63–104.

— *The Royal Dockyards 1690–1850* (Aldershot, 1989).

— *Dymchurch Martello Tower* (London, 1990).

— 'The Development and Organization of Plymouth Dockyard 1689–1815' in Duffy, *New Maritime History of Devon*, Vol. I, pp. 192–200.

— 'New Ideas and New Materials: Their Impact on the Royal Dockyards during the French Revolutionary and Napoleonic Wars 1793–1815' in Merwe, *Science and the French and British Navies*, pp. 88–98.

— *The Portsmouth Block Mills: Bentham, Brunel and the Start of the Royal Navy's Industrial Revolution* (Swindon, 2005).

— *Support for the Fleet: Architecture and Engineering of the Royal Navy's Bases 1700–1914* (Swindon, 2013).

— and Lewis, P. N., 'The Later Fortifications of Dover', *Post-Medieval Archaeology*, Vol. 16 (1982), pp. 141–96.

Coats, Ann, 'Efficiency in Dockyard Administration 1660–1800: A Reassessment' in N. Tracy (ed.), *The Age of Sail: The International Annual of the Historic Sailing Ship*, Vol. I (London, 2002), pp. 116–32.

— 'The Block Mills: New Labour Practices for New Machines?', *Transactions of the Naval Dockyards Society*, Vol. 1 (2006), pp. 59–84.

— 'Rosia Water Tanks, Gibraltar', *Transactions of the Naval Dockyards Society*, Vol. 2 (2006), pp. 81–7.

— '"Launched into Eternity": Admiralty Retribution or the Restoration of Discipline?' in Coats and MacDougall, *Naval Mutinies of 1797*, pp. 209–25.

— and MacDougall, Philip (eds.), *The Naval Mutinies of 1797: Unity and Perseverence* (Woodbridge, Suffolk, 2011).

Cobban, Alfred, 'British Secret Service in France 1784–1792', *English Historical Review*, Vol. 69 (1954), pp. 226–61.

Cock, Randolph, 'The Cost of Re-Coppering', *Mariner's Mirror*, Vol. 85 (1999), p. 93.

— '"The Finest Invention in the World": The Royal Navy's Early Trials of Copper Sheathing 1708–1770', *Mariner's Mirror*, Vol. 87 (2001), pp. 446–59.

Cohen, Emmeline W., *The Growth of the British Civil Service 1780–1939* (London, 1941; repr. 1965).

Colchester, Lord (ed.), *The Diary and Correspondence of Charles Abbot, Lord Colchester, Speaker of the House of Commons 1802–1817*, 3 vols. (London, 1861).

Cole, Gareth, 'Gunpowder Manufacturers and the Office of Ordnance 1793–1815' in Andreas Gestrich and Margrit Schulte Beerbühl (eds.), *Cosmopolitan Networks in Commerce and Society 1660–1914* (German Historical Institute, London, 2011), pp. 293–314.

— *Arming the Royal Navy 1793–1815: The Office of Ordnance and the State* (London, 2012).

Colley, Linda, *Britons: Forging the Nation 1707–1837* (New Haven and London, 1992).

— 'The Reach of the State, the Appeal of the Nation: Mass Arming and Political Culture in the Napoleonic Wars' in Lawrence Stone (ed.), *An Imperial State at War: Britain from 1689 to 1815* (London, 1994), pp. 165–84.

Collinge, J. M., *Navy Board Officials 1660–1832* (London, 1978).

— *Foreign Office Officials 1782–1870* (London, 1979).

Collins, Bruce, *War and Empire: The Expansion of Britain 1790–1830* (London, 2010).

Colvin, H. M., *The History of the King's Works*, Vols. V and VI (London, 1976–82).

Comfort, Sim, 'Comments Regarding the Awarding of Badges of Valour by the Lloyd's Patriotic Fund (1803–1809)', www.lloydsswords.com.

— *Naval Swords and Dirks: A Study of British, French and American Naval Swords, Cutlasses and Dirks used during the Age of Fighting Sail*, 2 vols. (London, 2008).

Condon, Mary Ellen, 'The Administration of the Transport Service during the War against Revolutionary France' (University of London Ph.D. thesis, 1968).

— 'Living Conditions On Board Troopships during the War against Revolutionary France 1793–1802', *Journal of the Society for Army Historical Research*, Vol. 49 (1971), pp. 14–19.

— 'Surveying, Measuring and Valuing British Transports during the War against Revolutionary France', *Mariner's Mirror*, Vol. 58 (1972), pp. 331–6.

Congreve, William (the Elder), *Statement of Facts Relative to the Savings which have Arisen from Manufacturing Gunpowder at the Royal Powder Mills and the Improvements Made since 1783* (London, 1811).

Congreve, William (the Younger), *The Details of the Rocket System* (London, 1814).

Consolvo, Charles, 'The Prospects and Promotion of British Naval Officers 1793–1815', *Mariner's Mirror*, Vol. 91 (2005), pp. 137–59.

Conway, Stephen, and Sanchez, Rafael Torres (eds.), *The Spending of States: Military Expenditure during the Long Eighteenth Century: Patterns, Organization and Consequences 1650–1815* (Saarbrucken, Germany, 2011).

Cookson, J. E., *The Friends of Peace: Anti-war Liberalism 1793–1815* (Cambridge, 1982).

— 'Political Arithmetic and War in Britain 1793–1815', *War and Society*, Vol. 1 (1983), pp. 37–60.

— 'The English Volunteer Movement of the French Wars 1793–1815: Some Contexts', *Historical Journal*, Vol. 32 (1989), pp. 867–91.

— *The British Armed Nation 1793–1815* (Oxford, 1997).

— 'Service without Politics? Army, Militia and Volunteers during the American and French Revolutionary Wars', *War in History*, Vol. 10 (2003), pp. 381–97.

— 'Regimental Worlds: Interpreting the Experience of British Soldiers during the Napoleonic Wars' in Forrest et al., *Soldiers, Citizens and Civilians*, pp. 23–42.

Cooper, Richard, 'William Pitt, Taxation and the Needs of War', *Journal of British Studies* Vol. 22 (1982), pp. 94–103.

Cope, S. R., 'The Goldsmids and the Development of the London Money Market during the Napoleonic Wars', *Economica* (1942), pp. 180–206.

— *Walter Boyd: A Merchant Banker in the Age of Napoleon* (Gloucester, 1983).

Corbett, Julian S., *The Campaign of Trafalgar* (London, 1919; repr. 1976).

— 'Napoleon and the British Navy after Trafalgar', *Quarterly Review*, Vol. 237 (1922), repr. in Richard Harding (ed.), *Naval History 1650–1850* (Aldershot, 2006), pp. 1–16.

Cormack, William S., *Revolution and Political Conflict in the French Navy 1789–1794* (Cambridge, 1995).

Cornwallis-West, G., *The Life and Letters of Admiral Cornwallis* (London, 1927).

Craig, Hardin, 'Letters of Lord St Vincent to Thomas Grenville 1806–1807' in Christopher Lloyd (ed.), *Naval Miscellany*, Vol. IV (Navy Records Society, No. 92, 1952), pp. 470–93.

Cranmer-Byng, J. L., 'Essex Prepares for Invasion', *Essex Review*, Vol. 60 (1951), pp. 127–34, 184–93; Vol. 61 (1952), pp. 43–7, 57–74.

Crawford, Captain A., *Reminiscences of a Naval Officer: A Quarter-Deck View of the War against Napoleon* (London, 1851; repr. 1999).

Creswell, John, *Generals and Admirals: The Story of Amphibious Command* (London, 1952).

Creveld, Martin van, *Supplying War: Logistics from Wallenstein to Patton* (Cambridge, 1977).

Crimmin, Patricia K., 'Admiralty Relations with the Treasury 1783–1806: The Preparation of Naval Estimates and the Beginnings of Treasury Control', *Mariner's Mirror*, Vol. 53 (1967), pp. 63–72.

— 'The Financial and Clerical Establishment of the Admiralty Office 1783–1806', *Mariner's Mirror*, Vol. 55 (1969), pp. 299–309.

— 'Royal Trinity House Volunteers Artillery', *Mariner's Mirror*, Vol. 70 (1984), p. 92.

— 'French Prisoners of War on Parole 1793–1815: The Welsh Border Towns' in *Guerres et paix 1660–1815* (Vincennes, 1987), pp. 61–71.

— 'The Impact of the Exchange of Prisoners of War on the Defense of Shipping in the American War 1812–1814' in Clark G. Reynolds (ed.), *Global Crossroads: The American Seas* (Missoula, Montana, 1988), pp. 145–54.

— 'The Channel's Strategic Significance: Invasion Threat, Line of Defence, Prison Wall, Escape Route', *Studies on Voltaire and the Eighteenth Century* (The Voltaire Foundation, 1991), pp. 67–79, 292.

— 'War and Peace: England and Spain: The Incarceration of Spanish Prisoners of War in Britain 1793–1816' in Berkeley, *New Lights on the Peninsular War*, pp. 231–41.

— 'Prisoners of War and British Port Communities 1793–1815', *Northern Mariner*, Vol. 6 (1996), pp. 17–27.

— 'The Sick and Hurt Board and the Health of Seamen, c. 1700–1806', *Journal of Maritime Research* (1999), e-journal.

— 'Sir Thomas Troubridge c. 1749–1807' in LeFevre and Harding, *Contemporaries of Nelson*, pp. 295–321.

— 'The Supply of Timber for the Royal Navy c. 1803–c. 1830', *Miscellany*, Vol. VII (Navy Records Society, 153, 2008), pp. 191–234.

— 'The Sick and Hurt Board: Fit for Purpose?' in David Haycock and Sally Archer (eds.), *Health and Medicine at Sea 1700–1900* (Woodbridge, Suffolk, 2009), pp. 90–107.

Crook, J., and Port, M. H., *The History of the King's Works*, Vol. VI (London, 1973).

Crook, Malcolm, *Toulon in War and Revolution: From the Ancien Régime to the Restoration 1750–1820* (Manchester, 1991).

Cross, Anthony, *By the Banks of the Neva: Chapters from the Lives and Careers of the British in Eighteenth-Century Russia* (Cambridge, 1997).

Crouzet, François, 'War, Blockade and Economic Change in Europe 1792–1815', *Journal of Economic History*, Vol. 24 (1964), pp. 567–88.

— 'Towards an Export Economy: British Exports during the Industrial Revolution', *Explorations in Economic History*, Vol. 17 (1980), pp. 48–93.

— 'America and the Crisis of the British Imperial Economy 1803–1807' in McCusker and Morgan, *Early Modern Atlantic Economy*, pp. 278–315.

Crowhurst, Patrick, *The French War on Trade: Privateering 1793–1815* (Aldershot, Hants, 1989).

Cruikshank, George, *A Pop-Gun Fired off by George Cruikshank in Defence of the British Volunteers of 1803* (London, 1806).

Crumplin, Michael, 'Surgery in the Royal Navy during the Republican and Napoleonic Wars' in Haycock and Archer, *Health and Medicine at Sea*, pp. 63–89.

Currie, Ann, *Henleys of Wapping: A London Shipowning Family 1770–1830* (London, 1988).

Daly, Gavin, 'Merchants and Maritime Commerce in Napoleonic Normandy', *French History*, Vol. 15 (2001), pp. 26–50.

— 'English Smugglers, the Channel, and the Napoleonic Wars 1800–1814', *Journal of British Studies*, Vol. 46 (2007), pp. 30–46.

— 'Napoleon and the City of Smugglers 1810–1814', *Historical Journal*, Vol. 50 (2007), pp. 333–52.

Dancy, Jeremiah R., 'British Naval Manpower during the French Revolutionary War 1793–1802' (Oxford D.Phil., 2012).

Daunton, M. J., *Trusting Leviathan: The Politics of Taxation in Britain 1799–1814* (Cambridge, 2001).

Davey, James, 'Within Hostile Shores: Victualling the Royal Navy in European Waters during the French Revolutionary and Napoleonic Wars', *International Journal of Maritime History*, Vol. 21 (2009), pp. 241–60.

— 'The Repatriation of Spanish Troops from Denmark 1808: The British Government, Logistics, and Maritime Supremacy', *Journal of Military History*, Vol. 74 (2010), pp. 689–707.

— 'The Advancement of Nautical Knowledge: The Hydrographical Office, the Royal Navy and the Charting of the Baltic Sea, 1795–1815', *Journal of Maritime Research*, Vol. 13 (2011), pp. 81–103.

— 'Securing the Sinews of Sea Power: British Intervention in the Baltic 1780–1815', *International History Review*, Vol. 33 (2011), pp. 161–84.

— 'Supplied by the Enemy: The Royal Navy and the British Consular Service in the Baltic 1808–12', *Historical Research*, Vol. 85 (2012), pp. 1–19.

— *The Transformation of British Naval Strategy: Seapower and Supply in Northern Europe 1808–1812* (Woodbridge, Suffolk, 2012).

Davies, D. W., *Sir John Moore's Peninsular Campaign 1808–1809* (The Hague, Netherlands, 1974).

Davies, Huw J., 'British Intelligence in the Peninsular War' (University of Exeter Ph.D., 2006).

— 'Integration of Strategic and Operational Intelligence during the Peninsular War', *Intelligence and National Security*, Vol. 21 (2006), pp. 202–23.

— 'Naval Intelligence to the British Army in the Peninsular War', *Journal of the Society for Army Historical Research*, Vol. 86 (2008), pp. 34–56.

— 'Diplomats as Spymasters: A Case Study of the Peninsular War 1809–1813', *Journal of Military History*, Vol. 76 (2012), pp. 37–68.

— *Wellington's Wars: The Making of a Military Genius* (New Haven, 2012).

Davis, Godfrey, 'The Whigs and the Peninsular War 1808–1814', *Transactions of the Royal Historical Society*, 2nd Series, Vol. 4 (1919), pp. 114–31.

Davis, Ralph, *The Industrial Revolution and British Overseas Trade* (Leicester, 1979).

Day, John, 'British Admiralty Control and Naval Power in the Indian Ocean 1793–1815' (Exeter Ph.D., 2012)

Deane, Phyllis, and Cole, W. A., *British Economic Growth 1688–1959: Trends and Structure* (Cambridge, 1964).

Derrick, Charles, *Memoirs of the Rise and Progress of the Royal Navy* (London, 1806).

Dixon, Peter, *Canning: Politican and Statesman* (London, 1976).

Dobson, C. R., *Masters and Journeymen: A Pre-History of Industrial Relations 1717–1800* (London, 1980).

Dodd, A. H., *The Industrial Revolution in North Wales* (Cardiff, 1951).

Doe, Helen, 'The Thames Merchant Yards in the Napoleonic Wars' in Roger Owen (ed.), *Shipbuilding and Ships on the Thames* (London, 2006), pp. 10–21.

— 'Challenging Images: Mrs. Mary Ross of Rochester, Nineteenth-century Business Woman and Warship Builder', *Journal of Maritime Research* (May 2006).

— *Enterprising Women and Shipping in the Nineteenth Century* (Woodbridge, Suffolk, 2009).

Douet, James, *British Barracks 1600–1914: Their Architecture and Role in Society* (London, 1998).

Downer, Martyn, *Nelson's Purse* (London, 2004).

Drabble, Stuart, 'Templar & Parlby: Eighteenth-Century Engineering and Building Contractors', *Proceedings of the Institution of Civil Engineers: Engineering History and Heritage*, Vol. 163 (August 2010), pp. 1–10.

Dropmore, Historical Manuscripts Commission, *Report on the MSS of J. B. Fortescue, Esq., Preserved at Dropmore*, 9 vols. (London, 1892–1915).

Dudley, William S., *The Naval War of 1812: A Documentary History*, 2 vols. (Washington, D.C., 1985, 1992).

Duffy, Michael, '"A particular service": The British Government and the Dunkirk Expedition of 1793', *English Historical Review*, Vol. 91 (1976), pp. 529–54.

— *Soldiers, Sugar and Seapower: The British Expeditions to the West Indies and the War against Revolutionary France* (Oxford, 1987).

— 'Pitt, Grenville and the Control of Foreign Policy in the 1790s' in J. Black (ed.), *Knights Errant and True Englishmen: British Foreign Policy 1660–1800* (Edinburgh, 1989), pp. 151–77.

— 'Devon and the Naval Strategy of the French Wars 1689–1815' in Duffy, *New Maritime History of Devon*, Vol. I, pp. 182–91.

— 'British Naval Intelligence and Bonaparte's Egyptian Expedition of 1798', *Mariner's Mirror*, Vol. 84 (1998), pp. 278–90.

— 'World-wide War and British Expansion 1793–1815' in Marshall, *British Empire*, pp. 184–207.

— *The Younger Pitt* (London, 2000).

— 'Sir Samuel Hood' in LeFevre and Harding, *Contemporaries of Nelson*, pp. 323–45.

— 'British Intelligence and the Breakout of the French Atlantic Fleet from Brest in 1799', *Intelligence and National Security*, Vol. 22 (2007), pp. 601–18.

— 'Festering the Spanish Ulcer: The Royal Navy and the Peninsular War 1806–1814' in Bruce A. Ellerman and S. C. M. Paine (eds.), *Naval Power and Expeditionary Warfare: Peripheral Campaigns and New Theatres of Naval Warfare* (London, 2011), pp. 15–28.

— et al. (eds.), *The New Maritime History of Devon*, 2 vols. (London, 1992, 1994).

Dugdale, George S., *Whitehall through the Centuries* (London, 1950).

Dupin, Charles, *Narratives of Two Excursions to the Ports of England, Scotland and Ireland in 1816, 1817 and 1818* (London, [n.d.]).

Durey, Michael, 'The British Secret Service and the Escape of Sir Sidney Smith from Paris in 1798', *History*, Vol. 84 (1999), pp. 437–57.

— 'Lord Grenville and the "Smoking Gun": The Plot to Assassinate the French Directory in 1798–1799', *Historical Journal*, Vol. 45 (2002), pp. 547–68.

— 'William Wickham, the Christ Church Connection and the Rise and Fall of the Security Service in Britain 1793–1801', *English Historical Review*, Vol. 121 (2006), pp. 714–45.

— '"Black Bob" Craufurd and Ireland 1798–1804', *War in History*, Vol. 16 (2009), pp. 133–56.

— *William Wickham, Master Spy* (London, 2009).

Earle, James, *Commodore Squib: The Life, Times and Secretive Wars of England's First Rocket Man 1772–1827* (Newcastle upon Tyne, 2010).

East, W. G., 'England in the Eighteenth Century' in H. C. Darby, *An Historical Geography of England before AD 1800* (Cambridge, 1961), pp. 465–528.

Eastwood, David, '"Amplifying the Province of the Legislature": The Flow of Information and the English State in the Early Nineteenth Century', *Historical Research*, Vol. 62 (1989), pp. 276–94.

— 'The Age of Uncertainty: Britain in the Early Nineteenth Century', *Transactions of the Royal Historical Society*, 6th Series, Vol. 8 (1998), pp. 91–115.

Ehrman, John, *The Younger Pitt. Vol. I: The Years of Acclaim. Vol. II: The Reluctant Transition. Vol. III: The Consuming Struggle* (London, 1969, 1983, 1996).

Elliott, Colin, 'Some Transactions of a Dartmouth Privateer during the French Wars at the End of the Eighteenth Century' in Stephen Fisher (ed.), *Studies in British Privateering, Trading Enterprise and Seamen's Welfare 1775–1800* (Exeter, 1987), pp. 19–40.

Ellis, Geoffrey, *Napoleon's Continental Blockade: The Case of Alsace* (Oxford, 1981).

Ellis, Kenneth, *The British Post Office in the Eighteenth Century: A Study in Administrative History* (Oxford, 1958).

— 'British Communications and Diplomacy in the Eighteenth Century', *Bulletin of the Institute of Historical Research*, Vol. 31 (1958), pp. 159–67.

Elting, John R., *Swords around a Throne: Napoleon's Grande Armée* (New York, 1988).

Emsley, Clive, *North Riding Naval Recruits: The Quota Acts and the Quota Men 1795–1797* (North Yorkshire County Record Office Publications No. 18, 1978).

— *British Society and the French Wars 1793–1815* (1979).

— 'The Military and Popular Disorder in England 1790–1801', *Journal of the Society for Army Historical Research*, Vol. 61 (1983), pp. 10–21, 96–112.

— 'The Volunteer Movement' in Guy, *Road to Waterloo*, pp. 40–47.

—, Crossley, Ceri, and Small, Ian (eds.), *The French Revolution and British Society* (Oxford, 1989).

Epin, Christian, *Les Ouvriers des arsenaux de la marine sous Napoléon: vivre et survivre en travaillant pour l'État* (Montreuillon, 1990).

Esdaile, Charles, *The Peninsular War* (London, 2002).

— *Napoleon's Wars: An International History 1803–1815* (London, 2007).

Esteban, Javier, 'Dimensions of Britain's Regulated Trade with Asia 1765–1812' in Sanchez, *War, State and Development*, pp. 69–86.

Evans, Chris, *Debating the Revolution: Britain in the 1790s* (London, 2006).

Evans, David, *Arming the Fleet: The Development of the Royal Ordnance Yards 1770–1945* (Gosport, 2006).

Fay, C. R., *Huskisson and His Age* (London, 1950).

Fedorak, Charles John, 'In Defence of Great Britain: Henry Addington, the Duke of York and Military Preparations against Invasion by Napoleonic France 1803–1804' in Philp, *Resisting Napoleon*, pp. 91–110.

Feldbaek, Ole, *The Battle of Copenhagen 1801* (Copenhagen, 1985; trans. 2002).

Ferguson, Kenneth, 'The Army in Ireland from the Restoration to the Act of Union' (Trinity College Dublin Ph.D., 1980).

Ferguson, Niall, *The House of Rothschild. Vol. I: Money's Prophets 1798–1848* (London, 1999).

Fernyhough, Thomas, *Military Memoirs of Four Brothers* (London, 1829; repr. 2002).

Fewster, Joseph M., *The Keelmen of Tyneside: Labour Organization and Conflict in the North East Coal Industry 1600–1830* (Woodbridge, Suffolk, 2011).

Findlay, Ronald, and O'Rourke, Kevin, *Power and Plenty: Trade, War and the World Economy in the Second Millennium* (Princeton, 2007).

Fisher, Susanna, 'Captain Thomas Hurd's Survey of the Bay of Brest during the Blockade in the Napoleonic Wars', *Mariner's Mirror*, Vol. 79 (1993), pp. 293–304.

Flavell, Julie, and Conway, Stephen (eds.), *Britain and America Go to War: The Impact of War and Warfare in Anglo-America 1754–1815* (Gainesville, Florida, 2004).

Flayhart, William Henry, *Counterpoint to Trafalgar: The Anglo-Russian Invasion of Naples 1805–1806* (Columbia, South Carolina, 1992).

Fletcher, Ian, *The Waters of Oblivion: The British Invasion of the Rio de la Plata 1806–1807* (Stroud, Gloucestershire, 2006).

Fone, J. F., 'The Naval Yard at Yarmouth in the Napoleonic Wars', *Norfolk Archaeology*, Vol. 41 (1992), pp. 351–8.

Fontana, V. J. L., 'The Political and Religious Signficance of the British/Irish Militia Interchange 1811–1816', *Journal of the Society for Army Historical Research*, Vol. 84 (2006), pp. 131–57.

Foreman, Amanda, *Georgiana, Duchess of Devonshire* (London, 1998).

Forrest, Alan, Hagemann, Karen, and Rendall, Jane (eds.), *Soldiers, Citizens and Civilians: Experiences and Perceptions of the Revolutionary and Napoleonic Wars 1790–1820* (Basingstoke, 2009).

Fremantle, Anne (ed.), *The Wynne Diaries: The Adventures of Two Sisters in Europe* (Oxford, 1952).

Frost, Alan, *Arthur Phillip 1738–1814: His Voyaging* (Melbourne, 1987).

Furber, Holden, *Henry Dundas, First Viscount Melville, 1742–1811: Political Manager of Scotland, Statesman, Administrator of British India* (Oxford, 1931).

Fussell, G. E., and Goodman, Constance, 'Eighteenth Century Traffic in Livestock', *Economic History*, Vol. 3 (1937), pp. 214–36.

Galpin, W. Freeman, 'The American Grain Trade to the Spanish Peninsula 1810–1814', *American Historical Review*, Vol. 28 (1922), pp. 24–44.

— *The Grain Supply of England during the Napoleonic Era* (Michigan, 1925; repr. New York, 1977).

Gardiner, Robert, *Frigates of the Napoleonic Wars* (London, 2000).

Gates, David, 'The Transformation of the Army 1783–1815' in Chandler and Beckett, *Oxford History of the British Army*, pp. 132–60.

— *The Napoleonic Wars 1803–1815* (London, 2003).

Gee, Austin, *The British Volunteer Movement 1794–1814* (Oxford, 2003).

Gilbert, K. R., *Henry Maudslay* (London, 1971).

Glete, Jan, *Navies and Nations: Warships, Navies and State Building in Europe and America 1500–1800*, 2 vols. (Stockholm, 1993).

Glover, Michael, '*A Very Slippery Fellow': The Life of Sir Robert Wilson 1777–1849* (Oxford, 1977).

Glover, Richard, *Peninsular Preparation: The Reform of the British Army 1795–1809* (Cambridge, 1963; repr. 2008).

— 'The French Fleet, 1807–1814: Britain's Problem and Madison's Opportunity', *Journal of Military History*, Vol. 34 (1967), pp. 233–54.

— *Britain at Bay: Defence against Napoleon 1803–1814* (1973).

Godechat, Jacques, 'The Internal History of France during the Wars 1793–1814' in C. W. Crawley (ed.), *The New Cambridge Modern History*, Vol. IX (Cambridge, 1965), pp. 275–306.

Goodwin, A., 'War Transport and "Counter-Revolution" in France in 1793: The Case of the Winter Company and Financier Jean-Jacques de Beaune' in M. R. D. Foot (ed.), *War and Society: Historical Essays in Honour and Memory of J. R. Western 1928–1971* (London, 1973), pp. 213–24.

Goodwin, John, *The Military Defence of West Sussex* (Easebourne, Midhurst, Sussex, 1985).

Gore, John (ed.), *Creevey's Life and Times: A Further Selection from the Correspondence of Thomas Creevey* (London, 1934).

Grainger, John D., *The Amiens Truce: Britain and Bonaparte 1801–1803* (Woodbridge, Suffolk, 2004).

Granville, Countess (ed.), *Lord Granville Leveson Gower: Private Correspondence 1781–1821*, 2 vols. (London, 1916).

Gray, Douglas, *Spencer Perceval, the Evangelical Prime Minister, 1762–1812* (Manchester, 1963).

Green, Geoffrey, *The Royal Navy and Anglo-Jewry 1740–1820* (London, 1989).

Greenleaf, W. H., 'The Commission of Military Enquiry 1805–1812', *Journal of the Society for Army Historical Research*, Vol. 41 (1963), pp. 171–81.

Gregory, Desmond, 'British Occupations of Madeira during the Wars against Napoleon', *Journal of the Society for Army Historical Research*, Vol. 66 (1988), pp. 80–96.

Gregory, Jeremy and Stevenson, John, *The Longman Companion to Britain in the Eighteenth Century 1688–1820* (London, 2000).

Grocott, Terence, *Shipwrecks of the Revolutionary and Napoleonic Eras* (London, 2002).

Guy, Alan, 'A Good Man at Falmouth: Captain Philip Melvill, Defender of Pendennis Castle 1796–1811' in Guy, *Road to Waterloo*, pp. 111–25.

— (ed.), *The Road to Waterloo: The British Army and the Struggle against Revolutionary and Napoleonic France 1793–1815* (London, 1990).

Gwyn, Julian, *Ashore and Afloat: The British Navy and Halifax Naval Yard before 1820* (Ottawa, 2004).

Hagemann, Karen, '"Unimaginable Horror and Misery": The Battle of Leipzig in October 1813 in Civilian Experience and Perception' in Forrest et al., *Soldiers, Citizens and Civilians*, pp. 157–78.

Hague, William, *William Pitt the Younger* (London, 2004).

— *William Wilberforce* (London, 2008).

Hall, Christopher D., 'Addington at War: Unspectacular but not Unsuccessful', *Bulletin of the Institute of Historical Research*, Vol. 61 (1988), pp. 306–16.

— *British Strategy in the Napoleonic War 1803–1815* (Manchester, 1992).

— *Wellington's Navy: Seapower and the Peninsular War 1807–1814* (London, 2004).

Hamilton, C. I., 'John Wilson Croker: Patronage and Clientage at the Admiralty 1809–1857', *Historical Journal*, Vol. 43 (2000), pp. 49–77.

— 'Expanding Naval Powers: Admiralty Private Secretaries and Private Offices 1800–1945', *War in History*, Vol. 10 (2003), pp. 125–56.

— *The Making of the Modern Admiralty: British Naval Policy-making 1805–1827* (London, 2011).

Hamilton, Sir Richard Vesey (ed.), *Journals and Letters of Admiral of the Fleet Sir Thomas Byam Martin*, 3 vols. (London, Navy Records Society, No. 12, 1896; No. 19, 1900; No. 24, 1902).

— and Laughton, John Knox (eds.), *Recollections of James Anthony Gardner, Commander R.N. (1775–1814)* (London, Navy Records Society, No. 31, 1906).

Hampson, Norman, *The Perfidy of Albion: French Perceptions of England during the French Revolution* (London, 1998).

Hanger, Colonel George, *Reflections on the Menaced Invasion* (London, 1804).

Harcourt, Revd Leveson (ed.), *The Diaries and Correspondence of the Right Honourable George Rose*, 2 vols. (London, 1860).

Harding, Richard, *Seapower and Naval Warfare 1630–1830* (London, 1999).

— 'Expeditionary Armies and Naval Power: The North German Campaign 1805–1806', *Trafalgar Chronicle*, Vol. 16 (2006), pp. 63–75.

— *Naval History 1680–1850* (Aldershot, Hants, 2006).

— and Ferri, Sergio Solbes (eds.), *The Contractor State and Its Implications 1659–1815* (Las Palmas, 2012).

Harling, Philip, *The Waning of 'Old Corruption': The Politics of Economical Reform in Britain 1779–1846* (Oxford, 1996).

— 'A Tale of Two Conflicts: Critiques of the British War Effort 1793–1815' in Philp, *Resisting Napoleon*, pp. 19–40.

— and Mandler, Peter, 'From "Fiscal-Miltary" State to Laissez-faire State 1760–1850', *Journal of British Studies*, Vol. 32 (1993), pp. 44–70.

Harris, J. R., *The Copper King: A Biography of Thomas Williams of Llanidan* (Liverpool, 1964).

— 'The Transfer of Technology between Britain and France and the French Revolution' in Ceri Crossley and Ian Small (eds.), *The French Revolution and British Culture* (Oxford, 1989), pp. 156–86.

— 'Industrial Espionage in the Eighteenth Century' in Harris, *Essays in Industry and Technology in the Eighteenth Century: England and France* (Basingstoke, 1992), pp. 164–75.

Harrison, Leslie, 'Privateers on the East Coast 1796–1797', *Mariner's Mirror*, Vol. 64 (1978), pp. 301–8.

Harvey, A. D., 'The Ministry of All the Talents: The Whigs in Office, February 1806 to March 1807', *Historical Journal*, Vol. 5 (1972), pp. 619–48.

— *Collision of Empires: Britain in Three World Wars 1793–1945* (Hambledon, 1992).

Hattendorf, John B., 'Sea Power as Control: Britain's Defensive Naval Strategy in the Mediterranean 1793–1815' in *Français et anglais en Méditerranée de la révolution française à l'indépendance de la Grèce (1789–1830)* (Vincennes, 1992), pp. 203–20.

— *Saint-Barthélemy and the Swedish East India Company: A Selection of Printed Documents* (New York, 1994).

—, Knight, R. J. B., Pearsall, A. W. H., Rodger, N. A. M., and Till, Geoffrey (eds.), *British Naval Documents 1204–1960* (Navy Records Society, No. 131, 1993).

Haycock, David, and Archer, Sally (eds.), *Health and Medicine at Sea 1700–1900* (Woodbridge, Suffolk, 2009).

Haythornthwaite, Philip, 'Militia Insurance', *Journal of the Society for Army Historical Research*, Vol. 54 (1976), p. 57.

— 'The Volunteer Force 1803–1804', *Journal of the Society for Army Historical Research*, Vol. 64 (1986), pp. 193–204.

Heizen, Jasper, 'Transnational Affinities and Invented Tradition: The Napoleonic Wars and Hanoverian Memory 1815–1915', *English Historical Review*, Vol. 127 (2012), pp. 1,367–1,403.

Henwood, Phillipe, *Bagnards à Brest* (Rennes, 1986).

Hewitt, Rachel, *Map of a Nation: A Biography of the Ordnance Survey* (London, 2010).

Hicks, Peter, 'Napoleon, Tilsit, Copenhagen and Portugal', *Trafalgar Chronicle*, Vol. 18 (2008), pp. 126–37.

Hill, Richard, *The Prizes of War: The Naval Prize System in the Napoleonic Wars 1793–1815* (Stroud, Gloucestershire, 1998).

Hilton, Boyd, 'The Political Arts of Lord Liverpool', *Transactions of the Royal Historical Society*, 5th Series, Vol. 38 (1988), pp. 147–70.

— *A Mad, Bad and Dangerous People? England 1783–1846* (Oxford, 2006).

Hinde, Wendy, *George Canning* (London, 1973).

Hogg, O. F. C., *The Royal Arsenal: Its Background, Origin and Subsequent History*, 2 vols. (Oxford, 1963).

Holberg, Tom, 'France: Decrees on Trade 1793–1810' (2008), pp. 1–6, www.napoleon-series.org.

Hope, Trevor J., 'Britain and the Black Sea Trade in the Late Eighteenth Century', *Revue roumaine d'études internationale*, Vol. 24 (1974), pp. 159–74.

Horn, D. B., *The British Diplomatic Service 1689–1789* (Oxford, 1961).

Houlding, John, *Fit for Service: The Training of the British Army 1715–1795* (Oxford, 1981).

Howard, Martin R., *Walcheren 1809: The Scandalous Destruction of the British Army* (Barnsley, South Yorkshire, 2012).

Hughes, Edward, *The Private Correspondence of Admiral Lord Collingwood* (Navy Records Society, No. 98, 1957).

— *North Country Life in the Eighteenth Century. Vol. II: Cumberland and Westmorland* (Oxford, 1965).

Hunt, Giles, *The Duel: Castlereagh, Canning and Deadly Cabinet Rivalry* (London, 2008).

Huskisson, William, *The Speeches of the Right Honourable William Huskisson*, 3 vols. (London, 1831).

Ilchester, Countess of (ed.), and Stavordale, Lord, *The Life and Letters of Lady Sarah Lennox 1745–1826*, 2 vols. (London, 1901).

Ilchester, Earl of, *The Journal of Elizabeth Lady Holland (1791–1811)*, 2 vols. (London, 1908).

Ingram, Edward (ed.), *Two Views of British India: The Private Correspondence of Mr Dundas and Lord Wellesley 1798–1801* (London, 1970).

— *Commitment to Empire: Prophecies of the Great Game in Asia 1797–1800* (Oxford, 1981).

James, William, *The Naval History of Britain*, 6 vols. (London, 1878).

Jane, Charles W. A., *Shirley Heights: The Defence of Nelson's Dockyard* (St John's, Antigua, 1982).

Jenks, Timothy, *Naval Engagements: Patriotism, Cultural Politics and the Royal Navy 1793–1815* (Oxford, 2006).

Jennings, Louis J. (ed.), *The Croker Papers: Correspondence and Diaries of the late Right Honourable John Wilson Croker (1809–1830)*, 3 vols. (London, 1884).

Joyce, Herbert, *History of the Post Office* (London, 1893).

Jupp, Peter, *Lord Grenville 1759–1834* (Oxford, 1985).

— (ed.), *The Letter Journal of George Canning 1793–1795* (London, 1991).

Kaplan, Herbert, *Russian Overseas Commerce with Great Britain during the Reign of Catherine II* (Philadelphia, 1995).

Kaplan, Stephen Laurence, *Provisioning Paris: Merchants and Millers in the Grain and Flour Trade during the Eighteenth Century* (Ithaca, NY, and London, 1984).

Kerrigan, Paul M., 'The Shannonbridge Fortifications', *Irish Sword*, Vol. 11 (1974), pp. 234–5.

Kert, Faye, 'Cruising in Colonial Waters: The Organization of North American Privateering in the War of 1812' in Starkey et al., *Pirates and Privateers*, pp. 141–54.

Kitchen, Frank, 'Napoleonic War Coastal Signal Stations', *Mariner's Mirror*, Vol. 76 (1990), pp. 337–44.

Knight, Jane, 'Nelson's Old Lady: Merchant News as a Source of Intelligence, June to October 1796', *Journal of Maritime Research* (May 2005), e-journal.

— 'Lieutenant J. H. E. Hill's Account of the Shipwreck of the *Valke*, 10 November 1799', *Mariner's Mirror*, Vol. 95 (2009), pp. 207–14.

Knight, Roger, 'The Introduction of Copper Sheathing into the Royal Navy 1779–1786', *Mariner's Mirror*, Vol. 59 (1973), pp. 200–309.

— 'The Building and Maintenance of the British Fleet during the Anglo-French Wars 1688–1815' in Acerra, Merino and Meyer, *Les Marines de guerre européennes*, pp. 35–50.

— *Portsmouth Dockyard Papers 1774–1783: The American War* (Portsmouth, 1987).

— *Shipbuilding Timber for the British Navy: Parliamentary Papers 1729–1792* (New York, 1993).

— 'The Royal Navy's Recovery after the Early Phase of the American Revolutionary War' in George J. Andrepolis and Harold E. Selesky (eds.), *The Aftermath of Defeat: Society, Armed Forces and the Challenge of Recovery* (New Haven and London, 1994), pp. 10–25, 160–62.

— 'The Maritime Legacy of Empire' in J. B. Hattendorf (ed.), *Maritime History. Vol. II: The Eighteenth Century and the Classic Age of Sail* (Malabar, Florida, 1997), pp. 211–73.

— 'From Impressment to Task Work: Strikes and Disruption in the Royal Dockyards 1688–1788' in Lunn and Day, *Labour Relations in the Royal Dockyards*, pp. 1–20.

— 'Richard, Earl Howe' in LeFevre and Harding, *Precursors of Nelson*, pp. 279–99.

— 'Devil Bolts and Deception? Wartime Naval Shipbuilding in Private Shipyards 1739–1815', *Journal of Maritime Research* (2003), e-journal.

— *The Pursuit of Victory: The Life and Achievement of Horatio Nelson* (London, 2005).

— 'The Fleets at Trafalgar: The Margin of Superiority' in David Cannadine (ed.), *Trafalgar in History: A Battle and Its Afterlife* (Basingstoke, Hants, 2006), pp. 61–77.

— 'Politics and Trust in Victualling the Navy 1793–1815', *Mariner's Mirror*, Vol. 94 (2008), pp. 133–49.

— 'The Spending and Accounting Performance of the British Victualling Board 1793–1815' in Conway and Sanchez, *The Spending of States*, pp. 181–200.

— and Alan Frost (eds.), *The Journal of Daniel Paine 1794–1797* (Sydney, 1983).

— and Martin Wilcox, *Sustaining the Fleet 1793–1815: War, the British Navy and the Contractor State* (London, 2010).

Kraehe, Enno E., 'Wellington and the Reconstruction of the Allied Armies during the Hundred Days', *International History Review*, Vol. 11 (1989), pp. 84–97.

Krajeski, Paul C., *In the Shadow of Nelson: The Naval Leadership of Admiral Sir Charles Cotton 1753–1812* (Westport, Connecticut, 2000).

Lambert, Andrew, 'Strategy, Policy and Shipbuilding: The Bombay Dockyard, the India Navy and Imperial Security in Eastern Seas 1784–1869' in Bowen, Lincoln and Rigby, *The Worlds of the East India Company*, pp. 137–51.

— 'The War of 1812 and the Defence of British Floating Trade', *Trafalgar Chronicle*, Vol. 22 (2012), pp. 12–25.

Langford, Paul, *A Polite and Commercial People: England 1727–1783* (Oxford, 1989).

Laughton, Sir John Knox (ed.), *Letters and Papers of Charles, Lord Barham, 1758–1813*, 3 vols. (Navy Records Society, 1906, 1909, 1910).

— *Naval Miscellany*, Vol. II (Navy Records Society, No. 40, 1910).

Lavery, Brian, *The Ship of the Line*, 2 vols. (London, 1983–4).

— *We Shall Fight Them on the Beaches: Defying Napoleon and Hitler 1805 and 1940* (London, 2009).

LeFevre, Peter, and Harding, Richard (eds.), *Precursors of Nelson: British Admirals of the Eighteenth Century* (London, 2000).

— *British Admirals of the Napoleonic Wars: The Contemporaries of Nelson* (London, 2005).

Lewis, Michael, *A Social History of the Navy 1793–1815* (London, 1960).

Lieven, Dominic, *Russia against Napoleon: The Battle for Europe 1807 to 1814* (London, 2009).

Lin, Patricia Y. C. E., 'Caring for the Nation's Families: British Soldiers' and Sailors' Families and the State 1793–1815' in Forrest et al., *Soldiers, Citizens and Civilians*, pp. 99–117.

Linch, Kevin B., '"This Exposed Maritime County": East Sussex and the Preparations for Invasion 1803–1804', *Trafalgar Chronicle*, Vol. 16 (2006), pp. 50–62.

— '"A Citizen and Not a Soldier": The British Volunteer Movement and the War against Napoleon', in Forrest et al., *Soldiers, Citizens and Civilians*, pp. 205–21.

— *Britain and Wellington's Army: Recruitment, Society and Tradition 1807–1815* (Basingstoke, 2011).

Linklater, Andro, *Why Spencer Perceval Had to Die: The Assassination of a British Prime Minister* (London, 2012).

Lloyd, Christopher (ed.), *The Keith Papers*, Vols. II and III (Navy Records Society, No. 90, 1950; No. 96, 1955).

— *Mr Barrow of the Admiralty: A Life of Sir John Barrow* (London, 1970).

— and Coulter, J. S., *Medicine and the Navy 1200–1900. Vol. III: 1714–1815* (London, 1961).

— and Craig, Hardin, 'Congreve's Rockets' in Lloyd (ed.), *Naval Miscellany*, Vol. IV (Navy Records Society, No. 92, 1952), pp. 424–68.

Lloyd, Clive L., *A History of Napoleonic and American Prisoners of War 1756–1816: Hulk, Depot and Parole* (Woodbridge, Suffolk, 2007).

London, David W., 'What Really Happened On Board HMS *London*?' in Coats and MacDougall, *Mutinies of 1797*, pp. 61–78.

Lowry, John, 'Sir Home Riggs Popham and the Invasion of Rio de la Plata in 1806' (University of Greenwich M.A. thesis, 2009).

Lunn, Ken, and Day, Ann (eds.), *A History of Work and Labour Relations in the Royal Dockyards* (London, 1999).

Lyon, David, *The Sailing Navy List: All the Ships of the Royal Navy – Built, Purchased and Captured – 1688–1850* (London, 1993).

Macartney, Sylvia, and West, John, *The Lewisham Silk Mills* (London, 1998).

McCord, Norman, 'Some Labour Troubles of the 1790s in North-East England', *International Review of Social History*, Vol. 12 (1968), pp. 366–83.

— 'The Impress Service in North-East England during the Napoleonic War', *Mariner's Mirror*, Vol. 54 (1968), pp. 163–80.

McCusker, John, and Morgan, Kenneth (eds.), *The Early Modern Atlantic Economy* (Cambridge, 2000).

Macdonald, Janet, *Feeding Nelson's Navy: The True Story of Food at Sea in the Georgian Navy* (London, 2004).

— 'The Victualling Yard at Gibraltar and Its Role in Feeding the Royal Navy in the Mediterranean during the Revolutionary and Napoleonic Wars', *Transactions of the Naval Dockyards Society*, Vol. 2 (2006), pp. 58–64.

— *The British Navy's Victualling Board 1793–1815: Management Competence and Incompetence* (Woodbridge, Suffolk, 2010).

MacDougall, Ian, *All Men are Brethren: Prisoners of War in Scotland 1803–1814* (Edinburgh, 2008).

MacDougall, Philip, 'The Changing Nature of the Dockyard Dispute 1790–1840' in Lunn and Day, *Labour Relations in the Royal Dockyards*, pp. 41–65.

McGrigor, Mary, *Wellington's Spies* (Barnsley, South Yorkshire, 2005).

McGuffie, T. H., 'Peninsular Prize Money', *Journal of the Society for Army Historical Research*, Vol. 24 (1946), p. 143.

Mackesy, Piers, *The War in the Mediterranean 1803–1810* (London, 1957).

— *Statesmen at War: The Strategy of Overthrow 1798–1799* (London, 1974).

— *War without Victory: The Downfall of Pitt 1799–1802* (Oxford, 1984).

— '"Most sadly bitched": The British Cádiz Expedition of 1800' in Edward Freeman (ed.), *Les Empires en guerre et paix 1793–1860* (Vincennes, 1990), pp. 41–56.

— *British Victory in Egypt: The End of Napoleon's Conquest* (London, 1995).

— 'Problems of an Amphibious Power: Britain against France', *Naval War College Review* (1978), repr. in Richard Harding (ed.), *Naval History 1650–1850* (Aldershot, 2004), pp. 117–26.

Macranie, K. D., *Admiral Lord Keith and the Naval War against Napoleon* (Gainesville, Florida, 2006).

Makepeace, Margaret, *The East India Company's London Workers: Management of the Warehouse Labourers 1800–1858* (Woodbridge, Suffolk, 2010).

Mallinson, Howard, *Send It by Semaphore: The Old Telegraphs during the Wars with France* (Ramsbury, Marlborough, 2005).

Malmesbury, Earl of (ed.), *Diaries and Correspondence of James Harris, First Earl of Malmesbury*, 4 vols. (London, 1844).

Manderson, James, *Twelve Letters Addressed to the Right Honourable Spencer Perceval* (London, 1812).

Markham, Sir Clements, (ed.) *Selections from the Correspondence of Admiral John Markham, 1801–4 and 1806–7* (Navy Records Society, No. 28, 1904).

Marsden, William, *A Brief Memoir of the Life of William Marsden, Written by Himself, with Notes from His Correspondence* (London, 1838).

Marsh Family website, *The Diary of George Marsh*, www.jjhc.info/marsh-george1800diary.htm.

Marshall, P. J. (ed.), *The Oxford History of the British Empire. Vol. II: The Eighteenth Century* (Oxford, 1998).

Marshall, William, *The Review and Abstract of the County Reports to the Board of Agriculture. Vol. V: Southern and Peninsular Departments* (London, 1818; repr. [n.d.], Newton Abbot, Devon).

Marzagalli, Silvia, 'The French Wars and North Sea Trade: The Case of Hamburg' in Lars U. Scholl and David M.Williams, *Crisis and Transition: Maritime Sectors in the North Sea Region 1790–1940* (Bremen, 2005), pp. 20–31.

— 'Napoleon's Continental Blockade: An Effective Substitute to Naval Weakness?' in Bruce A. Elleman and S. C. M. Paine, *Naval Blockades and Seapower: Strategies and Counter-Strategies 1805–2005* (London and New York, 2006), pp. 25–33.

Mead, Hilary, 'The Martello Towers of England', *Mariner's Mirror*, Vol. 34 (1948), pp. 205–17.

Melville, Louis (ed.), *The Huskisson Papers* (London, 1931).

Merino, Jose P., 'Graving Docks in France and Spain before 1800', *Mariner's Mirror*, Vol. 71 (1985), pp. 35–58.

Merwe, Pieter van der (ed.), *Science and the French and British Navies 1700–1850* (London, 2003).

Miller, David, 'In Support of Wellington's Army: The Royal Navy's Contribution to the Waterloo Campaign', *Journal of the Society for Army Historical Research*, Vol. 86 (2008), pp. 304–24.

Milton, Rosemary, and Callaghan, Richard, *The Redoubt Fortress and Martello Towers of Eastbourne 1804–2004* (Eastbourne, 2004).

Mitchell, B. R., and Deane, Phyllis, *An Abstract of British Historical Statistics* (Cambridge, 1962).

Mitchell, H., 'Francis Drake and the comte d'Antraigues: A Study of the Dropmore Bulletins 1793–1796', *Bulletin of the Institute of Historical Research*, Vol. 29 (1956), pp. 123–44.

Moody, T. W., Martin, F. X., and Byrne, F. J., *A New History of Ireland*, 9 vols. (Oxford, 1976–2005).

Moreira, Maria Cristina, 'Tracking Down Signs of the Portuguese Fiscal-Military State 1762–1816' in Sanchez, *War, State and Development*, pp. 251–75.

— 'Portuguese State Military Expenditure: British Support of the Peninsular War Efforts of the Erário Régio (Royal Treasury) from 1809 to 1811' in Conway and Sanchez, *The Spending of States*, pp. 109–27.

— and Eloranta, Jari, 'Contracts and the Role of the State: Portuguese Military Preparations Supply Systems in the Early Nineteenth Century' in Harding and Ferri, *Contractor State*, pp. 199–221.

Mori, Jennifer, *William Pitt and the French Revolution 1785–1795* (Edinburgh, 1997).

Morieux, Renaud, '"An Inundation from Our Shores": Travelling across the Channel around the Peace of Amiens' in Philp, *Resisting Napoleon*, pp. 217–40.

Morrison, James H., *Les systémes de communication militaires britanniques á Halifax et dans l'Empire* (Ottawa, 1982).

Morriss, Roger, 'Labour Relations in the Royal Dockyards 1801–1805', *Mariner's Mirror*, Vol. 62 (1976), pp. 337–46.

— 'Samuel Bentham and the Management of the Royal Dockyards 1796–1807', *Bulletin of the Institute of Historical Research*, Vol. 54 (1981), pp. 226–40.

— *The Royal Dockyards during the Revolutionary and Napoleonic Wars* (Leicester, 1983).

— 'St Vincent and Reform', *Mariner's Mirror*, Vol. 69 (1983), pp. 269–90.

— 'Industrial Relations at Plymouth Dockyard 1770–1820' in Duffy et al., *New Maritime History of Devon*, Vol. I, pp. 216–23.

— 'Government and Community: The Changing Context of Labour Relations 1770–1830' in Lunn and Day, *Labour Relations in the Royal Dockyards*, pp. 21–40.

— *Naval Power and British Culture 1760–1850: Public Trust and Government Ideology* (Aldershot, 2004).

— 'The Office of the Inspector-General of Naval Works and Technical Innovation in the Royal Dockyards', *Transactions of the Naval Dockyards Society*, Vol. 1 (2006), pp. 21–9.

— 'Colonization, Conquest and the Supply of Food and Transport: The Reorganization of Logistics Management 1780–1795', *War in History*, Vol. 14 (2007), pp. 310–24.

— *The Foundations of British Maritime Ascendancy: Resources, Logistics and the State 1755–1815* (Cambridge, 2010).

— '"High Exertions and Difficult Cases": The Work of the Transport Agent at Portsmouth and Southampton 1795–1797' in Richard Harding and Helen Doe (eds.), *Naval Leadership and Management 1650–1950* (Woodbridge, Suffolk, 2012), pp. 95–107.

— and Saxby, Richard, *The Channel Fleet and the Blockade of Brest* (Navy Records Society, No. 141, 2001).

Moss, Michael, 'From Cannon to Steam Propulsion: The Origins of Clyde Marine Engineering', *Mariner's Mirror*, Vol. 98 (2012), pp. 467–88.

Muir, Rory, *Britain and the Defeat of Napoleon 1807–1815* (New Haven, 1996).

— *At Wellington's Right Hand: The Letters of Lieutenant-Colonel Sir Alexander Gordon 1808–1815* (Army Records Society, 2003).

—, Burnham, Robert, Muir, Howie, and McGuigan, Ron, *Inside Wellington's Peninsular Army 1808–1814* (Barnsley, South Yorkshire, 2006).

— and Esdaile, C. J., 'Strategic Planning in a Time of Small Government: The Wars against Revolutionary and Napoleonic France' in C. M. Woolgar (ed.), *Wellington Studies 1* (Southampton, 1996), pp. 1–90.

Murphy, John A. (ed.), *The French are in the Bay: The Expedition to Bantry Bay 1796* (Dublin, 1997).

Murphy, Orville T., *Charles Gravier, comte de Vergennes: French Diplomacy in the Age of Revolution 1719–1787* (Albany, New York, 1982).

Musson, A. E., 'Industrial Motive Power in the United Kingdom 1800–1900', *Economic History Review*, 2nd Series, Vol. 29 (1976), pp. 415–26.

Naish, John, 'Joseph Whidbey and the Building of the Plymouth Breakwater', *Mariner's Mirror*, Vol. 78 (1992), pp. 37–56.

Namier, Lewis and Brooke, John, *The House of Commons 1754–1790*, 3 vols. (London, 1985).

Navickas, Katrina, 'The Defence of Manchester and Liverpool in 1803: Conflicts of Loyalism, Patriotism and the Middle Classes' in Philp, *Resisting Napoleon*, pp. 61–73.

Nelson, Ivan F., *The Irish Militia 1793–1802: Ireland's Forgotten Army* (Dublin, 2007).

Nelson, R. R., *The Home Office 1782–1801* (Durham, North Carolina, 1969).

Newman, Jon, '"An Insurrection of Loyalty": The London Volunteer Regiments' Response to the Invasion Threat' in Philp, *Resisting Napoleon*, pp. 75–89.

Norman, C. B., *The Corsairs of France* (London, 1887).

Norris, John, *Shelburne and Reform* (London, 1963).

Norway, Arthur, *History of the Post Office Packet Service between the Years 1793 and 1815* (London, 1895).

Nye, John V. C., 'The Political Economy of British Taxation 1660–1815', *Economic History Review*, Vol. 41 (1988), pp. 1–32.

— *War, Wine and Taxes: The Political Economy of Anglo-French Trade 1689–1900* (Princeton, 2007).

O'Brien, P. K., '"Inseperable Connections": Trade, Economy, Fiscal State and the Expansion of Empire 1688–1815' in Marshall, *British Empire*, pp. 53–77.

— 'Merchants and Bankers as Patriots or Speculators? Foreign Commerce and Monetary Policy in Wartime 1793–1815' in McCusker and Morgan, *Early Modern Atlantic Economy*, pp. 250–77.

— 'The Triumph and Denouement of the British Fiscal State: Taxation for the Wars against Revolutionary and Napoleonic France 1793–1815' in Christopher Storrs (ed.), *The Fiscal-Military State in Eighteenth-Century Europe: Essays in Honour of P. G. M. Dickson* (Farnham, Surrey, 2009), pp. 187–200.

— and Duran, Xavier, 'Total Factor Productivity for the Royal Navy from Victory at Texel (1653) to Triumph at Trafalgar' in Richard W. Unger (ed.), *Shipping and Economic Growth 1350–1850* (Leiden, 2011), pp. 279–307.

— and Engerman, S. L., 'Exports and the Growth of the British Economy from the Glorious Revolution to the Peace of Amiens' in Barbara L. Solow (ed.), *Slavery and the Rise of the Atlantic System* (Cambridge and New York, 1991).

Olson, Alison Gilbert, *The Radical Duke: The Career and Correspondence of Charles Lennox, Third Duke of Richmond* (Oxford, 1961).

Oman, Carola, *Sir John Moore* (London, 1953).

Paget, Sir Augustus (ed.), *The Paget Papers: Diplomatic and Other Correspondence of the Right Honourable Sir Arthur Paget 1797–1807*, 2 vols. (London, 1896).

Pakenham, Thomas, *Pakenham Letters* (privately printed, 1914).

Palmer, Charles John, *The History of Great Yarmouth*, 2 vols. (Great Yarmouth and London, 1856).

Palmer, Sarah, 'Shipbuilding in Southeast England 1800–1913' in Simon Ville (ed.), *Shipbuilding in the United Kingdom in the Nineteenth Century: A Regional Assessment* (St John's, Newfoundland, 1993), pp. 45–74.

—'"Injury, Loss and Damage": London's Waterfront Businesses and the Introduction of the Docks in the Early Nineteenth Century' (unpublished paper, 2006).

Parker, Charles Stuart, *Sir Robert Peel, from His Private Papers*, 3 vols. (London, 1891).

Parkinson, Cecil Northcote (ed.), *The Trade Winds: A Study of British Overseas Trade during the French Wars* (London, 1948).

— *Britannia Rules: The Classic Age of Naval History 1793–1815* (London, 1977; repr. Stroud, Gloucestershire, 1987).

Parris, Henry, *Constitutional Bureaucracy* (London, 1969).

Parsons, George Samuel, *Nelsonian Reminiscences* (London, 1843; repr. 1973).

Pasley, C. W., *Essay on the Military Policy and Institutions of the British Empire* (London, 1810).

— *Course of Military Instruction* (London, 1817).

Pearce, A. J., 'The Hope–Baring Contract: Finance and Trade between Europe and the Americas 1805–1808', *English Historical Review*, Vol. 124 (2009), pp. 1,324–52.

Pearsall, Alan, 'The Royal Navy and the Protection of Trade in the Eighteenth Century' in *Guerres et paix 1660–1815* (Vincennes, 1987), pp. 149–62.

Peaty, John, 'Architect of Victory: The Reforms of the Duke of York', *Journal of the Society for Army Historical Research*, Vol. 84 (2006), pp. 330–48.

Pellow, George (ed.), *The Life and Correspondence of the Right Honourable Henry Addington, First Viscount Sidmouth*, 3 vols. (London, 1847).

Perrin, W. G. (ed.), 'Charles Chambers: A Brief Chronological Journal of Remarkable Occurrences On Board His Majesty's Ship *Prometheus*' in *Naval Miscellany*, Vol. III (Navy Records Society, No. 63, 1927), pp. 369–466.

— (ed.), 'The Letters of Lord Nelson 1804–1805', *Naval Miscellany*, Vol. III (Navy Records Society, No. 63, 1928), pp. 175–90.

Petersen, Thomas Munch, *Defying Napoleon: How Britain Bombarded Copenhagen and Seized the Danish Fleet in 1807* (Stroud, Gloucestershire, 2007).

Philips, C. H., *The East India Company 1794–1834* (Manchester, 1940; repr. 1961).

Philp, Mark, *Resisting Napoleon: The British Response to the Threat of Invasion 1797–1815* (Aldershot, 2006).

Pimlott, J. L., 'The Administration of the British Army 1783–1793' (Leicester Ph.D., 1975).

Pocock, Tom, *A Thirst for Glory: The Life of Admiral Sir Sidney Smith* (London, 1996).

Polgieter, T. D., 'At the Cross-Roads of the World: The Cape of Good Hope and the First British Occupation 1795' in *Proceedings of the XXIV International Congress of Military History* (Lisbon, 1998), pp. 517–33.

Ponsford, C. N. (ed.), *Shipbuilding on the Exe: The Memoranda Book of Daniel Bishop Davy, 1799–1874, of Topsham* (Exeter, 1988).

Pool, Bernard, *Navy Board Contracts 1660–1832* (London, 1966).

— *The Croker Papers 1808–1857* (London, 1967).

Pope, Dudley, *The Great Gamble: Nelson at Copenhagen* (London, 1972).

Popham, Hugh, *A Damned Cunning Fellow: The Eventful Life of Rear-Admiral Sir Home Popham, K.C.B., K.C.H., K.M., F.R.S., 1762–1820* (Tywardreath, Cornwall, 1991).

Pugh, R. B., 'The Early History of the Admiralty Record Office' in J. C. Davies (ed.), *Studies Presented to Sir Hilary Jenkinson* (London, 1957), pp. 320–37.

— 'Charles Abbot and the Public Records: The First Phase', *Bulletin of the Institute of Historical Research*, Vol. 39 (1966), pp. 69–85.

Randall, Adrian, *Riotous Assemblies: Popular Protest in Hanoverian England* (Oxford, 2006).

Ravenhill, William, 'The Honourable Robert Edward Clifford 1767–1817: A Cartographer's Response to Napoleon', *Geographical Journal*, Vol. 160 (1994), pp. 159–72.

Redgrave, T. M. O., 'Wellington's Logistical Arrangements in the Peninsular War 1809–1814' (University of London Ph.D., 1979).

Reese, M. M., *Goodwood's Oak: The Life and Times of the Third Duke of Richmond, Lennox and Aubigny* (London, 1987).

Rickard, Gillian, *Kent Enrolments under the Navy Act 1796* (Canterbury, 1996).

Ritchie, G. S., *The Admiralty Chart: British Naval Hydrography in the Nineteenth Century* (1967; repr. Bishop Auckland, Durham, 1995).

Robertson, Frederick, *The Evolution of Naval Armament* (London, 1921; repr. 1968).

Robertson, Ian, *A Commanding Presence: Wellington in the Peninsula 1808–1814 – Logistics: Strategy: Survival* (Stroud, Gloucestershire, 2008).

Robertson, J. D. M., *The Press Gang in Orkney and Shetland* (Orkney, 2011).

Robinson, Howard, *Carrying British Mails Overseas* (London, 1964).

Robson, J. O., 'Rockets in the Napoleonic War: The Diary of William Laycock', *Journal of the Society for Army Historical Research*, Vol. 26 (1948), pp. 147–150.

Robson, Martin, *Britain, Portugal and South America in the Napoleonic Wars: Alliances and Diplomacy in Economic Maritime Conflict* (London, 2011).

Rodger, N. A. M., *The Wooden World: An Anatomy of the Georgian Navy* (London, 1986).

— 'Mobilizing Seapower in the Eighteenth Century' in *État, marine et société: hommage à Jean Meyer* (Paris, 1995), pp. 365–74; repr. in Rodger, *Essays in Naval History from Medieval to Modern* (Farnham, Surrey, 2009).

— 'Seapower and Empire 1688–1793' in Marshall, *British Empire*, pp. 169–83.

— 'Navies and the Enlightenment' in Merwe, *Science and the French and British Navies*, pp. 5–23.

— *The Command of the Ocean: A Naval History of Britain 1649–1815* (London, 2004).

— 'British Blockades in the Great Wars 1793–1815', *Trafalgar Chronicle*, Vol. 19 (2009), pp. 27–37.

— 'War as an Economic Activity in the "Long" Eighteenth Century', *International Journal of Maritime History*, Vol. 22 (2010), pp. 1–18.

— 'From the Military Revolution to the "Fiscal-Naval" State', *Journal of Maritime Research*, Vol. 13 (2011), pp. 119–28.

Rogers, Nicholas, 'The Sea Fencibles, Loyalism and the Reach of the State' in Philp, *Resisting Napoleon*, pp. 41–59.

— *The Press Gang: Naval Impressment and Its Opponents in Georgian Britain* (London, 2007).

Rose, George, *Observations Respecting the Public Expenditure and the Influence of the Crown* (London, 1810).

Rose, John Holland, *William Pitt and the Great War* (London, 1911).

— *Pitt and Napoleon: Essays and Letters* (London, 1912).

— 'Did Napoleon Intend to Invade England?' in *Pitt and Napoleon* (London, 1912), pp. 114–46.

— 'British West Indian Commerce as a Factor in the Napoleonic War', *Historical Journal*, Vol. 3 (1929), pp. 34–46.

— and Broadley, Alexander Meyrick, *Dumouriez and the Defence of England against Napoleon* (London, 1908).

Rosebery, the Earl of (ed.), *The Windham Papers*, 2 vols. (1903).

Rosier, Barrington, 'Fleet Repairs and Maintenance 1783–1793', *Mariner's Mirror*, Vol. 84 (1998), pp. 328–33.

Ross, Charles (ed.), *Correspondence of Charles, First Marquis Cornwallis*, 3 vols. (London, 1859).

Rumsby, John H., 'A Militiaman Captured by the French', *Journal of the Society for Army Historical Research*, Vol. 51 (1973), p. 251.

Sack, J. J., *The Grenvillites 1801–1829: Party Politics and Factionalism in the Age of Pitt and Liverpool* (Urbana, Illinois, 1979).

Sainty, J. C., *Treasury Officials 1660–1870* (London, 1972).

— *Officials of the Boards of Trade 1660–1870* (London, 1974).

— *Admiralty Officials 1660–1870* (London, 1975).

— *Home Office Officials 1782–1870* (London, 1975).

— *Colonial Office Officials 1794–1870* (London, 1976).

— 'The Evolution of the Parliamentary and Financial Secretaryships of the Treasury', *English Historical Review*, Vol. 91 (1976), pp. 566–84.

Sale, Kirkpatrick, *The Flower of His Genius: Robert Fulton and the American Dream* (New York, 2001).

Sanchez, Rafael Torres (ed.), *War, State and Development: Fiscal-Military States in the Eighteenth Century* (Pamplona, Spain, 2007).

Saunders, A. D., *Fortress Britain: Artillery Fortifications in the British Isles and Ireland* (Liphook, 1989).

— 'Upnor Castle and the Gunpowder Supply of the Navy 1801–1804', *Mariner's Mirror*, Vol. 91 (2005), pp. 160–74.

Schaffer, Simon, ' "The charter'd Thames": Naval Architecture and Experimental Spaces in Georgian Britain' in Lissa L. Roberts, Simon Schaffer and Peter Dear (eds.), *The Mindful Hand: Inquiry and Invention from the Late Renaissance to Early Industrialization* (Chicago, 2008), pp. 279–305.

Schofield, Philip, 'British Politicians and French Arms: The Ideological War of 1793–1795', *History*, Vol. 77 (1992), pp. 183–201.

Schom, Alan, *Trafalgar: Countdown to Battle 1803–1815* (London, 1980).

Schroeder, Paul W., *The Transformation of European Politics 1763–1848* (Oxford, 1994).

Scott, Hamish, 'The Importance of Bourbon Naval Construction to the Strategy of Choiseul after the Seven Years War', *International History Review*, Vol. 1 (1978), pp. 18–35.

— *British Foreign Policy in the Age of the American Revolution* (Oxford, 1990).

Le Service historique de la Marine, *Pierres de Mer: la patrimoine immobilier de la marine nationale* (Vincennes, 1996).

Semmel, Stuart, *Napoleon and the British* (New Haven, 2004).

Seth, Ronald, *The Spy in Silk Breeches: The Story of Montagu Fox, Eighteenth-Century Admiralty Agent Extraordinary* (London, 1968).

Seymour, W. A., *A History of the Ordnance Survey* (Folkestone, Kent, 1980).

Sheldon, Matthew, 'A Tale of Two Cities: The Facilities, Work and Impact of the Victualling Office at Portsmouth', *Transactions of the Naval Dockyards Society*, Vol. 1 (2006), pp. 35–45.

Sherwig, John M., *Guineas and Gunpowder: British Foreign Aid in the Wars against France 1793–1815* (Cambridge, Mass.,1969).

Solar, Peter M., and Klovland, Jan Tore, 'New Series for Agricultural Prices in London 1770–1914', *Economic History Review*, Vol. 64 (2011), pp. 72–87.

Sondhaus, Lawrence T., 'Napoleon's Shipbuilding Program at Venice', *Journal of Military History*, Vol. 53 (1989), pp. 349–62.

Sparrow, Elizabeth, 'The Alien Office 1792–1806', *Historical Journal*, Vol. 33 (1990), pp. 361–84.

— 'Secret Service under Pitt's Administrations 1792–1806', *History*, Vol. 83 (1998), pp. 280–94.

— *Secret Service: British Agents in France 1792–1815* (Woodbridge, 1999).

Starkey, David J., 'Devon's Shipbuilding Industry 1786–1970' in Duffy et al., *New Maritime History of Devon*, Vol. II, pp. 78–90.

— 'A Restless Spirit: British Privateering Enterprise 1739–1815' in Starkey et al., *Pirates and Privateers*, pp. 126–40.

— 'The British Seafaring Workforce: Size and Occupational Composition 1707–1828' in Harald Hamre et al. (eds.), *Ninth North Sea History Conference: Maritime People* (Stavanger, 2011), pp. 8–26.

—, Heslinga, E. S. van Eyck van, and Moor, J. A. de (eds.), *Pirates and Privateers: New Perspectives on the War on Trade in the Eighteenth and Nineteenth Centuries* (Exeter, 1997).

Stephenson, Charles, *The Admiral's Secret Weapon: Lord Dundonald and the Origins of Chemical Warfare* (Woodbridge, 2006).

Stern, Walter, 'The Bread Crisis in Britain 1795–1796', *Economica*, Vol. 31 (1964), pp. 168–87.

Strachan, Hew, '"The First World War": Review Article', *Historical Journal*, Vol. 43 (2000), pp. 889–903.

Sussex, Vivien J., *Continental Mail Service 1793–1815, especially by Yarmouth Packet Boats* (Colchester East Anglian Postal History Study Circle, 1978).

Sutcliffe, Robert, 'Bringing Forward Shipping for Government Service: The Indispensable Role of the Transport Service 1793–1815' (University of Greenwich Ph.D., 2012).

Syrett, David, *Shipping and the American War 1775–1783: A Study of British Transport Organization* (London, 1970).

— 'Christopher Atkinson and the Victualling Board 1775–1782', *Historical Research*, Vol. 64 (1996), pp. 129–42.

— *The Royal Navy in European Waters during the American Revolutionary War* (Columbia, South Carolina, 1998).

— 'Towards Dettingen: The Conveyance of the British Army to Flanders in 1742', *Journal of the Society for Army Historical Research*, Vol. 84 (2006), pp. 316–26.

Szostak, Rick, *The Role of Transportation in the Industrial Revolution: A Comparison of England and France* (Montreal and Kingston, Canada, 1991).

Talbott, John E., *The Pen and Ink Sailor: Charles Middleton and the King's Navy 1778–1813* (London, 1998).

Taylor, Stephen, *Storm and Conquest: The Clash of Empires in the Eastern Seas 1809* (New York, 2007).

Thomas, R. N. W., 'Wellington in the Low Countries 1794–1795', *International History Review*, Vol. 11 (1989), pp. 1–30.

Thompson, Neville, 'Lord Bathurst and the Administration of the Peninsular War 1812–1814' in Berkeley, *New Lights on the Peninsular War*, pp. 157–64.

— *Earl Bathurst and the British Empire* (Barnsley, South Yorkshire, 1999).

Thorne, R. G., *The House of Commons 1790–1820*, 5 vols. (London, 1986).

Tissot-Pontabry, Anaïs, 'Les Espions au service de la France sous le consulat et l'Empire' (Sorbonne M.A. thesis, 2005).

Tombs, Robert, *France 1814–1914* (London, 1996).

Tomlinson, Howard, 'Wealden Gunfounding: An Analysis of Its Demise in the Eighteenth Century', *Economic History Review*, Vol. 29 (1976), pp. 383–400.

Torrance, J. R., 'Sir George Harrison and the Growth of Bureaucracy in the Early-Nineteenth Century', *English Historical Review*, Vol. 83 (1969), pp. 52–88.

— 'Social Class and Bureaucratic Innovation: The Commissioners for Examining the Public Accounts 1782–1787', *Past & Present*, Vol. 78 (1978), pp. 56–81.

Tracy, Nicholas, 'British Assessments of French and Spanish Naval Construction 1763–1768', *Mariner's Mirror*, Vol. 61 (1975), pp. 73–85.

— (ed.), *The Naval Chronicle: The Contemporary Record of the Royal Navy at War 1793–1815*, 5 vols. (London, 1999).

Trinder, Ivan, *The Harwich Packets 1635–1834* (Colchester, 1998).

Unger, Richard W., 'The Tonnage of Europe's Merchant Fleets 1300–1800', *American Neptune*, Vol. 52 (1992), pp. 247–61.

Urban, Mark, *The Man Who Broke Napoleon's Codes: The Story of George Scovell* (London, 2001).

Vale, Brian, 'The Conquest of Scurvy 1793–1800: A Challenge to Current Orthodoxy', *Mariner's Mirror*, Vol. 94 (2008), pp. 160–79.

Vane, Charles, Marquess of Londonderry, *Memoirs and Correspondence of Viscount Castlereagh*, 4 vols. (London, 1850).

Verner, William, *Reminiscences (1782–1871) Seventh Hussars (Journal of the Society for Army Historical Research* Occasional Publications, No. 8, 1965).

Verney, Sir Harry (ed.), *Journals and Correspondence of General Sir Harry Calvert, Bart., G.C.B. and G.C.H.* (London, 1853).

Vesey, Richard Hamilton (ed.), *Journals and Letters of Admiral of the Fleet Sir Thomas Byam Martin*, 3 vols. (Navy Records Society, No. 24, 1902; No. 12, 1896; No. 19, 1900).

Ville, Simon P., *English Shipowning during the Industrial Revolution: Michael Henley & Son, London Shipowners, 1770–1830* (Manchester, 1987).

Vine, P. A. L., *London's Lost Route to the Sea* (London, 1965).

— *The Royal Military Canal* (Newton Abbot, 1972).

Voelcker, Tim, *Admiral Saumarez versus Napoleon: The Baltic 1807–1812* (Woodbridge, 2008).

Ward, J. R., *The Finance of Canal Building in Eighteenth Century England* (Oxford, 1974).

Ward, Peter, 'Admiral Peter Rainier and the Command of the East Indies Station 1794–1805' (Exeter Ph.D. thesis, 2010).

Ward, S. G. P., 'Defence Works in Britain 1803–1805', *Journal of the Society for Army Historical Research*, Vol. 27 (1949), pp. 18–37.

— *Wellington's Headquarters: A Study of the Administrative Problems in the Peninsula 1809–1814* (Oxford, 1957).

— 'The War with Revolutionary France and the Napoleonic Empire 1793–1815' (unpublished paper, July 1977, copy in the National Army Museum).

Ward, W. R., 'Some Eighteenth-Century Civil Servants: The English Revenue Commissioners 1754–1798', *English Historical Review*, Vol. 70 (1955), repr. in Rosalind Mitchison (ed.), *Essays in Eighteenth-Century History from the English History Review* (London, 1966), pp. 201–30.

Wareham, Tom, *Frigate Commander* (Barnsley, South Yorkshire, 2004).

Watson, Graham, *Militiamen and Sappers: A History of the Royal Monmouthshire Engineers (Militia)* (Monmouth, 1996).

Watson, Steven J., *The Reign of George III, 1760–1815* (Oxford, 1960).

Webb, P. L. C., 'The Naval Aspects of the Nootka Sound Crisis', *Mariner's Mirror*, Vol. 61 (1975), pp. 133–54.

— 'The Rebuilding and Repair of the Fleet 1783–1793', *Bulletin of the Institute of Historical Research*, Vol. 50 (1977), pp. 194–209.

— 'Seapower in the Ochakov Affair of 1791', *International History Review*, Vol. 11 (1980), pp. 13–33.

— 'Construction, Repair and Maintenance in the Battlefleet of the Royal Navy 1793–1815' in Jeremy Black and Philip Woodfine (eds.), *The British Navy and the Use of Naval Power in the Eighteenth Century* (Leicester, 1988), pp. 207–19.

Wells, Roger, 'Dearth and Distress in Yorkshire 1793–1802', *Borthwick Papers*, Vol. 52 (1977), pp. 1–49.

— 'The Militia Mutinies of 1795' in J. Rule (ed.), *Outside the Law: Studies in Crime and Order 1650–1850* (Exeter, 1982), pp. 35–64.

— *Insurrection: The British Experience 1795–1803* (Gloucester, 1983).

— *Wretched Faces: Famine in Wartime England 1793–1801* (Gloucester, 1988).

Western, J. R., *The English Militia in the Eighteenth Century: The Story of a Political Issue 1660–1802* (London, 1965).

Wheeler, H. F. B., and Broadley, Alexander Meyrick, *Napoleon and the Invasion of England: The Story of the Great Terror*, 2 vols (London, 1908).

White, Colin, *1797: Nelson's Year of Destiny* (Stroud, Gloucestershire, 2001).

Whitefield, Andrew, *Mr Hilhouse of Bristol: Shipbuilder for the Navy 1745–1822* (Bristol, 2010).

Whyman, Susan E., *The Pen and the People: English Letter Writers 1660–1800* (Oxford, 2009).

Wilcox, Martin, '"This Great Complex Concern": Victualling and the Royal Navy on the East Indies Station 1780–1815', *Mariner's Mirror*, Vol. 97 (2011), pp. 32–48.

— '"The Mystery and Business" of Navy Agents, *c.* 1700–1820', *International Journal of Maritime History*, Vol. 23 (2011), pp. 1–28.

Wilkin, F. S., 'The Contribution of Portsmouth Royal Dockyard to the Success of the Royal Navy in the Napoleonic War', *Transactions of the Naval Dockyards Society*, Vol. 1 (2006), pp. 47–58.

Wilkinson, D., 'How Did They Pass the Union? Secret Service Expenditure', *History*, Vol. 82 (1997), pp. 223–51.

— 'The Pitt–Portland Coalition of 1794 and the Origins of the "Tory" Party', *History*, Vol. 83 (1998), pp. 249–64.

— *The Duke of Portland: Politics and Party in the Age of George III* (London, 2003).

Willis, Richard, 'William Pitt's Resignation in 1801', *Bulletin of the Institute of Historical Research*, Vol. 44 (1971), pp. 239–57.

— 'Fox, Grenville and the Recovery of Opposition 1801–1804', *Journal of British Studies*, Vol. 11 (1971), pp. 24–43.

Winfield, Rif, *British Warships in the Age of Sail, 1793–1817: Design, Construction, Careers and Fates* (London, 2005).

Wood, Stephen, '"In Defence of the Commerce of Great Britain": A Group of Swords Presented to Officers of the British Royal Navy in the 1790s' in R. D. Smith (ed.), *International Committee of Museums and Collections of Arms and Military History: Papers on Arms and Military History 1957–2007* (Leeds, 2007), pp. 171–206.

Woodman, Richard, 'The Royal Trinity House Volunteer Artillery', *Mariner's Mirror*, Vol. 69 (1983), pp. 393–4.

— *The Victory of Seapower: Winning the Napoleonic War 1806–1814* (London, 1998).

— *A History of the British Merchant Navy. Vol. II: Britannia's Realm – In Support of the State 1763–1815* (Stroud, Gloucestershire, 2009).

Wright, J. F., 'British Government Borrowing in Wartime 1750–1815', *Economic History Review*, Vol. 52 (1999), pp. 355–61.

Yarker, Gwen, *Georgian Faces: Portrait of a County* (Dorchester, 2010).

Yonge, C. B., *The Life and Administration of Robert Banks Jenkinson, Second Earl of Liverpool, K.G.*, 3 vols. (London, 1868).

Young, Arthur, *General View of the Agriculture of the County of Sussex* (London, 1813; repr. 1970).

Zamoyski, Adam, *1812: Napoleon's Fatal March on Moscow* (London, 2004).

— *Rites of Peace: The Fall of Napoleon and the Congress of Vienna* (London, 2007).

Ziegler, Philip, *Addington* (London, 1965).

Notes

Full citations for each note can be found in the Bibliography.

Foreword

1. Cookson, 'Political Arithmetic', p. 50.
2. Heizen, 'Napoleonic Wars in British and Hanoverian Memory', pp. 1,404–16.
3. Bell, *First Total War*, p. 7.
4. Collins, *War and Empire*, p. viii.
5. Mackesy, *War in the Mediterranean*; *Statesmen at War*; *War without Victory*; *British Victory in Egypt*; Ehrman, *The Younger Pitt*.
6. Muir, *Britain and the Defeat of Napoleon*; Hall, *British Strategy in the Napoleonic War*; *Wellington's Navy*; Cookson, *The British Armed Nation*.
7. Lieven, *Russia against Napoleon*.
8. Winfield, *British Warships in the Age of Sail*; Burnham and McGuigan, *British Army against Napoleon*.
9. Thorne, *The House of Commons 1790–1820*; Sainty and Collinge, Office-Holders in Modern Britain series.

Introduction: A Hard-Working Generation

1. Parker, *Peel*, Vol. I, p. 29.
2. 7 Feb. 1794, Jupp, *Canning Letter Journal*, p. 64.
3. Collinge, *Navy Board Officials*, p. 8.
4. Colvin, *King's Works*, Vol. V, p. 363.
5. 29 Aug. 1786, *Marsh's Diary*; Colvin, *King's Works*, Vol. V, p. 366.

6. Duffy, *Younger Pitt*, pp. 89–90.
7. 30 Sept.–15 Oct. 1787, Laughton, *Papers of Lord Barham*, Vol. II, pp. 264–79.
8. Hamilton, *Papers of Byam Martin*, Vol. III, p. 381.
9. Ehrman, *Younger Pitt*, Vol. I, pp. 324–5, 326, quoting Rylands Eng. MS 678, 1 Sept. 1789.
10. Ibid., p. 324; Ward, 'English Revenue Commissioners', pp. 229–30.
11. Marsden, *Memoir*, pp. 40–60.
12. Lloyd, *Barrow*, pp. 17–18.
13. Durey, *Wickham*, p. 9.
14. 21 Apr. 1794, Jupp, *Canning Letter Journal*, p. 88.
15. Ibid., 1 Feb. 1795, p. 198.
16. Knight, *Pursuit of Victory*, pp. 458, 638.
17. Ibid., p. 10.
18. Jupp, *Canning Letter Journal*, pp. 91–2, 109–10.
19. Castlereagh to Lady Elizabeth Pratt, [n.d.] 1795, HRC, Londonderry MSS.
20. Bew, *Castlereagh*, p. xxi.
21. To Lady Elizabeth Pratt, *c.* 1792, HRC, Londonderry MSS; Bew, *Castlereagh*, p. 5.
22. Durey, *Wickham*, p. 32.
23. Ferguson, *House of Rothschild*, pp. 45, 49.
24. Davies, *Wellington*, p. 4.
25. Harry Calvert to John Calvert, 26 Apr. 1793, Verney, *Calvert*, pp. 69–70.
26. Knight, *Pursuit of Victory*, p. 80.
27. Hamilton, *Byam Martin*, Vol. I, pp. 180–82.
28. Schroeder, *European Politics*, p. 277.

PART ONE: THE EVER-PRESENT THREAT

1 The Arms Race and Intelligence 1783–1793

1. Hamilton, *Byam Martin*, Vol. I, pp. 139–140.
2. Black, *British Foreign Policy*, p. 12.
3. Blanning, *French Revolutionary Wars*, pp. 38–41; Knight, 'Royal Navy's Recovery', pp. 15, 20.
4. Strachan, 'First World War', pp. 889–903.
5. Quoted in Murphy, *Vergennes*, p. 399.
6. Ehrman, *Younger Pitt*, Vol. I, pp. 118–27; Hague, *Pitt*, pp. 135–52; Duffy, *Pitt*, pp. 18–23.

7. Black, *British Foreign Policy*, p. 16.
8. Scott, 'Bourbon Naval Construction', pp. 18–35; Tracy, 'British Assessments', pp. 73–85; *Navies, Deterrence and American Independence*, pp. 118–58.
9. Baugh, 'British Naval Failure', pp. 236–46.
10. Webb, 'Rebuilding of the Fleet', pp. 198–9, quoting A. Aspinall (ed.), *The Later Correspondence of George III* (Cambridge, 1962–70), Vol. I, No. 271, 1 Jan. 1786.
11. Ibid., pp. 196–7.
12. Ibid., pp. 196–9; Glete, *Navies and Nations*, Vol. I, p. 275.
13. Webb, 'Rebuilding the Fleet', pp. 210, 209.
14. Cobban, 'British Secret Service', pp. 233–4.
15. WLC, Sydney Papers, 6 June 1789.
16. Ibid., 24 May 1785.
17. Seth, *Spy in Silk Breeches*, pp. 49–57; Fraser to Stephens, 17, 15, 25 Oct. 1784, Admiralty in-letters, TNA, ADM 1/415.
18. Frost, *Arthur Phillip*, pp. 131–3.
19. WLC, Sydney Papers, accounts paid to Nepean by George Rose, 11 Nov. 1784.
20. Pitt to Middleton, 26 Sept. 1787, NMM, Middleton Papers, MID/1/149; Howe to Curtis, 26 Sept., HL, Howe Papers, HO 58; 20 Oct. 1787, HO 59; 22 Feb. 1788, HO 63; 1 Dec. 1788, 25 June 1789, HO 68.
21. Service historique, *Pierres de Mer*, p. 27; Cormack, *French Navy*, p. 30.
22. Cobban, 'British Secret Service', pp. 240–41, quoting BL, Add. MSS 28061, fol. 162, Carmarthen to Eden.
23. Pocock, *Sir Sidney Smith*, p. 9.
24. 18 Aug. 1787, Laughton, *Barham Papers*, Vol. II, pp. 255–7.
25. Howe to Sir Roger Curtis, 1 Dec. 1788, HL, Howe Papers, HO 68.
26. 4 June 1789, NMM, Hood Papers, HOO/2/109.
27. Cormack, *Revolution and French Navy*, p. 30; Service historique, *Pierres de mer*, p. 27.
28. Black, *British Foreign Policy*, pp. 144–53.
29. Ehrman, *Younger Pitt*, Vol. I, pp. 520–36.
30. 23 July, 8 Aug., 13, 28 Sept., 20 Nov. 1787, WLC, Sydney Papers.
31. Ehrman, *Younger Pitt*, Vol. I, p. 520; Black, *British Foreign Policy*, p. 154.
32. Pitt to Hood, 1 Oct. 1787, NMM, Hood Papers, HOO/2/176a.
33. 9 Oct. 1787, WLC, Melville Papers, Vol. III.
34. Black, *British Foreign Policy*, p. 154.
35. Webb, 'Rebuilding and Repair', p. 195, quoting *Parliamentary History*, Vol. XXVI, 27 Nov. 1787.

36. TNA, Admiralty List Books, ADM 8/64, 1788.
37. July 1788, sent on to Carmarthen, 2 Sept. 1788, Foreign Office General Correspondence, TNA, FO 27/29, 31.
38. 19 Feb. 1788, WLC, Sydney Papers, disbursements.
39. 21 Nov. 1788, WLC, Sydney Papers, disbursements.
40. Thorne, *House of Commons*, Vol. V, p. 144.
41. 'Detective's report on the movements of Richd Brinsley Sheridan from noon until 1.30 a.m., 6 Dec. 1788', WLC, Sydney Papers.
42. Crook, *Toulon*, pp. 78–96.
43. Cormack, *Revolution and French Navy*, pp. 85–7.
44. Cobban, 'British Secret Service', p. 251; Feb., May 1790, TNA, WO 1/395, Thomas Dumaresq.
45. Ehrman, *Younger Pitt*, Vol. I, pp. 385–6.
46. Ibid., Vol. I, p. 562; Black, *British Foreign Policy*, p. 236.
47. Webb, 'Nootka Sound', p. 142.
48. Ibid. pp. 138–9.
49. Ibid., pp. 140–42.
50. Black, *British Foreign Policy*, p. 246; Webb, 'Nootka Sound', p. 139.
51. Webb, 'Nootka Sound', pp. 133, 136, 143–4.
52. Black, *British Foreign Policy*, p. 251; Webb, 'Nootka Sound', p. 150.
53. Ehrman, *Younger Pitt*, Vol. II, p. 7.
54. Davey, 'Securing the Sinews', pp. 163–5; Webb, 'Ochakov Affair', p. 13.
55. Scott, *British Foreign Policy*, pp. 293–303; Syrett, *European Waters*, pp. 95–132.
56. Hope, 'Black Sea Trade', pp. 168, 170.
57. Hattendorf, *St Barthélemy and the Swedish West India Company*, pp. 20–23. For the Admiralty intelligence report see 6 Aug. 1784, Admiralty in-letters, TNA, ADM 1/3969.
58. Black, *British Foreign Policy*, p. 286, quoting Alexander Straton, secretary of the legation in Vienna, 9 Feb. 1791, TNA, FO 7/24, fol. 88.
59. Black, *British Foreign Policy*, p. 281, also pp. 278–85; Ehrman, *Younger Pitt*, Vol. I, pp. 502–9; *Younger Pitt*, Vol. II, pp. 3–41; Webb, 'Ochakov', pp. 14–16; Kaplan, *Russian Overseas Commerce*, pp. 151–7.
60. Black, *British Foreign Policy*, p. 299.
61. Webb, 'Ochakov Affair', p. 22.
62. Black, *British Foreign Policy*, pp. 300–318.
63. Hope, 'Black Sea Trade', pp. 171–2.
64. Black, *British Foreign Policy*, p. 318, quoting Williamwood, p. 157, Ewart Papers, 24 May 1791.

65. Acerra, Merino and and Meyer, *Marines*, pp. 71, 74; Cormack, *Revolution and the French Navy*, pp. 291–302.
66. TNA, Admiralty List Books, ADM 8/65, 1789.
67. Duffy, *Pitt*, p. 180.

2 Pitt's Investment 1783–1793

1. Deane and Cole, *British Economic Growth*, p. 8.
2. Unger, 'European Merchant Tonnage', p. 261.
3. O'Brien and Engerman, p. 184, quoting Crouzet, 'British Exports', pp. 51, 61.
4. Deane and Cole, *British Economic Growth*, pp. 52, 59.
5. Davey, 'Sinews of War', pp. 163–4.
6. Duffy, *Sugar and Sea Power*, pp. 3–33.
7. Findlay and O'Rouke, *Power and Profit*, p. 262.
8. Bamford, *Forests and French Sea Power*, pp. 185–95.
9. Knight and Wilcox, *Sustaining the Fleet*, p. 2.
10. Baker, *Government and Contractors*, p. 188.
11. *ODNB*; Ward, *Wellington's Headquarters*, p. 15.
12. Goodwin, 'Jean-Jacques de Beaune', pp. 213–24.
13. Cooper, 'Pitt and Taxation', p. 94.
14. Ehrman, *Younger Pitt*, Vol. I, pp. 269–71; Ward, 'Revenue Commissioners', pp. 128–30; Daunton, *Trusting Leviathan*, pp. 34–5.
15. Harling and Mandler, '"Fiscal Military" State' p. 54, quoting Commission on Public Accounts, *Seventh Report*, 18 June 1782, pp. 41, 430.
16. Harling, 'Old Corruption', p. 64.
17. Ibid., p. 62.
18. Breihan, 'Pitt', p. 81.
19. Webb, 'Rebuilding and Repair', pp. 197–8; Mitchell and Deane, *Historical Statistics*, p. 580.
20. Baugh, 'British Command of the Seas', pp. 153–9; Knight, 'Royal Navy's Recovery', pp. 15, 20; Webb, 'Rebuilding of the Fleet', p. 206.
21. TNA, Navy Board Standing Orders to the Dockyards, ADM 106/2509, 1783–4.
22. TNA, ADM 106/2509: 30, 6 Feb. 1783; 133, 24 June 1783; 129, 20 June 1783; 136, 30 June 1783; Knight, *Portsmouth Dockyard*, p. xl.
23. Knight, *Portsmouth Dockyard*, pp. 8–9; Blake, *Evangelicals in the Navy*, p. 43.
24. Talbott, *Pen and Ink Sailor*, pp. 122–6.

25. Jervis to Nepean, 5 May 1797, BL, Nepean Papers, Add. MSS 36708.
26. *Marsh Diary*, p. 48.
27. Knight and Wilcox, *Sustaining the Fleet*, p. 50.
28. Talbott, *Pen and Ink Sailor*, pp. 100–101.
29. Knight, 'Impressment to Task Work', pp. 1–20; Morriss, 'Industrial Relations', pp. 216–23.
30. TNA, Navy Board Standing Orders to the Dockyards, ADM 106/2509, 172, 4 Aug. 1783.
31. 11 Sept. 1783, Navy Board to Admiralty, NMM, ADM BP/4; Knight, *Portsmouth Dockyard Papers*, pp. 62–3.
32. Morriss, *Royal Dockyards*, p. 93.
33. Derrick, *Progress of the Navy*, p. 179.
34. Navy Board Standing Orders to the Dockyards, TNA, ADM 106/2509, 272, 30 Jan. 1784; 222, 29 Oct. 1783; 336, 3 Dec. 1784; 160, 24 July 1783; 272, 30 Jan. 1784; Talbott, *Pen and Ink Sailor*, pp. 90–114.
35. TNA, Navy Board Standing Orders to the Dockyards, ADM 106/2509, 272, 30 Jan. 1784.
36. Talbott, *Pen and Ink Sailor*, p. 102.
37. Coad, *Royal Dockyards*, pp. 103–6; Morriss, *Royal Dockyards*, pp. 39–44.
38. Talbott, *Pen and Ink Sailor*, pp. 100–103.
39. Coad, *Royal Dockyards*, pp. 130–34.
40. Knight, *Portsmouth Dockyard*, pp. 159–65.
41. Lyon, *Sailing Navy List*, pp. 70–72, 104, 236.
42. Drabble, 'Templar and Parlby', pp. 1–2.
43. Coad, *Royal Dockyards*, p. 100; *Block Mills*, pp. 27–8; *Support for the Fleet*, p. 95.
44. Morriss, *Royal Dockyards*, p. 44.
45. Merino, 'Graving Docks', pp. 48–9.
46. Cormack, *French Navy*, p. 46.
47. Cock, 'Early Trials of Copper Sheathing', pp. 446–59.
48. Knight, 'Copper Sheathing', p. 304.
49. Harris, *Copper King*, p. 49.
50. Ibid., pp. 177–8.
51. Knight, 'Copper Sheathing', p. 307.
52. Webb, 'Navy and British Diplomacy', p. 143; Rosier, 'Fleet Repairs', pp. 328–33; Cock, 'Cost of Re-Coppering', p. 93.
53. Harris, 'Industrial Espionage', p. 170, quoting Archives Navales T591, 4 and 5.
54. Knight, *Shipbuilding Timber*, pp. 11–19.

55. 24 Mar. 1786, NMM, Middleton Papers, MID/1/169.

56. Knight, *Shipbuilding Timber*, pp. 32–3.

57. Middleton to Pitt, 12 Dec. 1785, Laughton, *Barham Papers*, Vol. II, pp. 194–5.

58. 7. Oct. 1787, NMM, Middleton Papers, MID/1/196.

59. Knight and Wilcox, *Sustaining the Fleet*, pp. 32, 218.

60. Syrett, 'Christopher Atkinson', p. 141; Knight, 'Politics and Trust', pp. 133–4.

61. Knight, 'Politics and Trust', p. 134; Knight and Wilcox, *Sustaining the Fleet*, pp. 17–18, 24, 196, 207.

62. Baker, 'Open Contracting', pp. 453–4.

63. Norris, *Shelburne*, pp. 226–7.

64. Steven Watson, *George III*, p. 580.

65. Cole, *Arming the Navy*, pp. 11–13.

66. Evans, *Arming the Fleet*, pp. 33–5.

67. Hogg, *Arsenal*, Vol. I, p. 493; Vol. II, p. 1,289.

68. Jupp, *Grenville*, p. 45.

69. Olson, *Radical Duke*, pp. 12, 13, 95.

70. Ibid., p. 74.

71. Seymour, *Ordnance Survey*, p. 47, quoting TNA, WO 46/18; MR, 1385.

72. Douet, *Barracks*, p. 56.

73. Olson, *Radical Duke*, p. 82; Saunders, *Fortress Britain*, p. 126.

74. Cole, *Arming the Navy*, p. 17.

75. Jane, *Shirley Heights*, pp. 21–2.

76. Cole, *Arming the Navy*, pp. 60–61, 78–9.

77. Evans, *Arming the Fleet*, pp. 39–43.

78. Congreve, *Royal Powder Mills*, Appendix 1.

79. Tomlinson, 'Wealden Gunfounders', p. 388.

80. Baker, *Crisis in Ordnance*, p. 2.

81. Ibid., p. 31, quoting Blomefield to the Ordnance Board, 14 Mar. 1792.

82. Ibid., pp. 38–44.

83. Harris, 'Industrial Espionage', p. 171, quoting Faujas de Saint-Fond, *A Journey through England and Scotland to the Hebrides in 1784* (Sir A. Geikie (ed.), 1907), Vol. I, p. 151, Vol. II, p. 348.

84. Robertson, *Naval Gunnery*, p. 168.

85. Reese, *The Duke of Richmond*, pp. 203, 207; Bailey and Harding, 'India Pattern Musket', pp. 48–57.

86. Hewit, *Map of a Nation*, p. 103.

87. Seymour, *Ordnance Survey*, pp. 8–24, 47; Hewit, *Map of a Nation*, p. 103.

88. Thorne, *House of Commons*, Vol. V, p. 665.

89. Muir and Esdaile, 'Strategic Planning', pp. 3, 6.
90. Houlding, *Fit for Service*, pp. 70–71, 395.
91. Ibid., p. 89.
92. Ibid., pp. 75–89.
93. Pimlott, 'Administration of Army', p. 79.
94. Ibid., p. 359.
95. Ehrman, *Younger Pitt*, Vol. I, p. 562; Pimlott, 'Administration of Army', pp. 311, 319, 361, 341, Appendix 7, quoting 'Return of the Regiments Embarked On Board His Majesty's Fleet as Marines, 7 November 1790', TNA, WO 25/1146.
96. Pimlott, 'Administration of Army', pp. 311–12, 321–6.
97. Thorne, *House of Commons*, Vol. III, p. 582.
98. Douet, *Barracks*, pp. 58–9.
99. Ibid., p. 67.
100. Ibid., p. 62, quoting 13 June 1792, TNA, HO 42/20.
101. Ibid., pp. 63–5.
102. Joyce, *Post Office*, p. 246.
103. Ehrman, *Younger Pitt*, Vol. I, pp. 294–8.
104. Joyce, *Post Office*, p. 290.
105. Whyman, *Pen and People*, pp. 57, 58.
106. Whyman, *English Letter Writers*, p. 57.
107. Joyce, *Post Office*, p. 281.
108. Whyman, *Pen and People*, p. 58; Ehrman, *Younger Pitt*, Vol. I, pp. 293–8; Harling, 'Old Corruption', p. 70.
109. Barrow, *Life of Howe*, p. 182.
110. Joyce, *Post Office*, pp. 274–9.
111. 15 Mar. 1790, *Marsh Diary*, pp. 46–8.
112. Cormack, *Revolution and the French Navy*, pp. 109–42.

PART TWO: HOLDING THE LINE

3 The First Crisis 1795–1798

1. pp. 45–7. Quoted in Schofield, 'Ideological War', p. 195.
2. Ward, 'French Revolutionary and Napoleonic Wars', p. 6, quoting TNA, WO 30/64.
3. Schofield, 'Ideological War', p. 191, fn. 36, 192, quoting *Parliamentary Register*, Vol. XXXIV, pp. 45–51, 57–60, 390r.
4. Cookson, *Armed Nation*, p. 26.
5. Hampson, *Perfidy of Albion*, pp. 96–7.

6. To Colonel Sir Hew Dalrymple, 17 June 1794, Verney, *Calvert*, pp. 234–8, 254.

7. James, *Naval History*, Vol. I, p. 181.

8. Barrell, *Spirit of Despotism*, pp. 44–5.

9. Rogers, *Press Gang*, pp. 52–3.

10. Duffy, 'Control of Foreign Policy', pp. 151–77.

11. Bickley, *Sylvester Douglas*, Vol. I, p. 81.

12. Cookson, *Armed Nation*, p. 33.

13. 5 July 1794, Duffy, 'Dunkirk Expedition', p. 537n.

14. Ehrman, *Younger Pitt*, Vol. I, p. 132.

15. Jupp, *Canning Letter Journal*, pp. 28–9.

16. Ziegler, *Addington*, p. 56, quoting Liverpool to Lord Auckland, 4 Apr. 1807.

17. Verney, *Calvert*, p. 18.

18. Foreman, *Georgiana, Duchess of Devonshire*, p. 198.

19. Ilchester, *Lady Holland*, Vol. I, p. 100.

20. Foreman, *Duchess of Devonshire*, pp. 197–8, 279; see also the *ODNB* entry by E. A. Smith.

21. Sherwig, *Guineas and Gunpowder*, pp. 88, 365–8.

22. Duffy, 'Dunkirk Expedition', p. 531.

23. 'Minutes of Conversation with Mr Pitt 10 April 1793', TNA, WO 30/81.

24. To Major General Sir Hew Dalrymple, 9 Nov. 1794, Verney, *Calvert*, p. 385.

25. Calvert to Dalrymple, 12 Oct. 1794, ibid., pp. 359–60.

26. Duffy, *Sugar and Seapower*, p. 44.

27. Duffy, 'World-wide War', p. 188.

28. Thomas, 'Wellington in the Low Countries', p. 15.

29. Ibid., p. 30.

30. Dec. 1794, Jupp, *Canning Letter Journal*, p. 163.

31. Jupp, *Canning Letter Journal*, p. 184.

32. Barrell, *Spirit of Despotism*, pp. 32–3, 45–6.

33. Ehrman, *Younger Pitt*, Vol. II, pp. 412–13, quoting 9 July 1794, TNA, PRO 30/8/157.

34. Rosebery, *Windham Papers*, Vol. I, p. xxii.

35. Bourne, *Palmerston*, p. 115.

36. Thorne, *House of Commons*, Vol. V, pp. 613, 634.

37. Ibid., p. 634, quoting Chatsworth MSS [12 Apr. 1795].

38. Cornwallis-West, *Cornwallis*, p. 266; Tracy, *Naval Chronicle*, Vol. I, pp. 133–8.

39. Duffy, *Sugar and Seapower*, pp. 168–9.

40. 29 Jan. 1798, Corbett, *Spencer Papers*, Vol. II, p. 240; Mackesy, *Strategy of Overthrow*, p. 16.
41. Ingram, *Commitment to Empire*, p. 33, quoting National Archives of Scotland, GD/51/1/769/1, Huskisson to Dundas, 11 Sept. 1798.
42. St Vincent to Nepean, 28 Aug. 1800, BL, Nepean Papers, Add. MSS 36708.
43. Duffy, *Sugar and Seapower*, pp. 183–95.
44. Philips, *East India Company*, pp. 87–8.
45. Duffy, *Sugar and Seapower*, pp. 203–4.
46. BL, Add. MSS 33048, fol. 342.
47. Duffy, *Sugar and Seapower*, p. 139.
48. Potgeiter, 'Cape of Good Hope', pp. 524–7.
49. See Chapter 5. Ehrman, *Younger Pitt*, Vol. II, p. 562; Durey, *Wickham*, p. 51.
50. Duffy, *Sugar and Seapower*, p. 195.
51. Ibid., pp. 332–3.
52. Consolvo, 'British Naval Officers', pp. 147, 155.
53. Starkey, 'British Seafaring Workforce', p. 21.
54. Hughes, *North Country Life*, Vol. II, pp. 189–94.
55. 2 Feb. 1795, Jupp, *Canning Letter Journal*, p. 198.
56. Rickard, *Navy Act 1796*, pp. 1–8.
57. Dancy, 'British Naval Manpower', pp. 240–52, 273–6.
58. Knight and Wilcox, *Sustaining the Fleet*, p. 223.
59. Duffy, *Sugar and Seapower*, pp. 173–4.
60. Bartlett and Jeffrey, *Military History of Ireland*, p. 249.
61. Colley, 'Reach of the State', p. 168; Cookson, *Armed Nation*, p. 41; Philp, *Resisting Napoleon*, p. 6.
62. Fernyhough, *Military Memoirs*, pp. 5–6.
63. To John Calvert, 22 July 1794, Verney, *Calvert*, p. 281.
64. Duffy, *Sugar and Seapower*, p. 283, quoting 13, 20 Mar. 1797, War Office in-letters, TNA, WO 1/86.
65. Cookson, 'English Volunteer Movement', p. 883.
66. Cookson, *Armed Nation*, pp. 106–7, 118.
67. Jupp, *Canning Letter Journal*, pp. 109, 259.
68. Gloucester to William Windham, 31 Oct. 1798, Rosebery, *Windham Papers*, Vol. II, pp. 81–2.
69. Western, *English Militia*, p. 444; Randall, *Riotous Assemblies*, pp. 35–43.
70. Bartlett, 'Irish Militia', p. 63, quoting 5 July 1793, TNA, HO 100/40/102–4.

71. Ibid., p. 43.
72. Cookson, *Armed Nation*, p. 9.
73. Clammer, 'Dorset Volunteers', p. 10, quoting 34 Geo. III, c. 31.
74. Duffy, *Pitt*, pp. 154–5.
75. Cookson, 'English Volunteer Movement', pp. 879–80.
76. Thorne, *History of Parliament*, Vol. IV, p. 391.
77. Clammer, 'Dorset Volunteers', p. 10, quoting *Somerset and Dorset Notes and Queries*, Vol. XX (1930), pp. 58–9.
78. Durey, *Wickham*, p. 46.
79. Schofield, 'Ideological War', pp. 197–8.
80. Ehrman, *Younger Pitt*, Vol. II, p. 645.
81. Rodger, *Command of the Ocean*, pp. 436–7.
82. 11 Nov. 1796, Corbett, *Spencer Papers*, Vol. II, p. 71; Knight, *Pursuit of Victory*, pp. 203–4.
83. Mitchell and Deane, *British Historical Statistics*, pp. 577, 580.
84. Ehrman, *Younger Pitt*, Vol. II, p. 619; Cope, *Boyd*, pp. 120–30.
85. Ehrman, *Younger Pitt*, Vol. II, p. 639.
86. Daunton, *Trusting Leviathan*, p. 44; Cope, 'Pitt and Taxation', pp. 96–102.
87. Rodger, 'Blockade', p. 34.
88. George III to Spencer, 16 Aug. 1795, Morriss and Saxby, *Channel Fleet*, p. 110.
89. 14 Jan. 1797, HRC, Londonderry MSS.
90. Bradley, *Bantry Bay*, pp. 31–2.
91. Nelson, *Irish Militia*, pp. 164–5.
92. Bartlett and Jeffrey, *Military History of Ireland*, pp. 249, 270.
93. Nelson, *Irish Militia*, p. 152.
94. Bartlett, 'Bantry Bay', quoting 10 Jan. 1797, Public Record Office of Northern Ireland, T3229/2/19.
95. Durey, 'Crauford', p. 138.
96. Bartlett and Jeffrey, *Military History of Ireland*, p. 271.
97. Bartlett, 'Bantry Bay', quoting TNA, HO 100/69/1, fols. 28–30.
98. Daley, 'City of Smugglers', pp. 337–8.
99. Sherwig, *Guineas and Gunpowder*, pp. 12, 88.
100. Hanger, *Menaced Invasion*, pp. 7–17, 128.
101. The most authoritative of the military appreciations of the threat of invasion in the 1790s are quoted by Ward, 'French Revolutionary and Napoleonic Wars', fn. 5: duke of Richmond, 10 Feb. 1794 (TNA, Home Office papers on armed forces and Ireland, HO 50/371); General David Dundas [n.d., but before Feb. 1797] (TNA, War Office, military

correspondence, WO 30/64, 1–60) and Feb. 1798 (TNA, WO 30/68, 1–72).

102. Ward, 'French Revolutionary and Napoleonic Wars', quoting Dundas to Spencer, 20 Jan. 1798, TNA, WO 30/64.

103. Rodger, *Command of the Ocean*, pp. 456–7.

104. Ibid., p. 448, quoting Jervis, 4 May 1797, Corbett, *Spencer Papers*, Vol. II, p. 399.

105. London, 'H.M.S. *London*', pp. 76–7.

106. Coats, 'Admiralty Retribution', pp. 221–4.

107. Corbett, *Spencer Papers*, Vol. II, pp. 149–50.

108. Ibid., 14 June 1797, p. 155.

109. Camperdown, *Duncan*, p. 176.

110. Durey, 'Crauford', p. 142.

111. Nelson, *Irish Militia*, pp. 217–24.

112. Bradley, *Bantry Bay*, pp. 182, 198–9.

113. 3 Oct. 1798, BL, Nelson Papers, Add. MSS 34907, fol. 351.

114. 18 Nov. 1798, *Dropmore*, Vol. IV, pp. 381.

115. Ehrman, *Younger Pitt*, Vol. II, p. 650.

116. Schroeder, *Transformation of European Politics*, p. 199.

117. Knight, *Pursuit of Victory*, p. 295.

118. Coad and Lewis, 'Fortifications at Dover', pp. 153–4.

119. Mitchell and Deane, *British Historical Statistics*, p. 577.

4 Whitehall at War 1793–1802

1. Quoted in Harvey, *Collision of Empires*, p. 39.

2. Aylmer, 'Office Holding to Civil Service', pp. 91, 106–7.

3. *Parliamentary Papers*, 1830–31 (92): *Public Office Employment*, pp. 2–3. They were not amalgamated until 1909.

4. See Appendix 1, from *Parliamentary Papers*, 1830–31 (92): *Public Offices Employment*, pp. 2–3.

5. Bartlett, 'Development of the Army', pp. 31–2.

6. Duffy, *Pitt*, pp. 69–70.

7. Ibid., p. 115.

8. Jupp, *Canning Letter Journal*, p. 220, 7 Mar. 1795; pp. 274–6, 15 June 1796.

9. Canning to Leveson Gower, 1 Sept. 1799, Granville, *Leveson Gower Correspondence*, Vol. I, p. 257.

10. Duffy, *Pitt*, p. 68.

11. 16 Feb. 1797, Bickley, *Sylvester Douglas*, p. 128.
12. Hague, *Pitt*, p. 210, quoting Joseph Farington, *Diary*, Vol. V, p. 162.
13. Duffy, *Pitt*, p. 76.
14. Harvey, *Collision of Empires*, pp. 187–8.
15. Lady Stafford to Leveson Gower, 5 Aug. 1794, Granville, *Leveson Gower Correspondence*, Vol. I, p. 97.
16. Duffy, *Pitt*, p. 204.
17. Bickley, *Sylvester Douglas*, p. 126.
18. Furber, *Dundas*, p. 123.
19. Mackesy, *War without Victory*, p. 92; Philips, *East India Company*, p. 90.
20. 24 Apr. 1800, Rosebery, *Windham Papers*, Vol. II, p. 152.
21. Young to C. M. Pole, 21 July 1798, NMM, WYN/104.
22. Rodger, *Command of the Ocean*, pp. 515–16.
23. Ibid., pp. 508–18.
24. 2 June 1800, Marsden, *Brief Memoir*, pp. 97–8fn.
25. Gardiner, *Frigates*, p. 90.
26. Ritchie, *Admiralty Chart*, p. 30.
27. *The Times*, 28 Feb. 1801, quoted in Dudley Pope, *Great Gamble*, p. 159.
28. Harvey, *Collision of Empires*, pp. 115–16; Muir and Esdaile, 'Strategic Planning', pp. 26–7.
29. Verney, *Calvert*, p. 452.
30. To Major General Sir Hew Dalrymple, 12 Oct. 1794, ibid., p. 360.
31. Jupp, *Canning Letter Journal*, p. 204, 10 Feb. 1795.
32. Ibid., pp. 174–6, 30 Dec. 1794; p. 210, 20 Feb. 1795.
33. Ibid., p. 198, 1 Feb. 1795.
34. Ibid., p. 278, 23 June 1795.
35. Melville, *Huskisson*, pp. 24–5.
36. Jupp, *Canning Letter Journal*, p. 34, 3 Dec. 1793.
37. Chalus, 'Elite Women', p. 686.
38. Marsden, *Brief Memoir*, p. 99fn., 6 July 1800.
39. Harling, '*Old Corruption*', p. 65.
40. Thorne, *House of Commons*, Vol. V, pp. 45–52. The fellow MP was John William Ward.
41. Boscawen to Thomas Grenville, 30 Sept. 1806, HL, STG 136 (9).
42. Ward, 'English Revenue Commissioners', p. 207.
43. *Gentleman's Magazine*, 1811, p. 501; *ODNB*.
44. Thorne, *House of Commons*, Vol. V, p. 186.
45. Ibid., Vol. III, p. 228, quoting Joseph Jekyll to Bond, 2 July [1813], Dorset Record Office, Bond MSS D367.
46. St Vincent to Nepean, 29 July 1796, NMM, NEP/7.

47. Windham to Thomas Grenville, 17 Oct. 1806, HL, STG 168 (59).
48. 15 July 1798, Melville, *Huskisson*, p. 35.
49. Duffy, 'French Atlantic Fleet', p. 601.
50. Marsden, *Brief Memoir*, p. 99fn., 17 Sept. 1800; p. 97fn, 11 Mar. 1799.
51. Nelson, *Home Office*, p. 50.
52. The Transport Board was expected to work a five-day week, but had to continue on Saturdays throughout the French Revolutionary War. Morriss, *British Maritime Ascendancy*, p. 340.
53. Lord Chatham to Middleton, 11 Jan. 1794, NMM, MID/1/141.
54. Commission of Naval Revision, *Ninth Report*, p. 7. See Appendix 2.
55. Lloyd, *Prisoners of War*, p. 334.
56. Crimmin, 'Spanish Prisoners of War', p. 235, quoting Transport Board to Admiralty, 12 Jan. 1796, TNA, 98/107.
57. Durey, *Wickham*, p. 101, quoting Denization and Naturalisation Office: General Correspondence 1798–1811, TNA, HO 1/4.
58. Crimmin, 'Spanish Prisoners of War', pp. 231–5.
59. Ibid., p. 231, quoting numerous volumes from TNA, ADM 103.
60. To John Harrison, 27 Oct. 1797, BL, Althorp Papers, Add. MSS 75813.
61. Cole, *Arming the Navy*, pp. 38–40, 54.
62. Crimmin, 'Admiralty Relations with the Treasury', pp. 70–72.
63. 13 Dec. 1800, Rosebery, *Windham Papers*, Vol. II, p. 162.
64. E.g., 18 Apr. 1793, 'Memorial from the Clerks in the Navy Office', NMM, ADM BP/3; 6 June 1794, 'Shortage of Clerks . . . on Account of the Accumulation of Business', BP/4.
65. *Parliamentary Register*, Third Series, 1798, pp. 277–8.
66. Nelson, *Home Office*, pp. 62, 63.
67. Navy Board to Admiralty, 29 Nov. 1802, NMM, ADM BP/22B.
68. Nelson, *Home Office*, pp. 52, 54.
69. *ODNB*, quoting Glenbervie Diaries MSS, fols. 16–17; Harling, 'British War Effort', p. 127.
70. Harling, '*Old Corruption*', p. 73, quoting *Parliamentary Sessional Papers*, Vol. CXIII, p. 85.
71. George Hartwell, John Kingdom, Charles Derrick to the first lord of the Admiralty, 18 July 1800, NMM, ADM BP/20b.
72. Morriss, *Royal Dockyards*, p. 106.
73. MacDougall, 'Dockyard Dispute', pp. 47–8.
74. Morriss, *Royal Dockyards*, pp. 123, 128.
75. Commissioner Hope, Chatham, to Navy Board, 24 Aug. 1802, NMM, ADM BP/22b.
76. Gwyn, *Ashore and Afloat*, pp. 73–4, 330.

77. Cookson, 'Political Arithmetic', p. 38.
78. Eastwood, 'Information Flow', pp. 289–90.
79. Cookson, 'Political Arithmetic', pp. 41–2.
80. Eastwood, 'Information Flow', pp. 280–81.
81. East, 'Eighteenth Century', p. 471.
82. Deane and Cole, *Economic Growth*, p. 65.
83. Marsden, *Brief Memoir*, p. 100.

5 Intelligence and Communications 1793–1801

1. Duffy, 'Control of British Foreign Policy', p. 156, quoting *Dropmore*, Vol. V, p. 215.
2. To Burke, 7 Nov. 1793, Rosebery, *Windham*, Vol. I, p. 170; Ehrman, *Younger Pitt*, Vol. II, pp. 567–9.
3. Sparrow, *Secret Service*, p. 84.
4. E.g. TNA, ADM 1/6037, 109 folios of classified index to intelligence, Feb. 1794–Apr. 1796.
5. Duffy, 'French Atlantic Fleet', pp. 602–3, quoting 4 Apr. 1798, Corbett, *Spencer Papers*, Vol. II, p. 305.
6. Ibid., p. 602, quoting ibid., 27 Apr. 1798, p. 326.
7. E.g. Thomas White and Thomas Tayler sending extracts of letters to Philip Stephens, 18 May 1792, 12 Jan. 1794, 30 Jan. 1795, TNA, ADM 1/5120/1.
8. Knight, Jane, 'Merchant News', May 2005.
9. Ellis, *Post Office*, pp. 67–75, 138–9.
10. Durey, *Wickham*, p. 36, fn. 83, quoting Bland Burges to Grenville, 13 Oct. 1793, *Dropmore*, Vol. II, p. 445.
11. 23. Oct. 1796, Granville, *Leveson Gower Correspondence*, Vol. I, 131.
12. 7. Oct. 1798, NMM, NEP/2.
13. Paget to Lord St Helens, 18 Sept. 1801, Paget, *Paget Papers*, Vol. II, p. 15.
14. Durey, *Wickham*, p. 33; see Chapter 1.
15. Sparrow, 'Alien Office', p. 362.
16. Durey, *Wickham*.
17. Ibid., pp. 38–9, 42–3; Sparrow, 'Alien Office', p. 365.
18. Durey, *Wickham*, p. 45, quoting Portland to Wickham, 8 Sept. 1794, Hampshire Record Office, WP, 38M49/1/40/1.
19. Ibid., p. 46.
20. Ibid., pp. 41–4.
21. Sparrow, 'Secret Service', p. 368.

22. 10 Jan. 1798, Admiralty in-letters, TNA, ADM 1/4175, extract from Spiridion Foresti to Lord Grenville, Corfu, 8 Nov. 1797.
23. Secret service accounts, 'Government Account with the Rt Hon. Henry Dundas', 2 Mar. 1795, NMM, NEP/3.
24. Sparrow, 'Secret Service', p. 286.
25. Ibid., pp. 291–2.
26. Office for Auditing the Public Accounts, 1 Apr. 1801, HL, STG 187 (23).
27. Bew, *Castlereagh*, pp. 137–9.
28. NMM, NEP/4, 16 Dec. 1797, 19 Feb., 2 Mar. 1798.
29. Ibid., 30 July 1798.
30. Ibid., 3 June 1797.
31. Durey, *Wickham*, p. 75; Mitchell, 'Dropmore Bulletins', p. 142.
32. Pocock, *Smith*, p. 2.
33. Durey, 'Escape of Smith', p. 443.
34. 5, 16 May 1798, NMM, NEP/3.
35. Durey, *Wickham*, pp. 49, 53, 57–62, 100, 151.
36. Ellis, 'Communications and Diplomacy', pp. 169–72.
37. Ellis, *Post Office*, p. 34.
38. Durey, 'Grenville and the Smoking Gun', p. 563.
39. Abstracts of logs 1793–1794, TNA, ADM 7/575, a sample of twelve ships in each year.
40. To his father, the earl of Uxbridge, 1 Dec. 1800, Paget, *Paget Papers*, Vol. I, p. 287.
41. Ibid., Keith to Paget, 18 Dec. 1800, p. 289.
42. Grocott, *Shipwrecks*, p. 84, quoting *The Times*, 13 Nov. 1799.
43. Abstracts of logs 1793–1794, TNA, ADM 7/575.
44. Boyden, *British Army Postal Service*, p. 4.
45. Knight and Wilcox, *Sustaining the Fleet*, p. 192.
46. 'Reasons Assigned by Capt. Bridge Why Cuxhaven is Preferable to Bremerhale' [n.d.], TNA, POST/43/9.
47. Clowes, *Royal Navy History*, Vol. II, p. 412.
48. 18 May, 31 July 1797, TNA, Post Office records, POST 43/134, fols. 95–9.
49. Robinson, *British Mails*, pp. 311–12; Trinder, *Harwich Packets*, pp. 50–51.
50. 11 Oct. 1800, 10 Jan., 17 Apr., 1 May, 16 July 1801, *Prince of Wales*'s log, in the author's possession.
51. Ibid., 28 Sept. 1800–15 Aug. 1802. The shipwreck was sighted on 16 Mar. 1801.
52. Mackesy, *Strategy of Overthrow*, pp. 54, 62.

53. Hunter to Nelson, 26 Sept. 1804, NMM, CRK/7/106.

54. 14 Apr. 1800, Captains' in-letters, TNA, ADM 1/1922.

55. Barker and Gerhold, *Road Transport*, p. 24.

56. Mallinson, *Semaphore*, p. 82.

57. Ibid., pp. 76–8.

58. 4 Feb. 1796, Colchester, *Diary*, Vol. I, p. 30.

59. TNA, PRO 30/8/259.

60. [n.d. but July 1801], NMM, CRK/14/107.

61. 4 Aug. 1801, NMM, CRK/13/52.

62. Kitchen, 'Coastal Signal Stations', pp. 337–41.

63. Navy Office to Nepean, 19 Sept. 1796, NMM, ADM BP/16b.

64. Instructions to Lieutenants of Signal Posts, 22 Aug. 1798, NMM, ADM BP/18b.

65. Grocott, *Shipwrecks*, quoting *The Times*, 27 Feb. 1793.

66. Crowhurst, *French War on Trade*, pp. 199–202.

67. Harrison, 'Privateers on the East Coast', pp. 301–6.

68. Grocott, *Shipwrecks*, p. 85, quoting *Naval Chronicle*, pp. 3, 76.

69. NMM, HNL/13/10: 79, 27 Nov. 1799.

70. Mornington to Melville, 4 Sept. 1798, WLC, Melville Papers; Ward, 'Rainier', pp. 72, 75, 100.

71. Cleghorn to Dundas, 14 Feb. 1795, TNA, WO 1/361; Ehrman, *Younger Pitt*, p. 562n.; Durey, *Wickham*, pp. 41, 51.

72. Cleghorn to Dundas, 24 Oct. 1795, TNA, WO 1/361.

73. Ibid., 17 June, 20 July, 14 Oct. 1795; 14 July 1797.

74. Durey, *Wickham*, pp. 84–5.

75. Duffy, 'Egyptian Expedition Intelligence', p. 279.

76. Canning to Nepean, 24 Apr. 1798, enclosing Jackson's letter, TNA, ADM 1/4176; WLC, Melville Papers, Nepean's enclosure to Dundas, actions 29 Apr.–24 July 1798.

77. 'Buonaparte's Expedition to Egypt and the Means of Delivering that Country from the French', précis of fifty intelligence despatches received 20 Apr. 1798–10 May 1799, WLC, Melville Papers.

78. Ingram, *Commitment to Empire*, p. 42, quoting Eton to Dundas, 25 Apr. 1798, SRO, GD/51/1/768/3; Wood to Dundas, 26 Apr. 1798, TNA, WO 1/1101.

79. Ward, 'Rainier', pp. 92, 98.

80. Day to St Vincent from Genoa, 13 Apr. 1798, NMM, CRK/18/4; Duffy, 'Egyptian Expedition Intelligence', p. 283.

81. Duffy, 'Egyptian Expedition Intelligence', pp. 282–3.

82. Corbett, *Spencer Papers*, Vol. II, p. 445.

83. WLC, Melville Papers, Nepean's enclosure to Dundas, actions 29 Apr.–24 July 1798; Mackesy, *Strategy of Overthrow*, p. 22.
84. Knight, *Pursuit of Victory*, p. 279.
85. 28 May 1798, BL, Add. MSS 34906, fol. 426.
86. Knight, *Pursuit of Victory*, p. 284.
87. See letter of 29 Apr. 1798 to St Vincent, Corbett, *Spencer Papers*, Vol. III, pp. 437–41.
88. St Vincent to Nepean, 3 July 1798, NMM, NEP/4, fol. 121.
89. Précis of correspondence, 20 Apr. 1798–10 May 1799, WLC, MelvillePapers.
90. 28 Sept. 1798, *Dropmore*, Vol. IV, p. 328.
91. Melville, *Huskisson Papers*, pp. 38–9.
92. Précis of correspondence, 20 Apr. 1798–10 May 1799, WLC, Melville Papers.
93. Duffy, 'French Atlantic Fleet', pp. 603–4.
94. Ibid., pp. 609–11.
95. Rodger, *Command of the Ocean*, p. 462.
96. Huskisson to Home Popham, 16 July 1799, WLC, Melville Papers.
97. 26 Oct., 3, 21 Nov. 1796, 25 May 1798, 19 June, 18 Sept. 1800, NMM, NEP/2.
98. Durey, 'Assassination of the French Directory', pp. 551–5.
99. Durey, *Wickham*, p. 101.
100. Ibid., p. 100.
101. Durey, 'Escape of Smith', p. 438.
102. Rodger, *Command of the Ocean*, p. 466.
103. 8, 13 Jan. 1801, NMM, NEP/2; Knight, *Pursuit of Victory*, pp. 364, 388.
104. Duffy, 'French Atlantic Fleet', p. 614.

6 Feeding the Armed Forces and the Nation 1795–1812

1. James Whitworth to his wife, HMS *Portia*, 7 May 1812, NMM, WHW/1/4.
2. 2 Apr., 5 May 1812, logbook of the *Portia*, TNA, ADM 51/2626; Mar. 1811–Apr. 1818, muster book, ADM 37/3128.
3. Coad, *Royal Dockyards*, p. 275.
4. Macdonald, *Feeding Nelson's Navy*, p. 13.
5. Vale, 'Conquest of Scurvy', pp. 160–79.
6. Morriss and Saxby, *Channel Fleet*, pp. 13–14.

7. Cookson, *Armed Nation*, p. 5.
8. Knight, 'Politics and Trust', p. 136; Knight and Wilcox, *Sustaining the Fleet*, pp. 47, 51–2.
9. Rodger, 'War as an Economic Activity', p. 5.
10. Deane and Cole, *British Economic Growth*, p. 8.
11. Lloyd, *Prisoners of War*, p. 201.
12. Knight and Wilcox, *Sustaining the Fleet*, Appendix 4.
13. Ibid., Appendices 4 and 5.
14. Ibid., pp. 51, 52, 221.
15. Stern, 'Bread Crisis', pp. 171–2.
16. Knight and Wilcox, *Sustaining the Fleet*, 74–6
17. Randall, *Riotous Assemblies*, p. 224.
18. Knight and Wilcox, *Sustaining the Fleet*, p. 75.
19. Galpin, *Grain Supply*, pp. 13–14.
20. Bowen, *Business of Empire*, p. 51, quoting Stephen Lushington to Pitt, 25 June 1795, BL, India Office Records L/P and S/1, Vol. IX, fols. 190v–1.
21. Secret Committee, Minute, 30 Sept. 1795, BL, India Office Records, L/P and S/5/583 (reference provided by Alan Frost).
22. Bowen, *Business of Empire*, p. 51, quoting BL, India Office Records B/123, 236, 337, 589; B/124, 886.
23. Knight and Wilcox, *Sustaining the Fleet*, p. 74.
24. Charlesworth, *Atlas of Rural Protest*, pp. 101–2.
25. Wells, *Dearth in Yorkshire*, pp. 19, 23.
26. Vane, *Memoirs of Castlereagh*, Vol. IV, pp. 78–9.
27. Wells, *Wretched Faces*, p. 35.
28. Knight and Wilcox, *Sustaining the Fleet*, p. 77, quoting Wells, *Wretched Faces*, p. 1, from 11 Oct. 1800, BL, Add. MSS 38311, fols. 166–9.
29. Secret Letters of the Commissariat 1799–1806, TNA, WO 58/170.
30. Knight and Wilcox, *Sustaining the Fleet*, Appendix 3.
31. Ibid., pp. 121–2, 127–8.
32. www.nmm.ac.uk, 'Sustaining the Empire' database.
33. Knight and Wilcox, *Sustaining the Fleet*, pp. 149–51, 155–76.
34. Ibid., p. 5.
35. Ibid., pp. 16–17.
36. Armstrong, 'Coastal Shipping', p. 23.
37. Szostak, *Transportation in the Industrial Revolution*, pp. 54–9.
38. Chaloner, 'Salt in Cheshire', pp. 103–4, 112, 117.
39. Ward, *Canal Building*, pp. 26–73.
40. Randall, *Riotous Assemblies*, p. 80.

41. Kaplan, *Provisioning Paris*, p. 84.

42. Ward, *Canal Finance*, p. 136.

43. Nye, *War, Wine and Taxes*, p. 82.

44. Bonser, *Drovers*, p. 37.

45. Fussell and Goodman, 'Traffic in Livestock', pp. 217, 219, 221, 225.

46. Davey, 'Within Hostile Shores', p. 248, quoting memorandum, 24 July 1808, NMM, MKH/112.

47. To Benjamin Hallowell, 28 Jan. 1809, Hughes, *Collingwood Correspondence*, p. 265.

48. O'Brien, 'Triumph and Denouement', p. 197.

49. Brandon, 'South Downs', p. 46.

50. Marshall, *County Reports*, Vol. V, pp. 465–6, 498.

51. Ibid., pp. 474–5.

52. Vine, *London's Lost Route*, pp. 33–4, 50–51.

53. Knight and Wilcox, *Sustaining the Fleet*, pp. 46, 59.

54. Davey, 'Within Hostile Shores', p. 252.

55. 25 June 1795, Corbett, *Spencer Papers*, Vol. I, p. 46.

56. Morris, *Royal Dockyards*, pp. 46–7; Cross, *Banks of the Neva*, p. 207.

57. Knight and Wilcox, *Sustaining the Fleet*, pp. 59–60.

58. Coad, *Block Mills*, p. 35.

59. Coats, 'Rosia Water Tanks', pp. 83–5; Macdonald, 'Victualling Yard at Gibraltar', p. 58.

60. Knight and Wilcox, *Sustaining the Fleet*, pp. 58–63.

61. Armstrong, 'Coastal Shipping', pp. 23–32.

62. 23 Sept. 1795, with draft reply, BL, Add. MSS 75779; McCranie, *Lord Keith*, pp. 44–8.

63. Davey, 'Within Hostile Shores', p. 251.

64. *Hansard*, 1808, Vol. XI, cols. 879–81.

65. Morriss and Saxby, *Channel Fleet*, pp. 18–19, 132–4.

66. Mackesy, *Victory in Egypt*, pp. 38–48.

67. Motz to Treasury, 15 Mar. 1801, letters relating to army victualling, TNA, ADM 109/104.

68. Victualling Board minutes, 10 Feb., 9 June 1801, TNA, ADM 111/159.

69. Davey, 'Within Hostile Shores', pp. 248–50, 253.

70. Ibid., p. 241, quoting 16 Oct. 1808, TNA, ADM 1/7/278–80.

71. Ibid., p. 255.

72. Knight and Wilcox, *Sustaining the Fleet*, p. 213; Knight, *Pursuit of Victory*, pp. 489, 493.

73. Knight, *Pursuit of Victory*, p. 510.

7 Transporting the Army by Sea 1793–1811

1. HL, STG 168 (64).
2. Muir and Esdaile, 'Strategic Planning', p. 21.
3. Navy Board to Admiralty, 23 Aug. 1794, NMM, ADM BP/14.
4. Condon, 'Surveying and Measuring', pp. 334–5; Morriss, 'Colonization, Conquest', p. 313.
5. Morriss, 'Colonization, Conquest', p. 313.
6. Duffy, *Sugar and Seapower*, pp. 166–70.
7. Morriss, 'Colonization, Conquest', p. 317.
8. Condon, 'Administration of Transports', p. 281.
9. Sutcliffe, 'Bringing Forward Merchant Shipping', pp. 110, 202–3.
10. Thomas Hamilton to Thomas Grenville, 20 Feb. 1807, HL, STG 152 (19).
11. Currie, *Henleys of Wapping*, p. 13.
12. Morriss, 'Colonization, Conquest', pp. 316–17.
13. Blanning, *French Revolutionary Wars*, p. 209.
14. Mitchell and Deane, *British Historical Statistics*, p. 217; Duffy, *Sugar and Seapower*, p. 387; Parkinson, *Trade Winds*, p. 83; Morriss, *Foundations of Maritime Ascendancy*, p. 83.
15. TNA, MT 23/1, N/N/1797.
16. Currie, *Henley's of Wapping*, p. 17.
17. Ville, *English Shipowning*, pp. 124–6.
18. Syrett, 'British Army to Flanders 1742', p. 317.
19. 23 Dec. 1802, Markham, *Markham Letters*, p. 16.
20. E.g., 5 Mar. 1798, NMM, ADM BP/18a; 16 July 1805, BP/25B.
21. *Cobbett's Parliamentary Debates*, Vol. XVII, 1810, cols. 99–100, 113.
22. Condon, 'Living Conditions', p. 14.
23. Currie, *Henleys of Wapping*, p. 12.
24. 'A Proportion of Stores to be Provided by the Owners of Three Months' Transports', TNA, MT 23/2, N/N/1812.
25. Davey, *Transformation of British Naval Strategy*, pp. 92–4, 96.
26. 26 Nov. 1795, TNA, ADM 1/3730.
27. Hamilton and Laughton, *Gardner*, p. 250.
28. Ville, *English Shipowning*, p. 77, quoting NMM, HNL/48/16.
29. Ibid., quoting Sept. 1808, NMM, HNL/99/27.
30. Ibid., pp. 12–13.
31. Barney, 'North Sea and Baltic Convoy', pp. 433, 435, quoting NMM, HNL 59/34, 99/20.
32. Hamilton and Laughton, *Gardner*, pp. 265, 250.

33. E.g., Chandler, 'Undergroom at War', p. 218.

34. Burnham and McGuigan, *British Army Against Napoleon*, pp. 157–8.

35. Austen, *English Provincial Posts*, p. 81.

36. Carnock, *Cavalry*, pp. 5–7.

37. Castlereagh to his stepbrother, Charles Stewart, 25 Nov. 1808, HRC, Londonderry MSS.

38. Sutcliffe, 'Bringing Forward Merchant Shipping', p. 275, quoting 'Correspondence Relating to the Expeditions to Spain and Portugal ...', *Parliamentary Papers*, 1809 (66), p. 59.

39. Rodger, *Command of the Ocean*, p. 435.

40. Verney, *Calvert*, pp. 22–3.

41. Verner, *Reminiscences*, p. 12.

42. Admiral Berkeley to C. P. Yorke, 29 Sept. 1810, Yorke Papers, NMM, YOR/2.

43. Grocock, *Shipwrecks*, p. 84, quoting *The Times*, 13 Nov. 1799.

44. 25 Apr. 1801, Pakenham, *Letters*, p. 13.

45. 'Transports in 1801', HL, STG 147 (40).

46. Grocock, *Shipwrecks*, pp. 133–4, quoting *The Times*, 27 Nov. 1802.

47. Harvey, *Collision of Empires*, p. 133.

48. Oman, *Peninsular War*, Vol. I, p. 596; Verner, *Reminiscences*, p. 19.

49. Grocock, *Shipwrecks*, pp. 310–11, quoting the *Naval Chronicle*, Vol. XXVIII, 1811, p. 331.

50. Verner, *Reminiscences*, pp. 19–20.

51. Condon, 'Administration of Transports', p. 311.

52. Gregory, 'Madeira', pp. 80–96.

53. Baugh, '"Blue-Water" Policy', pp. 54, 56–8.

54. Rupert George to Lord Barham, 19 June 1805, NMM, MID/1/74.

55. Flayhart, *Counterpoint to Trafalgar*, pp. 89–93, 172.

56. Harding, 'Victory and Defeat', p. 25, quoting Lieutenant-General Beckwith to Lord Liverpool, 9 Feb. 1810, TNA, CO 318/40.

57. 21 June 1796, Admiralty in-letters, TNA, ADM 1/3731.

58. Morriss, 'Colonization, Conquest', p. 315.

59. Navy Board to Admiralty, 9 June 1798, NMM, ADM BP/18a; Winfield, *British Warships*, pp. 107, 114, 126–8.

60. Rupert George to Lord Spencer, 3 Oct. 1796, Althorp Papers, BL, Add. MSS 75792.

61. 'Men of War employed as Troop Ships in 1800 and 1801, exclusive of Men of War which were not fitted for that purpose, but occasionally received troops', HL, STG 147 (20); Winfield, *British Warships*, *passim*; 16 Nov. 1806, 'Monies Voted by Parliament', HL, STG 148 (16).

62. Bunbury, *Narratives*, p. 93.

63. 9 Dec. 1798, WLC, Melville Papers.

64. Bunbury, *Narratives*, pp. 55, 34.

65. Mackesy, *Strategy of Overthrow*, p. 237.

66. Ibid., p. 320; Morriss, *Foundations of Maritime Ascendancy*, p. 341.

67. Mackesy, *Strategy of Overthrow*, p. 246.

68. 3 Dec. 1799, 'Account of the amount of tonnage in the Transports Expedition to Holland', Dundas letter-book, SCC.

69. Spencer to Pitt, 2 Sept. 1799, Dundas letter-book, SCC.

70. Grey to Dundas, 15 Sept. 1799, Dundas letter-book, SCC.

71. Mackesy, *War without Victory*, p. 86.

72. Memorandum by Dundas, 31 Mar. 1800, Hattendorf et al., *British Naval Documents*, pp. 344–50.

73. Holland Rose, *Pitt and Napoleon*, pp. 266–71.

74. Huskisson to Dundas, 30 Nov. 1799, Dundas letter-book, SCC.

75. Pitt to Dundas, 2 Dec. 1799, Dundas letter-book, SCC.

76. Morriss, *Foundations of Maritime Ascendancy*, pp. 348–9; Ville, *English Shipowning*, p. 153.

77. Creswell, *Generals and Admirals*, p. 96.

78. 5 June 1800, Lloyd, *Keith Papers*, Vol. II, pp. 110–11.

79. Mackesy, 'Cádiz', p. 43, quoting General Doyle to Brownrigg, 24 Oct. 1800, BL, Add. MSS 38736.

80. Quoted in Mackesy, 'Cádiz', pp. 41, 50–53.

81. 27 Dec. 1800, Lloyd, *Keith Papers*, Vol. II, p. 150; 27 Dec. 1800, Richmond, *Spencer Papers*, pp. 140–43.

82. Transport Office to Keith, 8 Mar. 1800, NMM, KEI/1, pp. 143–5.

83. Mackesy, *Victory in Egypt*, p. 15.

84. Chandler, *Napoleonic Wars*, p. 72.

85. Lloyd, *Keith Papers*, Vol. II, pp. 268–9.

86. Muster book of the *Inflexible* 1800–1801, TNA, ADM 36/15106.

87. Muster book of the *Thisbe* 1800–1802, TNA, ADM 36/14088.

88. Mackesy, *Victory in Egypt*, pp. 15–16, quoting Dalhousie's journal, SRO, GD45/4/22, fol. 125.

89. Log of the *Peterel* 1800–1801, TNA, ADM 51/1364.

90. 30 Dec. 1801, log of the *Peterel*, TNA, ADM 51/1364.

91. Commander Inglis to Lieutenant Young, 18 Jan. 1801, Laughton, *Naval Miscellany*, Vol. II, p. 339.

92. Parsons, *Nelsonian Reminiscences*, p. 81.

93. Mackesy, *Victory in Egypt*, p. 16, quoting Dalhousie's journal, SRO, GD45/4/22, fol. 133.

94. 4 Feb. 1801, Lloyd, *Keith Papers*, Vol. II, p. 263.

95. Mackesy, *Victory in Egypt*, p. 49; Chandler, *Napoleonic Wars*, p. 72.

96. Log of the *Peterel*, TNA, ADM 51/1364.

97. Mackesy, *Victory in Egypt*, p. 62.

98. Chandler, *Napoleonic Wars*, p. 73.

99. Bunbury, *Narratives*, pp. 94–5.

100. BL, Add. MSS. 8807, quoted by Melville in his speech in the Lords, 21 May 1810.

101. Mackesy, *Victory in Egypt*, p. 76.

102. Laughton, *Miscellany*, Vol. II, p. 344.

103. To Buckingham, 25 Dec. 1806, 1 Apr. 1807, HL, STG 37 (39, 50); Munch-Petersen, *Copenhagen*, pp. 57–8.

104. Palmer, *Great Yarmouth*, Vol. II, p. 286.

105. Munch-Petersen, *Copenhagen*, p. 99.

106. Ibid., pp. 99, 152–3, 170, 199.

107. Oman, *Peninsular War*, Vol. I, p. 596; James Bowen to the Transport Board, 28 Jan. 1809, HL, STG 136 (21).

108. Carnock, *Cavalry*, p. 28.

109. Verner, *Reminiscences*, p. 16.

110. Copy of Bowen's report to the Transport Board, 28 Jan. 1809, HL, STG 136 (21).

111. *Cobbett's Parliamentary Debates*, Vol. XVII, 1810, col. 90.

112. Copy of Bowen's report to the Transport Board, 28 Jan. 1809, HL, STG 136 (21).

113. Muster book of the *Barfleur* 1808–9, TNA, ADM 37/1151.

114. Muster book of the *Ville de Paris* 1808–9, TNA, ADM 37/2265.

115. Muster book of the *Audacious* 1808–9, TNA, ADM 37/1103.

116. Carnock, *Cavalry*, p. 31.

117. Coad, 'Hurst Castle', p. 74.

118. Quoted in Robertson, *Commanding Presence*, pp. 88–9.

119. Ackroyd et al., *Advancing with the Army*, p. 33.

120. Robertson, *Commanding Presence*, pp. 88, 96.

121. Duffy, 'Hood', p. 341, quoting Lady Sarah Spencer to Robert Spencer, 6 Feb. 1809, in M. Wyndham (ed.), *Correspondence of Sarah Spencer, Lady Lyttleton 1787–1870* (London, 1912), p. 60.

122. Rodger, *Command of the Ocean*, p. 556; Glover, *Britain at Bay*, p. 24.

123. *ODNB*, quoting Graham Moore from H. Maxwell, *Creevey Papers*, p. 95; Creswell, *Generals and Admirals*, p. 106; James, *Naval History*, Vol. IV, p. 7.

124. Bond, *Grand Expedition*, p. 18, quoting C. Greenhill Gardyne, *The Life of a Regiment* (London, 1929), p. 171.

125. Charles Worsley Boys to James Boys, 25 Aug. 1809, Laughton, *Miscellany*, Vol. II, pp. 389, 391.

126. Bond, *Grand Expedition*, pp. 145–6, 179.

127. Ibid., p. 21.

128. To Charles Stewart, 31 July 1809, HRC, Londonderry MSS.

129. Bond, *Grand Expedition*, pp. 179–80.

130. Muir, *Defeat of Napoleon*, pp. 100–102.

131. Graham Moore to Creevey, 9 Jan. 1810, Creevey, *Life and Times*, p. 46.

132. Howard, *Walcheren*, pp. 164–6, 199, 201–2.

133. Information from Michael Crumplin and Robert Malster.

134. Ackroyd et al., *Advancing with the Army*, pp. 33–4.

135. 'Rupert George', 18 Sept. 1809, Syrett and Dinardo, *Commissioned Naval Officers*.

136. Duke of York to Windham, 18 Mar. 1806, Glover, *Britain at Bay*, p. 224.

137. Harvey, *Collision of Empires*, pp. 133–7.

138. Mackesy, 'Amphibious Power', p. 24.

PART THREE: DEFENDING THE REALM

8 Political Instability and the Conduct of the War 1802–1812

1. Quoted in Hunt, *Duel*, p. 143.

2. *Political Register*, Vol. 30, Letter V, to the People of the United States of America, quoted in Harvey, *Collision of Empires*, pp. 184–5.

3. Harvey, *Collision of Empires*, pp. 174–5.

4. Ehrman, *Younger Pitt*, Vol. III, pp. 495–6; Jupp, *Canning*, pp. 97–9.

5. See Appendix 2.

6. Breihan, 'Addington Party', p. 171.

7. Crimmin, 'Troubridge', p. 315; Thorne, *House of Commons*, Vol. V, p. 416.

8. Grenville to Buckingham, 4 Oct. 1806, HL, STG 37 (28).

9. Knight and Wilcox, *Sustaining the Navy*, p. 225.

10. 2 Oct. 1801, WLC, Melville Papers.

11. Schroeder, *Europe*, p. 226.

12. Ibid., p. 241; Grainger, *Amiens*, pp. 181–5.

13. Daly, 'English Smugglers', p. 43.

14. Balleine, *D'Auvergne*, pp. 96–100, 109–10.

15. 29 Apr. 1803, Paget, *Paget*, Vol. II, p. 77.

16. Glover, *Britain at Bay*, p. 43; Grainger, *Amiens*, p. 110.

17. 'Account of the Number of Ships in Commission and Complements', DHC, Addington Papers, 152M/c1802/ON18.

18. 1 Apr. 1803, DHC, Addington Papers, 152M/c1803/ON54.

19. Secret Orders, Admiralty Board to Bickerton, 7 Mar. 1803, TNA, ADM 2/1360.

20. Knight, *Pursuit of Victory*, pp. 442–3, quoting 19 Mar., 24 Apr. 1803, TNA, ADM 1/407.

21. Ziegler, *Addington*, p. 81.

22. Grenville to Buckingham, 18, 20 Oct. 1802, HL, STG 36 (9) and (8).

23. McCord, 'Impress Service', pp. 166–8.

24. Durey, *Wickham*, pp. 172–7.

25. Ibid., p. 170, quoting the *Weekly Political Register*, 20 Aug. 1803.

26. Hall, 'Addington Party', p. 315.

27. Morieux, 'Travelling across the Channel', p. 230.

28. Thorne, *House of Commons*, Vol. III, p. 238.

29. Ravenhill, 'Clifford', pp. 163–8.

30. Morieux, 'Travelling across the Channel', p. 236.

31. Thorne, *House of Commons*, Vol. IV, p. 143; Morriss, *Naval Power and Culture*, p. 162.

32. Breihan, 'Addington Party', p. 172.

33. Morriss, *Royal Dockyards*, pp. 82, 179.

34. Barrow, *Autobiography*, p. 257; Marsden, *Brief Memoir*, p. 103.

35. Arbuthnot to Paget, 12 Mar. 1804, Paget, *Paget Papers*, Vol. II, pp. 97–8.

36. Breihan, 'Addington Party', p. 174; Knight, 'Devil Bolts and Deception', p. 5.

37. Hague, *Pitt*, pp. 541–7.

38. 25 Sept. 1804, WLC, Melville Papers.

39. Knight, 'Fleets at Trafalgar', p. 69; see Chapter 12.

40. Rodger, *Command of the Ocean*, p. 531; Wareham, *Frigate Commander*, pp. 254–5; Ehrman, *Younger Pitt*, Vol. III, pp. 703–5.

41. Barrow, *Autobiography*, p. 260.

42. See Chapter 11.

43. Barrow, *Autobiography*, p. 269.

44. Hague, *Wilberforce*, p. 323.

45. Ehrman, *Younger Pitt*, Vol. III, pp. 757–8.

46. Ibid., p. 765, quoting 17 Apr. 1805, BL, Loan MS 72, Vol. 55.

47. Barrow, *Autobiography*, pp. 276–7.

48. Hague, *Pitt*, p. 565; Ehrman, *Younger Pitt*, Vol. III, pp. 825–6.

49. Hague, *Pitt*, p. 566.

50. Duffy, *Pitt*, pp. 227–8.

51. Jupp, *Grenville*, p. 345.

52. Ehrman, *Younger Pitt*, Vol. III, pp. 832–5.

53. Harvey, 'Ministry of All the Talents', pp. 619, 623.

54. Ibid., pp. 630–35.

55. Fernihough, *Military Memoirs*, p. 74.

56. Rodger, *Command of the Ocean*, pp. 550–51.

57. Harvey, 'Ministry of All the Talents', p. 637.

58. Atkinson, 'River Plate Expedition', pp. 69–76.

59. Fletcher, *Waters of Oblivion*, pp. 121–2, quoting Major General S. F. Whittingham, *A Memoir . . .* (1868), pp. 23–4.

60. Ibid., p. 137.

61. Hall, *British Strategy*, p. 131.

62. Beckett, 'Militia', p. 37.

63. Harvey, 'Ministry of All the Talents', p. 628; 15 July 1806, Colchester, *Diary and Correspondence*, Vol. II, p. 77.

64. 30 May 1806, Rosebery, *Windham*, Vol. II, p. 310.

65. Cookson, *Armed Nation*, p. 123; Hall, *British Strategy*, p. 133.

66. Glover, *Britain at Bay*, p. 139.

67. Ibid., p. 143; Glover, *Peninsular Preparation*, p. 240; Emsley, 'Volunteers', p. 47.

68. Glover, *Peninsular Preparation*, p. 242.

69. Harvey, 'Ministry of All the Talents', p. 628, quoting Wilberforce, *Life* (1838), Vol. III, p. 268.

70. Holmberg, 'French Decrees on Trade', p. 2.

71. Marzagalli, 'Continental Blockade', pp. 26–7.

72. Hicks, 'Napoleon, Tilsit', pp. 129–35.

73. Sack, *Grenvillites*, p. 99, quoting 28 Feb. 1804, Horner Papers, Vol. II, LSE.

74. 8 Aug. 1806, HL, STG 37 (18).

75. 'Appointments of Commissioned Officers', HL, ST 103.

76. 'Book of Promotions', HL, ST 21; 'Book of Applications', ST 102.

77. To Buckingham, 25 Dec. 1806, HL, STG 37 (39); Knight and Wilcox, *Sustaining the Fleet*, p. 222.

78. 6 Mar. 1807, HL, STG 37 (44).

79. Grenville to Buckingham, 5 Dec. 1806, HL, STG 37 (36).

80. Grenville to Buckingham, 1 Apr. 1807, HL, STG 37 (50).

81. Jupp, *Grenville*, pp. 409, 412.

82. Glover, *Peninsular Preparation*, pp. 247–52.

83. Hicks, 'Napoleon, Tilsit', p. 134, quoting Napoleon's *Correspondance*, No. 12,848.
84. Muir, *Defeat of Napoleon*, pp. 22–3.
85. Ibid., p. 25.
86. Cookson, *Armed Nation*, p. 53, quoting 16 Sept. 1807, Richmond MSS, National Library of Ireland, MS 70/1338.
87. Robson, *Portugal and South America*, pp. 168–9.
88. NMM website, 'Sustaining the Empire' database, from List Books, TNA, ADM 8.
89. Croker to C. P. Yorke, 23 Oct. 1811, NMM, YOR/3.
90. Winfield, *British Warships*, p. 291; see also Chapter 12.
91. NMM website, 'Sustaining the Empire' database, from List Books, TNA, ADM 8.
92. Knight and Wilcox, *Sustaining the Fleet*, p. 222.
93. Davey, 'Within Hostile Shores', pp. 244, 260.
94. Mackesy, *War in the Mediterranean*, pp. 398–9.
95. Collins, *War and Empire*, p. 247.
96. Hattendorf, 'Mediterranean', pp. 213–16.
97. Muir, *Defeat of Napoleon*, pp. 34, 37–40.
98. Ibid., p. 42; Davies, *Wellington's Wars*, p. 89.
99. Davey, 'Repatriation', p. 705.
100. Hall, *Wellington's Navy*, p. 30.
101. Muir, *Defeat of Napoleon*, pp. 54–8.
102. Krajeski, *Cotton*, p. 117.
103. Glover, 'French Fleet', pp. 233–4.
104. Thorne, *History of Parliament*, Vol. V, p. 486.
105. Brown, *Palmerston*, pp. 64–5.
106. Castlereagh to Charles Stewart, 12 May 1809, HRC, Londonderry MSS.
107. Hunt, *Duel*, pp. 132–8.
108. Thorne, *History of Parliament*, Vol. III, p. 399.
109. Grey, *Perceval*, p. 339.
110. Muir, *Defeat of Napoleon*, pp. 110–12.
111. Ibid., p. 123, quoting 7 Mar. 1810, Raglan Papers, Gwent County Record Office, n. 101.
112. Castlereagh to Charles Stewart, 8 Apr. 1812, HRC, Londonderry MSS.
113. *ODNB*, quoting Apr. 1810, Aspinall, *Later Correspondence of George III*, Vol. V, p. 573.
114. Muir, *Defeat of Napoleon*, p. 109.
115. Harcourt, *Rose Diaries*, Vol. II, p. 165.

116. Thorne, *History of Parliament*, Vol. V, pp. 668, 672.

117. Barrow, *Autobiography*, pp. 310–11.

118. Thorne, *History of Parliament*, Vol. V, p. 672.

119. James, *Naval History of Britain*, Vol. V, pp. 231–2.

120. Thorne, *House of Commons*, Vol. V, pp. 81–2.

121. Esdaile, *Peninsular War*, p. 339.

122. To the marquis of Buckingham, 14 Feb. 1812, Buckingham and Chandos, *Memoirs of the Court of George III*, p. 233.

123. Muir, *Defeat of Napoleon*, p. 198.

124. Gray, *Perceval*, pp. 448–69.

125. Harvey, *Collision of Empires*, quoting Lord Holland, *Further Memoirs of the Whig Party 1807–1821*, Lord Stavordale (ed.) (1905), p. 133.

126. Hilton, 'Political Arts of Lord Liverpool', p. 148; *Dangerous People*, p. 286.

127. Yorke to Liverpool, 22 May 1812, NMM, YOR/10 (5).

128. Thorne, *House of Commons*, Vol. I, p. 235.

9 The Invasion Threat 1803–1812

1. Wheeler and Broadley, *Napoleon and Invasion*, Vol. II, pp. 104–5, quoting Cruikshank, 'Volunteers', p. 11.

2. Coad and Lewis, 'Fortifications at Dover', p. 153, quoting TNA, WO 30/68; the same words are used in Verney, *Calvert*, pp. 501, 503.

3. Schom, *Trafalgar*, pp. 123–7.

4. Bunbury, *Narratives*, pp. 172–3.

5. Glover, *Britain at Bay*, p. 14.

6. Feb. 1801, DHC, 152M/c1804/OM10.

7. Linch, 'East Sussex and Invasion', p. 52, quoting Lieutenancy Papers, East Sussex County Record Office, LCG/3/EW1.

8. Ward, 'Defence Works', p. 19; Cookson, *Armed Nation*, pp. 4–13.

9. Boyden, 'Fire Beacons', pp. 127–30.

10. Ann Taylor to Jane Taylor at Lavenham, property of Robin Gilbert.

11. Watson to Addington, 10 Nov. 1803, commissary-general's secret letter-book, TNA, WO 58/170.

12. Burnham and McGuigan, *British Army against Napoleon*, pp. 7–9.

13. Ward, 'French Revolutionary and Napoleonic Wars', p. 18, quoting TNA, WO 30/68, 1–72; 30/76, 106–203.

14. Glover, *Britain at Bay*, pp. 151–8, quoting York to Keith, 18 Oct. 1803, TNA, WO 30/75; Keith to York, 21 Oct. 1803.

15. Cookson, *Armed Nation*, pp. 42–4.
16. 19 Aug. 1803, Ross, *Cornwallis*, Vol. III, p. 500; Cookson, *Armed Nation*, pp. 42–4.
17. Hanger, *Menaced Invasion*, p. 73.
18. Cookson, *Armed Nation*, p. 46, quoting York to Hobart, 25 Aug. 1803, National Archives of Scotland, Melville Papers, GD 51/1/982, 1.
19. Wheeler and Broadley, *Napoleon and Invasion*, Vol. II, p. 129.
20. Ward, 'Defence Works', p. 21, quoting duke of York to Lord Hobart, 25 Aug. 1803, TNA, WO 30/76.
21. Bunbury, *Narratives*, pp. 176–7; Ward, 'Defence Works', p. 2.
22. Fedorak, 'In Defence of Great Britain', p. 92.
23. Linch, 'East Sussex and Invasion', pp. 53, 56, quoting 23 Aug. 1803, TNA, HO 58/88, 23.
24. Colley, *Britons*, pp. 378–81.
25. Rodger, *Command of the Ocean*, p. 639.
26. Rodger, 'War as an Economic Activity', pp. 5–6.
27. Jupp, *Grenville*, p. 369; Muir, *Defeat of Napoleon*, pp. 14.
28. Cookson, *Armed Nation*, p. 50; Fedorak, 'Defence of Great Britain', p. 96.
29. Linch, 'East Sussex and Invasion', p. 53, quoting Military General Meeting, 14 Jan. 1803, East Sussex Record Office, LCG/EW 1.
30. Fontana, 'British/Irish Militia', p. 131.
31. Haythornthwaite, 'Militia Insurance', p. 57.
32. Muir, *Defeat of Napoleon*, quoting Fortescue, *County Lieutenancies*, pp. 196–7; Linch, *Wellington's Army*, p. 50.
33. Hall, 'Addington at War', p. 308.
34. See Colley, *Britons*, pp. 314–15, for the progress of the Buckinghamshire Militia.
35. Digest of Services 1803–1908, West Essex Militia, TNA, WO 68/257.
36. Militia Pay Lists, TNA, WO 13/2123.
37. Haythornthwaite, 'Volunteer Force', p. 193; Cookson, *Armed Nation*, pp. 77–80.
38. Clammer, 'Dorset Volunteers', pp. 10, 14.
39. Haythornthwaite, 'Volunteer Force', pp. 193–5.
40. Rogers, 'Sea Fencibles', p. 53; Cookson, *Armed Nation*, p. 9; Colley, 'Reach of the State', pp. 170–72, 181; Newman, 'London Defence Volunteers', p. 82.
41. Glover, *Britain at Bay*, pp. 44, 46.

42. Harvey, *Collision of Empires*, p. 180; Wheeler and Broadley, *Napoleon and Invasion*, Vol. II, p. 131, both quoting *Gentleman's Magazine*, 1803, pp. 974–7.

43. Glover, *Peninsular Preparation*, p. 57, quoting 6 Apr. 1804, HO 50/397.

44. Fedorak, 'In Defence of Great Britain', pp. 101, 103; Glover, *Peninsular Preparation*, pp. 52–8.

45. Ward, 'Defence Works', p. 19, quoting TNA, WO 30/70, p. 235.

46. Glover, *Britain at Bay*, p. 210, quoting 14 Mar. 1804, TNA, HO 50/397.

47. Linch, 'British Volunteer Movement', p. 212.

48. Yarker, *Georgian Faces*, pp. 64–5; Clammer, 'Dorset Volunteers', p. 11.

49. Royal Monmouth and Brecon Order Book, 23 Apr. 1808.

50. Hudson, 'Volunteers in Sussex', pp. 167, 170.

51. Vine, *London's Lost Route*, pp. 36–7.

52. Linch, 'East Sussex and Invasion', p. 56.

53. Ibid., p. 57, quoting 23 Sept. 1803, Lord Gage Papers, Sussex Archaeological Society Collection, East Sussex Record Office, SAS/GM/26.

54. Ibid., quoting 7 Dec. 1803, East Sussex Record Office, SHR 91; Hudson, 'Volunteers in Sussex', pp. 167, 173.

55. Linch, 'East Sussex Volunteers', p. 58; Hudson, 'Volunteers in Sussex', p. 173.

56. Rogers, 'Sea Fencibles', p. 45, quoting 43 Geo. III, c. 62, 24 June 1803.

57. Ibid., pp. 44–5.

58. *Steel's Navy List*, corrected to Nov. 1804, p. 42.

59. Rogers, 'Sea Fencibles', p. 43.

60. Ibid., p. 46, quoting TNA, ADM 1/581, fols. 19, 53, 71.

61. 18 Sept. 1805, Lloyd, *Keith Papers*, Vol. III, p. 153.

62. 1 Sept. 1803, NMM, ADM BP/23b.

63. 13 Sept. 1803, Croker Papers, NMM, CRK/13/45.

64. 18 Oct. 1803, NMM, ADM BP/23b.

65. Haythornthwaite, 'Volunteer Force', p. 199.

66. Annual Pay and Musters, Somerset Place Volunteers, 1804, TNA, WO 13/4465.

67. Woodman, 'Trinity House Volunteer Artillery', pp. 393–4.

68. Crimmin, 'Trinity House Artillery', p. 92.

69. Cookson 'Service without Politics?', p. 351.

70. Makepeace, *East India Company's London Workers*, p. 126; Bank of England, M6/32 papers from Freshfields.

71. 'Soldiers and Soldiering' website, Keith Oliver, quoting TNA, HO 50/357, and Shropshire Record Office, Leeke Papers, 81/323.

72. Glover, *Peninsular Preparation*, p. 237.

73. Hanger, *Menaced Invasion*, pp. 147–8.
74. Wheeler and Broadley, *Napoleon and Invasion*, Vol. II, pp. 105–6.
75. Guy, 'Pendennis Castle', p. 119; Boyden, 'Fire-Beacons', p. 131.
76. Glover, *Britain at Bay*, p. 210, quoting General Fox to Calvert, 14 Mar. 1804, TNA, HO 50/397.
77. 18 Dec. 1803, Ross, *Cornwallis*, Vol. III, p. 509; Glover, *Peninsular Preparation*, p. 237.
78. Newman, 'London Volunteer Regiments', p. 75.
79. Collins, *War and Empire*, pp. 234–5.
80. Navickas, 'Manchester and Liverpool in 1803', p. 64.
81. Hanger, *Menaced Invasion*, pp. 139–42.
82. Cookson, 'English Volunteer Movement', p. 875; Navickas, 'Manchester and Liverpool in 1803', p. 62.
83. Newman, 'London Volunteer Regiments', p. 85, quoting Anon., *A Few Lines Relative to the Parish of Hackney*, Hackney Archives Department M3598.
84. Fedorak, 'In Defence of Great Britain', p. 99, quoting 1 July 1803, TNA, WO 1/625.
85. Cookson, *Armed Nation*, p. 33, quoting *Dropmore*, Vol. IV, pp. 47–8.
86. Bunbury, *Narratives*, p. 177.
87. Linch, 'East Sussex and Invasion', p. 60; Bunbury, *Narratives*, p. 176.
88. Douet, *Barracks*, p. 75.
89. 24 Mar. 1805, Paget, *Paget Papers*, Vol. II, p. 169.
90. Bunbury, *Narratives*, p. 179fn.
91. 9. Sept. 1804, Thorne, *House of Commons*, Vol. V, p. 496.
92. Watson to Sturges Bourne, 4 Oct. 1805, commissary-general's secret letter-book, TNA, WO 58/170.
93. Hicks, 'Napoleon, Tilsit', pp. 126–7.
94. Glover, *Britain at Bay*, quoting from *Correspondance de Napoléon 1er*, Nos. 13,708, Mar. 1808; 16,916, 17 Sept. 1810; 18,039, 16 Aug. 1811; *The Times*, 11 July 1811.
95. Ward, 'Defence Works', p. 27.
96. Seymour, *Ordnance Survey*, p. 24; Ward, 'Defence Works', p. 21, quoting Ross, *Cornwallis*, Vol. II, p. 507.
97. Saunders, *Fortress Britain*, pp. 142–4.
98. Ward, 'Defence Works', p. 20.
99. Ibid., quoting Chatham to Camden, 30 Dec. 1804, TNA, WO 783.
100. 43 Geo. III, c. 55, sec. 10, quoted in Ward, 'Defence Works', p. 22; Oman, *Moore*, Chapter 8.

101. Ward, 'Defence Works', p. 24.
102. Ward, 'French Revolutionary and Napoleonic Wars', p. 26.
103. Ward, 'Defence Works', p. 28.
104. Holland Rose and Broadley, *Dumouriez and the Defence of England*, p. 216.
105. Knight, *Pursuit of Victory*, pp. 408–16.
106. Ward, 'French Revolutionary and Napoleonic Wars', p. 22, quoting TNA, WO 68, pp. 97–107.
107. Ward, 'Defence Works', p. 31.
108. Ibid., p. 32; Mead, 'Martello Towers', p. 213.
109. Saunders, *Fortress Britain*, pp. 141–3; Coad, *Dymchurch Martello Tower*, pp. 10–12; Clements, *Martello Towers*, pp. 22–30.
110. Ward, 'French Revolutionary and Napoleonic Wars', p. 14.
111. Ward, 'Defence Works', pp. 30, 33.
112. 'Soldiers and Soldiering' website, Richard Dickens, quoting TNA, WO 13.
113. J. Beckett, Whitehall, to Francis Moore, 4 May 1808, TNA, WO 13/4564.
114. Ward, 'Defence Works', p. 25.
115. Vine, *Military Canal*, pp. 62–5.
116. Ibid., p. 74.
117. 20 Oct. 1805, Pellow, *Addington*, Vol. II, p. 396.
118. Evans, *Arming the Fleet*, pp. 35, 248–9.
119. Cookson, *Armed Nation*, pp. 61–2.
120. Ward, 'Defence Works', p. 30.
121. Ibid., p. 27; Saunders, *Fortress Britain*, pp. 144–5.
122. Coad and Lewis, 'Fortifications at Dover', p. 155; Saunders, *Fortress Britain*, pp. 139–41.
123. Ibid., p. 154, quoting 30 June 1797, TNA, WO 55/778.
124. Ibid., p. 177, quoting 23 Sept. 1813, TNA, WO 55/779; Saunders, *Fortress Britain*, p. 141.
125. Cornwallis to Lieutenant-General Ross, 23 July 1804, Ross, *Cornwallis*, Vol. III, p. 514.
126. 'Digest of Services of the Tipperary Royal Field (Reserve) Artillery, formerly 1st, or South Tipperary, Artillery (Militia)', TNA, WO 68/68.
127. Kerrigan, 'Shannonbridge', pp. 235, 238–41; Saunders, *Fortress Britain*, pp. 149–50.
128. Cookson, *Armed Nation*, p. 58; Clements, *Martello Towers*, pp. 69–89.
129. Kerrigan, 'Shannonbridge', pp. 244–5.

130. Ward, 'French Revolutionary and Napoleonic Wars', p. 23, quoting 26 June 1804, TNA, WO 30/62.
131. Ibid., p. 24, quoting Wellington to General Sir James Murray, 6 Nov. 1845, TNA, WO 80/5.
132. 1 Jan. 1811, TNA, WO 30/80.
133. Cookson, *Armed Nation*, p. 65.

10 Intelligence, Security and Communications 1803–1811

1. Gray, *Perceval*, p. 164, quoting Perceval Papers, now in BL, Add. MSS 49173–95.
2. Durey, *Wickham*, p. 136.
3. Sparrow, *Secret Service*, p. 293.
4. Ibid., p. 299.
5. Durey, *Wickham*, pp. 89–90; Tissot-Pontabry, 'Les Espions au service de la France', pp. 46–67.
6. Elting, *Swords around a Throne*, p. 85.
7. 3 Aug. 1805, TNA, WO 43/292.
8. Durey, *Wickham*, pp. 135–7; Sparrow, *Secret Service*, p. 306.
9. Durey, *Wickham*, pp. 179, 189–95.
10. Marsden, *Brief Memoir*, p. 104.
11. E.g., the secretary of state's correspondence with the Admiralty for 1804; see TNA, ADM 1/4195, 4198, 4199; for indexes for 1807, ADM 12/34.
12. Davies, 'Intelligence', pp. 26, 29, 31.
13. Ibid., pp. 38–9.
14. Balleine, *D'Auvergne*, pp. 96–100, 109–10.
15. Daly, 'English Smugglers', p. 31.
16. Daly, 'City of Smugglers', p. 343, quoting 1 July 1811, TNA, CUST 54/25.
17. Glover, *Britain at Bay*, p. 161, quoting 17 Feb. 1804, TNA, HO 50/396.
18. Ward, 'French Revolutionary and Napoleonic Wars', pp. 28–9.
19. 30 Apr. 1811, TNA, ADM 1/4073.
20. Daly, 'City of Smugglers', pp. 342–3, quoting 1 July 1811, TNA, CUST 54/25.
21. Glover, *Britain at Bay*, p. 162, quoting 11 Sept. 1811, TNA, ADM 1/226; p. 163, quoting [n.d.], TNA, ADM 1/224.
22. Mackesy, *War in the Mediterranean*, p. 405, Appendix 6; Rodger, *Command of the Ocean*, p. 550.

23. Quoted in Mackesy, *War in the Mediterranean*, p. 396.

24. Ibid., pp. 360–61.

25. Robinson, *Carrying British Mails*, pp. 313–14.

26. Trinder, *Harwich Packets*, p. 155; Robinson, *Carrying British Mails*, p. 103.

27. Robinson, *Carrying British Mails*, p. 99, quoting POST/Falmouth letter-books, Vol. III, p. 215.

28. Dr von Hesse to Mr Stanhope, comptroller of the Foreign Department of the Post Office, 25 Apr. 1806, TNA, FO 33/36.

29. Trinder, *Harwich Packets*, pp. 53, 55.

30. *Prince of Wales* log, 13 Feb., 16 Mar. 1805.

31. 18 July 1804, 17, 18, 21, 22 July 1808, TNA, POST 43/7; postmaster-general to the Treasury, 12 Oct. 1804, TNA, T1/929.

32. Trinder, *Harwich Packets*, pp. 111–13.

33. Ibid., *Harwich Packets*, p. 104.

34. Freeling to Croker, 31 Dec. 1810, TNA, ADM 1/4073.

35. J. P. Morier to Freeling, 14 Sept. 1814, TNA, POST 43/9.

36. 20 Mar. 1813, TNA, POST 43/8; 5 Feb., 29 July 1814, TNA, POST 43/9.

37. Woodman, *Britannia's Realm*, p. 20.

38. Robinson, *Carrying British Mails*, pp. 80–81; Woodman, *Britannia's Realm*, pp. 228–30.

39. 3 Oct. 1810, NMM, YOR/7.

40. 1 Apr. 1815, Melville, *Huskisson Papers*, p. 101.

41. 15 Oct., 6 Nov., 10 Nov. 1807, TNA, ADM 7/589.

42. Ibid., Barrow to Admirals, etc., 2 May, 27 Aug. 1809.

43. Ibid., 24 Nov. 1810.

44. Ibid., Croker to Admirals, etc., 14 July 1810.

45. 15 Apr. 1812, TNA, ADM 1/4073.

46. Mallinson, *Semaphore*, p. 136.

47. Glover, *Britain at Bay*, p. 165, quoting Collingwood to W. W. Pole, secretary to the Admiralty, 20 July 1809, TNA, ADM 1/415.

48. W. W. Pole to D'Auvergne, 13 Feb. 1809, TNA, FO 95/623.

49. Dundonald, *Autobiography*, pp. 163–7; Mallinson, *Semaphore*, pp. 131–2.

50. Admiralty Rough Minutes, 7, 18 June 1804, TNA, ADM 3/150.

51. W. W. Pole to Vice-Admiral Bowen, Dublin, 8 Dec. 1807, TNA, ADM 7/589.

52. Kitchen, 'Signal Stations', pp. 337–43.

53. Log of the *Warning*, 30 Mar. 1811–31 Mar. 1812, TNA, ADM 51/2974.

54. Hamilton and Laughton, *Gardner*, pp. 252–3.
55. Mallinson, *Semaphore*, pp. 69, 161.
56. Ibid., pp. 81, 87.
57. Hawkesbury to Treasury, 3 July 1804, TNA, T/1/925.
58. Morrison, *Systèmes de communication*, pp. 32–4.
59. Barrow, *Autobiography*, p. 289; also Mallinson, *Semaphore*, pp. 190–91.
60. Grenville to the marquis of Buckingham, 25 Aug. 1807, HL, STG 38 (3).
61. Munch-Petersen, *Copenhagen*, pp. 86–8, 98–106.
62. Ibid., pp. 107–8, quoting Castlereagh to Admiralty, 18 July 1807, TNA, WO 6/14.
63. Munch-Petersen, *Copenhagen*, p. 209.
64. Ibid., pp. 117–41.
65. Hinde, *Canning*, p. 175, quoting 15 Nov. 1807, *Dropmore,* Vol. IX, pp. 144–5.
66. Ibid., p. 180, quoting 22, 26 Aug. 1807, Harewood MSS.
67. John Campbell to Lord Mulgrave, 27 Sept. 1807, 'Précis of Papers on Scheldt', TNA, ADM 1/3987.
68. Rodger, *Command of the Ocean*, p. 562.
69. Epin, *Ouvriers des Arsenaux*, p. 16.
70. Sondhaus, 'Napoleon's Shipbuilding', p. 361.
71. Epin, *Ouvriers des Arsenaux*, pp. 9–10, 81–5.
72. Henwood, *Bagnards à Brest*, pp. 18, 69.
73. Bond, *Grand Expedition*, p. 16, quoting 1 Mar. 1810, *Parliamentary Debates*, Vol. XV, Appendix, col. 522; Bew, *Castlereagh*, pp. 250–51.
74. Minute, 25 Mar. 1809, TNA, ADM 1/3975.
75. Bond, *Grand Expedition*, p. 16, quoting 3 June 1809, *Castlereagh's Correspondence*, pp. 270–71.
76. TNA, ADM 1/3975: file on naval Scheldt intelligence, 65 items, including Lieutenant John Campbell to Lord Mulgrave, 27 Sept. 1807; Decrès to Napoleon, intercepted 7 Dec. [1808]; Campbell to Mulgrave, 17 Jan. 1809.
77. Bond, *Grand Expedition*, p. 17, quoting 1 July 1809, TNA, ADM 1/3987.
78. Davies, 'Intelligence', p. 38, quoting Don to Charles Smith, 20 May 1811, TNA, FO 27/82.
79. Captain John Hancock to Sir Joseph Yorke, 24 April 1811, NMM, YOR/20.
80. 27 Apr. 1811, NMM, YOR/20.

81. 6 May, 1 Sept. 1811, NMM, YOR/20; also 21 Dec. 1811, TNA, ADM 1/3976.

82. 20 June 1811, NMM, YOR/20.

83. Captain Robert Mansel to Yorke, 12, 19 Sept. 1811, NMM, YOR/11.

84. Glover, *Britain at Bay*, pp. 189–90, quoting *Correspondance de Napoléon 1er*, No. 19,488, 23 Jan. 1813.

85. Epin, *Ouvriers des Arsenaux*, pp. 170, 177–80.

86. 15–16, 4 Aug. 1814, Vesey Hamilton, *Byam Martin*, Vol. III, p. 338.

11 Government Scandal and Reform 1803–1812

1. Harcourt, *Rose Diaries*, Vol. II, pp. 336, 338.

2. p. 169.

3. Ward, 'French Revolutionary and Napoleonic Wars', p. 25

4. Harling, *'Old Corruption'*, pp. 105, 134; Harling and Mandler, '"Fiscal-Military" State', p. 46.

5. Harling, *'Old Corruption'*, p. 133.

6. Parris, *Constitutional Bureaucracy*, p. 47.

7. Morriss, *Royal Dockyards*, p. 182.

8. Cole, *Arming the Navy*, p. 38; Evans, *Arming the Fleet*, pp. 33–5.

9. Commission of Military Enquiry, *Sixth Report*, p. 300.

10. Gray, *Perceval*, p. 328, quoting BL Herries MSS, letter-books, Vol. III, p. 117.

11. *Parliamentary Papers*, 1830–1831 (92), p. 3.

12. Hogg, *Arsenal*, Vol. I, p. 493; Vol. II, p. 1,289.

13. Sheldon, 'Victualling Office at Portsmouth', p. 43.

14. Morriss, *Royal Dockyards*, p. 106.

15. Wilkin, 'Portsmouth Dockyard', p. 54.

16. Gwyn, *Ashore and Afloat*, p. 127, quoting NMM, ADM BP/34b.

17. NMM, Dockyard Lists.

18. Crook and Port, *King's Works*, pp. 537–41.

19. Holl to Wellesley-Pole, 28 Sept. 1809, NMM, ADM BP/29B; Coad, *Royal Dockyards*, pp. 34–5, 72.

20. Duke of York to Castlereagh, 3 Aug. 1805, TNA, WO 43/292; Holl to William Wellesley-Pole, 27 Sept. 1809, NMM, ADM BP/29B.

21. 3 Dec. 1805, HL, STG 148 (21). See Appendix 2.

22. Commission of Naval Revision, *Tenth Report*, p. 14.

23. Crook and Port, *King's Works*, quoting TNA, WORKS 1/10.

24. Gray, *Perceval*, p. 325.
25. Commission of Military Enquiry, *Thirteenth Report*, p. 9.
26. 15 July 1803, NMM, ADM BP/23B.
27. 12 Mar. 1806, HL, STG 147 (5); 16, 19 Sept. 1806, 167 (38 and 39).
28. 5 Oct. 1806, HL, STG 151 (24).
29. 14 Nov. 1806, NMM, ADM BP/26.
30. 22 Aug.1807, NMM, ADM BP/27; 28 Dec. 1807, 28 Mar. 1808, BP/28.
31. Barrow, *Autobiography*, p. 258.
32. Ashworth, 'System of Terror', p. 68.
33. Morriss, 'St Vincent and Reform', p. 270.
34. Ibid., p. 274, quoting Melville Papers, National Archives of Scotland, GD/51/2/940, 1804.
35. Barrow, *Autobiography*, p. 256.
36. Marsden, *Brief Memoir*, p. 99fn.
37. Ibid., 13 Dec. 1802, p. 103fn.
38. Ziegler, *Addington*, pp. 169–70, quoting Tucker's *Memoirs of St Vincent*, p. 156.
39. Markham, *Markham*, pp. 11–25.
40. Thorne, *House of Commons*, Vol. IV, p. 842; Bonner-Smith, *St Vincent's Letters*, Vol. II, pp. 32–4.
41. Thorne, *House of Commons*, Vol. IV, p. 392.
42. Morriss, *Royal Dockyards*, p. 170.
43. Currie, *Henleys of Wapping*, p. 10, quoting Commission of Naval Enquiry, *Ninth Report*, p. 14.
44. Morriss, *Royal Dockyards*, p. 198.
45. 20 Oct. 1803, NMM, ADM BP/23b.
46. Barrow, *Autobiography*, pp. 252, 254–5.
47. Archbishop of York (Markham's father) to Pitt, 22 Sept. 1805, Chatham Papers, TNA, PRO 30/8/156, fols. 19–20.
48. Middleton to Pitt, NMM, MID/2/40 [35]; Morriss, *Naval Power and Culture*, p. 177.
49. Morriss, *Naval Power and Culture*, p. 172.
50. Laughton, *Barham Papers*, Vol. III, p. ix.
51. Blake, *Evangelicals in the Navy*, p. 48.
52. Greenleaf, 'Military Enquiry', p. 177, quoting *Morning Herald*, 25 June 1805.
53. Sainty, 'Secretaries', pp. 566–84.
54. Sainty, *Treasury Officials*, pp. 12–13; Gray, *Perceval*, pp. 310–12.
55. 20 May 1806, Colchester, *Diary and Correspondence*, Vol. II, p. 63.

56. Jupp, *Grenville*, p. 365.
57. Ibid., p. 366; Harvey, 'Talents Ministry', p. 639.
58. Crimmin, 'Sick and Hurt: Fit for Purpose?', p. 106.
59. Morriss, *Naval Power*, p. 173.
60. Memorandum by Middleton to Grenville, 4 Dec. 1806, HL, STG 157 (51).
61. Grenville to Thomas Boulden Thompson, 20 Jan. 1807, HL, STG 19 (2).
62. Morriss, *Royal Dockyards*, p. 205.
63. Ibid., p. 204.
64. Ibid., quoting NMM, MID/1/18/3.
65. Commission of Naval Revision, *Eleventh Report*, pp. 40, 156.
66. Knight, 'Victualling Spending and Accounting', pp. 194–200.
67. Davey, *British Naval Strategy*, p. 160, and Chapter 7 generally.
68. Ashworth, 'System of Terror', pp. 77–8, quoting 27 June 1812, NMM, ADM BP/32b.
69. Morriss, *Royal Dockyards*, pp. 205–8.
70. 25 Mar. 1813, petition of Eliza Payne, NMM, ADM BP/33A.
71. 3 June 1811, NMM, ADM BP/31B.
72. Navy Board to Admiral Domett, 8 Oct. 1813, NMM, ADM BP/33C.
73. See Appendix 2.
74. E.g., Commission of Military Enquiry, *Thirteenth Report*, pp. 42, 44.
75. Commission of Military Enquiry, *First Report*, p. 39.
76. Bartlett, 'British Army', pp. 46–8.
77. To George Harrison, Treasury, 17 Dec. 1806, TNA, WO 58/170.
78. *Hansard*, Vol. VIII, col. 843, 18 Feb 1807.
79. Thorne, *History of Parliament*, Vol. III, p. 582.
80. Downer, *Nelson's Purse*, pp. 345–50.
81. Commission of Military Enquiry, *Ninth Report*, pp. 314–15.
82. Crook and Port, *King's Works*, p. 82.
83. Major General Alexander Hope to Bunbury, 11 Oct. 1809, Bunbury, *Memoir*, p. 44.
84. Major General Sir Robert Brownrigg to Bunbury, 1 Nov. 1809, Bunbury, *Memoir*, p. 54.
85. Bartlett, 'British Army', pp. 74, 72.
86. Bourne, *Palmerston*, pp. 97–8.
87. Ibid., p. 115.
88. Brown, *Palmerston*, pp. 64–6.
89. Harling, 'Old Corruption', p. 78; Thorne, *House of Commons*, Vol. IV, pp. 266–7.
90. Pool, *Croker Papers*, p. 15.

91. Harling, *'Old Corruption'*, p. 78; Thorne, *House of Commons*, Vol. V, p. 453.

92. Knight, 'Politics and Trust', p. 142.

93. Knight, 'Victualling Spending and Accounting', p. 198.

94. Jupp, *Grenville*, pp. 350–51.

95. Marsden, *Brief Memoir*, p. 125.

96. Robert Ward, 31 Oct. 1807, Thorne, *House of Commons*, Vol. V, p. 513.

97. Rodger, *Command of the Ocean*, pp. 483–4, quoting Jennings, *Croker Papers*, Vol. I, p. 20.

98. Bourne, *Palmerston*, p. 94.

99. Thorne, *House of Commons*, Vol. IV, p. 745.

100. Knight, 'Politics and Trust', p. 139, quoting Laughton, *Barham Papers*, Vol. III, p. 82.

101. 30 Jan. 1806, Middleton Collection, NMM, MID/1/84.

102. Lieutenant Thomas Wilkes to his cousin, 21 June 1800, NMM, AGC/W/2.

103. Barrow, *Autobiography*, p. 300.

104. Hamond to George Rose, 6 Dec. 1809, Harcourt, *Rose Diaries*, Vol. II, p. 359.

105. Memoir by John Marsh, NMM, BGR/35.

106. Collinge, *Navy Office*; Knight, 'Politics and Trust', pp. 145–6.

107. Ritchie, *Admiralty Chart*, p. 111.

108. 21 Mar. 1809, *Parliamentary Debates*, Vol. XIII, col. 755.

109. Cohen, *Growth of the British Civil Service*, p. 59; Morriss, *Royal Dockyards*, p. 148; 17 Feb. 1802, HL, STG 147 (22).

110. Harling, *'Old Corruption'*, pp. 118–19.

111. Morriss, *Royal Dockyards*, p. 135.

112. 4 Feb. 1809, Harcourt, *Rose Diaries*, Vol. II, p. 337.

113. Morriss, *Naval Power and Culture*, pp. 228–9.

114. Harling, *'Old Corruption'*, p. 102, quoting 7 Nov. 1812, *Political Register*, Vol. XXII, col. 605.

115. Grenville to Buckingham, 4 Sept. 1808, HL, STG 38 (12).

116. Harling, *'Old Corruption'*, p. 126.

117. Ibid., p. 119, quoting *Hansard*, 27 Mar. 1809, Vol. XIII, col. 821; 27 Apr. 1809, Vol. XIV, cols. 268–71.

118. Laughton, *Barham Papers*, Vol. III, pp. 200–202.

119. Gray, *Perceval*, p. 327.

120. Information from Stephen Wood.

121. Gray, *Perceval*, pp. 327, 328, quoting TNA, T1/1024/1151; 1 May 1812, BL, Herries MSS, letter-books, Vol. II, pp. 144–5; TNA, T1/4044.

122. Redgrave, 'Wellington's Logistics', p. 25.

123. 12 Nov 1804, BL, Add. MSS 41079.

124. Pugh, 'Admiralty Record Office', p. 330.

125. Crimmin, 'Admiralty Relations with Treasury', p. 66; Knight, 'Victualling Spending and Accounting', p. 192.

126. 19 Feb., 12 Mar., 28 Apr., NMM, ADM BP/32B; 8 Jan. 1812, BP/32c, 30 Oct., BP/32a.

127. Lin, 'Soldiers and Sailors' Families', pp. 101, 100, quoting Patrick Colquhoun, *A Treatise on Wealth* ... (London, 1815), pp. 124–7.

128. Lin, 'Soldiers' and Sailors' Families', p. 107, issued by the War Office, 25 Mar. 1810.

129. Rodger, *Wooden World*, pp. 131–2.

130. 10 Jan. 1788, Commission on Fees, *Fourth Report*, p. 138.

131. 16 Oct. 1809, Rose, *Diaries*, Vol. II, p. 411; 18 Sept. 1814, pp. 513–14.

132. Hill, *Prizes of War*, pp. 235, 240.

133. Phillip Ottey to [Charles Grey], 18 Oct. 1816, HL, STG 159 (15), 18.

134. Wilkin, 'Portsmouth Dockyard', p. 50.

12 The Defence Industries 1800–1814

1. Knight, 'Trafalgar Fleets', p. 74, quoting WLC, Melville Papers.

2. Dupin, *Narratives*, p. 3.

3. Ibid., p. 2.

4. Rodger, 'War as an Economic Activity', pp. 16–18.

5. Musson, 'Motive Power', pp. 425–6.

6. Coad, *Royal Dockyards*, pp. 225–6.

7. Palmer, 'London's Waterfront', p. 1; Harvey, *Collision of Empires*, pp. 35–7.

8. Morriss, *Royal Dockyards*, p. 54.

9. Gilbert, *Maudslay*, pp. 18–30.

10. Grocott, *Shipwrecks*, p. 349, quoting *The Times*, 1 Jan. 1813.

11. Coad, *Royal Dockyards*, p. 219.

12. Coad, 'Chatham Ropeyard', pp. 163–5.

13. Knight, *Pursuit of Victory*, pp. 139, 520.

14. Corbett, *Trafalgar*, p. 53.

15. Glover, *Peninsular Preparation*, pp. 73–5.

16. Lloyd and Craig, 'Congreve's Rockets', pp. 447–56.

17. Ibid., 12 Oct. 1806, p. 456.

18. Blake, 'Siege of Flushing', p. 34, quoting Sir Richard Hennegan, *Seven Years' Campaigning in the Peninsula* (London, 1846), p. 78.

19. Earle, *Commodore Squib*, p. 123, quoting Chambers, 'Chronological Journal', p. 392.

20. Robson, 'Laycock', p. 150.

21. Young to Yorke, 4 Oct. 1811, NMM, YOR/20.

22. 19 Sept. 1811, TNA, FO 95/623.

23. Earle, *Commodore Squib*, p. 180.

24. Congreve, *Rocket System*, Introduction.

25. Burnham, 'Bridging Operations', p. 255.

26. Schaffer, 'The Charter'd Thames', pp. 299–301.

27. *Parliamentary History of England*, Vol. XXXVI, cols. 687–8, 13 May 1802.

28. Castlereagh to Sidney Smith, 19 Sept. 1805, Vane, *Castlereagh*, Second Series, Vol. I, pp. 91–4.

29. Sale, *Fulton*, pp. 95–105.

30. Stephenson, *Secret Weapon*, pp. 30–32.

31. Morriss, *Royal Dockyards*, p. 106.

32. Webb, 'Construction', p. 211, quoting Middleton to John Deas Thompson, 19 Nov. 1803, NMM, MID/13/1.

33. *Naval Chronicle*, Vol. V, 1801, pp. 130–31.

34. Troubridge to Nelson, 19 May [1803], NMM, CRK/13.

35. Knight, 'Trafalgar Fleets', pp. 73–4, quoting WLC, Melville Papers, 2 Feb. 1806.

36. Doe, 'Thames Shipbuilding', p. 16.

37. Gardiner, *Frigates*, pp. 11–12.

38. Barnard, *Wooden Walls*, p. 70; Doe, *Enterprising Women*, pp. 184–5; Whitefield, *Hilhouse*, pp. 120–36.

39. Doe, *Enterprising Women*, p. 176.

40. Contract of 17 May 1812, NMM, SPB/29.

41. Doe, 'Mary Ross', pp. 3–6.

42. Gardiner, *Frigates*, p. 20.

43. Webb, 'Construction', p. 215.

44. Doe, 'Mary Ross', p. 2; Morriss, *Royal Dockyards*, pp. 97, 106.

45. Keith to John Markham, 6 Mar. 1804, Markham, *Markham Correspondence*, p. 159.

46. Dockyard Lists, NMM.

47. Fone, 'Naval Yard at Yarmouth', p. 356.

48. Knight and Wilcox, *Sustaining the Fleet*, pp. 192–209.

49. *Parliamentary Papers*, 1805 (193), Vol. VIII, p. 185.

50. Starkey, 'Devon Shipbuilding', p. 85, quoting the *Exeter Flying Post*, 23 Apr. 1807.

51. Gardiner, *Frigates*, p. 191; Doe, *Enterprising Women*, p. 180.

52. Doe, 'Mary Ross', p. 5.

53. Ponsford, *Davy*, pp. 72, 77, quoting the *Exeter Flying Post*, 9 Aug. 1804.

54. Ibid., p. 71.

55. Aspinall, *Prince of Wales Correspondence*, Vol. IV, p. 536.

56. Doe, *Enterprising Women*, p. 178, quoting Minutes of the Evidence on Petitions Relating to East India Built Shipping, *Parliamentary Papers*, 1813–14, Vol. VIII, pp. 470–73.

57. Brenton, *St Vincent*, Vol. II, pp. 159–61; Lavery, *Ships of the Line*, Vol. II, pp. 134–9; Barrow, *Autobiography*, p. 263.

58. Winfield, *British Warships*, pp. 10–12.

59. 24 Jan. 1805, Marsden, *Brief Memoir*, p. 111.

60. Morriss, *Royal Dockyards*, p. 88; *Naval Power and Culture*, p. 164.

61. Albion, *Forests and Sea Power*, pp. 320–23.

62. Knight and Frost, *Daniel Paine*, p. 95, quoting Navy Board in-letters, 12 Mar. 1805, TNA, ADM 106/1791.

63. Gardiner, *Frigates*, p. 38.

64. Ibid., pp. 72–83; Lambert, 'Seppings', p. 10.

65. Lambert, *Bombay Dockyard*, pp. 141, 146; Winfield, *British Warships*, pp. 77, 158.

66. Cole, *Arming the Navy*, pp. 180, 218.

67. Ibid., pp. 183–4.

68. Moss, 'Cannon to Steam', p. 475.

69. Cole, 'Gunpowder Manufacturers', pp. 308–9; Moss, 'Cannon to Steam', pp. 479–82.

70. Moss, 'Cannon to Steam', pp. 478–81.

71. Cole, 'Gunpowder Manufacturers', p. 295.

72. Cole, *Arming the Navy*, pp. 163–5; Glover, *Peninsular Preparation*, pp. 68–9; Cole, 'Gunpowder Manufacturers', pp. 304–5.

73. Sherwig, *Guineas and Gunpowder*, p. 186.

74. Taylor, *Storm and Conquest*, p. 336.

75. Cole, 'Gunpowder Manufacturers', p. 298.

76. Cole, *Arming the Navy*, p. 148.

77. Glover, *Peninsular Preparation*, p. 67.

78. Cole, 'Gunpowder Manufacturers', p. 302, quoting Select Committee on Finance, *Third Report*, *Parliamentary Papers*, 1817.

79. Harvey, *Collision of Empires*, p. 101.

80. Glover, *Peninsular Preparation*, p. 61, quoting Commission of Military Enquiry, *Fifteenth Report*, Appendix 9.
81. Collins, *War and Empire*, p. 250, quoting Commission of Military Enquiry, *Fifteenth Report*, p. 383.
82. Macartney and West, *Lewisham Silk Mills*, pp. 37–45, 97–103.
83. Glover, *Peninsular Preparation*, p. 67, quoting Commission of Military Enquiry, *Sixteenth Report*, Appendix 9.
84. Grocott, *Shipwrecks*, p. 287, quoting the *Sherborne and Yeovil Mercury*, 1 Jan. 1810.
85. Evans, *Arming the Fleet*, pp. 50–52, quoting numerous references from TNA, WO 55.
86. Hogg, *Royal Arsenal*, Vol. I, pp. 500, 526.
87. Evans, *Arming the Fleet*, pp. 30–32, 50; Cole, 'Gunpowder Manufacturers', p. 302.
88. Saunders, 'Upnor', p. 167.
89. Evans, *Arming the Fleet*, pp. 34–49.
90. Bew, *Castlereagh*, p. 319, quoting Public Record Office of Northern Ireland, Castlereagh Papers, D3030/3312.
91. Lieven, *Russia Against Napoleon*, pp. 30–31.
92. Cornwallis to Lieutenant-General Ross, 8 Dec. 1803, Ross, *Cornwallis*, Vol. III, p. 507.
93. Barrow, *Autobiography*, p. 304.
94. Thorne, *History of Parliament*, Vol. V, p. 512, quoting BL, Add. MSS 37309, 41852.
95. Coad, *Block Mills*, pp. 49, 73.
96. Coats, 'Block Mills', p. 60.
97. Pool, *Navy Board Contracts*, p. 121.
98. Coad, *Block Mills*, p. 51.
99. Gilbert, *Maudslay*, pp. 18–19.
100. Coad, *Block Mills*, p. 64; *Support for the Fleet*, pp. 121–30.
101. Coats, 'Block Mills', p. 61.
102. Ibid., p. 62; Navy Board to Admiralty, 14 Nov. 1804, enclosing the Taylors' letter, NMM, ADM B/217.
103. Pool, *Navy Board Contracts*, pp. 129–30.
104. Navy Board to Admiralty, [?] 1805, NMM, ADM BP/25a; Coats, 'Block Mills', p. 81.
105. Wilkin, 'Portsmouth Dockyard', p. 56, quoting Rees, *Naval Architecture* (London, 1819–20), p. 174; Coats, 'Block Mills', p. 72.
106. Coats, 'Block Mills, p. 79.
107. Wilkin, 'Portsmouth Dockyard', p. 53; Morriss, 'Inspector-General', p. 25.

108. Wilkin, 'Portsmouth Dockyard', p. 53.
109. Coad, *Block Mills*, p. 101, quoting Book 17, 17 Feb. 1807, Science Museum, Goodrich Collection.
110. Coad, *Royal Dockyards*, p. 155, quoting 1 July 1807, NMM, ADM B/232.
111. Commission of Naval Revision, *Fourth Report*, p. 12.
112. Coad, *Royal Dockyards*, pp. 32–8.
113. Breihan, 'Addington Party', p. 168.
114. Feb. 1806, Craig, 'Letters of St Vincent'.
115. 4 July 1810, NMM, Yorke Papers, YOR/2.
116. Boucher, *Rennie*, pp. 128–33.
117. Morriss, *Royal Dockyards*, pp. 53, 55–7; Rennie's Report to the Commission of Naval Revision, BL, Add. MSS 27884.
118. 4 Dec. 1804, Marsden, *Brief Memoir*, p. 111.
119. Boucher, *Rennie*, p. 131.
120. Warren to Lord Spencer, [n.d], BL, Althorp Papers, Add. MSS 75847; Hurd to Lord Howick, 23 May 1806, HL, STG 154 (7).
121. Bridport to Spencer, 6 Aug. 1797, Morriss and Saxby, *Channel Fleet*, p. 262; St Vincent to Markham, 15 Sept. 1806, Brenton, *St Vincent*, Vol. II, p. 310; Mar. 1806, Markham, *Markham Correspondence*, pp. 43, 28.
122. 'Remarks On Board the *Defiance*' by John Tapson, 28 July 1806, WLC; Manderson, *Twelve Letters*, pp. 101–2.
123. Morriss, *Royal Dockyards*, p. 56.
124. 21 Nov. 1806, Brenton, *St Vincent*, Vol. II, p. 329.
125. Barrow, *Autobiography*, p. 314.
126. Morriss, *Royal Dockyards*, p. 57.
127. Brenton, *St Vincent*, Vol. II, p. 387.
128. Dupin, *Narratives*, p. 65.
129. Ibid., pp. 57–69.
130. Coad, *Support for the Fleet*, pp. 105–6.

13 Blockade, Taxes and the City of London 1806–1812

1. Harling, 'Old Corruption', p. 132, quoting BL, Add. MSS 4277b, fol. 267.
2. Sherwig, *Guineas and Gunpowder*, p. 4; Harling, 'Old Corruption', quoting Emsley, 'Impact of War', p. 60.
3. Hilton, *Dangerous People*, p. 115.
4. Gray, *Perceval*, p. 323.

5. O'Brien, 'Political Economy', p. 4; Findlay and O'Rourke, *Power and Plenty*, pp. 349–50.
6. Daunton, *Trusting Leviathan*, p. 44.
7. O'Brien, 'Inseparable Connections', p. 66.
8. Creevey, *Life and Times*, pp. 27–8.
9. O'Brien, 'Triumph and Denouement', pp. 169–72, 179–84.
10. O'Brien, 'Political Economy', pp. 13, 17, 22.
11. Sherwig, *Guineas and Gunpowder*, pp. 345, 367–8.
12. Hansard, *Parliamentary Debates*, Vol. XX, 1811, p. xv.
13. Cope, 'Goldsmids and the Money Markets', p. 181; O'Brien, 'Inseparable Connections', pp. 65–6.
14. Rose, *Observations*, pp. 27–8.
15. Torrance, 'George Harrison', p. 58.
16. Gray, *Perceval*, p. 321, quoting *Parliamentary Debates*, Vol. IX.
17. O'Brien, 'Patriots or Speculators', pp. 251–2.
18. Aaslestad, 'Continental System', p. 121.
19. Schulte Beerbühl, 'Transnational Networks', p. 23.
20. Schulte Beerbühl, 'Rothschild', pp. 46–7; Ferguson, *House of Rothschild*, Vol. I, p. 59.
21. Cope, 'Goldsmids and the Money Markets', p. 184, quoting *Public Characters* (1802/3), p. 50.
22. Ibid., p. 188.
23. O'Brien, 'Patriots or Speculators', pp. 260, 267, 269.
24. Arthur, *War of 1812*, p. 17.
25. Sherwig, *Guineas and Gunpowder*, p. 4; Davis, *Industrial Revolution*, pp. 25, 27.
26. Makepeace, *East India Company's London Workers*, p. 22; Bowen, *Business of Empire*, p. 266. The inherent risks in this trade are illustrated by the East Indiaman *Henry Addington*, setting out from Portsmouth in Dec. 1798, carrying a cargo of guns, shot, shells and anchors. The ship completed only a few miles of her journey to India, for, at high tide and in thick fog, she drifted on to the Bembridge ledge to the east of the Isle of Wight. Her dense, heavy cargo caused her hull to split immediately, her masts went overboard and within two days the ship became a total loss. Another disastrous voyage was that of the *Elizabeth*, 650 tons, not a Company ship, which set out from London in Oct. 1810, bound for Madras and Bengal with 372 passengers and crew, but also carrying iron, copper, lead, beer, glass and other sundries. She became separated from the East India convoy and put into Cork, after which she was swept up the Channel and driven ashore at Dunkirk, two months after leaving

London, with the loss of 350 lives. Napoleon exceptionally allowed a cartel to take the 22 survivors back to Britain (Grocott, *Shipwrecks*, pp. 64, 304, quoting *The Times*, 14, 18 Dec. 1798, 28 Jan. 1811).

27. Duffy, 'World-wide War', p. 202.

28. Esteban, 'Fiscal Dimensions', p. 79.

29. Bowen, 'Mobilizing Resources', pp. 90–110.

30. Crimmin, 'Search for Timber', p. 195.

31. 17 Nov. 1806, HL, STG 37 (33); Chatham Officers to Navy Board, 12 Sept. 1803, Hattendorf et al., *British Naval Documents*, pp. 505–6.

32. Albion, *Forests and Sea Power*, pp. 355, 420–21; Åström, 'North European Timber', pp. 92–7.

33. Munch-Petersen, *Defying Napoleon*, p. 46.

34. Davey, 'British Intervention in the Baltic', pp. 164, 177.

35. Voelcker, *Saumarez*, pp. 86–8.

36. Galpin, *Grain Supply*, p. 180.

37. Navy Board to Admiralty, 2 Jan. 1808, NMM, ADM BP/28.

38. Crimmin, 'Search for Timber', p. 213.

39. 27 Sept., 9, 11 Nov., 2 Dec. 1808, NMM, ADM BP/28.

40. Davey, 'Sinews of Sea Power', pp. 171–2, 178.

41. Rodger, *Command of the Ocean*, pp. 559–60; Arthur, *War of 1812*, p. 17.

42. Crowhurst, *Privateering*, pp. 203–4.

43. Losses of British merchantmen from French privateers are computed in 1803 to have totalled 22; 1804, 387; 1805, 507; 1806, 519; 1807, 559; 1808, 469; 1809, 571; 1810, 619; 1811, 470; 1812, 475; 1813, 371; 1814, 145. These figures do not include losses from Danish and Norwegian privateers after 1807, nor Dutch, nor from American privateers between 1812 and 1814 (Norman, *Corsairs of France*, p. 453).

44. Rodger, *Command of the Ocean*, pp. 559–60; Woodman, *Britannia's Realm*, p. 187.

45. Woodman, *Victory of Seapower*, p. 61.

46. Grocott, *Shipwrecks*, p. 276, quoting the *Sherbourne and Yeovil Mercury*, 13 Feb. 1809.

47. Norman, *French Corsairs*, appendices.

48. Pearsall, 'Protection of Trade', pp. 155, 162.

49. Mackesy, *War in the Mediterranean*, p. 115; Woodman, *Britannia's Realm*, p. 187.

50. Muir, *Defeat of Napoleon*, p. 165.

51. Grocott, *Shipwrecks*, pp. 306–7, quoting the *Annual Register*, 1811, pp. 6–7.

52. 18, 27 July 1810, Jennings, *Croker Papers*, Vol. I, pp. 33–4.

53. Between 1803 and 1815 only 175 privateers were fitted out, although 1,800 merchant ships optimistically took out 'Letters of Marque' (the document enabling a merchant ship to take a prize lawfully), and thus equipped these ships sailed over 5,000 voyages. Letters of Marque were issued to 509 ships sailing from London, and 401 from Liverpool, with the rest spread through many different British and colonial ports (Starkey, *Privateering*, Appendix 8).

54. Woodman, *Britannia's Realm*, pp. 146–8.

55. Wilcox, 'Navy Agents', pp. 25–7.

56. Hill, *Prizes of War*, pp. 139–54.

57. The army received prize money for captured enemy equipment and other booty, but in far smaller amounts than the navy. The prince regent approved prize money in six payments for the Peninsular War for periods of service or for a particular action, broken down into six classes from general officers to the rank and file. For example, the third payment was for service in the capture of Ciudad Rodrigo and Badajoz in Jan. and Apr. 1812. Payments for the six classes were: general officers, £134.9s.10d.; field officers, £68.8s.1d.; captains, £11.2s.10d.; subalterns, £4.14s.1d.; sergeants, £2.10s.11d.; corporals, drummers, and rank and file, 7s.6d. (McGuffie, 'Peninsular Prize Money', p. 143).

58. The figure of 46.3 per cent has been calculated by Professor Dan Benjamin; private communication, 20 Feb. 2012.

59. Rodger, *Command of the Ocean*, p. 546.

60. Comfort, 'Lloyd's Patriotic Fund', www.lloydsswords.com.

61. Aaslestad, 'Continental System', p. 118.

62. Daley, 'Merchants in Normandy', p. 37.

63. Duffy, *Sugar and Seapower*, pp. 389–90; Ellis, *Continental System*, p. 287.

64. Hattendorf et al., *British Naval Documents*, p. 352.

65. Holmberg, 'French Decrees on Trade', p. 2.

66. Licences could be issued by government officials abroad or by senior officers commanding British fleets. In 1806, 849 licences were issued, rising to 1,491 in 1807 and further increases took place in following years. Between 1806 and 1808, when Spain became an ally, 277 licences were issued for the import and export of goods to South America, for neutral ships leaving or calling at neutral ports such as Lisbon or Hamburg (Schulte Beerbühl, 'Transnational Networks', p. 25, quoting Privy Council Records, TNA, PC 1/3867).

67. Daley, 'English Smugglers', p. 41.

68. Sparrow, 'Alien Office', pp. 382–3.

69. Aaslestad, 'Continental Blockade', p. 119.

70. Information from Dr Jan Ruger.

71. Schulte Beerbühl, 'Rothschild', pp. 43, 45.

72. Marzagalli, 'Hamburg', pp. 29–30.

73. Aaslestad, 'Continental System', pp. 122–3.

74. Ibid., pp. 119–20.

75. Ferguson, *House of Rothschild*, Vol. I, pp. 56–7.

76. Daley, 'City of Smugglers', p. 337.

77. Holmberg, 'French Decrees on Trade', p. 4.

78. Davey, *British Naval Strategy*, pp. 190–91.

79. Sherwig, *Guineas and Gunpowder*, p. 12.

80. Pearce, 'Hope–Baring Contract', p. 1,326.

81. Bordo and White, 'Two Currencies', pp. 303–16.

82. Pearce, 'Hope–Baring Contract', pp. 1,324–45; Schulte Beerbühl, 'Transnational Networks', pp. 29–31.

83. D. W. Davies, *Moore's Peninsular Campaign*, p. 67.

84. Gray, *Perceval*, pp. 331–5.

85. Fay, *Huskisson*, p. 69, quoting TNA, T/64/329.

86. Gray, *Perceval*, p. 331, quoting TNA, T1/999/2628.

87. Ibid., p. 337, quoting 2 Oct. 1808, Perceval MSS.

88. Ibid., p. 331, quoting *Commons Accounts and Reports*, 1812 (198), Vol. IX, p. 60.

89. Ibid., pp. 338–40.

90. Ibid., p. 341, quoting TNA, T27/64/490, 502; T29/102/119; T29/108/372.

91. Ibid., p. 324, quoting 9 Aug. 1812, Commissariat letter-books, BL, Herries MSS, Vol. III, pp. 150–51; TNA, T1/65/123.

92. Galpin, *Grain Supply*, p. 193.

93. Daley, 'City of Smugglers', pp. 336, 349.

94. According to a French ministerial report, in 1812 smugglers took goods from Gravelines to England to the value of 4.5 million francs. Lace was the single most valuable item. Silk products made up a quarter of its value, while alcohol made up a third, of which French brandy was the most important (Daley, 'City of Smugglers', p. 350).

95. Ferguson, *House of Rothschild*, Vol. I, p. 87.

96. Sherwig, *Guineas and Gunpowder*, p. 273, quoting TNA, FO 65/76.

97. Muir, *Defeat of Napoleon*, p. 111; Sherwig, *Guineas and Gunpowder*, pp. 4, 345–64, 365–8, 288, quoting *Hansard*, Vol. XXVII, 1814, col. 134.

98. Huskisson, *Speeches*, Vol. I, pp. 214–15.

99. Thorne, *House of Commons*, Vol. I, p. 141; Green, *Navy and Anglo-Jewry*, p. 98.
100. Muir, *Defeat of Napoleon*, p. 158, quoting the *Annual Register*.
101. Galpin, *Grain Supply*, pp. 74–5, quoting *Parliamentary Papers*, 1812, No. 210, p. 365.
102. West Essex Militia, Digest of Services, 1803–1908, TNA, WO 68/257.
103. Aaslestad, 'Continental System', pp. 127–8.
104. Holland Rose, 'West Indies Trade', p. 46.
105. Ferguson, *House of Rothschild*, Vol. I, pp. 83–4.
106. Ibid., pp. 67, 85.
107. Ibid., p. 89.
108. Sherwig, *Guineas and Gunpowder*, pp. 326–8.
109. Ibid., p. 342.
110. Ferguson, *House of Rothschild*, Vol. I, pp. 88–9.

PART FOUR: THE TABLES TURNED
14 Russia and the Peninsula 1812–1813

1. Muir, *Alexander Gordon*, p. 140.
2. Letter 48, HRC, Londonderry MSS, pp. 257–8.
3. Esdaile, *Peninsular War*, pp. 328, 330.
4. Ibid., pp. 378–9; Urban, *Scovell*, p. 131; Davies, *Wellington's Wars*, p. 141; 'Diplomats as Spymasters', p. 44.
5. Muir, *Defeat of Napoleon*, p. 216.
6. Lieven, *Russia Against Napoleon*, pp. 135–7.
7. Ibid., pp. 138, 194, 203, 212–13.
8. Zamoyski, *1812*, pp. 358–500.
9. Lieven, *Russia Against Napoleon*, pp. 278–82.
10. *ODNB* entry on Wellington.
11. Harvey, *Collision of Empires*, pp. 159–60, quoting from Marmont to Jourdan, 26 Feb. 1812, Marmont's *Mémoires du maréchal Marmont, duc de Raguse*, 9 vols. (Paris, 1857), Vol. IV, p. 345.
12. Lieven, *Russia Against Napoleon*, pp. 102, 337–8.
13. Ibid., p. 262.
14. Ibid., pp. 30–31, 337; Sherwig, *Guineas and Gunpowder*, p. 282.
15. Davies, 'Whigs and the Peninsula', p. 123.
16. *ODNB* entry on Liverpool.
17. Davies, *Wellington's Wars*, p. 124, quoting 10 Sept. 1810, BL, Add. MSS 38325.

18. Harling, '*Old Corruption*', p. 134, quoting 29 Oct. 1811, BL Add. MSS 38196.

19. 27 Oct. 1812, Yonge, *Liverpool*, Vol. I, pp. 440–42.

20. Davies, *Wellington's Wars*, p. 124.

21. Thompson, 'Bathurst', p. 160, quoting Nov. 1812, BL, Bathurst Papers, Vol. LX.

22. 22 Dec. 1812, Yonge, *Liverpool*, Vol. I, pp. 448–9.

23. Lieven, *Russia Against Napoleon*, pp. 307, 340, 350–51.

24. Thompson, 'Bathurst', pp. 163–4.

25. Hall, *British Strategy*, pp. 184–90.

26. Sherwig, *Guineas and Gunpowder*, pp. 365–8.

27. Moreira, 'Portuguese Fiscal-Military State', p. 267.

28. Moreira, 'Portuguese State Military Expenditure', pp. 112–13, 116, 122–4.

29. Hall, *British Strategy*, pp. 36–7; *Wellington's Navy*, pp. 111–15.

30. Hall, *Wellington's Navy*, p. 112, quoting Convoy Lists, TNA, ADM 7/64.

31. Redgrave, 'Peninsular Logistics', pp. 57–60; Knight and Wilcox, *Sustaining the Fleet*, p. 54; Galpin, 'American Grain Trade', p. 25.

32. Galpin, 'American Grain Trade', p. 42.

33. Redgrave, 'Peninsular Logistics', pp. 61, 66.

34. Hall, *British Strategy*, pp. 34–5.

35. Lieven, *Russia Against Napoleon*, p. 455.

36. Esdaile, *Peninsular War*, p. 454.

37. Duffy, 'Festering the Spanish Ulcer', p. 16, quoting Gurwood, *Wellington's Dispatches*, pp. 9, 363; 10, 162, 479–80.

38. Ward, *Wellington's Headquarters*, p. 87; Hall, *Wellington's Navy*, p. 114.

39. Gates, *Napoleonic Wars*, pp. 189–92.

40. Davies, *Wellington's Wars*, pp. 164–5; 'Naval Intelligence', p. 52; Robertson, *Commanding Presence*, pp. 214–15.

41. Duffy, 'Festering the Spanish Ulcer', p. 24, quoting from Hamilton, *Byam Martin*, Vol. II, p. 409; Hall, *Wellington's Navy*, pp. 232–4.

42. Urban, *Napoleon's Codes*, pp. 127–30, 202–4, 224–5.

43. Davies, 'Diplomats as Spymasters', pp. 45–6.

44. Davies, 'Naval Intelligence', p. 56.

45. Ibid., pp. 34, 47, 56.

46. Harvey, *Collision of Empires*, pp. 149–53.

47. Ibid., p. 150.

48. Gray, *Perceval*, p. 349.

49. Redgrave, 'Peninsular Logistics', p. 132, quoting Wellington to Bathurst, 21 Apr. 1813.
50. Harvey, *Collision of Empires*, p. 148; Sherwig, *Guineas and Gunpowder*, p. 255.
51. Davies, *Wellington's Wars*, p. 204.
52. Lieven, *Russia Against Napoleon*, p. 458.
53. Hagemann, 'Leipzig', pp. 168, 170, 174.
54. Lieven, *Russia Against Napoleon*, pp. 479–93, 494–5, 516.
55. Ward, *Wellington's Headquarters*, p. 62.
56. 17 Mar. 1813, Pellow, *Sidmouth*, Vol. III, p. 97.
57. Barrow, *Autobiography*, p. 320.
58. Harling, 'Old Corruption', p. 135; Thorne, *History of Parliament*, Vol. IV, p. 188.

15 The Manpower Emergency 1812–1814

1. Hamilton, *Byam Martin*, Vol. II, p. 368.
2. Bickham, *Weight of Vengeance*, pp. 62–5.
3. Arthur, *War of 1812*, p. 22; Bickham, *Weight of Vengeance*, pp. 27–8.
4. Muir, *Defeat of Napoleon*, p. 233.
5. Bickham, *Weight of Vengeance*, pp. 63, 78.
6. Dudley, *Naval War of 1812*, pp. 26–34.
7. Bellesiles, 'Experiencing the War', p. 208.
8. Kert, 'Cruising in Colonial Waters', p. 152.
9. Lambert, 'War of 1812', pp. 18–20, quoting Admiralty to Warren, 2 Dec. 1812, TNA, ADM 2/1107.
10. Arthur, *War of 1812*, p. 200; Muir, *Defeat of Napoleon*, pp. 235–40.
11. Muir, *Defeat of Napoleon*, pp. 306–9.
12. Bamford, 'Manpower', pp. 29–31.
13. Linch, *Wellington's Army*, p. 16.
14. Rodger, *Command of the Ocean*, p. 639.
15. Arthur, *War of 1812*, pp. 41, 74–5.
16. Glover, 'French Fleet', p. 246, quoting Pellew to Croker, 20 Jan. 1813, TNA, ADM 1/424; 12 Feb. 1813, ADM/2,926.
17. Glover, *Peninsular Preparation*, pp. 219–31; Bamford, 'Manpower', p. 43.
18. Linch, *Wellington's Army*, p. 38.
19. Glover, *Britain at Bay*, p. 224, quoting from 18 Mar. 1806, George III's MSS, Royal Library, Windsor, 12407–18.
20. Cookson, *Armed Nation*, pp. 100–101.

21. Arnold, 'Column versus Line', p. 207.
22. Ibid.
23. Regimental Orders, 18 Aug. 1807, Monmouth Castle, RMRE/12/2; Watson, *Militiamen and Sappers*, p. 48.
24. Cookson, *Armed Nation*, p. 119.
25. Muir, *Defeat of Napoleon*, pp. 155–6.
26. Bamford, 'Manpower', p. 38, quoting Castlereagh to Lord Clancarty, TNA, WO1/198, pp. 217–19.
27. Linch, *Wellington's Army*, p. 38, quoting *Parliamentary Debates*, 1812–1813, Vol. XXIV, col. 258.
28. Ibid., p. 122, quoting 1 Jan. 1811, TNA, WO30/80.
29. Cookson, *Armed Nation*, p. 119.
30. Linch, *Wellington's Army*, p. 114, quoting 30 Aug. 1813, TNA, WO 25/3225.
31. Cookson, *Armed Nation*, p. 119.
32. Linch, *Wellington's Army*, p. 114.
33. Bamford, 'Manpower', p. 26, quoting Army Digests in TNA, WO 17/2814.
34. Cookson, *Armed Nation*, p. 119.
35. Linch, *Wellington's Army*, pp. 151–2.
36. Muir, *Defeat of Napoleon*, p. 309.
37. Fontana, 'British/Irish Militia Exchange', pp. 141, 157.
38. 31 Aug. 1813, Monmouth Castle, RMRE/12/14; Watson, *Militiamen and Sappers*, p. 49.
39. Crimmin, 'Prisoners of War and Port Communities', p. 19.
40. Crowhurst, *French War on Trade*, p. 209.
41. Crimmin, 'Incarceration of Spanish Prisoners of War', p. 231; MacDougall, *Prisoners of War in Scotland*, p. 708, both quoting *Parliamentary Papers*, Vol. IX, 1812, col. 301.
42. Chamberlain, 'Marching into Captivity', p. 222.
43. Registers of Prisoners aboard the *Vanguard* and *Temeraire* prison ships, TNA, ADM 103/430 and 438.
44. TNA, ADM 103, Index; Crimmin, 'Exchange of Prisoners', p. 148.
45. Lloyd, *Prisoners of War*, pp. 296–7; Chamberlain, *Hell upon Water*, pp. 238–40.
46. MacDougall, *Prisoners of War in Scotland*, pp. 567–8, 820.
47. Crimmin, 'Prisoners of War and Port Communities', p. 22.
48. Harvey, *Collision of Empires*, p. 198, quoting Roy Bennett, 'French Prisoners of War on Parole in Britain 1803–1814' (London Ph.D., 1964), pp. 201–10, 252–77, 345.

49. Daley, 'English Smugglers', p. 35, quoting list of French prisoners of war who had broken their parole up to 20 Nov. 1811, Archives Nationale, FF2 50; Daley, 'City of Smugglers', pp. 346–7.
50. Crimmin, 'Prisoners of War and Port Communities', pp. 17, 19.
51. MacDougall, *Prisoners of War in Scotland*, pp. 104–7, 110, 114–15.
52. Arthur, *War of 1812*, pp. 225–6.
53. Ibid., pp. 106, 199, 221–6.
54. Bartlett and Smith, 'Cochrane's Naval Campaign', pp. 180–86, 191.
55. Bickham, *Weight of Vengeance*, p. 258, quoting 9 Nov. 1814, Wellington's *Supplementary Despatches* (London, 1858–72), Vol. IX, pp. 424–6.
56. Bickham, *Weight of Vengeance*, pp. 258–60.
57. 27 Dec. 1814, Pellow, *Sidmouth*, Vol. III, p. 122.

16 Final Victory

1. Muir, *Defeat of Napoleon*, p. 338, quoting Wellington, *Supplementary Despatches*, Vol. IX, p. 494.
2. Lieven, *Russia Against Napoleon*, p. 516.
3. 31 Dec. 1813, Cookson, *British Armed Nation*, p. 39, quoting Wellington, *Supplementary Despatches*, Vol. VIII, pp. 450–52.
4. Bew, *Castlereagh*, p. 360.
5. Muir, *Defeat of Napoleon*, pp. 325–6.
6. Zamoyski, *Rites of Peace*, pp. 211–12; Bew, *Castlereagh*, p. 366.
7. Zamoyski, *Rites of Peace*, pp. 209–10.
8. Muir, *Defeat of Napoleon*, p. 330.
9. Zamoyski, *Rites of Peace*, p. 211.
10. Coad, *Block Mills*, p. 103, reproduction of *The Times*, 27 June 1814.
11. Zamoyski, *Rites of Peace*, p. 217.
12. Sherwig, *Guineas and Gunpowder*, pp. 326–7.
13. Lady Sarah Napier to Lady Susan O'Brien, Dec. 1814, Ilchester and Stavordale, *Lady Sarah Lennox*, Vol. II, p. 263.
14. Hogg, *Royal Arsenal*, Vol. II, p. 592.
15. Crook and Port, *King's Works*, p. 319, quoting 29 June 1814, *Parliamentary Debates*, 1814, cols. 420–22.
16. Zamoyski, *Rites of Peace*, pp. 173–4.
17. Schroeder, *European Politics*, p. 502.
18. Muir, *Defeat of Napoleon*, p. 337.
19. Schroeder, *European Politics*, p. 535.

20. Ibid., p. 550.

21. Ibid., p. 551.

22. Kraehe, 'Reconstruction of the Allied Armies', pp. 88–90, 96–7.

23. Muir, *Defeat of Napoleon*, p. 353.

24. Davies, *Wellington's Wars*, p. 241.

25. Collins, *War and Empire*, p. 358.

26. Muir, *Defeat of Napoleon*, pp. 363, 365.

27. 4 Dec. 1815, HRC, Londonderry MSS.

28. Voelcker, *Saumarez*, pp. 198–220.

29. Mackesy, 'Amphibious Power', p. 122.

30. Esdaile, *Peninsular War*, p. 505.

31. See Appendix 2.

32. Sherwig, *Guineas and Gunpowder*, pp. 345–69.

33. Bell, *First Total War*, Introduction.

34. Esdaile, *Napoleon's Wars*, p. 6.

35. Duffy, *Sugar and Seapower*, pp. 1–16.

36. Knight and Wilcox, *Sustaining the Fleet*, pp. 8–16, 37–47.

37. Galpin, *Grain Supply*, pp. 168–71.

38. Gray, *Perceval*, p. 470.

39. See Appendix 1.

40. Schroeder, *European Politics*, p. 551.

41. Muir, *Defeat of Napoleon*, p. 381.

Aftermath

1. Lieven, *Russia Against Napoleon*, p. 259, quoting Sir Robert Wilson, *The French Invasion of Russia* (Bridgnorth, 1996), p. 234; see also Glover, *Very Slippery Fellow*, p. 130; Rodger, *Command of the Ocean*, p. 574.

2. Tombs, *France*, p. 337.

3. Hilton, *Dangerous People*, pp. 237, 251.

4. Harling and Mandler, '"Fiscal-Military State"', pp. 66–7.

5. Rodger, *Command of the Ocean*, p. 639.

6. Lewis, *Navy in Transition*, pp. 69, 84.

7. Glete, *Navy and Nations*, Vol. II, p. 422; Duffy, 'World-wide War', p. 204; Hilton, *Dangerous People*, p. 238.

8. Collins, *War and Empire*, p. 407.

9. Burnham and McGuigan, *British Army Against Napoleon*, pp. 217, 232.

10. Cookson, *Armed Nation*, p. 246.

11. 'Public Offices Employment . . . 1805, 1810, 1815, 1819 and 1827', *Parliamentary Papers*, 1830–31 (92), pp. 2–3.
12. Ibid., p. 253.
13. Hilton, *Dangerous People*, pp. 251–2.
14. *ODNB*, quoting J. Greig, *The Farington Diaries*, Vol. VIII, 1928, p. 243.
15. Durey, *Wickham*, p. 194.
16. Brenton, *St Vincent*, Vol. II, p. 375.
17. Marsden, *Brief Memoir*, p. 133.
18. Lloyd, *Barrow of the Admiralty*, p. 86.
19. Ibid., pp. 124–65.
20. Beamish, *Brunel*, pp. 131–8, 168–75.
21. Bew, *Castlereagh*, p. 557, quoting Robert and Samuel Wilberforce, *The Life of William Wilberforce* (London, 1848), Vol. V, p. 135.
22. Collins, *War and Empire*, pp. 402–3; Day, 'Naval Power in the Indian Ocean', pp. 323, 325.
23. Duffy, 'World-wide war', p. 206.
24. Hilton, *Dangerous People*, p. 244.

Index

Individuals are here shown with their final naval or military rank.

Abbot, Charles, Baron Colchester
  (1757–1829) xxxiv, 116–17,
  137, 170, 225, 232, 328,
  499, 507
Abercromby, General Sir Ralph
  (1734–1801) 73, 74–5, 78, 86–7,
  93, 172–3, 192, 196–8, 200, 500
Aberdeen *see* Hamilton-Gordon
Abergavenny, Wales 447
Aboukir Bay, Battle of (1798)
  92, 147
Aboukir Bay, landing at (1801) 200
Act of Union (1801) 127, 214
Adams, James, MP (1752–1816) 486
Addington, Henry, Viscount
  Sidmouth (1757–1844) xix, 98,
  103, 280, 338
  as Prime Minister 103, 214–15,
  218–20, 222–3, 233, 249, 251,
  271–3, 287–8, 320, 322, 324,
  345, 387, 475
  as Lord Sidmouth 229, 432,
  448, 483
Addington, John Hiley, MP
  (1759–1818) 476–7, 448, 484,
  494
Adjutant-General 49, 255, 263, 277,
  417, 441, 432, 440, 472
Admirals' mutiny (1795) 186

Admiralty *see* British government:
  departments
Adour, French river 356
Adriatic Sea 200
Aegean Sea 200
Affleck, Vice-Admiral Philip
  (1726–1799) 485
agents, naval 398
agents, prize 333, 398–9
agriculture 96, 120, 141, 160, 162,
  164, 438, 463, 466, 469
Agriculture, Board of 120, 168
Aix Roads, Battle of (1809) 468
Ajaccio, Corsica 118
'Alarmists' *see* Portland Whigs
Alcock, Thomas, Treasurer of the
  Ordnance 497
Aldeburgh, Suffolk 278
Aldridge, John, MP (?1737–1795)
  497
Alexander, Tsar of Russia
  (1777–1825) 305, 420, 430,
  449–52, 454–5
Alexandria, Egypt 118, 142–3,
  147, 200
Alien Act (1793) 125, 289
Alien Office *see* British government:
  departments
Alresford, Hampshire 447

Ambleteuse 252
American privateers *see* privateers
American Revolutionary War
  (1775–1783) xxxi, xxxvi, 3–5,
  7–8, 17–18, 23–4, 27–8, 33–4,
  37–40, 43–5, 52, 56, 87–8,
  110, 154, 206, 346
Amherst, Jeffrey, General Baron
  (1717–1797) 93, 492
Amiens, Peace of (1802–1803) xxiv,
  xxxviii, 118, 120, 134–5, 151,
  155, 163, 183, 189–90, 215,
  217, 229, 233, 252, 276,
  285, 315, 320, 374, 387, 399,
  401, 464
amphibious (or conjunct) operations
  94, 109, 159, 160, 176, 188,
  189–92, 196–7, 201, 205,
  210, 227, 364, 427,
  459–60, 463
Amsterdam 303, 406, 414
Angers, French Royal Academy of
  Equitation xxxvi
Anglesey 36, 166, 379
Anguish, Thomas, parliamentary
  commissioner 504
Anholt, Island of 174
Antigua *see* English Harbour,
  Antigua
Antwerp 311, 312, 450
  shipbuilding 205–8, 240, 283,
  308–10, 312, 461
Arbuthnot, Charles, MP
  (1767–1850) xxxiii, 222, 231,
  345, 477, 480
Archbishop of Canterbury 236
army
  Barrack Master-General 332
  barracks 24, 42, 44, 52, 185, 209,
  261–2, 281–2, 332

Commissariat 97, 155, 159, 195,
  254–5, 315, 344–5, 357, 413,
  420, 462
Commissaries-General 159, 172,
  254, 273, 408
Comptroller of Army
  Accounts 326
Estimates 49, 223, 232, 314, 467
hospitals 205, 209, 218
Medical Board 209
Paymasters-General 335
Quartermaster-General xxxvii,
  255, 261, 273, 275, 279, 287
Quartermaster-General's
  Department 49, 91, 185, 195,
  255, 259, 279, 326, 335
recruiting 233
Storekeeper-General 24
army regiments
  Dragoons 50, 63, 302
  Hussars 78, 185, 188, 204
  Foot xxxvi, 428
  Foot Guards 232, 265, 356
  Highland 231
  Chasseurs Britannique 78
  Corps de Chartres 78
  Duc de Castre's Corps 78
  Green Howards 468
  King's German Legion 188, 202,
  306, 439, 456
  de Mortemarte 78
  Life Guards 70
  Prince Charles of Levenstein's
  Corps 78
artillery *see* Ordnance Department
Arun, River 168
Ashby de la Zouche 411
Ashley, Cropley (later Ashley
  Cooper), MP (1768–1851)
  496–7

Aspern–Essling, Battle of (1809) 309
Association of Friends of the People 66
Atkinson, Christopher, MP, wheat contractor (1739–1819) 39–40, 160, 163
Auckland *see* Eden
Augur, Captain, volunteer captain 279
Aust, George, Foreign Office civil servant 480
Austen, Jane (1775–1817)
Austerlitz, Battle of (1805) 228, 420
Austria 17, 20, 52, 61, 66–7, 82, 93, 136, 145, 149, 194, 227–8, 245, 273, 293, 305, 309–10, 389, 405, 409, 424, 430, 439, 449–51, 454–6, 458, 463
Austrian Netherlands 67, 82

Badajoz, Spain, siege of (1812) 418, 427–8, 446
Bagot, Charles, MP (1781–1843) 480
Baillie, Thomas, Clerk of Deliveries, Ordnance 497
Baird, Andrew, Inspector of Naval and Prison Hospitals 491
Baird, General Sir David (1757–1829) 204, 230
Baldwin, George, British Consul in Alexandria (1744–1826) 142–3, 147
Ball, Rear-Admiral Sir Alexander (1757–1809) xxxvii
Ballina, Co. Mayo, Ireland 91
Ballinamuck, Co. Longford, Ireland 91
Baltic region 4, 7, 14, 16–19, 150–51, 159, 173–4, 192, 238, 240, 295, 304, 306, 363, 371, 395, 403
  naval stores 17–18, 22, 38, 174, 194, 249, 304, 394–5
  grain imports from 157, 426
British Baltic Fleet 156, 173–4, 202, 236, 240, 247, 300, 306, 310, 330, 404, 447, 458
Bank of England xxvi, 84, 87, 224, 269, 390, 392, 409
Bankes, Henry, MP (1756–1834) 507
Bantry Bay, southern Ireland xxxv, 85–6, 144, 146
Barcelona 136, 292
Barham *see* Middleton
Baring, Sir Charles, banker 406
Baring, Sir Francis, banker (1740–1810) 406, 410, 414, 506
Barley 136, 160, 164, 165
Barnard's, shipbuilders 362
Barne, Snowden, MP (1756–1825) 477
Barrow, Sir John, Admiralty civil servant (1764–1848) xxxiii, 226, 247, 291, 303, 320, 324, 341, 351, 360, 367, 375, 383, 397, 432, 465, 472, 487
Basle, Switzerland 144
Basque Roads, action (1809) 291
Batavia 142
Bathurst, Benjamin, diplomat (1784–1809) 481
Bathurst, Henry, Earl, MP, government minister (1762–1834) 249, 422–4, 440, 450, 454, 456, 479, 491, 501
Battersea, London 165, 472
Bay of Biscay 396
Baylen, Battle of (1808) 242

Bayonne, France 356, 444
Bayonne Decree (1808) 401
Beachcroft, Samuel, parliamentary
    commissioner 504
Beaufort, Colonel the Duke of
    264, 439
Beaufoy, Henry, MP
    (1750–1795) 502
Beaune, Jean-Jacques de, French
    merchant, 25
Beckett, John, civil servant 483
Beckwith, Colonel F., parliamentary
    commissioner 512
Bellingham, John, bankrupt and
    assassin (d. 1812) 249
Belt, Greater, off Denmark 173, 395
Belt, Little, off Denmark 173
Bennett, Charles, Earl Tankerville
    (1743–1822) 108
Bennot, John Bennet, Inspector of
    Packets 134, 503
Bentham, Jeremy (1748–1832) 170
Bentham, Samuel (1757–1831)
    169–70, 320, 341, 376, 378,
    380, 451, 462, 487, 489
    technological innovations 34,
    170–71, 353, 377–9
    management theories 368,
    380–81
Beresford, General William Carr
    (1768–1856) 425
Bergen-op-Zoom, attack on (1814)
    441, 469
Berkeley, Admiral George Cranfield,
    Baron (1753–1818) 187, 267,
    381, 434, 496
Berlin 18, 135–6
Berlin Decrees (1806) 234, 400,
    402, 461
Bermuda 236, 363, 381

Bernstorff, Count, Danish
    negotiator 135
Berthier, Marshal, French war
    minister (1753–1815) 252
Bessborough, Lady 125
Bickerton, Admiral Sir Richard, MP
    (1759–1832) 218
Birmingham 36, 47, 50, 52, 62, 157,
    280, 357, 372
Biscuit 24, 39, 86, 144, 156, 160,
    173–4, 254, 426
Bishop's Waltham, Hampshire 447
Blachford, Barrington Pope, MP
    (d. 1816) 486
Black Sea 4, 18–19
Blackwall 276, 353
Blair, Robert, Sick and Hurt
    commissioner 490
Bland Burges, Sir James, MP
    (1752–1824) 124, 480
Blane, Sir Gilbert, Sick and Hurt
    commissioner 490
block mills, Portsmouth 376–8, 451,
    472–3
Blomefield, Lieutenant-General Sir
    Thomas (1774–1822) 46–7,
    370, 498
Board of Control see British
    government: departments
Board of Trade see British
    government: departments
Bombay 118, 142, 145, 162, 363, 370
Bompard, Commodore Jean-
    Baptiste, French naval
    officer 92
Bonaparte see Napoleon
Bonaparte, Joseph, King of Spain
    (1768–1844) 418
Bond, Nathaniel, MP (1754–1823)
    476, 501

Bonds 84, 414

Bordeaux 22

Boringdon, John Parker, Baron, later
Earl of Morley (1772–1840) 70

Borodino, Russia, Battle of (1812)
419, 439

Bosanquet, Charles, parliamentary
commissioner 513

Boscawen, William, Victualling
commissioner (1752–1811) 107

Boschetti, Juan Maria, building
contractor, Gibraltar 171

Bouching (cannon repair) 46

Boughton Hill, near Canterbury 255

Boulogne 10, 140, 252, 274, 277,
301, 354, 356, 446

Boulton, Matthew, engineer
(1728–1809) 353

Bourbon monarchy 4, 5, 11, 14,
130, 286, 444–5, 453, 467

Bourne see Sturges-Bourne

Bouverie, Edward, MP
(1760–1824) 108

Bouverie, William Pleydell, MP,
later Viscount Folkestone and
Earl of Radnor
(1779–1869) 244

Bowen, Rear-Admiral James,
Transport commissioner
(1751–1835) 179, 182,
203–4, 488

Boyd, Walter, City banker
(1753–1837) 84, 127, 220

Boys, Captain Charles, RN
(d. 1809) 207

Bradshaw, L., parliamentary
commissioner 513

Bragge, Charles (later Bragge-
Bathurst), MP (1754–1831)
244, 488, 493

Bragge, William 494

Brandon, Suffolk 48

Brazil 239, 308

Brent, Samuel and Daniel,
shipbuilders 367

Brentford, Middlesex 254

Brest 6–8, 10, 14–16, 69, 83–5, 88,
92, 123, 141, 148–9, 151, 155,
174, 193–6, 223, 234, 274,
303, 309–10, 382

breweries 164–5, 352

Bridgwater, Captain, Monmouth
Regiment 264

Bridport see Hood

Bridport, Dorset 205

Briggs, Sir John Thomas, Admiralty
civil servant (1781–1865) 325,
329, 510

Brill, Holland 133

Bristol 54, 155, 362–3, 391, 444

British government
accounting xxiii, 25–7, 32–3, 40,
103, 114, 120, 163, 243,
296–7, 314, 318, 323, 326,
327–8, 330, 331–2, 335–7,
346, 349, 393, 425, 462
auditing 27, 127, 314, 330, 332,
335, 414
cabinet xxii, xxxi, xxxii, 11, 15,
19, 41, 44, 64–5, 71–2, 82,
83–4, 92, 97–100, 123, 125–6,
130, 146, 150, 152, 156, 177,
192, 196–8, 201, 206, 213,
224, 229, 236–9, 241, 244–7,
249, 251, 271, 288, 304,
306–7, 309–10, 322, 338, 408,
423–4, 454, 465
departments: Admiralty xxx,
xxxi, xxxiii, 6–7, 9–12, 16, 19,
30–32, 37–41, 51, 71–3, 85,

British government – *cont.*
88–9, 92, 97–8, 102–3, 106,
108, 110–12, 117, 120, 122–3,
126–8, 137, 140, 144–6,
148–9, 156, 163, 170, 172,
174, 177–9, 181–2, 187,
190–92, 206, 214–15, 217–19,
221–3, 226–7, 230, 234–7,
246–7, 250, 266–7, 288, 291,
298–303, 310–11, 313, 317,
319–22, 324, 328–9, 331–2,
334, 337–9, 344, 346, 348–9,
355, 359, 362, 367–9, 375,
377–80, 383, 394–5, 397,
432–3, 436–7, 460, 464, 469,
471; Admiralty, Hydrographic
Office 103, 151, 317, 341;
Admiralty, Record Office 346;
Alien Office xxv, 125–6, 142,
285, 287–9; Barrack Master-
General 333; Board of Control
26, 64, 101, 190, 388; Board of
Trade 470; Customs xxxii, 26,
97, 119, 179, 290–91, 315,
328, 342, 345, 347; Excise 25,
96–7, 315, 328, 342, 347;
Foreign Office xxxiii, 6, 98,
126, 128, 131, 222, 244, 246,
249, 395; Home Office xxxv, 6,
12, 71, 126, 259, 263, 431;
Ireland 80, 86–7; Navy Office
xxx–xxxi, 16, 28–30, 33, 36–8,
41, 55, 103, 108, 110, 112,
115, 117–18, 136, 156, 177,
179, 221, 267–8, 315, 319,
321–4, 330–31, 340–41, 343,
346, 350, 359, 360–63, 365,
367, 376, 378–80, 394–5; Navy
Pay Office 112, 268, 343, 348;
Office of Works 96, 317, 334;
Post Office 53–5, 124, 132–4,
287–8, 291, 293–4, 296–8,
300, 328, 389; Secretary of
State for War 49, 64, 71, 104,
110, 122, 156, 177–8, 275,
277, 288, 326, 335; Sick and
Hurt Office xxx, 30, 111, 318,
328; Transport Board 108–11,
155–6, 160, 164, 176–82,
190–93, 196, 203, 207, 210,
318, 324, 325, 328, 343, 425,
427, 445–7; Treasury 25, 40,
54, 97–8, 107, 155, 413, 110,
112, 114, 124, 156, 177, 179,
245, 275, 297, 303, 315,
326–8, 333–8, 342, 345, 353,
387, 390, 407, 409, 413–14,
425, 465; Treasury,
Commissariat 97, 155, 195,
254, 315, 344–5, 357, 413,
426, 462; Victualling Office 24,
30, 39–40, 107, 112, 154–7,
160, 162, 164, 171–3, 268,
317, 323, 330, 338, 340–42,
344, 357, 462 (*see also*
victualling yards); War Office
49, 51, 72, 97, 110, 112, 243,
259, 335–6, 461
expenditure 5–6, 27, 83, 127,
150, 335, 346, 349, 370, 387,
389, 411, 425, 452; income 22,
83–4, 94, 119, 387–9, 411;
pensions 342–3, 347–8;
sinecures 25, 43, 96, 106–7,
229, 314, 343–4, 462; travel
allowances 136
officials: ambassadors xxxii,
xxxiii, xxxiv, 16, 62, 143, 217,
222, 231, 245–6, 428, 440;
Chief Secretary to the Viceroy/

Lord Lieutenant, Ireland xxxiv, 219, 227, 287–8, 320, 328, 470; Treasury, Assistant Secretary 327, 390, 472; Treasury, Commissary-General 159, 173; Treasury, Commissary-in-Chief xxxv, 318, 326, 335, 344, 413, 469–70; Treasury, Secretary to the Board xxxii, xxxiii, 108–9, 273, 326, 339, 345, 348; Inspector of Telegraphs, Admiralty 103; Inspector-General of Fortifications and Works 275; Inspector-General of Naval Works 103, 170, 320, 376, 378, 380; Inspector-General of Recruiting 232, 263

British merchant shipping 174, 210, 392, 398

Brodrick, Thomas (d. 1795) 483

Brodrick, William, MP (1763–1819) 476–7, 502

Broke, Rear-Admiral Sir Philip (1776–1841) 435

Brooks's, Whig club 13

Brown, Lieutenant-Colonel John 277, 279

Brown, Nicholas, Victualling commissioner 330, 344

Brownrigg, Lieutenant-General Sir Robert (1755–1833) 273, 277, 287, 310, 335

Bruce, John, MP (?1745–1826) 502

Bruix, Eustache, French admiral (1759–1805) 148–9, 151

Brunel, Marc Isambard (1769–1849) 376–8, 472–3

Brussels 303, 456, 457

Buckingham House 70

Buckingham, Marquess of, see Grenville

Buckinghamshire 167, 233, 471

Buckinghamshire, Earl of, see Hobart

Budge, William, Victualling commissioner 223, 341

Buenos Aires 231, 273, 316, 345

Buller, James, MP (1772–1830) 486

bullion 290, 297, 404, 406–9

Bunbury, Lieutenant-General Sir Henry Edward (1778–1860) 191–2, 201, 259, 272–3, 288–9, 334–5, 424, 440–41, 465, 472, 492

Bure, River, Norfolk 164

Bureau des Renseignments 287

Burke, Edmund, MP (1730–1797) xxx, 20, 40, 43, 62, 82

Burrard Neale, Admiral Sir Harry, MP (1765–1840) 485

Busaco, Battle of (1810) 439

cabinet see British government

Cádiz 14–16, 92, 127, 128, 144, 146–47, 149, 175, 197, 224, 227, 355, 418, 427–8

Calais 10, 133, 220, 274, 295, 396, 446

Calcraft, John, MP (1765–1831) 496

Calder, Admiral Sir Robert (1745–1818) 303–4

Caldiero, Battle of (1805) 227

Call, Sir John, MP, parliamentary commissioner 507

Calvert, General Sir Harry (1763–1826) xxxvi, 62, 65, 67, 78, 186, 263, 270, 273, 277, 310, 441, 465, 472, 492

Camden *see* Pratt

Camperdown, Battle of (1797) 90, 150, 190

Canada 75, 154, 157, 303, 394, 424, 435–6, 444, 448

canals, 154, 164–5, 168, 280, 352, 374, 402, 469

  Grand Junction 165

  Grand Union 165, 280, 374

  Wey and Arun 168

  Royal Military 277, 279–80, 281

  Grand Canal, Ireland 282

Canning, George (1770–1827) xxix, xxxiii–xxxiv, 65, 69–70, 79, 98, 105–6, 125, 225, 245, 268, 299, 344, 464–5, 470, 482, 488, 494

  as Undersecretary, Foreign Office 98, 126, 131, 480

  as Foreign Secretary 237, 239, 244, 286, 304–8, 479

cannon, 42, 45–7, 182, 201, 275, 279, 357, 370–71, 372, 463, 469

  Blomefield's new pattern 370

cannon foundry, Nantes 37

  French commercial espionage 47

Cannon Row, Westminster 177

Cape of Good Hope 75, 118, 142, 172, 188, 216, 230–31, 273, 300, 324, 450, 474

Cape St Vincent, Battle of (1797) 88

Carhampton *see* Luttrell

Caribbean *see* West Indies

Carleton, General Sir Guy, later Baron Dorchester (1724–1808) 504

Carlisle 262

Carlton House 355, 453

Carnock, Major Lord 204

Carron Company, cannon founders, Scotland 46–7, 370–71

carronade 134, 182, 354, 370

Cartagena, Spain 427

cartels 111, 146, 396, 445

cast iron 46

Castlebar, Co Mayo, Ireland 91

Castlereagh *see* Stewart

Cathcart, General William Schaw, Earl (1755–1843) 202, 238, 481, 500

Catherine the Great (1729–1796) 4, 17, 125

cattle 24, 39, 156, 159–60, 163, 165–8, 272, 357, 445, 463

caulkers 31, 118, 361, 363–4

cavalry xxxiv, 63, 78, 80–81, 86, 159, 176, 185–6, 195, 201, 203, 210, 219, 232, 262–5, 270, 272, 274, 335, 424, 431, 457, 459

Cavendish-Bentinck, William Henry, Marquess of Titchfield, MP (1768–1854) 271, 477

Cavendish, Georgiana, Duchess of Devonshire (1757–1806) 66, 72, 106

Cavendish, William, Duke of Devonshire (1748–1811) 13

Cavendish-Bentinck, William, Duke of Portland (1738–1809) 4, 13, 70–71, 97

  as Home Secretary 71, 87, 98, 105, 115, 126, 483

  as Prime Minister 100, 206, 237, 244–5, 309, 333, 338–9, 386, 465, 476

Cawdor, John Pryse Campbell, Baron (1755–1821) 87

Census (1801) 119, 260, 438

Ceylon 75, 142–3, 216, 468, 474

Chambers, Charles, naval
surgeon 355

Chancery Lane, London 398

Channel, the 8, 11, 72, 74, 84, 144,
171–2, 187, 204, 219, 230,
240, 251–2, 272, 277, 289,
290–91, 294, 396, 402, 409,
446, 450, 456

Channel Fleet 14, 19, 73, 85, 93, 146,
149, 155, 172, 236, 240, 433

Channel Islands 148, 216

Chapman, Frederick af, Swedish
shipbuilder (1721–1808) 8

chartering 109–10, 176, 179,
180–81, 184, 191, 469

Chatham see Pitt, John

Chatham Chest 323

Chatham Dockyard see dockyards

Chatham Lines 281

Cheesemonger's Company 141

Chelmsford, Essex 209, 261

Chelsea Hospital 51

chemical warfare 357

Cherbourg 8–9, 56, 274, 384, 446

Cherry, George, Chairman of the
Victualling Board 163, 490

Cherson, Black Sea port 18

Chesapeake Bay 236

Cheshire 37, 159, 164

Chesil Bank 74

Chester 374

Chesterfield see Stanhope

Chichester see Pelham

Chichester, Sussex 79, 157, 185, 209

Chinnery, William, civil servant
(1766–1834) 337

Christ Church, Oxford xxix, xxxiii,
xxxiv, 70, 116, 125–6, 287,
326, 470

Christchurch, Hampshire 107

Christian, Rear-Admiral Sir Hugh
Cloberry (1747–1798) 73, 110,
177–8, 488

Cinque Ports xxxiv, 259

Cintra, Convention of 242

City of London xxx; Chapter 13
passim

Ciudad Roderigo, Spain, siege of
(1812) 418, 127

civil servants xxii, 68, 96, 325,
343–4, 466

Clancarty see Trench

Clarence, Duke of, later William IV
(1765–1837) 450

Clarke, Mary Ann, mistress of the
Duke of York (1776–1852)
242, 344

Clarke, William, Home Office
agent 13

Cleghorn, Hugh (1752–1837)
142–3

Clerk of the Ordnance 338, 375

Clerke's Acts (1782) 40

clerks, government 114, 115, 117,
313–14, 319, 329–30, 343–5
Admiralty 123, 299, 319, 346
Barrack Department 332
dockyards 29, 316, 323, 370
Home Office 115–16
Marine Pay Office 319
Navy Office xxx, 55, 109, 117,
123, 315, 318–19
Ordnance Department 315, 370
Transport Office 328
Treasury 97, 326–7
Treasurer of the Navy 348–9
Victualling Office 40, 163,
317, 337
War Office 97, 346

Clifford, Robert Edward,
    cartographer 220–21
Clinton, General Sir William Henry
    (1769–1846) 492
Clive, Edward, Earl Powis
    (1754–1839) 498
coal 29, 168, 192, 264, 323, 351,
    395, 463
coal trade 77, 141, 181, 219, 365
Coalition, First (1793–1797)
    66, 69, 93
Coalition, Second (1799–1801) 93,
    130, 149
Coalition, Third (1805) 227, 228
Cobbett, William, radical journalist
    (1763–1835) 213–14, 220, 232,
    243, 271, 314, 345
Cochin 142
Cochrane, Admiral Alexander, MP
    (1758–1832) 447
Cochrane, Admiral Thomas, MP,
    later Earl of Dundonald
    (1775–1860) 301, 343, 357,
    407, 468
Cochrane, Basil, provisions
    contractor 162
Cochrane Johnstone, Colonel
    Andrew, MP (1767–1833) 407
Cockburn, Admiral Sir George
    (1772–1853) 447
Cockburn, Alexander, British
    Consul in Tonningen
    (1776–1852) 305
Cockburn, Sir James (1771–1852) 492
Coffin, Admiral Sir Isaac (d. 1839) 118
Coffin, Thomas Ashton,
    Commissary-in-Chief 344, 479
Colchester, Essex 209, 253
Collingwood, Vice-Admiral
    Cuthbert, Baron (1750–1810)

156, 167, 230, 241, 292, 299,
    301, 397, 458
Colpoys, Admiral Sir John
    (1742–1821) 85–6, 89, 223
Combination Act (1799) 94
Commander-in-Chief, army 49, 51,
    93, 104, 242–3, 254, 275, 277,
    336, 347, 437, 441, 472
    Ireland 86–90
    Maritime Provinces 303
    Mediterranean 196
    Spain 424
Commander-in-Chief, navy 172
    Channel 93
    Downs 137, 141
    East Indies, 145
    North America 447
    North Sea 255, 363
    Plymouth 303
    Portsmouth 9, 11
    Mediterranean 93, 196, 292
Commissariat see army
Commissary-in-Chief see British
    government: officials
Commissioner of the Salt Tax 107
Congreve, General Sir William
    Congreve (1743–1814) 44–5,
    371, 498
Congreve, Sir William (1772–1828)
    354–6, 452–3, 473, 498
conjunct expeditions see
    amphibious operations
Consolidation Act (1787) 25
Continental blockade 234, 394–5
Continental System 402–3, 412,
    434, 464
contractors, government 23, 26, 37,
    42, 112, 115, 181, 317–18,
    321, 323, 335, 357, 370–71,
    381, 390, 462

army 279, 335
barrack 52
dockyard 33–4, 222, 380, 383–4
ordnance 24, 42, 45–7, 371–2
packet 53
shipbuilding 223, 350, 357, 359,
   367, 369, 376, 378
victualling 23–4, 160–62, 169,
   175, 330, 337, 463
transports 155
convicts, 42, 316, 369
French 309
convoys 74, 110, 119, 147–8, 154,
   172–5, 180–84, 190, 240, 330,
   364, 389, 394–6, 398–9,
   426, 436
Cooke, Edward, civil servant
   (1755–1820) 80, 86, 158, 480,
   491, 499
Copenhagen, Battle of (1801)
   151, 187
Copenhagen, bombardment of
   (1807) 201–2, 237–8, 285, 294,
   304–8, 372, 375, 458–60
copper 38, 46, 171, 393, 463
bolts 37, 137, 378
rolling mill 36
sheathing 12, 35–6, 38, 181,
   378–9
Corfu 126, 149, 474
Cork, Ireland 15, 78, 86, 132, 160,
   182, 199, 241, 282, 465
Corn 39, 120, 158, 162, 167–8, 445
Corn Laws 470
Cornish, Rear-Admiral Sir Samuel
   Pitchford (d. 1816) 16
Cornwallis, Admiral Sir William,
   MP (1744–1819) 72, 155, 223
Cornwallis, General Charles,
   Marquess (1738–1805) 41, 91,

107–8, 197, 215, 256, 270,
   275, 282, 375, 495, 498, 500
Corsica 69, 75, 83, 118, 143, 276
Corunna, Spain xxxiv, 185, 188,
   202–3, 205–9, 242, 427, 460
cotton trade 22, 352, 392–3
Courtenay, John, MP
   (1738–1816) 477
Courtenay, Thomas, MP
   (1782–1841) 502
Coutts Bank 224, 402
Coventry 52, 79
Cox, Samuel C., parliamentary
   commissioner 512
Craig, General Sir James
   (1748–1812) 75, 175, 189
Craufurd, Major General Robert
   (1764–1812) 91, 93
Crawfurd, Gibbs, Clerk of the
   Ordnance, MP
   (1732–1793) 496
Crawley ironworks, Newcastle 41
Crediton, Devon 447
Creevey, Thomas, MP (1768–1838)
   292, 388, 502
Crew, Robert H., Secretary to the
   Board of Ordnance 497
Crewe, John, MP (1742–1829) 105
Crewe's Act 1782 40
Crockness, Orkney 278
Croker, John Wilson, MP, Secretary
   of the Admiralty (1780–1857)
   291, 298, 300, 337, 339, 355,
   397, 432, 465, 472, 486
Cromer, Norfolk 275
Crown Street, Westminster 318
Cruikshank, George (1792–1878)
   251, 270
Cuffe, John Otway, Earl of Desart,
   MP (1788–1820) 477

Cunninghame, Lieutenant-General Robert 500

Curtis, Admiral Sir Roger (1746–1816) 7–9, 92, 146, 325, 510

Custance & Stone, Great Yarmouth shipbuilders 364

customs, foreign 403–4, 412

customs collectors, Dover 290–91

Customs Department see British government: departments

customs duties 22, 25, 389, 393, 394, 402

Cuxhaven, Germany 131, 133–4, 136, 294, 298

Czartoryski, Prince Adam, Tsar's Polish adviser (1770–1861) 450

d'Albert, Comte, French naval officer 12

d'Antraigues, Comte, British agent (1753–1812) 307

D'Auvergne, Rear-Admiral Philippe (1754–1816) 9, 123, 128, 148, 289, 291, 301, 355

Dalhousie, Major General George Ramsay, Earl of (1770–1838) 199–200

Dalrymple, Alexander, Hydrographer of the Navy (1737–1808) 103, 341–2, 487

Dalrymple, General Sir Hew (1750–1830) 242

Dance, Commodore Sir Nathaniel, East India Company (1748–1827) 399–400

Danzig oak plank 394

Dardanelles 231

Dartmoor Prison see prisoner-of-war depots

Dartmouth see Legge

Dartmouth, Devon 261, 365

Davison, Alexander, army contractor (1750–1829) 333–4, 400, 497

Davy, Robert, Devon shipbuilder 365–6

Day, Captain William, RN, 146

Deal, Kent 39, 137, 207, 209, 267, 290, 300, 303, 446

Deane, Captain Anthony, packet ship commander 135, 295–6

Decrès, Denis, French Minister of Marine (1761–1820) 238, 274, 310, 312

Defence Act (1803) 275

De Lancey, Colonel Oliver, Barrack Master-General 52, 332–3

Delaware, United States 426

Den Helder, expedition to (1799) 133–4, 143, 149, 159, 192–3, 206, 326

Den Helder, Holland 83

Denmark 18, 173, 201–2, 238, 241–2, 285, 293–4, 298, 304–7, 389, 402, 453, 458, 460

Depillion signal system 301

Depot for Military Knowledge 287

Deptford 77, 373

Deptford Dockyard see dockyards

Deptford Victualling Yard see victualling yards

Derby 411

Derrick, Charles, Navy Office clerk 32

devil bolts 366

Devon 259, 364, 365, 445, 446

Devonshire see Cavendish

Devonshire House 66

Dick, Sir John, parliamentary commissioner 478, 505

Fort Pitt, Chatham 281
Foster, John, MP (1740–1828) 477
Foulness Marshes, Essex 302
Fox, Charles James, MP
    (1749–1806) 4, 11, 13, 65, 70,
    216, 220, 228–30, 234, 270,
    338, 465, 479
Fox, General Henry (1755–1811)
    263, 270, 493, 500
Foxford, Co. Mayo, Ireland 91
Frankfurt xxxvi, 391, 402–3,
    412, 414
Frankland, William, MP
    (1761–1816) 486
Fraser, William, civil servant xxxii
Frederick William III, King of
    Prussia (1770–1840) 10,
    449–51
Frederickstown, Nova Scotia 303
Freeling, Sir Francis, Secretary of the
    Post Office (1764–1836) 298,
    300, 502
Fremantle, Vice-Admiral Sir
    Thomas, MP (1765–1819)
    236, 485
Fremantle, William Henry, MP
    (1766–1850) 328, 478
French
    'Army of England' 251
    Atlantic Fleet 14
    Channel ports 72, 84, 251, 396
    Directory 82, 125, 129–30, 144,
        150, 180
    Ministry of the Interior 403
    National Assembly 15
    royalists 72, 123, 128–30, 151,
        285–6
    Windward Islands 68
Frere, John Hookham (1769–1846)
    xxxiii–xxxiv, 480, 482

Friedland, Battle of (1807) 230,
    305–6
Frinton, Essex 302
Fulham 254
Fulton, Robert, American inventor
    (1765–1815) 356

Gage, Viscount, Sussex landowner
    (1761–1808) 265
Galway Bay 282, 303
Gambier, Admiral James, Baron
    (1756–1833) 202, 306,
    468, 485
Gambier, Samuel, Navy Board
    commissioner (1752–1813) 268
Gamble, Revd John (1762–1811)
    137
Ganteaume, Honoré, French
    admiral (1755–1818) 151
Gardner, Alan, Admiral Lord, MP
    (1742–1808) 485
Gardner, Commander James
    Anthony (d. 1846) 183,
    185, 302
Garlike, Benjamin, diplomat
    (1766–1815) 305
Garthshore, William, MP
    (1764–1806) 486
Gentleman's Magazine 107, 263
George III (1738–1820) xxx, xxxvi,
    42, 49, 70–71, 74, 85, 97–8,
    100, 108, 115, 130, 142, 202,
    214, 232, 237, 244–7, 253,
    262, 268, 306, 337, 339,
    443, 461
George, Prince of Wales later
    George IV (1762–1830) 13,
    107–8, 237, 245, 248, 326,
    336, 345, 354, 356–7, 423,
    443, 450–52, 457, 464, 47

Dickinson, Captain Thomas, RN,
    Inspector of Ordnance
    Shipping 498
Dickinson, William, MP
    (1771–1837) 486
Dniester, River 18
docks xxxii, 33–5, 37, 163, 279,
    352–3, 377, 381
dockyard 'chips' 31–2
dockyards xxx, 16, 18, 23–4, 28–9,
    31–6, 38–9, 41, 52, 117, 160,
    170, 191, 202, 215, 222, 236,
    267, 316–17, 319, 320–21,
    323, 329, 330–31, 343, 352–3,
    359–60, 363, 367–9, 379,
    380–81, 396, 462–3
    Bombay 118, 363, 370
    Chatham 117, 170, 281, 353, 367
    Deptford xxxi, 8, 38, 179, 180,
        182, 222, 381
    French 12, 14–16, 18, 35, 129,
        193, 220, 308–9, 311–12
    Pembroke 381
    Plymouth 43, 170, 323, 374, 367
    Portsmouth 45, 171, 267, 350,
        356, 362, 377–8, 378–9, 451
    Sheerness, xxxi, 89, 118, 302,
        317, 381
    Woolwich 267, 329, 353, 360,
        363, 369
    officers xxxi, 177, 180, 222, 235,
        268, 316, 323, 340, 342, 362,
        394; Timber Master 368–9;
        Clerk of the Cheque 348
Dodds, William, Master 184
Domett, Admiral Sir William
    (1752–1828) 325, 485, 510
Dominica 44, 107, 407
Don, General Sir George
    (1756–1832) 289, 311

Dorchester 374
Dorset 266, 446
Douarnenez Bay, France 193
Douglas, Captain Sir Andrew Snape,
    RN (1761–1797) 9
Douglas, Sylvester, MP, later Lord
    Glenbervie (1743–1823) 98–9,
    101, 116, 494, 499, 501
Douglas, William, Duke of
    Queensberry (1723–1810) 13
Douro, river in Portugal 427
Dover 77, 133, 199, 207, 259, 267,
    281, 290–91, 295, 397, 450,
    452, 455
Dover Castle 94, 251, 259, 281
Downing Street xxix, 11, 20, 63
Downs, anchorage off Deal, Kent
    16, 19, 89, 132, 137, 141, 171,
    187, 192, 207, 397
Drake, Francis, diplomat
    (1764–1821) 128, 482
Dresden, Battle of (1813) 312
Drinkwater, Lieutenant-General Sir
    John (1762–1844) 326, 345,
    478, 512
drovers 166, 463
Drummond, Commissary-
    General 429
Drummond, George 504
Dublin 78, 158, 219, 280–82,
    287, 303
Dublin Castle see British government:
    departments: Ireland
Duckworth, Admiral Sir John
    Thomas (1748–1817) 196, 231
Duke of York see York
Duncan, Admiral Adam, Viscount
    (1731–1804) 90, 93, 143
Duncan, Captain Henry, RN
    (c. 1735–1814) 268

Dundas, General Sir David
(1735?–1820) 242, 310, 472
early career xxxvi, 276
Quartermaster-General 61, 91,
253, 255, 259, 273, 275,
277, 493
Commander-in-Chief 243,
335–6, 492
Dundas, General Frank 324
Dundas, Henry, 1st Viscount
Melville (1742–1811)
xxix–xxx, xxxii, xxxv, 26, 43,
64, 99, 101, 105, 196, 271–2,
465, 488, 501
as Home Secretary 52, 71, 115,
126, 332, 483
as Secretary of State for War
66–9, 73–4, 78, 83, 88, 104,
122–3, 142–3, 145, 147–9,
157, 159, 190–91, 193–5,
197–8, 214–15, 251, 491
as First Lord of the Admiralty
223, 277–8, 321, 324, 484
Dundas, Lady Jane
(1766–1829) xxix
Dundas, Robert Saunders, 2nd
Viscount Melville (1771–1851)
334, 485, 499, 501
Dundas, William, MP (1762–1845)
486, 493
Dundee, Scotland 352, 447
Dunkirk 10, 67–8, 83, 396,
409, 446
Dunlop, Ralph, British seaman 291
Dunsterville, Bartholomew,
blockmaking contractor 376
Dupin, Charles, French naval
engineer (1784–1873) 351–2,
383–4
Dutch Crisis (1787) xxxi, 17, 39, 50

Dutch East India Company 142
Dymchurch 187, 275, 279
dysentery 174, 205, 209, 430

East India Company xxxiii, 22, 38,
47, 64, 74, 84, 115, 142–3,
145, 147, 158, 190, 269, 300,
353, 360, 370–71, 393, 399
East Indies 10, 50, 75, 154, 300, 318
East Indies Station 118, 145,
156, 162
Eastbourne 266, 275, 279
economic warfare 233–4, 392, 400
Eden, Sir Morton Frederick, later
Baron Henley, diplomat
(1752–1830) 481
Eden, William, Baron Auckland
(1744–1814) 501
Edinburgh 164, 259, 301, 447
Edwardes, William, Baron
Kensington, MP
(1777–1852) 486
Egremont see Wyndham
Egypt 92, 144–51, 181, 198, 200,
217–18, 231, 276, 288,
426, 459
Elba, island of 217, 449, 455, 465
Elbe, River 131, 134–5, 233–4
Eliot, Edward James, MP
(1758–1797) 476
Ellenborough see Law, Edward
Ellenborough, Lady 108
Elliot, Gilbert, Baron Minto 72,
143, 481, 501
Elliot, William, MP
(1766–1818) 499
Elphinstone see Keith
embezzlement 29, 336
Emmet, Robert, Irish nationalist
(1778–1803) 219–20

Enghien, Duc d', French royalist 286
engineers see Ordnance Department
English Harbour, Antigua xxxi,
44, 474
Erskine, John 478
Étaples 252
Etches, Richard Cadman, British
secret agent 125, 129, 150–51
Exchequer bills 249, 389, 390
Excise Department see British
government: departments
excise duties 25, 389, 393
Exe, River 365

Fairlight, Sussex 302
Falmouth 134, 160–61, 171, 185,
270, 293–4, 298, 382–3
Fane, John, Earl of Westmorland
(1759–1841) 498
Fanshawe, Captain Robert, MP
(d. 1823) 268
Faversham, gunpowder mill 42,
44, 372
Fawcett, Lieutenant-General Sir
William (1727–1804) 49, 492
Feluccas 200
Fernhurst, West Sussex 374
Ferrol, Spain 14, 136, 197
Fife, Scotland 259, 279
Finch Hatton, Edward 484
Finchley Common 270
Finisterre 15, 294
Finlaison, John, civil servant
(1783–1860) 325, 330, 346
Firle, Sussex 265
First Fleet to Australia (1787–8) 7,
12, 266
First Lord of the Admiralty see
British government:
departments: Admiralty

First of June, Battle of (179
Fisher, Edward, civil servant
Fishguard, South Wales 87
Fitzgerald (later Vesey Fitzger
William, MP (?1782–184.
FitzGerald, Lord Edward
(1763–1798) 144
Fitzgerald, Lord Robert Stephen
diplomat (1765–1833) 482
Fitzherbert, Alleyne, Baron St
Helens, diplomat (1753–1839
481–2
Fitzpatrick, General Richard, MP
(1748–1813) 493
Fitzwilliam, William Wentworth,
Earl Fitzwilliam
(1748–1833) 498
Flanders xxxvi, 67, 104
Flower, Sir Charles, provisions
contractor (1763–1834) 161
Floyd, Lieutenant-General Sir John
(1748–1818) 500
Flushing, Cornwall 298
Flushing, Holland 205, 208,
290–91, 308, 310–11, 355
Folkestone see Bouverie
food prices 63, 117, 159,
411, 445
food shortages xxviii, 53, 157, 410
Ford, Colonel William, engineer 281
Ford, John, parliamentary
commissioner 508
Fordyce, John, MP (1735–1809)
xxxii, 325, 329, 507, 510
Foreign Office see British
government: departments
Fort Charlotte, Shetland Islands 43
Fort Clarence, Chatham 281
Fort Monkton, Portsmouth
Harbour 43

George, Sir Rupert, Chairman of the
Transport Board (d. 1823) 110,
178, 183, 190, 207, 210, 488
Ghent, Treaty of (1814) 448,
454, 470
Gibraltar xxxi, 7–8, 47, 50, 68, 75,
83, 132, 144, 163, 171, 182,
196, 198, 206, 300, 396,
426, 474
Gill, Thomas, Admiral (d. 1874)
302
Glasgow 391
Glenbervie see Douglas
Gloucester, William Henry, Duke of
(1743–1805) 80
Goddard, Charles, civil servant
(1769–1848) 106
Gold Standard 87
Golding, Edward, MP (1746–1818)
235, 476
Goldsmid, Abraham, banker
(1756–1810) 391, 410
Goldsmid, Benjamin, banker
(1753–1808) 391, 410
Goodrich, Simon, engineer
(1773–1847) 378–9, 451
Gordon & Murphy, London
merchants 407
Gordon Riots (1780) 50
Gordon, Lieutenant-Colonel Sir
Alexander 417
Gordon, General Sir James
Willoughby (1753–1851)
xxxvii, 291, 310, 335, 344,
479, 492–3
Gordon, Lady Georgiana 106
Gordon Theodore, Inspector-
General of Army Hospitals 495
Gothenburg, Sweden 18, 239,
294–6, 298, 391, 395

Goulburn, Henry, MP (1784–1856)
340, 448, 470, 484, 491
Gower see Leveson Gower
Graham, General Thomas, MP, later
Baron Lynedoch (1748–1843)
198, 436, 441
Graham, James, Duke of Montrose
(1755–1836) 501
grain 39, 69, 79, 157–8, 164, 393,
395, 403, 410, 426, 463
see also wheat
Grand National Jubilee
(1814) 452
Grant, Charles, MP
(1778–1866) 477
Gravelines 10, 291, 409
Gravesend, Kent 90, 381
Great Yarmouth 90, 133–6, 153,
164, 171, 187, 202, 237, 241,
259, 276, 293–4, 300, 303,
306, 319, 363–4, 374–5
Green Park, London 452
Greenock 363
Greenwich Hospital 323
Greenwich marshes 276
Gregory, William, Irish civil
servant 499
Grenville, George Nugent-Temple,
1st Marquis of Buckingham
(1753–1813) 235–7, 273,
305, 328
Grenville, Richard, Earl Temple, MP
(1776–1839) 501
Grenville, Thomas, MP
(1755–1846) 219, 248, 305,
307, 343, 471, 501
early career 127, 135, 481
as First Lord of the Admiralty
178, 202, 234–7, 319, 329,
383, 394, 460, 484

Grenville, William Wyndham,
Baron, (1759–1834) 65–6, 223,
228, 243, 246, 248, 272–3,
307, 471
early career xxxiii, 43, 64
as Foreign Secretary 66, 69, 92,
98–9, 122, 124–6, 127–9,
131,145, 148–9, 194, 479
as Prime Minister 176, 229,
232–3, 237, 327–8, 338, 345,
355, 376, 386, 465, 476
Greville, Charles (1762–1832) 483
Grey, Charles, later Lord Howick,
later 2nd Earl Grey
(1764–1845) 65–6, 223, 228,
230, 234, 243, 246, 248, 329,
381, 421, 471, 479, 484
Grey, General Charles, 1st Earl Grey
(1729–1807) 68, 73, 193–4, 225
Grey, Thomas de, MP, later Baron
Walsingham, Joint Postmaster-
General (1748–1818) 53, 502
Guadeloupe 189
Guernsey 48, 292
Guildford, Surrey 185, 275
gun barrels 372
gunboats 7–8, 173, 223, 240, 256,
291, 302, 355, 362
gun-brigs 153, 240, 289, 354, 361,
364–6, 397
gunlocks 354, 372
Gunning, John, Surgeon-General of
the Army (d. 1798) 495
gunsmiths 47, 357, 372, 463, 466
Gustavus Adolf IV, King of Sweden
(1778–1837) 239

Hackness, Orkney 278
Hadden James, Surveyor-General of
the Ordnance 496

Haiti 22
Halifax, Nova Scotia xxxi, xxxvii,
118, 132, 161, 303, 316,
363, 474
Hamburg 131, 142, 159, 294, 298,
391, 402–3, 406, 412, 414
Hamilton, Alexander, Marquess of
Douglas and Clydesdale, MP
and diplomat (1767–1852) 481
Hamilton, Sackville, Undersecretary,
Dublin Castle 499
Hamilton, Sir William, diplomat
(1731–1803) 143
Hamilton, Vice-Admiral Thomas
(d. 1815) 178–9, 350
Hamilton, William Richard,
diplomat (1777–1859) 480
Hamilton-Gordon, George, Earl of
Aberdeen (1784–1860) 481
Hammond, George, Undersecretary
Foreign Office
(1763–1853) 480
Hamond, Captain Sir Andrew
Snape, RN, MP (1738–1828)
221, 321, 333, 340–41,
360, 489
Hamond's Knoll, off Happisburgh,
Norfolk 135
Hampden see Trevor
Hancock, Samuel, Admiralty civil
servant 348
Hanger, Colonel George, later Baron
Coleraine, military writer
(1751–1824) 87–8, 256,
269, 271
Hanover xxxvi, 62, 66, 124, 219,
233, 355, 389, 452
Hardenberg, Karl von, Prussian
Chancellor (1750–1822)
449–50, 454–5

hardwoods 17, 369, 394–5
Hardy, Admiral Sir Thomas
  Masterman (1769–1839) 136
Hare, James, MP (1747–1804) 105
Harness, John, Sick and Hurt
  commissioner 490
Harrington see Stanhope
Harris, James, Earl of Malmesbury,
  diplomat (1746–1820) xxxii,
  82, 481
Harris, James Edward, Viscount
  FitzHarris, MP
  (1778–1841) 476
Harrison, Sir George, Treasury civil
  servant (1767–1841) 327, 335,
  390, 465, 472, 478
Harvey, Admiral Sir Henry
  (d. 1810) 75
Harwich 133, 207, 209, 261, 275,
  293–4, 295–8
Hastings, General Francis Rawdon,
  Marquess Moira (1754–1826)
  333, 496
Heatley, David, agent victualler at
  Lisbon 163
Heligoland 134–5, 294, 381,
  402, 412
Hellevoetsluis, Holland 293, 413
Henley, Michael, shipowner
  (1742–1813) 141, 181, 184
Hennem, Jonathan, small arms
  contractor, 47
Henslow, Sir John, Surveyor of the
  Navy (1730–1815) 340, 489
Herbert, Lieutenant-General George
  Augustus, Earl of Pembroke,
  MP and diplomat (1759–1827)
  304, 481
Heron, Sir Robert, MP
  (1765–1864) 432

Herries, Charles, volunteer colonel
  and banker 127, 345, 494
Herries, John Charles (1778–1855)
  xxxv, 333, 345, 413–14, 465,
  470, 472, 478–9
Herries, Robert & Co., bankers 143
Hervey, Frederick William, MP
  (Earl of Bristol from 1803)
  (1769–1859) 480
Hewett, General Sir George
  (1750–1840) 493–4, 500
Hilhouse, James Martin, Bristol
  shipbuilder (1749–1822) 362
Hill, Edmund, gunpowder
  manufacturer 371
Hobart, Robert, Earl of
  Buckinghamshire (1760–1816)
  217–18, 271, 491, 499, 501–2
Hobhouse, Benjamin, MP
  (1757–1831) 502
Hobson, William, government
  building contractor 277–8
Hoche, General Lazare, French
  general 72, 85, 144
Holford, George, MP (1767–1839)
  502
Holl, Edward, architect 317,
  487, 489
Holland xxxvi, 3, 10–11, 18, 22, 45,
  62, 66–7, 69, 82, 93, 104, 130,
  142, 149–50, 186–7, 189, 192,
  205, 209, 290, 293, 355, 406,
  408, 412–13, 436, 440–41,
  450, 453, 468
Holland, Lady, Elizabeth Vassal Fox
  (1771?–1845) 66, 72
Holy Roman Empire 230
Holywell, River Dee 36–7
Home Office see British
  government: departments

Hood, Admiral Alexander, Viscount Bridport (1727–1814) 85, 149, 325

Hood, Admiral Samuel, Viscount (1724–1816) 9, 11, 16, 18–19, 68–9, 85, 93, 129, 276, 485

Hood, Vice-Admiral Sir Samuel (1762–1814) 84, 203, 205, 298

Hope, Admiral Sir William Johnstone, MP (1766–1811) 485

Hope, Colonel Alexander 256, 335

Hope, Lieutenant-General Sir John (1765–1836) 204, 310, 500

Hope, Rear-Admiral George Johnstone 485

Hope & Co., Amsterdam bankers 406

Hope–Baring contract 406

Hopkins, Richard, MP (?1728–1799) 476

Horner, Francis, MP (1778–1817) 234

Horse Guards 49, 104, 121, 185, 207, 243, 275, 277, 287, 317–18, 336

horse mills 352

Houghton chalk pits, Sussex 168

House of Commons xxxiv, 19, 40, 82, 112, 116, 127, 206, 214–15, 219, 221–2, 244, 249, 277, 314, 334, 346–7, 410, 423, 455

House of Lords xxxvi, 181, 204, 221, 228, 356

Howe, Admiral Richard, Earl (1726–1799) xxxi, 5, 9, 11, 14–16, 19, 30–31, 33, 38, 54–5, 85, 89, 93, 140, 235, 321, 325, 349

Howe, General Sir William (1729–1814) 496

Howick see Grey

Hudson Bay Company 184

Hull 141, 160–61, 167, 259, 262, 352, 363, 402

Hull, William, Governor of Michigan 435

Hungarians 78

Hunt, Henry, radical politician (1773–1835) 470

Hunt, Joseph, MP and civil servant (?1762–1816) 336, 497

Hurd, Captain Thomas, Hydrographer of the Navy (1747–1823) 342, 382, 487

hurricane season 163

Hurst Castle 204

Huskisson, William, MP (1770–1830) xxxv, 109, 410, 484

as Undersecretary of State for War 73, 105, 109, 148–9, 194–5, 491

as Junior Secretary at the Treasury 245, 297, 390, 407–8, 465, 478

Husum, Denmark 294, 297

Hutchinson, Lieutenant-General John Hely, Baron Hutchinson (1757–1832) 481

Hyde Park, London 52, 262, 452

Hydrographic Office see British government: departments: Admiralty

Hythe, Kent 255

Ibbetson, John, Admiralty civil servant

income tax see tax: income

India xxii, 3–4, 22, 45, 92, 141,
143, 145, 147, 158, 172, 188,
216, 246, 370–71, 393–5
'individual responsibility' 320,
324, 381
Indonesia 188
industrial espionage 37
industrial recession 158
Industrial Revolution 353, 462
Inglis, Charles, Captain, RN (d.
1877) 199
intelligence
British 144, 311, 402; Chapters 5
and 10 passim
French 287
military 286, 289
invasion scares 150, 248, 253, 274,
276, 282
invasion threat 69, 104, 143–4, 219,
223, 240, 265, 273, 283–4,
302, 308, 388, 450, 461;
Chapter 9 passim
invasion threats, Ireland xxxv, 12,
83, 85–6, 90–92, 143–6,
148–50, 240, 246, 274, 282–3,
285, 308
Ionian Islands 189, 396
Ireland 21, 49, 51, 68, 78, 80, 86–7,
115, 155, 158–60, 166, 184,
217, 301, 303, 318, 345, 348,
411, 438, 443
Irish parliament 127
Irish rebellion (1798) 87, 90–91,
124, 144, 191
Irish troops 77, 91, 443
Irving, Thomas, customs civil
servant xxxii, 119
Irving Reid, London bankers 407
Isle of Dogs 352
Isle of Wight 48, 209, 255, 259

Jackson, Cyril, Dean of Christ
Church, Oxford (1746–1819)
xxix, xxxiii–xxxiv
Jackson, Francis James,
diplomat 481
Jackson, Thomas, diplomat 145
Jamaica xxxi, 12, 16, 22, 75, 132,
316, 474
Jedda 142
Jefferson, Thomas, US President
(1743–1826) 434–5
Jenkinson, Charles, 1st Earl
Liverpool (1729–1808) 159,
226, 500
Jenkinson, Charles Cecil Cope, MP
(1784–1851) 484, 491
Jenkinson, Robert Banks (Lord
Hawkesbury 1796–1808), 2nd
Earl Liverpool (1770–1828) 65,
79, 101, 271
as Foreign Secretary 479
as Home Secretary 226, 238, 483
as Secretary of State for War 491,
288, 335, 422
as Prime Minister xxxiv–xxxv,
100, 249–50, 327, 476, 386,
413, 422–3, 426, 448–9,
454–5, 465, 470
Jersey 6, 48, 123, 289, 292, 301,
311
Jervis, Admiral John, Earl St Vincent
(1735–1823) 325, 369, 381–3
on active service 73, 83, 85, 88,
92–3, 127–8, 144, 146–8, 172,
175, 225, 471, 482
as First Lord of the Admiralty
103, 108, 118, 163, 181, 214,
218, 221–3, 320–22, 361, 369,
381, 484
Johnstone, James 7

Jones, John Paul (1747–1792) 170
Junot, Jean-Andoche, French
    general (1784–1860) 239
justices of the peace 77, 259

Karlskrona 8, 35
Kattegat 298
Keate, Thomas, Surgeon-General of
    the Army (1745–1821) 495
Keats, Admiral Sir Richard
    Goodwin (1756–1834) 93,
    202, 242, 428
Keith, Admiral George Keith
    Elphinstone, 1st Viscount
    (1746–1823) 75, 93, 172, 344
    Commander-in-Chief,
        Mediterranean 132, 149, 156,
        173, 196–200
    Commander-in-Chief, North Sea
        and Channel 255, 266–7,
        363, 433
Kent, Edward, Duke of
    (1767–1820) xxxvii, 303
Kherson, Battle of (1788) 170
Killala, Co. Mayo, Ireland 91
King, John, MP (1759–1830) xxxiv,
    126, 288, 478, 483
King, John, shipbuilder 362
King's Bounty 76
King's German Legion see army
    regiments
King's Messengers 131, 135–6, 292
Kingston, Surrey 185
Kirkcaldy, Scotland 447
Knight, Edward, wheat
    contractor 161
Knight, Francis, Inspector-General
    of Army Hospitals
    (d. 1832) 495
Knights of St John 147, 216

Kronstadt 35
Kutuzov, Prince Mikhail, Russian
    Field Marshal (1747–1813)
    421, 467

L'Orient, France 123, 289
Lagos Bay 174
Lake, Lieutenant-General Gerard
    (1744–1808) 90, 500
Lambeth, south London 353, 377
Lancashire 36–7, 80, 157–8, 441
Land's End 140
Law, Edward, Baron Ellenborough
    (1750–1818) 81, 229, 280,
    333, 476
Law, Ewan, MP (1747–1829) 322,
    508
Laycock, William, Ordnance
    non-commissioned officer 355
Le Geyt, Captain 7
Leakes, John Martin 478
Leeds 50, 158
Leeds, Francis Osbourne, Duke of
    (1751–1799) 116
Leeward Islands 12, 132, 161, 217
Legge, George, Earl of Dartmouth
    (Viscount Lewisham
    1755–1801) (1755–1810) 501
Legge, Henry, Pitt's private secretary
    100
Leghorn 15, 136, 145
Leicester 50, 411
Leicester see Townshend
Leipzig, Battle of (1813) 356, 430, 459
Leipzig University xxxv, 345
Leith, Scotland 160–61, 363–4
Lennox, Charles, 3rd Duke of
    Richmond (1735–1806) 11,
    42–5, 47–8, 52, 55, 67, 253,
    259, 264–5, 495

Lennox, Charles, Earl of March, MP (later 4th Duke of Richmond) (1791–1860) 238, 304, 451, 498

Levant 146, 394

Levant Company 19

Leveson Gower, George Granville, MP, Earl Gower, later 1st Duke of Sutherland, Joint Postmaster-General (1758–1833) 502

Leveson Gower, Lord Granville, MP (1773–1846) 125, 476, 481, 493

Lewisham *see* Legge

Lewisham, south London 372–3

licences 401–4, 409, 426

Lieven, Countess, Russian Ambassador's wife (1743–1828) 451

Ligny, Battle of (1815) 457

Lille, France 82, 137, 303

Linois, Durand, French admiral 399–400

Lisbon 53, 83, 118, 127, 134, 163, 175, 188, 239, 245, 298–9, 308, 418, 425–9, 460

Littlehampton, Sussex 168, 276

Liverpool 50, 164, 271, 280, 301, 363, 391–2, 411, 470

Liverpool, Lady 106

Liverpool, Lord *see* Jenkinson

Lizard, Cornwall 188

Lloyd, James Martin, MP (1762–1844) 497

Lloyd's Coffee House 124, 300, 398

Lloyd's Insurance 400, 406

Lloyd's Patriotic Fund 399–400

London 13–14, 16, 50, 54, 63, 70, 81, 89, 105, 110, 125, 140, 146, 159, 164–7, 184, 254, 256, 259, 262, 270, 280, 302–3, 313–18, 345, 347, 352, 363, 451–2, 469

London, City of xxxiii, 5, 25, 38, 87–8, 413, 429; Chapter 13 *passim*

London Corn Exchange 39, 158, 162

London Corresponding Society 125

London docks 156, 163, 279, 352

London Tavern 268

Long, Charles, MP, later Baron Farnborough (1760–1838) 99, 108–9, 173, 222, 326, 476, 478, 494, 499

Lords Lieutenant 253, 259, 232, 263

Lough Foyle, Ireland 282

Lough Swilly, Ireland 282

Louis XVI of France (1754–1793) 4, 8, 20

Lowndes, William, civil servant xxxii, 25

Lowther, William (later Viscount Lowther), MP (1787–1872) 477, 486

Loyalist Associations 61

Loyalty Loan (1796) 84

Lushington, Stephen Rumbold, MP (1776–1868) 478

Luttrell, Lieutenant-General Henry Lawes, Earl of Carhampton (1743–1821) 86, 500

Macartney, George, Lord (1737–1806) 324

Macbride, Captain John, RN, MP (c. 1735–1800) 9

McGrigor, Sir James, Director-General of Army Medical Board (1771–1858) 205, 495

M'Cleay, Alexander, Secretary to the Transport Board 488
McMahon, John, MP (c. 1754–1817) 497
Madeira 188
Madison, James, US President (1751–1836) 434–5
Madras 118, 143, 145, 162
Madrid xxxiv, 15–16, 136, 241, 406, 418, 423, 428, 465
Maitland, Lieutenant-General Frederick 436
Malta xxxvii, 118, 132, 143, 147, 149, 167, 173, 188–9, 198–9, 216, 218, 241, 316, 371, 381, 396, 402, 474
Man, Vice-Admiral Robert (d. 1813) 485
Manchester 52, 271, 391, 402, 412, 470
Manderson, Captain James (d. 1837) 382
manpower reserves 51, 76–8, 82, 119, 221, 311–12, 347, 424, 431, 452, 456, 459–60; Chapter 15 passim
March see Lennox
marine barracks 52
Markham, Osbourne, Navy Board commissioner 321, 324, 494
Markham, Rear-Admiral John, MP (1761–1827) 215, 321–2, 382, 485
Marmaris, Bay of, Turkey 199–200
Marmont, Auguste, French Marshal 304, 420
Marquand, John, civil engineer 33
Marsden, Alexander, Irish civil servant 219, 499

Marsden, William, Secretary to the Admiralty (1754–1836) xxxiii
  as Second Secretary 102, 106, 109, 120, 320–21, 487
  as First Secretary 222, 230, 237, 320, 324, 339, 368, 382, 471, 486
marsh fever 209, 310
Marsh, George, Navy Board commissioner (1722–1800) 30, 55
Marsh, John, Chairman of the Victualling Board 163, 341, 490
Martello Towers 276, 281–3, 302
Martin, Admiral Sir Thomas Byam, MP (1753–1854) xxxvii, 3, 312, 427
Martin, Captain Sir Henry, Comptroller of the Navy (d. 1794) xxxi, 489
Martinique 118, 189
Massena, André, French Marshal (1758–1817) 417
Maudslay, Henry, engineer (1771–1831) 353, 376–7
Mauritius 145, 188, 316, 450
Meadows, General Sir William 500
Meares, John, naval officer and shipowner (1756–1809) 14
Mediterranean 7, 12, 74, 83, 92, 132, 141, 145–6, 148, 155, 173, 175, 189, 194, 197, 230, 298, 396–7, 452
Mediterranean Fleet (British) 83, 85, 88, 92–3, 144, 149, 198, 218, 241, 292, 299, 301, 437, 458
Mediterranean Fleet (French) 7
Medway, River xxxi, 362, 374, 381
Melville see Dundas

merchant shipping 13, 76, 89, 109,
    111, 140, 160, 164, 174–6,
    220, 234, 293, 300, 392, 395,
    397–8, 399, 401, 408, 410,
    425, 427, 434–5, 447, 463;
    Chapter 7 *passim*
Merry, Anthony, diplomat
    (1756–1835) 15, 125, 217
Messina, Sicily 189
Metternich, Count von Klemens
    (1771–1859) 449–51, 454
Metz, France 303, 311
Meuron, Colonel the Compte de,
    Swiss soldier 142–3
Middleton, Admiral Sir Charles,
    MP, later Baron Barham
    (1726–1813) 19, 38, 324, 346,
    359, 506
  as Comptroller of the Navy
    xxx–xxxiii, 9, 29–33, 38–9, 55,
    190, 349
  as Admiralty commissioner 72–3,
    110, 170, 177, 180, 222, 485
  as First Lord of the Admiralty
    226–7, 325, 328, 340,
    378, 484
  as Chairman of the Commission
    of Naval Revision 325,
    329, 510
militia 78–80, 87, 111, 154, 157,
    159, 217, 238, 248, 255–6,
    259, 261–2, 270–71, 283–4,
    332, 335, 411, 437, 439–41,
    443–5
militia, Ireland 78, 80, 85–6,
    91, 443
Militia Acts 79, 80–81, 232,
    260–61, 265, 439
militia ballots 233, 238, 259, 469
militia substitutes 80, 261

militia regiments
  East Suffolk 281
  Fife 279
  Gloucestershire 79
  Herefordshire 157
  Hertfordshire 79
  Leicestershire 411
  Montgomeryshire 281
  Northamptonshire 79, 411
  Nottinghamshire 411
  Oxfordshire 79
  Royal Monmouth and Brecon
    264, 439, 443
  Rutland 411
  Somersetshire 444
  Sussex 262
  Warwickshire 411
  West Essex 261, 411
Miller, Colonel Sir John Riggs,
    Sussex volunteer officer 265
Miller, Lieutenant-Colonel James,
    Inspector of Small Arms 372, 498
mines, underwater weapons 356
Minorca 118, 132, 188, 196, 198,
    276, 355
Minto see Elliot, Gilbert
Miranda, General Francisco de,
    South American patriot 14, 241
Mitchell, Admiral Sir Andrew
    (1757–1806) 192
Moira see Hastings
Molleson, William 478, 505
Mona copper mines, Anglesey 36
Mondego Bay, Portugal 242, 460
Montagu, Admiral Sir George
    (d. 1829) 299
Montagu, John, 5th Earl of
    Sandwich, Joint Postmaster-
    General (1744–1814) 502
Montevideo 231, 273, 316

Moody, Robert Sadleir, Victualling Board commissioner 341

Moore, Lieutenant-General Sir John Moore (1761–1809) 91, 93, 197, 203, 239, 275, 290

Moore, Thomas, smuggler 446

Moorsom, Captain Robert, MP (1760–1835) 485, 496

Morning Chronicle 213, 422

Morning Herald 326

Mornington, Earl of, *see* Wellesley, Richard

Morres, Lodge Evans, Undersecretary, Dublin Castle 499

Morse, General Robert, military engineer (1742–1818) 275, 277

Moscow, burning of (1812) 419

Moscow, Napoleon's retreat from 284, 419–20, 439, 467

Motz, Commissary-General 173

Mulgrave *see* Phipps

Murray, George Revd Lord (1761–1803) 137

Murray, Sir Patrick, MP (1771–1837)

musket cartridges 371, 375

muskets 47–8, 81, 182, 263, 357, 371–5, 393, 410, 421

muskets, East India Pattern 48, 393

Mylor, Cornwall 383

Nantes 22, 37

Napier, Lady Sarah Lennox (1745–1826) 452

Naples 143–4, 146–7, 189, 216, 227

Napoleon
    peace negotiations with Britain 82, 215–16, 249
    relations with government ministers 310, 312, 354
    strategy and tactics 92, 210, 217, 219, 228–9, 233–4, 238–9, 242, 248, 272–4, 277, 283, 305, 307, 400, 404–5, 418, 457

National Convention, Paris 62

national debt 25, 87, 386, 389, 463, 467

navy
    Comptroller of the Navy xxx, xxxi, xxxvii, 6, 29–30, 41, 221–2, 321, 340, 360
    Estimates 5, 339
    hospital ships 74, 186, 201, 328, 445
    hospitals 34, 205, 328
    impressment 62–4, 76–7, 219, 260, 264–8, 298, 397, 433
    regulating officers 63
    stations 32, 162
    stores xxx, 18, 23, 32, 220, 395, 396; *see also* Baltic region: naval stores
    Treasurer of the Navy xxix, 13, 101, 107, 112, 224, 325, 348

Neave, Richard, parliamentary commissioner 504

Neerwinden, Battle of (1793) 67

Nelson, Vice-Admiral Horatio, Viscount (1758–1805) xxxiv, xxxvii, 92, 94, 140, 144, 146–7, 151, 156, 169, 174, 214, 227, 229, 277, 292, 333, 366

Nepean, Sir Evan, MP and civil servant (1752–1822) xxxii, xxxiii, 152, 333
    as Undersecretary at the Home Office xxxv, 6–7, 10, 13, 80, 106, 109, 125, 127, 483

as Undersecretary of State for
War 109,127, 491
as Secretary of the Admiralty
125–6, 128, 145, 147–9, 150,
218, 320, 486
as Chief Secretary, Ireland 227,
320, 499
as Admiralty commissioner 227, 486
Nesslerode, Count Charles, Russian
minister (1780–1862) 456
Netherlands see Holland
Neuchâtel 142
New Orleans, Battle of (1815) 448
Newark on Trent 411
Newcastle 41, 63, 78, 160, 164,
186, 262
Newfoundland 12, 188, 365
Nicholls, Admiral Sir Henry
(d. 1829) 389, 508
Nieuport, surrender of (1794) 78
Nile see Aboukir Bay
Nock, Henry, small arms contractor
47–8
Nootka Sound crisis 1790 3, 13, 15, 51
Nore 140, 167, 240
Nore Mutiny (1797) 89–90, 143, 191
Norfolk 72, 166, 233, 266, 275,
301, 364
Norfolk, Virginia 433
Norman Cross see prisoner-of-war
depots
North, George, Frederick, Earl of
Guilford (1732–1792) 4, 25
North Africa 175, 218, 396
North Downs 275
North Foreland 140–41, 397
North Sea 53, 74, 90, 131, 133,
134–5, 141, 153, 171, 187,
240, 255, 290, 292–5, 303,
363, 402, 412

North Shields 63
North Tawton, Devon 447
Northfleet, proposed dockyard
at 381
Northumberland 259, 471
Norwich 52, 164
Norwood, south London 256
Nottingham 50, 52, 248, 411
Nova Scotia xxxi, 12, 132,
187, 474
Nunhead, south London 256

Oakes, General Sir Hildebrand 326,
496, 512
Ochakov Crisis (1791) 17–19
Office of Works see British
government: departments
Oporto, Portugal 427
Orange, Prince of 75
Orange, Princess of 10
orders-in-council 234, 327,
343, 434
Ordnance Department 41, 44, 46–7,
52, 112, 315, 317–18, 337,
371–2, 469
Artillery 41–2, 44, 67–8, 78, 91,
137, 176, 185–6, 232, 262,
264–5, 268, 270, 274, 279,
316, 354, 427, 457
Board of 41–2, 45, 47, 90,178,
275, 318, 371–3
Engineers xxxvi, 41, 195
Master-General 11, 41–5, 47–8,
55, 107–8, 177, 247, 275, 277,
282, 291, 318, 333, 356, 375
Ordnance depots
Great Yarmouth 374
Horsea 374
Purfleet, Essex 45
Priddy's Hard 42, 45

Ordnance depots – *cont.*
  St Budeaux 374
  Stamshaw 374
  Tipner Point 45
  Tower of London 48, 318, 373
  Upnor Castle 42, 374
  Weedon Bec 280
Ordnance gunpowder mills
  Faversham 42, 44, 372
  Waltham Abbey 42, 45, 372
Ordnance manufacture and testing
  Artillery Inspectorate 370
  Brass Foundry, Woolwich 46
  Lewisham 372
  Royal Laboratory, Woolwich
    44–5, 354, 371, 373, 452
  Temporary Laboratory,
    Plymouth 373
  Temporary Laboratory,
    Portsmouth 373
  Woolwich Arsenal 42, 280, 316,
    353, 371, 373–4, 452
Ordnance Survey 42, 48, 137, 276, 318
Oreston, near Plymouth 383
Osborn, John, MP (1772–1848) 486
Ostend 69, 88
Ouvrard, Gabriel-Julien, French
  banker (1770–1846) 406
Oxford University, Chancellor 471

packet service *see* Post Office
Paddington Basin 280
Paget, Berkeley, MP (1780–1842) 477
Paget, General Henry William, Lord
  Paget, later Marquess of
  Anglesey (1768–1854) 273
Paget, Sir Arthur, diplomat
  (1771–1840) 125,132, 217,
  222, 481
Palermo, Sicily 198

Pall Mall 70, 318
Palliser, Admiral Sir Hugh
  (1723–1796) 108
Palmer, John, Post Office employee
  54–5
Palmerston *see* Temple
Pamplona, Spain 444
Paris, Treaty of (1783) 3
Paris, Treaty of (1814) 450
Paris, Treaty of (1815) 467
Parish, David, banker 406
Parish, John, Hamburg merchant 402
Parker, Richard, Nore mutineer 89
Parlby, Thomas, dockyard building
  contractor (1727–1802) 34
parliament xxx, 4, 5, 14, 25, 40–41,
  44, 49, 55, 61–2, 70, 72, 76,
  79, 89, 94, 104–5, 107, 114,
  126, 132, 158, 165, 172, 206,
  214, 220, 222–3, 225, 228,
  232, 235, 238, 245, 247–9,
  260, 307, 314, 321, 323, 329,
  335, 338, 343, 346, 349,
  387–8, 390, 412, 432, 436,
  440, 452, 455, 462, 464–7
  see also House of Commons;
  House of Lords
parliamentary commissions
  into the administration of the
    Woods and Forests 38, 325
  Commission of Military Enquiry
    313, 326, 334–5, 328, 336–7,
    343, 345, 370, 373
  Commission of Naval Enquiry 214,
    224, 322–3, 325, 328, 331–2, 462
  Commission of Naval Revision
    324, 462, 328–30, 335, 341,
    343, 346, 380–81
  Commission on Fees 26, 55, 103,
    115–16, 314, 327, 348

Committee on Public Accounts
    25–6
  see also Appendix 2
Parliamentary Committee on Public
    Expenditure (1807) 335
parliamentary reform 243, 470
Parliamentary Select Committee on
    Finance 117
parole see prisoners of war
Parsons, George, Commander
    (d. 1854) 199
Pasley, Lieutenant-General Sir
    Charles William
    (1780–1861) 210
patronage xxxiii, 41, 43, 55, 102,
    112, 116, 313, 326, 332, 354,
    356, 452, 462
Patton, Admiral Philip 485
Paulet, Rear-Admiral Lord Henry
    (1767–1832) 485
Paymasters-General see army
Payne, John, Navy Office clerk
    330–31
peace preliminaries (1801) 135, 215
peace negotiations (1796) 82, 84, 125
Peace of Amiens see Amiens, Peace of
Peake, Sir Henry, Surveyor of the
    Navy 236, 489
Peel, Sir Robert, MP (1788–1850)
    xxix, xxxiv, 340, 470, 491, 499
Pelham, Thomas, MP, later Lord
    Pelham (1801) and Earl of
    Chichester (1805) (1756–1826)
    105, 483, 499, 502
Pellew, Admiral Edward, Viscount
    Exmouth (1757–1833) 94, 223,
    382, 432, 437
Pembroke see Herbert
Penang 316, 363
Penge Common, south London 256

Pepys, Sir Lucas, Physician-General of
    the Army (1742–1830) 209, 495
Perceval, Charles George (later Lord
    Arden), MP (1756–1840) 486
Perceval, Spencer, MP
    (1762–1812) 233
  as Chancellor of the Exchequer
    245, 285, 333, 345, 383, 390,
    407, 412, 476
  as Prime Minister 100, 246–7,
    249, 327, 334, 337, 340,
    344–5, 386, 412, 464–5, 476
Percy, George, Lord Lovaine, MP
    (1778–1807) 476
Peterloo Massacre (1819) 470
Peters, Henry, parliamentary
    commissioner 513.
Petty, Lord Henry, MP (1780–1763)
    314, 388, 476
Petworth House, West Sussex 168,
    264, 451
Pevensey, East Sussex 88, 266, 278
Philippon, General Armand, French
    governor of Badajoz
    (1761–1836) 446
Phillip, Arthur, Admiral
    (1738–1814) 7, 266
Phipps, Edmund, MP (1760–1837) 497
Phipps, General Henry, Earl
    Mulgrave (1755–1831) 247,
    356, 470, 479, 496
  as First Lord of the Admiralty
    181, 237–8, 246, 310, 313,
    329, 341, 343–4, 348, 484
Pichegru, Jean-Charles, French
    general (1761–1804) 130, 286
Piggott, Arthur, parliamentary
    commissioner 504
Pigou, Charles, gunpowder
    manufacturer 371

pigs 39, 159, 165, 357
Pinkerton, Thomas, provisions
    contractor 161–2
Pitcher's shipbuilding yard,
    Gravesend 381
Pitt, General John, Earl of Chatham
    (1756–1835)
    as First Lord of the Admiralty 19,
    55, 72, 85, 110, 484
    as Master-General of the
    Ordnance 41, 247, 275, 277,
    375, 495–6
    command at Walcheren 206–9
Pitt, William, MP (1759–1806)
    xxxii, 4, 464–5, 473
    as Prime Minister (1783–1801)
    xxix, xxxi–xxxiii, 4–6, 8,
    10–20, 61–2, 64–7, 69–72, 76,
    82, 84, 87, 90, 97–101, 105–7,
    115, 122, 126–8, 140, 149,
    157–8, 165, 168, 191, 193–5,
    213–14, 387, 475; Chapter 2
    passim
    in Opposition 215, 219, 222–3,
    268, 271
    as Prime Minister (1804–6) 108,
    223, 225–8, 277–9, 324–6,
    340, 369
Plymouth xxxii, 12, 43, 52, 79, 87,
    88–9, 141, 154, 159, 182, 205,
    259, 298, 300, 303, 373, 376,
    444–5, 476
    Breakwater 247, 383–4
    Dock Water Company 170
    Sound 8, 141, 161, 167, 457
Plymouth Dockyard see dockyards
Poland 18–19, 157, 450, 453–5
Pole, Admiral Sir Morice, MP
    (1757–1830) 322, 485
Poleacres 200

Pole-Carew, Reginald, MP
    (1753–1835) 484
Pollock, William, Chief Clerk at the
    Home Office 115–16
Poor Employment Act (1817) 469
Popham, Admiral Sir Home
    (1762–1820) 88, 149, 206,
    208, 222–3, 231–2, 426, 428
population, Great Britain 77, 119,
    155, 259–60, 262, 438, 440
Population Bill 119
Portland, Dorset 34, 266
Portland, Duke of, see
    Cavendish-Bentinck
Portland Whigs 71, 97, 105
Portsmouth 9, 11–12, 52, 74, 79, 88,
    137, 140–41, 159, 185, 168, 182,
    205, 207, 259, 261, 299–300,
    303, 398, 409, 445, 451
Portsmouth Dockyard see
    dockyards
Portugal 127, 238–40, 242, 308,
    425, 429, 458, 460
Portuguese Army 418, 425, 439
Postmaster-General 53, 134, 291
Post Office 132–3, 288, 292–4, 298
    packets to Lisbon and West Indies
    132, 293, 298
    packets, North Sea 53, 132–4,
    293–4, 297–8
    Foreign Department 291
Powis see Clive
Praed, William Mackworth,
    parliamentary
    commissioner 508
Pratt, John Jeffrey, Marquess
    Camden (1759–1840) 86–7,
    222, 277, 476, 491, 498
press gangs see navy: impressment
Preventative Water Guard 290

Prince Regent *see* George, Prince
    of Wales
prisoner-of-war depots 111
    Dartmoor 155, 170, 444–5
    Esk Mills, Scotland 447
    Forton, Gosport 445
    Millbay, Plymouth 445
    Norman Cross 155, 411
    Perth, Scotland 445, 447
    Porchester Castle 155
    Stapleton, Bristol 155, 444–5
    Valleyfield, Scotland 447
prisoner of war
    French parole 129
    hulks 155, 444–5, 447
    parole towns 111, 446–7
    American 444
    British 111, 124, 220, 290, 311, 402
    French 111, 444, 446
    other nationalities 444
privateers
    American 43, 240, 278, 292–3,
        435–6
    British 76, 401
    Danish 240, 293, 298, 396
    Dutch 240, 293, 396
    French 111, 129, 134, 140–41,
        168, 184, 240, 280, 289, 293,
        302, 389, 394, 396–7, 444
    Spanish 293
Privy Council 157, 225
Proby, John Joshua, Earl of
    Carysfort, diplomat
    (1751–1828) 481
provisions, military and naval
    beer 155–6, 160, 163, 165, 168,
        388
    bread 155–6, 160, 172
    biscuit 24, 39, 86, 144, 155–6,
        173–4, 254, 426

butter 153, 155–6, 160
cheese 153,156
flour 24, 172, 254
fresh meat, live cattle and
    vegetables 24, 156, 173–4
hay 159, 167
molasses 158
oats 155, 159, 421
olive oil 158
pease 156
rice 158, 162, 254, 393
rum 158
rye 159
salt beef 39, 86,155–6, 163, 254
salt pork 39, 86,156, 163, 254
vinegar 156, 160, 254
water 85, 153, 168–71, 174, 200
wine and spirits 156, 158, 169,
    298, 388, 425, 428
Prussia xxxvi, 10, 17, 20, 52, 61, 66,
    93, 136, 214, 230, 293, 305,
    375, 389, 405, 410, 421, 430,
    449–50, 452, 454–6, 459, 463
Pulteney, General Sir James Murray,
    MP (1753–1811) 493
Purbeck, Isle of, Dorset 262
Pybus, Charles Small, MP
    (1766–1810) 476, 486

Quakers 261
Quebec 115, 303, 394
Queensberry *see* Douglas
Quota Acts (1796) 77, 260

Radnor *see* Bouverie
Rainier, Peter, Admiral
    (1741–1808) 145
Ramsden, Jesse, scientific
    instrument-maker
    (1735–1800) 48

Ramsgate, Kent 208, 397
Raven, Edward, Home Office
    clerk 115
Ravensbourne, Kentish river 372
Reading 165
Red Sea 142, 145
Reform Act (1832) 470–71
Regency Crisis (1788) 12
Rennie, John, engineer (1761–1821)
    170, 276, 279, 317, 352, 356,
    379, 381–3
Reynolds, Major Thomas
    Vincent, 276
Rhineland 216
Rhodes, island of 199
Richmond see Lennox
Ringmer, Sussex 265
Rio de Janeiro 316
Robinson, Frederick John, MP
    (1782–1859) 477, 486, 492,
    494, 501
Rochefort 84, 123, 172, 236
Rochester, Kent 261, 275, 277
Rockets, Congreve 186, 354–6
Roe, William, parliamentary
    commissioner 504
Rogers, Augustus, Secretary to the
    Board of Ordnance 497
Roman Catholics 80, 214, 220, 237,
    246, 261, 443, 470
Romana, Marquis de, Spanish Army
    officer 241
Romford, Essex 185
Romney Marsh 167, 187, 279
ropery, Chatham dockyard 353
Rose, George, MP (1744–1818)
    xxxiii, 107, 221, 268, 344, 390,
    494, 501
    as Secretary of the Treasury xxxii,
        99, 109, 173, 477

as Treasurer of the Navy 313,
    348–9, 386, 488
Rosia Bay, Gibraltar 171
Ross, General Alexander
    (1742–1827) 256, 270, 496
Ross, Mary, Rochester
    shipbuilder 362
Rother, River, Sussex 168, 279
Rothschild, Nathan Meyer
    (1777–1836) xxxv, 391–2,
    402, 409, 412–14, 424
Roy, General Sir William
    (1726–1790) 48
Royal Laboratory, Woolwich see
    Ordnance manufacture and
    testing
Rule, Sir William, Surveyor of the
    Navy 360, 489
Rush, John, Inspector-General of
    Regimental Infirmaries
    (d. 1801) 495
Russell, John, Duke of Bedford, MP
    (1766–1839) 498
Russell, Lord William, MP
    (1767–1840) 486
Russia 4, 16–19, 83, 92–3, 149,
    170, 189, 214, 216, 227–8,
    231, 238–9, 242, 248–9,
    273–4, 283, 307, 346, 375,
    378–9, 389, 395, 404–5, 410,
    412, 435, 447, 449–50, 451–6,
    459–60, 463–4, 467–8, 473
Russian Army 149, 189,192, 228,
    305, 412, 418, 439, 456, 467;
    Chapter 14 passim
Russian Navy 151, 170, 242, 346,
    378, 395; hemp 394–5
Ryder, Dudley, MP, later Earl of
    Harrowby (1762–1847) 479,
    481, 488, 494, 501, 507

Ryder, Richard, MP (1795–1830) 248, 477
Rye, Sussex xxxiv, 446

St Andrew's University 142
St Barthélemy, West Indies 18
St Helena 399, 458
St Helens *see* Fitzherbert
St Helens, Lancashire 36
St Helens, eastern end of the Solent 140
St James's Park, London 453
St James's Square 333
St Jean de Luz 413, 424
St Lucia 75, 204, 450
St Malo, France 292, 396
St Osyth, Essex 278
St Petersburg 391, 410, 414
St Vincent *see* Jervis
Salamanca, Spain, Battle of (1812) 303, 418, 439
salt 107, 164
salt beef and salt pork *see* provisions
saltpetre 22, 45, 371, 393–4
San Domingo 22–3, 217, 220
San Domingo, Battle of (1806) 230, 458
San Juan, Puerto Rico 75
San Sebastián, Spain, taking of (1813) 428–9
Sandwich *see* Montagu
Santander, Spain 242, 426, 430
Sardinia 66, 93, 128, 144, 389
Sargent, John, MP (1750–1831) 478, 496
Saumarez, Admiral James, Baron (1757–1836) 93, 156, 167, 174, 239–40, 395, 404, 458
Saxony 450, 453–5

Saxton, Captain Sir Charles (1732–1808) 268
Saxton, Sir Charles, Undersecretary, Dublin Castle 499
Scheldt, River 206–8, 240, 309–11, 450, 461
School of Naval Architecture, Portsmouth dockyard 356
Scotland 26, 46–7, 64, 77, 81, 111, 159, 255, 274, 348, 357, 370, 445, 447
Scotland Yard, near Whitehall 177, 317
Scott, Claude, wheat contractor 157–8
Scovell, General Sir George (1774–1861) 428
Scurvy 154, 172, 174–5, 218
Sea Fencibles 266–7
Seaford, Sussex 79, 278
seamen
    British merchant 63, 74, 76, 182, 188, 199, 266, 323, 398, 466
    British naval 12, 20, 62, 76, 89, 132, 154–6, 168, 171–5, 201, 204, 217–18, 240–41, 291, 323, 333, 347–9, 398, 400, 433–4, 436–7, 468–9
    French 9, 14, 56, 123, 221, 308, 444, 446
    Spanish 15
Searle, Captain John Clarke,, RN, Chairman of the Victualling Board 344, 490
Secret Committee of the East India Company 145
secret service xxii, 125, 151
secret service money 12, 124, 126–9, 151–2

Secretary at War *see* British
  government: departments: War
  Office
Secretary of State for War *see* British
  government: departments
semaphore 301–3
Seppings, Sir Robert, Surveyor of
  the Navy (1767–1840) 247,
  341, 369, 489
Serle, Ambrose, Transport
  commissioner (1742–1812)
  325, 488, 510
Seven Years War 4, 7, 34, 93
Seymour, Admiral Lord Hugh
  (1759–1801) 485
Shannonbridge, Ireland 282
Shee, Sir George (1758–1825) 484, 491
Sheerness 261
Shells 354
Sheridan, Richard Brinsley, MP
  (1751–1816) 13, 44, 65–6, 72,
  223, 228, 246, 421, 471, 488
ship's blocks 376–8
shipbuilding 24, 174
  naval 41, 170, 215
  contractors 24, 28, 359–67, 463,
    466, 469
  French 240, 461
  iron 38, 368
  timber 369, 394
shipping licences *see* licences
ships, British merchant
  Apus of London (rowing galley)
    291
  Black Joke 148
  Cumberland 397
  Dispatch 188
  Eagle 184
  Lady Juliana 180
  Lord MacArtney 132

Marquis of Granby 141
Prince of Wales (packet) 134,
  295–6
Roebuck 187
Smallbridge 188
Swan (revenue cutter) 396
Trinity (yacht) 268
ships, British naval
  Ajax (74) 367
  Audacious (74) 204
  Bellerophon (74) 457
  Bonetta (sloop) 132
  Caledonia (120) 367
  Champion (frigate) 135
  Crane (schooner) 364
  Defence (74) 247
  Delight (sloop) 365
  Diana (frigate) 406
  Fury (sloop) 14
  Guerrière (frigate) 435
  Hero (74) 247
  Hound (sloop) 14
  Immortalité (38) 289
  Imperieuse (40) 301
  Impregnable (74) 450
  Inflexible (64) 199
  Invincible (74) 135
  Java (frigate) 435
  Le Caton (hospital ship) 328
  Leopard (frigate) 434
  Locust (gunboat) 291
  London (90) 89
  Lutine (frigate) 134
  Lynx (sloop) 132
  Macedonian (frigate) 435
  Melampus (frigate) 14, 433–4
  Minden (74) 370
  Northumberland (74) 458
  Nautilus (sloop) 141
  Peterel (sloop) 199–200

Pigeon (schooner) 364
Portia (sloop) 153
Prometheus (fireship) 355
Quail (schooner) 364
Ranger (sloop) 365
Royal William (100) 140
St George (98) 247
Salsette (frigate) 370
Sampson (prison ship) 444
Shannon (frigate) 435
Shark (sloop) 132
Southampton (frigate) 9
Temeraire (prison ship) 444
Thais (fireship) 365
Thisbe (frigate) 199
Vanguard (prison ship) 444
Venerable (74) 90
Ville de Paris (110) 204
Vryheid (Dutch prize) 187
Warning (signal station vessel)
   302
Zebra (sloop) 14
ships, French merchant
Rebecca 148
ships, French Navy
Algésiras (74) 175
Vengeur de People (74) 62
ships, US Navy
Chesapeake (frigate) 433–5
United States (frigate) 435
shipwrecks 135, 178, 187–8
shipwrights
   British 24, 29, 31, 117, 236, 316,
      330, 361, 363–5, 368–9, 394
   Danish 305
   French 23, 311–12
Shirley, Lieutenant-General Sir
   Thomas, colonial governor
   (1727–1800) 44
Shorncliffe Camp, Kent 275, 290

Shrapnel, Henry, Lieutenant-General
   (1761–1842) 47
shutter telegraph 137, 139, 140, 303
Sicily 45, 132, 144, 147, 189, 198,
   218, 241, 371, 389, 394, 427
Sick and Hurt Office *see* British
   government: departments
Sidmouth *see* Addington
signal books 125, 299–300
signal stations 140, 299–301, 303
Simcoe, General John Graves
   (1752–1806) 220
Sinclair, Sir John, MP (1754–1835)
   21, 120
Singleton, Mark, MP (1762–1840)
   107–8, 497
Skaggerrak 298
Slade, Benjamin, purveyor of
   Deptford Dockyard 38
small arms manufacture xxxviii, 24,
   42, 47, 154, 280, 317, 372,
   375, 469
Smith, Adam (1723–1790) 71, 142
Smith, Admiral Sir Sidney
   (1764–1840) 9, 128–9, 239
Smith, Charles Culling, Foreign
   Office civil servant
   (1775–1853) 480
Smith, William, dissenting, MP
   (1756–1835) 221
Smith, William, Treasurer of the
   Ordnance (d. 1803) 497
Smithfield market 167
Smiths 31, 67, 370
Smolensk, Russia 419
smuggling 23, 50, 124, 266,
   290–91, 298, 308, 401–4, 409,
   412, 446
Smyth, John, MP (1748–1811)
   98–9, 476, 486

Smyth, John Henry, MP
(1780–1822) 484
Snodgrass, Gabriel, East India
Company Surveyor 360, 369
Society for the Improvement of
Naval Architecture 356
Solent 8, 88, 140, 361–2
Solly, Isaac, Baltic merchant
(1769–1853) 395
Somerset 167
Somerset, Lord Charles, MP
(1767–1831) 494
Somerset House xxix–xxxi, 6, 39,
55, 64, 101, 105, 112, 160, 164,
178, 263, 268, 317, 347, 398
Soult, Nicolas, French marshal 203
South Africa 369
South Downs, Sussex 167
South Midlands 158
South Shields 363
Spa Fields Riot (1816) 469
Spain xxxiv, 3–5, 13–16, 66, 68, 75,
83, 93, 136, 146, 162, 175,
186, 205, 217, 241–3, 303–4,
308, 311, 355, 389, 405,
417–18, 420–21, 423, 425–6,
429, 436, 439, 453, 460, 463
Spanish Army 186, 241–2, 242,
303, 373, 418, 425, 430, 439
Spanish colonies 15, 17, 75, 111,
188, 194, 216, 231
Spanish dollars 136, 224, 405–8,
412, 429
Spanish Navy 7, 14–16, 34, 43, 51,
83, 88, 128, 149, 174–5, 224,
227, 242
specie xxxv, 22, 87, 132, 173, 245,
404–9, 412, 424, 429
Spencer, George, Marquess of
Blandford, MP (1766–1840) 477

Spencer, George John, 2nd Earl
(1758–1834), First Lord of the
Admiralty 71–4, 83, 85–6, 88,
90, 98, 102–3, 106, 108–9, 112,
123, 146–7, 149, 170, 172, 178,
186, 191, 193, 197, 214, 320,
235, 471, 483, 484, 502
Spencer, John Charles, Viscount
Althorp, later 3rd Earl Spencer
(1782–1845) 477
Spencer, Lady Lavinia 102
Spencer, Lord Henry John, MP and
diplomat (1770–1795) 481
Spithead 15–16, 74, 132, 167, 187,
204, 242
Spithead Mutiny (1797) 88–9,
140, 191
Staines 254
Stamps and Excise Office 25
Stanhope, General Charles, Earl of
Harrington (1733–1829) 500
Stanhope, Philip, Earl of
Chesterfield, Joint Postmaster-
General (1755–1815) 502
Stapleton see prisoner-of-war depots
steam dredgers 353, 382
steam power 8, 37, 157, 164,
352–3, 356, 372, 377–8, 381,
385, 468
steam pumps 171, 279, 353, 377
Steel's Navy List 266
Steele, Thomas, MP (1753–1823) 494
Stephens, Sir Philip, MP, Admiralty
civil servant and commissioner
(1723–1809) 12, 108–9, 226,
339, 486
Stephenson, Major General Sir
Benjamin, parliamentary
commissioner 334, 513
Stewart see Vane

Stewart, Admiral George, Viscount
    Garlies, MP (1768–1834) 485
Stewart, Robert, Viscount
    Castlereagh and Marquess of
    Londonderry (1769–1822)
    early career xxxiv–xxxv, 85, 101,
        158, 499, 501
    as Secretary of State for War
        202–3, 206–7, 237–8, 239,
        243–5, 261, 287–8, 309–10,
        408, 459, 465, 491
    as Foreign Secretary 246, 249, 312,
        410, 413, 417, 440, 449–51,
        453–6, 458, 465, 473, 479
Stiles, William, customs official xxxii
Stockholm 16, 396
Stokes Bay, Solent 185
Strachan, Admiral Sir Richard
    (1760–1828) 206, 208, 361
Strand, London xxix, xxxiii, 398
Strasbourg 303
Strood, Kent 261
Stuart, General Sir Charles
    (1753–1801) 196
Stuart, John, Earl of Bute, diplomat
    (1744–1814) 482
Stuart, Sir Charles, later Baron
    Stuart de Rothesay, diplomat
    (1779–1845) 428, 482
Sturges-Bourne, William, MP
    (1769–1845) 273, 326, 477
subsidies xxxviii, 66, 87, 388–9,
    405, 413–14, 456, 465
subsidies, Treaty of (France and
    Spain, 1803) 405
Suffolk 48, 79, 88, 108, 164, 185,
    262, 278
sugar 403, 404
sugar trade 22–3, 68, 158, 163,
    406, 412

Sullivan, John, MP (1749–1839) 491
sulphur 45, 357, 371, 394
Sunderland 104, 141, 219, 262
Surveyor-General of Crown
    Lands 325
Surveyor-General of the King's
    Works 334
Surveyor of the Navy xxx, 236,
    340–41, 360
Surveyor of Telegraphs 137
Sweden 4, 16–18, 133, 167, 173,
    239, 242, 294, 296, 355, 375,
    389, 394–5, 410, 453, 463
Swinburne, Henry, Agent for
    Transports (1743–1803) 129
swords 182, 375, 399–400
Sydenham, Thomas, diplomat
Sydney, Australia 474

Talbot, James, British secret agent 150
Talib, Abu, Persian diplomat 106
Talleyrand, Charles-Maurice de
    (1754–1838) 125, 151, 453
Tankerville see Bennett
Tanner, Benjamin, Dartmouth
    shipbuilder 361, 365
Tavistock, Devon 445
tax xxii, 10, 25, 83–4, 94, 97, 116,
    119, 165, 245, 343, 347, 352,
    388, 436; Chapter 13 passim
    assessed 84, 116, 389
    income 84, 94, 387–9
    property 388, 468
Taxes, Board of 25, 97
Taylor, Ann (1782–1866) 253
Taylor, Henry, block-maker 376
Taylor & Co, gunpowder
    manufacturer 371
Tees, River 301
telegraph see shutter telegraph

Telford, Thomas, civil engineer (1757–1834) 352

Tellichery, India 143

Templar, James, dockyard building contractor (1722–1782) 34

Temple see Grenville

Temple, the, prison in Paris 286

Temple, Henry, Viscount Palmerston, MP (1784–1865) 243, 271, 335–6, 340, 346, 440, 465, 470, 473, 486, 493

Templeman, Giles, parliamentary commissioner 512

Texel 90, 150, 153, 184, 193, 220, 248, 289

Thames, River 12, 42, 88, 90, 164–5, 171, 184, 255–6, 268, 276, 301, 316, 361

Thames yards xxxi, 118,160, 280, 362–3, 374, 381, 451

Thompson, John Deas 510

Thompson, Vice-Admiral Sir Thomas Boulden, MP (1766–1828) 340, 350, 489

Thornton, Samuel, MP (1754–1838) 410

Thornton, Sir Edward (1766–1852) diplomat 481

Thornton & Power, Hamburg merchants 159

Thoroton, Thomas, Clerk of Deliveries, Ordnance 497

Thurlow, Edward, Baron (1731–1806) 11

Thynne, Lord George, MP (1770–1838) 476

Tierney, George, MP (1761–1830) 101, 244, 246, 268, 488, 501

Tilbury 90, 268

Tilsit, Treaty of (1807) 214, 230, 238, 273–4, 305, 307–8, 404, 461

Times, The, newspaper 103, 132, 274

tobacco 290, 298, 412

Tobago 450

Todd, Anthony, Secretary of Post Office (1718–1798) 54, 502

Tone, Wolfe, Irish nationalist (1763–1798) 90

Tonningen, southern Denmark 294, 305, 402

Topsham, Devon 365

Torbay 8, 15, 85, 93, 171–2, 382–3, 458

Torrens, Major General Sir Henry (1779–1828) 492

Torres Vedras, Lines of 418, 420, 423, 460

Toulon 6–7, 10, 12, 14–15, 35, 68–9, 92, 129, 144, 146, 218, 220, 230, 241, 292, 301, 310, 437

Tower of London 48, 156, 318, 373

Townshend, George, Earl of Leicester, Joint Postmaster-General (1788–1807) 502

Townshend, John Thomas, MP (1764–1831) 476, 486

Townshend, Lord John (1757–1833) 494

Towry, George Phillips, Victualling Board commissioner (1729–1817) 40, 112, 163–4, 268, 317, 342, 490

Trafalgar, Battle of (1805) 175, 206, 227–8, 241, 273, 351, 354, 361, 372, 458, 468

Trail, James, Undersecretary, Dublin Castle 499

Transport Board see British government: departments

Treasonable Practices Act 117
Treasurer of the Navy *see* clerks, government
Treasury *see* British government: departments
Treaty of San Ildefonso (1796) 83
Trench, Richard le Poer, Earl of Clancarty 501, 502
Trevor, John Hampden, later Viscount Hampden, diplomat (1748–1824) 128, 482
Trigge, General Sir William 496
Trincomalee, Ceylon 75, 118, 143, 474
Trinidad 75, 216
Trinity House 90, 268
troopships 147, 171, 181, 191–2, 198, 200
Trotter, Alexander, civil servant 224
Trotter, John, army contractor 24
Troubetskoi, Prince, Russian diplomat 307
Troubridge, Admiral Sir Thomas (1758–1807) 92–3, 140, 146, 214, 360, 485
Tucker, Benjamin (1762–1829) 320–22, 324, 487
Tucker, Joseph, Surveyor of the Navy 489
Tullamore, Ireland 443
Tunbridge Wells 109, 465
Turin 128, 145, 303
Turkey 4, 17–19, 92, 170, 173, 199–200, 231
Turner, J. M. W. (1775–1851) 216, 264
Twiss, General William, military engineer (1745–1827) 277, 281
Typhus 205, 209, 430
Tyson, John, Nelson's secretary (d. 1816) 267

Udney, John, British consul in Leghorn 145, 147
Ulm, Battle of (1805) 227
uniforms 24, 185, 199, 263–4, 267–8, 357, 425, 462, 466
United States 3–4, 23, 123, 162, 217, 236, 356, 392, 401–2, 406, 411, 424, 426, 433–7, 444, 447, 449, 468
see also privateers: American
Upnor Castle *see* Ordnance depots
Ushant 15, 154

Valmy, Battle of (1792) 20
Vancouver Island 13
Vane (formerly Stewart), Lieutenant-General Charles William, MP (later 3rd Marquess of Londonderry, Castlereagh's stepbrother) (1778–1854) 85, 207, 243, 246, 417, 458, 481–2, 492
Vansittart, Nicholas, MP, later Lord Bexley (1766–1851) 345, 476–8, 499
Vauxhall, London 165
Vendée, royalists 72, 83, 122–3, 128, 228
Venice 142, 216, 303, 309, 437
Vera Cruz, Mexico 406, 408
Verderer of the New Forest 107
Vergennes, Charles Gravier, Comte de (1717–1787) 4
Vice-Admiralty Court 399
victualling yards 155, 160, 165, 169, 215, 463
    Chatham 160
    Deal 39
    Deptford 39, 117, 160–61, 164, 178, 316, 330

victualling yards – *cont.*
  Dover 39
  Plymouth 39
  Portsmouth 39, 160–61, 168, 316
Vienna 125, 136, 217, 222, 305, 414
Vienna, Congress of (1814–1815)
    448, 449–50, 452–3, 455,
    466, 470
Vigo, Spain 203
Villeneuve, Pierre-Charles de, French
    admiral (1763–1806) 169
Villiers, George, MP and Paymaster
    of Marines (1759–1827) 337
Villiers, John Charles, Earl of
    Clarendon, diplomat
    (1757–1838) 482
Vimeiro, Battle of (1808) 242
Vincent, Sir Francis (1780–1809) 480
Vinegar Hill, Battle of (1798) 91
Vitoria 372
volunteer regiments
  Bank of England 269
  Buckinghamshire Yeomanry 233
  Dorset Volunteer Rangers 263
  Hackney and Stoke Newington 271
  Halifax 263
  Islington 271
  Lincolns Inn 81
  London and Westminster Light
    Horse 263, 270, 345
  Manchester 271
  Norfolk 4th Battalion 233
  North Pevensey Infantry 265
  Pendennis Artillery 270
  Piddleton Town Infantry 81
  Portsmouth Dockyard 267
  Royal East India Company 269
  Royal Trinity House Artillery 268
  Somerset Place Regiment 263,
    268, 279

South Lewes 265
South Pevensey Legion 265
Sussex 264
Sussex Yeomanry Horse
    Artillery 264
Woodley Cavalry 219
Woolwich Dockyard 267
volunteers 76, 80–82, 154, 159,
    233, 238, 251, 253, 255–6,
    259–60, 262–3, 265–7, 269–72,
    274, 279, 470

Wagram, Battle of (1809)
    312, 439
Walcheren expedition (1809) 171,
    205, 207–10, 240, 244,
    247, 311, 330, 355, 408,
    438, 459
Walker, Samuel of Rotherham,
    cannon founder 47, 370
Wallace, Thomas, MP
    (1768–1844) 486
Walmer Castle 278
Walpole, George, MP
    (1758–1835) 480
Walpole, Horatio, Lord Walpole,
    MP (1783–1858) 486
Walpole, Robert, diplomat
    (1736–1810) 482
Walsingham *see* de Grey
Waltham Abbey, gunpowder mill
    42, 45, 372
Wapping 181
War Office *see* British government:
    departments
Ward, Robert, MP (1755–1846)
    486, 496
Wardle, Colonel Gwyllym, MP
    (?1761–1833) 242–3
Warre, Henry, Rear-Admiral 12

Warren, Admiral Sir John Borlase,
MP (1753–1852) 72, 92–3,
382, 435, 437, 481
Warrender, Sir George, MP
(1782–1849) 432, 486
Washington, burning of (1814) 447
Waterloo, Battle of (1815) 355, 372,
414, 457, 466–8
Watson, Sir Brook, MP
(1735–1807) 159, 254, 273
Watt, James (1736–1819) 216, 353
Wealden gunfounding 45
Weaver Navigation 164
Wedgwood, Josiah (1730–1795) 13
Weevil, Portsmouth Harbour 154
Weir, John, Director-General of the
Army Medical Board (d. 1819)
491, 495
Wellesley, Field-Marshal Arthur,
1st Duke of Wellington
(1769–1852)
early career xxxvi, 69, 202, 499
in the Peninsula 155, 241–2, 408,
417–18, 420, 422–9, 431, 436,
441, 444, 465
Vienna and Waterloo 455–7, 466,
480
later career 283, 448, 450,
470–71, 473
Wellesley, Henry, MP and diplomat
(1773–1847) 428, 477, 482
Wellesley, Richard, Marquess (Lord
Mornington 1781–1799)
(1760–1842) 63, 246, 249,
393, 410, 476, 477, 479, 482
Wellesley-Pole, William, later Lord
Mornington (1763–1845) 237,
246, 339, 341, 346, 375, 477,
486, 496, 499
Wellington see Wellesley

Welshpool, Wales 447
West Indies 14, 16, 18, 22, 23, 44,
49–51, 68–9, 73–8, 134, 141,
156, 158–9, 163, 177, 180,
182–3, 188–90, 196, 217, 221,
225, 227, 273, 292, 298, 300,
316, 334, 368, 393, 396, 449,
459
Western Approaches 8, 15, 383
Western Heights, Dover 281
Wharton, Richard, MP
(c. 1764–1828) 478
wheat 22, 39, 120, 157–61, 163–4,
167, 172, 241, 357, 390, 395,
403–4, 426, 426, 463
wheat prices 157, 215, 426
Whidbey, Joseph, naval engineer
(1757–1833) 329, 362, 383
Whitbread, Samuel, MP (1764–1815)
225, 244, 246, 329, 421
Whitby 363
White, George, Master Shipwright,
Portsmouth Dockyard 39
Whitehall xxx–xxxi, 11, 63, 105,
131, 137, 273, 288, 303,
317–18, 389, 451, 466;
Chapter 4 passim
Whitehaven, Cumberland 76, 160
Whitelocke, Lieutenant-General Sir
John (1757–1833) 231–2, 493
Whitworth, Charles, Earl
Whitworth, diplomat (1752–
1825) 217, 480–81, 498
Whitworth, James, seaman 153
Wickham, William, MP
(1761–1840) xxxiv, 82, 125–6,
128–9, 142–3, 150, 287, 483–4
as Chief Secretary, Ireland 219,
288, 499
later career 328, 471, 477

Wilberforce, William, MP (1759–
1833) 222, 225, 228, 233, 238,
473
Wilkes, Joseph, British secret agent
128
Willes, Sir Francis, cryptographer
130–31
Williams, John, Secretary to the
Commission of Naval
Enquiry 509
Williams, Thomas, MP industrialist
(1737–1802) 36, 41, 379
Wilson, Colonel Sir Robert
(1777–1849)
Wimbledon 52, 99–100, 109, 195
Wimereux 252, 409
Windham, William, MP
(1750–1810) 61, 70, 277, 342
as Secretary at War 71–2, 101,
106, 112, 122, 128, 215, 228,
461, 493
as Secretary of State for War 176,
229–30, 232–3, 244, 247,
260, 279, 326, 438, 461,
465, 491
Wolters, Margrete, British secret
agent in Holland 7
Woodbridge, Suffolk 185, 262
Woolwich, Royal Laboratory see
Ordnance manufacture and
testing
Woolwich Arsenal see Ordnance
manfacture and testing
Woolwich Dockyard see dockyards
Woolwich Warren see Ordnance
manufacture and testing:
Woolwich Arsenal
Wordsworth, William
(1770–1850) 216

Wright, Captain John Wesley, RN
(1769–1805) 129, 286
Wyndham, George O'Brien, Earl of
Egremont (1751–1837) 168,
264, 452
Wynn, Charles Watkin Williams,
MP (1775–1850) 484

Xebecs 200

Yare, River, Norfolk 364, 374
Yarmouth see Great Yarmouth
Yellow fever 175
Yonge, Sir George, MP
(1732–1812) 49, 52, 493
York, Duke of, Field-Marshal
Frederick (1763–1827) xxxvi,
13, 67–9, 192, 206, 461, 472
as Commander-in-Chief 43, 93,
103–4, 137, 186, 210, 229,
233, 242, 254–6, 259, 262,
273, 277, 279, 287, 347, 357,
437–8, 441, 492
Yorke, Admiral Sir Joseph, MP
(1768–1831) 432, 485
Yorke, Charles Philip, MP
(1764–1834) 247–9, 263, 271,
287, 298, 311, 331, 339, 355,
383, 483, 485
Yorke, Philip, Earl of Hardwicke
498
Yorkshire 80, 158, 167, 263, 301,
441
Young, Admiral Sir William
(1751–1821) xxxvii, 73, 92,
102, 109, 240, 311, 355, 485
Young, Arthur (1741–1820)
120, 167
Ystad, southern Sweden 167